# LLVM Code Generation

A deep dive into compiler backend development

**Quentin Colombet**

‹packt›

# LLVM Code Generation

**Portfolio Director:** Kunal Chaudhari

**Relationship Lead:** Samriddhi Murarka

**Project Manager:** Ashwin Dinesh Kharwa

**Content Engineer:** Sujata Tripathi

**Technical Editor:** Rohit Singh

**Copy Editor:** Safis Editing

**Indexer:** Hemangini Bari

**Production Designer:** Vijay Kamble

**Growth Lead:** Vinishka Kalra

First published: May 2025

Production reference: 4030925

Published by Packt Publishing Ltd.

Grosvenor House

11 St Paul's Square

Birmingham

B3 1RB, UK.

ISBN 978-1-83763-778-2

www.packtpub.com

*To my wife, Luce, and my three sons, Clovis, Mathias, and Gabriel, for supporting and encouraging me throughout this project. I may not have been the most present dad during this time, and your patience with me has been noticed and appreciated. With love.*

*– Quentin Colombet*

# Foreword

At first glance, it might seem like only a few people ever work on LLVM backends. After all, the number of backends in upstream LLVM is limited, and most of them are already stable and functioning well. So, why would they need significant changes?

In reality, LLVM has become the de facto standard for code generation—not just for CPUs but also for increasingly diverse compute engines such as GPUs and other accelerators. When a new CPU or accelerator needs code generation support, the default choice is often to adopt LLVM and implement a backend.

Furthermore, the existing upstream backends are under constant improvement. They're regularly updated to support new CPU instructions, refine and enhance optimizations, introduce additional security-hardening features, and much more.

Beyond development in industry and by enthusiasts, LLVM is also a top choice in academia for systems and compiler research. Many innovations in performance tuning, security, and other areas require modifying LLVM backends to enable experimentation.

These are just a few scenarios where someone might need to create or modify LLVM backends—and I'm sure there are many more. But even considering just these three, it's clear that thousands of developers need to do at least some LLVM backend development, and they need high-quality documentation to do it well.

While the LLVM project offers extensive documentation and tutorials, there continues to be a gap in documenting very clearly everything you need to know to become proficient in backend development.

Effectively working on LLVM backends often requires reverse engineering and internalizing their architecture. Historically, the most efficient way to learn has been to find an expert and engage in long, detailed conversations to piece everything together. Of course, not everyone has access to such experts. Even though the LLVM community makes a huge effort to share expert knowledge—through comprehensive documentation (`https://llvm.org/docs/`), hundreds of recorded talks and presentations (`https://llvm.org/devmtg/`), and programs such as office hours and online sync-ups (`https://llvm.org/docs/GettingInvolved.html#office-hours`)—the learning curve remains steep.

A few years ago, I had a conversation with Quentin at one of the LLVM Developers' Meetings about this very topic. I thought then (and still do!) that Quentin is one of the most knowledgeable LLVM backend engineers out there. I was thinking out loud, *"Wouldn't it be amazing if all of your knowledge—especially about LLVM backend development—could be made easily available to the entire LLVM community? Just imagine how much easier and faster backend development would become if your insights were accessible in a book..."*

I'm thrilled that our conversation helped inspire Quentin to write this fantastic book. It distills deep insights and practical knowledge into a single, well-organized resource—ideal for anyone starting or continuing their journey in LLVM backend development. I hope that everyone working on backends reads it, and that it fuels even more innovation and progress in the LLVM ecosystem.

Thank you, Quentin, for writing all this down!

*Kristof Beyls*

*Senior Technical Director and Fellow, Arm*

# Contributors

## About the author

**Quentin Colombet** is a veteran LLVM contributor who focuses on the development of backends. He is the architect of the new instruction selection framework (GlobalISel) and code owner of the LLVM register allocators.

He has more than two decades of experience working on different compiler backends for various architectures (GPU, CPU, microcontroller, DSP, and ASIC, among others) and compiler frameworks (Open64, LLVM, IREE, and Glow, to name the main ones). He joined the LLVM project when he started at Apple in 2012 and has worked on the x86, AArch64, and Apple GPU backends and all the products that include these processing units. Since starting on the LLVM infrastructure, he has helped interns and new hires onboard the LLVM infrastructure at Apple, Meta, and Google, as well as, more recently, his own company, Brium, while contributing to the projects using that technology in these companies.

*I want to thank Bruno Cardoso Lopes, who inspired me to write this book and introduced me to the Packt team. Thank you to the Packt team for their support and continuous feedback, more specifically, Aditi Chatterjee, Ashwin Dinesh Kharwa, Samriddhi Murarka, and Sujata Tripathi, who all worked closely with me to make this project a reality. Thanks to my technical reviewer, Shuo Niu, who brought a different perspective to the book and helped me clarify the content, resulting in a better experience. And, of course, thank you to my wife, Luce, who encouraged me to get started on this project and supported me along the way.*

# About the reviewer

**Shuo Niu** holds a Master of Engineering in computer engineering from the University of Toronto. With six years of experience in LLVM compiler development, specializing in middle-end and backend optimizations for FPGA HLS compilers, Shuo is now extending his expertise to building AI compilers for low-power AI chips. Committed to fostering a stronger LLVM community, Shuo also served as a technical reviewer for *Learn LLVM 17, Second Edition*.

# Table of Contents

# Chapter 3: Compiler Basics and How They Map to LLVM APIs      **55**

## Chapter 15: Instruction Selection: The IR Building Phase      417

## Chapter 16: Instruction Selection: The Legalization Phase      441

## Chapter 17: Instruction Selection: The Selection Phase and Beyond    459

## Chapter 21: Getting Started with the Assembler     553

## Chapter 22: Unlock Your Book's Exclusive Benefits     567

## Other Books You May Enjoy     570

## Index     575

# Preface

Welcome to *LLVM Code Generation*

The LLVM infrastructure is a set of libraries that can be composed to build various tools that manipulate **intermediate representations** (**IRs**) and in particular compilers – that is, tools that translate an input language (for instance, C++) into an output language (for instance, x86 assembly code) while preserving the semantics of the input language. One of the most known LLVM-based projects is the Clang C++ toolchain.

In this book, we focus on the usage of the LLVM infrastructure to write compiler **backends** – that is, the part of the compiler that is responsible for producing the assembly code for a specific architecture such as the AArch64 or x86 **central processing units** (**CPUs**) for writing backends.

An LLVM backend hinges around two main Irs: the LLVM IR and the Machine IR. The differences between these representations do not matter at this point; what matters is that you must learn how to manipulate both to be able to write a backend in LLVM.

The LLVM IR has been extensively covered in literature already, but the Machine IR (the parts that are closer to the assembly representation) has not.

This book proposes to close that gap with explanations of how things work and concrete examples that illustrate the implementation of concepts. We will also cover the LLVM IR and the related mechanism to give you a complete picture of the LLVM infrastructure and help you understand how things connect in a fully functional backend that goes from the LLVM IR to the assembly code.

To summarize, to fully appreciate the capabilities of the LLVM infrastructure, this book covers every component that is involved in emitting assembly code, including the LLVM IR, the pass pipeline, TableGen (LLVM's own **domain-specific language** (**DSL**)), and the relevant TableGen backend, the Machine IR, and some part of the **machine code** (**MC**) layer.

# Who this book is for

This book is for people who want to use the LLVM infrastructure to write new backends or modify/ extend existing ones.

We crafted this book for people who have zero knowledge of compiler backends. This means that all the concepts used are first introduced and explained such that no prior compiler backend knowledge is necessary. We believe this book is a good introduction for anyone who wants to get started with the **code generation (codegen)** part of a compiler toolchain, whether they are familiar with compilers and LLVM or not. In particular, the concepts introduced in this book apply to every compiler, and LLVM is just one possible implementation of such concepts. In other words, we argue that the content of this book may be useful to students and compiler practitioners beyond LLVM. Of course, a lot of the content of this book is still LLVM-specific.

To summarize, whether you are new to compilers, new to LLVM, or new to LLVM backends, we believe you will find something useful in this book.

# What this book covers

*Chapter 1, Building LLVM and Understanding the Directory Structure*, introduces the LLVM project, how to build it, and explains how the whole project is organized. This will allow you to get started with the LLVM project and is a key step to start on the right foot.

*Chapter 2, Contributing to LLVM*, guides you into engaging with the open source community and gives you concrete steps that you can take to contribute to the project. In particular, this chapter gives you concrete elements on how to seek help from the open source community.

*Chapter 3, Compiler Basics and How They Map to LLVM APIs*, introduces the concepts used in compilers and teaches you which LLVM **application programming interfaces (APIs)** you can use to manipulate them. This chapter is fundamental to a good understanding of the rest of the book, as it gives you the core knowledge of what you manipulate in a compiler such as LLVM.

*Chapter 4, Writing Your First Optimization*, teaches you how to create your own optimizations using the LLVM infrastructure. Additionally, it introduces advanced compiler concepts that you must know when working with optimizations.

*Chapter 5, Dealing with Pass Managers*, explains how to understand, debug, and build your own sequence of optimizations with both the legacy and the new pass manager. LLVM comes with pre-existing pass pipelines, and to be able to extend them or build a new one, it is important to understand how the pass managers work. This knowledge is key to building your own optimizing compiler.

*Chapter 6, TableGen - LLVM Swiss Army Knife for Modeling*, teaches you about the TableGen syntax, how it integrates with the rest of the LLVM infrastructure, and gives you guidelines on how to debug it. From command-line options to the encoding of the instructions, the definition of intrinsics, the description of the register classes, and so on, Tablegen is a pervasive tool used throughout the entire LLVM infrastructure. Thanks to this chapter, you will confidently approach the modeling tasks that are required in the later chapters.

*Chapter 7*, *Understanding LLVM IR*, provides an overview of the LLVM IR and how to understand it. The LLVM IR is the backbone of the LLVM infrastructure and, as such, understanding it is the first step to being able to optimize it or more generally transform it.

*Chapter 8*, *Survey of Existing Passes*, gives you an overview of the optimizations and analyses that the LLVM infrastructure provides. This chapter also points out the key APIs that you may need to implement to get the most out of the related optimizations and analyses. Thanks to this knowledge, you will be able to reuse everything the LLVM infrastructure has to offer to craft the perfect optimization pipeline.

*Chapter 9*, *Introducing Target-Specific Constructs*, goes into the details of how the LLVM infrastructure can be augmented with target-specific information and, in particular, how to add a new backend in the infrastructure. This chapter is key in setting up the connections between the LLVM infrastructure and your backend such that LLVM can start producing elements that are specific to your backend.

*Chapter 10*, *Hands-On Debugging LLVM IR Passes*, describes the mechanisms available to help you debug with the LLVM IR passes, including how to use the logging mechanism, the tools to automatically reduce the size of your inputs, and how to interact with the LLVM infrastructure in a debugger.

*Chapter 11*, *Getting Started with the Backend*, teaches you about the Machine IR and shows you how to implement the key pieces of your backend to get started with the codegen process. This information is key to interacting with the Machine IR.

*Chapter 12*, *Getting Started with the Machine Code Layer*, introduces the MC layer and shows you how to augment the description of the instructions of your backend with encoding information that is ultimately used to produce the final object file.

*Chapter 13*, *The Machine Pass Pipeline*, teaches you about the default codegen pipeline that the LLVM infrastructure provides, the different stages that the Machine IR goes through, and how to inject your own optimizations in that pipeline. Thanks to this information, you will be able to customize the codegen pipeline to your needs.

*Chapter 14*, *Getting Started with Instruction Selection*, introduces the LLVM frameworks responsible for translating the LLVM IR to the Machine IR, shows you how to connect each of them to your codegen pipeline, shows how to manipulate their internal IRs, and teaches you how to create a skeleton of an instruction selector using these frameworks.

*Chapter 15*, *Instruction Selection - The IR Building Phase*, goes into the details of the lowering of the LLVM IR into the generic IR of the instruction selection frameworks. This includes showing you how to lower the **application binary interface** (ABI) of your backend.

*Chapter 16*, *Instruction Selection - The Legalization Phase*, teaches you how to transform the generic IR of the instruction selection frameworks into something that your target supports.

*Chapter 17*, *Instruction Selection - The Selection Phase and Beyond*, wraps up the instruction selection process with the final stage of this transformation by showing you how to produce target-specific instructions and how to take advantage of some of the capabilities of the instruction selection frameworks to debug and optimize the instruction selection pipeline.

*Chapter 18*, *Instruction Scheduling*, teaches you how to leverage the instruction scheduling infrastructure to produce highly optimized code sequences.

*Chapter 19*, *Register Allocation*, introduces the representations used in LLVM that touch on the concept of register liveness and teaches you how to provide the key pieces to allow the LLVM infrastructure to perform the allocation of the registers. This part of the implementation is key in producing code for programs that are more than toy examples.

*Chapter 20*, *Lowering of the Stack Layout*, guides you in implementing the lowering of the stack layout of your backend. The stack layout is an important piece of the ABI of your target, and its implementation is a mandatory step to support again anything beyond toy examples. This chapter also touches on corner cases that you inevitably run into when lowering your stack, such as running out of registers when expanding the stack offsets, and the kind of helpers the LLVM infrastructure provides to get you out of these situations.

*Chapter 21*, *Getting Started with the Assembler*, finishes this book by showing you how what you implemented comes together to produce the final object file and teaches you how to implement the concepts specific to this part of the compiler toolchain, such as the relocations. The introduced concepts open you up to the fascinating world of binary tools and conclude your journey in the compiler backend world.

# To get the most out of this book

The chapters are self-contained and, aside from the compiler concepts introduced in *Chapters 3* and *4*, you should be able to jump to any of them and get started. If you are new to the codegen space, we still recommend that you follow the chapters in order as they follow the natural flow of a compiler backend from the input IR progressively lowering it to assembly code. If you are new to compilers, we still recommend that you read at least *Chapters 3* and *4* first.

For people with a compiler background but new to backends or wanting to refresh or refine their knowledge of the backends, you can use the *Quiz time* sections at the end of each chapter to first check your knowledge against what the chapter covers to decide whether the chapter may cover something that you may not know before reading it.

Finally, we are firm believers that practicing something helps to digest it; therefore, we recommend you spend time doing the coding exercises and implement your own solutions without looking at the provided solutions.

| Software covered in the book | Operating system requirements |
|---|---|
| LLVM 20 | Windows, macOS, or Linux |

If you are using the digital version of this book, we advise you to type the code yourself or access the code from the book's GitHub repository (a link is available in the next section). Doing so will help you avoid any potential errors related to the copying and pasting of code.

Note that the code snippets and APIs are based on the open source release of LLVM 20.1.1 from February 2025. All the code has been tested solely on macOS but should work equally well on Windows and Linux. The code snippets are also available for the LLVM 19.0.1 release from September 2024 in the `release_llvm_19_0_1` branch of the repositories listed in the next section.

## Download the example code files

You can download the example code files and exercises for this book from GitHub at `https://github.com/PacktPublishing/LLVM-Code-Generation`. If there's an update to the code, it will be updated in the GitHub repository. Additionally, the book comes with a second companion repository at `https://github.com/PacktPublishing/LLVM-Code-Generation-by-example`. This is a fork of LLVM that is used throughout the book to illustrate how to develop a full backend.

We also have other code bundles from our rich catalog of books and videos available at `https://github.com/PacktPublishing/`. Check them out!

## Download the color images

We also provide a PDF file that has color images of the screenshots/diagrams used in this book. You can download it here: `https://packt.link/gbp/9781837637782`.

## Conventions used

There are a number of text conventions used throughout this book.

`Code in text`: Indicates code words in text, database table names, folder names, filenames, file extensions, pathnames, dummy URLs, user input, and X/Twitter handles. Here is an example: "Since the SDISel framework is a single `MachineFunctionPass` instance, the only way to augment it is through the hooks provided by the various `TargetXXX` classes of your backend."

A block of code is set as follows:

```
SelectionDAG has 9 nodes:
  t0: ch,glue = EntryToken
      t2: i16,ch = CopyFromReg t0, Register:i16 %0
      t4: i16,ch = CopyFromReg t0, Register:i16 %1
    t5: i16 = add t2, t4
  t7: ch,glue = CopyToReg t0, Register:i16 $r1, t5
  t8: ch = H2BLBISD::RETURN_GLUE t7, Register:i16 $r1, t7:1
```

Warnings or important notes appear like this.

Tips and tricks appear like this.

# Get in touch

Feedback from our readers is always welcome.

**General feedback:** Email feedback@packtpub.com and mention the book's title in the subject of your message. If you have questions about any aspect of this book, please email us at questions@packtpub.com.

**Errata:** Although we have taken every care to ensure the accuracy of our content, mistakes do happen. If you have found a mistake in this book, we would be grateful if you reported this to us. Please visit http://www.packtpub.com/submit-errata, click **Submit Errata**, and fill in the form.

**Piracy:** If you come across any illegal copies of our works in any form on the internet, we would be grateful if you would provide us with the location address or website name. Please contact us at copyright@packtpub.com with a link to the material.

**If you are interested in becoming an author:** If there is a topic that you have expertise in and you are interested in either writing or contributing to a book, please visit http://authors.packtpub.com/.

# Share your thoughts

Once you've read *LLVM Code Generation*, we'd love to hear your thoughts! Scan the QR code below to go straight to the Amazon review page for this book and share your feedback.

https://packt.link/r/1837637784

Your review is important to us and the tech community and will help us make sure we're delivering excellent quality content.

# Part 1

# Getting Started with LLVM

In this part, we start with an introduction to the LLVM ecosystem, its community, and the various parts that make up the LLVM infrastructure.

This part assumes that you have no prior experience with LLVM and little to no experience with compilers.

More specifically, in this part, you will learn the following:

- How to set up your environment to build and test the different projects that the LLVM infrastructure offers
- How to interact with the LLVM community and, in particular, how to seek help and contribute
- About the basic concepts used in compilers and how to manipulate them through the LLVM **application programming interfaces (APIs)**
- How to write your first optimization pass and the things to consider while optimizing your program
- How to build and customize your optimization pipeline
- How TableGen, LLVM's **domain-specific language (DSL)**, fits into the LLVM infrastructure

By the end of this part, you will have a complete picture of the overall structure of the LLVM infrastructure and will be ready to dive into its inner workings.

This part of the book includes the following chapters:

- *Chapter 1, Building LLVM and Understanding the Directory Structure*
- *Chapter 2, Contributing to LLVM*
- *Chapter 3, Compiler Basics and How They Map to the LLVM APIs*
- *Chapter 4, Writing Your First Optimization*
- *Chapter 5, Dealing with the Pass Managers*
- *Chapter 6, TableGen - The LLVM Swiss Army Knife for Modeling*

# 1

# Building LLVM and Understanding the Directory Structure

The **LLVM** infrastructure provides a set of libraries that can be assembled to create different tools and **compilers**.

*LLVM* originally stood for **Low-Level Virtual Machine**. Nowadays, it is much more than that, as you will shortly learn, and people just use LLVM as a name.

Given the sheer volume of code that makes the LLVM repository, it can be daunting to even know where to start.

In this chapter, we will give you the keys to approach and use this code base confidently. Using this knowledge, you will be able to do the following:

- Understand the different components that make a compiler
- Build and test the LLVM project
- Navigate LLVM's directory structure and locate the implementation of different components
- Contribute to the LLVM project

This chapter covers the basics needed to get started with LLVM. If you are already familiar with the LLVM infrastructure or followed the tutorial from the official LLVM website (https://llvm.org/docs/GettingStarted.html), you can skip it. You can, however, check the *Quiz time* section at the end of the chapter to see whether there is anything you may have missed.

# Getting the most out of this book — get to know your free benefits

Unlock exclusive **free** benefits that come with your purchase, thoughtfully crafted to supercharge your learning journey and help you learn without limits.

Here's a quick overview of what you get with this book:

## Next-gen reader

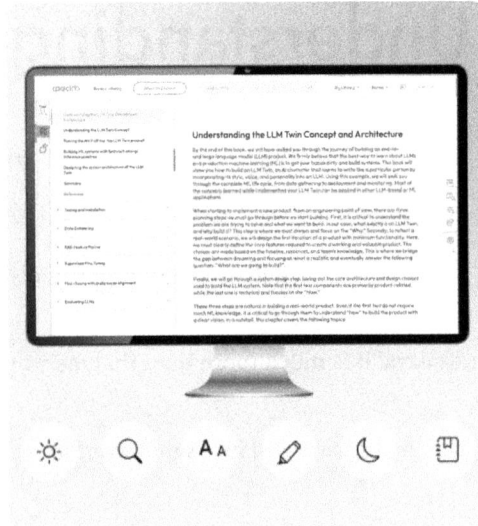

Our web-based reader, designed to help you learn effectively, comes with the following features:

⌁ **Multi-device progress sync**: Learn from any device with seamless progress sync.

📑 **Highlighting and notetaking**: Turn your reading into lasting knowledge.

🔖 **Bookmarking**: Revisit your most important learnings anytime.

☀ **Dark mode**: Focus with minimal eye strain by switching to dark or sepia mode.

*Figure 1.1: Illustration of the next-gen Packt Reader's features*

## Interactive AI assistant (beta)

Our interactive AI assistant has been trained on the content of this book, so it can help you out if you encounter any issues. It comes with the following features:

✦ **Summarize it**: Summarize key sections or an entire chapter.

✦ **AI code explainers**: In the next-gen Packt Reader, click the **Explain** button above each code block for AI-powered code explanations.

*Note: The AI assistant is part of next-gen Packt Reader and is still in beta.*

*Figure 1.2: Illustration of Packt's AI assistant*

## DRM-free PDF or ePub version

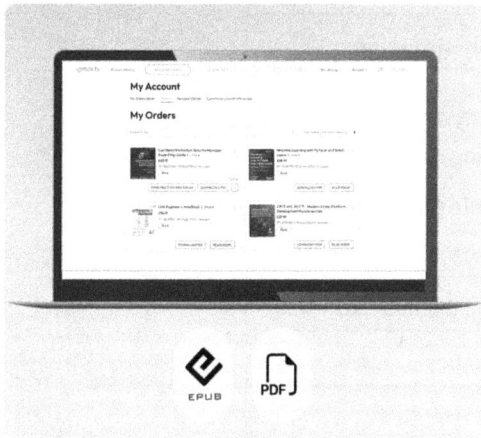

Learn without limits with the following perks included with your purchase:

📄 Learn from anywhere with a DRM-free PDF copy of this book.

📖 Use your favorite e-reader to learn using a DRM-free ePub version of this book.

*Figure 1.3: Free PDF and ePub*

### Unlock this book's exclusive benefits now

Take a moment to get the most out of your purchase and enjoy the complete learning experience.

*Note: Have your purchase invoice ready before you begin.*

UNLOCK NOW

https://www.packtpub.com/unlock/9781837637782

# Technical requirements

To work with the LLVM code base, you need specific tools on your system. In this section, we list the required versions of these tools for the latest major LLVM release: 20.1.0.

Later, in *Identifying the right version of the tools*, you will learn how to find the version of the tools required to build a specific version of LLVM, including older and newer releases and the LLVM top-of-tree (that is, the actively developed repository). Additionally, you will learn how to install them.

With no further due, here are the versions of the tools required for LLVM 20.1.0:

| Tool | Required version |
|---|---|
| Git | None specified |
| C/C++ toolchain | >=Clang 5.0 |
| | >=Apple Clang 10.0 |
| | >=GCC 7.4 |
| | >=Visual Studio 2019 16.8 |
| CMake | >=3.20.0 |
| Ninja | None specified |
| Python | >=3.8 |

*Table 1.1: Tools required for LLVM 20.1.0*

Furthermore, this book comes with scripts, examples, and more that will ease your journey with learning the LLVM infrastructure. We will specifically list the relevant content in the related sections, but remember that the repository lives at `https://github.com/PacktPublishing/LLVM-Code-Generation`.

# Getting ready for LLVM's world

In the *Technical requirement* section, we already listed which version of tools you needed to work with LLVM 20.1.0. However, LLVM is a lively project and what is required today may be different than what is required tomorrow. Also, to step back a bit, you may not know why you need these tools to begin with and/or how to get them.

This section addresses these questions, and you will learn the following in the process:

- The purpose of each required tool
- How to check that your environment has the proper tools
- How to install the proper tools

Depending on how familiar you are with development on Linux/macOS, this setup can be tedious or a walk in the park.

Ultimately, this section aims to teach you how to go beyond a fixed release of LLVM by giving you the knowledge required to find the information you need.

If you are familiar with package managers (e.g., the apt-get command-line tool on Linux and Homebrew (https://brew.sh) on macOS), you can skip this part and directly install Git, Clang, CMake, Ninja, and Python through them. For Windows, if you do not have a package manager, the steps provided here are all manual, meaning that if you pick the related Windows binary distribution of the related tools, it should just work. Now, for Windows again, you may be better off installing these tools through **Visual Studio Code (VS Code)** (https://code.visualstudio.com) via the VS Code's extensions.

In any case, you might want to double-check which version of these tools you need by going through the *Identifying the right version of the tools* section.

## Prerequisites

As mentioned previously, you need a set of specific tools to build the LLVM code base. This section summarizes what each of these tools does and how they work together to build the LLVM project.

This list of tools is as follows:

- **Git:** The software used for the versioning control of LLVM
- **A C/C++ toolchain:** The LLVM code base is in C/C++, and as such, we will need a toolchain to build that type of code
- **CMake:** The software used to configure the build system
- **Ninja:** The software used to drive the build system
- **Python:** The scripting language and execution environment used for testing

*Figure 1.1* illustrates how the different tools work together to build an LLVM compiler:

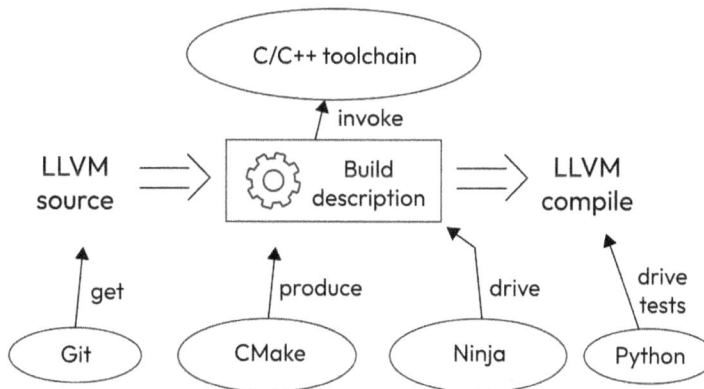

*Figure 1.1: The essential command-line tools to build an LLVM compiler*

Breaking this figure down, here are the steps it takes:

1. Git retrieves the source code.
2. CMake generates the build system for a particular driver, such as Ninja, and a particular C/C++ toolchain.
3. Ninja drives the build process.
4. The C/C++ toolchain builds the compiler.
5. Python drives the execution of the tests.

## Identifying the right version of the tools

The required version of these tools depends on the version of LLVM you are building. For instance, see the *Technical requirements* section for the latest major release of LLVM, 20.1.0.

To check the required version for a specific release, check out the **Getting Started** page of the documentation for this release. To get there, perform the following steps:

1. Go to `https://releases.llvm.org/`.
2. Scroll down to the **Download** section.
3. In the documentation column, click on the link named `llvm` or `docs` for the release you are interested in. For instance, release 20.1.0 should bring you to a URL such as `https://releases.llvm.org/20.1.0/docs/index.html`.
4. Scroll down to the **Documentation** section.
5. Click on **Getting Started/Tutorials**.
6. Find the **Software** and the **Host C++ Toolchain[...]** sections. For instance, for release 20.1.0, the **Software** section lives at `https://releases.llvm.org/20.1.0/docs/GettingStarted.html#software`.

To find the requirements for LLVM top-of-tree, simply follow the same steps but with the release named **Git**. This release should have a release date of **Current**.

You learned how to identify which version of the tools you need to have to be able to work with LLVM. Now, let's see how to install these versions.

> Note
>
> Ninja is the preferred driver of the build system of LLVM. However, LLVM also supports other drivers such as Makefile (the default), Xcode, and, to some extent, Bazel. Feel free to choose what works best for you.

# Installing the right tools

Depending on your **operating system (OS)**, you may have already all the necessary tools installed. You can use the following commands to check which version of the tools are installed and whether they meet the minimum requirements that we described in the previous section:

| Tool | Checking the availability |
|------|---------------------------|
| Git | `git -version` |
| C/C++ toolchain (LLVM) | `clang -version` |
| CMake | `cmake -version` |
| Ninja | `ninja -version` |
| Python | `python3 -version` |

*Table 1.2: Commands to install the right tools*

If any of the commands from this table fails or if any of the versions do not meet the minimum requirements, you will have to install/update the related tools.

Assuming you are missing some of the tools, here are the steps to install them from the official websites. Feel free to use your own package manager if you do not want to do this manually.

In a nutshell, you need to do the following:

1. Go to the official website for the tool.
2. Go to the **Downloads** page.
3. Download the proper package for your OS.
4. Unpack/install the package to a location of your choice.

The official websites are as follows:

| Tool | Where to get it |
|------|-----------------|
| Git | `https://git-scm.com/downloads` or `https://git-scm.com`, and then click on **Downloads** |
| C/C++ toolchain (LLVM) | `https://releases.llvm.org` or `https://www.llvm.org`, and then click on **All Releases** |
| CMake | `https://cmake.org/download/` or `https://cmake.org/`, and then click on **Downloads** |

| Tool | Where to get it |
|------|------------------|
| Ninja | `https://github.com/ninja-build/ninja/releases` or `https://ninja-build.org`, and then click on **download the Ninja binary** |
| Python | `https://www.python.org/downloads/` or `https://www.python.org`, and then click on **Downloads** |

*Table 1.3: Websites where you can find the required tools*

Note that, on macOS, Git and Clang come with the Xcode CLI package. To install them on this OS, please run the following command:

```
$ xcode-select --install
```

> 💡 **Quick tip**: Enhance your coding experience with the **AI Code Explainer** and **Quick Copy** features. Open this book in the next-gen Packt Reader. Click the **Copy** button (**1**) to quickly copy code into your coding environment, or click the **Explain** button (**2**) to get the AI assistant to explain a block of code to you.
>
> ```
>                                                              Copy        Explain
> function calculate(a, b) {
>   return {sum: a + b};                                        1            2
> };
> ```
>
> 🔒 **The next-gen Packt Reader** is included for free with the purchase of this book. Unlock it by scanning the QR code below or visiting `https://www.packtpub.com/unlock/9781837637782`.
>
>

To make things easier, you will find a script that can help you set up the environment for macOS in the `ch1` directory of the Git repository of this book.

If you do not have Git, you can get this script with the following command:

```
$ curl --location https://raw.githubusercontent.com/PacktPublishing/LLVM-Code-
Generation/main/ch1/setup_env.sh --output setup_env.sh
```

If you have Git, simply run the following command:

```
$ git clone https://github.com/PacktPublishing/LLVM-Code-Generation.git
$ cd LLVM-Code-Generation/ch1
```

After you get the script one way or another, run the following command:

```
$ bash setup_env.sh ${INSTALL_PREFIX}
```

`INSTALL_PREFIX` is the path where you want the tools to be installed.

At this point, you know how to identify the required version of the tools to build LLVM. You also acquired a basic understanding of how these tools interact with each other during the build process.

From this point forward, we will assume that you have all the necessary tools available at one of the directories recorded in the `PATH` environment variable. In other words, you can use these tools without having to explicitly set their path on the command line.

Now that we have taken care of the setup of the environment, we can start playing with LLVM.

# Building a compiler

In this section, we will introduce the different parts of what makes a compiler and how they relate to the LLVM code base. In the process, you will do the following:

- Understand the overall architecture of a compiler
- Learn how to build Clang from the source
- Be able to decide which components of LLVM you need to build

If you are already familiar with the components of a compiler toolchain and want to jump straight into the action, skip directly to the *Building LLVM* section.

## What is a compiler?

The definition of a compiler means different things for different people. For instance, for a student in their first year of computer science, a compiler may be seen as a tool that translates a source language into executable code. This is a possible definition, but it is also a very coarse-grain one.

When you look closer at a **compiler**, you will find that it is a collection of different tools, or libraries, working together to achieve this translation. That's why we talk about a **compiler toolchain**.

To go back to the previous coarse-grain definition, a compiler, such as Clang, is a compiler **driver**: it invokes the different tools in the right order and pulls the related dependencies from the standard library to produce the final executable code.

The LLVM code base reflects the composability of these tools. It is organized as a set of libraries that you can use to build a variety of tools and, in particular, a compiler toolchain.

To get a better understanding of which tools are right to build for your particular project, let us see which components are involved with a concrete example: **Clang**.

# Opening Clang's hood

To build an executable from a C file, Clang, a C/C++ compiler built on top of LLVM, orchestrates three different components: the frontend, the backend, and the linker. Additionally, Clang has to pull in dependencies that are expected by the system/language, such as the standard library, so that the following happens:

- The frontend has access to the standard headers, for instance, what the prototype of the `printf` function is.
- The linker has access to the standard implementations, for instance, the actual implementation of `printf`.

The following picture gives a high-level view of the different parts of a compiler and the different LLVM projects involved in building such a compiler.

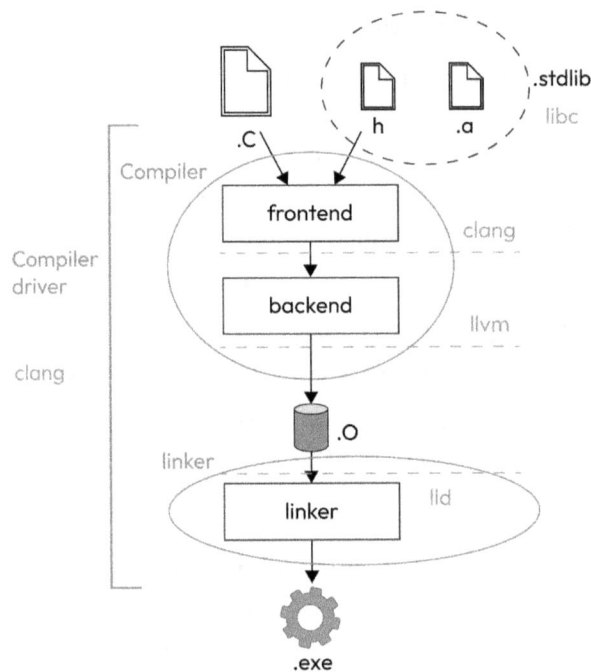

*Figure 1.2: The different components of a compiler*

When building a C file, Clang acts as a driver for a series of tools. It invokes the frontend (Clang project in LLVM), then passes down the result to the backend (LLVM project) that produces an object file that gets linked with the standard library (the `libc` project in LLVM) by the linker (the `lld` project in LLVM).

The takeaway is building Clang alone will not be enough to have a properly functioning compiler. To get there, you will need to build at least the linker and the standard library, which come respectively under the lld and the libc/libcxx projects in LLVM. Otherwise, your compiler toolchain will have to rely on what the host provides.

> **Note**
>
> You may have noticed that we did not mention the frontend and backend in this list. This is because, when building the Clang project, these are always included.

In any case, the focus of this book is LLVM backends, so, why are we spending so much time on Clang?

The reason is simple: Clang offers a familiar way to interact with LLVM constructs. By using the Clang frontend, you will be able to generate the LLVM **intermediate representation** (**IR**) by simply writing C/C++. We believe this is a gentler way to start your journey with LLVM backends.

As we progress through the book, we will have fewer and fewer C/C++ inputs and more and more LLVM IR ones.

## Building Clang

As already mentioned, here, we are only interested in Clang's frontend capabilities. As such, the following instructions focus only on building this part of LLVM. You will learn more about the possible customizations of the build system in the *Building LLVM* section.

Assuming LLVM_SRC is the path where you want to have the LLVM source code and CLANG_BUILD is the path where you want the build of Clang to happen, please run the following:

```
$ git clone https://github.com/llvm/llvm-project.git \
    ${LLVM_SRC}
$ mkdir -p ${CLANG_BUILD}
$ cd ${CLANG_BUILD}
$ cmake -DLLVM_ENABLE_PROJECTS=clang -GNinja -DCMAKE_BUILD_TYPE=Release ${LLVM_SRC}/llvm
$ ninja clang
```

This will check out the LLVM sources from GitHub, create a build directory, move there, configure the build system for building clang with Ninja, and finally, build Clang.

If you run into any issues, make sure you have all the required tools in PATH (see the *Installing the Right Tools* section).

When the build finishes, you should have a shiny new clang executable at ${CLANG_BUILD}/bin.

# Experimenting with Clang

If you ever look deeper into Clang, you will find out that it is composed of many more phases than the frontend, backend, and linker. By playing with Clang's command-line options, you can expose the intermediate results of some of these phases.

Here is the list of these phases:

1. **Frontend**: This validates that the input file is syntactically and semantically correct and produces the LLVM IR.

   - **Preprocessor**: This expands macros (e.g., #include).
   - **Sema**: This validates the syntax and semantics of the program.
   - **Codegen**: This produces the LLVM IR.

2. **Backend**: This translates the LLVM IR to target specific instructions.

   - **Middle-end optimizations**: LLVM IR to LLVM IR optimizations.
   - **Assembly generation**: Target-specific IR to assembly code.

3. **Assembler**: This translates assembly code to an object file.

Here are the options to inspect their results:

| To stop | Command |
|---|---|
| After the preprocessor | `clang -E` |
| After syntax checking | `clang -fsyntax-only` |
| After LLVM IR code generation | `clang -O0 -emit-llvm -S` |
| After the middle-end optimizations<br>(pick the level you want) | `clang -O<1\|2\|3\|s\|z> -emit-llvm -S` |
| After assembly generation<br>(i.e., see the textual representation of the assembly) | `clang -S` |
| After the assembler<br>(i.e., see the object file representation) | `clang -c` |

*Table 1.4: Checking the results after each phase*

Note

For the commands using -emit-llvm, you can use -c instead of -S if you want to see the binary representation of the LLVM IR, called **bitcode**, instead of its textual form.

LLVM also offers different tools to reproduce these steps. These tools have different purposes and levels of control, and we will explore them in due time.

Now, you know which components are involved in a compiler toolchain and which part of the LLVM infrastructure covers which component. You scratched the surface of the LLVM build system by building Clang and, in the process, gained a valuable tool to play with the different compilation stages.

Next, let us dive deeper into the LLVM build system by learning how to build the core of components.

# Building LLVM

This is where your journey as a backend developer starts: you will learn how to build the core LLVM project.

Instead of just dropping a bunch of commands for you to run (we will do some of that too, we promise), you will discover the most relevant knobs that you can use to tailor the build process to your needs.

We believe this is important knowledge to gain as it will help you optimize your development process and increase your productivity by focusing on what you need to build/run for your use cases.

To set the context, the core LLVM project contains all the necessary pieces to build an optimizing backend from LLVM IR down to assembly code/an object file for 20+ different architectures. This is a lot of code and chances are that you do not care about all these architectures. Therefore, at the very least, learning how to build only the ones you care about will save you compile time and down the road will improve your development speed.

## Configuring the build system

LLVM's official build system is CMake, and everything you know about CMake applies here. If you do not know about CMake, do not worry, we will cover enough to get you going.

CMake comes with some built-in variables that can be used to customize some key aspects of the build process. You will recognize these because their name starts with CMAKE_. We will not go over all of them but instead mention the most useful ones in this context. You can learn more about their meaning or discover new ones by looking directly at the CMake documentation (https://cmake.org/documentation/).

CMake also supports command-line options, but for all intent and purposes, we will mention only three here:

- -D<var>=<value>: This defines the value of a CMake variable.
- -G<generatorName>: This generates a build system for the specified generator.
- -C<pathToCacheFile>: This preloads a cache file; cache files are useful for sharing specific configurations and avoiding setting all the variables manually. In a nutshell, this is useful to pre-set some CMake variables.

With this knowledge, here is one of the simplest commands you can run from your build directory to configure the LLVM's build system:

```
$ cmake -GNinja -DCMAKE_BUILD_TYPE=Debug ${LLVM_SRC}/llvm
```

Your system is now ready for development, albeit things are going to be slow:

1.  All the ~20 non-experimental backends will be built.
2.  Everything that is built will use the Debug configuration, meaning that the experience is centered around smooth debugging sessions.

Regarding *Step 2*, building for Debug, it may be exactly what you want while you develop the compiler, but this is not something you want the end users to experience!

Here is a list of knobs, all CMake variables, that you should use to speed things up:

| Variable | Value | Meaning |
| --- | --- | --- |
| **Standard options** | | |
| CMAKE_BUILD_TYPE | Debug | Build for a smooth debug experience: Assertions: Enabled Optimizations: Disabled Debug info: Enabled Produces a large and slow compiler. |
| | Release | Build an optimized compiler: Assertions: Disabled Optimizations: Enabled Debug info: Disabled Produces a smaller and faster compiler. |
| CMAKE_C_COMPILER | <path> | Specify the path to the C compiler. This is particularly useful when bootstrapping or cross-compiling the compiler. We will not cover these topics, but at least you know where to look if you are interested in this. |
| CMAKE_CXX_COMPILER | <path> | Specify the path to the C++ compiler. |
| CMAKE_INSTALL_PREFIX | <path> | Specify where to install the final artifacts. |

| Variable | Value | Meaning |
|---|---|---|
| **Faster build time** | | |
| `LLVM_TARGETS_TO_BUILD` | `Target1;...` | Specify the list of backends to build (semicolon separated).<br><br>`Target1`, and so on, must match the directory name of one of the backends in `${LLVM_SRC}/llvm/lib/Target`.<br><br>Default to the `all` special value, which builds all the ~20 non-experimental LLVM backends. |
| `LLVM_OPTIMIZED_TABLEGEN` | `BOOL` | Specify whether or not to build TableGen in optimized mode.<br><br>We will cover TableGen in more detail in the dedicated chapter but the gist of it is unless you are developing a TableGen backend, you will likely want to set this variable to speed up your build. |
| **Notably useful** | | |
| `BUILD_SHARED_LIBS` | `BOOL` | Build libraries as shared libraries.<br><br>This avoids the link steps for the different executables, but this means they are not self-contained anymore and you have to "ship" the shared libraries alongside them. For local development, this may be worth it, although the debug experience may not be that great. |
| `LLVM_ENABLE_ASSERTIONS` | `BOOL` | Enable or disable assertions.<br><br>Using this option, you can for instance enable the assertions in a release build, which can be useful to diagnose some issues while not paying the price of a full debug build. |
| `LLVM_ENABLE_PROJECTS` | `Project1;...` | Build `Project1`, and so on, on top of the LLVM core.<br><br>The project names must match the directory names at the root of `${LLVM_SRC}` (e.g., `clang;mlir` will build both Clang and MLIR with the rest of LLVM). |

*Table 1.5: CMake Variables and what they mean*

With all these knobs available to you, here is our recommendation for a faster build time that still features a debugger-friendly compiler:

```
$ cmake -GNinja -DCMAKE_BUILD_TYPE=Debug -DLLVM_TARGETS_TO_BUILD="X86;AArch64"
-DLLVM_OPTIMIZED_TABLEGEN=1 ${LLVM_SRC}/llvm
```

To break the command down, we are building the core LLVM project in the Debug mode with just the X86 and AArch64 backends and with the TableGen tool being optimized.

Make sure to adapt the backends-to-build to your needs.

Note that if you want more information on the available options, you can run the following command:

```
$ cmake -LH ${LLVM_SRC}/llvm
```

The L option lists the available variables, and the H option prints the help information for each of them. You can also add the A option if you want to see all the advanced variables as well. Be aware that it prints a lot of text!

> **Note**
>
> At one point, you may have several build directories around. If you don't remember which is which, you can open the CMakeCache.txt file in the root of the related directory to check how the variables were set.

Now that your build directory is properly configured, we are almost ready to trigger a build, but we are missing a primer on Ninja, which can help you speed up your development cycle even more.

## Crash course on Ninja

**Ninja** is a tool that drives a build system. It makes sure that artifacts are built following the order of the dependencies described in this build system.

> **Note**
>
> You will have a crash course on how to describe these dependencies with CMake when you get to the point of adding your code to LLVM.

Back to Ninja, its usage is as follows:

```
$ ninja [options] [buildTarget1] [buildTarget2] ...
```

buildTargetX represents the names of the artifacts described in the build system. In that context, an artifact is often a file, but it can also be just a name that is tied to specific actions. The point is that by knowing the available targets, you can focus your development time on what you care about.

Consider the build dependencies described in *Figure 1.3*:

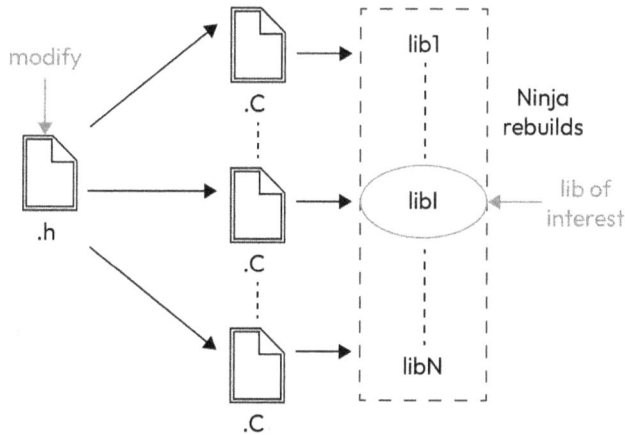

*Figure 1.3: Build dependencies in action*

Modifying a header used by several files in different libraries will trigger a rebuild of all the libraries. If you care only about specific libraries, to speed up your build time, consider using the specific build targets of these libraries.

In this example, you are modifying a header file that is referenced by several libraries, but you only care about one of them for now.

Ninja will rebuild all the libraries that reference this header file in their dependencies. You may not want your computer to waste time rebuilding libraries that you do not care about at this point. After all, you would be wasting some of your time if you were to do that. Instead, you can tell Ninja to only build the library you care about by specifying its build target on the command line.

To get a list of all the available build targets in a previously configured build directory, you can use the special help target:

```
$ ninja help
```

> **Note**
>
> Ninja also has a help option. The help option starts with a dash (-), explains how to use Ninja, and lists the available options.

A couple of additional options that are worth mentioning are as follows:

- -v: This prints the executed commands.
- -j N: This runs the build command in parallel with a max of *N* parallel execution. It is useful to use, for instance, -j 1 with -v to get better visibility of what is happening when you try to reproduce something manually.

- -k N: This keeps running the build system until it hits *N* errors. This is useful with N == 0 (which means infinity in this case) to see how far your build can go and if you want to have a grasp of how many different errors you will have to fix.

> **Note**
>
> The tooling around build systems is large and we only scratched the surface here. For instance, **Ccache** (https://ccache.dev/) can improve the build time and is relatively easy to set up.

At this point, you are finally ready to build LLVM.

# Building the core LLVM project

In this section, you will learn the commands to build LLVM from the previously configured build directory.

First things first, the simplest way to build LLVM is to run:

```
$ ninja
```

This is it!

Yes, this is really it, but there are a couple of build targets that you may want to know, namely the following:

- opt: Build the driver for the LLVM IR to LLVM IR optimizations.
- llc: Build the driver for the LLVM IR to assembly/object file pipeline.
- llvm-mc: Build the tool to play with the assembling/disassembling mechanism.
- check: Run all the core LLVM unit tests. This target will rebuild automatically all the tools that are involved in the unit tests, including the aforementioned targets.

The opt, llc, and llvm-mc targets produce binaries with the same name in ${BUILD_DIR}/bin. These are going to be the main tools that you will use for the rest of this book.

At this point, my recommendation is to make a habit of running the check target until you get accustomed to the various parts of LLVM and make sure that it comes back clean, meaning that you do not get any unexpected failures.

A clean report should look like this:

```
$ ninja check
Total Discovered Tests: 57407
  Skipped          :     45 (0.08%)
  Unsupported      : 21191 (36.91%)
  Passed           : 36111 (62.90%)
  Expectedly Failed:    60 (0.10%)
```

This quick introduction to testing ends this section, where you have learned about the following:

- How to control the build system via the main CMake variables to build exactly what you need?
- How to interact with Ninja, the driver of the build system, to cut down on your build time, print the executed command, or discover the relevant build targets?
- How to build the core LLVM project and produce your first LLVM artifacts?

In the next section, we deepen the topic of compiler testing that we just barely touched on here.

# Testing a compiler

In the previous section, you have learned how to run the core LLVM unit tests, but this is only the beginning of the story. There are two big missing pieces:

- How do you understand and reproduce a failing unit test?
- How do you go beyond unit testing?

Let us answer these questions in the following sections. However, first, we need a primer on some of the tools/infrastructure used for testing in LLVM.

## Crash course on the Google test infrastructure

LLVM uses the **Google test infrastructure (gtest)** for some of its unit tests.

The tests based on gtest are regular C++ codes and produce regular executables. If you open one of the source files of the tests using this framework, you will find gtest-specific directives (e.g., EXPECT_EQ, TEST, etc.) but nothing complicated beyond that.

Running the related executable will directly reproduce whatever issue you may want to investigate and all the techniques you know for debugging C++ code apply.

You can find more information on gtest at https://google.github.io/googletest/.

## Crash course on the LLVM Integrated Tester

The **LLVM Integrated Tester** (lit) drives a lot of the LLVM testing infrastructure.

In a nutshell, this tester does the following:

- Discovers the tests to be run
- Runs them concurrently
- Prints a summary of failure/success at the end

You have already seen lit in action when you ran ninja check.

In this section, we will focus on how you can describe what a test does and the capabilities of the lit driver for running tests. Later in this book, when learning how to add tests, you will learn, superficially, how lit picks up new tests.

If you want to dig into lit right now, feel free to use the online documentation at https://llvm.org/docs/CommandGuide/lit.html.

Note that if you ever build a compiler-like project, consider using lit to drive your testing infrastructure. This is a great tool and will save you a bunch of time instead of reinventing the wheel.

## Testing in lit

Let us assume that lit recognized that a file is a test. Again, we will not describe how lit does this.

lit will scan this file for directives from the comments for this type of file, meaning that lit adapts to the input file to derive what needs to be done.

For instance, if the test file is an LLVM IR file (identified by its .ll extension), lit searches the directives in the lines that start with ;, similarly, for a **Multi-Level Intermediate Representation** (MLIR) file (identified by its .mlir extension), it will look at the lines that start with //.

Using these directives, lit determines the following:

1. **Requirements**: Does this test need to be run?
2. **Command**: How is this test run?
3. **Status**: At the end of the run, is this result a pass or a failure?

The test file itself can also be the input of the run commands of that test file. This is not strictly required but is the most common, if not the only, pattern that you will see in the LLVM unit tests.

## Directives

Here are the directives that are used the most within the LLVM project:

| Directive | Meaning |
| --- | --- |
| RUN: <command> | Describe how to run this test. |
| | You can put as many RUN directives as you want. lit will run them in order. |
| | A test is successful when all the RUN lines are. The testing will stop on the first one that fails. A run line fails when it returns non-zero (i.e., bash style). |
| | For the command lines themselves, lit offers some substitution capabilities that we cover later. |
| REQUIRES: <config> | Only run this test if the following requirement is fulfilled. |
| | For instance, using arm-registered-target as config will execute the RUN commands of this test only if the backend in the llvm/lib/Target/ARM directory has been built. |

| Directive | Meaning |
|---|---|
| `XFAIL: <config>` | This means that the RUN commands of this test are expected to fail for this config. This will be reported as expected failures in the final report. Note that if the RUN commands work for this test, it will be an unexpected success. |

*Table 1.6: Commonly used directives*

Regarding the available configurations for `<config>`, this depends on how the internals of lit are initialized. If you are curious, you can look, for instance, at how `config.available_features` is initialized in `${LLVM_SRC}/ llvm/test/lit.cfg.py`. For now, just look at how the existing tests set that directive and replicate what you see and need.

Plumbing new configuration is not particularly difficult, but also not particularly interesting, especially without a motivating example. For instance, the solution will look different if you need to plumb that through CMake, or if it is something you want/can do in Python or any other programming language.

## Describing the RUN command

As already stated, it is common for the test file to also be the input of its RUN line. Similarly, sometimes it is useful to be able to create a temporary file while running a test. If you want to support such features while allowing tests to run concurrently and from any path, as a build directory can be instantiated anywhere, it gets tricky quickly.

Fortunately, lit comes with such capabilities out of the box. lit exposes special sequences of characters, called **macros**, which are substituted by the proper string when the test gets to run.

Here are some of the most common substitutions in LLVM:

| Macro | Substitution |
|---|---|
| `%s` | Source file: The path to the current file |
| `%S` | Source directory: The parent directory of the current file |
| `%t` | Temporary file: The path to a unique temporary file |

*Table 1.7: Common substitutions*

Consider a test file named `myFile.ll` with a RUN directive of the form:

```
; RUN: echo %s %t
```

When lit consumes `myFile.ll`, it will spawn an environment that will execute this command and print the following:

```
<fullPathTo>/myFile.ll <fullPathToTemporaryCreated>/myFile.ll.tmp
```

However, note that this command will only work if echo is in your path. So, what happens if you want to test something that you are building as part of your build process? lit allows you to specify your own substitutions. If you are testing the tools already built by LLVM, lit is already properly configured to handle all that. If you are building a new tool, you may want to add your own custom substitutions. For that, look at how config.substitutions is initialized in ${LLVM_SRC}/ llvm/test/lit.cfg.py.

## The lit driver – llvm-lit

When building LLVM, you also build the lit driver, llvm-lit, as part of the default build target or the check target.

This executable is what drives the execution of most of the tests in LLVM and by using it directly, you can selectively rerun the tests.

For instance, let us say you want to run only the GlobalISel tests of the AArch64 backend. You can do this by launching the following command from your build directory:

```
$ ./bin/llvm-lit test/CodeGen/AArch64/GlobalISel/
```

This should print all the tests that are executed as well as their status as lit makes progress through them:

```
-- Testing: 610 tests, 4 workers --
PASS: LLVM :: CodeGen/AArch64/GlobalISel/fold-global-offsets-target-features.mir
(1 of 610)
PASS: LLVM :: CodeGen/AArch64/GlobalISel/gisel-commandline-option.ll (2 of 610)
PASS: LLVM :: CodeGen/AArch64/GlobalISel/arm64-pcsections.ll (3 of 610)
[...]
```

As you can see, this prints a lot of information, and you may not care about these details. Hence, you will want to use the -s option.

More generally, here are a few useful options:

| Option | Effect |
|--------|--------|
| -s | Silent: Only print a progress bar and the final report |
| -v | Verbose: Print the RUN lines and the output of a test on failure |
| -a | Print all: Same as verbose but for all tests, not just the failing ones |

*Table 1.8: Some useful options and their effect*

When using lit directly, you may want to make a habit of using the following command:

```
$ ./bin/llvm-lit -sv <tests>
```

This will give you a concise report while producing all the commands required to reproduce the tests that failed.

# Crash course on FileCheck

FileCheck is the last piece of infrastructure you need to learn before being able to confidently approach the LLVM tests.

FileCheck is a tool that reads a file that describes patterns. This file is called check-file and checks that these patterns happen on an input file (by default, the standard input). If all the patterns are matched, it returns success (0); if not, it returns failure (non-zero) and prints where the match failed.

Like lit, FileCheck's patterns are described through directives that live in the comment of check-file. These directives start with a customizable prefix, which is CHECK by default, and can be enhanced with special semantics using a dash (-) followed by a keyword (e.g., CHECK-NEXT).

FileCheck is a powerful tool and can be overwhelming at first. To make it more approachable, we prepared some examples for you to look at in ch1/FileCheckExamples of the repository of this book. In any case, we strongly recommend reading the full documentation eventually, which is available at https://llvm.org/docs/CommandGuide/FileCheck.html.

Here are a handful of directives to get you started:

| Directive | Meaning |
|---|---|
| CHECK: <pattern> | Match <pattern>. |
| CHECK-NEXT: <pattern> | Match <pattern> on exactly the next line of the previously matched pattern. |
| CHECK-SAME: <pattern> | Match <pattern> on the same line as the previously matched pattern. |
| CHECK-NOT: <pattern> | Fail if <pattern> is matched. The pattern is not looked for as soon as the next CHECK directive is matched. |
| CHECK-LABEL: <pattern> | Sort of a <pattern> anchor used to structure the matches in a file. Note that FileCheck assumes that this pattern appears only once in the input file. If that is not the case, you may anchor yourself in an unpredictable location. |
| CHECK-DAG: <pattern> | All patterns matched with continuous DAG directives can be matched in any order. This is useful for producing patterns that are resilient on output reordering. |
| CHECK-COUNT-<Num>: <pattern> | Succeed if <pattern> is matched <Num> times. |

*Table 1.9: Important directives*

In all cases, `<pattern>` can be the following:

- **Straight text:** An exact match is expected, albeit `FileCheck` ignores space differences (i.e., all spaces are collapsed into just one).
- **Regular expression (regex):** Regex can be used but needs to be specified within the following markers: `{{` and `}}`. For instance, `{{[0-9]+}}` matches any number.
- **Variable:** A match can be stored in a variable. The syntax to define a variable is `[[VAR:<pattern>]]` and to use a variable is `[[VAR]]`. A variable cannot be used before it is defined. You can define and use a variable on the same line. When using regex in the definition of variables, you do not need to use the `{{` and `}}` markers. For instance, `[[VAR:[0-9]+]]` will match a number in `[[VAR]]`.
- A mix of all of the above.

Remember, the `CHECK` prefix is also customizable, and you can also use several prefixes within the same `FileCheck` invocation. The prefixes are specified with the `--check-prefixes=<pref1>,<pref2>,...` option.

## FileCheck by example

To make things more concrete, this section expands on one of the examples provided in the repository of this book. The example is located in `ch1/FileCheckExamples/ex3`.

At this point, the `FileCheck` executable should already be available in the `bin` directory of your build directory. If this is not the case, you can also build it directly using `ninja FileCheck`. In any case, make sure `FileCheck` is in your `PATH` if you want to use the `run.sh` script available for this example.

This example uses a simple `FileCheck` invocation:

```
$ FileCheck --input-file input.txt check-file.txt
```

The content of `input.txt` and `check-file.txt` are respectively:

| input.txt | check-file.txt |
|---|---|
| I feel<br><br>great<br>today<br><br>How about    you?<br>This line doesn't matter<br>as well as this one<br>I don't know<br><br>Meh<br><br>The       end<br><br>or is it? | CHECK: I<br>CHECK-SAME: feel<br>CHECK: great<br>CHECK-NEXT: today<br>CHECK:    How about you?<br>CHECK-DAG: Meh<br>CHECK-DAG: I don<br><br>CHECK-NOT: or is it<br>CHECK: The end<br>CHECK: or is it |

The input is only plain text. Notice how we purposely put random spaces everywhere, including empty lines, both in the input file and the check file. The point is that they do not matter unless you use SAME or NEXT.

For instance, notice how the first line of the input, I feel, is matched through two different directives CHECK: I and CHECK-SAME: feel. Since we used SAME here, we expect feel and I to be on the same line. You can try to replace CHECK-SAME with just CHECK and see how it affects the matching (or not), then move the feel word onto a different line and repeat your experience.

Similarly, look at the CHECK-NEXT: today directive. This will succeed only if today is exactly on the next line. Try to add more line spacing or put today on the same line as great.

Next, the CHECK: How about you? directive demonstrates that the spacing does not matter one way or the other:

- The related input line has more spaces between about and you than what is matched
- The related match line has more spaces before How than the related input line

Before looking at the DAG directives, notice how the This line doesn't matter and as well as this one lines are completely ignored. Anything that is not matched is implicitly ignored. So, if there is something you explicitly do not want to see in the output, make sure to use the CHECK-NOT directive.

Then, comes the DAG directive. This one is interesting for producing robust tests when the output is somewhat brittle but consistent. For instance, if you want to match the output of different threads and you know what each thread will produce, but you cannot predict in which order their output will be serialized, the DAG directives may be the solution.

The way it works is as follows:

- All the continuous DAG directives form a block. The continuity is obtained by writing DAG directives one after the other, with non-directive lines between them. As soon as you use a non-DAG directive, the block ends. Then, the next DAG directive will be part of a new block.
- The block is matched in every order (it is not as brute force as this, but this is the idea).
- FileCheck variables defined/used in this block form data dependencies that are honored. This means that even if you define and use a FileCheck variable within the same DAG block, you will not run into problems where your variable is used before being defined. However, be aware that to honor this dependency, FileCheck might find the beginning of the sequence you are looking for in a completely different place.

Back to the block of DAG directives of this example. Notice how the block states Meh first then I don, whereas the input file has these patterns in the reverse order. Thanks to the DAG directive, the order does not matter. Also, notice how I don still matches with I don't know. This is a feature in FileCheck: the matching happens on the substring.

Try it for yourself: replace I don by I do and notice how the test still passes.

The bottom line is be careful when you write your CHECK patterns or your tests may pass on inputs that you would have liked to reject.

Finally, here comes the CHECK-NOT: or is it directive. It makes sure that this particular line does not occur between the previous match (the DAG block in this case) and the next match (CHECK: The end). After the next match, it is completely okay to have the pattern occur and, indeed, you can see it in the input file after The end. Try to move the CHECK-NOT directive after CHECK for The end and remove the final CHECK: or is it line and see what happens.

At this point, you know all the different tools and frameworks involved in the testing of LLVM. Let us see how they articulate together to test the compiler.

## LLVM unit tests

LLVM unit tests are primarily focused on testing small parts of the compiler, such as a specific optimization or the specific behavior of a class.

There are two kinds of unit tests in LLVM that are logically separated into two different folders of your build directory:

- unittests: This contains the tests that are directly generated from the related directory of the LLVM source (${LLVM_SRC}/llvm/unittests). These tests are written using gtest.
- test: This contains the output scripts used by lit. The actual tests live in the related directory of the LLVM source (${LLVM_SRC}/llvm/test).

When you execute ninja check, you effectively run all the unit tests.

> **Note**
>
> If you built another project, you could use the check-<project> build target to run the unit tests of that project. For instance, use check-clang and check-mlir if you have built Clang and MLIR, respectively. You can also run the unit tests of all the built projects with check-all.

So, now, what should you do if some of them are failing?

First, if you have zero local changes, do the following:

- Check whether your build is configured correctly. For instance, if you did not enable the backend of your current computer, some tests may fail because they have nothing to run against. When this happens, this is admittedly a bug in the build configuration of LLVM, but some of these bugs may still exist.
- If you are building LLVM top-of-tree (as opposed to a release of LLVM), check whether LLVM itself is broken by looking at the status of the buildbots (from https://llvm.org, click on **Buildbot** and/or **Green Dragon**). Look for a configuration close to what you have and check if this one is green (passes) or red (fails). If it fails, that means that the issue will likely be fixed soon, otherwise, this is likely an issue with your local setting, or you might have uncovered a bug. In any case, follow up with the community (see *Chapter 2* for that) to see what is going on and/or report the issue.

Second, if you do have local changes: At this point, this means you want to reproduce the issue to be able to dig deeper. Let us see how to find the input of a test and run it manually.

## Finding the source of a test

Let us assume you ran the check build target, and you have a bunch of failing tests. At the end of the entire run of ninja check, you should see a report that looks like this:

```
Failed Tests (2):
  LLVM-Unit :: MI/./MITests/LiveVariablesTest/recomputeForSingleDefVirtReg_
handle_undef2
  LLVM :: CodeGen/AArch64/aarch-multipart.ll
```

The beginning of each line tells you which project fails. Here, it is LLVM, but it could be, for instance, Clang if you built and run Clang's unit tests.

Then, for unit tests that are written with gtest, you will see -Unit right after the project name. Test lines with no suffix are pure lit tests.

Therefore, in this example, the first failing test is written with gtest and the second with lit.

In any case, everything that is after :: identifies the specific test.

- For gtest, the name looks like <path>/<exeName>/<testSuiteName>/<testName>. Here, <path>, for LLVM, is relative to ${BUILD_DIR}/unittests. (For other projects, such as Clang or MLIR, <path> is relative to ${BUILD_DIR}/tools/<project>/unittests.) The source files of such tests are usually at ${LLVM_SRC}/llvm/unittests/<path>/.To identify which exact source file to look at, you need to search for the TEST macro that matches both <testSuiteName> and <testName>. Therefore, the failing test in this example is the executable located at ${BUILD_DIR}/unittests/ MI/MITests. That executable comes from the source files located in ${LLVM_SRC}/unittests/ MI, and the file that defines TEST(LiveVariablesTest, recomputeForSingleDefVirtReg_ handle_undef2) is LiveIntervalTest.cpp.
- For lit, the name is simply the path of the source file from the root of the related lit entry point. For LLVM, that entry point is ${LLVM_SRC}/llvm/test. (For other projects, this entry point is ${LLVM_SRC}/<project>/test.) So, in this example, the file that describes the test is located at ${LLVM_SRC}/llvm/test/ CodeGen/AArch64/aarch-multipart.ll.

At this point, we know which file to look at, so, let's see how we can run the related test manually.

## Running unit tests manually

As already mentioned in *Crash course on gtest*, running a gtest manually means simply invoking the related executable. Since you have learned how to find the source file of a test in the previous section, this means you are down to a regular C++ debugging session at this point.

Remember that to regenerate the executable for your unit test, it is sufficient to run the following:

```
$ ninja <executableName>
```

Now, let us focus on the lit tests. To rerun a particular lit test, you can run it from your build directory:

```
$ ./bin/llvm-lit -sv test/<testName>
```

Where <testName> is the relative path that was reported in the final report of ninja check.

Note that for other projects, such as Clang or MLIR, the lit entry point in the build directory is slightly different than the LLVM project. This difference is reflected in the command line that you need to use to rerun a specific test:

```
$ ./bin/llvm-lit -sv tools/<project>/test/<testName>
```

Notice how in the previous command, test/<testName> became tools/<project>/test/<testName> to account for this change in the entry point.

> **Note**
>
> When you use llvm-lit like this, <testName> can also be a directory name. When this is the case, all the tests in this directory and recursively in the child directories of this directory are run.

Until this test is fixed, this should produce an output with lines starting with RUN. These lines are what you need to run to reproduce the issue manually. At this point, you can use whatever is appropriate to debug and fix the issue.

Here is an example of such output:

```
FAIL: LLVM :: CodeGen/AArch64/aarch-multipart.ll (1 of 1)
******************** TEST 'LLVM :: CodeGen/AArch64/aarch-multipart.ll' FAILED
********************
Exit Code: 2

Command Output (stderr):
--
RUN: at line 1: ${BUILD_DIR}/bin/llc < ${LLVM_SRC}/llvm/test/CodeGen/AArch64/
aarch-multipart.ll -o - | ${BUILD_DIR}/bin/FileCheck ${LLVM_SRC}/llvm/test/
CodeGen/AArch64/aarch-multipart.ll
[...]
```

So, to reproduce the issue you would need to run the following:

```
$ ${BUILD_DIR}/bin/llc < ${LLVM_SRC}/llvm/test/CodeGen/AArch64/aarch-multipart.
ll -o - | ${BUILD_DIR}/bin/FileCheck ${LLVM_SRC}/llvm/test/CodeGen/AArch64/
aarch-multipart.ll
```

Depending on what is wrong in this case, you would need to do either of the following:

- Fix something in `llc`
- Fix the IR in the input file (`${LLVM_SRC}/llvm/test/CodeGen/AArch64/aarch-multipart.ll`)
- Fix the patterns checked by `FileCheck` in the input file
- A combination of all of the preceding

Also, remember that some tests have more than one `RUN` line. Therefore, make sure to run all the lines to find the one that does not work before going too deep in debugging.

As soon as you fix your issue, the `lit` command should not print the `RUN` lines anymore. Instead, it should come with a clean output similar to the following output:

```
  Passed: 1 (100.00%)
```

As briefly mentioned in *Crash course on FileCheck*, remember that you can still use the a option to print the `RUN` lines of a passing test. For instance, with our running example, this would look like this:

```
$ ./bin/llvm-lit -sav test/CodeGen/AArch64/aarch-multipart.ll
```

In any case, remember that most `lit` tests in LLVM use the same pattern where the test file is both the input file of the commands to run and `check-file` used by `FileCheck` to match the output of the run commands. Putting everything together, a typical `lit` test in LLVM can be summarized in *Figure 1.4*:

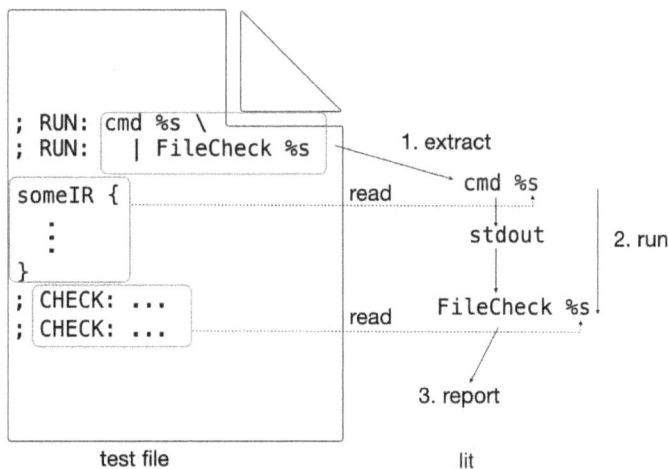

*Figure 1.4: A typical lit test in LLVM*

The test file describes the commands to run through the RUN directives. llvm-lit (1) extracts these commands, (2) runs them, and (3) produces a report. The run typically consists of executing some LLVM tools (e.g., llc, opt) and checking their output against some patterns described within the test file itself with FileCheck. In other words, a test file contains a) the commands to run; b) the input IR; and c) the patterns to match, as highlighted in the three blocks.

## The unit tests pass, what now?

The unit tests are only the bare minimum when it comes to compiler testing. At this point, what was tested is as follows:

- We tested that specific patterns are generated for specific inputs by specific optimizations/ backends
- We tested that certain classes behave a certain way for certain inputs

While this gives some initial confidence that the compiler is correct, this fundamentally lacks end-to-end testing with proper functional testing. Indeed, we have not run any of the code produced by the compiler so far.

Let us see how we can address that in the next section.

## LLVM functional tests

The wonderful thing about testing a compiler is that, for the most part, you do not have to write functional tests. Indeed, the rest of the world did it for you when they wrote correctness tests for their applications. As such, functionally testing a compiler means checking that an application is correct when compiled with your compiler.

With that in mind, you can start compiling any applications that are important for your use cases and check that they still pass their conformance tests.

This is a nice property, but it does not really help you to get started. Where would you look for relevant applications? How do you run them for correctness testing?

Fortunately, LLVM also features a test suite that can be used for correctness and performance testing.

> Note
>
> We will not go into details for performance testing as this is highly application- and backend-specific. Put differently, unlike correctness testing, a lot of applications do not come with well-established performance testing, or at least not one that makes sense for what you may want to measure when working on a backend compiler.

We will summarize how to use this test suite hereafter, but for the full documentation, please see https://llvm.org/docs/TestSuiteGuide.html. Specifically, this document also covers how to use the test suite for cross-compilation and remote execution (build on one machine, run on another).

## The LLVM test suite

The LLVM test suite is a set of standalone C/C++ applications, which means the following:

1. You need to be able to plug your backend from a C/C++ frontend such as Clang to be able to use it. With what you learned in *Configuring the build system*, this is no problem for you! (Spoiler: just add -DLLVM_ENABLE_PROJECTS="clang" to your CMake command.)

2. You must create a separate build directory and configure the build system with CMake for them.

First things first, to get the LLVM test suite, run the following:

```
$ git clone https://github.com/llvm/llvm-test-suite.git ${TESTSUITE_SRC}
```

Create a build directory:

```
$ mkdir -p ${TESTSUITE_BUILD_DIR}
$ cd ${TESTSUITE_BUILD_DIR}
```

Then, configure it:

```
$ cmake -GNinja -DCMAKE_C_COMPILER=${BUILD_DIR}/bin/clang ${TESTSUITE_DIR}
```

This will set up the test suite with your Clang compiler and the default compilation option. If you want to specify your own set of compiler flags, use the standard CMAKE_C_FLAGS and CMAKE_CXX_FLAGS CMake variables for that. Also, the test suite comes with several pre-configured sets of compilation options. You can use them by sourcing the relevant CMake cache like the following:

```
$ cmake -GNinja -DCMAKE_C_COMPILER=${BUILD_DIR}/bin/clang -C${TESTSUITE_DIR}/
cmake/caches/<specificOption>.cmake ${TESTSUITE_DIR}
```

For instance, here is the same command if you want to use -O3 as a compilation option:

```
$ cmake -GNinja -DCMAKE_C_COMPILER=${BUILD_DIR}/bin/clang -C${TESTSUITE_DIR}/
cmake/caches/O3.cmake ${TESTSUITE_DIR}
```

In any case, look at ${TESTSUITE_DIR}/cmake/cache/ to see what is available.

Next, you need to build the test suite:

```
$ ninja
```

In typical LLVM fashion, the LLVM test suite is also driven by lit. Therefore, to run it, from ${TESTSUITE_BUILD_DIR}, simply use this command:

```
$ ${BUILD_DIR}/bin/llvm-lit -sv .
```

If you want to run a specific (set of) tests, just provide the path to the test(s) you want to run. For instance, to run the MultiSource sqlite3 application and all of the SingleSource tests, run:

```
$ ${BUILD_DIR}/bin/llvm-lit -sv MultiSource/Applications/sqlite3 SingleSource
```

Of course, everything that you love about lit also applies to the test suite, so if you want to find the run command of a particular test, use the -a option.

## The functional tests fail – what do you do?

Quickly enough, you will have your first bug in the compiler. If you are lucky, the bug will fail the compilation. For instance, it will crash the compiler, and in this case, you are back to debugging a regular C++ application except the application is your compiler. If you are less fortunate, you may have to deal with a **miscompile**: the compilation process worked fine, but the application fails its correctness test.

When tracking down a miscompile, there are different things to consider:

- Do you know which compiler changes introduced the issue?
- Do you know which application changes introduced the issue?

Essentially, you need to establish a baseline and bisect the changes to minimize the difference in the final assembly code.

> **Note**
>
> When bringing up a new backend, you have zero baselines. This is why you must write comprehensive unit tests, otherwise, you may have to deal with many miscompiles and will have no idea where to start!

Now, let us say you have identified the compiler change, but you still do not know what causes the issue and the application still has too many differences in the final assembly.

At this point, you are in a relatively good position: you have a working and a non-working compiler. Assuming you are not building the application with link-time optimizations then, by design, all the produced compiler artifacts are interchangeable.

What this means is you can build your application twice: once with the working compiler and once with the failing compiler, and then you can mix and match the artifacts together. Now, you can just bisect the artifacts to find the one with a defect.

For instance, let us say that the application is made of five different object files put together. You can produce the final executable of the application by linking half of the object files from compiler A and the other half from compiler B. Then, you can test whether this application works:

- If not, then take more objects from compiler A than compiler B
- If yes, then take more objects from compiler B than compiler A

Rinse and repeat until adding any artifacts from the non-working compiler will produce an error.

At this point, you narrowed down the issue from the full application down to just one file. There are ways to further reduce the difference down, but this will require some modifications of the compiler. We will sketch this method in *Chapter 10*.

The following list summarizes what you need to do:

- **Try to pin down a compiler change**: The idea is to have one working and one non-working compiler. This could also be one set of options versus another set of options. The problem is if the sets are too different, even if you identify a culprit input file, the difference may still be too big to easily find the issue. Ideally, you would want an option that says, *enable suspected culprit change*.

- **Check which object files are different**: md5 is your friend but beware of the changes that come from having different source paths for instance. This can create artificial differences due to different debug information.

- Using a custom link command (or if you feel adventurous, by changing the build system of the application), assemble different executables while bisecting the set of object files that were different until you narrow down the issue to just one file.

- Look at the difference in that one file.

> Note
>
> If you know the culprit change, you can further reduce the difference by introducing a command-line option/environment variable to control how many times this change is applied. Then, you can bisect based on the number of times this change is applied. Be careful to have deterministic runs between different build invocations. For instance, you do not want to pair that with a multithreaded environment such as Ninja, but you may want to pair that with the single command line of your culprit file. If your environment has indeterminism, you may not be able to converge on something that makes sense.

Finally, remember that you have other tools to help you, such as the sanitizers for undefined behavior or invalid address accesses. We will talk about that in *Chapter 10*. Also, remember that it is possible that the application is broken, and your change merely just exposed the issue. Again, the sanitizer tools should help you triage any issue you encounter and in any case, when in doubt regarding the semantics of the inpout language refer back to the related standard specification!

At this point, you know how to build and test LLVM. You have a basic understanding of the tools and frameworks used during this process, namely gtest, lit, and FileCheck. You can confidently run the LLVM unit tests and know how to reproduce any issue that may arise with them. You also gained some insights on the steps you can take to narrow down compiler issues with larger tests or, more generally, when compiling big projects.

With all this knowledge, you must be eager to start contributing to the project. Before we cover this aspect, we will explain briefly how the LLVM directory structure works. This will help you shape your contributions in a way that matches the philosophy behind LLVM.

# Understanding the directory structure

In this section, you will learn the basics of how the LLVM folders are organized. This knowledge will come in handy when you start contributing to LLVM. This will help you shape patches that follow the philosophy behind the directory structure and hence, help you avoid unnecessary rounds of reviews where you would have to fix that.

## High-level directory structure

At a high level, the LLVM code base is organized into projects: Clang, MLIR, the **LLVM debugger** (**LLDB**), and many more. Each project has its own directory, and its name matches the name of the related project in lowercase: `clang`, `mlir`, `lldb`, and so on.

You need to use these directory names in the `LLVM_ENABLE_PROJECTS` CMake variable to build the related projects.

The common theme around these projects is that they use or contribute to a part of the LLVM infrastructure.

## Focusing on the core LLVM project

Unsurprisingly, the core LLVM project lives in the `llvm` directory.

The core of LLVM is primarily composed of several libraries and, although not immediately apparent, this is reflected in the directory tree.

First thing first, diving into the `llvm` folder, the main interesting pieces are as follows:

- `include`: The include files, also known as the public includes or public headers, that are exposed by the LLVM project
- `lib`: The different libraries
- `tools`: Developer-facing tools
- `unittests` and `test` are the tests for all the tools and libraries
- `utils`: Various utility tools such as `FileCheck` and `llvm-lit`

Now, if you list the content of the `lib` directory, you will see that this list is replicated almost one-to-one in the `include/llvm`, `unittests`, and `test` directories.

For instance, under `lib`, you will find an `Analysis` folder. Now, look under `include/llvm`, and you will find the same folder. Likewise, you will find an `Analysis` folder under `test` and `unittests`.

Again, this is not a one-to-one mapping, but this is the general idea of how it works. Therefore, if you create a new library under `lib`, you will want to do the following:

1. Put your public headers under `include/llvm/<yourLib>`.
2. Add your `lit` tests under `test/<yourLib>`.
3. Create your gtest tests under `unittests/<yourLib>`.

# A word on the include files

As already mentioned, for the LLVM project, public headers live in `<project>/include/<project>`, so naturally two questions come to mind:

1. Where do the private headers go? In other words, where can you declare the **application programming interfaces (APIs)** that you want to share within a component while not exposing it to the outside world?

2. Why is there a `<project>` directory under include? (E.g., llvm/include/llvm.)

Let us find out!

## Private headers

**Private headers** live in the related library directory.

For instance, look into llvm/lib/CodeGen. There, you will find header files, such as SplitKit.h, that are used exclusively within the CodeGen library.

Looking at the source code, you can easily identify which headers are private and which ones are public by looking at the include path:

- Public headers start with `<project>/<libname>/<filename>`
- Private headers are simply `<filename>`

## What is the deal with `<project>/include/<project>`?

Looking at the paths of the public headers, one could wonder why we repeat `<project>` twice.

While this observation is true, the reason for this is to make the attribution easier and avoid conflict when cross-referencing headers from different LLVM projects due to the way the include paths are configured in the whole LLVM code base.

The include paths start under the include directory of the related project. In other words, headers included from, for instance, LLVM and Clang are described relative to llvm/include and clang/include, respectively.

So, if Clang includes headers that come both from LLVM and Clang, as in clang/lib/CodeGen/CGBuiltin.cpp, this materializes with the following:

```
#include "clang/..."
#include "llvm/..."
```

Therefore, the source project is immediately obvious and naming conflicts are not possible (e.g., having Utils.h in both LLVM and Clang will result in different include paths in the source code).

# What is include/<project>-c?

A few LLVM projects have `include/<project>-c` directories. These folders contain the C API for the related projects and libraries.

This API is a wrapper around the related C++ implementations and provides an easier way to integrate LLVM projects by shielding external consumers from the ever-changing C++ API.

Although the C API may change, there is a strong push from the community to keep it stable as much as possible. Put differently, if there is a change in the C API, you can expect a heads-up in the release note and/or a schedule for deprecating the old one.

On the other hand, the C++ API can change at every commit, and it can be a daunting task to keep up with all the changes. The C API, however, is less feature-rich than the C++ API.

The key takeaways are as follows:

- Consider using the C API if you are an external user of LLVM
- Be prepared to maintain any new C API that you propose for a long time
- Expect pushbacks when suggesting changes to the C API

To learn more about the expectations around the C API, please read the online document at `https://llvm.org/docs/DeveloperPolicy.html#c-api-changes`.

# Overview of some of the LLVM components

Going through the whole LLVM code base and listing what lives where is not particularly interesting or useful. You will build this knowledge as you practice and you will learn about the important ones for building an LLVM backend through this book. Nevertheless, it can be interesting to know about a few main components, so that you can start looking at some code on your own and even contribute to code review!

## Generic LLVM goodness

LLVM provides a lot of carefully optimized data structures and utilities that can be reused as is.

You can find containers for link lists, maps, and so on, as well as portable implementations for arbitrary-sized integer types in `ADT`.

Similarly, you can find wrappers for string and file system manipulations, error handling, and so on in `Support`.

## Working with the LLVM IR

The LLVM IR is the archstone of the LLVM infrastructure. You will learn more about it in *Chapter 7*. For now, just remember that this is the main exchange format for everything built around LLVM. It lives in the `IR` directories (both `include/llvm/IR`, and `lib/IR`).

Optimizations transforming/analyzing the IR live in `Analysis` and `Transforms`. We will have a closer look at this in *Chapter 8*.

Handling of the binary and textual representation of the IR is done in `Bitcode`, `IRReader`, and `IRWriter`.

### Generic backend infrastructure

The backbone of the backend infrastructure lives in `CodeGen`.

You will find what is required to model registers, instructions, and functions and key optimizations such as instruction scheduling or register allocation.

### Target-specific constructs

Target-specific constructs, irrespective of whether they touch the LLVM IR or the lower part of the stack, live in the related `lib/Target/<backendName>` directory.

As we progress through the book, we will go into more detail about what lives in the different libraries and thus, what exactly you will find in a particular directory. For now, the goal is to grasp the split between what is exposed to the external world (public headers) and what is not and give you an idea of what you can find in the LLVM code base.

To wrap things up, in this section, you learned how the LLVM directory structure is organized, what lives where, and, in particular, where public and private headers are stored. By understanding these aspects, you will naturally comply with the expectations around the structure of your future contributions to the LLVM project and thus, speed up your ability to contribute to LLVM, which is conveniently the topic of our next chapter!

# Summary

In this chapter, you learned how to set up your development environment and how to find the required version of the different tools to build the different versions of the LLVM infrastructure, including the open-source repository. This is a necessary step to be able to get started with building the LLVM infrastructure.

Next, you discovered the main components that make a compiler toolchain, namely the driver, frontend, backend, linker, and standard library, and which LLVM project they map to. This information will come in handy when you decide what you want to build out of the LLVM infrastructure.

After that, you dove into the build configurations of the core LLVM project and learned how to tweak the CMake variables to tailor the build to your needs while balancing the debuggability of the produced artifacts and the build time. You also learned how to use Ninja, the driver of the build system, efficiently to reduce the turnaround time between development, building, and testing.

Following the trails of testing, you learned how to run, locate, and reproduce failures with `lit`, the LLVM integrated tester, and how the unit tests are articulated around a key tool called `FileCheck`. This knowledge is necessary to investigate the failures that will inevitably arise when developing your own compiler. Going beyond unit testing, you learned how to use the LLVM test suite and got a taste of how to tackle miscompiles in applications.

Next, you learned about the general structure of the LLVM directory tree. This knowledge will help you find the implementation of the different components, but, more importantly, it will give you a framework to shape the practical details of where your future open source contributions should live.

The next chapter will help you get started with your open-source contributions, but first, let us solidify your learning with a quiz!

# Quiz time

Now that you have completed reading this chapter, answer the following questions to test your knowledge:

1.  You have a pristine clone of the LLVM code base and yet the build fails with weird compiler errors. What could be the reason?

    The most likely reasons are as follows:

    *   The LLVM code base is temporarily broken.
    *   Check the build bots at `https://lab.llvm.org/buildbot/`.
    *   Your environment is not properly set up.
    *   Check that your tools meet the expected minimal requirements. See *Installing the right tools*.

2.  You have a C file, and you are curious about what the LLVM IR looks like without optimization. How can you print this IR using Clang?

    You can run the following:

    ```
    $ clang -S -O0 -emit-llvm myFile.c -o -
    ```

    See *Experimenting with Clang*.

3.  You want to build LLVM for just the AMDGPU and X86 backends. Which CMake variable should you set and how do you set it?

    You want to set the variable that controls the list of backends that are built: `LLVM_TARGETS_TO_BUILD`.

    On your CMake command, that means adding `-DLLVM_TARGETS_TO_BUILD="AMDGPU;X86"`.

    See *Configuring the build system*.

4.  Your build of LLVM is failing and you would like to prefetch all the compilation errors in one
    go instead of stopping on the first one. Which Ninja option can you use to do that?

    You can use the *keep running* option to do that:

    ```
    $ ninja -k 0 <yourBuildTarget>
    ```

    See *Crash course on Ninja*.

5.  Write a set of `FileCheck` directives to match the exact lines of `input.txt` while ignoring the
    ones starting with #.

    Note that the input file lives at `ch1/quiz/ex8-9` of the repository of this book:

    ```
    input.txt

    This is an example of match
    # Do not want to see that
    with FileCheck
    This line needs to happen exactly after "With FileCheck"

    # Neither this
    Over
    ```

    The set of `FileCheck` directives are as follows:

    ```
    check-file.txt

    CHECK: This is an example of match
    CHECK: with FileCheck
    CHECK-NEXT: This line needs to happen exactly after "With
    FileCheck"
    CHECK: Over
    ```

    Run the following:

    ```
    $ FileCheck --input-file input.txt check-file.txt
    ```

    See *Crash course on FileCheck*.

    Note that `check-file` lives at `ch1/quiz/ex8-9` of the repository of this book.

6. Write a set of `FileCheck` directives to match the exact lines of `input.txt` and reject the match if the text starting with # appears between the non-# lines.

   The set of `FileCheck` directives, after rejecting the match if the text starting with # appears between the non-# lines, are as follows:

   ---
   **check-file.txt**

   ---
   ```
   CHECK: This is an example of match
   SECOND-CHECK-NOT: Do not want to see that
   CHECK: with FileCheck
   CHECK-NEXT: This line needs to happen exactly after "With
   FileCheck"
   SECOND-CHECK-NOT: Neither this
   CHECK: Over
   ```
   ---

   Then, run the following:

   ```
   $ FileCheck --input-file input.txt check-file.txt --check-
   prefixes='CHECK,SECOND-CHECK'
   ```

   See *Crash course on FileCheck*.

   Note that this will fail since the faulty lines are in the input.

   You can run the test without the faulty lines by modifying `input.txt` or filtering out them directly on the command line:

   ```
   $ grep -v '^#' input.txt | FileCheck check-file.txt --check-
   prefixes='CHECK,SECOND-CHECK'
   ```

7. Let us say `ninja` check reports the following failing test: `LLVM :: Transforms/InstCombine/add.ll`. Where would you find the file that describes the test?

8. The test lives at `${LLVM_SRC}/test/Transforms/InstCombine/add.ll`. See *Finding the source of a test*.

9. Using the test from the previous question, how would you find the command to reproduce the failure?

   Simply run the `lit` driver with the `-a` option from your build directory:

   ```
   $ ./bin/llvm-lit -a test/Transforms/InstCombine/add.ll
   ```

   Then, look at the RUN lines in the output.

   See *Running unit tests manually*.

10. You have an application with 100+ C files that compiles fine with your compiler but fails its conformance tests when you enable your local changes. The differences in the final binary file are massive and span pretty much all the files. What steps could you take to narrow down the difference?

    In a nutshell, bisect the object files by tweaking the link command such that you combine a mix of the object files produced by both a compiler with your changes and a compiler without your changes. Do this until you narrow down the changes to just one object file. Then, bisect how many times your changes are applied to this one file until you cannot reduce the problem anymore. Finally, examine the remaining differences in the assembly file and try to understand what is wrong.

    See *The functional tests fail – what do you do?*

11. When would it be appropriate to use the LLVM C API?

    If you are using LLVM as a dependency for an external project. The stability provided by the C API makes the integration of LLVM easier. See *What are these include/<project>-c?.*

---

**Unlock this book's exclusive benefits now**

This book comes with additional benefits designed to elevate your learning experience.

*Note: Have your purchase invoice ready before you begin.*

https://www.packtpub.com/unlock/9781837637782

# 2

# Contributing to LLVM

After going through *Chapter 1*, you have enough knowledge to start contributing to LLVM. While this may surprise you, given you did not even write a single line of code, contributing to LLVM is more than sending patches.

Contributing to an open source project can take many forms. Here are a few examples that we will cover in this chapter:

- Reporting issues
- Engaging in conversations in the public forum
- Reviewing code
- Contributing patches

Before diving into the details, the idea is to get your feet wet and build your confidence to a point where you feel you can contribute patches.

The LLVM community is supportive and welcoming, and you will not be alone on this journey.

To stay this great, the LLVM community abides by a strict code of conduct that you can find on the official website (https://llvm.org/docs/CodeOfConduct.html). We strongly recommend you read it and make sure to follow it whenever you engage with the community. The code of conduct is straightforward and should not surprise you. The gist of it is to apply common sense and be polite in your interactions. In any case, go read it; there is important information in there.

Let us see how you can do your first of a long series of contributions!

## Reporting an issue

LLVM is software and even compilers are not exempt from bugs.

One of the ways you can start contributing to the LLVM project is by reporting issues.

For example, if you find a crash in Clang, it will instruct you how to report this issue and provide you with a reproducer.

If you find an issue in any component while using it, the issue potentially being as simple as missing or incorrect documentation, file an issue (or fix it directly!) in the GitHub tracker at `https://github.com/llvm/llvm-project/issues`.

In any case, make sure your report is actionable in the following ways:

- Include the configuration:
    - The version of LLVM
    - The OS
    - How LLVM was built
    - Anything that you think may be relevant (e.g., host CPU, etc.)
- Upload the reduced input
- Provide the steps to reproduce
- Explain how the observed behavior departs from the expected behavior
- Add labels to help identify which component is at fault if you can

An example of a bad report would be *LLVM is slow, please fix it.*

On the other hand, an example of a better report would include the following points:

Built LLVM in release mode at <hash> on Windows 11. Clang takes XX minutes to compile my huge example. I narrowed down the issue to YY optimization that seems to be quadratic when <description of something specific>.

To reproduce:

1. **Download** `myCoupleTensOfLines.ll`
2. **Run** `opt -passes=YY myCoupleTensOfLines.ll`
3. Measure the compile time
4. **Download** `myCoupleTensOfLinesWithASmallTweak.ll`
5. **Run** `opt -passes=YY myCoupleTensOfLinesWithASmallTweak.ll`
6. Measure the compile time
7. Notice how the small tweak increases the compile time by 10x

I have uploaded the huge example at `myHugeExample.E`

**Expected behavior:** The small tweak has a barely noticeable impact on compile time.

> **Note**
>
> Do not file issues for things that you can fix yourself, such as missing documentation or typos. Feel free to directly submit a patch for that: refer to the *Contributing patches* section. When in doubt, file an issue anyway! The idea here is to avoid flooding the bug tracker with things that take more time to file than fixing them.

The takeaway is the more effort you spend on your report, the more likely it is that it can be fixed quickly. Another way to see it is that all the effort that you put in is someone else's saved effort, and given that you have more context, you will be more effective at filling in the initial blanks.

Good bug reports are invaluable for improving the quality of the project and do not require deep knowledge of the LLVM infrastructure to be actionable. Therefore, they are a great way to get started with your contributions and get to know people.

As you progress through your understanding of the LLVM code base, you will be able to do the following:

- Help narrow down issues to specific components
- Suggest possible solutions
- Provide workaround and fixes
- Screen incoming/existing issues

All these activities are important for the health of the project and are too often neglected. We need you!

In this section, you saw how to report an issue about the LLVM project. With this type of involvement, you can contribute to LLVM right now. Indeed, initially, this activity doesn't involve a deep understanding of the LLVM infrastructure. Then, you saw how, as you accumulate knowledge, you can deepen your involvement around handling these issues until, ultimately, you become part of the community yourself.

In the next section, you will discover a complementary way to contribute to LLVM.

# Engaging with the community

LLVM features a set of mediums to engage with the rest of the community. Things such as asking/answering questions, discussing software design, planning the next release, etc., all happen in the open and you can be part of that starting right now!

Join the Discord server at `https://discord.com/invite/xS7Z362` (or go to `https://llvm.org` and click on **Discord**) to watch and participate in interactions between members and grow into a part of the community yourself. Start by doing things such as asking questions and offering pointers. Slowly but surely, you will gain the confidence and knowledge to engage in deeper conversations.

Similarly, join the Discourse forum (`https://discourse.llvm.org/`) to get to know what is happening in the project. Start, for instance, with the **Announcements** channel to see when the releases are coming out or when the next developers' meeting is being held. Then, dive into the topics that interest you by following the channels that are relevant to you. For example, the **Code generation** channel is a good start for backend developers.

Also, remember that the GitHub issues are also a place where you can engage. You can try to reproduce issues, reduce the input, narrow down the problem, and comment on your findings. Anything that motivates you is an effective way to start. Find where that place is for you.

Finally, feel free to join the LLVM office-hour sessions. There, you can have live conversations with LLVM contributors, including the author of this book, and can ask anything about LLVM. Look at the dedicated section of the **Getting Involved** page of the LLVM documentation for more details (`https://llvm.org/docs/GettingInvolved.html#office-hours`).

In any case, do not be shy! Remember that every LLVM developer started from knowing nothing about the project.

Engaging with the community will be a tremendous boost to your productivity. This will help you get unstuck by asking questions in the right place and to the right person and will allow you to build some name recognition, which may come in handy in unexpected ways, such as when trying to rally people around a design or landing a new job.

The bottom line is although contributing patches is an important way to contribute, do not neglect the other ways too!

Speaking of underrated contributions, in the next section, we will cover code reviews!

## Reviewing patches

Reviewing patches is a significant part of the work in open source. Without reviewers, nobody can land patches and/or the quality of the code may degrade over time. As such, the LLVM project has its own guidelines for reviewing patches at `https://llvm.org/docs/CodeReview.html`.

More concretely for you, now that the LLVM project is fully integrated with GitHub, it is easier than ever to help review patches. You can start looking at ongoing **pull requests** (**PRs**) at `https://github.com/llvm/llvm-project/pulls`. Then, you can jump in as a reviewer on any of them. If you do not know where to start, that is okay. Focus on a specific theme or path and start reviewing that.

Start small:

- Look for typos
- Report stylistic issues, according to the LLVM coding standard (`https://llvm.org/docs/CodingStandards.html`)
- Ask for appropriated comments/tests
- Ask questions! If something is not clear to you, it may not be for others either

While at it, think about the following:

- How would you have implemented this patch?
- Does the contribution make sense?
- Is there a better way to do this?
- Is this even necessary? Maybe something already solves that problem elsewhere.
- Learn the surrounding code.
- Understand how things connect together.

Feel free to approve a PR while mentioning that the contributor should wait for someone more experienced for the final approval.

As time goes on, you will build the knowledge and confidence to be the final approver yourself.

In this section, you saw how important reviewing PRs is. You understood that the open source community cannot survive on patch contributions alone. You learned how to grow into a reviewer yourself and that you can start doing it today!

Next, you will learn about the most obvious form of contributions, writing code!

# Contributing patches

Now, you feel confident enough to contribute patches – great!

Remember that you do not have to start with hard-to-fix problems. You can start by fixing small issues or typos! Whatever helps get you started with the process is a good learning experience.

LLVM features a label **good first issue** that you can use to search for issues that are supposed to be simple enough to get started. Just remember that this label is manually set, and it is possible that the person who set it has misjudged the difficulty of the problem. The bottom line is that it is okay to feel that even starter tasks are too difficult sometimes.

To get you started, feel free to reach out on the LLVM Discord server (https://discord.com/invite/xS7Z362) to existing contributors. Often, contributors will be happy to mentor you in looking into specific issues. Look at the CODE_OWNERS.TXT file for a list of people that you can reach out to for various components. You can also check the list of authors using Git on the paths that you may modify to get a sense of who has been active in this space recently.

You can use the following Git command in your LLVM repository to list who the latest authors are:

```
$ git log --pretty=format:"%aN<%ae> (%as)-%h %s" -- <
pathToTheFilesThatNeedAReviewer>
```

This will print who changed the file, their email address, the date of the change, the hash of the change, and the title of the commit. In other words, all the context you need to figure out if that person touched the file recently and what they did with it.

For instance, an author with a commit marked as **non-functional change** (NFC) may not be the best reviewer because this change may be a mechanical update of the whole LLVM code base and the author may have no clue about what this file does.

If you are interested only in the list of authors, use a shorter print format:

```
$ git log --pretty=format:"%aN" -- <pathToTheFilesThatNeedAReviewer>
```

We do not recommend this method since you lack the context to decide whether the contributions of the authors are relevant enough for them to be added as reviewers.

That said, if you are unsure, add someone as a reviewer no matter what. These people can always decline after the fact.

# Understanding patch contribution in a nutshell

The process of contributing a patch is now completely integrated with GitHub. The latest instructions can be found in the official LLVM user guides at `https://llvm.org/docs/GitHub.html`.

You need to follow these steps to make your contribution:

1. Fork the LLVM repository:

    1. Go to `https://github.com/llvm/llvm-project`.
    2. Click on **Fork** on the right in the top banner.
    3. Click **Create fork** on the next page.

2. Clone either the main repository or your fork:

    ```
    $ git clone https://github.com/llvm/llvm-project.git ${LLVM_SRC}
    ```

3. Make your changes.

4. Rebase the `main` branch from the open source repository:

    ```
    $ git rebase https://github.com/llvm/llvm-project.git main
    ```

5. Push your changes in your fork:

    ```
    $ git push <yourGitHubForkURL> main:<myChange>
    ```

6. Create a pull request to the main repository:

    1. Go to `https://github.com/llvm/llvm-project`.
    2. Click on **Pull requests** in the top bar.
    3. Click on **New pull request**.
    4. Click on **compare across forks**.
    5. Choose the official LLVM repository as the **base repository** and main as the **base**.
    6. Choose your fork as the **head repository** and myChange as the **compare**.
    7. Click **Create pull request**.

When you create a pull request, remember the following regarding your changes:

- They must be as small and incremental as possible. Avoid massive changes unless you agree with the community beforehand that this is the right thing to do, for instance, through a **request for comment** (RFC) on Discourse. More details on when to do an RFC can be found at `https://llvm.org/docs/DeveloperPolicy.html`.
- They must contain a test that exercises the code being added/modified in a reasonable way. See the *A word on adding tests* section later in this chapter for more details.
- They will be squashed together when the PR is approved. In other words, they will collapse into one single commit. If you want to keep your changes logically separated, you will need to create different PRs and wait for each one of them to be merged separately.

Also, make sure to assign reviewers to your PR. The LLVM project has a lot of traffic, and it is easy to miss a PR if it is not pinned to particular reviewers. To find suitable reviewers, use the same tips as for finding people to mentor you: use `CODE_OWNERS.TXT` or look at the authors with Git.

## Following up with your contribution

If you do not get any reply within one week, ping the reviewers, try to add more context as well, reach out on Discord, etc. In any case, make sure to wait at least one week before pinging the PR again. This is part of the LLVM policy and pinging more often than that may seem rude. Everybody is busy; we know it can be frustrating, but it will get there.

When receiving feedback, assume good intent and try to comply as much as possible with the reviewers' requests. It is okay to push back but do so with good intent as well. For instance, if a reviewer asks you about the compile time impact of your change, it is expected that you have or will measure it.

At the end of the day, everybody's goal is to make LLVM better and this requires supporting or doing things in a way you may not have anticipated.

When your PR is finally merged, keep an eye on the LLVM buildbots (`https://lab.llvm.org/buildbot/`, or go to `https://llvm.org` and then click on **Buildbot**). If your change breaks any of them, you (or someone else) may have to revert your change. This is perfectly fine to revert changes. Take the time to fix whatever was broken and resubmit your PR with fixes and additional tests.

When reverting your change, make sure to mention in the commit message why this change needed to be reverted. A link to the buildbot failure or a GitHub issue is a welcome addition to such messages.

## A word on adding tests

With rare exceptions, every change made must come with a test case. Obviously, the test needs to fail without your change, otherwise you are not testing the right thing.

The test case must convey the intent of the test and be as small as possible, both in terms of its input and what it is testing.

For instance, let us say that you are fixing an issue in optimization XX that is only exposed when the user runs the compiler with the O3 optimization level. While it is okay to have a test where you run the whole compiler at O3, you also need a test that specifically runs optimization XX alone. The rationale is to make the test robust against future changes.

To put it simply, issues are often tied to the form in which the **intermediate representation** (IR) reaches the faulty optimization. For instance, let's say that the issue crashes the compiler when this specific IR construct a = b * 2 reaches optimization XX. Now, suppose that the O3 optimization level is being reworked by another contributor in open source. After their contribution, O3 runs a new optimization before optimization XX and this new optimization modifies a = b * 2 into a = 2 * b. At this point, the faulty pattern does not reach optimization XX anymore when run as part of O3. As a result, a test that solely checks the absence of the issue in O3 is useless with respect to this issue. Therefore, the issue might creep in again unless a more targeted test is added.

Later in this book, we will cover tools to shrink the size of the inputs of your tests and ways to clean them up. Just remember that the tests that you add may be modified by someone else and that you need to give them all the information to update the test if it were to fail. This is why it is important to describe what is being tested and what the expected output is.

In this section, you learned how to contribute patches. You discovered the life of a pull request, how to make sure the review moves forward, and what to do after your change has landed. With this knowledge, you have now all the pieces to confidently navigate this process.

# Summary

In this chapter, you learned the various ways you can contribute to the LLVM project and you saw that not all contributions are patches, but these contributions are equally important.

As you can imagine, this was not an exhaustive list of how you can get more involved in the community. For instance, we did not cover meet-ups or LLVM developers' meetings. The latter can be a tremendous opportunity to find people with the same interests as you. Consider doing a lightning talk about the topic you are working on to get the word out and gather people to help you.

At the end of the day, remember that an open source project is built around a community. To become more productive with the project, we recommend that you aim to be a part of this community and actively contribute back. Think of it this way: whatever you contribute to the project may help someone else and can also be improved and maintained by someone else!

At this point, you should be itching to write some code with the LLVM infrastructure. Before we can get to that, we need to introduce a few core compiler concepts to comfortably interact with the LLVM APIs. We will cover these concepts and the related LLVM APIs in the next chapter.

# Quiz time

Now that you have completed reading this chapter, try answering the following questions to test your knowledge:

1.  Before starting to interact with the LLVM community, what piece of documentation should you read?

    The answer is the code of conduct of the LLVM community (`https://llvm.org/docs/ CodeOfConduct.html`). This document describes the expectations around interaction with the community – you would not want to start from the wrong foot, would you?

    See the introduction of this chapter for more details.

2.  When reporting an issue, what can you do to make it more likely to be fixed by the community?

    In a nutshell, reduce the size of the input(s) required to reproduce the problem as much as possible. Include as many relevant details as possible, as in, *this happens only on macOS, this started to fail after the release of 17.0.1*, etc.

Essentially all the effort you put in will save someone else's time, and the less time this other person must dedicate to understand or reproduce your issue, the more time they have to dig into it, and thus solve it!

More details on this in the *Reporting an issue* section.

3. What can you expect from the LLVM office hours?

   LLVM office hours are for you an opportunity to ask any questions related to LLVM to some active LLVM contributors. See the *Engaging with the community* section for more details.

4. Why is reviewing patches important for the project?

   If people only submit patches but nobody is reviewing them, then the project cannot make progress since nothing can land (unless you do not care about code quality and consistency!). Hence, having an active pool of reviewers is crucial to the health of the project. See the *Reviewing patches* section.

5. Imagine that you would like to make a big change to the LLVM project. How should you approach that?

   The exact details are available in the developer policy (`https://llvm.org/docs/DeveloperPolicy.html`) but essentially, you need to start with an RFC and get buy-in from the stakeholders. More details can be found in the *Understanding patch contribution in a nutshell* section.

---

## Unlock this book's exclusive benefits now

This book comes with additional benefits designed to elevate your learning experience.

*Note: Have your purchase invoice ready before you begin.*

`https://www.packtpub.com/unlock/9781837637782`

# 3

# Compiler Basics and How They Map to LLVM APIs

This chapter introduces the fundamental concepts of working on a compiler and shows how they map to **Low Level Virtual Machine (LLVM)** **application programming interfaces (APIs)**. In this chapter, you will do the following:

- Familiarize yourself with the vocabulary used in compilers
- Build a mental model of what these concepts are used for
- Learn how to manipulate these concepts through LLVM APIs

To help you solidify your knowledge, you will write a couple of programs that build some **intermediate representation (IR)** from scratch.

Before we get started, let us review the software that you will need for this chapter.

## Technical requirements

You will find the complete code of what we are building in this chapter in the ch3 folder of the GitHub repository of this book: https://github.com/PacktPublishing/LLVM-Code-Generation.

What we build will depend on a few LLVM libraries. Therefore, these libraries will need to be available for linking the final executable code.

You can get them in either of the following ways:

- Building the LLVM core project yourself while making sure you build the backend that matches your computer architecture. Check out the *Configuring the build system* section in *Chapter 1* if you forgot how to do that or have not done so yet, and remember to set the right value for LLVM_TARGETS_TO_BUILD!
- Downloading the latest LLVM release from https://releases.llvm.org/. Beware that depending on your **operating system (OS)** and computer, a release may not be available, and you may have to resort to the method described in the first bullet point to get the desired libraries.

The project we build in this chapter is a C++ project, and we will use the same tools as what is needed to build LLVM, namely, a C/C++ compiler toolchain, CMake, and Ninja. Please refer to the *Installing the right tools* section in *Chapter 1* on how to fulfill these requirements.

# A word on APIs

In this chapter, we will discuss a few APIs. You will likely find that these references are too few and imprecise to be able to leverage them properly.

This is by design!

We believe we expose enough of them to give you an overview of what you need and that you can figure the rest out by yourself/with the support of the community.

In other words, these references give you an entry point in the relevant APIs, and you should be able to extract what you need from there.

Do not worry – there are plenty of resources to help you in your survey of the APIs.

First, chances are you are using an **integrated developer environment** (IDE) that can help you navigate these APIs. In other words, by only knowing the main classes you can work your way around.

Second, the whole LLVM code base is documented in *Doxygen*.

> Doxygen
>
> Doxygen is a documentation tool that allows the production of rich documentation experiences from comments in the source code. The usage of Doxygen is documented for LLVM at `https://llvm.org/docs/CodingStandards.html#doxygen-use-in-documentation-comments`.

Thanks to Doxygen and LLVM **continuous integration** (CI), you can find up-to-date and interactive documentation of LLVM APIs at `https://llvm.org/doxygen/` (or go to `https://llvm.org/` and click on **doxygen**). For past releases, go to the release page `https://releases.llvm.org/` (or go to `https://llvm.org/` and click on **All Releases**), then click on **Download** next to the release you are interested in. Depending on how recent that release is, you will either end up on the GitHub page of that release (for example, for LLVM 17.0.6, this is `https://github.com/llvm/llvm-project/releases/tag/llvmorg-17.0.6`) and will download the LLVM Doxygen tarball from there (for example, `https://github.com/llvm/llvm-project/releases/download/llvmorg-17.0.6/llvm_doxygen-17.0.6.tar.xz`) or end up on the dedicated section on the download page (for example, for LLVM 10.0.0, `https://releases.llvm.org/download.html#10.0.0`), where you will find a link to a tarball named LLVM Doxygen (`https://github.com/llvm/llvm-project/releases/download/llvmorg-10.0.0/llvm_doxygen-10.0.0.tar.xz`).

At first, the Doxygen pages may be a little confusing to navigate but we give you an example next. In the long run, we are sure you will figure out ways that work best for you!

Back to navigating the Doxygen pages.

Let us say that you look for the Module class:

1.  Hover over **Classes** in the top toolbar
2.  Click on **Class List**
3.  On the new page, click on the llvm namespace
4.  You will end up on a page with a list of the following:

    1.  Sub-namespaces in alphabetical order

    2.  Classes in alphabetical order, and the Module class should be there

5.  Click on **Module**
6.  Alternatively, when hovering over **Classes**, you can use **Class Index**, which is faster

One of the nice features of Doxygen is that it produces an interactive diagram of the inheritance graph for each class.

Hopefully, these directions give you concrete steps on how to dive into the LLVM APIs that you will see throughout this book; nevertheless, if this is not enough, fear not because you will find concrete examples of how to use some of the APIs presented in this chapter in the repository of this book, as already mentioned in the *Technical requirements* section. Make sure to look at the README.md file of the related chapter to learn more about these examples.

Before we let you dive into the compiler jargon, here are a couple of things that apply to the content of the whole chapter:

*   Unless otherwise specified, the presented APIs live in the llvm namespace. As you learned in the *Understanding the directory structure* section in *Chapter 1*, you will find the related public headers under ${LLVM_SRC}/llvm/include/llvm/<relatedLibary>, where ${LLVM_SRC} is the path to your clone of the LLVM Git repository. If you use an LLVM release, the path will be slightly different: ${INSTALL_PREFIX}/include/llvm/<relatedLibrary>.
*   The core LLVM infrastructure has different levels of IR. In this chapter, we focus on the main ones: the LLVM IR and the Machine IR. You will learn more about these IRs and their purpose in the dedicated chapters, respectively *Chapters 7* and *11*, but this gives you a quick introduction to these IRs. The only thing to remember at this point is that the LLVM IR offers a higher level of abstraction than the Machine IR.

Now, let us start with compiler terms that you will inevitably encounter in your LLVM journey.

# Understanding compiler jargon

In this section, you will learn about terms that are commonly used in compilers. With this knowledge, you will be able to comfortably approach discussions around compilers.

# Target

In compilers, a **target** is the hardware architecture that a program will run on. You will see that we use this term as a verb too when talking about implementing/specializing features for a particular target. For instance, the targeting of instruction selection means that we will modify the instruction selection transformation so that it supports a specific target.

# Host

A **host** is the device that runs the compiler. In a lot of cases, the host and target are the same, but when they are different, we talk about cross-compilation. For example, you can run a compiler that produces code for an AArch64 target (for instance, used in a phone) on an x86 host (a desktop device).

# Lowering

When working on and reading about compilers, you will encounter the term **lowering**. Behind this term is the notion that as your input program is being compiled, it goes through various stages that progressively lower its level of abstraction all the way down to the final assembly of the target machine.

In other words, the process of lowering makes some input representations closer and closer to the target.

# Canonical form

Throughout the LLVM code base and documentation, you will see the term **canonical form**. This is about the recommended way of representing something.

For instance, consider the following expressions: a = b + 2 and a = 2 + b. These expressions compute the same results but offer different ways to represent their computations. Conceptually, as you add more terms to these expressions, the number of ways to represent them will grow exponentially. Agreeing on a canonical form means that the compiler will strive to generate expressions in only one way. For instance, a rule could be to put the constants on the right-hand side of binary operators.

Other forms are, of course, supported, but if your code does not follow the canonical form, it is possible that the quality of the generated code will suffer.

For the most part, you do not have to worry about the canonical form because LLVM offers APIs to canonicalize your IR. However, it is still important to know what canonical form and canonicalization are about.

# Build time, compile time, and runtime

When it comes to performance evaluation, compilers are subjected to criteria that do not apply to most other software. As a result, some terms can become ambiguous for compilers. For instance, when talking about runtime, are we talking about the time it takes to run a binary produced by the compiler or the time it takes for the compiler to produce this binary?

So, we use the following definitions to disambiguate this:

- **Build time:** The time it takes to build the compiler; for example, the time it takes for Ninja to complete the build of LLVM.

- **Compile time:** The time it takes for the compiler to process a file; for example, the time it takes for Clang to produce an object file from the source file.
- **Runtime:** The time it takes for the final binary to execute; for example, the time it takes to run the binary produced by Clang.

To put things differently, the runtime of the compiler is the compile time of your application.

## Backend and middle-end

As you discovered in the *Building a compiler* section in *Chapter 1*, a compiler is not a monolith. Two of the main components are the frontend and the backend. Sadly, the term **backend** is slightly overloaded, and depending on your point of view, it may mean different things.

In this book, you will be exposed to two of these meanings.

The first one is what you already know: the component that processes what a frontend, such as Clang, produces.

Now, if you zoom in on this backend, you will find target-agnostic transformations followed by target-specific transformations. The target-specific part is, in this context, called the backend of this target; for example, the x86 backend. The target-agnostic part, which happens roughly before the target-specific part, is called the **middle-end** because it sits between the frontend and a target-specific backend.

## Application binary interface

The **application binary interface** (ABI) describes how your functions talk to each other at a low level. This means that an ABI defines how and where the arguments of a function are set on the caller side so that they can be retrieved on the callee side.

In LLVM, the ABI taints the whole compiler stack because it affects the function signature (for example, small enough structures may be split into individual arguments), which is usually determined by the frontend, all the way down to the backend, which must set the right stack alignment, reserve dedicated registers, and so on.

If you are writing your own backend, you must define your own ABI. We recommend using an existing one and derive yours from that because ABI design is hard and easy to do wrong!

For a given target, there may be several ABIs, but for a given **calling convention** (CC), there is only one matching ABI. The CC depends on the programming language and is set by the frontend for the backend.

ABIs are extremely important as they provide the glue between functions. In other words, they formalize how the handshake happens between the caller and the callee. For instance, the ABI prescribes where the input arguments should be set by the caller and, thus, where the callee can expect to find its input arguments.

Then, as long as compilers follow the rules of the ABI, a function compiled with a compiler can talk to a function compiled with a different compiler.

Therefore, the ABI is the only thing that keeps artifacts produced by different compilers capable of interacting with each other.

# Encoding

**Encoding** describes the way your program is eventually assembled in a binary format that makes sense for your target. More specifically, encodings describe which bits define which operands of your instructions, how memory addresses are represented, the size limit of your immediate values (that is, your literal constants), and so on.

Encodings are target-specific and are usually provided by the hardware vendor through their **Instruction Set Architecture (ISA)** document.

At the middle-end level, encodings can be ignored, but the lower you go in the backend, the more you must think about it.

The bottom line is encodings are something that creates constraints for the backend, and as a compiler writer, you will have to deal with these constraints!

For instance, consider the following C statement:

```
a = b + c;
```

Imagine that you want to lower this statement to a target that only supports 2-address-like encoding, as with x86 in the early days. 2-address means that instructions can only accommodate up to 2 operands, including the definition. In other words, to do a binary operation, you must fold one of the arguments with the definition. Put differently, you must rewrite your input in the following C statement equivalent:

```
a = b;
a += c;
```

Other types of encoding constraints include the following:

- Particular operands have to live in specific registers
- Constants bigger than a given number of bits need to live in a register
- Inputs' operands need to be in contiguous registers

Now that you are familiar with the day-to-day terms of a compiler engineer, you will have a better understanding of the comments and APIs you will read across the LLVM code base.

In the next section, you will learn about basic structures that you will manipulate throughout your compiler journey.

# Working with basic structures

In this section, you will learn about the prevalent structures used to represent a program. In other words, whatever you build with the LLVM infrastructure, chances are you will have to manipulate these structures.

Thanks to this knowledge, you will be able to build an intuition of which APIs hold which information and offer which capabilities for manipulating a program. Naturally, this is only the beginning, and you will sharpen your knowledge of the APIs as you progress through the book.

This introduction will help you get started with the LLVM code base and give you a thread to follow when starting to explore LLVM APIs on your own.

We follow a top-down approach. We start from the constructs with the largest logical scope and then progressively zoom in on concepts with narrower scopes. What this means is that when you see a concept not defined yet, it will be presented in the following section.

# Module

A **module** is a container for the program currently being compiled. To put it succinctly, a module is roughly equivalent to the input file that you give to the compiler. It contains all global variables, function definitions, metadata, and so on that you will need to process this input.

The concept of a module is not specific to LLVM, but in the literature, it often appears with other names such as **translation unit (TU)** or **compilation unit (CU)**.

## A module at the LLVM IR level

At the LLVM IR level, the concept of a module maps directly to the `Module` class that lives in the `IR` library (albeit the vented library is called `LLVMCore`). Again, if you do not know how to locate a library in the directory tree, please refer to the *Understanding the directory structure* section in *Chapter 1*.

In the backend, the module is typically handed over by some sort of frontend, hence you rarely need to create one by yourself. However, for education purposes, or if you want to create your own tool/frontend, as we are doing in some examples of this chapter, here is how you create an LLVM IR module from scratch:

```
LLVMContext Context;
Module MyModule("MyModule", Context);
```

Alternatively, you can initialize your module directly from LLVM IR serialized formats. Indeed, the LLVM IR can be stored in a file (or memory) with either a textual or binary representation. You will learn more about these representations in *Chapter 7*. Anyway, assuming you have such a serialized format handy in a file, you can use the APIs defined in `IRReader.h`, also from the `IRReader` library, to load your module directly from that file. In this case, you will use the `parseIRFile` function:

```
LLVMContext Context;
SMDiagnostic Err;
std::unique_ptr<Module> MyModule = parseIRFile("MyIRFile", Err, Context);
```

Similarly, you can create a module from a single string containing the textual form of the LLVM IR, which again you will explore in more detail in *Chapter 7*, using the `parseAssemblyString` function from the `AsmParser` library:

```
LLVMContext Context;
SMDiagnostic Err;
std::unique_ptr<Module> MyModule = parseAssemblyString(InputIR, Err, Context);
```

> **Note**
>
> The `parseIRFile` API supports both textual and binary serialization formats of the LLVM IR. The files holding the textual representation usually have the `.ll` extension, while the binary files have the `.bc` extension.

In all cases, notice how you must first create an `LLVMContext` object. You will see that the `LLVMContext` class is required in a lot of APIs. The `LLVMContext` class is responsible for rendering unique (we also say *uniquing*) certain information that holds for the entire compiler/tool you are building. For instance, when you create literal constants, the `LLVMContext` instance will make sure that constants with the same type (for example, `int`, `float`, …) and value (for example, `2`, `1.0`, …) are bound to the same underlying object. That way, checking that two constants are equal is as easy and efficient as checking that the addresses of the objects are the same.

> **Note**
>
> If you want to use different `LLVMContext` instances for different purposes, beware that the *uniquing* property will obviously not work across them.

At this point, you can manipulate the module directly through its member functions. For instance, you can inspect or create global variables (variables accessible from anywhere within a module) with `Module::getGlobalVariable(StringRef Name)` and `Module::insertGlobalVariable(GlobalVariable *GV)` respectively.

More importantly, a module holds a list of all **functions** that are defined or used within this module. For now, let us assume that the module has been populated with the IR that represents a C program with two functions in it, `foo` and `main`; you can obtain the `foo` function through `Module::getFunction(StringRef Name)`, with `Name` being equal to `foo`. More generally, you can iterate through all the functions within a module by using the begin and end iterators through a range loop, as illustrated in the following snippet:

```
for(Function &MyFunction: MyModule) {
    // Do something with MyFunction.
}
```

The order of the functions matches what is displayed when you print the module.

Let us now see how this concept of a module maps at the Machine IR level.

## A module at the Machine IR level

In short, the Machine IR level does not have the concept of a module.

The code that deals with the Machine IR is usually limited to the scope of only one function at a time. When a module scope is required, it is articulated around the `Module` class of the LLVM IR through the `MachineModuleInfo` API.

When you require access to the whole module while working at the Machine IR level, you do not need to create a MachineModuleInfo object yourself, if you use the regular pass pipeline mechanism that LLVM offers. We will cover this mechanism in *Chapter 5*.

Now, if you want to handle a module directly at the Machine IR level, you can try to instantiate a MachineModuleInfo object yourself, but the reality is this object is not meant to be handled directly; instead, you must go through MachineModuleInfoWrapperPass to do the heavy lifting. In *Chapter 5*, we will cover the mechanism that allows us to get such an object.

Beware that the MachineModuleInfo API offers only a mapping from an LLVM IR Function to a MachineFunction. It does not provide any capabilities to translate one to the other. If you use the MachineModuleInfo API directly, you will have to handle this translation yourself. You can do that by mapping an existing LLVM IR Function object to an empty MachineFunction object using MachineModuleInfo::getOrCreateMachineFunction(Function &F), then populate the resulting MachineFunction instance manually.

All the described Machine IR APIs of this section live in the CodeGen library.

We have been talking a lot about the LLVM IR Function class and the MachineFunction class without properly introducing them. Let us fix that in the next section.

# Function

A **function** is exactly what you would picture in any programming language. This is a named entity that encompasses some computations and can be called from various points as long as you comply with its signature/prototype. It has some properties, such as a list of arguments, a returned type, a set of attributes (for example, noinline), and so on.

In LLVM, we do not make any distinction between what in C++ we would call functions, member functions, procedures, lambdas, and so on. From the backend perspective, everything is a function. The only difference is how they get called. For example, various kinds of functions may have distinct CCs; in other words, the compiler may use different sequences of instructions when it lowers calls to them.

> Note
>
> When it comes to functions, the backend is straightforward. This is only possible because the frontend does most of the heavy lifting. For instance, it is the frontend's responsibility to produce additional parameters that are not visible in the source language, such as how the this pointer is added to every member function, or to generate additional code to express the polymorphism of a virtual function, such as how to load a **virtual table** (**vtable**) and look up the address of the related function for the current instance of an object.

The backend makes one distinction when it comes to functions: is this function implemented in this module or is it implemented in a different one? Put differently, is it a function definition or a function declaration?

Unless the function declaration is used within the module, it is dropped from the list of functions in that module: when it comes to generating code, this function declaration is useless and can safely be dropped.

## A function in the LLVM IR

LLVM exposes the concept of function at the LLVM IR level through the Function class. This class lives in the IR library. This API exposes everything you need to query the return type (Type *Function::getReturnType()), the list of arguments (arg_iterator Function::arg_begin() and arg_iterator Function::arg_end()), the attributes (AttributeList Function::getAttributes()), and so on.

At this level, the distinction between a function definition and a function declaration is whether the related Function object has a body.

You will not find a body field in this class; instead, you can check if the Function object is empty (bool Function::empty()). If this is true, this means it does not have a body and thus, this is a declaration. Alternatively, the GlobalValue class, which is one of the ancestors of the Function class, exposes a method named isDeclaration that also answers the question of whether a function is a declaration or a definition.

Next, by using Function::getParent(), you can access the module that encompasses the related function.

Focusing on functions with a body, the content of a function's body is split across different **basic blocks**. You can access these constructs through the begin() and end() methods:

```
for(BasicBlock &MyBasicBlock: MyFunction) {
    // Do something with MyBasicBlock.
}
```

## A function in the Machine IR

At the Machine IR level, a function is represented with the MachineFunction class. This class is in the CodeGen library.

Unlike the LLVM IR Function class, the MachineFunction class offers little information about the function itself. For instance, all the APIs around the return type and so on are nonexistent here. Instead, the MachineFunction class exposes a pointer to the LLVM IR Function object that it mirrors (Function &MachineFunction::getFunction()). Therefore, this kind of metadata remains accessible, albeit through a pointer indirection. Nevertheless, if you look at the MachineFunction API, you will notice methods to query some properties of the MachineFunction class. These properties are relevant to the low-level processing of the related function and hence, it would not make sense to expose them in the LLVM IR APIs. For instance, you can query if a function still has virtual registers (NoVRegs) as opposed to physical registers, which is something the LLVM IR does not deal with. We will cover these properties in the chapter dedicated to the Machine IR, *Chapter 11*.

As with the LLVM IR Function class, the MachineFunction class' body is split across basic blocks, and you access them directly through the begin() and end() methods:

```
for(MachineBasicBlock &MyMachineBB: MyMachineFunction) {
  // Do something with MyMachineBB.
}
```

For both the Function class and the MachineFunction class, the order of the basic blocks in this list matches the order printed on the screen. Put differently, without any optimization, this list follows the original order of the source program.

We saw that basic blocks are the building blocks of a function, but we did not introduce them. Let us fix this in the next section.

## Basic block

A **basic block** is a **single-entry single-exit** (SESE) region of code where the entry point is at the beginning of the region and the exit point at the end. Behind SESE is a simple concept. A basic block is a sequence of continuous instructions. The key word here is *continuous*. This implies that when you hit an instruction, by definition, all the instructions before this instruction within the same block have been executed, and all the instructions remaining in this basic block will be executed.

Since basic blocks are used a lot around the compiler code base, they are often simply referred to as blocks.

As long as the code region remains SESE, there is no limit on how you form a basic block. However, generally, basic blocks are formed such that they are maximal. This means that it is impossible to find a longer sequence of instructions that would meet the SESE criteria. *Table 3.1* illustrates how some code can be split into basic blocks:

| Input C program | One of the possible configurations of basic blocks | Basic blocks in maximal form |
|---|---|---|
| ```int foo(int a) {   int b = bar();   int c = baz();   if (c == a)     goto IF;   else     goto END; IF:   b += a * bar(); END:   return b; }``` | ```BB1:   int b = bar(); BB2:   int c = baz(); BB3:   (c == a)     goto IF; BB4:   goto END; IF:   b += a * bar(); END:   return b;``` | ```BB1:   int b = bar();   int c = baz();   (c == a)     goto IF; BB2:   goto END; IF:   b += a * bar(); END:   return b;``` |

*Table 3.1: Different configurations of basic blocks for the same input program*

Before we explain the content of this table, let us clarify something that you may have noticed. In the second and third columns, we dropped the if and else keywords. C programs are not directly suitable for a representation with basic blocks, because if keywords have a semantic of jumps; that is, they redirect the execution of the program to somewhere else. To work around this, we use a predicated notation of the form cond  goto. This means this goto is executed only if cond is true. Also, the start of each basic block is represented with a label of the form name:; for example, BB1: and IF:.

Back to the explanation - The second column shows how we can split the input program into many basic blocks where each block is almost just one instruction. The third column shows the same program with the basic blocks in maximal form. If you try to change the boundaries of any of the basic blocks of the third column, you will break the SESE property. For instance, adding goto  END to the IF block will produce a basic block with two entry points: one at BB2 and one at IF. Similarly, extending BB1 to include goto  END will produce a basic block with two exit points: one at goto  IF and one at goto END. Finally, notice that SESE regions have a single-entry point (respectively single-exit point), but that point can be reached through several paths (respectively can jump to different paths). For example, see how BB1 can either jump to IF or fall through to BB2 and how END can be reached from the end of BB2 and the end of IF.

> Note
>
> While the maximal property ensures that you do not end up with arbitrary boundaries between instructions, it is sometimes not applied. For instance, let us say you have an algorithm with a complexity that is quadratic in the number of instructions within a basic block. It is correct to split that block into several blocks to reduce the compile time. In other words, not satisfying the maximal property is perfectly fine, but by doing that, you will nevertheless limit the capabilities of other optimizations, so make sure to stitch the blocks back together!

## A basic block in the LLVM IR

Unsurprisingly, the concept of basic blocks is represented with the BasicBlock class from the IR library.

Similarly to the Function class, the BasicBlock class offers a BasicBlock::getParent() method to access its encompassing scope; in other words, the instance of the Function class that owns the related basic block.

Diving into the content of a basic block, you can walk through its body using the begin() and end() methods. This returns iterators to the **instructions** that make the basic block.

The order of the instructions matches a top-to-bottom traversal of the basic block. Hence, the loop in the following snippet would traverse the instructions in the same order as they would be executed:

```
for (Instruction &MyInstr: MyBasicBlock) {
  // Do something with MyInstr.
}
```

LLVM IR basic blocks have additional constraints:

- They must have exactly one terminator instruction, which is a special instruction that defines the possible destinations of this basic block.
- For instance, in the rightmost column of *Table 3.1*, the terminator instruction of BB2 is goto END.
- They must end with a terminator instruction.
- Certain special instructions must appear first, if any.

Putting everything together, a basic block is a non-empty list of instructions with some special instructions at the beginning and a terminator at the end.

You can access the first instruction after the special instructions using BasicBlock::getFirstNonPHI(), and you can access the terminator by using BasicBlock::getTerminator(). Typically, when making changes local to a basic block, you should iterate through the instructions in this range: getFirstNonPHI(), getTerminator().

> **Note**
>
> The constraints may be temporarily violated, for instance, while constructing a basic block. However, if an ill-formed basic block is fed to the LLVM verifier, it will fail to pass the checks.

Looking at the bigger picture, the BasicBlock API does not offer access to the list of **predecessors**, the basic blocks that may jump to this instance, and the list of **successors**, the basic blocks this instance may jump to.

This information needs to be queried separately. We will cover this in the *Control flow graph* section.

## A basic block in the Machine IR

Similarly to the LLVM IR level, the concept of basic blocks maps to MachineBasicBlock.

You will find the same APIs: begin(), end(), and getParent(). However, they will be mapped on their Machine IR counterparts: MachineInstruction and MachineFunction.

There are a couple of differences compared to the BasicBlock class:

- MachineBasicBlock instances can have zero or several terminator instructions.
- MachineBasicBlock instances offer a direct API to traverse their predecessors and successors through predXXX and succXXX methods.

Both the BasicBlock and MachineBasicBlock classes can be turned into an iterator to the parent's list using getIterator(). This means that you can, from an instance of one of these classes, get to the next or previous basic block in the list of basic blocks from the related parent function.

Finally, since terminators are optional in MachineBasicBlock instances, depending on the sequence of code at the end of a MachineBasicBlock instance, the execution of the related program may fall through to the next basic block in the serialization order. The serialization order is represented by the list of MachineBasicBlock in the related MachineFunction object.

What this means is moving the blocks within that list does the following:

- Changes the order they are printed on the screen/file.
- May change the execution of the final executable code, if you do not insert the proper terminators, since you may be changing the execution that follows the fall-through paths.

We will cover these aspects in more detail in *Chapter 11*.

## Instruction

An **instruction** is the smallest piece of computation that can be represented in the IR.

When looking at a C program, you can think of an instruction as a simple statement. Complex statements would produce several instructions.

For instance, consider the following statement:

```
b += a * bar();
```

This statement would be broken down into the following instructions:

```
temp0 = bar();
temp1 = a * temp0;
b = b + temp1;
```

The granularity of what can be represented with a single instruction depends on the actual IR.

Looking into the details of an instruction (for example, temp1 = a * temp0), you can see that it is defined by three main pieces:

- **Its definitions**: The results produced by this instruction, here temp1.
- **Its arguments, or uses, also called operands**: The input of this instruction, here a and temp0.
- **Its operation code, or opcode for short**: A unique identifier that carries the semantics of this instruction, here *.

> **Note**
>
> The words *argument* and *operand* are both overloaded in LLVM parlance. Depending on the context, they may mean different things. For now, we will stick with the word *argument* and use it to describe the input of an instruction. This will help clear out some of the confusion when looking at the MachineInstr::getOperand method for the Machine IR API.

In the LLVM IR and the Machine IR, an instruction is usually printed using the following format:

```
def0, def1, … = opcode arg0, arg1, …
```

# An instruction in the LLVM IR

You may have guessed it, but an instruction in the LLVM IR is represented by the `Instruction` class from the IR library.

In this class, you will find methods to query the main characteristic of an instruction:

- **Its definition:** The `Instruction` object is the definition itself. More on that hereafter.
- **Its arguments:** The `getOperand(unsigned index)` method, where `index` is a number between zero and the number of arguments minus one, `op_begin()`, and `op_end()`. This API is inherited from the `User` class. We will cover inheritance graphs in *Chapter 4*.
- **Its opcode:** The `getOpcode()` method.

It may be surprising to you that the instruction itself is the definition, but at the LLVM IR level, everything is managed through pointers. Therefore, the arguments of an instruction are simply pointers to the instructions (or, more precisely, an instance of the `Value` class) defining them. As a result, an instruction can only define one value. At this level of IR, if you need an instruction that defines multiple values, you need to define a single value with several fields (as with a structure in C).

Additionally, you will find all the methods to move an instruction around, potentially to a different basic block (`moveBefore`, `moveAfter`, `insertBefore`, and so on), query some properties about the instruction itself (you can find some examples of that in *Chapter 4*), and a pointer to its parent `BasicBlock` object (`Instruction::getParent()`).

# An instruction in the Machine IR

Instructions are represented with the `MachineInstr` class from the `CodeGen` library.

The `MachineInstr` class is more flexible than the `Instruction` class but is less intuitive to work with. You will learn about its details when reading *Chapter 11*. For now, let us highlight the way you can get the main characteristics of a `MachineInstr` class:

- **Its definitions:** The `getOperand(unsigned index)` method, where `index` is a number between zero and the number of operands minus one. In this context, *operands* means all the arguments and definitions of the instruction.
- **Its arguments:** The `getOperand(unsigned index)` method. This is not a typo; this is the exact same API as the instruction's definitions. You have to unbox the returned `MachineOperand` object to know if you are dealing with a definition or an argument. Again, you will learn more about this in *Chapter 11*.
- **Its opcode:** The `getOpcode()` method.

Aside from the expected methods to move the instruction around, query its property, and get to the parent basic block, the `MachineInstr` class offers some helper functions to iterate through its definitions (`MachineInstr::defs()`) and arguments (`MachineInstr::uses()`). However, you still need to unbox the related `MachineOperand` objects, and again, we will not cover this here.

Finally, as with the classes of the basic block family, you can morph instances of the `Instruction` and `MachineInstr` classes into an iterator of the parent list (`getIterator()`). This gives you a convenient way to look at the surrounding instructions of the one you already have.

At this point, you have had an overview of all the classes that are used to represent a program at different levels of IR. Before we wrap this section, let us see how the piece connects to represent how that program executes or, put differently, how the program flows!

## Control flow graph

The term **control flow** describes the order of execution of the instructions. In a basic block, for instance, this is a straight line from top to bottom.

A **control flow graph** (CFG) is a way to represent a function as a graph. It is an important concept to master, even if you do not go deep in compilers. Indeed, even the concepts of predecessors and successors, which you saw in the *Basic block* section, are, in fact, derived from the CFG.

A CFG is defined by a set of nodes N (also called vertices in the literature) and a set of directed edges E that each connect two nodes from N.

For a function F, the set of nodes N is equal to F's basic blocks, and there is an edge between two nodes src and dst if and only if src may jump to dst. Put differently, there is a control flow edge when the control flow may get transferred from src to dst. We used the word *may* in the previous sentence because some of these edges can be predicated by a set of conditions, meaning we may take them at runtime or not. For instance, the jump of an `if` statement produces two edges: one when the execution follows the `true` condition and one when it follows the `false` condition.

*Figure 3.1* shows the CFG for the program from *Table 3.1* with the basic blocks in the maximal form:

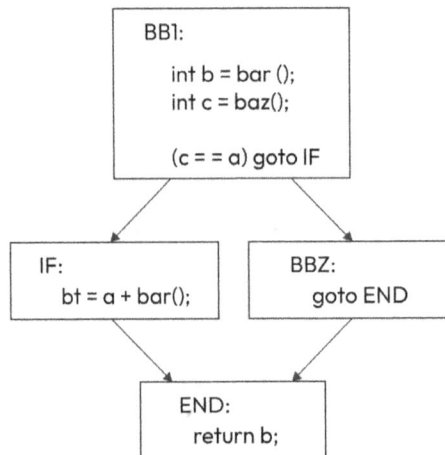

*Figure 3.1: The CFG of the rightmost column of Table 3.1*

The first node executed in a CFG is called the entry point, and the last possible ones are called exit points. The entry point maps to the entry of a function and the exit points map to all return points of a function.

> **Note**
>
> It is sometimes easier to reason about a CFG with only one exit point. It is always possible to emulate a unique exit point by creating a fake basic block and have all the exit blocks flow into it. This exit point can also be properly generated instead of just faked, but this exercise is left to the reader.

There are a few patterns and concepts around CFGs that are worth mentioning since you will see them a lot in the compiler literature and the LLVM code base. Moreover, these patterns have certain properties that will help you solve compiler-specific problems when you know what to look for. Therefore, it is important to know that they exist.

## Reverse post-order traversal

A **reverse post-order (RPO)** traversal defines an order in which the nodes of a CFG are visited. This order guarantees that you will traverse the graph in a topological order. To put it simply, in a well-formed program (that is, where all the variables are defined before being used), by following the topological order, you encounter the definitions before their uses.

LLVM offers an API, named `ReversePostOrderTraversal`, to use RPO on your functions out of the box. This API is part of the `ADT` library.

> **Note**
>
> If you are curious, the algorithm to build RPO is relatively simple, and to put it in fancy terms, it is a post-order (you visit the current node after visiting all its children) depth-first-search traversal where you invert the visiting order at the end, hence you reverse the post-order.

Here is an example of using an RPO traversal in the LLVM IR:

```
ReversePostOrderTraversal<Function *> RPOT(&MyFunction);
For (BasicBlock *BB: RPOT) {
  // Do something in topological order.
}
```

The following snippet shows the use of an RPO traversal in the Machine IR:

```
ReversePostOrderTraversal<MachineFunction *> RPOT(&MyMachineFunction);
For (MachineBasicBlock *MBB: RPOT) {
  // Do something in topological order.
}
```

# Backedge

Intuitively, a **backedge** is a control flow edge that goes backward. In other words, this is an edge that takes you back in the execution of your program. Hence, you re-execute something that you have already executed. At this point, you may realize that a backedge is part of what you would call a loop in a programming language.

This definition is a bit loose, but you get the idea:

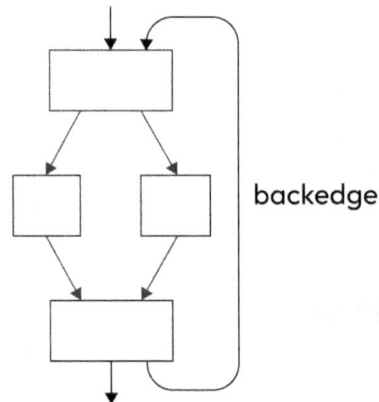

*Figure 3.2: A backedge in a CFG*

A proper definition of backedges is edges that do not respect the topological order. So, if you were to number basic blocks using a topological order, such as RPO, a backedge would jump from a source with a higher number than the number of the destination.

To put things together, identifying backedges is important to identify loops. Identifying loops is important since loops are where most programs spend most of their runtime, hence, they are the primary focus for compiler optimizations.

# Critical edge

A **critical edge** is a control flow edge that connects a source with multiple successors and a destination with multiple predecessors, as illustrated in the left part of *Figure 3.3*:

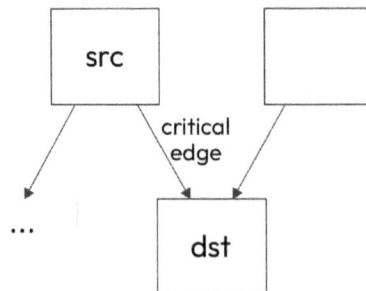

*Figure 3.3: A critical edge in a CFG*

Critical edges are an important concept because if you want to optimize or generate something specific for the path taken by this edge (src, dst), you cannot do so without affecting the other successors of src or the other predecessors of dst.

In other words, changes made around a critical edge affect the whole region around it. As a result, certain optimization needs to be extra careful around such edges, as illustrated in *Figure 3.4*:

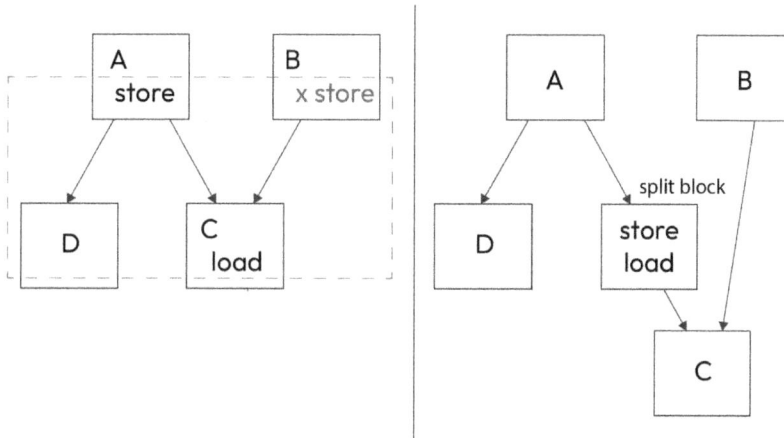

*Figure 3.4: Region affected by critical edges and how to break them*

On the left of *Figure 3.4*, the edge (A, C) is critical. Because of that, inserting a store in A and reloading in C means that the whole dotted region needs to play nicely with this memory location. Concretely, this means that on the execution path going through the edge (A, D), the store is useless, and on the execution path going through the edge (B, C), a store needs to be added.

That said, it is possible to break critical edges, as illustrated in the right part of *Figure 3.4*, by creating a new basic block on this edge, named *split block* here. In that case, we say that we split the critical edge from (src, dst) to (src, newBB) (newBB, dst). Splitting a critical edge usually comes with a cost. For instance, you may create additional indirections (jumps) in the CFG that may have a performance impact on the final generated code.

At the IR level, you can check if an edge is critical using the isCriticalEdge function from the Analysis library.

## Irreducible graph

The notion of graph reducibility gives some information about whether a CFG is well structured. Conceptually, well structured means that loops within the CFG are perfectly nested. Conversely, loops not properly nested will produce irreducible CFGs.

This is important to know when you deal with **irreducible graphs** because some analysis provided by the LLVM infrastructure may give you surprising results on such graphs, and you may misinterpret them and generate incorrect code.

For instance, consider the following snippet and its CFG representation in *Figure 3.5*:

```
extern void someFct();

int irreducible(int shouldSkip1stCall) {
  int i = 0;
  if (shouldSkip1stCall)
    goto SKIP;
  do {
    someFct();
    SKIP:;
  } while (++i < 7);
  return 32;
}
```

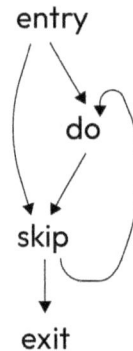

*Figure 3.5: An irreducible CFG*

Although this snippet has conceptually only one loop, it has two loop headers; you can enter the loop (do..while) through two different points (do and SKIP). We will cover the jargon around loops specifically in *Chapter 4*.

The bottom line is, if your optimization behaves strangely with some loops, check if you are not dealing with irreducible graphs as they can easily throw off some potentially implicit assumptions you were making in your code.

You can use the templated containsIrreducibleCFG API from the IR library to check if the CFG of a function is irreducible. The template parameters allow you to use this API for both the LLVM IR and the Machine IR levels, but they require that you provide the RPO iterator and the LoopInfo analysis for your Function/MachineFunction class.

Before we wrap up this section, we need to at least give a proper definition of an irreducible graph.

A CFG is reducible if and only if you can reduce it to a single basic block by applying the following rules until you cannot make any changes:

1.  Remove self-edges; that is, remove all e (src, dst) from E where src = dst.

2.  If basic block A has only one predecessor, merge it with its predecessor; that is, do the following:

    •   Delete A

    •   Delete the unique edge (src, A)

    •   Update all edges (A, dst) to (src, dst)

If you cannot make any progress and your CFG is not a single basic block, then it is irreducible.

You can find an example of how this algorithm is applied in the *Quiz time* section.

> Note
>
> Irreducible graphs can cause nasty bugs when you do not handle them correctly. However, most optimization/analysis/tools work just fine with these constructs. If irreducible graphs are a problem for you, LLVM provides a transformation that turns irreducible graphs into reducible ones through the FixIrreduciblePass API, which is part of the TransformUtils library. This transformation only works at the LLVM IR level.

In this section, you learned the basic concepts (module, function, basic block, instruction, and CFG) that you will manipulate while working on a compiler. You saw how these concepts map to key LLVM APIs and had a brief overview of how to use these APIs.

Let us now put that into practice by building some IR directly.

# Building your first IRs

In this section, you will put to the test what you just learned by building an IR both at the LLVM IR and the Machine IR levels. The goal of this exercise is twofold:

1.  Manipulate the APIs to create instances of the classes Module, Function, MachineFunction, and so on.

2.  Get a sense of what a frontend has to put with when it comes to producing an IR.

This exercise remains however artificial in the sense that at this point, you lack a lot of knowledge to build any complex IR. You will build this knowledge along the way, namely in *Chapters 4, 7,* and *10,* but this gives you a good introduction to what is ahead and helps you solidify your current learning.

In this exercise, you will build the IR for the following snippet:

```
extern int baz();
extern void bar(int);
void foo(int a, int b) {
  int var = a + b;
```

```
    if (var == 0xFF) {
        bar(var);
        var = baz();
    }
    bar(var);
}
```

By default – in other words, when you do not enable optimizations in your compiler toolchain or when you run with -O0 – local variables are not optimized. What this means is each local variable is stored on the current function's stack. In other words, from a frontend perspective, all accesses to local variables, reads, and writes go through the memory that has been allocated for the stack of this function.

What this implies concretely is the following:

- You need to reserve some space on the stack for each local variable
- Each read of a variable goes through a load from the related stack location
- Each write of a variable goes through a store to the related stack location

In this exercise, we will follow the same convention. Therefore, make sure to allocate memory space for var and access it exclusively through loads and stores.

Do not worry – we will point out which instructions you have to use to achieve these patterns.

## Building your first LLVM IR

In this section, you will practice building an LLVM IR for the previously presented C snippet. To complete this exercise, you can dig into the APIs of the various classes that you discovered in the early sections (Module, Function, and so on).

To make your task more approachable, let us start by pointing out most of the APIs that you need.

## A walk over the required APIs

To create function declarations (bar and baz here), you can use one of the Module::getOrInsertFunction methods. These methods require that you have an instance of a Module class, but you already know how to create a Module object (see the *Module* section if you do not remember).

Zooming into the Module::getOrInsertFunction methods, you need to define the type of the function to create it. The function type is represented with the FunctionType class and you can instantiate an object of this class using one of the FunctionType::get static methods. The API is simple: you need to provide the return type and an array with a type for each input argument.

For this exercise, you need three types: void, int, and ptr. You can create the first two types with the related static function of the Type class: Type::VoidTy(LLVMContext &) and Type::getInt32Ty(LLVMContext &), respectively. For the third one, similarly to the FunctionType class, you need to use the static get method from the PointerType class. When using this method, do not worry about the AddressSpace argument and just put 0. We will cover what this represents in *Chapter 7*. You should know how to get/create an LLVMContext object at this point, but for the sake of this exercise, we provide it as an input of your function because its lifetime needs to be longer than the Module object that you are building!

To create a function definition, you can use one of the static Create methods of the Function class. These methods need a FunctionType instance as well as a LinkageType instance and a Module instance. For this exercise, the linkage type does not matter; you can pick whatever enum value you want – for example, GlobalValue::ExternalLinkage.

Now that you have your Function instance, you need to populate it with basic blocks. As you learned in the *Basic block* section, there is no right or wrong way to do this splitting, but we recommend aiming for maximal basic blocks.

First, focus on creating the basic blocks, irrespective of how they are connected. The CFG and, thus, the connections between the blocks will be created automatically when you add branch instructions.

You have guessed it – to create BasicBlock objects, you can use the static BasicBlock::Create method. Make sure to set the Function argument to your Function instance; otherwise, the BasicBlock class will be an orphan (that is, will not have a parent).

At this point, you have the skeleton of your function; the only remaining thing is to populate each basic block with the related instructions. This is, nevertheless, not as straightforward as it may seem at first. Indeed, remember that you must do the following:

- Allocate some memory space on the stack for var; you can do that by using AllocaInst.
- Instantiate every read of var with a load from the allocated stack slot by reusing the returned Value object from AllocaInst in a LoadInst object.
- Do the same thing for every write to var using the StoreInst object.

For the a and b variables, these come straight from the arguments of the Function object, and you already know how to access them. We let you dig into the Function APIs to find out how to access them without using the arg_xxx iterators that we already mentioned in the *A function in LLVM IR* section.

You almost have everything you need to complete this exercise. You miss only three kinds of instructions:

- The return instruction to materialize the terminator instruction in the exit block (remember – each basic block must end with a terminator): ReturnInst.
- The integer comparison instruction to materialize var == 0xFF: ICmpInst. For the 0xFF constant, use the ConstantInt::get static method.
- The branch instruction, also a terminator instruction, to jump to different basic blocks: BranchInst. You will see that you can create both conditional and unconditional branches. In other words, branches with two possible destinations are chosen with a predicate such as the one produced with the ICmpInst instruction, and branches with only one destination.

For all your instructions, you can use the IRBuilder helper class to create them.

## Your turn

Go to ch3/llvm_ir/your_turn/populate_function.cpp and populate the function called buildIR. This function returns a (unique) pointer to the instance of the Module class that represents the snippet you should build. Follow the steps in README.md to build and run your example, and feel free to look at ch3/llvm_ir/solution /populate_function.cpp to see an example of how to build this IR.

Note

You can use `ch3/input.c` with Clang, as explained in *Chapter 1*, to see the IR that Clang produces (use the `-S`, `-O0`, and `-emit-llvm` options). You will see that the produced IR is even more verbose than what we proposed to build. This is because we simplified how the arguments were accessed since they are only read.

# Building your first Machine IR

The Machine IR is target-specific, so depending on which architecture you target, the lowering may be different. For this exercise, we will assume that we build for the AArch64 target and that we only care about a partially lowered IR.

What this means for you is you do not have to know the AArch64 ISA to be able to do this exercise. However, this flexibility comes with a cost: you will have to produce additional types for your IR to be valid.

In any case, the goal here is to make you manipulate the Machine IR API, so do not overthink the actual details. We will dive into these in *Chapter 10* and onward.

Before we go through the APIs you may need to complete this exercise, we need to define a simplified ABI that you must follow:

- 32-bit arguments are passed through registers: w0, w1, ...
- 32-bit returned values are passed through registers: w0, w1, ...

What this means is the following:

- The foo function's input arguments are provided through, respectively, w0 for a and w1 for b
- The bar function's input argument must be provided through w0
- The baz function's returned value is provided through w0

Let us dive into the meat of the Machine IR creation!

# A walk over the required APIs

Since the Machine IR level only represents one function at a time, you do not have to worry about the function declarations of bar and baz.

Then, to create the foo function's skeleton, you need to instantiate the basic blocks using `MachineFunction::CreateMachineBasicBlock`. Be careful that although this method creates the basic blocks, it does not insert them in `MachineFunction`, so make sure to call `MachineFunction::push_back` with the newly created blocks. Also, remember that the order in the list of basic blocks determines the serialization order and, by extension, the fall-through paths that you can use.

Next, unlike at the LLVM IR level, you need to explicitly create the CFG. For that, you can use the `MachineBasicBlock::addSuccessor` method.

What is left at this point is to populate your basic blocks. For this exercise, you will use the `MachineIRBuilder` class from the `GlobalISel` library. This offers a higher-level API than the `MachineInstrBuilder` class from the `CodeGen` library and hides some of the Machine IR details that you do not know yet and that you will discover in *Chapter 10*.

When you instantiate your `MachineIRBuilder` object, you need to give it some context that will be used as the default insertion point for your new instructions. We recommend using `MachineIRBuilder::MachineIRBuilder(MachineBasicBlock &, MachineBasicBlock::iterator)` for this exercise with the iterator argument set to `YourBlock.end()`. That way, you can populate your block following a top-down approach without having to change the insertion point as you go.

The `MachineIRBuilder` class supports different forms for instantiating instructions. For this exercise, you will use only one of them, where you will do the following:

- Pass the type of the result value
- Pass the input arguments as instances of the `Register` class
- Get back the result value as an instance of the `Register` class

What this means is all your calls to your `MachineIRBuilder` object should look like this:

- Here is the call for instructions that define a result:

    ```
    Register Result = MIBuilder.buildXXX(ResultType, RegArg0, RegArg1, …).getReg(0);
    ```

- This is the call for instructions that do not define a result:

    ```
    MIBuilder.buildXXX(RegArg0, RegArg1, …);
    ```

Regarding the type of your results, we provided some boilerplate code that instantiates them for you. Therefore, you just have to use the code provided here:

- `I1` for the bool type
- `I32` for the int type
- `VarAddrLLT` for the type of the stack slot for `var`

Now, in terms of methods, here are all the methods you need to instantiate the proper instructions:

- `MachineIRBuilder::buildAdd`: Binary add.
- `MachineIRBuilder::buildBr`: Unconditional branch.
- `MachineIRBuilder::buildBrCond`: Conditional branch.
- `MachineIRBuilder::buildConstant`: Constant (0xFF, for instance.)
- `MachineIRBuilder::buildCopy`: Copy value around; required to set and read from `w0` and `w1`.
- `MachineIRBuilder::buildICmp`: Integer comparison.
- `MachineIRBuilder::buildFrameIndex`: Materialize the stack slot for `var`; use the provided `VarAddrLLT` and `FrameIndex` variables as arguments. Creating a stack slot is outside of the scope of this exercise.

- `MachineIRBuilder::buildLoad`: Load a value from an address; for example, a frame index of a stack slot.
- `MachineIRBuilder::buildStore`: Store a value to an address.

If you have been paying attention, you should have noticed that we are missing two kinds of instructions: the call instruction and the return instruction. These instructions are target-specific and cannot be instantiated with one of the generic methods. Instead, you have to manually specify the target opcode for them using the `MachineIRBuilder::buildInstr` method. The short version is you cannot do that the right way at this point, so instead, we will use inline assembly to materialize instructions that would resemble the real ones:

- For the call to `bar`, run the following:

```
MIBuilder.buildInstr(TargetOpcode::INLINEASM, {}, {})
    .addExternalSymbol("bl @bar")
    .addImm(0)
    .addReg(W0, RegState::Implicit);
```

- For the call to `baz`, run the following:

```
MIBuilder.buildInstr(TargetOpcode::INLINEASM, {}, {})
    .addExternalSymbol("bl @baz")
    .addImm(0)
    .addReg(W0, RegState::Implicit | RegState::Define);
```

- For the return instruction at the end of the function, run the following:

```
MIBuilder.buildInstr(TargetOpcode::INLINEASM, {}, {})
        .addExternalSymbol("ret")
        .addImm(0);
```

Before we open the floor for you, here is a last constraint to be aware of: for the most part, instructions built with the `MachineIRBuilder` API do not accept non-register arguments; this is why you must materialize the constant (`0xFF`) in a register first. Similarly, physical registers, such as `w0` and `w1`, should be avoided in this API, except for the `MachineIRBuilder::buildCopy` API. Hence, make sure to copy to and from `w0` and `w1` as needed in your IR.

## Your turn

Populate the function named populateMachineIR in ch3/machineir/your_turn/populate_function. cpp. This function gives you a `MachineModuleInfo` object and a `Function` class to instantiate your `MachineFunction` class. It also provides two `Register` variables, `W0` and `W1`, that you can use to satisfy the ABI requirements.

At the beginning of this function, you will also find, as already mentioned, variables that hold the **low-level type (LLT)** required for the call to `MachineIRBuilder::buildXXX` as well as some other variables that you will need to use for the load and store builders.

Complete this function, and when you are ready, look at the README.md file in ch3/machineir to run your code. The main function of this exercise builds the IR with your solution and the provided solution (located in ch3/machineir/solution/populate_function.cpp) and, in both cases, prints the built functions and checks that they pass the verifier (MachineFunction::verify). Try to have your IR pass the verifier without issue.

> **Note**
>
> If you look at the implementation in ch3/machineir/solution/populate_function. cpp, you will see that we created one block with two terminators and one block with no terminator. The block with no terminator just falls through to the next one, as we already explained in the *A basic block in the Machine IR* section. However, when you think about the block with two terminators, it violates the SESE constraint. This is a design choice in the Machine IR. The SESE constraint can be violated within the terminators' region to save some memory space. Indeed, it is possible to generate a version of the Machine IR that does not violate this constraint (by creating a fall-through block with just one unconditional branch in it), but that means allocating one more MachineBasicBlock object for just one instruction. This trade-off is shown in *Table 3.2*.

| BB1 violates SESE | More code is required to respect SESE |
|---|---|
| ```<br>BB1:<br>  G_BRCOND predicate, BB2<br>  G_BR BB3<br>``` | ```<br>BB1:<br>  G_BRCOND predicate, BB2<br>BBTmp:<br>  G_BR BB3<br>``` |

*Table 3.2: SESE can be violated in the Machine IR in the terminator region*

This concludes your hands-on experience with manipulating some IR at both the LLVM IR and Machine IR levels. In the process, you saw firsthand what it takes to instantiate such IRs and had a glimpse at some of the APIs that you can leverage to do that.

Next, we summarize what you learned throughout this chapter.

# Summary

In this chapter, you learned basic jargon and concepts that you will manipulate in your day-to-day job as a compiler engineer. Things such as module, function, basic block, instruction, CFG, have no secret for you now.

You also learned how these concepts map to LLVM APIs, both at the LLVM IR and the Machine IR levels. While you only scratched the surface of these APIs, you now have a mental model of what offers what and have a few concrete pointers to start digging more into them.

Your next stop is with more advanced compiler concepts that will allow you to go deeper into the LLVM infrastructure and give you an idea of what it takes to write your first optimization. Before you go there, you have guessed it – it is quiz time!

## Quiz time

Now that you have completed reading this chapter, try answering the following questions to test your knowledge:

1.  Draw the CFG for the following C program:

    ```c
    int foo(int b) {
      int res = 0;
      for (int i = 0; i < b; ++i) {
        if (i % b == 0) {
          res + = bar(i);
        } else {
          res -= baz(i);
        }
      }
      return res;
    }
    ```

    The answer is the following:

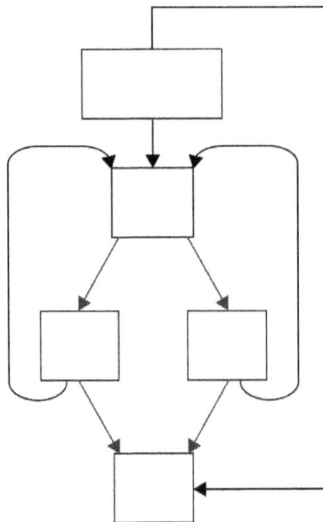

    Please refer to the *Control flow graph* section for the definition of a CFG.

2. Is the following CFG reducible?

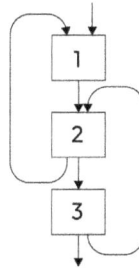

Yes!

Please use the algorithm described in the *Irreducible graph* section.

You can reduce it with the following sequence:

- 3 has only one predecessor: Merge 2 and 3
- 2 has now a self-edge: Remove it
- 2 has now only one predecessor: Merge 1 and 2
- 1 has now a self-edge: Remove it

If only the basic block 1 remains, the graph is irreducible.

3. Given the following irreducible CFG, how could you make it reducible?

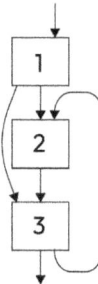

Technically, we did not teach you how to do that (aside from calling `FixIrreduciblePass`), and the goal of this exercise was to force you to think about how you would solve such problems.

The idea is to collect the headers of the loop and create a condition in a block called a guard to fall back to what LLVM calls a natural loop with only one header.

The guard block will dispatch to the right loop using the following predicate:

- Coming from 1: Use 1's condition to jump to either 2 or 3
- Coming from 2: Set predicate to jump to 3
- Coming from 3: Set predicate to jump to 2

All in all, the CFG looks like this:

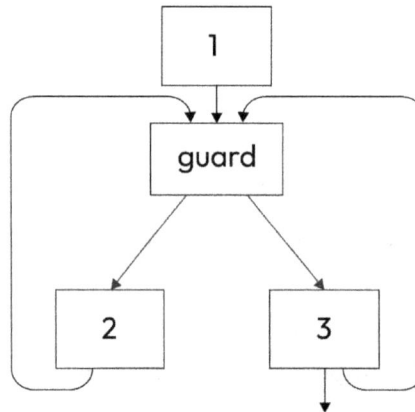

You can check that this is indeed reducible.

4. Point out the critical edges in the original CFG from *question 3*.

   Edges (1, 2) and (1, 3) are critical edges (1 has several successors, and both 2 and 3 have several predecessors).

   See the *Critical edge* section for more details about critical edges.

5. Name a kind of topological traversal of a CFG offered by LLVM APIs.

   RPO. See the *Reverse post-order traversal* section.

6. How can you find all the backedges in a CFG?

   See how you can identify backedges with RPO as defined in the *Backedge* section.

7. What would you call the time spent by your compiler to compile an input file?

   Compile time. See the *Build time, compile time, and runtime* section.

# 4

# Writing Your First Optimization

This chapter introduces advanced compiler topics that you will need to work with the LLVM infrastructure and compilers in general. Similar to *Chapter 3*, you will see how these concepts map to LLVM **application programming interfaces (APIs)**.

To help you build confidence in writing your own programs, we will build a program together that performs a simple optimization called constant propagation. If you are not familiar with this optimization, do not worry – this is mainly an excuse to manipulate LLVM APIs, and we will explain it in due time.

This chapter will cover the following key topics:

- The concepts involved in a modern compiler framework like LLVM to write optimizations
- How to write an optimization in LLVM

Before we get started, let us review the software that you will need for this chapter.

## Technical requirements

You will find the complete code of what we are building in this chapter in the ch4 folder of the repository of this book: https://github.com/PacktPublishing/LLVM-Code-Generation.

The technical requirements are otherwise the same as in *Chapter 3*. In other words, you will need a C/C++ compiler toolchain, CMake, and Ninja.

Finally, if you use a toolchain that does not have Clang, consider building your own Clang compiler as this will come in handy to produce the input of our program. Check out the *Building Clang* section in *Chapter 1*, for a method to generate your own Clang compiler.

Now that we have taken care of the logistics for this chapter, let us dive into our first concept: value!

# The concept of value

A value is an entity that bears a certain meaning at a given time. While this definition may be hard to grasp, you are likely already familiar with this concept with your background in computer science.

For instance, consider the following snippet:

```
a = b + c;
a = a + d;
```

The first statement assigns a value to a (b + c), and the next statement assigns a different value to a (a's previous value + d).

This example highlights that values and variables are two different concepts.

The concept of value is interesting because if you can pin the value of a variable, it opens the door to many optimizations/analyses.

Consider the following example:

```
void foo(int a, int b) {
  int var = a + b;
  if (var == 0xFF) {
    bar(var);
    var = baz();
  }
  bar(var);
}
```

In this snippet, it is trivial to see that in the call to bar in the first if statement, it is possible to replace var with the 0xFF constant.

In general, this is not that easy. We would need to perform a reachability analysis (which of var's definitions reaches this particular use of var) and unbox the related definition(s) to see what optimization opportunities we have.

Now, imagine that the concept of value is directly part of the **intermediate representation** (IR). This is possible with the **static single assignment** (SSA) form that is used extensively throughout LLVM.

Let us see what SSA is about.

# SSA

SSA is a way to represent values directly in an IR. The idea is straightforward: rename all variables such that each variable holds exactly one value statically. The term *statically* means that a variable is lexicographically defined at most once in the related function. In other words, a variable can be defined in a loop, hence it will hold different values during its lifetime at runtime, but statically it appears only once in the IR.

You may realize that although the concept is simple, there is a fundamental problem: how can you represent variables that are defined through distinct paths? Put differently, let us say that we rename all variables such that all assignments within a function use a different name. The question is: How do you reconcile uses of the original variable that may be defined by distinct values?

For instance, look back at the previous snippet. If we rename var in its first assignment to var1 and var2 in its second assignment (within the if statement), which variable should you use in var's last use at the end of the function?

This problem is solved with the introduction of a special instruction called phi (f). A phi instruction is used when different values are joined conditionally through several paths to produce a new value. *Figure 4.1* illustrates what SSA looks like when constructed on the previous snippet:

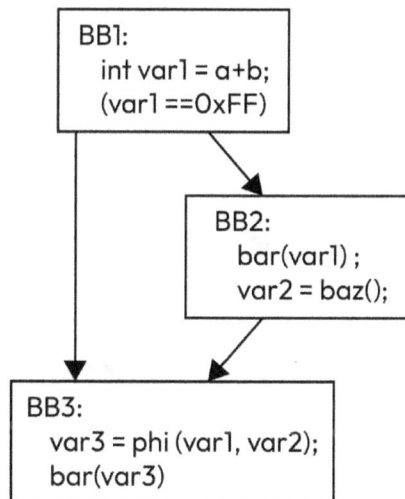

*Figure 4.1: A program in SSA form*

A phi instruction copies the input value from the related control flow edge to the definition of the phi. For instance, in *Figure 4.1*, when the control flow goes from BB1 to BB3 (that is, the left edge – the first value of the phi), var1 is copied into var3. When the control flow goes from BB2 to BB3, the second value, var2, is copied into var3.

To put it differently, phi instructions act as if a copy were inserted on the related incoming edge.

In the LLVM IR and Machine IR levels, phi instructions are grouped together at the beginning of the basic blocks. It is invalid to insert non-phi instructions before phi instructions.

Phi instructions are mapped to the PHINode class, which is a subclass of the Instruction class, in the LLVM IR and to the MachineInstr class with getOpcode() == PHI in the Machine IR.

> **Note**
>
> There are different ways to represent the join point of values. Phis are the most common ones, but if you look at the **multi-level IR (MLIR)**, you will see that they use an argument-passing style. We will not cover this in this book, but the exact same principles apply.

SSA offers a lot of interesting properties that you will discover in the next sections. But first, let us see how you get the program in SSA form.

## Constructing the SSA form

To get your program in SSA form, you need to take a non-SSA program and rewrite it in SSA form: renaming the variables, inserting the phi instructions in the right place, and so on.

We will not go into the details of how to do that. While the details are interesting, it is unlikely you will need to reimplement this part yourself since, unsurprisingly, LLVM already offers such a capability. If you are curious about implementing your own construction of the SSA form from a non-SSA representation, there is plenty of literature on that. For instance, we recommend *Simple and Efficient Construction of Static Single Assignment Form* by *Braun et al.*, published in *Compiler Construction* in 2013.

In the LLVM IR, the Instruction class can only represent values, so technically, you can only build SSA programs. However, users do not write in SSA form, so you need a mechanism to close this gap when going from the frontend to the backend. The way to do that is to use memory locations.

Memory locations are not in SSA form in the LLVM IR because memory locations obtained by different means (that is, through different values) can end up referencing the same address. In that case, we say that the memory locations or the addresses are aliases (we also use alias as a verb: they alias). This concept of aliasing is exactly what SSA prevents: it disambiguates values from variables.

Anyhow, memory locations in the LLVM IR have the same expressiveness as a non-SSA program and, as a result, this is what a frontend will use.

Putting things together, a frontend, such as Clang, generates programs in the LLVM IR that rely heavily on memory and will let the backend optimize memory accesses.

Using the same code snippet as the previous section, a frontend generates an IR that resembles what is depicted in *Figure 4.1*. Notice all the alloca instructions that create some space on the stack of the function and the load and store instructions to read and write the values. (You will learn how to read the LLVM IR in *Chapter 7*.)

Then, the backend will optimize away the memory accesses to construct the SSA form depicted back in *Figure 4.1*:

```
define void @foo(i32 noundef %arg, i32 noundef %arg1) {
bb1:
  %i = alloca i32, align 4
  %i2 = alloca i32, align 4
  %i3 = alloca i32, align 4
  store i32 %arg, ptr %i, align 4
  store i32 %arg1, ptr %i2, align 4
  %i4 = load i32, ptr %i, align 4
  %i5 = load i32, ptr %i2, align 4
  %i6 = add nsw i32 %i4, %i5
  store i32 %i6, ptr %i3, align 4
  %i7 = load i32, ptr %i3, align 4
  %i8 = icmp eq i32 %i7, 255
  br i1 %i8, label %bb2, label %bb3
bb2:
  %i10 = load i32, ptr %i3, align 4
  call void @bar(i32 noundef %i10)
  %i11 = call i32 @baz()
  store i32 %i11, ptr %i3, align 4
  br label %bb3
bb3:
  %i13 = load i32, ptr %i3, align 4
  call void @bar(i32 noundef %i13)
  ret void
}
```

The optimization in the LLVM IR responsible for promoting memory locations to SSA values is called `mem2reg`. This optimization lives in the `TransformsUtils` library and can be called through the `createPromoteMemoryToRegisterPass` API (more details on how to use that in *Chapter 5*). You can also use the underlying logic of this optimization by directly calling the `PromoteMemToReg` API. You will see that this API takes three arguments: the list of `alloca` instructions that define the memory locations you want to promote to register, the dominator tree, and the assumption cache. The assumption cache can be obtained directly through the `Function` class, but the dominator tree needs to be constructed.

Before looking at the dominator tree, the subject of our next section, know that `mem2reg` is useful when you want to go from a non-SSA form to an SSA form. However, this is a heavy hammer when it comes to updating a program already in an SSA form. For these cases, depending on the kind of transformations you do, you should either maintain the SSA form yourself or use the `SSAUpdater` helper class, which also lives in the `TransformsUtils` library.

Regarding the Machine IR, there is no equivalent of `mem2reg` at this level. Generally, the Machine IR is built directly from an LLVM IR representation in SSA form, so it inherits its SSA properties by default. Also, note that the Machine IR level can deal with both SSA and non-SSA forms, so the requirements around being in SSA form are looser. The Machine IR also provides a `MachineSSAUpdate` helper class in the `CodeGen` library.

Finally, it is possible to also have some SSA properties on memory locations. To get this, you will need to leverage the `MemorySSA` analysis from the `Analysis` library. Beware that memory locations are trickier to work with, and while the `MemorySSA` analysis alleviates a lot of the pain, you must remember that it must be correct with respect to aliasing rules. Hence, the result may not be as smooth as one could initially expect.

Let us go back to the dominator tree by introducing an important property around SSA values: the concept of dominance.

## Dominance

The concept of dominance in a **control-flow graph** (CFG )is a property that arises from the layout of the nodes. Let us imagine two nodes d and n in a CFG; d dominates n if all the paths from the entry point to n must go through d. *Figure 4.2* summarizes this concept, where the wiggling arrows represent all the possible execution paths that lead to a particular node in the CFG:

entry

• d

• n

*Figure 4.2: d dominates n*

This concept is interesting in the compiler world because values follow this property: to be able to use a value, you need to define it first. Therefore, a definition must dominate its uses.

> Note
>
> It is possible to write programs where the use of a variable happens before the variable's definition. While such programs are broken in their own way, a compiler still needs to accurately represent them. This type of program is well-supported and well-defined with the concept of value and dominance. We simply produce undefined or, more precisely, poisoned values on the related execution paths. We will explain the difference between undefined and poisoned values in *Chapter 7*.

Here are a couple more notions that are used within LLVM and in compilers in general:

- d strictly dominates n if d dominates n and d is not n.
- The **immediate dominator**, or **idom**, of a node n is the node that dominates n but does not dominate any of the other nodes that dominate n. To put it simply, idom(n) is the last/closet node that dominates n.

You now have enough background to understand the concept of the dominator tree that we briefly mentioned in the previous section.

A **dominator tree** is a tree rooted in the entry block of the CFG, where the children of a node are the nodes that are immediately dominated by their parent.

For example, consider the CFG from the previous snippet, as shown on the left-hand side of *Figure 4.3*:

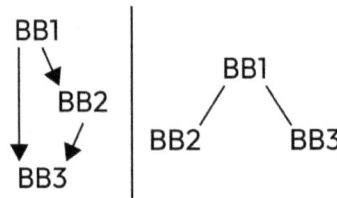

*Figure 4.3: A CFG on the left and its dominator tree on the right*

The resulting dominator tree, on the right-hand side of the diagram, has as many nodes as the original CFG, but notice how the edges are different. More specifically, notice how BB2 has no edge connecting it to BB3. If this does not directly make sense to you, try to think of this representation in terms of values. Where can you define a value used in BB3 such that this value will be defined on all paths that lead to BB3? Defining such a value in BB2 will not be valid because if the program goes from BB1 to BB3, this value will not be defined. Also, remember that a value is not a variable; you can only define it once (statically). In other words, you cannot insert two definitions (one in BB1 and one in BB2) of the same value; otherwise, this is not a value anymore. Indeed, by definition, a value holds only one value!

As you probably already realize, immediate dominators and, by extension, dominator trees are especially useful when doing compiler optimizations, such as code motion, that require some rewrite of the values. By using the dominator tree, you can quickly find the insertion point in your CFG, hence your program, where materializing the definition of a new value will properly reach all its uses.

Another important notion related to dominance is post-dominance.

**Post-dominance** depicts the same concept as dominance but with the exit node. A node p post-dominates a node n if all the paths from n to the exit node must go through p. The same notion of idom applies to post-dominators and is called **immediate post-dominator** (**ipdom**).

Using the same notation as *Figure 4.2*, *Figure 4.4* depicts the post-dominator relationship between p and n:

*Figure 4.4: p post-dominates n*

> **Note**
>
> Remember that, as already mentioned, for CFGs with more than one exit node, you can always create a fake unique exit node.

This notion of post-dominance can be handy, for instance, when you want to optimize the release of resources, as with some managed memory. However, beware that dominance and post-dominance properties can be a little surprising when applied to basic blocks in loops.

Consider the following snippet where some resources are used within a loop, and you want to correctly place allocation and deallocation points:

```
while (1) {
  if (catchExit())
    return;
  // use resource
}
```

Naively, you could think that it would be enough to allocate the resources you need in a basic block that dominates the uses of the resources and deallocate them in a basic block that post-dominates them.

While this is true for a CFG without loops, these constraints are not sufficient when loops are involved.

Consider the incorrect placement as shown next:

```
while (1) {
  // allocate resource
  // deallocate resource
  if (catchExit())
   return;
  // use resources
}
```

The problem is while the deallocation post-dominates the code that uses the resources (after using the resources, the program must go through `deallocate` before it can reach the return behind the `catchExit` condition), the deallocation also dominates the use of the resources, so when reaching the use of the resources, they would be already unavailable.

The takeaway from this example is to be careful with loops!

## Def-use and use-def chains

**Def-use** and **use-def** chains are a natural consequence of the concept of value. The concept of a def-use chain is a fancy way to say that by knowing the definition of a value, you can find all its uses, and vice versa for the use-def chain.

What this means concretely is you will find APIs in LLVM that given a value, enable you to do the following:

1.  Access all its uses
2.  Access its unique definition

For instance, imagine that your program is written such that all variables are values. By knowing the name of your variable, you can easily find its definition and all its uses by scanning the text of your program. Of course, the LLVM infrastructure uses a much more efficient way to build and maintain this information, but you get the idea.

### Def-use and use-def chains in the LLVM IR

At the LLVM IR level, def-use and use-def chains are maintained automatically. In other words, you do not have to worry about updating any sort of data structure on the side for this information to remain correct.

Almost all the classes that make the IR derive from the `Value` class from the `IR` library. This class represents the value itself – for instance, the actual instruction that defines this value. As such, when you have a handle on a value, you already know the definition. For instance, if you obtain an instance of the `Function` class (for example, through `Module::getFunction(StringRef Name)`), the pointer that you get represents conceptually the definition of the related function.

Using the handle you have of a value, you can use the family of Value::useXXX() methods (where XXX means that several endings are possible; for example, uses, use_begin, use_end, and so on) to get iterators on the use list of that value.

These iterators return instances of the Use class. You can use Use::get() or Use::operator*() to access the instance representing the value being used and Use::getUser() to access the user of the value. The Use::getOperandNo() iterator also gives the index at which the value is used in this user. The returned user is of the User class, which is also a subclass of Value, and that notably exposes methods to get and set operands, respectively User::getOperand(unsigned i) and User::setOperand(unsigned i, Value *Val). In other words, a User object is a kind of Value object that uses Value objects as inputs.

To put everything together, given an object of the Use class, MyUse, MyUse.get() is equal to MyUse.getUser()->getOperand(MyUse.getOperandNo()).

It is possible to use a different set of iterators if you want to traverse only the users of a value and not its uses. For this, use the methods of the form Value::userXXX().

The difference between a use and a user can be puzzling at first, so let us spend some time refining your understanding.

Essentially, the Use class represents the link between an instance of the Value class and its users, themselves represented with the User class. *Figure 4.5* illustrates the relationship and differences between a Value object, its Use objects, and its User objects:

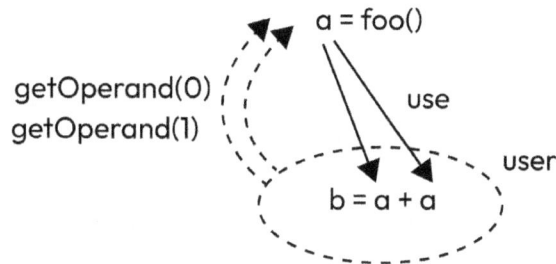

*Figure 4.5: The difference between the Use and User classes*

The value a is the returned value of the foo function and is represented with one of the derived classes of Value (CallInst in this case). The value a has two uses – 1) b at operand 0 and 2) b at operand 1 – but only one user: b.

> **Note**
>
> As you saw with Module::getFunction and the input argument, not all instances of the Value class are represented with an instruction. While this is obvious in this case, it is easy to end up with non-instruction values while walking through the use-def chain of the operand of an instruction. Similarly surprising at first, depending on the kind of value you are looking at, it is possible to jump around different functions when traversing the list of uses/users. Be careful about that in the algorithm you write, or you may inadvertently impact code in a different scope than intended.

*Table 4.1* gives an example of code where the code snippet on the right would jump from the scope of bar to the scope of foo, simply by following the use-def chain starting at bar_res:

| Input IR | A program using LLVM APIs |
|---|---|
| <pre>extern char *global;<br>char **other_global = &global;<br><br>char foo() {<br>  char foo_res = global[0];<br>  return foo_res;<br>}<br>char bar() {<br>  char bar_res = global[0];<br>  return bar_res;<br>}</pre> | <pre>Value *Global = BarRes.<br>getOperand(0);<br>for (User *UserOfGlobal : Global-<br>>users()) {<br>  auto *UserInstr = dyn_<br>cast<Instruction><br>(UserOfGlobal);<br>  if (!UserInstr) {<br>    errs() << "Found a non-<br>instruction use of global: " <<<br>*UserOfGlobal<br>              << '\n';<br>    continue;<br>  }<br>  Function *UserFunc = UserInstr-<br>>getParent()->getParent();<br>  if (UserFunc != BarFunc)<br>    errs() << "Went from bar to "<br><< UserFunc->getName() << '\n';<br>}</pre> |

*Table 4.1: Code sequence showing an implicit change of function scope*

Let us detail what happens in *Table 4.1*:

1. The code starts from the definition of bar_res (we omitted the code to get this value for conciseness, but a full example can be found at ch4/ implicit_func_scope_change).

2. We get the definition of global: Value *Global = BarRes.getOperand(0).

3. We walk the users of global: for (User *UserOfGlobal: Global->users()).

4. We try to dynamically cast this user to an instruction: auto *UserInstr = dyn_cast<Instruction>(UserOfGlobal).

5. For other_global, this cast returns nullptr, and we print the first error, Found a non-instruction…, which illustrates that not all users are instructions.

6. For bar_res and foo_res, the cast succeeds, and we look for the parent of the parent of this definition (hence, we get the basic block first (->getParent()), and from there, the function second (->getParent()).

7.  Finally, we check if that function is the same as bar, and for foo_res's function, this prints the second error, Went from bar to…, which illustrates that while walking def-use and use-def chains, it is possible to go from an instruction in a function to an instruction in another function.

> **Warning**
>
> Depending on how this example runs, you may notice that the order of the error messages may change. This is expected and is the last takeaway from this section: the lists of uses and users do not follow any specific order. Make sure your code is resilient with respect to order; for instance, even if all the users are within the same basic block, it is incorrect to expect that these users will be handed to you in the topological order (top to bottom) of this block.

To summarize, you can walk the def-use chain using the Value::useXXX and Value::userXXX family of methods. You can walk the use-def chain by using the User::getOperand method.

> **Note**
>
> To get used to navigating LLVM APIs, we encourage you to locate the Value class in the Doxygen documentation. When you access the page for the Value class, you will see the inheritance diagram of this class at the very top of the page. The link to this page for the open source repository is https://llvm.org/doxygen/classllvm_1_1Value.html.

## Def-use and use-def chains in the Machine IR

The Machine IR also automatically maintains information around def-use and use-def chains. This information is maintained in a side data structure represented by the MachineRegisterInfo class from the CodeGen library. Each MachineFunction instance has its own MachineRegisterInfo instance that you can access through the MachineFunction::getRegInfo() API. Any modification to a MachineFunction instance's content (through MachineInstr or MachineOperand, for instance) automatically updates MachineRegisterInfo.

Zooming in on the MachineRegisterInfo class, its API is not strictly about the def-use or use-def chain. It instead covers a grouping and mapping of definitions and uses of an entity that may contain a value. This entity is called a register and is represented by the Register class, also from the CodeGen library.

We will go into more details of what a register is in *Chapter 11*. For now, assume that a register is like a variable in your favorite programming language. Variables can be values if they are uniquely defined, but not all variables are values.

Back to the MachineRegisterInfo class – its API does the following:

1.  Operates on registers
2.  Gives you a def-use/use-def chain when the input register is uniquely defined

These two properties raise a few questions:

1. **Register:** How do you get such an instance from the Machine IR?
2. **Unique definition:** How do you find out that a register is uniquely defined?
3. **Non-unique definition:** What do you get in this case?

Getting a register requires unboxing an instance of the MachineOperand class. You have already learned how to get a MachineOperand instance through a MachineInstr instance (reminder: use MachineInstr::getOperand). Now, to get to a register, you have to do the following:

1. Check that this operand is a register using MachineOperand::isReg().
2. Unbox the MachineOperand instance to get the register, using MachineOperand.getReg().
3. (optional) Check whether this operand is a definition (MachineOperand::isDef()).

Do not worry about the other kinds of MachineOperand instances; you will discover them in *Chapter 11*.

Using the previously obtained register, you can use MachineInstr *MachineRegisterInfo::getUni queVRegDef(Register Reg) to try to obtain the unique definition of this register.

If the returned MachineInstr instance is not nullptr, then you can do one of the following:

- If Reg was a use (MachineOperand::isDef() == false), then you just obtained its definition, so you effectively followed its use-def chain.
- If Reg was a def, you can use MachineRegisterInfo::use_operands(Register Reg) for a range iterator on all MachineOperand instances that use Reg, or MachineRegisterInfo::use_ instructions(Register Reg) for a range iterator on all MachineInstr instances that use Reg (you should recognize the distinction between the Use and User classes, which we explained in the *Def-use and use-def chains in the LLVM IR* section).

If the returned MachineInstr instance is nullptr, then you are not dealing with a value, and MachineRegisterInfo::use_operands and MachineRegisterInfo::use_instructions will give you range iterators over the list of all the uses/users of this variable. In other words, you do not have an easy way to link a use to its definition(s). Depending on what you are after at this point, you will need to either reconstruct the SSA form, perform a reachability algorithm, or use a different data structure called LiveInterval, which we will present in *Chapter 16*. Before doing any of that, check that you are not dealing with a physical register (Register::isPhysical()) since these can never be put in SSA form. We will cover them properly in *Chapter 11*.

> **Note**
>
> If you feel you must reconstruct SSA, step back and check if whatever you want to do can be done earlier in your pipeline, where SSA is still maintained.

To summarize, MachineRegisterInfo does not care whether your registers are values or not. This is your responsibility to interpret what it returns to you. Also, you will notice that this class offers a lot more methods to iterate through various flavors of instructions, operands, and so on. You will learn about their use later in *Chapter 11*.

This concludes our section on the concept of value. You saw how it simplifies some compiler optimizations and analyses and how it is implemented in the middle-end and backend through the SSA form. In the process, you have learned important concepts used throughout LLVM, such as dominance and def-use/use-def chains.

At this point, you have enough background to start experimenting with the different IR levels. Our next section will teach you the concepts and the related helper structures you can use when writing optimizations.

# Tackling optimizations

A lot of the work of a backend compiler engineer is about improving the performance of the generated code – in other words, write optimizations.

Although you could write any optimization you want from scratch, the LLVM infrastructure provides many APIs to help you in this endeavor.

This section has two goals:

1. Teach you some of the basics of compiler optimizations
2. Show you how to leverage LLVM to do the heavy lifting

Let us start with our first concept: legality!

## Legality

The concept of legality is prevalent in every aspect of the work of a compiler engineer. The question you should ask yourself when coming up with new optimization is: Is this legal? In other words, does this optimization preserve the semantics of the program?

If the answer is yes, great – you only have to worry about the profitability aspect described in the next section!

If the answer is no, think about what you need to prove to be able to apply your optimization and whether this proof can be done at compile time or if it requires some information at runtime.

For instance, let us say you want to write an optimization that turns a sequence of half-precision floating-point additions into a smaller sequence of additions by combining constant terms together; for example, `3.0 + a + 3.0` becomes `a + 6.0`.

Pause for a second and think about it.

The problem here is that although the math looks sound, you may be hitting rounding errors.

Using `alive`, a tool that checks if your transformation is likely correct based on an input source LLVM IR and a target LLVM IR, you can easily find a counter-example. See `https://alive2.llvm.org/ce/z/eBV7vs`.

Therefore, such optimization is not generally legal.

Several APIs can help you decide whether something is legal. However, depending on what you are trying to achieve, the information you seek may not be directly accessible. Here, we list a few of these APIs to give you an idea of the information you can leverage when checking for legality.

## Integer overflow/underflow

The **No Unsigned Wrap** (NUW) and **No Signed Wrap** (NSW) flags allow us to determine the behavior of an instruction when integer overflow/underflow (when you go out of the range of the representable integer) occurs. When this flag is present, this means the related instruction will have an **undefined behavior** (UB) (meaning the program may not function properly at this point) on unsigned or signed overflow/underflow, respectively. While this may sound scary, this is the bread and butter of compiler optimizations. If a value goes into UB territory, then your optimization is correct as long as it is valid while the value is in the defined behavior range. In other words, if your optimization behaves improperly only when the value would have been undefined, this is okay since anything can happen when you are in the undefined range.

When the NSW flag is absent, the semantic of integer overflow/underflow is well defined. The related integer instruction wraps around its result following a $2^n$ modulo. For the exact details, check out the related section in the language reference: `https://llvm.org/docs/LangRef.html#id89`.

Let us take an example to make this more concrete.

Consider the optimization that tries to replace x * 2 == 2 with x == 1; that is, you divide both sides of the comparison by two.

This optimization is only legal when x * 2 has the NSW flag. Indeed, let us assume it does not have this flag; this means that when x is greater than `INT_MAX / 2`, x * 2 will wrap around the maximum representable number. Using this property, we can choose a value of x such that ((x * 2) % 2^32) == 2 but (x % 2^32) != 1; for instance, x = 0x80000001 (that is, 2^31 + 1).

Now, assuming that the NSW flag is set, the optimization becomes valid because the troublesome values would be in the undefined range since this flag tells us that x * 2 is not supposed to require wrapping to be computed correctly. For your information, here are the alive proofs with NSW (`https://alive2.llvm.org/ce/z/WP8rwF`) and without NSW (`https://alive2.llvm.org/ce/z/DdwJpB`).

In terms of API, you can query the presence or absence of these flags:

- **At the LLVM IR level:** `bool Instruction::hasNoUnsignedWrap()` and `bool Instruction::hasNoSignedWrap()`
- At the Machine IR level: `bool MachineInstr::getFlag(MIFlag Flag)` with the `MIFlag::NoUWrap` and `MIFlag::NoSWrap` values

## Fast-math flags

**Fast-math flags** (FMF) describe the assumption you can make on specific instructions. For instance, having the `ninf` flag on an instruction means that this instruction will not have to deal with infinity values. If an infinity value is fed to this instruction at runtime, then the behavior is undefined. A full list of FMF is available at `https://llvm.org/docs/LangRef.html#fast-math-flags`.

These flags can be queried as follows:

- **At the LLVM IR level:** There is a method for each flag; for example, bool `Instruction::hasNoInfs()`.
- **At the Machine IR level:** bool `MachineInstr::getFlag(MIFlag Flag)` with the appropriate `MIFlag::FmXXX` enumerator.

Going back to our example, 3.0 + a + 3.0 becomes a + 6.0. The transformation would be valid if the related instructions had the reassoc flag, which allows doing reassociation on math expressions, irrespective of the impact this may have on the precision of the result.

## Side effects

Side effects are things that happen indirectly when executing something. For instance, consider the following sequence of C statements:

```
val1 = A[0];
B[1] = val2;
val3 = A[0];
```

In this sequence, is it legal to replace val3 directly with val1?

The answer depends on which memory location B[1] points to. If the address of B[1] is equal to or overlaps with A[0] (in other words, if B[1] and A[0] alias), then this is not legal. Writing to B[1] produces a memory side effect, and you have to determine which memory locations are affected to be able to safely perform the val1/val3 replacement.

Side effects are either known – that is, pin to a specific resource such as memory, flag register (for example, for comparison, add-carry, and so on) – or unknown. When a side effect is unknown, that means that it is not explicitly represented or deductible with the IR alone. In this case, we say that the side effect is unmodeled. When dealing with unmodeled side effects, tread conservatively.

For known side effects, you can leverage the following APIs:

- **At the LLVM IR level:** You can directly check if the instruction deals with memory location by checking the opcode of the related instruction (load, store, atomic, and so on), use bool `Instruction::mayWriteToMemory()`, and so on methods, or use bool `Instruction::mayHaveSideEffects()` methods.
- **At the Machine IR level:** bool `MachineInstr::mayLoad()`, bool `MachineInstr::mayStore()`, bool `MachineInstr::mayRaiseFPException()`, and so on.

On the other hand, unmodeled side effects are flagged with the following APIs:

- **At the LLVM IR level:** bool `Instruction::mayHaveSideEffects()`
- **At the Machine IR level:** bool `MachineInstr::hasUnmodeledSideEffects()`

To disambiguate memory side effects, you can use the alias analysis and/or the MemorySSA analysis available in the Analysis library. Although these analyses are only available at the LLVM IR level, it is possible to query them at the Machine IR level through MachineMemoryOperand. We will go into more detail in *Chapter 11*.

Note

The body of a function can contain any kinds of instructions. This means calls to arbitrary functions must be conservatively modeled as having side effects. To avoid unnecessarily constraining optimizations, known functions, such as functions from the standard libraries, are tagged, when appropriate, with specific attributes that you can query to decide whether something is legal or not. For instance, the `Function` class exposes a `getMemoryEffects()` method that describes the memory effects (represented with the `MemoryEffects` class) of the related function. Using the returned object, you can check the type of accesses that may be made. For instance, `bool MemoryEffects::doesNotAccessMemory()` tells you whether the memory is accessed at all. When a function has no side effect, and different calls to this function with the same inputs yield the same outputs, we say that the function is pure.

This was a quick survey of the kind of API you can leverage to do your legality checks when modifying a program. This is not exhaustive, and, for instance, we did not mention things that you must always guarantee, such as the dominance property of a definition over its uses.

At this point, we assume you determined that your optimization is valid, but is it worth it? Put differently, will your transformation improve the quality/performance of the generated code?

The next section tackles exactly these questions by introducing the concept of profitability.

## Profitability

The next big thing that you need to answer is whether your transformation is profitable.

In other words, legality is about whether you can do your transformation, but profitability is about whether you should.

Unfortunately, there is no silver bullet to decide whether something is profitable. Answering the profitability question depends on what you are trying to achieve. What is profitable in one case may be the opposite of what you would like to do in another case.

For instance, consider the inlining optimization. This optimization replaces calls to functions with the content of their body. By inlining the code of a function into its caller (the function that calls it), you remove the overhead of executing the call, you expose more optimization opportunities by breaking the boundaries of the call, and so on. If you are optimizing for performance, you should always inline a callee in its caller; easy, right?

This is not that simple; inlining may increase the code size of your final executable and thrash your instruction cache. Similarly, later optimizations may be pushed in corner cases, and you may end up oversubscribing the physical registers. In both cases, this is averse to our original performance goal since this may slow down the runtime of the final executable code compared to a non-inlined version of the executable code.

Let us consider another scenario. We listed the negative effects of inlining, and they were all around code size. Therefore, if we were to optimize for minimum code size (identified with the `minsize` function attribute and queried with `bool Function::hasMinSize()`), meaning we want to produce the smallest executable code possible, we would not use inlining. This time, that was easy, right?

This is not generally the best option either. Sometimes inlining produces smaller executable code because you can specialize the body of the callee to the context of the caller and, similarly, the body of the caller may become smaller because of the additional context from the body of the callee, as illustrated in *Table 4.2*:

| Original code | After inlining | After further optimizations |
|---|---|---|
| ```int bar(int a) {
    // Fast path.
    if (a == 1)
        return 0;
    // Lengthy
handling.
    return 1;
}
int foo() {
    int barRes =
bar(1);
    if (barRes) {
        // Lengthy
handling
        return 1;
    }
    return 0;
}``` | ```int bar(int a) {
    // Fast path.
    if (a == 1)
        return 0;
    // Lengthy handling.
    return 1;
}
int foo() {
    if (1 == 1) {
        barRes = 0;
    } else {
        // Lengthy
handling.
        barRes = 1;
    }
    if (barRes) {
        // Lengthy
handling
        return 1;
    }
    return 0;
}``` | ```int bar(int a) {
    // Fast path.
    if (a == 1)
        return 0;
    // Lengthy
handling.
    return 1;
}
int foo() {
    return 0;
}``` |

*Table 4.2: Inlining enables other optimizations*

As shown in the rightmost column of *Table 4.2*, inlining can shrink the code size.

The point of this example was to show you that profitability is hard to predict. This is especially true for a modern compiler that emphasizes modularity over monolithic design. This is not a criticism of modern compiler design, only a reflection on the implications.

Going back to the example in *Table 4.2*, if you stop the compiler right after inlining (middle column), then it would be the right thing to disable inlining to optimize for minimal code size. Indeed, at this point, the code takes more space. However, if you run a later dead code elimination pass, the code shrinks. Therefore, to accurately model the profitability of one transformation, this transformation would need to know exactly which transformations are still to be run and what they do. Obviously, this is not practical.

Instead, each transformation must rely on a proxy to make its decisions. We call such a proxy a **cost model**.

A cost model defines an objective function that a transformation needs to maximize or minimize depending on the goal to achieve. To get to the best/sufficiently good solution, various techniques can be used (for example, dynamic programming, integer linear programming, heuristics, and so on), and this part is totally in your hands. The method to use depends on the problem, your compile-time budget, and so on. In other words, you will need to do your own research and experimentation and talk to the community and people in general!

That said, the LLVM infrastructure offers a few APIs that you can use to build your own cost model.

Let us describe a few of them.

## Instruction lowering — TargetTransformInfo and TargetLowering

The `TargetTransformInfo` class from the `Analysis` library abstracts at the LLVM IR level what the **codegen** passes (the transformations that work on the code generation part of the compiler) do. The `TargetTransformInfo` instances are often held in variables named `TTI`.

It is used by the LLVM IR passes to get an estimate of the cost of LLVM IR instructions. The cost is represented by the `InstructionCost` class, which is part of the `Support` library. This class encapsulates the standard operations you need to handle costs (+, -, comparisons, and so on.) and exposes an `InstructionCost::isValid()` method to check if the related construct is even valid. The actual value of the cost depends on the target implementation, and in general, you should avoid unboxing it. In other words, you should manipulate the `InstructionCost` class through the dedicated APIs instead of using the actual values underneath them because how to interpret these values is target-specific. At the end of the day, if you are writing your own backend, you will have to populate these costs yourself, so how you handle them is up to you. Generally speaking, however, users of these APIs will not look past the `InstructionCost` abstraction.

The main API is `InstructionCost TragetTransformInfo::getInstructionCost(const User *U, TargetCostKind CostKind)`.

The `CostModelPrinterPass` class from the `Analysis` library can be used to print the estimated cost for each instruction in a function. Assuming you have an LLVM IR representation handy, you can see it in action with the following command line:

```
$ ${LLVM_BUILD_DIR}/bin/opt -passes="print<cost-model>" -cost-kind=${COST_KIND}
input.ll
```

Here, `${COST_KIND}` can be throughput, latency, code size, or size.

The printed costs change based on which target is defined in the `triple` field. You will get more information on the `triple` field in *Chapter 7*.

This information is used throughout the LLVM IR passes to build their cost model. For instance, the inliner, loop vectorizer, loop unroller, and **straightline program (SLP)** vectorizer build their cost model on top of this information.

The `TargetLowering` class fills a similar goal to `TargetTransformInfo` but is used by lower-level APIs. In other words, `TargetTranformInfo` is aimed at generic LLVM IR transformations, whereas the `TargetLowering` API is used by target-specific transformations, typically toward the end of the middle-end. This is reflected in the location of this API: it lives in the `CodeGen` library. This class is often named `TLI` in the LLVM code base but must not be confused with the `TargetLibraryInfo` class, which is our next topic.

## Library support – TargetLibraryInfo

The `TargetLibraryInfo` class from the `Analysis` library provides information about which library functions are supported for the current target and whether specific optimized versions of a library call are available. Instances of this class are often named `TLI`, which is the same as `TargetLowering`, so beware of the context!

For instance, you can use this API to check, using `TargetLoweringInfo:: isFunctionVectorizable (StringRef F, const ElementCount &VF)`, if a particular function F ((for instance the cosf function from the mathematic library (libm))) has a variant that supports a specific vector size VF, meaning that it can process a given number of elements in parallel.

## Datatype properties – DataLayout

The `DataLayout` class from the `IR` library provides an API to query how different datatypes are aligned, how much space they take in memory, and so on and so forth.

The information provided here has all sorts of implications; for instance, if you want to read from memory the content of a big structure in one go, you may want to check that the size of the structure fits your largest possible load (`TypeSize DataLayout::getTypeSizeInBits(Type *Ty)`).

That said, most of the time, you may want to query directly the `TargetTransformInfo` API, which itself depends on an instance of the `DataLayout` class to provide you with an `InstructionCost` instance.

Instances of the `DataLayout` class generally appear with a variable named `DL`.

## Register pressure

The idea behind register pressure is to keep track of all resources that may reside in the register and make sure that this number does not exceed the number of physical registers.

For instance, if you move some instructions around in your transformation, the related values will ultimately need to be available in some hardware storage. If by doing your transformation, you oversubscribe the registers, you will need to back up the additional values with memory, which is slower to access than registers.

Most of the LLVM IR passes do not care about how many physical registers are going to be used to lower the current IR. The assumption is the backend passes will do the right thing.

As such, the concept of register pressure is not available at the LLVM IR level. It is relatively easy, though, to estimate it by keeping track of which values are going to be used at any program point by following the dominator tree (remember the **reverse post-order** (RPO) traversal!) and leveraging the DataLayout to know how much space is required for each value.

At the Machine IR level, the CodeGen library features a RegPressureTracker class to help you keep track of this information. This works through what we call register pressure sets, which can be obtained either through the MachineRegisterInfo or TargetRegisterInfo APIs, depending on what you are doing.

We will go into more detail about the register pressure sets and register pressure trackers in *Chapter 11*.

## Basic block frequency

To help guide decisions, it may be important to know how often different parts of the CFG are executed compared to others. The BlockFrequencyInfo and MachineBlockFrequencyInfo classes fill that gap. These APIs are respectively available in the Analysis library for the LLVM IR passes and the CodeGen library for the Machine IR passes.

The usage of these APIs is straightforward: you run the related pass, either BlockFrequencyAnalysis or MachineBlockFrequencyInfo (more on how to do that in the next chapter), then you use the resulting BlockFrequencyInfo instance or directly the MachineBlockFrequencyInfo instance to access the frequency of your blocks:

- **At the LLVM IR level:** BlockFrequency BlockFrequencyInfo::getBlockFreq(const BasicBlock *BB)
- **At the Machine IR level:** BlockFrequency MachineBlockFrequencyInfo::getBlockFreq(const MachineBasicBlock *MBB)

By default, the block frequencies are heuristically computed. For instance, a block before an if-then-else statement would have a frequency of 1, the then and else blocks a frequency of 0.5, and the block after the if-then-else-statement would have a frequency of 1.

The frequencies can also use profile-guided information if it is provided. Profile-guided information means that you compile your program once with some instrumentations enabled. This instrumentation collects the frequencies of the basic blocks of your program while you run it on representative examples. This information can then be fed back to the compiler to improve the accuracy of the cost models/heuristics. We will not cover how to enable this in this book, but you can search for **profile-guided optimization** (PGO) on the internet to get some insights into how to do that.

You can see the BlockFrequencyInfo class on the LLVM IR by using the following command:

```
$ ${LLVM_BUILD_DIR}/bin/opt -passes='print<block-freq>' input.ll
```

It is also possible to print this information at the Machine IR level, but the command is not as trivial, so we will cover it later in this book.

## More precise instruction properties — scheduling model and instruction description

During the lowering, the closer you get to the final executable code, the more information about the target you can leverage in your transformations.

At the Machine IR level and below, you have access to the instruction's description. This information is represented with the `MCInstrDesc` struct from the MC library, and it gives you access to a lot of low-level details about each instruction. For instance, using this struct, you can tell what kind of instruction you are dealing with (`MCInstrDesc::isCall()`, `MCInstrDesc::isBranch()`, and so on), its code size (`MCInstrDesc::getSize()`), and its scheduling class identifier (`MCInstrDesc::getSchedClass()`); that is, the identifier that allows getting to the scheduling class that describes how the instruction behaves with respect to the scheduling model.

You can access `MCInstrDesc` information directly from a `MachineInstr` instance using `MachineInstr::getDesc()` or by querying the `TargetInstrInfo` instance of a `MachineFunction` instance (`MachineFunction::getInstrInfo()`, then `MCInstrInfo::get(unsigned Opcode)`).

Going back to the scheduling model of the target, it is represented with the `MCSchedModel` struct and gives you for each scheduling class some information about the latency of the instructions in that class, their throughput, and so on. To access the scheduling model, you can, for instance, start with a `MachineFunction` instance, get the `TargetSubtargetInfo` information (`MachineFunction::getSubtarget()`; that is, the actual microarchitecture being targeted), and then the scheduling model from the sub-target (`MCSubtargetInfo::getSchedModel()`).

Then, using the `MCInstrDesc` instance of the instructions you are interested in, you can get the identifier of the related scheduling class and use it to query the model and get the underlying `MCSchedClassDesc` instance that holds the necessary information: `MCSchedModel::getSchedClassDesc(MyInstrDesc.getSchedClass())`.

We will go into more detail about scheduling models in *Chapter 15*.

Now that you have a sense of what you can leverage to do your own profitability checks, let us conclude this section around optimization with some terms that are used a lot in the optimization space.

## Transformation jargon

This section goes over a few terms commonly used when describing optimizations and that you will see in the LLVM code base or compiler literature.

### Instcombine

You will see that people use the term *instcombine* a lot. **Instcombine** refers to a certain class of optimization that essentially takes a pattern formed by some instructions and rewrites them in either a more efficient form or a canonical pattern. For instance, taking a = b * 2 and rewriting it into a = b << 1 is a sort of instcombine.

In LLVM, instcombine is also the name given to an optimization that does exactly this kind of transformation and has a strong focus on canonicalization. We will go into more detail about this in *Chapter 8*.

More generally, optimizations that perform instcombine-like transformations are called peephole optimizations.

## Fixed point

Some transformation aims at reaching a **fixed point**. What this means is the transformation is applied repeatedly until nothing changes, hence it reaches a fixed point. **Fixed-point optimizations** (**FPOs**) are rarely used in practice in LLVM because if for one reason or another your changes oscillate (that is, do not have a proper fixed point), the compiler would never stop. Therefore, it is common to put a maximum number of iterations while trying to reach a fixed point. Unless reaching a fixed point is required for correctness, this is a sensible thing to do in your optimization.

## Liveness

A value is said to be alive at a given program point when its definition reaches this point, and use of that value is still reachable from this point. To put it simply, **liveness** is about whether a value needs to be kept around for future use.

This is an important concept because it affects the register pressure, but also things such as dead code elimination, and so on.

## Hoisting

The term **hoisting** refers to a transformation that moves something up in the CFG. For instance, if you pull up an invariant outside of a loop, you are hoisting this invariant outside of the loop.

## Sinking

The term **sinking** refers to the opposite transformation of hoisting. In other words, sinking is about pushing entities down the CFG. For instance, if you move the definition of a value before an if block into its then block, you are sinking the definition.

## Folding

**Folding** is a transformation that consists of taking several entities and producing a smaller number of entities. Folding can be seen as a special kind of instcombine. Indeed, not all instcombines reduce the number of instructions.

You are now armed with a better understanding of which LLVM APIs you can leverage to implement your own transformations. Next, we will do a quick refresher on loops and how to leverage the LLVM infrastructure to handle them.

# Loops

Loops are important structures to identify in the CFGs in order to generate efficient code. Indeed, most programs spend most of their time in loops, which means that the code generated in loops is especially critical to get right for performance.

We are sure you are already familiar with the concepts of loop, loop nest, inner loop, outer loop, and the like. However, it is less likely that you are familiar with some terminologies used in compilers and, especially, LLVM.

This section focuses on concepts that are likely new to you and, hence, does not reintroduce all of them. You can find a complete refresher on loops at `https://llvm.org/docs/LoopTerminology.html`.

## Terminology

Let us first start with a diagram representing the different elements of a canonical loop in LLVM, *Figure 4.6*, and we will define these terms one by one:

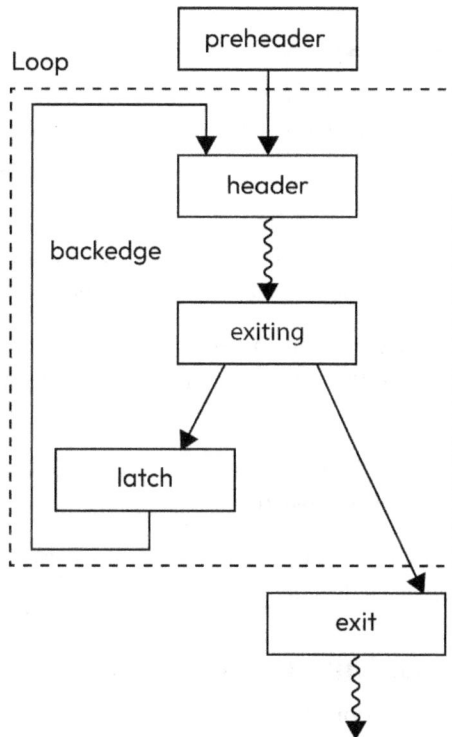

*Figure 4.6: A canonical loop in LLVM*

## Preheader

The preheader of a loop is a basic block that is not part of the loop but that dominates the loop. This is typically the basic block where you would put the initialization of your induction variables (the variables that are increased/decreased at each iteration of the loop).

## Header

This is the first basic block within the loop. It dominates all the basic blocks within the loop.

## Exiting block

The exiting block is a basic block within the loop that has successor blocks outside the loop.

## Latch

The latch is a basic block within the loop that carries a backedge to the header.

## Exit block

An exit block is a basic block outside of the loop that is a successor of an exiting block.

These different blocks make what a canonical loop in LLVM is. Blocks with these roles also always exist in a non-canonical loop but one block may assume different roles; for example, the exiting block may also be the header block.

## Where to get loop information

LLVM offers loop-related information through the derived classes of the `LoopBase` class. The `LoopBase` class lives in the `Support` library. Its LLVM IR specialization, the `Loop` class, lives in the `Analysis` library. The Machine IR specialization, the `MachineLoop` class, lives in the `CodeGen` library.

The API offered by the `LoopBase` class and its derived classes is a straightforward application of the terminology that you now know. Indeed, you will find methods to find the preheader (`LoopBase::getLoopPreheader()`), the loop header (`LoopBase::getHeader()`), and so on.

To get this information populated, you need to use the `LoopInfo` and `MachineLoopInfo` passes respectively for the LLVM IR level and the Machine IR level. You will learn how to run passes in the next chapter.

Throughout this section, you refreshed your memory around loops and learned how information about loops is presented in the LLVM infrastructure.

You have now all the necessary background to start writing your own optimizations, and the next section offers you a motivating example to start that!

# Writing a simple constant propagation optimization

To help you master LLVM APIs, this section offers a hands-on exercise where you will implement your own constant propagation optimization at the LLVM IR level.

To be able to complete this exercise, you will have to take a closer look at the APIs of the classes that we introduced earlier, mainly the `Module`, `Function`, `BasicBlock`, and `Instruction` classes, but believe it or not, you have been exposed to almost everything you need to be able to do that.

A possible solution is given in ch4/simple_constant_propagation, and the README.md file in this directory explains how to use your implementation in the provided framework.

Before we give you the few APIs that you need to complete this exercise, let us introduce the problem properly.

## The optimization

The constant propagation optimization is as simple as it sounds: you find constant values in your programs, and you try to form more constants by simulating the computations that appear in the program.

For instance, let us consider the following snippet:

```
a = 2
b = 3;
d = a + b + c + 3;
```

When we reach the assignment for d, we know that a is equal to 2, b is equal to 3, and that we add another constant, 3. Therefore, d is equal to 2 + 3 + c + 3; hence, 8 + c.

The goal of the constant propagation optimization is exactly that: simplify computations by replacing variables with constants and combining the constants to produce fewer computations.

## Simplifying assumptions

For this exercise, we made the following assumptions to keep the implementation trackable:

- Only integer types are constant propagated.
- Constant propagation is always legal and profitable.
- We give up on constants when the constant type changes; for instance, zero extension (for example, unsigned a = -3; long long b = a;).

In the *Going further* section, we hint at how to lift these assumptions, but the actual implementation is out of the scope of this chapter.

## Missing APIs

To be able to complete this exercise, here are a few APIs that you will need to use.

## The Constant class

The Constant class from the IR library is what is used to represent all sorts of constants in the LLVM IR. For this exercise, you will focus on one of its sub-subclasses: ConstantInt. This class holds the value of the constants you will need to propagate in your optimization.

Note

If you remember, everything in the LLVM IR is an instance of the Value class, so how do you get an instance of the ConstantInt class from a Value object? In a regular C++ program, you would use **run-time type information** (**RTTI**) to dynamically cast your Value instance to the desired class. However, LLVM explicitly disabled all RTTI support. Instead, it has its own RTTI support that essentially assigns an embedded unique identifier to each class and uses this identifier to statically (that is, without RTTI support) check if an instance is of a certain type. What you need to remember is that you will need to use LLVM's rolled-out RTTI constructs (isa<typename>(Obj), cast<typename>(Obj), and dyn_cast<typename>(Obj)) to get the type you want. More details about LLVM's RTTI are available at https://llvm.org/docs/HowToSetUpLLVMStyleRTTI.html.

The most generic way to get the actual constant value from ConstantInt is through const APInt &ConstantInt::getValue(). There are more direct ways to get a value (for example, uint64_t ConstantInt::getZExtValue()), but these are less generic in the sense that you have to first check that the value fits in the returned type. In other words, it is easy to shoot yourself in the foot if you are not careful.

## The APInt class

The APInt class from the ADT library abstracts arbitrary precision integers. Thanks to this class, you can perform integer arithmetic with integers of any bit-width (for example, 32-bit integer, 64-bit integer, but also 13-bit integer!). This is especially useful in compilers because your host may not have the same precisions as your target, so by using APInt for all your integer computations (APFloat for all your floating-point ones), you make sure that all the math you do at compile time reflects accurately what would have happened on the target.

## Creating a constant

You know how to get a constant and perform computation on it, so now we need to see how to create a ConstantInt instance from a constant.

Instances of ConstantInt are a bit particular because they do not have a definition per se. Instead, they are accessible everywhere in the module (Module class) and, if you remember, are uniqued across an LLVMContext instance. As a result, you can create a ConstantInt instance out of thin air (as opposed to requiring a parent scope, such as an instance of a Module or Function class), but you need to have an LLVMContext object around.

Putting things together, you can create ConstantInt objects by using one of the static methods this class offers – for instance, ConstantInt::get(LLVMContext &Context, const APInt &V).

## Replacing a value

You have now your shiny new constant, so let us see how you can modify the IR with it.

The immediate thing you may have thought of is to simply use the setter for the User object's operands: `User::setOperand(unsigned i, Value *Val)`. While this works, you will have to maintain your own map (`Value`, `NewConstant`) and update the operands as you go through them during your traversal of the IR or through the def-use chain.

As you can imagine, replacing a value with another one is a common operation, so the `Value` class offers a method to do that in one go so that you do not have to maintain your own map: `Value::replaceAllUsesWith(Value *NewVal)`.

## Your turn

At this point, your job is to fill out the `myConstantPropagation` function located in `ch4/simple_constant_propagation/your_turn/opt.cpp`.

The prototype of the function is the following:

```
bool myConstantPropagation(Function &F)
```

This function takes a `Function` object as input, modifies it in place, and returns `true` if any changes have been made and `false` otherwise.

When you are done with the implementation, follow the steps in the `README.md` file and run both your and the reference implementation to see if you can get the same simplifications.

## Going further

This section gives you ideas on what you could try to challenge yourself and push your optimization further.

## Legality

While legality is relatively easy with integer types, try to think about when it is legal to preserve the NSW and NUW flags in the process.

Next, think about how to support floating-point types.

Remember to check the FMF and leverage `APFloat`!

Finally, think about reassociation: how would you simplify something such as a = 3 + b + 3 when the constants do not appear in the same expression; that is, you have the following two different sequences:

```
tmp = b + 3
a = tmp + 3
```

Here is an alternative:

```
tmp = 3 + 3
a = tmp + b
```

## Profitability

You have guessed it – while constant propagation is profitable most of the time, it can be harmful in some specific cases depending on architectural constraints. For instance, imagine that materializing a constant in the final assembly requires 2 instructions and 1 register of storage when the constant does not fit in 16-bit.

Think how you could model that and the kind of trade-offs you would need to do.

For instance, consider the following sequence:

```
cst = 262144
a = cst + b
c = cst + 3
e = c + d
```

This will be lowered in as follows:

```
cst = load <low_part(262144)>
cst |= load <high_part(262144)>
a = cst + b
c = cst + 3
e = c + d
```

And now, here is the same sequence with constant propagation:

```
cst = load <low_part(262144)>
cst |= load <high_part(262144)>
a = cst + b
c = load <low_part(262144 + 3)>
c |= load <high_part(262144 + 3)>
e = c + d
```

Notice how the new sequence is longer than the default sequence.

If you want an idea of how to optimize for this sort of problem, look at `llvm/lib/Transforms/Scalar/ConstantHoisting.cpp`.

## Propagating constants across types

To propagate constants across type changes (for example, `int8_t` to `int32_t`), you can take a closer look at the API of `APInt`. This class offers type-changing methods such as `APInt::sext`, `APInt::trunc`, and so on that return a new `APInt` instance with the right value.

In this exercise, you were able to write your first optimization and directly manipulate the APIs used to modify the IR. You also had a few hints about the kind of problems you will have to solve as a compiler engineer, and we hope they demonstrate how fascinating this field is.

# Summary

You discovered the world of optimizations and the challenges you must solve when writing new optimizations. These challenges revolved around two concepts: legality and profitability. In the process, you learned about the helper structures that can be leveraged to build a cost model: something that can be used to reason about profitability.

Finally, you put all this knowledge into action by writing your own first optimization.

Your next stop is with the pass manager, where you will learn how to create a sequence of optimizations and reuse the existing ones. Before you go there, you have guessed it – it is quiz time!

# Quiz time

Now that you have completed reading this chapter, try answering the following questions to test your knowledge:

1.  What is the difference between a Use object and a User object in LLVM?

    A Use object represents the relationship between a definition and an operand of one of its users; that is the entity that uses that value. A user is represented with an instance of the User class.

    Put differently, a Use object represents the edge between a definition and a User object, and a definition can have several Use instances for one User object. For example, a = b + b: b has one user (the computation that produces a) and two uses (the first and second operands of the computation that produces a).

    See the *Def-use and use-def chains in the LLVM IR* section for more details.

2.  Point out the latch basic blocks in the following CFG:

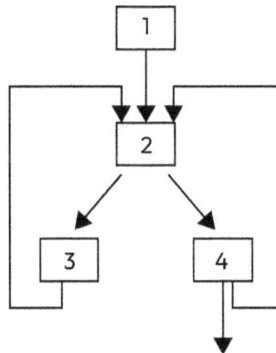

    3 and 4. 4 is also an exiting block, but blocks can assume several roles.

    See the *Loops* section for loop terminology.

3.  Does the definition of b dominate its use in this program?

    ```
    void foo(int a) {
       int b;
       if (a == 3)
          b = foo();
       else
          // do something else
       if (a == 3) // a has not been changed
          bar(b);
       else
          // do something else
    }
    ```

    Although b is always defined when reaching its use, its definition does not statically dominate its use. Indeed, it exits a path (first then block, then second then block) where b's use can be reached without going through its definition. While this path is not possible at runtime, it does not matter, because the concept of dominance is purely static.

    See the *Dominance* section for more details about dominance.

4.  Given the program from *question 3*, write it in SSA form:

    ```
    void foo(int a) {
       int b1;
       if (a == 3)
          b2 = foo();
       else
          // do something else
       b3 = phi(b2, b1)
       if (a == 3) // a has not been changed
          bar(b3);
       else
          // do something else
    }
    ```

    This can be further simplified into the following representation if you do not want to represent uninitialized variables (b1's definition):

    ```
    void foo(int a) {
       if (a == 3)
          b2 = foo();
       else
          // do something else
    ```

```
    b3 = phi(b2, poison)
    if (a == 3) // a has not been changed
        bar(b3);
    else
        // do something else
}
```

See the *SSA* section for more details about the SSA form.

5. Name two things you can leverage when doing your legality checks.

   Wrapping flags and FMF. See the *Legality* section for more details.

6. What is register pressure?

   Register pressure measures how many registers are required (or expected) for a particular region.

   See the *Register pressure* section for more details.

7. Given the following program and its IR, is the rightmost IR equivalent to the one in the middle?

| input.c | IR | Optimized IR |
|---|---|---|
| `int foo(int a) {`<br>`    a += 3;`<br>`    return ((unsigned)`<br>`a) + 3;`<br>`}` | `    %tmp = add nsw`<br>`i32 %a, 3`<br>`    %res = add i32`<br>`%tmp, 3` | `    %res = add nsw i32`<br>`%a, 6` |

The rightmost IR is not equivalent because the NSW flag has been incorrectly preserved. As a result, it is possible to find a counter-example that proves that this transformation is incorrect. If you set 2147483642 for a, the IRs are not equivalent (see `https://alive2.llvm.org/ce/z/E4Q02I` for the details).

In other words, this transformation is not legal.

For more details about legality and the NSW flag, please check the *Legality* and *Integer overflow/ underflow* sections.

8. Which API gives you at the Machine IR level the definition(s) of a register?

   The `MachineRegisterInfo` class.

   See the *Def-use and use-def chains in the Machine IR* section.

## Unlock this book's exclusive benefits now

This book comes with additional benefits designed to elevate your learning experience.

*Note: Have your purchase invoice ready before you begin.*

https://www.packtpub.com/unlock/9781837637782

# 5

# Dealing with Pass Managers

This chapter describes the pass manager framework. This framework is used to structure the work that the compiler does.

Throughout this chapter, you will do the following:

- Learn what a pass and a pass manager are
- Get first-hand experience in creating a pass and a pass pipeline
- Learn about the developer tools you can leverage to debug a pass pipeline

It is possible to use the LLVM infrastructure without working with passes and pass managers. However, if you want to reuse any of the compiler transformations that the LLVM project has to offer, you must manipulate these concepts.

The concept of the pass and the mechanism used to drive them, the pass manager, is core to the LLVM infrastructure and, as such, is well documented. Therefore, this chapter primes you for these concepts to make the existing documentation more approachable, and while it teaches you how to write a pass and a pass pipeline, it focuses on teaching what happens under the hood and how to leverage the existing tools to inspect what happens at compile time.

Let us get started with the technical requirements.

## Technical requirements

You will find the complete code of what we are building in this chapter in the ch5 folder of the repository of this book: https://github.com/PacktPublishing/LLVM-Code-Generation.

At this point, you know the drill with respect to the tools that you need to build a project that uses the LLVM infrastructure.

Therefore, let us dive right into the topic by defining what a pass is.

# What is a pass?

A lot of the interesting pieces of the LLVM infrastructure are articulated around the concept of a pass.

In a nutshell, a **pass** is a class that does the following:

- Encapsulates a transformation (for example, an analysis, an optimization, ...)
- Describes the dependencies of this transformation (for example, the transformation needs to have access to the dominator tree analysis)
- Returns the effect of this transformation on the **intermediate representation** (**IR**) (for example, the transformation modified the **control flow graph** (**CFG**))

A pass also applies to a scope, meaning it can only modify elements within this scope. For instance, a loop-scoped pass can only modify what is within the loop that the pass is currently processing. In other words, the pass can modify all the basic blocks and instructions that live within this loop, but it is not allowed to modify unrelated loops or its parent loop (if any) or parent function, for instance.

> Warning
>
> Although modifying something that is outside of the scope of a pass (for example, modifying a module from a function-scoped pass) might work, you must not do this. The LLVM infrastructure may not report any issue if you do that, but you may have nasty bugs lurking around analysis invalidation and so on. Therefore, make sure to always use the appropriate scope for the type of transformation you want to write.

The available scopes, from broad to narrow, are as follows:

- **Module:** The full IR of the current module.
- **CGSCC: Call-graph strongly connected component** (**CGSCC**) is a strongly connected subset of the functions within a module, where a call graph is the directed graph where the nodes are the functions, and the edges are the possible function calls from the caller and the callee. Strongly connected means that each function within this subset can reach all the other ones in this subset by following the call graph.
- **Function:** The IR representing a single function.
- **Loop:** The IR representing a single loop.
- **Region:** The IR representing a **single-entry single-exit** (**SESE**) region; for example, the IR of a single basic block.
- `MachineFunction`: The IR of a single function in Machine IR.

The last two scopes are usable only with the legacy pass manager.

> **Note**
>
> Although `MachineFunction` objects are conceptually functions, they are in their own category because they do not have access to the rest of the IR, as already mentioned in the *A module at the Machine IR level* section of *Chapter 3*.

Now that you have a basic understanding of what a pass is, let us see how you articulate them with a pass manager.

# What is a pass manager?

A **pass manager** is a driver for the set of passes that you want to run.

It fulfills three main functions:

- It provides a structure to run passes in a specific order.
- It makes sure that the dependencies of a pass are properly executed before the pass itself.
- It preserves or invalidates the various analyses based on the passes' effects.

When a pass manager invokes a pass, it also provides specific guarantees on the order in which the IR is visited.

These guarantees are as follows:

- For CGSCC-scoped passes, a pass manager invokes the pass on the leaf **strongly connected component (SCC)** regions first then moves up in the call graph.
- For loop-scoped passes, loops are visited following their nested level from innermost to outermost loops.
- For region-scoped passes, the nesting level is also used in a similar fashion: from the innermost region to the outermost regions.
- For other scopes, the order is not specified.

The takeaway is for scopes where some logical structure makes sense, the order follows a children-to-parents traversal. For scopes where no logical structure exists (that is, each element is independent), the order should not matter.

> **Note**
>
> If possible, refrain from using the region scope. It is expensive to compute, needs to be recomputed most of the time between passes, and you can, most of the time, define a similar algorithm using the more efficient dominator tree construct.

So far, you have seen a high-level picture of how passes and pass managers are structured. The next section goes into more detail by going through the two implementations that the LLVM project provides.

# The legacy and new pass manager

The LLVM infrastructure is in the middle of a several-years-long transition from the previous pass manager to the new one. While the goal is ultimately to use only the new pass manager, the reality is for the time being that you still must deal with both implementations. This is especially true for all the passes used for code generation (that is, `MachineFunction`-scoped) because the new pass manager does not provide any support for them.

In this section, you have the following:

- A comparison of pass managers' capabilities
- An overview of how they work internally
- A primer on the **application programming interface** (API) required by both pass managers

Let us start with the first bullet point: a comparison of their capabilities.

## Pass managers' capabilities

As already hinted, the new pass manager supports fewer scopes than the legacy one. This limitation is a calculated one. Aside from the `MachineFunction` scope, all the removed capabilities either have an equivalent implementation in the new pass manager or were deemed sufficiently irrelevant to not warrant an implementation in the new framework.

*Table 5.1* gives an overview of the supported scopes and the related API:

| Scope | Legacy pass manager | New pass manager |
|---|---|---|
| Module | `legacy::PassManager` | `ModulePassManager` |
| CGSCC | Implementation detail `CGPassManager` | `CGSCCPassManager` |
| Function | `legacy::FunctionPassManager` | `FunctionPassManager` |
| Loop | Implementation detail `LPPassManager` | `LoopPassManager` |
| Region | Implementation detail `RGPassManager` | Not available |
| `MachineFunction` | Implementation detail `MachineFunctionPass` | `MachineFunctionPassManager` Under development |

*Table 5.1: Pass manager APIs*

In *Table 5.1*, for the legacy pass manager, some scopes are marked as *Implementation detail*. What this means is you do not need to interact directly with these pass managers. Instead, you can focus on creating a pass with the right scope, and the top-level pass manager takes care of the plumbing. For instance, the `CGPassManager` class represents a nested pass manager that is implemented using the `ModulePass` class doubled with the `PMDataManager` class (used to manage analyses.)

When it gets executed by `legacy::PassManager` (that is, the module-scoped manager), `CGPassManager` builds the call graph of the SCC and calls the SCC passes accordingly. What this means for you is that with the legacy pass manager, you just need to register your pass with the top-level pass manager, and this manager will automatically add it to a properly scoped manager.

At this point, you see the different types of pass managers that exist, but you are still in the unknown with respect to what they exactly do and how to populate them. The next section covers the latter point as this will help introduce the inner workings of pass managers and hence explain what they do.

## Populating a pass manager

In essence, a pass manager is a simple object with a simple purpose: you add passes to it and it executes them in the provided order.

As already mentioned, what the pass manager brings is twofold:

- It feeds the passes the level of IR they expect.
- It makes the analyses you rely on available and current.

The technicalities of how these two mechanisms work will become clear after you learn how to create a pass of a particular scope. For now, let us assume you know how to create such a pass, and then populating a pass manager becomes trivial:

- For the legacy pass manager, you simply call the following: `legacy::PassManager::add(Pass *)`.
- For the new pass manager, you need to call something that resembles the following: `RelatedScopedManager.addPass(YourPass())`.

The actual method used for the new pass manager is difficult to capture in a one-line snippet because it relies on template specialization. For this call to `::addPass` to work properly, you need to do the following:

1. Use the rightly scoped pass manager to add your pass (that is, `FunctionPassManager` for a function-scoped pass, `ModulePassManager` for a module-scoped pass, and so on, although you can use adaptors to target a differently scoped pass manager).
2. Use the constructor of your pass directly in the `::addPass` method.

On the other hand, the legacy pass manager handles all the complexity behind the scenes, but this has several drawbacks:

1.  The implementation of the legacy pass manager is not straightforward.
2.  This creates several compile-time inefficiencies due to the untangling of the complexity and the heavy use of polymorphism.
3.  The implementation of a pass requires a lot more work than with the new pass manager.

Anyhow, after calling add/addPass with all the transformations you want to execute, you simply call ::run on the related pass manager and you are done: your pass pipeline is running!

Now that you know how to create a pass pipeline, let us see what happens under the hood.

## Inner workings of pass managers

This section goes into detail about how pass managers work. While the information here is not crucial for the use of the LLVM infrastructure, this will help you make better design choices when it comes to crafting your own pass pipeline. First, it will help you understand why certain analysis passes need to be (re)run, and second, it will help you fix compile-time issues by making an informed decision on whether you should preserve some analysis or tweak your pass pipeline.

At the high level, both the legacy and the new pass managers work the same way:

1.  Before running a pass, they check if the analyses that this pass relies on are available:
    a.  If yes, nothing needs to be done.
    b.  If no, they run these analyses beforehand.
2.  They run the pass.
3.  If the pass modified the IR, they check what kind of information the pass affects and preserves and invalidate the results of the analyses that are affected and not preserved.

One takeaway of this sequence is analyses and passes are treated differently. Passes are simply run, whereas analyses are carried around.

Going back to pass managers, one thing to remember is the new pass manager is more efficient.

First, the new pass manager gets rid of the overheads induced by polymorphism by using heavily templated code that leverages a technique called **curiously recurring template pattern** (CRTP). In a nutshell, this technique relies on a templated parent class P, which is then derived using the children themselves as the template argument (for example, class Child : public P<Child>). This eliminates the polymorphism by hardcoding the dispatching of the relevant methods through template instantiation. You will see which classes you need to use to leverage this technique for your passes in the *Writing a pass for the new pass manager* section.

Second, the new pass manager handles the available analyses as a cache and lazily runs them when a pass needs them. By contrast, the legacy pass manager handles the analyses as a scheduling problem. This means it must change the execution pipeline on the fly to (re)schedule analyses that have been invalidated. On top of that, the legacy pass manager must know beforehand all the dependencies, which impacts the effort you need to produce to write a pass. You will see this in action in the *Writing a pass for the legacy pass manager* section.

To summarize, a pass manager needs three things from a pass:

- Which analyses it requires
- What effects the pass has on the IR
- Whether the pass modified the IR

At this point, you know what a pass manager does, how to create your own pass pipeline, and how the two different flavors of pass managers work. You also discovered that pass managers make a distinction between regular passes and analyses. The next section teaches you how to create a pass or an analysis and points out which APIs you need to use.

# Creating a pass

The legacy and the new pass managers have different ways of creating passes. In this section, you will learn how to achieve that task with both frameworks.

In both cases, you will see that you must provide the three main bits of information that the related pass manager needs to perform its task:

1. What is the scope of a pass?
2. What analyses does this pass depend on?
3. What effect does this pass have on the input IR?

Let us see how you can provide this information, starting with the legacy pass manager.

## Writing a pass for the legacy pass manager

As already mentioned, there are three things that a pass needs to provide for the pass manager to do its job. Depending on what your pass does, some parts may be optional because the default implementation may do what you want. You will find what the default implementation is in the related sections later in the chapter.

Now, let us start with how to specify the scope of your pass.

## Using the proper base class

For the legacy pass manager, creating a pass for a specific scope implies inheriting from the related scoped pass class and implementing the runOnXXX method.

*Table 5.2* lists which parent class you must use for each scope and the method that you need to override:

| Scope | Inherit from | Method to override |
|---|---|---|
| Module | `ModulePass` | `bool runOnModule(Module&)` |
| CGSCC | `CallGraphSCCPass` | `bool runOnSCC(CallGraphSCC&)` |
| Function | `FunctionPass` | `bool runOnFunction(Function&)` |
| Loop | `LoopPass` | `bool runOnLoop(Loop*, LPPassManager&)` |
| Region | `RegionPass` | `bool runOnRegion(Region*, GPassManager&)` |
| MachineFunction | `MachineFunctionPass` | `bool runOnMachineFunction(MachineFunction&)` |

*Table 5.2: The base classes for the different scopes*

The Boolean returned by the `runOnXXX` method tells the pass manager whether the related pass made any changes to the IR fed to this method.

> **Note**
>
> The legacy pass manager does not make any distinction between a pass and an analysis. In other words, all analyses are also passes.

If you look at the inheritance graph of the `Pass` class from the IR library and, more specifically, the `ModulePass` class, you will notice a class named `ImmutablePass`. This class is worth mentioning because it is used to carry information around. What this means is this class is never run. Instead, it is only instantiated and cannot be invalidated. If this is a capability that interests you, look at the *Specificities of the Pass class* section to see the APIs you can leverage to populate the information of your own `ImmutablePass` class.

At this point, you know what the skeleton of your pass looks like:

```
class MyPass : public XXXPass {
public:
  bool runOnXXX(/*ProperIR arguments*/) override;
};
```

Your next stop will cover how you specify dependencies for your pass.

# Expressing the dependencies of a pass

To describe the dependencies of a pass (and, by extension, of an analysis) to the legacy pass manager, you must describe two elements:

1.  Which analyses the pass depends on
2.  How to initialize this class and its dependencies

You achieve the first element by overriding the `Pass::getAnalysisUsage(AnalysisUsage &AU)` method.

Using the provided `AnalysisUsage` object, you can describe the dependencies by calling `AnalysisUsage::addRequired</*PassClass*/>()` for each analysis.

Then, you will be able to use the related analysis in the `runOnXXX` method by calling `Pass::getAnalysis</*PassClass*/>()`.

> **Note**
>
> It is a mistake to try to access an analysis in `runOnXXX` while not adding it to the list of dependencies. However, this may work by accident if a pass A before yours needed that analysis and a pass B after yours needs that analysis, and this analysis has not been invalidated between A and B. Make sure you do not rely on this behavior, or you are exposing yourself to bugs!

The second element, which describes how this pass and its analyses are initialized, may feel redundant but is sadly mandatory when you write analysis passes. It is mandatory for analyses because this is how the legacy pass manager knows how to instantiate and run analyses before the passes that need them. For regular passes, you can skip this step, but we recommend that you still do it because it is what registers your pass with the pass manager and makes it discoverable and callable directly from the command-line interface of the related LLVM-provided developer tools (opt and llc).

Concretely, to tell the pass manager how your pass is instantiated, you need to use the following macros:

*   If your pass does not have any dependencies, use the following:

    *   `INITIALIZE_PASS(passName, arg, name, cfg, analysis)`

        Here, the following applies:

        *   `passName` is the C++ name of your class.
        *   `arg` is the string that will be used on the command line to invoke your pass.
        *   `name` is the string that is printed in the built-in debug capabilities of LLVM. This name can be overridden within your pass by writing your own `getPassName()` method.
        *   `cfg` is a Boolean that tells the pass manager whether your pass only looks at the CFG. For instance, an analysis pass building the dominator tree should set this to `true`.
        *   `analysis` is a Boolean that tells whether your pass is an analysis.

- If your pass has dependencies, use the macros in this order:

  1. `INITIALIZE_PASS_BEGIN(passName, arg, name, cfg, analysis)`, where the arguments are the same as `INITIALIZE_PASS`.

  2. `INITIALIZE_PASS_DEPENDENCY(passName)`: One entry per dependency. In other words, you should have as many of this macro as the number of `AnalysisUsage::addRequired` calls that you have in your `Pass::getAnalysisUsage` override.

  3. `INITIALIZE_PASS_END(passName, arg, name, cfg, analysis)`, where the arguments are the same as `INITIALIZE_PASS` and should match what is in `INITIALIZE_PASS_BEGIN`. In practice, these arguments are dropped.

> **Note**
>
> It is equivalent to using directly `INITIALIZE_PASS` or the `INITIALIZE_PASS_BEGIN` and `INITIALIZE_PASS_END` pair without any `INITIALIZE_PASS_DEPENDENCY` dependency in between. A lot of passes do that in LLVM, but we recommend using directly `INITIALIZE_PASS` when appropriated as it makes the code immediately clear that the related pass does not have any dependency.

Additionally, the legacy pass manager needs a specific identifier to register your pass. You provide this by adding a `static char ID` field to your class and initializing this field to any value (usually 0) outside of the class. You will notice that you need to provide this ID to the constructor of the parent class too (`ModulePass`, `FunctionPass`, and so on).

Finally, you need to declare somewhere the prototype of the `initializeXXX` function that is going to be generated with the macros. If you are developing directly in the LLVM tree, this prototype is usually added to the file at `${LLVM_SRC}/llvm/include/llvm/InitializePasses.h`. If you are developing outside of the LLVM tree, just put it at the beginning of your C++ file where you call the macros.

> **Note**
>
> When developing in the LLVM tree, if you add a new `.cpp` file for your class, make sure to add an entry in the `CMakeLists.txt` file that lives in the same directory.

In any case, the prototype needs to look like this:

```
namespace llvm {
void initialize##PassName##Pass(PassRegistry &);
}
```

Here, `##PassName##` is the name of the C++ class that implements your pass. Notice that the macro adds `Pass` at the end of the function name, so if your pass' name is, for instance, `MyPass`, the initialization function will end in `PassPass` (for example, `initializeMyPassPass`.) It is a detail but one that could cause a few minutes of debugging some missing symbol errors!

> Note
>
> The `INITIALIZE_PASS_DEPENDENCY` macro must capture all analyses that you might use. The `Pass::addRequired` calls need only to capture the ones that you actually use. What this means is at compile time, you can execute your calls to `addRequired` conditionally. For instance, maybe you require some analyses only when a certain command-line option is used.

Let us put everything together with an example.

Let us say that we have a pass called `MyOptim` and that it depends on analyses `A`, `B`, and `C`.

First, your pass needs to have an ID:

```
class MyOptim : public XXXPass {
  static char ID;
public:
  MyOptim() : XXXPass(ID) {}
  /*...*/
}
char MyOptim::ID = 0;
```

Next, the `getAnalysisUsage` method of `MyOptim` will look like this:

```
void MyOptim::getAnalysisUsage(AnalysisUsage &AU) {
  AU.addRequired<A>();
  AU.addRequired<B>();
  AU.addRequired<C>();
}
```

Then, somewhere, usually at the end of the same C++ file, you should have something resembling the following:

```
INITIALIZE_PASS_BEGIN(MyOptim, "my-cli-flag-for-myoptim", "My wonderful optim",
/*isCFGOnly=*/false, /*isAnalysis=*/false)
INITIALIZE_PASS_DEPENDENCY(A)
INITIALIZE_PASS_DEPENDENCY(B)
INITIALIZE_PASS_DEPENDENCY(C)
INITIALIZE_PASS_END (MyOptim, "my-cli-flag-for-myoptim", "My wonderful optim",
/*isCFGOnly=*/false, /*isAnalysis=*/false)
```

For these macros to expand correctly, you need to also declare the following prototype before calling this macro (or directly in the `InitializePasses.h` file in LLVM):

```
namespace llvm {
void initializeMyOptimPass(PassRegistry &);
}
```

Finally, if you want the registration process to happen properly, you must call this initializer from somewhere – for instance, the `main` function of your application. The recommended way requires more explanations and is the topic of our next paragraph.

If you are developing your pass in the LLVM tree, the directory where you put your pass should come with a file that contains an initializer for all passes in that directory. For instance, all passes that live under ${LLVM_SRC}/llvm/lib/Transforms/Scalar are initialized in the `initializeScalarOpts` function located at the root of this folder in `Scalar.cpp`. Similarly, all passes in ${LLVM_SRC}/llvm/lib/CodeGen are initialized in the `initializeCodeGen` function located at the root of this folder in `CodeGen.cpp`. Locate the file for your library and add a call to your initializer in the initializer of this library.

If you are developing out of the LLVM tree, either call your initializer directly from the `main` function or from your pass' constructor. Calling this function directly from the constructor is less principled in the sense that this means something must know that this pass exists to be able to register it, but in practice, a lot of passes do that because they are not used as an analysis and thus do not require to be pre-registered. In any case, the argument of this initializer is a `PassRegistry` object, and in both cases, you should use the `PassRegistry::getPassRegistry()` static method to get one. This method returns a singleton object that will be shared with the pass manager:

```
llvm::initializeMyOptimPass(*PassRegistry::getPassRegistry());
```

Now, your pass is properly registered and so are its dependencies. Next, let us see how to describe the effects of your pass on other analyses.

## Preserving analyses

Unless your `runOnXXX` method returns `true`, the pass manager assumes that your pass did not make any changes. Therefore, make sure the returned status accurately captures whether you made changes to the IR. Otherwise, you are in for some nasty bugs such as stall analyses used in passes that occur later in the pass pipeline.

By default, when your pass returns `true`, the pass manager assumes that each analysis is invalidated (this is technically more complicated than that, but this approximation suffices), meaning that if a later pass needs one of them, the pass manager will have to reschedule them to recompute them.

To override this behavior, you must explicitly mark in your `getAnalysisUsage` method which analyses you preserve. This is the same method used to describe your dependencies. You mark an analysis as preserved by calling `AnalysisUsage::setPreserved</*AnalysisPass*/>()`.

That's it!

Careful, however, that when you mark an analysis as preserved, it is indeed preserved by your implementation. In other words, this means that you know that the modifications you are doing are not affecting this analysis, or you update the analysis yourself within your pass. Some analyses provide some API to update them on the fly, such as the `DominatorTree` analysis; others do not.

Before we close this section on the legacy pass manager, there are a few specificities that are interesting to know to take advantage of everything that this pass manager has to offer.

## Specificities of the Pass class

The `Pass` class offers additional member functions that you can override to have better control of what happens during the lifetime of your pass.

This section lists a few of them and explains what you can achieve with them.

Let us start this list with the `bool doInitialization(Module &)` and `bool doFinalization(Module &)` methods from the `Pass` class.

The `doInitialization` method is called at the very beginning of the pass pipeline and `doFinalization` is called at the very end.

Compared to the related class' constructors and destructors, these methods provide you more context because you have access to the current module. Also, they are more flexible than the class constructor and destructor because they are called more often.

Indeed, your class constructor or destructor is called once during the compilation process, whereas these methods are called once per module. While this distinction is not particularly relevant for a classic compiler that compiles one module and then stops, this becomes important when your compiler may proceed with more than one module – for instance, when the compiler is used as a service for **just-in-time** (JIT) compilation.

As with the `runOnXXX` method, the returned Boolean specifies whether a change has been made to the IR. This Boolean, however, does not trigger any analysis invalidation since at this point, the pass pipeline does not yet run. This Boolean is mainly used for nested pass managers such as `LPPassManager`.

The next interesting method is `releaseMemory()`. This method is called when the pass manager determines that your pass is not used anymore. This method is used to release resources before reaching the end of the pipeline.

Putting `doInitialization`, `doFinalization`, and `releaseMemory` together, let us assume we have a pass pipeline with two passes, `PassA` and `PassB`, where `PassB` depends on `PassA`. The order in which these methods are called during the execution of the compiler for each module looks like this:

- `PassA::doInitialization`
- `PassB::doInitialization`
- `PassA::runOnXXX`
- `PassB::runOnXXX`
- `PassA::releaseMemory`

- `PassB::releaseMemory`
- `PassB::doFinalization`
- `PassA::doFinalization`

The `runOnXXX`/`releaseMemory` pair is called the same number of times. This means that if your pass is implemented with a `FunctionPass` class, `runOnXXX` and `releaseMemory` are called as many times as there are functions in the module. Notice also how the `doInitialization`/`doFinalization` pair for `PassB` is enclosed within the `doInitialization`/`doFinalization` pair for `PassA`.

The last method worth mentioning is `getAnalysisIfAvailable</*AnalysisName*/>()`. This method can be used in your `runOnXXX` method to access an analysis pass that may be available at this point. If the pass is available, then the pass manager will hand it to you; if not, it will give you `nullptr`. This method does not require declaring any dependency between your pass and this one, but the drawback is that your pass needs to be able to work without this analysis.

This can be useful when your pass can perform a little better if certain information is available, but the improvements of this pass alone with this information are not worth computing this information from scratch.

At this point, you know all the details around the legacy pass manager and the `Pass` class, the base entity used to represent a pass.

It is now time to learn how to represent a pass and everything around it in the new framework.

# Writing a pass for the new pass manager

Writing a pass for the new pass manager is much easier than with the legacy one. In essence, with the new pass manager, anything can be a pass as long as it implements a `run` method with the appropriate level of IR as input. We list the actual signatures for the different levels in the next section.

Now, in practice, your pass needs some boilerplate to fit nicely with the infrastructure (for example, a name,) but most of this boilerplate can be inherited from the following two structures:

- For passes: `PassInfoMixin<YourPass>`
- For analyses: `AnalysisInfoMixin<YourPass>`

The analyses require a different base class because, unlike passes, they need an identifier to be registered in the pass manager so that other passes can depend on them and can be (re)computed on the fly.

## Implementing the right method

As already stated, in the new pass manager, a pass must implement a `run` method with the appropriate inputs. *Table 5.3* shows what this signature looks like for each scope:

| Scope | Method signature |
|---|---|
| Module | `Result run(Module &M, ModuleAnalysisManager &AM)` |
| CGSCC | `Result run(LazyCallGraph::SCC &C,  CGSCCAnalysisManager &AM,`<br>`LazyCallGraph &CG, CGSCCUpdateResult &UR)` |
| Function | `Result run(Function &F, FunctionAnalysisManager &FAM)` |
| Loop | `Result run(Loop &L, LoopAnalysisManager &AM, LoopStandardAnalysisResults`<br>`&AR,  LPMUpdater &U)` |

*Table 5.3: Methods to implement for the different scopes*

The takeaways are that the `run` method does the following:

- Takes two main arguments: the input IR and an `XXXAnalysisManager` object. The `XXXAnalysisManager` object manages the analyses cache for this level of IR.
- Returns a result that is a templated type. This type is always `PreservedAnalyses` for regular passes and is whatever the analysis produces for analyses.

For scopes with additional arguments (that is, CGSCC and loop), these are used to get access to additional information and utility functions that help the pass manager keep track of how the IR has been modified.

We invite you to read the comments in the code on the related classes if you want more details on these.

Unlike the legacy pass manager, passes in the new framework do not have to describe their dependencies with the different analyses. Instead, the `XXXAnalysisManager` objects manage a cache of the analyses and recompute them when they are needed but stall.

For these caches to work, your analyses need to be registered in the related `XXXAnalysisManager` object. This is the topic of the next section.

## Registering an analysis

The registration process requires two things:

1. Your pass needs an identifier.
2. You need to tell the `XXXAnalysisManager` object how to build your pass.

For the first bullet point, you need to add a `static AnalysisKey Key` field to your pass.

For the second bullet point, you provide a function, usually a lambda, to `XXXAnalysisManager::registerPass`.

For instance, the following snippet is the skeleton of an analysis that works on function scope and produces some custom information held in a class called `MyAnalysisInfo`:

```
class MyAnalysis : public AnalysisInfoMixin<MyAnalysis> {
  friend AnalysisInfoMixin<MyAnalysis>;
  static AnalysisKey Key;
public:
  /// Provide the result typedef for this analysis pass.
  using Result = MyAnalysisInfo;
  MyAnalysisInfo run(Function &, FunctionAnalysisManager &);
};
```

Then you need to instantiate this class Key somewhere:

```
AnalysisKey MyAnalysis::Key;
```

And proceed to its registration, for instance, in your main function:

```
FunctionAnalysisManager FAM;
FAM.registerPass([]{ return MyAnalysisInfo(); });
```

> **Note**
>
> If you are building your analysis directly in the LLVM tree, you do not have to manually register your pass. Instead, you need to add an entry in `${LLVM_SRC}/llvm/lib/Passes/PassRegistry.def` that resembles `IRLevel_Type("passname", MyPass())` where `IRLevel` can be `MODULE`, `FUNCTION`, and so on and `Type` can be `ANALYSIS`, `PASS`, and so on. Make sure to add your entry in the right section (that is, `MODULE` with `MODULE`, `FUNCTION` with `FUNCTION`, and so on) and include the header file of your pass in `${LLVM_SRC}/llvm/lib/Passes/PassBuilder.cpp`.

You now know how to create your own analysis and register it with `XXXAnalysisManager`. The only thing left is for you to learn how to tell the pass manager the effects that your passes have on the analyses.

## Describing the effects of your pass

Only regular passes need to describe the effects that they have on the analyses. Analyses are assumed to leave the IR untouched.

The way you describe these effects is through the returned `PreservedAnalyses` object of your pass' `run` method. This object tells which set of analyses are preserved. It is more expressive than its legacy pass manager counterpart `AnalysisUsage` because analyses can more precisely define what changes affect them. In a nutshell, the pass manager provides keys that passes can mark as preserved, and your analysis can check these keys.

In its simplest form, the key is a specific analysis. Therefore, if your pass preserves a specific analysis, you can directly use something like the following:

```
PreservedAnalyses MyPass::run(/*some arguments*/) {
  /* do something */
  PreservedAnalyses PA;
  PA.preserveSet<MyAnalysis>();
  return PA;
}
```

For more details on how to check for a set of specific keys, look at `https://llvm.org/docs/NewPassManager.html#implementing-analysis-invalidation`.

This concludes this section on creating a pass. In this section, you learned how to create a pass both with the legacy and the new pass managers. You discovered which methods you need to implement to tell pass managers which scope of the IR your pass works on and how it interacts with the analysis passes.

In the next section, you will learn how to debug a pass pipeline and fix any potential inefficiencies.

# Inspecting the pass pipeline

As you grow your expertise in building passes and pass pipelines, you will inevitably run into issues – for instance, around compile time. In this section, you will learn how to inspect the pass pipeline and draw conclusions from that.

## Available developer tools

The LLVM infrastructure provides several tools and utilities to interact with the passes and the pass pipelines. The main ones are opt and llc, which are a driver for LLVM passes and a compiler from LLVM IR to assembly code (in textual or object form), respectively.

If you look at Clang's implementation of the *codegen* pipeline, you will find that it resembles opt's pipeline for the middle-end and llc's pipeline for the backend. In other words, you can reproduce Clang's behavior with a call to opt with the right options followed by a call to llc.

Before we present how to debug your pass pipeline irrespective of whether you followed Clang's way of building your pass pipeline, here is what you can leverage if you want your own pass pipeline to do something like Clang:

- To create your middle-end, use `PassBuilder::parsePassPipeline`, or if you already know the kind of pipeline you want, you can use some of the default pipeline implementations, such as `PassBuilder::buildPerModuleDefaultPipeline`, from the `Passes` library.
- To create your backend, use `TargetMachine::addPassesToEmitFile`. The difficult part here is to get `TargetMachine`, but you can look at the implementation of llc (`${LLVM_SRC}/llvm/tools/llc/llc.cpp`) or the main function in `ch3/machineir/main.cpp` in the repository of this book to get an idea of how to do that.

> **Note**
>
> If you look closely at the signature of these APIs, you will notice that, as already mentioned, the middle-end uses the new pass manager, whereas the backend still uses the legacy pass manager.

The next section will teach you how to connect the different pieces of the LLVM infrastructure to collect information about a pass pipeline and its passes.

# Plumbing up the information you need

Depending on the pass manager, it is more or less difficult to surface the information we need to inspect the pass pipeline.

On one hand, the legacy pass manager offers backed-in debug capabilities that are relatively easy to surface. On the other hand, the new pass manager requires an increasing amount of work depending on how much of the existing infrastructure you want or can reuse.

Going back to Clang, for instance, it exposes a command-line option (`-fdebug-pass-structure`) that prints out what the pass pipeline looks like both for the middle-end and the backend and another command-line option (`-ftime-report`) that prints out how much time is spent in each pass. We will see how to interpret these outputs in the next section. Additionally, you can pass an option (`-mllvm -print-pipeline-passes`) that prints out a list of options that need to be used to reproduce your (middle-end) pipeline with opt.

Now, if you do not use Clang, there are some steps you can take to get the same kind of information.

For the new pass manager, for the structure of the pass pipeline, you must rewire the pass instrumentation from scratch. If you use the `PassBuilder` class to build your pass pipeline, you can reuse some existing plumbing. That said, the principle and effort are about the same as doing everything without the `PassBuilder` class.

Concretely, before instantiating your pass manager, you need to hook up the `PassInstrumentationAnalysis` class with the logging capabilities enabled. You can achieve that with the following code sequence:

```
ModuleAnalysisManager MAM;
PassInstrumentationCallbacks PIC;
PrintPassOptions PrintPassOpts;
PrintPassOpts.Verbose = true;
PrintPassOpts.SkipAnalyses = false;
PrintPassOpts.Indent = true;
StandardInstrumentations SI(Context,
                            /*DebugLogging=*/true,
                            /*VerifyEachPass=*/false,
                            PrintPassOpts);
```

```
SI.registerCallbacks(PIC, &MAM);
MAM.registerPass([&] {
    return PassInstrumentationAnalysis(&PIC);
});
```

In detail, this snippet instantiates a StandardInstrumentations object from the Passes library with all the relevant logging options turned on. Then, by calling registerCallbacks, it populates the PassInstrumentationCallbacks PIC object with all the hooks that enable the logging capabilities. Finally, we register PIC with the PassInstrumentationAnalysis pass, which is a pass that ModuleAnalysisManager will run automatically for instrumentation purposes. Now, when this analysis runs, it will automatically call the callbacks from PIC, and this is going to produce the information we need to inspect the pass pipeline.

For the legacy pass manager and for the profiling capabilities, things are both easier and more restrictive. It is easier because you must only hook up the LLVM command-line options in your program and enable them, but it is more restrictive because as soon as you start hooking up the LLVM command-line options, all your command-line options need to go through LLVM, which may or may not be an option for you!

In any case, the command-line options we want to plumb through are the following:

- -debug-pass=<levelOfDetails> for the structure of the pass pipeline in the legacy pass manager
- -time-passes for the profiling information for both pass managers

To enable these command-line options, you have different alternatives:

1. Adopt the command-line options' API for your whole handling of command-line options. In a nutshell, this means that all your command-line options need to be declared with cl::opt, and you need to call cl::ParseCommandLineOptions(argc, argv) at the beginning of your main function to set them. More details at https://www.llvm.org/docs/CommandLine.html. When this is done, you can pass the related command-line options to your command line. In other words, you have access to the full set of LLVM command-line options.

2. Modify your version of LLVM and set these options manually. That is, add a cl::init(<DesiredDefaultValue>) instance (in this case, <DesiredDefaultValue> would be true) to the definition of the cl::opt PassDebugging global in ${LLVM_SRC}/llvm/lib/IR/LegacyPassManager.cpp for the structure of the pass pipeline of the legacy pass manager and the definition of the cl::opt EnableTiming global in ${LLVM_SRC}/llvm/lib/IR/PassTimingInfo.cpp. You can, of course, modify the source code differently if you prefer!

Finally, if you use several pass managers in your program, you may want to add a call to reportAndResetTimings between their runs to get the performance of each pass pipeline. Otherwise, you will automatically only get reports for pass pipelines produced with the new pass managers.

With the work you have done here, you can now see the detailed pass pipeline in action and how well it performs. In the next section, you will learn how to interpret the information printed by this plumbing.

# Interpreting the logs of pass managers

In the previous section, you learned how to get the logs that show you the structure of your pass pipeline and its time profile. Depending on the kind of inefficiencies you want to tackle, you may want to start with one or the other.

## The pass pipeline structure

The log for the pass pipeline structure helps you understand the following:

- How your IR goes through your passes
- When the analysis passes are (re)run

This log corresponds to the -debug-pass=Structure command-line option and the PassInstrumentationCallbacks object, which you discovered in the previous section.

The following output shows an example of such a log for the new pass manager:

```
Running pass: ModuleToFunctionPassAdaptor on [module]
  Running analysis: InnerAnalysisManagerProxy<FunctionAnalysisManager, Module>
on [module]
  Running pass: PassManager<Function> on foo (9 instructions)
    Running pass: FctPassA on foo (9 instructions)
      Running analysis: DominatorTreeAnalysis on foo
      ...
    Running pass: FctPassB on foo (9 instructions)
      Running analysis: TargetLibraryAnalysis on foo
      ...
  Running pass: PassManager<Function> on bar (10 instructions)
    Invalidating analysis: SomeAnalysis on bar
    Running pass: FctPassA on bar (10 instructions)
    ...
    Running pass: FctPassB on bar (10 instructions)
    ...
Running pass: ModulePassA on [module]
  Running analysis: ModuleAnalysisA on [module]
```

The log is straightforward to read, but there are a couple of things that are worth mentioning as they will help you fix potential inefficiencies.

The first one is that the log shows you when the analysis passes are run and invalidated. The information about the invalidation is straightforward with the new pass manager; you get a message that starts with Invalidating. For the legacy pass manager, this is not immediately obvious, though. Instead, you must make sure that the analysis passes run as often as they should and not more. In other words, if they get invalidated, you will see that they are rerun.

To improve the efficiency of your pipeline, double-check that you need all the analysis passes that are run and, if you do, try to preserve them across passes.

The second one is the structure of the pass pipeline itself. Here, for instance, we have a module with two functions, foo and bar, and a pass pipeline with three main passes: two function passes, FctPassA and FctPassB, and one module pass, ModulePassA. Notice how the IR flows through this pipeline:

- FctPassA is applied to foo
- FctPassB is applied to foo
- FctPassA is applied to bar
- FctPassB is applied to bar
- ModulePassA is applied to the whole module

In other words, the pass manager pushes through the current scope of IR as far as possible in the pipeline until it reaches a scope change. This structure is the recommended one. However, it is easy to produce a different structure where FctPassA goes through foo then bar, then FctPassB goes through foo then bar, then ModulePassA goes through the whole module.

Here is a snippet that builds the recommended structure of a pass manager when PRESERVE_FCT_SCOPE is defined; otherwise, it produces the simpler module-to-module order by leveraging XXXPassAdaptor. In both cases, this is the same order of passes, but the IR flows through it differently:

```
ModulePassManager NewPM;
#ifdef PRESERVE_FCT_SCOPE
FunctionPassManager FPMgr;
FPMgr.addPass(FctPassA());
FPMgr.addPass(FctPassB());
NewPM.addPass(
  createModuleToFunctionPassAdaptor(std::move(FPMgr)));
#else
NewPM.addPass(
  createModuleToFunctionPassAdaptor(FctPassA()));
NewPM.addPass(
  createModuleToFunctionPassAdaptor(FctPassB()));
#endif
NewPM.addPass(ModulePassA());
```

For the legacy pass manager, you need to go after the exact same inefficiencies: pass invalidation and non-scope-preserving structure.

Before going into how to spot these details, the following output gives a concrete example of a log:

```
...
  ModulePass Manager
    FunctionPass Manager
      AnalysisA
      ...
      FctPassA
      AnalysisB
      ...
      FctPassB
    ModuleAnalysisA
    ModulePassA
```

The bad news about the legacy pass manager's structure log, as with the preceding output, is that nothing in the log tells you which passes are analyses and which ones are regular passes. In other words, you know that AnalysisA is an analysis pass only if you know that this name represents an analysis. If the name is not descriptive enough, you are on your own! The second issue is there is no direct logging that a pass has been invalidated. Instead, you need to spot whether the name of an analysis pass keeps coming up in the pipeline. If it does, that means it has been invalidated since it needs to be rerun. Finally, you must infer how the IR flows through the pipeline by yourself. The indentation helps you identify a scope, but then you need to know that within one scope the IR flows all the way, as we already explained (that is, foo goes through the full FunctionManager class's passes before bar is fed to this part of the pipeline).

The good news with the legacy pass manager is that you get the recommended structure out of the box: the pass manager groups the passes together when they are from the same scope. The drawback is since all of this happens under the hood, it is easy to insert a module pass in the middle of a sequence of function passes without realizing it. Similarly, while it is possible, it is more complicated to break the predefined flow when you want (for example, you need to wrap your function pass in a module pass or create a dummy module pass to force a break in the automatic scoping mechanism). The bottom line is that this manager offers less control.

Note

In the legacy pass manager, analyses may be bound to a nested pass manager. For instance, when you add a function pass after a module pass (that is, you have a scope change), what the legacy pass manager does is first create a new function pass manager (which is itself a module pass) and register your pass with this nested manager. While this is mainly a technical detail, this can have dramatic implications on your ability to preserve analysis. Indeed, since you are starting with a fresh nested manager, it is likely that it will not have access to the previously computed analyses. If the information you need cannot be recomputed from scratch, then you must rethink your pass pipeline structure.

To summarize, for the legacy pass manager structure, pay attention to the different indentation levels (this means a break in the pass manager nested structure), and pay attention to the names of the passes that are repeated a lot. If these are analysis passes, you may want to preserve them.

Now that you are satisfied with the structure of your pass pipeline, let us see how you interpret its time profile.

## Time profile

When you enable the time profile (hooked up with the `-time-passes` command-line option), you end up with an output that resembles the following:

```
===-------------------------------------------------------------------------===
                      Pass execution timing report
===-------------------------------------------------------------------------===
  Total Execution Time: 0.0007 seconds (0.0007 wall clock)

   ---User Time---    --System Time--    --User+System--    ---Wall Time---
---Instr---    --- Name ---
   0.0004 ( 79.2%)    0.0001 ( 58.9%)    0.0005 ( 73.6%)    0.0005 ( 73.6%)
3312503   InstCombinePass
[...]
   0.0005 (100.0%)    0.0002 (100.0%)    0.0007 (100.0%)    0.0007 (100.0%)
4462553   Total


===-------------------------------------------------------------------------===
                      Analysis execution timing report
===-------------------------------------------------------------------------===
  Total Execution Time: 0.0002 seconds (0.0002 wall clock)

   ---User Time---    --System Time--    --User+System--    ---Wall Time---
---Instr---    --- Name ---
   0.0000 ( 35.5%)    0.0000 ( 66.2%)    0.0001 ( 45.3%)    0.0001 ( 45.9%)
692166   AAManager
[...]
```

For both the legacy and the new pass manager, you have the same overall structure, except that the legacy pass manager does not report the analysis passes in a dedicated section.

The report is self-explanatory; however, here are a few things to remember when you look at it:

1.  The time profile can change drastically between a *debug*, a *release with assertion enabled*, and a *release without assertions* builds. Make sure to profile what makes sense for your use case.

2.  The reported time is the cumulated time spent on a particular pass. A pass may end up being executed a lot and thus contributing a lot to the compile time just because it is invalidated all the time. Make sure to double-check the structure of the pipeline because you may be wasting time to optimize a particular pass.

> **Note**
>
> In the time profile, you will also find sections that go into detail on how time is spent within passes. We will not cover this in this book, but if you are interested in leveraging this, look at how the `NamedRegionTimer` class from the `Support` library is used; for instance, in `${LLVM_SRC}/llvm/lib/CodeGen/RegAllocGreedy.cpp`.

This concludes this overview of how to inspect the pass pipeline. In this section, you have learned the following:

*   How to instantiate your pass pipeline to match the behavior of the provided developer tools, `opt` and `llc`

*   How to connect the logging capabilities of different pass managers to the implementation of your pipeline

*   How to interpret and leverage logging information around the structure of the pass pipeline and its timing information

Now, it is time to put all your newly acquired knowledge together with some hands-on experience.

# Your turn

To help you solidify your understanding of what you learned throughout this chapter, we prepared two exercises that will put you to the test.

In the first one, you will create a pass with both the legacy pass manager and the new pass manager.

In the second, you will also interact with both managers, but this time, you will create a pass pipeline that can produce logging information.

## Writing your own pass

For this exercise, you will have to produce two implementations: one for the legacy pass manager, where you will fill in the blanks for a function called `createYourTurnPassForLegacyPM`, located in `ch5/your_first_pass/your_turn/passWithLegacyPM.cpp`, and one for the new pass manager, where you will have to implement the class called `YourTurnConstantPropagationNewPass` declared in `ch5/your_first_pass/your_turn/passWithNewPM.h` and whose implementation should live in `ch5/your_first_pass/your_turn/passWithNewPM.cpp`.

> **Note**
>
> The pointer that you hand over to the legacy pass manager when adding a pass must be dynamically allocated. The pass manager takes ownership of this pointer and will deallocate it at the right time.

For this exercise, your pass will simply reuse the simple constant propagation implementation from the previous chapter. The prototype of this function is given in the `.cpp` files you have to fill in, and the compilation and linking are taken care of for you. If you want to implement your own pass, feel free to do so!

To know how to run your example, look at the `README.md` file in `ch5/your_first_pass`. Also, if you want some inspiration, feel free to look at the provided solution at `ch5/your_first_pass/solution`.

You should be able to complete everything by calling the APIs you learned in this chapter.

Next, let us see if you can create a pass pipeline.

## Writing your own pass pipeline

In this exercise, you will manipulate both pass managers to create a simple pass pipeline consisting of three optimizations in this order: mem2reg, instcombine, and alwaysinline.

The mem2reg pass comes from the `TransformsUtils` library and can be instantiated with `createProm oteMemoryToRegisterPass` for the legacy pass manager and `PromotePass` for the new pass manager, respectively.

For `instcombine`, its implementation lives in the `Transforms` library, and its APIs are the following:

- `createInstructionCombiningPass` for the legacy pass manager
- `InstCombinePass` for the new pass manager

Finally, the `alwaysinline` pass is available from the `IPO` library with the following:

- `createAlwaysInlinerLegacyPass` for the legacy pass manager
- `AlwaysInlinerPass` for the new pass manager

In the case of the new pass manager, try to hook up the logging capabilities for the structure of the pass pipeline. The command-line options are already properly hooked up for you for both managers; you only have to worry about setting up the proper `PassInstrumentionCallbacks` options.

> **Note**
>
> We already prefetched all the necessary LLVM libraries in the `CMakeLists.txt` file of this exercise. However, if you want to play with different passes or if you want to learn how to do this for your own project, take a look at `https://llvm.org/docs/CMake.html#embedding-llvm-in-your-project` and, more specifically, at the definition of `llvm_map_components_to_libnames`, which is what you would need to update.

The files that you need to modify live at ch5/your_first_pipeline/your_turn/passPipelineWithNewPM. cpp and ch5/your_first_pipeline/your_turn/passPipelineWithLegacyPM.cpp. Look at the README. md file in ch5/your_first_pipeline to see how to build and run this example.

For the new pass manager, you will need to leverage the PassBuilder class to register the analysis passes that are required by the LLVM passes. This is straightforward; just use the following snippet to initialize your XXXAnalysisManager instances:

```
PassBuilder PB;
PB.registerFunctionAnalyses(FAM);
PB.registerModuleAnalyses(MAM);
```

Also, be careful with the order in which you create your XXXAnalysisManager instances. They need to be created from the narrower to the broader scope. For more details on why, look at https://llvm. org/docs/NewPassManager.html#just-tell-me-how-to-run-the-default-optimization-pipeline-with-the-new-pass-manager.

Finally, there are other pitfalls that you might fall into. Do not worry – this is part of the learning, and if you are stuck, feel free to look at a possible implementation in ch5/your_first_pipeline/solution.

Now that you have firsthand experience with everything related to passes and pass managers, we can conclude this chapter.

## Summary

In this chapter, you discovered the concept of passes and pass pipelines. You learned the difference between passes and analyses and the different scopes of IR they can operate on. You were able to get firsthand experience in implementing your own pass and pass pipeline. This knowledge and experience are the backbone of how LLVM-based compilers are traditionally built.

You also learned how to leverage the logging capabilities that the LLVM infrastructure has to offer with respect to the structure of your pass pipeline and its profiling information and saw how to navigate this information and act based on it.

Before you get started with the next chapter on TableGen, feel free to challenge yourself with the quiz below!

## Further reading

For a more in-depth understanding of the concepts covered in the chapter, we invite you to check out the following resources:

- Explanation of how to write a pass with the new pass manager: https://llvm.org/docs/ WritingAnLLVMNewPMPass.html
- Explanation of how to write a pass with the legacy pass manager: https://llvm.org/docs/ WritingAnLLVMPass.html
- Explanation of how the new pass manager works: https://llvm.org/docs/NewPassManager. html

# Quiz time

Now that you have completed reading this chapter, try answering the following questions to test your knowledge:

1. Would it be correct for a function pass to modify the definition of a global variable?

   No, it would not because passes are not supposed to modify elements of the IR that are outside of the scope that was provided to them. It is okay to look at the broader scope, but not modify it.

   Modifying a global variable would require a module scope since the variable is visible to the whole module.

   More details in the *What is a pass?* section.

2. Draw the CGSCC of the following snippet:

   ```
   void foo() {
     bar();
     baz();
   }
   void bar() {
     foo();
     baz();
   }
   void baz() {
     charlie();
   }
   ```

   To draw the CGSCC, first compute the call graph. This gives you the nodes of the call graph and its edges. Then, identify the regions that are strongly connected. The definition of strongly connected is available in the *What is a pass?* section.

   The result looks like this:

   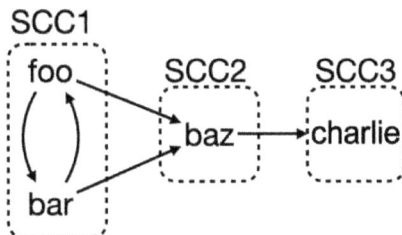

3.   When using the `Pass` class, should you always override the `releaseMemory()` method?

     No, this method is mainly useful for analysis passes. If you write a regular pass, you should do your memory allocation/deallocation in the `runOnXXX` method. For analysis passes, on the other hand, if you allocate memory dynamically in your `runOnXXX` method, it may be interesting to override this method.

     Check out the *Specificities of the Pass class* section to get more information on when the pass manager calls the different methods.

4.   Let us say that you find out that a pass gets invalidated too often. What can you do?

     You can inspect the pass structure to see which passes do not preserve this analysis, check if the related passes are not just missing to populate the `PreservedAnalysis/AnalysisUsage` information, and if all this was correct, teach the related passes how to preserve your analysis.

     For more details, check out the *Preserving analyses* section for the legacy pass manager and the *Describing the effects of your pass* section for the new pass manager.

5.   What logging capabilities do pass managers offer?

     Pass managers can print out a detailed view of both the structure of your pass pipeline and the time that each pass individually takes.

     More information on this can be found in the *Inspecting the pass pipeline* section.

# 6

# TableGen — LLVM Swiss Army Knife for Modeling

For every target, there are a lot of things to model in a compiler infrastructure to be able to do the following:

- Represent all the available resources
- Extract all the possible performance
- Manipulate the actual instructions

This list is not exhaustive, but the point IS that you need to model a lot of details of a target in a compiler infrastructure.

While it is possible to implement everything with your regular programming language, such as C++, you can find more productive ways to do so. In the LLVM infrastructure, this takes the form of a **domain-specific language (DSL)** called TableGen.

In this chapter, you will learn the TableGen syntax and how to work your way through the errors reported by the TableGen tooling. These skills will help you be more productive when working with this part of the LLVM ecosystem.

This chapter focuses on TableGen itself, not the uses of its output through the LLVM infrastructure. How the TableGen output is used is, as you will discover, TableGen-backend-specific and will be covered in the relevant chapters. Here, we will use one TableGen backend to get you accustomed to the structure of the TableGen output, starting you off on the right foot for the upcoming chapters.

Before getting started with TableGen, let's briefly discuss the technical requirements.

# Technical requirements

In this chapter, you will wrestle directly with the TableGen tooling that comes with the LLVM releases. At this point, you know the drill concerning the tools that you need to build a project using the LLVM infrastructure (Git, CMake, Ninja, and the C++ toolchain).

Additionally, you will find the code for the examples in this chapter in a folder named ch6, which can be found in the GitHub repository of this book: `https://github.com/PacktPublishing/LLVM-Code-Generation`.

Without further ado, let's start our journey with TableGen.

# Getting started with TableGen

The name **TableGen** stems from its original usage – generating tables. For instance, TableGen generates the table that represents all the registers of a target. TableGen outgrew this purpose and is now used to model a wide range of things, from Clang's command-line options to **multi-level intermediate representation (MLIR)** operations' boilerplate C++ code, or used directly within LLVM to generate the instruction selection tables, and so on.

Fundamentally, TableGen is a DSL to produce records. A **record** is an entity with a name and an arbitrary number of fields, where each field has its own type.

How these records are used and what output TableGen generates from them depends on the specific TableGen backend.

We will survey one of the TableGen backends used in this book in the *Discovering a TableGen backend* section, but you will learn how to use this backend and the other ones in the relevant upcoming chapters.

TableGen's strength lies in how you can structure the generation of your records such that you can factor out the repeated parts of records.

For instance, imagine that you want to produce records that hold the ages and names of people. Without even describing the TableGen syntax yet, this could look like the following snippet:

```
class Person<int age, string name> {
  int _age = age;
  string _name = name;
}
def A: Person<23, "A">;
def B: Person<64, "B">;
def /*Anonym*/: Person<43, "anonymous">;
```

Note how the boilerplate of our records is gathered in just one location, the Person class, and how easy it is to create a record for each person (A, B, etc.).

Then, you can process that input (saved in a file named person.td, in this case) through TableGen with the following command:

```
$ ${LLVM_INSTALL_DIR}/bin/llvm-tblgen person.td
```

Running this command will yield the following records:

```
def A {       // Person
  int _age = 23;
  string _name = "A";
}
def B {       // Person
  int _age = 64;
  string _name = "B";
}
def anonymous_0 {    // Person
  int _age = 43;
  string _name = "anonymous";
}
```

As you can see, TableGen's basic functionality expands a structured representation of your records into a mostly flat representation. The parts that do not get flattened are the fields with non-built-in types.

To summarize, TableGen is a sort of glorified string concatenation tool, at least for the frontend part.

The interesting bits happen when you enable a TableGen backend (through one of the --gen-xxx options of the llvm-tblgen tool). When a TableGen backend is enabled, TableGen feeds the records, after flattening them all, to the related backend. The backend then generates what is expected from these records, and this content is included in the related part of the LLVM infrastructure. Where and how things are included depends on the usage of the generated information, but the general mechanism remains the same for all of them, as illustrated in *Figure 6.1*.

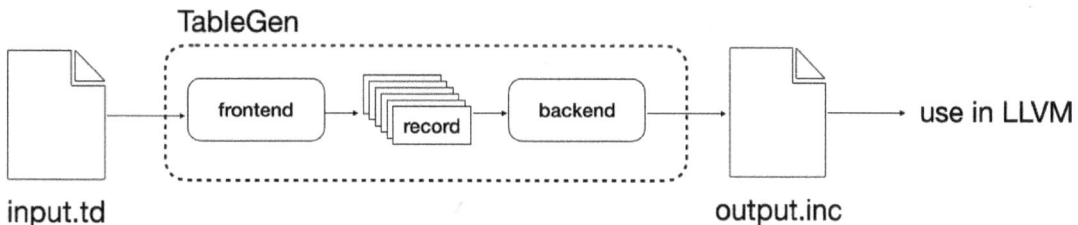

*Figure 6.1: Usage of TableGen in LLVM*

In *Figure 6.1*, an input file, usually with the .td suffix, which stands for **target description**, is fed to TableGen. The TableGen frontend generates flattened records and feds them to the desired backend. The backend generates its output in a file with a .inc suffix. That suffix indicates that this file needs to be included somewhere else to make sense. The type of output in the .inc file depends on the backend, but usually in LLVM, TableGen is used to produce C++ code.

The invocation of TableGen happens at **build time**. The content of certain LLVM files depends on the presence of the `.inc` files, and they are generated as part of the build process. This is why building TableGen in **release** mode, as described in *Chapter 1*, can help you speed up your build time even if you are interested in building your whole compiler in **debug** mode.

> **Note**
>
> Even if you are tempted to modify the content of a `.inc` file, do not! Although this is fine for exploration purposes, the `.inc` suffix is used as an indication that the related file has been automatically generated. In other words, if you want to modify it, you must modify its source; hence, find its related `.td` file.

In this section, you learned the basic mechanics of TableGen. You saw that it is used as a DSL to generate, at build time, information included by the rest of the LLVM infrastructure. You also learned that what is generated is TableGen-backend specific.

Before looking at the TableGen backends more closely, let's get a primer on the TableGen syntax.

# The TableGen programming language

In this section, we will offer a primer on the TableGen syntax. The goal here is not for you to become a TableGen programmer but to know enough so that you can understand what you read and write when working with TableGen in the rest of this book. For a more thorough explanation of the TableGen syntax, consult the *Further reading* section.

As you saw in the previous section, TableGen is a language used to generate records. It relies on two main constructs to describe its records:

- `class`: A way to structure, pre-fill, and specify a type for records
- `def`: An instantiation of a record

The general syntax to describe a record is as follows:

```
def [optionalName][: optionalClassA[<argN[, argM]*>][, optionalClassB[<argV[,
argW]*>]]*] [{
  [type fieldName [ = value];]*
}];
```

In this snippet, everything between [ and ] is optional, and the * character means, as usual for regular expression, that the previous expression is repeated zero or more times.

Additionally, `argX` are the potentially required arguments of the related class. They must match in type and number at least all the non-default arguments specified for this class (see the *Types* section for more details). Then, `value` is used to initialize `fieldName`, and it must have the same type as `type`. The syntax of `value` depends on `type`.

> **Note**
>
> When you use other records in your fields (e.g., when `value` is another record), TableGen creates a reference to the original record. In other words, records are never copied.

A record instantiated with `optionalClassX` inherits all the fields of the respective class or classes. You can assign as many classes as you want to a record, as shown in the following snippet:

```
def MyRecord: classA, classB;
```

The resulting record will have the following traits:

- Be usable as an instance of each of these classes (for example, `MyRecord` can be used in both `list<classA>` and `list<classB>` instances).
- Be the union of all the fields of all the classes.

> **Note**
>
> If two classes have a field with the same name and are used together to instantiate a record, only the last seen field is kept. Similarly, if a record declares a field of the same name, only this one is kept. In other words, unlike C++ inheritance, name collisions cannot be disambiguated, and the last instantiated one wins.

Note that a record does not need to be typed. In other words, a record can be instantiated with just a `def` statement.

Let's now focus on the available types in TableGen, the topic of our next section.

## Types

While a record may not be typed, every field in a record must be typed. The types can be either one of the built-in types or user-defined.

The built-in types are as follows:

- `int`: A 64-bit integer value
- `bit`: A zero or one
- `bits<size>`: A sequence of `size` of zeros and ones
- `string`: A sequence of arbitrary characters
- `list<type>`: A sequence of `type` elements
- `dag`: A structure that represents a **directed acyclic graph (DAG)**. Without going into details, you can view this as arbitrary nested lists where each list starts with an operator (e.g., `(add (mul a, b), (div c, d))` is the DAG that represents a math expression of the form `(a * b) + (c / d)`). This is useful, for instance, to describe instruction selection patterns.

To initialize the integer-like types (int, bit, and bits) you can use your preferred *C-style* syntax for decimal and hexadecimal numbers, or the TableGen binary format in the 0b form, followed by zeros and ones.

For strings, simply use the *C-style* string syntax.

On top of the built-in types, you can create your own types using the class keyword. A class offers a convenient way to structure your records and can be parametrized with optional arguments, using a syntax close to C++ templates.

Using the same convention as the definition of a record, the definition of a class resembles the following:

```
class ClassName[<type arg1[, type arg2]*>] [: superclass1[<argN[, argM]*>] [,
superclass2[<argV[, argW]*>]]*] [{
  [type fieldName [ = value];]*
}];
```

The class's arguments can be set to a default value and used in the body of the class.

For instance, we can modify our Person class from earlier to set a default name:

```
class Person<int age, string name = "anonymous"> {
  int _age = age;
  string _name = name;
}
```

With this snippet, the instantiation of a record of type Person does not need to set the name argument anymore. Instead, "anonymous" will be automatically filled in.

This concludes the primer on types in TableGen.

Next, let's introduce some of the programming capabilities that TableGen offers.

## Programming with TableGen

TableGen offers some basic programmability features to make the description of your records more compact. These are called bang operators, and they are all prefixed with the ! character (i.e., the bang operator in C, hence the name) – for example, !add and !range.

For instance, you can define a record with a list of integers from 0 to 10 without the number 5, and then count how many items there are in the list by using something like the following:

```
def MyRecord {
  list<int> ZeroTo10No5 =
      !filter(var, !range(0, 10), !ne(var, 5));
  int num = !size(ZeroTo10No5);
}
```

In this snippet, we define a list of integers from 0 to 10 by using the !range operator. We then give this list of integers to the !filter operator. This operator iterates through this list and checks whether the current element, stored in the variable named var (defined by the first argument of the operator), matches the predicate given as its third argument – in this case, the !ne operator. !ne checks that two values are not equal.

Note how you can reference other fields (here ZeroTo10No5) when defining another one (here, num).

You can find the complete list of the bang operators at https://llvm.org/docs/TableGen/ProgRef. html#bang-operators.

Before we finish with the TableGen syntax, there is one last important concept that you need to be aware of – multi-class. Let's cover this topic in our next section.

## Defining multiple records at once

With its obsession with compact code, TableGen offers a way to create a template for multiple records at once. You can use it with the multiclass keyword for the description of the template and the defm keyword for the instantiation of the records.

Before we dive into the syntax of these constructs, we want to highlight that, unlike classes, multi-classes are not types per se. You can instantiate a (multi-)record with a multi-class, but you cannot use a multi-class as the type parameter of list, for instance. We will illustrate this difference with an example, but first, let's lay down the syntax.

Using the same convention as before, here is what a multi-class definition looks like:

```
multiclass name[<type [arg1, type arg2]*>][: optionalMulticlassA[<argN[,
argM]*>][, optionalMulticlassB[<argG[, argH]*>]]* [{
  [def|defm recordSuffix  // full record definition]*
}]
```

In this snippet, you can see that you can only describe multi-classes through other multi-classes (i.e., the initialization list accepts only multi-classes), but you can put as many (multi-)records as you want in its body.

While the (multi-)record's definition in the multi-class body is the full record's body (i.e., it follows the syntax shown earlier), the record is not instantiated just yet. Instead, the records described in a multi-class are instantiated when a standalone defm statement is used.

Using the same convention as before, a defm statement looks like the following expression:

```
defm [optionalName] : multiclassA[<argN[, argM]*>][, multiclassB[<argV[,
argW]*>]]*[,classD[<argY[, argZ]*>]]*;
```

A defm statement instantiates multiple records at once. All the records from all the multiclassX templates are instantiated, and their names are, by default, prepended by optionalName. In other words, by using this snippet and the previous multi-class one, the resulting record's name will be optionalName followed by recordSuffix. Additionally, each record is augmented with the fields found in the union of all of classX.

> **Note**
>
> If you do not set a name for your record (in other words, if you leave a blank between the def or defm keyword and the body of the (multi-)record), TableGen will automatically assign a unique name to your record(s). You have actually already experienced that, in the very first example, where def  /*Anonym*/:  ... produced the record named def anonymous_0!

To make the `multiclass` and `defm` constructs more concrete, let's look at an example that uses them.

Consider the following snippet:

```
multiclass Bundle<string base> {
  def A {
    string name = !strconcat(base, "-", "A");
    int price = 12;
    int weight = 1;
  }
  def B {
    string name = !strconcat(base, "-", "B");
    string tag = "special";
  }
}

class ShippingPrice<int arg> {
  int shippingPrice = arg;
}

defm valuedBundle : Bundle<"valued">, ShippingPrice<5>;
```

In this snippet, we declare one multi-class (`Bundle`) and one class (`ShippingPrice`). The multi-class defines two records, A and B. When we instantiate this multi-class with `valuedBundle`, we immediately create two records, named `valuedBundleA` and `valuedBundleB` (i.e., the name given to the `defm` statement, prepended to the two definitions from within the multi-class). Moreover, these records end up with a `shippingPrice` field with a value of 5, due to the usage of `ShippingPrice<5>` at the end of the `defm` statement.

Note that you can see which records are generated for this example by following the `README.md` instructions in the `ch6` file for the `multiclass.td` example.

Now that you have a better grasp of what a multi-class is, you can understand why this is not the kind of type that can appear in a `list` definition. To clarify this, as you saw, a multi-class is a collection of records, not a type per se. Each of these records may have distinct types, and they are technically never held together.

In other words, the following snippet is invalid:

```
list<Bundle> // error
```

However, let's say we add a definition of type `Gift` under the name `C` in our `Bundle` multi-class. After the `defm` statement of our previous example, a `valuedBundleC` record exists and has the `Gift` type (defined earlier as a class). Now, this record can be used in a list of `Gift`:

```
def AnotherRecord {
   list<Gift> gifts = [valuedBundleC];
}
```

We are almost done with our survey of the TableGen programming language; we are missing just one thing relating to field assignment that is used a lot in the LLVM code base. Let's address that in the next section.

## Assigning fields

TableGen offers diverse ways to assign a value to a field. Some ways take precedence over others, and since they are all used extensively in the LLVM code base, it is important you know about them.

You already know two of them:

- Assignment via multi-class/class arguments
- Plain assignment (e.g., with a literal/argument)

There is a third way that you need to know; it uses the `let` keyword with or without the `in` keyword.

The `let` keyword allows to override the values of a list of fields for the specified context. Without the `in` keyword, the context is the current record or class.

When used in a record or class, the syntax of a `let` statement is as follows:

```
let fieldName1 = newVal1[, fieldName2 = newVal2]*;
```

When using a `let` keyword in a record or class, all `fieldNameX` instances must have been previously defined. The `let` keyword assigns `newValX` to `fieldNameX`.

Now, if you want to define a context for the effect of `let`, you use the following construct:

```
let FieldName1 = NewVal1[, FieldName2 = NewVal2]* in
```

Compared to the version without the `in` keyword, field names will be resolved in the context of the statement right after `in`. This means that `fieldNameX` can reference field names that are yet to be defined. Additionally, the statement right after the `in` keyword can be arbitrarily large by encompassing it with { and } characters.

This means you can override the values of many fields for many records at once.

Finally, let's define the order of evaluation of the ways of assigning a value. Since the `let` keyword is used for overriding, it is evaluated after the regular field assignments (i.e., any non-`let` assignments are resolved first). Now, if there are several `let`-statements that affect the same field in the same context, the last one, in a file order from top to bottom, wins.

To make this clearer, consider the following example:

```
class MyClass<string _alias=""> {
  string alias = _alias;
}


let alias = "let from out" in
def A: MyClass<> {}


def B: MyClass<> {
  let alias = "let from body";
}


def C: MyClass<"from arg">;


let alias = "alias from bigger scope" in {
let alias = "let from out" in
def D: MyClass<"from arg"> {
  let alias = "let from body";
}


def E: MyClass<"will be overridden">;
} // end "alias from bigger scope"
```

In this example, you see the different assignment mechanisms in action on the field named alias:

- For record A, `alias` is overridden with a `let`-statement right after the definition of the record. `alias` will have the `"let from out"` value.
- For record B, `alias` is overridden within the body of the record. It will have the `"let from body"` value.
- For record C, we use a regular assignment (`alias = _alias` from within `MyClass`) after passing the value we want, `"from arg"`, as a class argument.
- For record D, focus on the `let` statements, since they override everything else. Then, find the last one – `alias` will have the `"let from body"` value.
- Record E looks innocent at first, but note that we are still within the context of the `let` statement that started slightly before record D. As such, the value of `alias` will have the value of this `let` statement (i.e., `"alias from bigger scope"`).

This concludes the basic skills you need to navigate the `.td` files in the LLVM code base. You will see that TableGen offers some other constructs that you should be already familiar with, such as comments (`//` and `/* */`) and includes (`include "path"`), but you should already be familiar with these concepts.

> Note
>
> In TableGen, there is no concept of header files. As such, you will not find any guard construct (the `ifndef`/`define` construct in the C-world), and includes flow transitively in the included files. This means two things. First, if you include a file twice, even transitively (e.g., if A includes B and C, and B includes D, and C also includes D, it implies that A includes D twice (once through B and once through C)), you will end up with a lot of errors around redefined records/classes. If that happens, double-check your includes in the global context. Second, it is okay to assume that a bigger context includes what you need in your `.td` file and materialize the dependencies accordingly (e.g., for the previous example, you would have A includes B, C and D, B includes nothing, and C includes nothing; D needs to be included before B and C in A).

In this section, you learned how to read, write, and understand TableGen files. You got accustomed to the not-so-intuitive `multiclass` and `defm` constructs, and you saw how to leverage `let` statements to modify your records after the fact.

The next section will prime you on the usage of TableGen in the LLVM infrastructure by presenting a TableGen backend used in LLVM.

# Discovering a TableGen backend

Although we could have fun creating records all day long, there is not much point to it if we don't do anything with them. Therefore, in this section, you will discover one of the TableGen backends used to build LLVM – in other words, how records that you create are consumed and used in LLVM.

While the content of this section remains high-level, we believe understanding the purpose of the records that you will build makes you more effective at it. First, it will help you build a mental model of the inner workings of TableGen, and second, it will give you confidence in approaching new TableGen backends.

Let's start this section with some information that applies to all the TableGen backends that target LLVM.

## General information on TableGen backends for LLVM

If you are building several projects within the LLVM umbrella, you will see that different projects use different TableGen drivers. For instance, while LLVM proper has `llvm-tblgen`, Clang has `clang-tblgen`, and MLIR has `mlir-tblgen`.

The main difference between these drivers is the TableGen backends they offer. Otherwise, the frontend is the same for all of them, meaning that what you learned on the TableGen syntax applies to all of them as well.

In this book, you will interact solely with the `llvm-tblgen` tool (i.e., the driver of the LLVM project).

Using this tool, you can see all the available backends by running the following on the command line:

```
$ llvm-tblgen --help
```

This will print a list of all the command-line options supported by the tool and the `--gen-xxx` options that, by convention, represent the available backends.

From that point, you can start playing with the different backends.

Now, more realistically, you do not want to start playing with a specific backend from scratch. Indeed, you need to provide certain records for the backends to do what they are meant to do. (You will learn what these records are in the relevant upcoming chapters.) Moreover, these records rely on classes that are provided by the core LLVM infrastructure, and you do not want to rediscover where these live and so on. Put differently, you do not want to rediscover the build dependencies manually. Instead, you want to leverage the build system to provide you with the right command for a specific backend.

If you are dealing with an issue with TableGen, chances are your build system will fail while building the related `.inc` file, so you will get this command line easily. If not, you can rebuild this `.inc` file with the right build target, as explained in the *A Crash course on Ninja* section in *Chapter 1*.

For instance, here is the command line reported by the build system for the `lib/Target/AArch64/AArch64GenInstrInfo.inc` target (i.e., the `instr-info` backend when run for the AArch64 backend):

```
$ llvm-tblgen -gen-instr-info -I ${LLVM_SRC}/llvm/lib/Target/AArch64 -I${LLVM_
BUILD}/include -I ${LLVM_SRC}/llvm/include -I ${LLVM_SRC}/llvm/lib/Target
${LLVM_SRC}/llvm/lib/Target/AArch64/AArch64.td --write-if-changed -o lib/Target/
AArch64/AArch64GenInstrInfo.inc -d lib/Target/AArch64/AArch64GenInstrInfo.inc.d
```

Irrespective of how you get your `llvm-tblgen` command line, the point is that this is your starting point for further exploration or debugging.

For existing LLVM backends, you can further check how a `.inc` file fits in the overall picture by looking at how it's used.

For instance, the following command line, run at the root of `${LLVM_SRC}`, gives all the files that directly use `AArch64GenInstrInfo.inc`:

```
$ git grep -l 'AArch64GenInstrInfo\.inc"' -- llvm
```

Now, you know how to discover what backends exist and how to find the proper command-line invocation for them.

The next section takes you a little bit deeper into the world of a TableGen backend.

# Discovering a TableGen backend

Sadly, most TableGen backends are under-documented. The good news is that all of them are used by at least one open source target. Using this open source target, you can see what the related .inc file looks like, and you can forge a mental model of how the related .td files connect to this output.

This section presents what one TableGen backend generates. This information will help you build some reflexes of how to approach TableGen backends that you have never worked with. By seeing how a backend works, you will learn what to look for when approaching a new backend.

We focused on one of the backends you will use later in this book, but we did not document all the ones that you will use. However, you can use the same approach to reverse-engineer how all the TableGen backends work.

Let's now focus on the TableGen backend used to generate the information for the *intrinsics*.

## The implementation of intrinsics

At the LLVM **intermediate representation** (IR) level, **intrinsics** are special functions known by the compiler. They usually map to specific target instructions. For instance, the LLVM function named llvm.aarch64.ldxr is an intrinsic at the LLVM IR level that maps to the LDXRB instruction of the AArch64 backend.

The TableGen backend that we cover here generates the LLVM IR boilerplate to use this intrinsic. The mapping to the final instruction is outside of the scope of this backend. You can invoke this backend through the llvm-tblgen executable by using the -gen-intrinsic-impl option.

You can look at the generated boilerplate by opening ${LLVM_BUILD}/include/llvm/IR/IntrinsicImpl.inc.

Let's look at the content of this file.

## The content of a generated file

Looking into IntrinsicImpl.inc, the interesting bits are how the generated code is structured. The file is virtually split into several sections. Each section is guarded by a macro, #ifdef GET_[LLVM_]INTRINSIC_XXX, where XXX is, in this case, one of IITINFO, TARGET_DATA, NAME_TABLE, and so on. Each section has its own usage ,as described in *Table 6.1*:

| Name | Usage |
| --- | --- |
| GET_INTRINSIC_IITINFO | Gets the enumeration that describes the possible **Intrinsic Information Types (IITs)**. This is the enum type used in the list returned by Intrinsic::getIntrinsicInfoTableEntries. |

| Name | Usage |
| --- | --- |
| `GET_INTRINSIC_TARGET_DATA` | Gets the table that maps each target's namespace (identified in the intrinsic name, `llvm.<targetnamespace>`) to the range of indices that defines all the intrinsics for this namespace.<br><br>This is used underneath `Function::lookupIntrinsicID` to find `Intrinsic::ID`. |
| `GET_INTRINSIC_NAME_TABLE` | Gets the table that maps an `Intrinsic::ID` to the LLVM function name.<br><br>This is used by `Intrinsic::getBaseName`. |
| `GET_INTRINSIC_OVERLOAD_TABLE` | Gets the table that feeds into the `Intrinsic::isOverloaded` method. |
| `GET_INTRINSIC_GENERATOR_GLOBAL` | Gets the table of the IIT for each intrinsic.<br><br>This is used in `Intrinsic::getIntrinsicInfoTableEntri es` to produce the list of `IITDescriptor`. |
| `GET_INTRINSIC_ATTRIBUTES` | Gets all the code used to produce the information returned by `Intrinsic::getAttributes`. |
| `GET_LLVM_INTRINSIC_FOR_CLANG_ BUILTIN` | Gets the implementation that maps Clang's built-in names (as seen in a C program) to `Intrinsic::ID`. |
| `GET_LLVM_INTRINSIC_FOR_MS_ BUILTIN` | Gets the implementation that maps Microsoft's built-in names (as seen in a C program) to `Intrinsic::ID`. |

*Table 6.1: Macros that guard the generated output of the IntrinsicImpl TableGen backend*

If you look at the other TableGen backends used by LLVM, you will see the same structure – virtual sections enabled by different macros and included in various parts of the LLVM infrastructure.

For this TableGen backend, you can find these usages by looking at how `IntrinsicImpl.inc` is included throughout the LLVM code base.

Let's now look at what drives this backend.

## The source of a TableGen backend

The main source file used by the `IntrinsicImpl` TableGen backend in the LLVM build system is `${LLVM_SRC}/llvm/include/llvm/IR/Intrinsics.td`.

This file contains the classes and records that are used to define all the target-specific intrinsics.

The thing that may be difficult to untangle with TableGen is that the backend draws some information from specific classes and/or records. In other words, records can be more than just an instantiation of a class.

For instance, consider the following snippet from `Intrinsics.td`:

```
def IntrArgMemOnly : IntrinsicProperty;
def IntrInaccessibleMemOnly : IntrinsicProperty;
```

These two records have the same type (`IntrinsicProperty`) and carry the same field values. Therefore, you might think that they are interchangeable, but this is not true!

The name of certain records carries special significance for the related backend.

In this case, the `IntrinsicEmitter` class (located in `llvm/utils/TableGen`), which implements this TableGen backend, uses these records to classify the memory effects of the intrinsics and generates different C++ code based on that.

For instance, you can see from the following snippet from `IntrinsicsAArch64.td` how `IntrArgMemOnly` can be used to define a particular intrinsic:

```
def int_aarch64_settag : DefaultAttrsIntrinsic<[], [llvm_ptr_ty, llvm_i64_ty],
    [IntrWriteMem, IntrArgMemOnly, NoCapture<ArgIndex<0>>, WriteOnly<ArgIndex<0>>]>;
```

The takeaway is that by only looking at a `.td` file, it is impossible to determine what are considered built-in constructs for a specific backend and what are just the uses of these constructs!

To remediate that problem, the authoring of TableGen files in LLVM is structured such that important records and classes are in one main include file (here `Intrinsics.td`) and the instantiation of these concepts is in target-specific files (here `IntrinsicsXXX.td` where XXX is the name of the related backend.) What this means is the classes and records that you may find in `IntrinsicsXXX.td` are specific to these files and are not load-bearing for the TableGen backend itself. In other words, you can interpret them as regular records and classes (i.e., a way to share information between records). The records and classes defined in the generic files usually hold a lot of comments that will help you instantiate your own records.

What you saw in this section applies to all TableGen backends in LLVM. For instance, if you look at `${LLVM_BUILD}/lib/Target/AArch64/AArch64GenGlobalISel.inc`, which is the output of the GlobalISel selector (`-gen-global-isel`) TableGen backend, you will find the guarded sections (e.g., `GET_GLOBALISEL_PREDICATE_BITSET` and `GET_GLOBALISEL_TEMPORARIES_DECL`), the load-bearing records and classes (in `${LLVM_SRC}/llvm/include/llvm/Target/Target.td`), and the LLVM-backend-specific implementation (in `${LLVM_SRC}/llvm/lib/Target/AArch64/AArch64.td`).

In this section, you learned that, sadly, the best way to approach a TableGen backend is to look at what was implemented in another LLVM backend. However, by discovering the general principles behind each TableGen backend used in LLVM, you learned how to follow basic threads to forge an understanding of the main classes and records leveraged by the related backends.

The next section covers tips and tricks to help you troubleshoot issues with a TableGen backend.

# Debugging the TableGen framework

When you interact with TableGen, it may not be immediately obvious what part of TableGen fails you, or how you misused it!

In this section, you will learn ways to determine what goes wrong. The way to fix the problem may, however, be backend-specific, and given the sheer volume of TableGen backends, we will not cover this in this book. However, we give you general guidance on how to approach them.

Let's start with the basics!

## Identifying the failing component

As you learned in *Getting started with TableGen*, a TableGen workflow implies several components – the frontend, the backend, and the use of the generated output in LLVM.

To identify which component is at fault, you need to identify when the failure occurs:

- If the failure occurs while producing the `.inc` file, the problem is either with the TableGen frontend or backend, the syntax you used, or how you used the specific constructs (class or record) of this backend.
- If the failure occurs while building a part of LLVM that includes the `.inc` file, the problem is with the TableGen backend, how you used the specific constructs of this backend, or the code that uses that generated file.
- If the failure occurs while running the compiler, the problem is with the TableGen backend, the code that uses it, or how you used the specific constructs of this backend.

Most of the TableGen backends have been around for a while and used quite a lot. Therefore, if something breaks at build time but after the `.inc` file has been generated (case 2) or at runtime (case 3), chances are the issue is in how you described your records. If you cannot find the issue yourself or believe there is a bug in the related TableGen backend, engage with the LLVM community. You may, for instance, help future developers by making the related TableGen backend produce a warning for the problematic case, instead of generating something dubious!

This leaves us with case 1 – TableGen failing to generate the `.inc` file.

At this point, TableGen should report an error. Your job is to find out whether this error comes from the TableGen frontend or backend.

To easily identify whether you are dealing with a frontend or a backend error, do the following:

1. Find the command line that generates the `.inc` file (refer back to the *General information on TableGen backends for LLVM* section).
2. Remove the `-gen-xxx` options.
3. Add the `-print-records` option.
4. Run the resulting command.

If the error remains, you are dealing with a TableGen frontend error. In other words, your syntax is incorrect. Usually, the frontend errors come with a line and column number referencing the input file.

If the error disappears, you are dealing with a backend-specific error, which we will discuss in the next section.

## Cracking open a TableGen backend

Most of the time, the error reported by a TableGen backend gives you enough information to infer what you need to do to solve it.

For instance, imagine you want to use the GlobalISel selector backend and you get the following error:

```
error: The class 'HwMode' is not defined
```

This is straightforward – you miss a record of the HwMode class in your .td file for the backend to be able to operate.

To find this class, you can leverage git grep (see the following code snippet), or you can follow the include directory (-I option) to find the .td file where the important classes and records are defined (in this case, ${LLVM_SRC}/llvm/include/llvm/Target/Target.td):

```
$ cd ${LLVM_SRC}; git grep 'class HwMode' -- llvm/include/llvm | grep '\.td'
```

The previous command goes into the ${LLVM_SRC} directory, looks for the definition of the HwMode class, and filters the result such that only .td files are printed.

Then, later, let's say the next error is as follows:

```
input.td:13:1: error: Record `anonymous_7223', field `InstructionSet' does not
have a def initializer!
```

This time, this is a frontend error that tells us that the InstructionSet field is not initialized. In other words, this means we did not set a value for that field but we should have. (There is no default initializer in this case.) We just need to check what the type of InstructionSet is to see how to instantiate a record appropriately and move on.

After all that, if you still encounter errors that may not have an obvious fix and the community cannot help you, this is where the fun starts!

If you are lucky, the backend features a rich enough debug log for you to understand what is going on. To enable it, add -debug to the llvm-tblgen command line.

If this is not enough, you must dig into the C++ code of the related backend. All the backends live under ${LLVM_SRC}/llvm/utils/TableGen.

When looking at the code of a TableGen backend, here are a few things you should know:

- The entry point is usually a run method on the related XXXEmitter class.
- The load-bearing records and classes are usually collected through calls to RecordKeeper::getAllDerivedDefinitions; looking at the arguments of this function gives you the names of these records and classes.
- The helper structures used throughout the backends live in private headers under ${LLVM_SRC}/llvm/utils/TableGen/Common.

Overall, although what is generated by the TableGen backends may be complicated, following how they do the generation is relatively simple. First, they traverse some records stored in the main `RecordKeeper` object provided to them. Second, they generated the final output based on the values of the fields of these records.

In this section, you learned the basic skills required to approach an unknown TableGen backend. You saw that, if possible, you should use an existing user (i.e., an open source LLVM backend) of this backend as a template, and if this is not possible, you saw how to break down the problem into stages to isolate where the problem comes from. Finally, you got a few tips on how to approach the C++ code of a TableGen backend.

## Summary

While we could spend a lot more time describing TableGen and its backends, we believe this chapter gave you enough material for you to get started in this space. Also, while understanding how a TableGen backend works can be satisfying, it is not required to write an LLVM backend. Hence, you just learned the basic skills that are necessary to write the inputs of these backends.

At this point, you may not feel comfortable writing records for a specific backend or know how the TableGen output of a backend fits into the LLVM infrastructure, and this is expected. You will grow more confident and accumulate this knowledge in the respective chapters when targeting these backends. However, now, you should feel confident looking at TableGen files (`.td`), and although you may not understand what the records are meant for, you should be able to predict what their content is.

In conclusion, you learned the following in this chapter:

- What TableGen is and the general principle of how it is used in LLVM
- How to read and write your first TableGen inputs
- How the TableGen backends work and the basic structure of

    - their inputs, including where to find the load-bearing records and classes
    - their outputs, with their different sections guarded by macros

- How to deal with errors with TableGen

This chapter concludes the basic knowledge you need to efficiently develop a backend with the LLVM infrastructure. In the next chapter, we will start to go deeper into the world of compilers by focusing our attention on understanding the LLVM IR.

## Further reading

This chapter gave you a primer on TableGen. We did not cover things that you will probably never do, such as developing your own TableGen backend. If you want to explore TableGen-related topics in more detail, the LLVM's documentation, while not perfect, covers some of these.

You can refer to the following:

- An overview of TableGen at `https://llvm.org/docs/TableGen/`.
- The full specification of the TableGen language at `https://llvm.org/docs/TableGen/ProgRef.html`.
- The (succinct) documentation of the TableGen backends at `https://llvm.org/docs/TableGen/BackEnds.html`.
- How to develop a TableGen backend at `https://llvm.org/docs/TableGen/BackGuide.html`. This one is also interesting if you want to debug a TableGen backend, since it presents the main classes available to handle records.
- The command-line guide for the `llvm-tblgen` tool at `https://llvm.org/docs/CommandGuide/tblgen.html`.
- Finally, the compiler explorer website (`https://godbolt.org/`) features a TableGen mode for you to play with the TableGen syntax.

Before you finish this chapter, check out the quiz to test what you remember!

# Quiz time

Now that you have completed reading this chapter, try answering the following questions to test your knowledge:

1.  What does the following snippet do?

    ```
    def;
    ```

    This creates an empty record, and TableGen automatically assigns it a unique name.

    See the *The TableGen programming language* and *Defining multiple records at once* sections.

2.  What would happen if we took the snippet featured in the *Defining multiple records at once* section and replaced the definition of the `ShippingPrice` class with the following snippet?

    ```
    class ShippingPrice<int arg> {
      int price = arg;
    }
    ```

    We replaced the field named `shippingPrice` with a field named `price`. The new name now collides with the `price` field of record A. As a result, the value of record A's `price` will be overridden by the value of the `price` field of the `ShippingPrice` class.

    See the *The TableGen programming language* section for more information.

3.  How can you check whether a TableGen error comes from the frontend or the backend?

    First, frontend errors usually report the filename, the line, and column numbers. Second, the frontend errors are not affected by the presence of/lack of -gen-xxx options.

    See the *Identifying the failing component* section.

4.  How would you approach working with an existing TableGen backend for the first time?

    In a nutshell, you would look for another LLVM backend where this TableGen backend is used, read the comment in the main `.td` file that supports this TableGen backend, ask the community, and if necessary, look at the code of the TableGen backend.

    See the *Discovering a TableGen backend* section.

5.  How is the output of a TableGen backend typically structured?

    The output of a TableGen backend is usually saved in a `.inc` file that is later included in various LLVM C++ files. The content of the file features several sections, each guarded by an `ifdef` macro.

    See the *The content of a generated file* section.

# Part 2

# Middle-End: LLVM IR to LLVM IR

After getting an overview of the LLVM infrastructure, this part dives into what comes to most people's minds when thinking about LLVM: the middle-end and the LLVM **intermediate representation** (**IR**).

The middle-end is the backbone of the optimizing compilers based on LLVM. It encompasses an IR that optimizations work on and a set of readily available optimizations and analyses that you can reuse to build your own compiler.

In this part, we focus on four aspects:

- Giving you the tools to understand the LLVM IR and how it maps to a high-level language such as C++. This knowledge will both allow you to better manipulate the IR and give you an idea of how language frontends work.
- Presenting the main optimizations that the LLVM middle-end has to offer.
- Demonstrating how target-specific constructs fit in the middle-end.
- Teaching you how to debug LLVM passes.

By the end of this part, we will have uncovered the LLVM middle-end's secrets and you should be confident in manipulating the LLVM IR and the passes of the LLVM infrastructure and debugging the passes. This knowledge will set you on the right track to enter the world of the backend that starts when the LLVM IR gets converted to the Machine IR.

This part of the book includes the following chapters:

- *Chapter 7, Understanding LLVM IR*
- *Chapter 8, Survey of the Existing Passes*
- *Chapter 9, Introducing Target-Specific Constructs*
- *Chapter 10, Hands-On Debugging LLVM IR Passes*

# 7

# Understanding LLVM IR

In previous chapters, you learned how a compiler is structured around an **intermediate representation (IR)** and how IRs map to the C++ classes used in LLVM.

You are now ready to go even deeper into the LLVM infrastructure!

In this chapter, you will learn the syntax and semantics of the IR that powers most of the tools built with and around the LLVM infrastructure. This IR is so pervasive in the LLVM ecosystem that it is simply called LLVM IR.

The goal of this chapter is to give you enough knowledge to be able to do the following:

- Understand basic LLVM IR programs
- Find the information you need to understand what not-yet-seen LLVM IR constructs do
- Write simple LLVM IR programs

These skills are key to being able to think about the legality of the transformations you will write or modify. Indeed, by understanding what is representable in the IR, you will be able to think of ways to alter it while preserving the semantics or checking the right prerequisite to make these non-semantic-preserving changes legal. Finally, being able to write simple LLVM IR programs and understand how they map to higher-level languages such as C/C++ will help you to be more productive when it comes to testing your transformations.

While you will not become an expert at understanding LLVM IR in just a chapter, you will learn enough to confidently get to this point eventually!

# Technical requirements

In this chapter, you will use C/C++ programs to build your mental model of how LLVM IR is structured. To perform the translation, we will use the methods that you discovered in the *Experimenting with Clang* section in *Chapter 1*. As such, you will need an installation of Clang available. Refer to *Chapter 1* on how to get this.

Additionally, in the ch7 directory of the GitHub repository of this book, https://github.com/ PacktPublishing/LLVM-Code-Generation.git, we provide examples of how to perform this translation.

Now that your setup is in order, let us move to the section that introduces what an IR is.

# Understanding the need for an IR

Until this point, we have not properly defined what an IR is and why you need one in a compiler. In this section, we will answer these two questions.

## What an IR is

An IR is a data structure suitable for the tasks a compiler needs to do. The right IR depends on what the related compiler is expected to achieve.

For instance, if you build a tool that obfuscates the name of the variables of a C program by replacing them with random names, it might be enough to manipulate a string representing your program. Your transformation does not need to go too deep into the semantics of the input program, and since you support only C programs, you do not need to abstract away the syntax either. Similarly, imagine you build a compiler that translates C programs to assembly code for a specific X86 microarchitecture for a specific **operating system (OS)**. Given the requirement of this tool, there are a lot of things that you do not need to abstract away, such as the **endianness** of the target (how the bytes are laid out in the memory), the size of the pointer type, the format of the final object file, and so on.

While your IR can be more expressive than the inputs of your program, it should never be less expressive than them; otherwise, you lose potentially vital information too soon.

For instance, with the last example with the X86 compiler, LLVM IR is suitable for the job but can represent much more. Conversely, if your IR cannot represent the complete cohort of C inputs, your IR is doomed.

To summarize, your IR is a way to abstract the actual inputs of your tool and provide a suitable representation for the kind of manipulation your tool does, and its complexity depends on your use cases.

## Why use an IR?

Abstracting the inputs of a compiler is interesting because it exposes reusability across different use cases and languages. Indeed, you would not want to rewrite your backend compiler when targeting one OS or another.

By using a general-enough IR, such as LLVM IR, your compiler can use the same optimizations and infrastructure for a large variety of languages, such as C, Swift, JavaScript, and so on, targets such as X86, AArch64, and AMDGPU, and OSs such as Linux and Windows.

This may make the design of the transformations more complex, but the reusability across different tools and languages is worth the investment.

This section convinced you (hopefully!) of the need for an IR in a compiler by showing you what it does.

The next section introduces LLVM IR, the IR used in the LLVM middle-end.

# Introducing LLVM IR

You already had a taste of LLVM IR in the snippets of previous chapters. In this section, we will define how to read and understand this IR by using its textual representation.

LLVM IR also supports a binary representation called **bitcode**, which is more compact than the textual representation and comes with some backward compatibility guarantees. While we touch on this briefly in the *Textual versus binary format* section, we do not expect that you will actively use this representation and thus keep its description to a minimum. In other words, we focus on the textual representation in this section.

The syntax of LLVM IR is straightforward and we only describe it at a high level, skipping some of the details. Indeed, at this point, we will not describe all the decorators that you can add, such as function attributes, metadata, and so on. Instead, we will focus on the core IR and give you the ropes to understand the things that we do not cover. For the complete specification of the LLVM IR language, we invite you to read the language reference at `https://llvm.org/docs/LangRef.html`. With that being said, we recommend starting with this section because the language reference can be daunting at first.

With this disclaimer out of the way, let us start with the identifiers.

## Identifiers

In a regular programming language, an **identifier** is the name you give to a variable. In LLVM IR, there is no concept of a variable per se because this IR can only represent a program in **static single assignment (SSA)** form. Therefore, instead of manipulating variables, you manipulate the values that follow all the properties of the SSA form.

There are three classes of identifiers, which are as follows:

- **Local:** Used within a function, their name starts with the character %
- **Global:** Used anywhere in a module, their name starts with the character @
- **Metadata:** Used anywhere in a module, their name starts with the exclamation mark character (!)

The name of the identifier follows one of the three following rules:

- The named values use the following regular expression: `[-a-zA-Z$._][-a-zA-Z$._0-9]*`. In other words, this is a sequence of characters that does not start with a number and allows a few special characters, such as `-`, `_`, `.`, and `$`.

- The unnamed values, also called **implicit variables** for the local- and global-scoped identifiers, use an unsigned integer.

- The freeform names start with `"` and end with `"` and use anything in between. This naming scheme is not available for metadata.

> **Note**
>
> The identifiers of the implicit variables are assigned automatically by the LLVM infrastructure. Values use this naming scheme by default and this default is reflected in the API of the `IRBuilder` class, which is the helper class used to build LLVM IR. Indeed, in all the methods of this class, the `name` argument is optional and hence the unnamed scheme is used. The numbers used as identifiers must follow a strict increasing order following the top-down traversal of the function, starting with `%0` for the first unnamed value. It is a good practice to remove the implicit variables before editing a file manually. Otherwise, you may break the ordering of these variables and produce an invalid IR.

At this point, you know how to recognize the kind of value just by looking at its first character and you understand the naming scheme.

On the programming side, the local values are represented by various subclasses of the `Value` class and the global values by the `GlobalValue` subclasses. The `GlobalValue` class is also a subclass of the `Value` class.

For the metadata, they are in a distinct inheritance tree that is rooted in the `Metadata` class.

All these classes are part of the LLVM core library, which lives under the `IR` directory.

Let us make things more concrete by showing how these identifiers are used, starting with functions!

## Functions

LLVM IR offers two distinct ways to describe a **function** by using two different keywords:

- `declare`: This reflects the concept of a function declaration; that is, you only know the prototype of the function.

- `define`: This reflects the concept of a function definition; that is, you know the content of the function.

Then, like regular programming languages, you will find the result type and the list of arguments.

Putting everything together, and using the same notation as we used in *Chapter 6*, for regular expressions, a function declaration looks like this:

```
declare resultTy @funcName([argTy1 [%argName1][, argTyX [%argNameX]]*])
```

> 💡 **Quick tip**: Enhance your coding experience with the **AI Code Explainer** and **Quick Copy** features. Open this book in the next-gen Packt Reader. Click the **Copy** button (**1**) to quickly copy code into your coding environment, or click the **Explain** button (**2**) to get the AI assistant to explain a block of code to you.
>
> ```
>                                                      Copy    Explain
> function calculate(a, b) {
>   return {sum: a + b};                                1        2
> };
> ```
>
> 📖 **The next-gen Packt Reader** is included for free with the purchase of this book. Unlock it by scanning the QR code below or visiting `https://www.packtpub.com/unlock/9781837637782`.
>
>

Notice how the function name uses a global identifier; that is, it starts with an @. All the xxxTy words in this snippet are types. Types are described in the *Types* section.

A function definition follows a similar pattern except that it comes with a body enclosed between a { and }, as follows:

```
define resultTy @funcName([argTy1 [%argName1][, argTyX [%argNameX]]*]) {
  ; function body
}
```

> **Note**
>
> Comments in LLVM IR start with the semicolon character (;). Everything after a ; on the same line is a comment, like // comments in C++ programs.

As already described in the *A function in LLVM IR* section from *Chapter 3*, functions map to the `Function` class. We already covered the main **application programming interfaces (APIs)** of this class in that chapter.

Another piece of syntax that you will inevitably encounter is around the function attributes and argument attributes. **Attributes** are keywords added to the function and/or arguments that give more information about the related item or demand a certain behavior from the compiler.

For instance, the `noreturn` function attribute tells the compiler that this function should never normally return. If it does, then the behavior is undefined. Exceptions are still allowed since this is not a normal return.

Another example is `noinline`, which tells the compiler that this function must not be inlined in any of its callers.

Notice how `noreturn` defines a property of the function and `noinline` gives direction to the compiler.

Similar concepts (property and direction) apply to the function arguments.

The full list of supported attributes is available at `https://llvm.org/docs/LangRef.html#function-attributes` for the functions and `https://llvm.org/docs/LangRef.html#parameter-attributes` for the function arguments.

The syntax is, for the most part, straightforward, with plain text attributes right after the function's signature for the function's attributes and right after the type of the function argument for parameters, as illustrated by the following snippet:

```
define i32 @bar(ptr noalias nocapture %arg) noinline noreturn {
  ; ...
}
```

An alternative syntax is also supported for function attributes. It allows the reusability of a set of attributes across functions and can produce more compact textual IR. This is the syntax used by default and it looks like the following:

```
define i32 @bar(ptr noalias nocapture %arg) #0 {
  ; ...
}
attributes #0 = { noinline noreturn }
```

Attributes are grouped into sets and are assigned a number using the `attributes #num` syntax. This number is used instead of the list of attributes on the function's signature.

Let us now see the syntax of the content of the body of a function, which, as you already discovered in *Chapter 3*, is composed of basic blocks filled with instructions.

# Basic blocks

**Basic blocks** in LLVM IR are either implicit or named.

For the named basic block, the syntax is as follows:

```
BasicBlockName:
  ; content of the basic block
```

The name of the basic block follows the rules of the identifiers that we previously described but without any leading character.

For an implicit block, the name is automatically assigned by LLVM and follows the strict increasing numbering of the implicit variables.

When the blocks are implicit, you can find their boundaries by simply remembering that a basic block must end with a terminator instruction, such as `ret`, `br`, and `switch` (see https://llvm.org/docs/LangRef.html#terminator-instructions for the full list of terminator instructions). Hence, there are as many basic blocks as terminator instructions.

The content of a basic block is a list of instructions with a mandatory terminator instruction at the end.

The basic blocks map to the `BasicBlock` class, as we already covered in *Chapter 3*.

Let us now look at instructions.

# Instructions

**Instructions** are the smallest piece of computation that you can represent in the LLVM IR. By composing them, you create the complex semantics of your input program.

The list of supported instructions is fixed, in the sense that you cannot augment it within the LLVM IR language. Indeed, each instruction's mnemonic (its name, or **opcode**) is a keyword in LLVM IR.

The general syntax of an instruction is as follows:

```
%resultVal = opcode type1 %val1, type2 %val2, ...
```

In this syntax, you can find the expected characteristics of an instruction:

- Its definition, if any, is on the left-hand side of the assignment operator (=).
- Its opcode is the first thing after the = or the first thing if the instruction does not define any value.
- Its arguments, if any, come right after the opcode and are prefixed by their type when the type is not already obvious. In other words, the first argument is always typed, but the second may not be. The exact rules for putting a type in front of an argument depend on the opcode. The number of arguments depends on the opcode too.

The type of `%resultVal` is inferred from the arguments of the instruction and also depends on the opcode. When looking at examples, you will see that the types just make sense, but, if you are unsure, always refer to the language reference.

All instructions map to the same base class called `Instruction`. A lot of the instructions then use their own derived class; for instance, the `br` instruction is implemented by the `BranchInst` class, and the `phi` instruction is implemented by the `PHINode` class.

Some instructions share the same derived class, and you need to further explore the API of that class to find out what you are dealing with. The most notable instructions following that implementation are all the binary instructions (e.g., `add`, `sub`, `udiv`, etc.) that are implemented with the `BinaryOperator` class and do not have their own derived class. You need to use `BinaryOperator::getOpcode()` (or `Instruction::getOpcode()`) to know what you are effectively dealing with (after using the appropriate `isa`, `cast`, or `dyn_cast` conversion, as explained in *Chapter 4*).

Finding the right class is, for the most part, relatively easy: the opcode printed in the textual IR maps almost one-to-one to a C++ class with a similar name (e.g., the `BitCastInst` class is `bitcast`, the `IntToPtrInst` class is `int_to_ptr`, and so on). For the other cases, look around the code base or ask the community. You know the drill at this point!

We need to introduce one more element before we can go through an example. This element is how we describe types.

## Types

The LLVM IR offers a rich type system where you have built-in types that you can compose to produce your own types.

Most of the instructions, however, only work on the built-in types. This means you need to break down your types into these built-in types before being able to use the instructions. This is identical to what you do in C where you cannot use the operator + on a structure, but you can use that same operator on the fields of this structure as long as they are built-in types.

LLVM IR's types are split into three main categories:

- Single-value types
- The label type
- Aggregate types

Different instructions accept distinct kinds of types and ultimately, you must refer to the instructions' definition in the LLVM language reference to know what they support.

In the next few sections, we will describe each of these categories of types and you will see that their use just makes sense.

Before we describe each of these categories in their own section, let us mention a type that does not fall into any of these categories but that you will encounter a lot.

The void type, represented in LLVM IR with the `void` keyword, is used every time you syntactically need a type, such as for the return type of a function, but you want to express that you do not need one. In other words, `void` is a placeholder that means that you expect nothing.

Let us now go through the categories starting with the simplest types: single-value types.

# Single-value types

**Single-value types** are the most basic types you encounter in LLVM IR, and they capture the types of values that are commonly used during code generation (or codegen).

As such, pointers and vectors are considered single-value types. From a codegen perspective, a pointer is usually just an integer, and a vector (several elements batched together) is something the target may support out of the box. Vector types are used to represent the **Single Instruction Multiple Data (SIMD)** programming model, which is prevalent in modern architectures.

LLVM IR supports three main classes of types as base types: integer, floating-point, and pointer types. Their syntax and semantics are presented in *Table 7.1*.

| Type | Syntax | Semantics |
|------|--------|-----------|
| Integer | `iN` | An integer with `N` bits of precision. |
| | | For instance, `i1` is a Boolean and `i32` is a 32-bit integer. |
| | | The maximum bitwidth is practically illimited ($2^{23}$, i.e., ~`i8000000`), although the resulting codegen may not look pretty for a width not usually encountered in C-like programs. |
| Floating-point | `Half` | Half-precision floating-point. |
| | | This is a 16-bit width floating-point type that follows the IEEE-754-2008 specifications. |
| | `Float` | Single-precision floating-point. |
| | | 32-bit width follows the same IEEE specifications. |
| | `Double` | Double-precision floating-point. |
| | | 64-bit width follows the same IEEE specifications. |
| | `fp128` | 128-bit floating-point type. |
| | | Follows the same IEEE specifications. |
| | `Bfloat` | Brain floating-point. |
| | | 16-bit width type (7 significand). Popular type often featured under the name BF16 and used extensively in machine learning applications. |
| | | Additional floating types are supported, but these are the most common ones. Check `https://llvm.org/docs/LangRef.html#floating-point-types` for the complete list. |

| Type | Syntax | Semantics |
|------|--------|-----------|
| Pointer | `ptr addrspace(N)` | Pointer to the address space number, `N`.<br><br>The `addrspace(N)` part is optional and by default, the pointer will describe an address from the address space, `0`.<br><br>Prior to LLVM 15, the pointer could also be described with the pointed type using the syntax `type addrspace(N)*`. This syntax is deprecated, although it is still supported with the right command line options. |

*Table 7.1: The most common single-value types in LLVM IR*

### Address spaces

Most CPUs only have one address space. As such, this is a concept that you may be able to ignore in your compiler journey. However, the chances are that you will encounter a target that needs this concept sooner rather than later. For instance, GPUs require the compiler to handle this kind of concept. An address space captures the fact that the target has different sorts of memories with different sorts of requirements (e.g., different pointer sizes). For instance, a GPU may be able to access the memory it shares with the CPU but may also have its own separate memory. In this case, you need at least two different address spaces to differentiate the addresses that target one kind of memory or the other (e.g., global versus local memory). The numbers used to identify an address space are target-specific, though, by convention, `0` is usually the most general memory space (global memory).

Then, these base types can be used as the element type of the vector type.

The base syntax of a vector type is as follows:

```
<#elts x typeOfElts>
```

In this snippet, `#elts` is an integer literal (a statically defined constant integer) and `typeOfElts` is one of the base types.

For instance, `<4 x float>` represents a vector of four elements of single-precision floating-point elements.

Elements of vector types are accessed from left to right, meaning that the first element of a vector, which sits at index 0, is the leftmost value in the vector. This representation makes vectors close to C-style arrays and as such, their syntax and semantics should not surprise you.

> **Note**
>
> Although it is convenient to think of vector types as C-style arrays, this is not a perfect match. Indeed, the layout in memory of a vector type may not match what you expect. In other words, when thinking in terms of arrays, you may assume that the sequence of bytes is contiguous in memory. This is not necessarily true for vectors, and this depends on the endianness of your target. You will find more details on this in the *Data layout* section.

Vectors can also be scalable, meaning that the number of elements in the vector is a multiple of a constant that is set at runtime. This type of vector is called a **scalable vector** and, using the same convention as the previous snippet, it uses the following syntax:

```
<vscale x #elts x typeOfElts>
```

vscale is a keyword in the LLVM IR language that represents the constant that will be set at runtime.

The literals for these types look exactly as you would expect:

- Boolean (i1) can be defined with the literals true or false.
- iN uses a plain integer or a hexadecimal (0x) notation prefixed with an s or u to specify whether the value is signed or unsigned, respectively.
- Floating-point types support decimal, exponent, or hexadecimal notations.
- Pointer supports null.
- Vector types support <type literal0, type literal1, ...>; for example, we use <i32 1, i32 2, i32 25> for a literal representing a vector of three i32 elements, where the first element is 1, the second 2, and the third 25.

All types, except the label type (see the next section) and void type, can also use the constants undef and poison (e.g., i32 undef and ptr poison).

> **undef versus poison**
>
> undef is a bit of a misnomer because while it represents an undefined value (a random pattern of bit), it really means that we do not care about the content of this value. In other words, it has nothing to do with the undefined behavior. On the other hand, poison means that the value is poisoned, and you should never read it because otherwise the behavior is undefined.

Undefined values are represented by the UndefValue class, while poisoned values are represented by the PoisonValue class. Both classes offer a static get method that allows us to create such a value.

The full specifications of the literals can be found at https://llvm.org/docs/LangRef.html#simple-constants.

This concludes the section on single-value types. Our next section covers the label type.

# The label type

The **label type** represents the address of the basic block. This type is used in instructions that either affect the flow of the program, such as unconditional (br  label) and conditional (br  i1) branch instructions or are affected by the flow of the program, such as phi (phi) instructions.

Label values are represented by the basic block identifier prefixed with the % character and the label type is simply identified with the label keyword.

For instance, the following snippet does an unconditional jump to the basic block named nextBB:

```
br label %nextBB
```

Next comes the most complex types.

# Aggregate types

As their name indicates, **aggregate types** are types that aggregate other types together, including other aggregate types.

There are two main aggregate types:

- The structure type is a collection of fields of different types
- The array type is a statically sized collection of elements of the same type

## Structure type

The **structure type** can be as follows:

- **Named:** The type is given a name and that name can be used where you would syntactically expect a built-in type name. In LLVM, this type of syntax is referenced as **identified**.
- **Anonymous:** The structure type is used in line with the rest of the code. In LLVM, this syntax is called **literal**.

The following snippet shows how to create a named type and use it in an instruction:

```
%my.type = type { i32, ptr }

define void @useOfMyType(ptr %dst) {
  store %my.type zeroinitializer, ptr %dst
  ret void
}
```

Notice how the store instruction uses %my.type, which we defined on the first line of this snippet.

Now, the following snippet shows the same code but with an anonymous type:

```
define void @useUnknownType(ptr %dst) {
  store { i32, ptr } zeroinitializer, ptr %dst
  ret void
}
```

In this snippet, you see that we did not define a type name before using the structure type in the store instruction.

As you saw in these two snippets, the general syntax for a structure type is as follows:

```
{type1, type2, ...}
```

And if you want that type to be named, you add the type keyword in front of it and assign it a name:

```
%typeId = type {type1, type2, ...}
```

In this snippet, you just created a new type named %typeId.

> **Note**
>
> You can create a named type with any type, even single-value types; however, the LLVM tooling will fold away the names of all non-structure types and replace them with the actual type as soon as it parses this kind of input. In other words, although this is a valid syntax, you should not encounter it unless the LLVM IR has been written by hand.

Putting things together, here is a structure type with a simple field and two structure fields:

```
{i32, {ptr, half}, {i32, i1, i1}}
```

At this point, you may be wondering how to access a particular field since they are all unnamed. When looking at the LLVM language reference, you will see instructions specifically designed to work with aggregate types, such as extractvalue (https://llvm.org/docs/LangRef.html#extractvalue-instruction). The language reference does a good job of explaining the syntax and semantics of these instructions in particular, and all instructions in general, so we will not repeat that here.

Just to give you a sense of how it works, in a nutshell, you use a series of indices to describe which field you want to access for a specific structure type. For instance, to access the field with the half type in the previous snippet, you must use the following getelementptr instruction:

```
%addr_half_field = getelementptr inbounds %my.type, ptr %dst, i64 0, i32 1, i32 1
```

This snippet describes the address of the second field within the second field of a structure of type %my.type. In more detail, the address is built around &dst[0] (first i64 0), which yields an address in {i32, {ptr, half}, {i32, i1, i1}} (called %my.type here), then we want the second field of that structure (first i32 1), which yields {ptr, half}, and finally we want the second field of that structure (second i32 1), which yields half. We invite you to check the *Further reading* section for more in-depth documentation about accessing fields.

> **Note**
>
> Named types cannot be declared locally in a function. Therefore, all the definitions of the named structure types live directly in the module scope. Notice, however, that unlike global values, the identifiers for the types all start with % instead of @.

Let us move to the second, and last, aggregate type that we will present in this chapter.

## Array type

The **array type** represents contiguous elements of the same type in memory.

Unlike vector types, element types used in array types can be as complex as desired. For instance, it is perfectly valid to create an array of an array, whereas vector types can only use scalar types as vector elements – that is, non-vector single-value types.

The syntax of an array type is as follows:

```
[#elts x typeOfElts]
```

Here, #elts is a constant and typeOfElts is any type, including aggregate types.

> **Note**
>
> While the number of elements of an array type is specified statically, there is no restriction on how you can index in this array. In other words, it is syntactically perfectly valid to request access outside of the static bound of an array. This becomes problematic only if the actual allocated object is too small. What this means is that [0 x type], for instance, can be used to represent an array that is dynamically allocated.

To illustrate the syntax for an array, the following snippet initializes to zero an array of 12 arrays of 36 32-bit integer elements:

```
define void @useOfArrayType(ptr %dst) {
  store [12 x [36 x i32]] zeroinitializer, ptr %dst
  ret void
}
```

Before concluding this survey of the LLVM IR types, their syntax, and their semantics, let us give you an overview of how each of them maps to the LLVM IR API.

# Types in the LLVM IR API

All the LLVM IR types derive from the Type class, which you already briefly manipulated in *Chapter 3*.

This class offers static methods to create the most commonly used types (e.g., Type::getLabelType and Type::getInt1Ty).

For less frequently used types, you can leverage the static method named get of the class of the type you want. The names of the classes are self-explanatory: IntegerType, FunctionType, StructType, VectorType, PointerType, and so on.

The base Type class also exposes a lot of helper methods that allow you to get information on the derived type without having to cast your object to the derived class.

For instance, let us say that you want to check whether the type of an add instruction is a vector of the integer type.

The following snippet would work but is a bit complicated:

```
bool isVectorOfIntV1(Instruction &Add) {
  auto *VecTy = dyn_cast<VectorType>(Add.getType());
  return VecTy &&
    isa<IntegerType>(VecTy->getElementType());
}
```

This snippet gets the type of the given instruction and casts it to VectorType. If the cast fails, it returns false, and if it succeeds, it checks and returns whether the element type of the vector type is of the IntegerType class.

The same result can be obtained directly using the helper methods of the base Type class, like so:

```
bool isVectorOfIntV2(Instruction &Add) {
  Type *Ty = Add.getType();
  return Ty->isVectorTy() &&
    Ty->getScalarType()->isIntegerTy();
}
```

The logic in this snippet is fundamentally the same as the previous one, except we do not have to resort to explicit castings (dyn_cast or isa) or manipulate the derived types directly like VectorType. The benefits may not be obvious in this simple example, but for more complex code, this drastically simplifies the implementation and readability of the program.

You can find a use case of these methods in the check_vec_int_ty.cpp example of ch7 in the repository of this book.

The bottom line is that for most cases, you should not need to get to the derived type to get the information you need. We recommend checking the API of the Type class before looking at the API of the desired derived type. In any case, remember that you can look at these APIs through the LLVM **doxygen pages** (e.g., for the Type class, this is https://llvm.org/doxygen/classllvm_1_1Type.html).

This concludes the introduction to the LLVM IR types. There are other types that we did not mention, and you can find more information about them directly in the language reference document. The reason that we did not cover them is because they are rarely used in regular programs.

Now that you know the syntax of all the basic elements that make up LLVM IR, let us look at an example.

# Walking through an example

In this section, we will walk you through a complete example of a textual representation of LLVM IR.

For this example, we will use the following snippet:

```
define i32 @foo(i32, i32, i32 %arg) {
entry:
  %myid = add i32 %0, %1
  %31 = mul i32 %myid, 2
  %45 = shl i32 %31, 5
  %"00~random~00" = udiv i32 %45, %arg
  br label %46


  br label %47


47:
  ret i32 %"00~random~00"
}
```

In this example, you can see a function, foo, that produces a 32-bit integer value (i32) and takes three input arguments, all 32-bit integers (i32, i32, i32 %arg). The first two arguments use implicit naming and are automatically bound to the identifiers %0 and %1, respectively.

> **Note**
>
> The function's arguments and basic block names are the only identifiers that do not need to be explicitly set. For all other values, even if you use the naming scheme of unnamed values, you must write their (non-)name down.

After the list of arguments, the body of foo starts.

The first element is the name of the first basic block, called entry here. Then follows the content of this block until we reach the terminator instruction, br, which stands for branch and causes the control flow to branch from entry to the block named 46.

Here, you can taste the way implicit variables muddy the readability of the program. Can you find where the basic block 46 is?

In this case, this is simply the next line in this function. You can find this out by keeping track of the unnamed values. The last unnamed value was the instruction %45, then the next basic block is unnamed as well and LLVM assigns it the next available number, hence 46.

Generally, the IR is not as messy when it comes to implicit variables:

1.  The numbers are assigned consecutively, which makes them easier to follow (unlike here where we jump from %2 to %31, and from %31 to %45).
2.  The IR is dumped with comments that identify the names of the unnamed basic blocks.

That said, all these nicer properties fall apart as soon as you start modifying the IR file manually. The conclusion is, as already stated, before changing an LLVM IR file, manually make sure that you get rid of the implicit variables. You have been warned twice at this point!

> How to get rid of implicit variables
>
> The LLVM infrastructure offers an optimization pass, `InstructionNamerPass` from the `TransformsUtils` library, that you can use to get rid of implicit variables. To use it, simply run the command hereafter. This command gets rid of the function attribute called `optnone` (via the `sed` part of the command). This attribute prevents optimizations from altering the content of a function and since the `IntrusctionNamerPass` transformation is considered an optimization pass, it would block it. Then, the command feeds the resulting IR to the LLVM optimization driver (opt) while running the desired pass, registered under the name `instnamer`. The `-S` option makes sure that you get the textual representation of the IR.

The command to get rid of implicit variables is as follows:

```
$ cat input.ll | sed -e 's#optnone##g' | ${LLVM_BUILD}/bin/opt -S
-passes=instnamer -o -
```

Going back to the content of the entry block, the flow is easy to follow:

*   `add` performs a 32-bit addition
*   `mul` performs a 32-bit multiply
*   `shl` performs a 32-bit shift left
*   `udiv` performs an unsigned 32-bit division

Notice how most instructions do not care about whether the 32-bit operation is signed or unsigned. This is because the LLVM uses a two's complement representation for the integer and the result is modulo $2^n$. If you care about overflow or underflow, you must use the **No Signed Wrap (NSW)** or **No Unsigned Wrap (NUW)** flags to capture the semantics you would like (see the *Integer overflow/underflow* section in *Chapter 4* for more details). These flags are represented with the `nsw` and `nuw` keywords respectively and must be placed before the type of the first argument of the related instruction.

Going back to the syntax of these instructions, notice that the operands' type is set only on the first argument. The second argument is required to have the same type as the first one, and so is the result of the instruction.

Finally, notice the different naming schemes used for each instruction:

- **The named variant:** `%myid`
- **The unnamed variant:** `%31, %45`
- **The freeform variant:** `%"00~random~00"`

At this point, you have learned how to read (and write) simple LLVM IR programs. You saw how all the basic concepts, such as functions, basic blocks, instructions, and types, can be represented in LLVM IR.

Now that you have a basic understanding of LLVM IR, let us move on to more advanced topics and see how target-specific characteristics leak into the IR.

# Target-specific elements in LLVM IR

While the core of LLVM IR is target-agnostic, target-specific constraints leak in more or less subtle ways into the IR.

In this section, we will cover some of the elements that may make running an LLVM IR program difficult from one target to another.

This knowledge can help you to investigate issues across platforms and understand the limitations of such an approach.

Let us start this list with an obvious one, the intrinsic functions.

## Intrinsic functions

**Intrinsic functions**, or intrinsics for short, are built-in functions that map to low-level constructs, and potentially target-specific instructions.

When writing a frontend, you should aim to target the regular LLVM IR as much as possible. However, some constructs may be difficult to express, or it may be difficult to preserve the developer's intent with only regular instructions. This is when intrinsics come in handy because they allow you to cross the frontend-backend untouched. They are usually exposed as built-in functions in the source language.

For instance, let us take a horizontal addition, which is a vector operation where you take all the elements in a vector and add them together to reduce it to a single scalar value.

One way to express this construct for a vector of four elements could be with the following C snippet:

```
int hadd(const Vec4 *input) {
    return input->a + input->b + input->c + input->d;
}
```

If you use Clang to produce the LLVM IR for this snippet, you will see an IR that resembles the following:

```
load ; input->a
add ; add a
load ; input->b
add ; add b
...
```

The IR is messy and yet, for the purpose of the example, we already cleaned it up with mem2reg. At this point, the backend must analyze (e.g., pattern match) the IR to rebuild the intent behind this sequence of instructions, and the chances are this sequence will be obfuscated or destroyed by other optimizations.

Note that you can reproduce this example by following the instructions in the README.md file in the ch7 folder.

This is where intrinsics are useful and, in this case, ideally, you would like your input IR to look like the following:

```
%vec = load <4 x i32>, ptr %arg
%hadd = tail call i32 @llvm.vector.reduce.add.v4i32(<4 x i32> %vec)
```

Here, the intent is clear and if your target supports horizontal additions, you likely will get the expected hardware acceleration from this input.

With this lengthy introduction about what intrinsics are and how they are used complete, let us see how target information spills into the IR.

There are two kinds of intrinsics:

- The generic intrinsics can be reused across backends
- The target-specific intrinsics are bound to a specific backend

The name of intrinsic functions always starts with llvm. Target-specific intrinsics are then followed by the backend name. For example, llvm.vector.reduce.add.xxx is a generic intrinsic, and llvm.aarch64.ldxr is an intrinsic specific to the AArch64 backend.

Target-specific intrinsics cannot be reused across backends, unless you explicitly rewrite them into something that your backend understands.

On the implementation side, to know whether a function call (represented by the CallInst class, a derived class of the CallBase class) is a call to an intrinsic, you must first obtain the target of the call. The easiest way to get that is by using CallBase::getCalledFunction(). Then, you can use Function::isIntrinsic() to directly check whether this function is an intrinsic or Function::getIntrinsicID() and check that the resulting Intrinsic::ID is not Intrinsic::not_intrinsic. Finally, you can check whether the function is a target intrinsic either by using Function::isTargetIntrinsic() directly or, if you only have the Intrinsic::ID value, by using the static method, Function::isTargetInstrinsic(Intrinsic::ID).

At this point, you should feel comfortable identifying whether an intrinsic is generic or target-specific, both by inspecting the IR visually and programmatically.

Next, let us introduce the concept of a triple, which is also target-specific.

# Triple

A triple, represented by the `Triple` class from the `TargetParser` library, is a piece of information that is usually embedded in the IR and describes three main components:

- The target architecture, for instance, x86_64 or aarch64
- The vendor, for instance, Apple or Nvidia
- The OS, for instance, macOS or iOS

Additionally, the environment can be specified, such as pixel or msvc.

All this information affects the behavior of a backend in various ways that we cannot list exhaustively. The two obvious ones are as follows:

- The backend that is used; for instance, when the triple specifies i686 as the target, the backend used is X86.
- The **application binary interface (ABI)**. For instance, the ABI for X86 on Windows is different from X86 on Linux.

In LLVM IR, triples are represented by the following syntax:

```
target triple = "target-vendor-os[-environment]"
```

In this syntax, [ ] means that the environment is optional. The three other parts of the triple are mandatory but can be left empty.

For instance, all the triples in this snippet are valid:

```
target triple = "amdgcn--" ; only target is set.
target triple = "aarch64--linux-gnu" ; no vendor, gnu env.
target triple = "aarch64---" ; only target set, empty env.
target triple = "x86_64-pc-win32" ; full triple, no env.
target triple = "-apple-macosx14.0.0" ; no target.
```

For any component of the triple that is left blank, a default is applied. That default depends on how LLVM has been configured, but most likely this will match the configuration of your computer.

If the input IR has no triple, it is as if you set a triple with all the fields blank.

In this section, you saw how you can inject in the IR itself the target configuration that this IR was intended to. One of these pieces of information is the target architecture, and in the next section, you will see that the IR can even carry information about the intended microarchitecture.

# Function attributes

You already saw how function attributes can be used to instruct the compiler to do certain things. These things can be target-specific up to a point where you can tell the compiler to use (or not use) certain target features or tweak the codegen for a specific microarchitecture.

For instance, consider the following snippet that sets two sets of function attributes (#0 and #1):

```
attributes #0 = { "target-cpu"="x86-64" "target-features"="+sse,+sse2" }
attributes #1 = { "target-cpu"="x86-64" "tune-cpu"="sandybridge" }
```

In this example, `attributes` #0 instructs the compiler to enable specific instruction sets (SSE and SSE2) and `attributes` #1 tells the compiler to target the microarchitecture Sandybridge of the X86 architecture.

What this means for the related functions is as follows:

- Some things may be tied to these specific features, making running these functions on a different architecture/microarchitecture potentially problematic (for instance, an ABI mismatch: the caller sets the callee's floating-point arguments in regular registers, whereas the callee was compiled with an ABI that expects them in floating-point registers).
- If you are investigating a codegen bug, it is possible that playing with these features will hide/expose the issue.

Now that you have seen that function attributes can hold target-specific information, you will be aware of their potential impact on codegen and will adapt the way you approach debugging or porting LLVM IR programs.

Let us move on to one of the big, target-specific things that can be set in LLVM IR, the data layout.

# Data layout

You already had a glimpse of what the data layout, represented by the `DataLayout` class, does in the *Profitability* section in *Chapter 4*. In this section, you will see how it is represented in the LLVM IR, and you will understand how it impacts codegen.

Like the triple that you discovered previously, the data layout is an optional piece of information in the IR that, if not set, will default to what your default configuration is.

The data layout describes how much space in memory each type takes, the alignment of the pointer for different data types, the sizes of the pointer for the various address spaces, the sizes of integers that are natively supported, and so on. Based on this information, you can imagine how this may affect the optimizations.

For instance, if the data layout says that i32 is supported, this implies that the arithmetic instructions on this type have a cost of one, by default, and this pushes the cost model of the inliner in certain directions.

In LLVM IR, the data layout is represented by a string. In that string, each field is separated by a -
and the format of each field depends on what it describes. For instance, `i<size>:<abi>:[<pref>]`
describes the alignment in memory of the integer type with a bitwidth of `size`. That alignment must
be at least `abi` but, if possible, it should be set to `pref`. Both `abi` and `pref` are expressed in bits and
must be a multiple of a byte (i.e., eight.)

For instance, consider the following snippet:

```
define i32 @foo(ptr %src) {
  %res = load i32, ptr %src
  ret i32 %res
}
```

In this snippet, the load from `%src` has no alignment set since we have not yet enforced any constraint
on the IR with a data layout.

Now, let us say that we add the following line to this IR:

```
target datalayout = "i32:128"
```

This line tells LLVM that the i32 type must be aligned to 128 bits. As a result, pushing this IR through
LLVM (via opt) changes the load alignment to 16 bytes:

```
%res = load i32, ptr %src, align 16
```

You can play with the data layout and see how this affects the alignment of the load.

For instance, you can change the alignment to 8 bits using the following snippet:

```
target datalayout = "i32:8"
```

After applying this data layout, the load will now have the expected 1-byte alignment:

```
%res = load i32, ptr %src, align 1
```

The takeaway is that although you can drop the data layout to take some LLVM IR and compile it to
another target, this data layout may have spread the alignment requirements all over the IR. What this
means in practice is that even if you set your own data layout, all the alignments already set will not be
updated and this can result in worse codegen. For instance, let us say that a load to an i32 element is
marked as having an alignment of 1 byte, and your target only supports a minimum alignment of 4 bytes
to be able to load this type in one go. Having this alignment already set will force you to break down
this load into smaller pieces (likely pieces of 1 byte at a time) to be able to comply with the alignment.

The data layout allows you to change much more than the memory alignment and there are at least two things that you need to be aware of:

- The default address space
- The endianness

The default address space describes the kind of memory that is used by default when creating memory objects, such as stack objects (using the `alloca` instruction) or global objects. The effect of this default is subtle. It does not change the default address space in the existing IR, but instead, it affects objects created programmatically. In other words, if in the IR you use the default pointer syntax, `ptr`, this pointer points to address space 0. This does not change. However, if you create a `GlobalVariable` instance without specifying the address space within your optimization pass, that global variable will use the default global address space provided by the data layout.

The data layout allows to specify three default address spaces:

- One for the program itself: `P<address space>`
- One for the objects created with `alloca`: `A<address space>`
- One for the global objects: `G<address space>`

Similarly to the alignments, when changing the data layout, make sure that if you change the default address spaces, the existing `load`, `store`, `alloca`, and global objects are compatible with them.

Finally, the endianness is the last thing that can hit you hard when changing the data layout. The endianness is deeply connected to how the target architecture lays its bytes in memory and more often than not, it is not something that you control. However, the endianness can spill over into the IR as well. Although this is less likely, it is important to be aware of.

First, let us quickly define the two existing endianness modes, as follows:

- **Big-endian:** The most significant bytes are stored in the low addresses
- **Little-endian:** The least significant bytes are stored in the low addresses

Typically, when you think about binary representation, you think in terms of little-endian: the first bit holds the less significant one, and the last one holds the most significant one.

Consider the following 4-byte hexadecimal value in register `0x04030201`. *Figure 7.1* shows how this value is stored in memory based on the endianness.

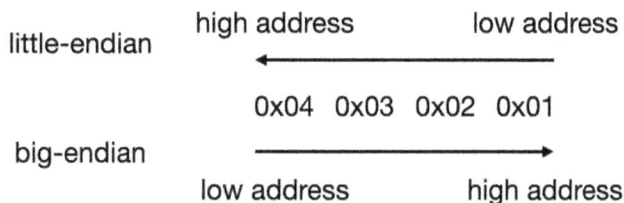

*Figure 7.1: 0x04030201 in memory with little/big-endian*

Since the endianness only affects the layout in memory and the target takes care of it, the leaking of this information in the IR is limited. Nevertheless, depending on how the IR has been produced, this layout may be visible directly in the program.

For instance, let us go back to the alignment issue with the 32-bit value that cannot be loaded in one go. If you get the IR after this breakdown, the endianness will be visible since you work with bytes at this point. Similarly, if the input program was doing bit manipulation from memory addresses, the developer may have written their code with an endianness model in mind, as shown in the following snippet:

```
int buildIntLittleEndian(const char *input) {
  int res = 0;
  for (int i = 0; i < sizeof(res); ++i) {
    res |= input[i] << (8 * i);
  }
  return res;
}


int buildIntBigEndian(const char *input) {
  int res = 0;
  for (int i = 0; i < sizeof(res); ++i) {
    res <<= 8;
    res |= input[i];
  }
  return res;
}
```

In this snippet, you see two functions for building a 4-byte integer from an array of four bytes. One is implemented using a little-endian memory layout (buildIntLittleEndian) and the other uses big-endian (buildIntBigEndian). You can imagine that the resulting IR will be much different depending on whether one or the other is used, and it is unlikely you can recover from the endianness spilling into the IR at this point.

How endianness affects vector values

When dealing with vector values, you are dealing with register-like values, hence they use a little-endian-like logic. This means that the first element of a vector is at the lowest address. Therefore, although the vector literal looks like `<i32 %first, i32 %second, ...>`, `%first` is on the right-hand side of the bit pattern of the whole vector in register; that is, the bit pattern of that register is from the most significant bit to the least significant bit, `... %second %first`. While this can be confusing, if you think about it, it is exactly how you write and think about arrays in C. Now, the endianness of the target can kick in when you start casting values from one type to another. LLVM offers a `bitcast` operation that creates a new value from a value of the same bitwidth but a different type. For example, the instruction `bitcast float %aFloat to i32` creates a new value out of `%aFloat` but keeps the exact same bit pattern. This is as if the bits were reinterpreted as a different type. The semantics of the `bitcast` operation are as if you were to store the input value in memory and reload it to create a new value. This process is a **no-op** (it does not change anything) for most types since their sizes are the same and the bytes are laid out the same way with respect to endianness. Problems arise when you change how sub-byte chunks are interpreted. This happens with vector types with sub-byte element types being bitcasted to a different bitwidth element type. At this point, the store/load semantics of `bitcast` expose the endianness of the data layout. The LLVM documentation has a nice explanation of this at `https://llvm.org/docs/LangRef.html#vector-type` that we will not repeat here

The endianness is expressed in the data layout string as E for big-endian and e for little-endian.

Keep in mind that a data layout is usually the manifestation of a triple. In other words, while you can change a data layout, what you describe in it must make sense for that triple; otherwise, the backend can behave in unexpected ways. To put it differently, even if you can modify a data layout, you should not!

This section concludes the introduction to the data layout and its implication for codegen. To know more about what can be modeled with the data layout and how, please read the full description in the language reference (`https://llvm.org/docs/LangRef.html#langref-datalayout`).

In the next section, you will learn about the last target-specific piece that can leak into the LLVM IR, the application binary interface.

## Application binary interface

The **application binary interface** (**ABI**) is also something that is dictated by the target triple; however, the input IR can carry ABI-specific decisions beyond the triple as early as right out of the frontend.

Note

If you do not remember what the ABI is, refer back to the section named *Application binary interface* in *Chapter 3*.

Try it for yourself. Write a few C/C++ snippets and look at the LLVM IR that is produced out of Clang for the same snippet but different targets (e.g., AMDGPU or arm) or OS (e.g., Linux or Windows).

For instance, take the following C snippet:

```
typedef struct {
  int a, b, c, d;
} BigStruct;


BigStruct bigStructReturned() {
  BigStruct big = {0, 0, 0, 0};
  return big;
}
```

Now compile this snippet for both AArch64 and X86 for macOS (if you run on macOS, you do not have to set the `-Xclang -triple=xxx` option):

```
$ clang -S -emit-llvm -O0 <input>.c -o x86.ll -arch x86_64 -Xclang
-triple=x86_64-apple-macosx14
$ clang -S -emit-llvm -O0 <input>.c -o aarch64.ll -arch arm64 -Xclang
-triple=aarch64-apple-macosx14
```

Looking at the resulting IRs, you see that aside from the different triple and function attributes, the signature of the `bigStructReturned` function itself is different:

```
; x86_64
define { i64, i64 } @bigStructReturned() {
...
; aarch64
define [2 x i64] @bigStructReturned() {
...
```

The X86 variant returns a struct {i64, i64}, whereas the AArch64 variant returns an array [2 x i64]. In this case, if you were to remove the triple and function attributes and feed the X86 IR to the AArch64 backend and vice versa, you would get the same codegen. However, this is not generally true.

To take a more drastic example, you can compile this program for a 32-bit target and a 64-bit, for instance using two processors from the Arm family, armv7 and aarch64.

For this example, we will use an embedded OS as an example since armv7 is for embedded targets, and thus, we must modify the command line to reflect that:

```
$ clang -S -emit-llvm -O0 <input>.c -o armv7.ll -arch armv7 -Xclang
-triple=armv7-apple-ios10
$ clang -S -emit-llvm -O0 <input>.c -o aarch64_ios.ll -arch arm64 -Xclang
-triple=aarch64-apple-ios10
```

Looking at the IRs, this time we would end up with an ABI breaking change if we were to compile the armv7 IR for aarch64 and vice versa. Indeed, for armv7, the frontend decides to pass the returned structure as an input address that the function then populates, whereas for aarch64 the structure is built in the function and returned by the value.

You can see this impact on the ABI directly on the signature of the produced IR:

```
; armv7
define void @bigStructReturned(ptr dead_on_unwind noalias writable sret(%struct.
BigStruct) align 4 %agg.result)
; aarch64
define [2 x i64] @bigStructReturned()
```

The armv7 variant in that snippet returns `void`, whereas the aarch64 variant returns `[2 x i64]`. You can reproduce this example by looking at the example named `impact_of_abi.c` in the `ch7` folder of the repository of this book.

The takeaway is that the ABI leaks potentially very early into the LLVM IR and you cannot expect to use the input of a particular triple for another triple.

In this section, you saw the various ways target-specific information can taint the LLVM IR. You discovered that some of these elements are easily identifiable, such as the target-specific intrinsics or the function attributes. Other elements are more subtle and affect the IR in a drastic way and cannot be recovered after the fact, such as the impact of the lowering of the ABI by the frontend on the signature of the LLVM IR functions. All these things put together sent you a clear message: LLVM IR is not a portable format!

Our next section touches on the portability aspect of LLVM IR by going through the difference between its textual and binary representations.

## Textual versus binary format

As already mentioned at the beginning of this chapter, the LLVM IR supports two formats: textual or human-readable and binary, also known as bitcode.

Aside from being more compact, the bitcode format offers some backward properties, meaning that a bitcode file created with an older version of LLVM will work with a new version of LLVM. There is no such guarantee for the textual format. What this means is that in theory, the human-readable syntax of LLVM IR can change all the time and IR written in the past may not work with a parser from a newer LLVM. In practice, the textual format is relatively stable but still breaks from time to time. When this happens, you can leverage the backward properties of the bitcode format by doing the following:

1. Saving your textual IR to bitcode using opt from the old LLVM
2. Loading your bitcode file using opt from the new LLVM and saving the output in textual format

This process is illustrated in *Figure 7.2*:

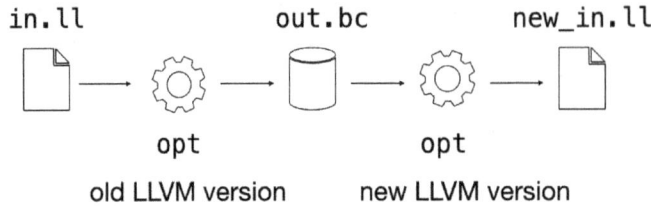

Figure 7.2: Updating the textual IR file when the LLVM syntax changes

You can reproduce the pipeline of this figure by using the right option for opt to output the bitcode (default) or the textual format (-S.) In other words, to reproduce this pipeline, you can run the following command:

```
$ ${OLD_LLVM_BIN}/opt in.ll -o - | ${NEW_LLVM_BIN}/opt -S -o new_in.ll
```

You may wonder why this works at all. After all, the bitcode format and the textual format represent the same thing but in a slightly different way.

The LLVM community promises that the bitcode format will be backward compatible unless major changes are made. On the other hand, the textual format is just a convenient tool for the developers, and as such, syntax-breaking changes are handled as best effort, meaning that unless it is relatively easy to be backward compatible, the old textual IR becomes incompatible with new textual IR.

To offer this backward-compatible support, the LLVM bitcode reader, implemented with the BitcodeReader class from the BitReader library (under the path Bitcode/Reader), features an auto-upgrade mechanism that converts the old format into the new format. What this means is that the reader applies rewrite rules from the old specifications to the new specifications.

Without going into the details, if you ever need to go down this path, the auto-upgrade functions are usually implemented in the AutoUpgrade.<h|cpp> files from the IR library and are called from the BitcodeReader class.

In this section, you learned the main differences between the textual and the binary representations of LLVM IR. The former is a tool used by developers and is not officially backward compatible, whereas the latter comes with guarantees of backward compatibility, making it a more robust format to base your tools on.

Before we conclude this chapter, we wanted to give you a cheat sheet of LLVM IR main APIs, the topic of our next section.

# LLVM IR API – cheat sheet

Now that you know the LLVM IR representation, we can use it to anchor the various APIs that you saw in this and previous chapters.

The result is the cheat sheet presented in *Figure 7.3*:

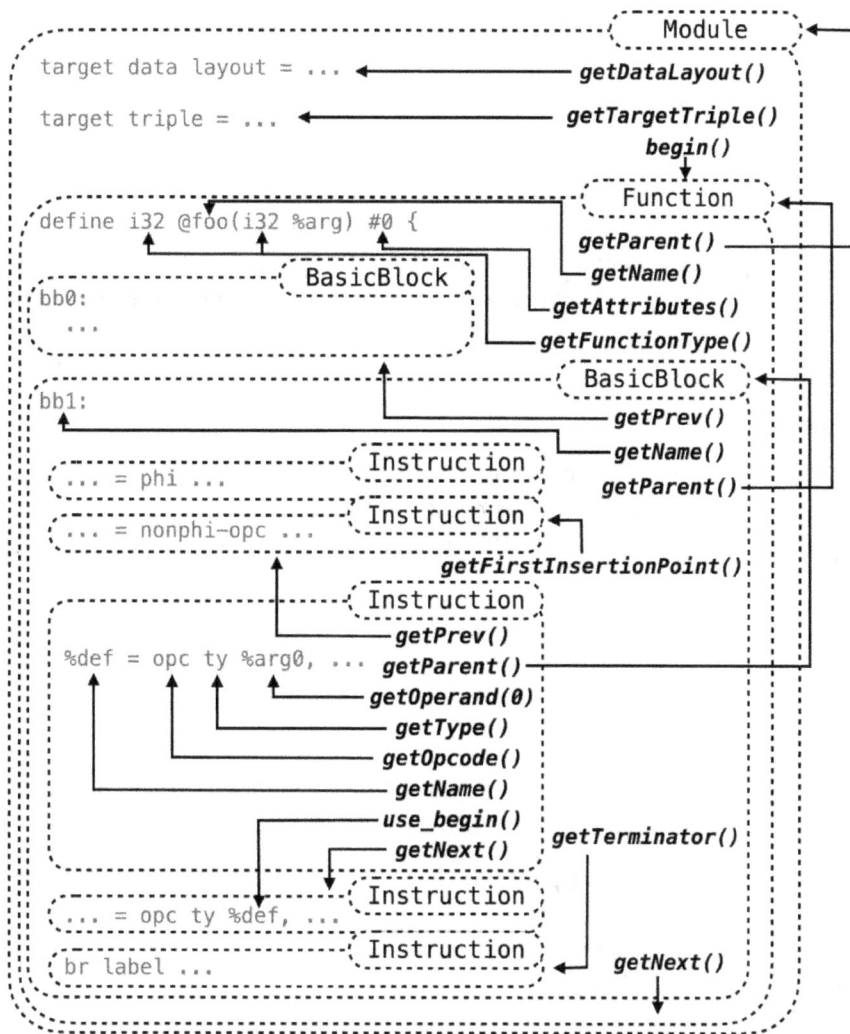

*Figure 7.3: LLVM IR API cheat sheet*

In *Figure 7.3*, we represented the scopes of the various classes, with their names framed in the top-right correct of the related scope. This cheat sheet shows four scopes, from innermost scope to outermost: Instruction, BasicBlock, Function, and Module. Within a scope, we showed a few methods, in italics, that you can call when you have a hold of the related instance, meaning you can call the methods in the BasicBlock scope if you hold a pointer on such an instance. The black arrows show what the results of the methods point to.

This cheat sheet is obviously not exhaustive, but we believe it should give you a better grasp of how LLVM IR is structured and how it maps to the related APIs.

From this point forward, you will build your own cheat sheet!

In this section, you gained a condensed view of the LLVM APIs that map directly to the LLM IR representation.

The next section summarizes the knowledge you obtained in this chapter.

# Summary

In this chapter, you gained enough knowledge to feel comfortable reading and writing the textual LLVM IR representation. You learned enough to dig into the full LLVM language reference specification if you ever get stuck or feel unsure about the syntax or semantics of some of the LLVM structures.

In the process, you learned the benefits of using an IR in a compiler and discovered that while LLVM IR can represent target-agnostic constructs, an actual instance of LLVM IR is likely tainted by some target-specific concepts starting with the ABI.

Finally, you were able to map the concepts and APIs learned in previous chapters to the textual IR representations. This knowledge should boost your ability to manipulate LLVM IR and further strengthen your mental model of how the IR is structured, making you a more productive compiler engineer in the long run.

The next chapter will go a little bit deeper into the LLVM infrastructure by giving you a survey of the existing passes, but more importantly, it will cover how to approach a pass that you do not know.

# Further reading

As already stated, this chapter gives you the intuition of the LLVM IR textual representation. To further deepen your expertise, we encourage you to read the following materials:

- `https://llvm.org/docs/LangRef.html`: The LLVM language reference that we mentioned time and time again! This is the full specification of the LLVM IR textual representation. In particular, you can find the full list of the supported generic intrinsics as well as how to interpret all the fields of the data layout string and so on.

- `https://llvm.org/docs/GetElementPtr.html`: This dedicated page gives a detailed explanation of one of the difficult-to-grasp LLVM instructions: `getelementptr` (or `gep` for short). In a nutshell, this instruction allows you to describe which field you want to access in an aggregate type. We already gave you the intuition of how this works, but we guarantee you that you will often forget how this instruction works and thus, how to give it the right parameters when building your own transformations.

- `https://llvm.org/devmtg/2020-09/slides/Lee-UndefPoison.pdf`: This presentation talks at length about the importance of having two representations of undefined: `undef` and `poison`. We already gave you a primer on this, but this presentation is a nice addition to further understand the deep technical reasons for this choice.

Before you move to the next chapter, please look at the quiz!

# Quiz time

Now that you have finished reading this chapter, try answering the following questions to test your knowledge:

1. Given the following input IR, why is opt returning the following error?

   The input is as follows:

   ```
   define i32 @add(i32 %0, i32 %1) {
     %2 = add i32 %0, %1
     ret i32 %2
   }
   ```

   The error is as follows:

   ```
   input.ll:2:3: error: instruction expected to be numbered '%3' or greater
     %2 = add i32 %0, %1
     ^
   ```

   This is because %2 is already used as the implicit name of the entry basic block.

   Check the *Basic blocks* section for more details, or follow the example in the *Walking through an example* section.

2. How could you fix the previous error with minimal changes?

   There are two things you could do in this case: rename %2 (for example, to %3) or change the name of the basic block. For this solution, we decided to go with the latter as it does not imply changing any other reference since the basic block is not explicitly used anywhere, unlike %2, which is used in the terminator of this block.

   The result is as follows:

   ```
   define i32 @add(i32 %0, i32 %1) {
   bb:
     %2 = add i32 %0, %1
     ret i32 %2
   }
   ```

3. How can you get rid of all the implicit variables?

   Firstly, if you are unsure about what an implicit variable is, look at the *Identifiers* section.

   To get rid of the implicit variables, you must change the identifiers from the unnamed-values scheme to the named-values scheme. This means that none of your identifiers should be integers only.

   The easiest way to do that is by using the command described in the *Walking through an example* section that leverages the InstructionNamerPass optimization.

4.   Are vector types aggregate types?

No, they are not.

Vector types are single-value types because of the following:

- They cannot use non-single value types as element types
- They usually map to simple low-level constructs such as a plain register used in a SIMD instruction

See the *Single-value types* section for more details.

5.   Is the LLVM IR bitcode format a portable format across architectures?

Generally, no, it is not.

LLVM IR, irrespective of whether it is the textual or the bitcode representation, often carries information that is tainted by the target, such as the intrinsics or the ABI.

Look at the *Target-specific elements in LLVM IR* section for more details.

# 8

# Survey of the Existing Passes

While this book is about building an LLVM backend, it is important to also know what the middle end has to offer. Indeed, although you can connect an LLVM backend right after a frontend and skip all the middle-end optimizations, you realistically do not want to re-implement all the optimizations that are perfectly doable in the middle end. For instance, there is zero benefit in reimplementing your own mem2reg pass; at best your implementation will be equivalent and at worst you'll introduce a bunch of bugs!

Sometimes it may make sense to reimplement something for your target's specific needs or do that transformation at a lower level of **intermediate representation (IR)**. However, you cannot make an educated decision if you do not know what is already available.

The deeper into the compiler pipeline you get, the more you are tied to the target, and the easier certain things are to do, but conversely, the harder other things are. Therefore, it is important to have a good comprehension of what exists in the different layers of your compiler so that you can use the right tool (transformation in this case) for the job and reuse what exists.

Note that we use the term transformation as a generalization of the concept of an LLVM pass.

Some things are clear-cut when it comes to deciding what level of IR and target-specific information makes sense to solve a problem. Sometimes, it is not as clear but having an idea of what is already in the middle end may at least give you a sense of what is feasible. You will see some of the properties you can use to decide where something should be implemented in the next chapter.

The goals of this chapter are as follows:

- To make you aware of what the middle end is capable of
- To teach you some of the ways you can approach a transformation that you do not know

While we cover some transformations in this chapter, we have kept the details at a minimum and focused only on the main ones. Therefore, it is important that you learn how to get a grasp of a new transformation by yourself.

# Technical requirements

In this chapter, we will leverage the LLVM developer tool named opt to discover the available transformations in the middle end.

To get it, either build it from the LLVM source or download an official LLVM release. Both methods are explained in *Chapter 1*.

We recommend using a version built from the sources because this will ensure that the information that you get out of opt is in sync with the sources that you have access to. Of course, you can also extract the right branch from the LLVM repository to be in sync with what you downloaded, or directly download the source from the related release (https://releases.llvm.org/).

Finally, in the ch8 directory of the GitHub repository of this book, https://github.com/PacktPublishing/LLVM-Code-Generation.git, we provide the examples that we use in the various sections.

Let us get started with how you even begin this journey of finding what the middle end has to offer.

# How to find the unknown

If we told you to look for a specific transformation, you would find it by looking for some keywords across the code base (using git grep, for instance). However, if you do not know what exists in the middle end, how do you even begin to look for it?

In this section, you will discover two main ways to approach the LLVM code base to find what it has to offer. This information is important as it allows you to reuse what exists instead of reimplementing everything.

The first approach leverages opt, an LLVM-provided developer tool, to present human-friendly information. We will show you how to dig into the code base using that information.

In the second approach, we flip the angle of attack by starting from the source files instead of the developer-facing tools. You will discover what to expect in each directory and how to extract the relevant information from the source files.

## Leveraging opt

The developer tool named opt acts as a driver for all the LLVM-IR-to-LLVM-IR passes. As such, it covers everything that exists in the middle end. Therefore, to get an overview of everything that is available there, you can simply leverage the help message offered by this tool. But there is a caveat.

This tool allows you to use both the legacy pass manager and the new one. Therefore, the default help message (available through the --help option) covers both managers indiscriminately. In other words, what is printed may go beyond the middle end since the legacy pass manager also drives the backends.

Try it yourself by running the following command:

```
$ ${LLVM_INSTALL_DIR}/bin/opt --help
```

This command describes how to use the opt tool and lists all the passes you can run, but it does not tell you which one runs with each pass manager. This is annoying in the sense that some passes may not be LLVM-IR-to-LLVM-IR passes, which means that they are technically not part of the middle end, and opt cannot run them (yes, opt is lying to you!). In other words, it may be complicated for you to leverage these passes for your needs. In any case, the information printed there is still useful, and you will see how to filter out the interesting bits in a minute.

In the previous command's output, locate the section right under the Optimizations available line. This should resemble something like the following:

```
Optimizations available (use '-passes=' for the new pass manager)
    --aa        - Function Alias Analysis Results
    --aa-eval - Exhaustive Alias Analysis Precision Evaluator
    --aarch64-O0-prelegalizer-combiner - Combine AArch64 machine instrs before
legalization
[...]
    --gvn       - Global Value Numbering
[...]
```

What you see in this output are the options to run the related pass with the legacy pass manager and a brief description of what this pass does.

For instance, the following command runs the **global value numbering (GVN)** pass, which is a standard compiler optimization, with the new pass manager:

```
$ ${LLVM_INSTALL_DIR}/bin/opt --passes=gvn input.bc -S -o -
```

Now, this is where things become tricky; if you try the same thing with aarch64-O0-prelegalizer-combiner, opt will tell you it does not know this pass. While in this case, it is clear that the pass is target-specific, since its name starts with aarch64, it may not always be that simple. For example, the aa pass is target independent and yet, running --passes=aa does not work with the new pass manager.

At this point, you need to use a second command to check which passes are indeed supported by the new pass manager:

```
$ ${LLVM_INSTALL_DIR}/bin/opt --print-passes
```

This command prints the names of all the passes that the new pass manager supports. For instance, here is a snippet of what it produces:

```
Module passes:
  always-inline
  attributor
```

```
    annotation2metadata
[...]
```

Using the list returned by this command, you can determine which passes work on which level of IR, and thus, by ignoring all passes that appear under the Machine XXX section, you get the list of the middle-end passes.

Then, you can intersect that list with the list returned by the help command to find out what each of them does.

For instance, in the previous output, you saw that the always-inline pass works at the Module level, and by using the --help output, you can find the purpose of this pass: Inliner for always_inline functions.

Now, using the description of this pass, you can find where it is implemented by running from your LLVM source directory something such as the following:

```
$ git grep "the short description of the pass" llvm
```

Alternatively, you can use the following method, which directly looks at the new pass manager registry from the option name:

```
$ git grep "pass-option-name" llvm/lib/Passes/PassRegistry.def
```

This command prints the line of the registration macros that you discovered in *Chapter 5*, for the pass registered under the option named pass-option-name (see the full example below with always-inline). Now you need to locate the class name used in the registration macros and look for that class name in the source files.

In the next command, we assume that the class name in the registration macro is className:

```
$ git grep -l "className" llvm
```

This command prints the paths of all the files where className is used. One of them should be the implementation of this class.

Here is what it would look like for the always-inline pass with the first method:

```
$ git grep -l "Inliner for always_inline functions" llvm
llvm/lib/Transforms/IPO/AlwaysInliner.cpp
```

Here is what it would look like with the second method:

```
$ git grep "always-inline" llvm/lib/Passes/PassRegistry.def
llvm/lib/Passes/PassRegistry.def:MODULE_PASS("always-inline",
AlwaysInlinerPass())
$ git grep -l "class AlwaysInlinerPass" llvm
llvm/include/llvm/Transforms/IPO/AlwaysInliner.h
```

While one method gives you the `.cpp` file and the other `.h`, both point to the same implementation, as you know from *Chapter 1*.

> **Note**
>
> While you may not be able to leverage a target-specific pass such as `aarch64-O0-prelegalizer-combiner` out of the box, the kind of transformation it performs may still be interesting to you. At this point, you can try to make it more generic so that it applies to your case or use it as an inspiration for your own pass.

At this point, you know how to find the implementation of the passes starting from the help message. Before we explain what you can do with this file, let us present a second way of approaching the problem by starting with the LLVM source code. Both methods will converge after this section.

## Using the LLVM code base

To discover what the middle end has to offer, you can scan through the files that are in the LLVM repository. In this section, we give you some guidance so that your search can be more focused and hence more productive.

Most of the LLVM IR generic passes live under two folders: `Analysis` and `Transforms` (with the respective `include/llvm` and `lib` prefixes, of course, as you learned in *Chapter 1*).

The `Analysis` directory holds all the analyses and the `Utils` subdirectory holds additional helper classes that are used by these analyses.

The `Transforms` directory has more subdirectories, which makes it easier to further narrow down what may be of interest to you.

These subdirectories, as identified by the name after each bullet point, contain, respectively:

- `AggressiveInstCombine`: A more aggressive version of instcombiner; see the `InstCombine` point that follows.
- `Coroutines`: Transformations around the lowering of coroutines. A coroutine is a function that can be resumed or suspended without locking the current thread. The lowering is usually highly specific to a source language.
- `HipStdPar`: Transformations to enable the HIP C++ standard parallelism support.
- `IPO`: **Interprocedural optimizations**, or **IPOs**, are transformations that apply across procedures, for instance, inlining, which takes the IR of the callee function and puts it in the IR of its caller.
- `InstCombine`: Transformations that apply simple rewrite patterns that are beneficial for all targets.

- **Instrumentation**: Transformations used for instrumentation purposes. These transformations add constructs to the IR to maintain specific data structures next to the original IR. These are used to collect information for performance purposes, such as **program-guided optimization (PGO)**, or for debugging purposes, like what a sanitizer would need to diagnose use-after-free issues or undefined behaviors.

- **Scalar**: Transformations that are non-vector-related. This includes many different optimizations, of which the loop optimizations are unrelated to vectorization (see the Vectorize bullet point below).

- **Utils**: Generally useful passes or helper functions used to transform the LLVM IR.

- **Vectorize**: Transformations that produce vectorized code, meaning code that follows a **single-instruction multiple-data** (SIMD) model. In other words, passes contained in this directory produce LLVM IR instructions that use vector types.

Using this high-level guidance to direct your search on a specific class of transformation, you can then look at the names of the different files in these folders and open the implementations that seem interesting to you.

Once you find something that seems relevant, you can use the information from the next section to help you dig in.

## Starting from the implementation

Now that you know the file where the pass you are interested in is implemented, open this file and look at the comment at the beginning of the file. Most passes have a detailed description of what a pass does. In the case of the always-inline pass, the description is underwhelming but sufficient to understand what it does. Some passes are more detailed; for instance, the description lists the research paper that this pass is based on.

You should also be able to locate the option name of the pass: either through the registration macros, as we explained in the *Leveraging opt* section earlier, or by finding the name in the INITIALIZE_XXX macros, as we explained in *Chapter 5*. Either way, using this name, such as always-inline, you can find the unit tests of this pass and run them by yourself with the **LLVM Integrated Tester (lit)**, as you learned in *Chapter 1*. Using lit, you can extract the command used to run the tests and play with the input IR to better understand what a pass does.

The following command gives you all the tests that exercise the always-inline pass more or less directly:

```
$ git grep -l 'RUN: .*always-inline' llvm/test
```

Using the list of files returned by this command, you can invoke lit to re-run a specific test or subset of the tests and see the pass in action by looking at the input IR and the output IR.

In this section, you will find out how to do the following:

- Determine whether a pass is part of the middle end
- Get a brief description of all the passes
- Find the implementation of the passes
- Get some more information on what a pass does
- Find the unit tests of a pass and play with the input IR to refine your understanding of what a pass does

While all this can seem lightweight, this gives you a handle to start digging into the transformation by yourself.

In the next section, we will show you some of the main transformations that are available in the middle end and describe what they do at a high level, starting with the helper passes.

# Survey of the helper passes

LLVM provides some helper passes that do not directly contribute to the compiler pipeline. These passes are completely optional and do not modify the IR at all. Yet, they are critical for every compiler writer because they allow them to inspect the compiler state (the IR) at various points, by inserting in the pass pipeline the related passes.

In this section, we will cover the two most useful passes:

- The verifier
- The printer

Let us start with the verifier.

## The verifier

The core LLVM library (in the IR directory) features a **verifier** that checks that the IR is well formed.

For instance, it checks that the definition of a value dominates all its uses so that the IR conforms to the **static single assignment** (**SSA**) form or that the input arguments of a fadd instruction, a floating-point addition, are both of the same type and that this type is of the floating-point family.

This pass is invaluable to narrow down when a transformation modified the IR in an illegal way. The llc developer tool runs with the verifier enabled by default at various points of the codegen pipeline (can be disabled with -disable-verify) and opt exposes an option, -verify-each, to automatically insert the verifier after each pass in your pipeline.

To enable that feature in the new pass manager, you just have to set the VerifyEachPass argument to true when you instantiate the StandardInstrumentations object, as shown in *Chapter 5*.

Now, if you want to hook up the verifier manually, you must add to your pass pipeline the following passes:

- For the legacy manager: `createVerifierPass(bool FatalErrors)`
- For the new pass manager: `VerifierPass(bool FatalErrors)`

If you do not remember how to do that, go back to the *Populating a pass manager* section in *Chapter 5*.

The verifier is registered under the name `verify`, hence you can invoke it with opt using `--passes=verify` (or `--verify` for the legacy pass manager).

Any time you encounter weird issues with some IR, make sure to run the verifier on it. If your IR is not valid, passes may behave in unexpected ways.

Let us now move on to the second helper pass, the printer.

# The printer

As its name suggests, the **printer passes** are a wrapper around the functionalities that print the IR. There is one printer pass per scope: module, function, and loop. Like the verifier, the printers are part of the IR library.

The printers are already embedded in both the legacy and new pass managers, and if you hooked up the parsing of the LLVM options (see *Chapter 5*), you can use them through the following command-line options:

- `-print-before-all`/`-print-after-all`: Print the IR before/after each pass.
- `-print-before`/`-print-after=passname`: Print the IR before/after the pass named `passname`, as identified by the name used in the registration process in the related pass manager (see *Chapter 5*).

You can add printers manually to your pass pipeline:

- **For the legacy pass manager:** Use `createPrintXXXPass`, where `XXX` is `Module`, `Function`, or `Loop`.
- **For the new pass manager:** By instantiating one of the `PrintXXXPass` classes, where `XXX` is `Module`, `Function`, or `Loop`.

> Instantiating a pass with the legacy pass manager
>
> Most of the non-analysis passes that are exposed to the legacy pass manager are implemented in anonymous namespaces. This means you cannot directly instantiate them using their constructor. Instead, you need to use the related `createXXXPass` function, where `XXX` is the name of the legacy pass. Going forward, we will only give the name of the legacy pass and not the name of the related `createXXXPass` function. We trust that you will find this function easily. Usually, it is implemented in the same source file as the legacy pass

The registration names are, for the legacy pass manager, `print-module`, `print-function`, and `print-`

loop. However, with a recent LLVM, chances are opt does not hook them up anymore and you have to use the new pass manager.

For the new pass manager, the registration name is print for all of them and what determines the one that is called depends on the scope of the current manager. In other words, if you invoke the print pass in a module scope, you get PrintModulePass, if you do this in a function scope, you get PrintFunctionPass, and so on.

> Understanding the new pass manager **command-line interface** (**CLI**)
>
> The scoping of the new pass manager is directly expressed in the **CLI** options. By default, the scope depends on the first pass that you run, meaning that the opt -passes=mypass command will run mypass with the pass manager that has the appropriate scope for mypass. You can specify the scope of your pipeline by using the module, function, or loop keyword, followed by the list of passes, in parentheses, you want to run in this nested pipeline. These constructs allow you to play with the structure of the pass pipeline, as we showed in the *The pass pipeline structure* section in *Chapter 5*, but there we were directly using the C++ **application programming interface** (**API**). Finally, some passes also support flags. You can pass these using < >. The flags are highly implementation-specific and may not be stable from one LLVM release to another.

Consider the following opt invocation:

```
$ ${LLVM_INSTALL_DIR}/bin/opt --passes='function(print,consthoist,loop(print),
instcombine<use-loop-info;max-iterations=3>),globaldce' myinput.ll -S -o -
```

This command will run myinput.ll through the following nested pipeline:

- Function-scoped, identified by function(...):

    - print: Given the scope, this is the registration name of PrintFunctionPass
    - consthoist: The constant hoisting function pass
    - Loop-scoped, identified by loop(...):
    - print: Given the scope, PrintLoopPass
    - instcombine: The instruction combiner pass instantiated with two specific arguments: use-loop-info and max-iterations=3

- Module-scoped:

    - globaldce: The global dead-code elimination pass

If you remember the exercise from *Chapter 5*, you can connect the dots between the function and loop keywords with the pass adaptor (XXXPassAdaptor).

To learn more about the capabilities of the CLI of the new pass manager, check the dedicated resource at https://llvm.org/docs/NewPassManager.html#invoking-opt.

In this section, you learned about two of the most useful passes to help you in your compiler journey. The first one, the verifier, validates that your IR is well formed and can help you spot transformations that behave incorrectly. The second one, or ones to be more precise, the printers, allow you to visually inspect the IR at various points of the pipeline. In the process, you learned how to hook these passes in your custom pass pipeline.

Now that you are armed with these tools, we can move on to presenting a few of the interesting analysis passes.

From this point forward, we will focus on only a few passes per category. You can build up your knowledge of the ones that we do not cover using the method presented earlier in this chapter.

# Analysis passes

The generic analysis passes, from the `Analysis` library, provide information that can be leveraged to perform certain algorithms (e.g., the dominance tree or the alias information), refine a cost model (e.g., block frequency or scalar evolution), and inject some target specific knowledge (e.g., target transform info or target library info).

We already described how you can use analyses in *Chapter 5*, so here, we'll focus only on pointing out some of the interesting ones and showing the APIs you need to use to leverage them.

We have already presented some of the results of the analyses in the previous chapters, namely the target transformation information (represented with the `TargetTransformInfo` class) and the loop information (represented with the `LoopInfo` class) in *Chapter 4*. However, we did not explicitly cover how to get these results. Therefore, let us start with these two so you can connect the dots between the results of the analyses and how you get them.

## Target transformation information

To get an instance of the `TargetTransformInfo` class, which encapsulates the costs of performing certain transformations on the current target, you need to get the result of the analysis named `TargetIRAnalysis` when using the new pass manager, and `TargetTransformInfoWrapperPass` with the legacy pass manager.

Doing this translates into the following snippet for the legacy pass manager:

```
TargetTransformInfo &TTI = getAnalysis<TargetTransformInfoWrapperPass>().getTTI(F);
```

In this snippet, the call to `getAnalysis` happens from your pass (which must inherit one of the derived `Pass` classes) and `F` is an instance of the `Function` class.

Similarly, with the new pass manager, this translates into the following snippet:

```
TargetTransformInfo &TTI = FAM.getResult<TargetIRAnalysis>(F);
```

In this snippet, we get the result of the `TargetIRAnalysis` pass from an instance of the `FunctionAnalysisManager` class, called `FAM` here. The `FunctionAnalysisManager` instance is either available directly as an argument of the `run` method of your pass or can be obtained from the `XXXAnalysisManager` instance that is passed to the `run` method.

Finally, the CLI name of the pass is `target-ir` (`tti` in the legacy pass manager), but as most analysis passes, there is no straightforward way to see what it does. You can request it in the pass pipeline using `require<target-ir>` within your pass description (i.e., with the `--passes` option) but in the end, if nothing uses it, you will not observe any change.

Going forward, we will not explicitly give the snippet to do the invocations for the respective managers. This is just an application of what you learned in *Chapter 5*, and this is very mechanical. We believe that after seeing it once, you will be able to replicate it easily with other passes.

## Loop information

The **loop information**, represented with the `LoopInfo` class, that we discussed in *Chapter 4*, in the *Where to get loop information* section, is available as the result of the `LoopAnalysis` class (or `LoopInfoWrapperPass` for the legacy pass manager).

This information is useful to check whether two basic blocks are within the same loop (i.e., they share the same loop header), to get to specific parts of the loop (e.g., if you want to move some code in the latch of the loop), and so on.

The loop information is registered under the name `loops` in the CLI. This is one of the few analyses that you can print directly with opt using `print<loops>` within your pipeline description, as illustrated by the following command:

```
$ ${LLVM_INSTALL_DIR}/bin/opt -passes='print<loops>' input.ll
```

This command creates a simple pass pipeline consisting only of the printing of the loop information (implemented underneath with the `LoopPrinterPass` class). The pass responsible for printing the loop information already correctly requires that the information has been computed.

## Alias analysis

The **alias analysis** provides critical information whenever you try to optimize programs that deal with pointers. The alias analysis is a bit unconventional in the sense that it is not just one analysis but a collection of analyses that augment each other. What this means is although the result of the alias analysis exposes a unique way to check whether two pointers are aliases, it gets this information by consolidating the result of several alias analyses.

For instance, let us say the alias analysis leverages two types of alias analyses: one based on the type of the pointed value, where under strict aliasing rules a floating-point pointer cannot alias with a pointer on an integer value, and the other analysis based on a range analysis that estimates, conservatively, the amount of memory a pointer can reach. The first analysis is cheap compared to the second one and therefore, if it is enough to answer whether the pointers overlap, then the second one is not used.

Because of this additional complexity, the best way to leverage the alias analyses (e.g., basic, type-based, etc.) is through the `AAManager` pass. This pass is responsible, as its name suggests, for managing the different alias analyses available. The available analyses depend on how you create your `AAManager`, and you can use `AAManager::registerFunctionAnalysis` to register additional alias analyses. Alternatively, if you build your pass pipeline using the `PassBuilder` class, it already takes care of adding the most common ones as well as the target-specific ones when using `PassBuilder::buildDefaultAAPipeline`.

On the legacy pass manager side, things are less flexible, and you only get what is available through the `AAResultsWrapperPass` pass. However, it should hold almost all the same passes as `PassBuilder::buildDefaultAAPipeline`.

The result of the `AAManager` pass is an instance of the `AAResults` class. Check the API of this class to see how to query whether two pointers overlap.

Finally, the name used in the CLI is aa.

## Block frequency info

As already mentioned in *Chapter 4*, in the *Basic block frequency* section, the LLVM infrastructure features a pass named `BlockFrequencyAnalysis` (`BlockFrequencyInfoWrapperPass` in the legacy pass manager) that produces estimates of the basic block frequencies, or put differently, how many times they are expected to be executed. This information is returned as an instance of the `BlockFrequencyInfo` class. On the command line, you can add this analysis to your pipeline by using `block-freq` (and the `require` keyword like all analyses), and you can print it through `print<block-freq>`. This analysis also exists at the machine IR level, as previously mentioned in *Chapter 4*, too.

## Dominator tree information

The **dominator tree information** is computed by the `DominatorTreeAnalysis` class, and the `DominatorTreeWrapperPass` class in the legacy pass manager. Its result is an instance of the `DominatorTree` class, which exposes a method to answer the question of whether A dominates B, where A and B are basic blocks, instructions, and so on.

This analysis is part of the `IR` library and not the `Analysis` library because it is deeply connected with the SSA properties, like you saw in *Chapter 4*, and used extensively throughout the LLVM ecosystem. As such, it is important to leverage the `DomTreeUpdater` helper class, featured in the `Analysis` library, to maintain this information yourself when applicable or possible.

The name of the dominator tree information in the CLI is domtree. Moreover, you can print it with `print<domtree>`, and verify that it is correct with `verify<domtree>`.

Similarly, you have access to the post-dominator tree information through the postdomtree name and the same kind of information at the machine IR level with machinedomtree and machinepostdomtree. The machine passes use the legacy pass manager and are available through the `MachineDominatorTree` and `MachinePostDominatorTree` classes, respectively.

## Value tracking

The last piece of infrastructure that is pervasively used in LLVM is a helper class named ValueTracking. While this is not an analysis pass, it lives in the Analysis library, and we believe it is important you know about its existence.

This class can be used to get some information about the actual value that is held by a value, and you can leverage that information to perform certain optimizations.

For instance, consider the following LLVM IR:

```
%a = and i64 %b, u0xfffffffffffffffc
%mod = urem i64 %a, 2
%cond = icmp eq i64 %mod, 0
```

In this snippet, although we do not know the value of %b, we know that because of the mask applied to produce %a, the first three least significant bits of %a will be zeros. Thanks to this information, we know that %mod will always be 0 and thus that %cond will always be true.

The ValueTracking class performs this kind of analysis for you. You give it a value and it will return the known bits pattern for this value. Its main API is KnownBits computeKnownBits(const Value *V, const DataLayout &DL, /*a bunch of other arguments*/). It is very easy to use and extremely powerful, although it can be compile-time intensive!

This concludes our section on some of the most useful analysis passes or helper classes. Using this information, you can start writing your own optimization that leverages them, instead of reinventing the wheel.

Of course, this list is nowhere near exhaustive, and we recommend you look closer at what the Analysis library has to offer. For instance, the scalar evolution analysis and the related framework are a fantastic tool for working with induction variables, that is, variables that control loops. You can use that framework to perform complicated optimizations. There are many more like this, and you should check them out!

In the next section, we will highlight some of the passes that you can use to perform some canonicalization steps.

# Canonicalization passes

**Canonicalization passes** are transformations that put the IR in a canonical form, that is, an agreed-upon way to represent expressions.

For instance, consider the C statement a = b - c. A frontend could produce the following two equivalent IRs:

- Version 1:

    ```
    %a = sub i64 %b - %c
    ```

- Version 2:

```
%neg_c = sub i64 0, %c
%a = add i64 %b, %neg_c
```

In both cases, the semantics are the same, but the first version is a more direct translation of the input C statement and is also more compact. The canonical form in LLVM of this expression is the first version. It is important to be aware of the tendency of the LLVM middle end to revolve around the canonical representation.

What this means is the following:

- With the standard pipeline, anything that is not canonical will be canonicalized
- Optimizations have been tested almost exclusively using the canonical form

The second point means that when you use existing optimizations on a non-canonicalized IR, the optimization may miss opportunities or have rough edges. In any case, patches are welcome to fix these!

You may wonder then, why not canonicalize the IR upon its construction or modification?

The answer is that what may be the preferred form for one target may be an adverse form for another. Hence, the LLVM infrastructure allows some freedom on what is representable. For instance, the second version of the previous IR may be a better representation of a target with no subtraction instruction, but with addition and negation instructions.

Putting everything together, canonicalization passes narrow down the various ways the same semantics can be expressed in the IR. This means that optimizations can optimize more easily since they can focus on supporting fewer variations. In other words, without canonicalization, a slight variation in the input IR (e.g., add i64 %a, 2 versus add i64 2, %a) may have a drastic impact on the quality of the generated code.

Unfortunately, there is no documented canonical representation or one true canonicalization pass. Instead, this representation is something that evolves over time and that you build a feel for. The rule of thumb is that canonical representation is the simplest way you can represent something.

With that said, the bulk of the canonicalization is embodied by the InstCombinePass class. However, this pass also does a lot of optimizations that are deemed universally beneficial.

In summary, what in LLVM constitutes the canonicalization passes depends on some subjective criteria. For this section, we retain and introduce the following passes:

- The instruction combiner
- The memory-to-register rewriter
- The converter to loop-closed-SSA form

Let us start with our first pass, the instruction combiner.

# The instruction combiner

The instruction combiner, or **instcombine** is, like you discovered in *Chapter 4*, a set of rewrite patterns that aims at canonicalizing the IR and making it more efficient.

Most passes do not worry about the canonical representation and rely on the fact that this pass is re-run from time to time in the pipeline to clean things up.

As a result, when building your own pipeline, you may have to insert this pass in a few places. Beware, however, that this pass can become a compile-time sink if you run it too often.

Additionally, when you start modifying the IR with target-specific constructs in mind, be aware that instcombine may put the IR back in the canonical form; remember what you saw with the sub i64 %b, %c versus add i64 %b, (sub i64 0, %c) example.

What this means is a typical compiler pipeline uses instcombine heavily in the middle-end pipeline until target-specific passes are introduced. At this point, instcombine is not invoked anymore.

> Note
>
> If you still need instcombine-like optimizations after introducing target-specific constructs but are afraid that going back to the canonical representation, that is, running instcombine, can undo your changes, you can use the simplifyXXXInst helper functions available in the Analysis library directly.

To provide a more concrete idea of what constitutes a canonical rewrite and an optimization, here are two examples.

## An example of a canonical rewrite

Let us look at the patterns tested in llvm/test/Transforms/InstCombine/load-bitcast32.ll.

This file exercises the canonicalization patterns that materialize the constraints carried by a target that supports only 32-bit pointers. Concretely, what these patterns do is expand the inttoptr instruction to make the changes in bit width explicit.

For instance, consider the following input IR from that file:

```
%b = load i64, ptr %x
%c = inttoptr i64 %b to ptr
```

This snippet loads a 64-bit value and casts it to a pointer type. Since the target only supports 32-bit pointers, this means this conversion implicitly truncates the 64-bit value to 32-bit.

When running instcombine on this example, the truncate is explicitly exposed:

```
%b = load i64, ptr %x
%b32 = trunc i64 %b to i32
%c = inttoptr i32 %b32 to ptr
```

This is a canonicalization pattern because its only purpose is to express `inttoptr` as a bit-width-neutral operation, meaning it does not implicitly change the bit width from the input type to the output type. In other words, the resulting code is as efficient as the original code. The interest of such rewrites is that other optimizations see the additional logic and can transform it. For instance, `trunc i64 (zext i32 to i64) to i32` can now be simplified into a no-op.

## An example of an optimization

The second class of rewrites that instcombine does is generically useful optimizations.

Consider the following snippet in an LLVM IR:

```
%res = xor i64 %x, %x
```

This snippet does a bitwise logical exclusive of both operands, which in this case is twice the `%x` value. This will always return 0 and instcombine catches this pattern and replaces all the values of `%res` with the constant 0.

This example is here to show you that instcombine remains an optimization pass and as such, you should not run it when your users compile with all the optimizations disabled (typically O0).

> **Note**
>
> Since instcombine is not typically run in the O0 compilation pipeline, you may wonder what happens to the canonical representation in this mode. The answer is the IR is mostly not in canonical form in this mode. This is okay because the expectation of an O0 pipeline is **garbage in-garbage out**, meaning the compiler does not try to improve the situation. With that said, this means your lowering passes, that is, the ones that must run irrespective of the optimization level, must run correctly even in a non-canonical form.

This is one of the many patterns that instcombine optimizes.

To find out more about what instcombine has to offer, you can scan through the source of the pass, which is in the files located in `llvm/lib/Transforms/InstCombine`.

Alternatively, you can look at the main tests available at `llvm/test/Transforms/InstCombine`. Be aware that we are talking about ~1,500 test files with around 32k definitions of IR functions, which roughly translates to as many unit tests.

Now, realistically, we recommend using it without going deeply into what it does. If you find that there are patterns that it does not optimize, consider whether this is beneficial for all targets (or a canonical way to represent something), and if yes, try to contribute it back to open source. If not, you must do that in your own target-specific pass.

## How to use instcombine

`InstCombinePass` is so important in the LLVM infrastructure that it comes in its own library, the `InstCombine` library. This library is located under the `Transforms/InstCombine` directory.

To add instcombine to your pass pipeline, you need to add an instance of the `InstCombinePass` class to your pass pipeline (`InstructionCombiningPass` for the legacy pass manager).

The CLI name of the pass is, you have guessed it, `instcombine`.

This section gave you a taste of what instcombine does. It would be too long, and not worth it, to try to cover it fully, and the bottom line is that it is a treasure trove of optimizations and simplifications, and it should be part of your pass pipeline.

In the next section, we will cover one of the passes that simplifies the job of and exposes optimization opportunities to all the transformations, the memory to register rewriter.

## The memory to register rewriter

The memory to register rewriter is the pass responsible for eliminating memory accesses and replacing them with SSA values. In the *Constructing the SSA form* section, in *Chapter 4*, you already discovered what this entails and had a glimpse of how to perform this transformation.

Now that you know the pass managers, we can give you the full details!

Promoting memory locations to register is performed by the `PromotePass` class (`PromoteLegacyPass` in the legacy pass manager), from the `TransformsUtils` library.

The CLI name of this pass is `mem2reg`.

Although this is not a canonicalization pass, we put it in this category because the IR produced by this pass is the starting point of any sane optimizations. Indeed, without this transformation, all the optimizations would need to track memory locations and use alias analyses to perform anything useful. Additionally, unless the memory locations are promoted to registers, you do not get any of the advantages of the SSA form, such as the def-uses chains and the dominance property. In other words, you would be stuck with a compiler technology of another age.

Therefore, you want to run this pass in your pipeline as soon as possible. However, you do not want to run it at O0.

The next section covers a pass that canonicalizes loops.

## The converter to loop-closed-SSA form

The **loop-closed SSA (LCSSA)** form is a representation that guarantees that no value defined inside a loop is used outside a loop. This form is obtained by defining new `phis` values in the exit blocks. In any case, the details of how to build that form are not particularly relevant to understand why such representation is interesting.

This form is interesting when you want to do loop transformations because now, you can directly separate the uses that are within the loop from the uses that are outside the loop.

For instance, consider the following LLVM IR snippet:

```
define i64 @def_in_loop_use_outside(i64 %src, i64 %upper_bound) {
entry:
  br label %loop

loop:
  %iv = phi i64 [0, %entry], [%iv_plus_1, %loop]
  %iv_plus_1 = add i64 %iv, 1
  %cond = icmp ult i64 %iv_plus_1, %upper_bound
  br i1 %cond, label %loop, label %end

end:
  %tmp = add i64 %iv_plus_1, %src
  %res = add i64 %tmp, %iv_plus_1
  ret i64 %res
}
```

In this snippet, we iterate from 0 to %upper_bound and compute a value based on the induction variable represented by the %iv and %iv_plus_1 values.

Notice how %iv_plus_1 is defined within the loop and used both inside and outside it. This means that if we were to walk through the def-uses chain of %iv_plus_1, we would obtain uses that are inside and outside the loop.

Turning this loop into LCSSA form provides a nicer way to get what is used inside and outside a loop:

```
define i64 @def_in_loop_use_outside(i64 %src, i64 %upper_bound) {
entry:
  br label %loop

loop:
  %iv = phi i64 [ 0, %entry ], [ %iv_plus_1, %loop ]
  %iv_plus_1 = add i64 %iv, 1
  %cond = icmp ult i64 %iv_plus_1, %upper_bound
  br i1 %cond, label %loop, label %end

end:
  %iv_plus_1.lcssa = phi i64 [ %iv_plus_1, %loop ]
  %tmp = add i64 %iv_plus_1.lcssa, %src
  %res = add i64 %tmp, %iv_plus_1.lcssa
  ret i64 %res
}
```

Thanks to the LCSSA form, you can now easily differentiate the uses outside of the loop, since they use the %iv_plus_1.lcssa value. The definition of %iv_plus_1.lcssa itself is a use of %iv_plus_1 outside of the loop, so technically, if you are interested only in the uses of %iv_plus_1 inside the loop, you must still filter this one out. However, you already moved all the other uses out of the way to %iv_plus_1.lcssa.

> **Note**
>
> We wanted to present the LCSSA form to you because, as we said, this is useful for some loop transformations, but it also has other use cases, and you may invent your own. For instance, looking back at the previous example, you see that %iv, and by extension %iv_plus_1, is initialized with a constant. Now imagine that this loop is run on a GPU-like architecture where a certain number of threads are run in locked steps. This means that within the loop, the induction variable has the same value across all threads. On some AMD **graphics processing units (GPUs)**, for instance, this means that you can store and compute this value into cheaper (shared) resources such as the scalar registers. However, in this case, the scalar register cannot be used outside of the loop because %upper_bound may be different for each thread, but this is perfectly captured by the definition of a new value: %iv_plus_1.lcssa.

To get your IR in LCSSA form, you need to add an instance of the LCSSAPass class (LCSSAWrapperPass in the legacy pass manager), from the TransformsUtils library.

The CLI name of this pass is lcssa.

The LCSSA form is ephemeral in the sense that it can be easily reverted by other optimizations. For instance, instcombine will get rid of the additional phi that has been added in the previous example. This means you must put the IR in LCSSA form in front of the pass that needs it. With that said, if you write a loop pass, the LoopAnalysisManager class gives you the guarantee, among others, that the instance of the loops provided as an argument of the run method of your pass are already in that form.

This concludes our survey of what we consider canonical passes. In the process, you learned about three different passes:

- instcombine: A pass that performs rewrites that are generally good for all targets.
- mem2reg: A pass that promotes memory accesses to SSA values and makes later transformations much easier to write.
- lcssa: A pass that transforms loops into the LCSSA form. This form makes certain optimization easier and opens up certain lowering capabilities that are otherwise not possible.

Moreover, in this section, you understood the reason for having a canonical representation and learned that this representation may clash with some of the things you may be trying to achieve for target-specific constructs.

In the next section, you will discover some of the transformations that LLVM offers in the middle end. Unlike the canonical passes presented here, these passes are solely focused on making the generated code run faster, but unlike something such as `instcombine` or `mem2reg`, these transformations may not even be relevant for your target!

# Optimization passes

In this section, you will discover some of the passes that you can leverage to improve the quality of the codegen of your target.

LLVM is a huge code base, so we cannot realistically cover all of the passes. This is why we again strongly recommend applying what you learned in the *How to find the unknown* section earlier in this chapter to discover what is available.

To help you in this task, the following sections give you a sort of identity card for a few of the passes available in the middle end. The sections are broken down following the directory structure of the LLVM code base.

The goal of these ID cards is to give you a single source of key information to use and understand a pass and that you can use as a quick reference in the future.

Feel free to complete this list by yourself or produce your own card format!

The identity card contains the following fields:

- **Pass name:** Human-readable pass name
- **Class pass name:** Name of the class to add in your pass pipeline, followed, if available, by the pass name in parentheses for the legacy pass manager or NA if not available
- **CLI name:** The name of the pass as identified in opt
- **Description:** A high-level explanation of what the pass does
- **In/Out:** An example of an input/output IR demonstrating the kind of transformation that the pass does
- **Explanation of the example:** Explains what is happening in the transformation from **In** to **Out**
- **Target-specific elements:** Describes whether this pass is influenced/controlled by any target-specific information

The fields are laid out using the structure shown in the following table:

| Pass name | |
|---|---|
| Class pass name (legacy pass name) | CLI name |
| Description | |
| In | Out |
| Explanation of the example | |
| Target-specific elements (if any) | |

Finally, each example given as input for each transformation is available in ch8/<cli_name>.ll. Look in the README.md file of this directory to find out how to run them by yourself.

## Interprocedural optimizations

In this section, we present the identity cards of a few of the IPO passes.

| Argument promotion | |
|---|---|
| ArgumentPromotionPass (NA) | argpromotion |

This pass tries to replace pointer arguments with regular values. In other words, it promotes an argument passed by reference to an argument passed by value.

This replacement is only possible if the function is internal to the module, meaning that it is okay to change its **application binary interface** (**ABI**) because the optimization sees all the uses of the function.

This transformation exposes opportunities to get rid of stack allocation and memory accesses.

```
define i64 @foo() {
  %local = alloca i64
  store i64 2, ptr %local
  %res = call i64 @bar(ptr
%local)
  ret i64 %res
}


define internal i64 @bar(ptr
%local) {
  %val = load i64, ptr %local
  %res = add i64 %val, 2
  ret i64 %res
}
```

```
define i64 @foo() {
  %local = alloca i64
  store i64 2, ptr %local
  %local.val = load i64, ptr %local
  %res = call i64 @bar(i64 %local.
val)
  ret i64 %res
}


define internal i64 @bar(i64
%local.0.val) {
  %res = add i64 %local.0.val, 2
  ret i64 %res
}
```

The argument pointer of @bar is replaced by a plain i64 value. This saves the load within @bar and now the load is in @foo. However, thanks to this change, a pass such as mem2reg can eliminate all the alloca and load and store instructions.

This pass uses TargetTransformInfo to check whether the produced function signature is compatible with what the target ABI supports.

| Dead argument elimination | |
|---|---|
| `DeadArgumentEliminationPass` (DAE) | `deadargelim` |

This pass removes from the function signature the arguments that are not used.

Similar to the argument promotion pass, this transformation can only happen if the optimization sees all the call sites of the related function.

```
define i64 @foo() {
  %local = alloca i64
  %local2 = alloca i64
  store i64 2, ptr %local
  store i64 2, ptr %local2
  %res = call i64 @bar(ptr
%local, ptr %local2)
  ret i64 %res
}


define internal i64 @bar(ptr
%local, ptr %local2) {
  %val = load i64, ptr %local
  %res = add i64 %val, 2
  ret i64 %res
}
```

```
define i64 @foo() {
  %local = alloca i64
  %local2 = alloca i64
  store i64 2, ptr %local
  store i64 2, ptr %local2
  %res = call i64 @bar(ptr %local)
  ret i64 %res
}


define internal i64 @bar(ptr %local) {
  %val = load i64, ptr %local
  %res = add i64 %val, 2
  ret i64 %res
}
```

In this example, the second parameter of `@bar` is unused. Thanks to the dead argument elimination pass, it can be removed. This opens some more opportunities to remove some dead code. Indeed, after this transformation, the `alloca` and `store` instructions for `%local2` in `@foo` can be removed.

Target-specific elements: None

| **Inliner** | |
|---|---|
| `InlinerPass` (NA) | `inline` |

This optimization takes call sites and tries to eliminate them by replacing them with the content of the functions being called (the callees).

This particular inliner uses the regions formed by the **call graph strongly connect component** (**CGSCC**) to determine the order in which inline decisions are made, starting from the leaves of the call graph and moving up to their parents.

If you want to have more flexibility on the order of the inlining decisions, you can use the sister optimization, `module-inliner`.

<table>
<tr><td>

```
define i64 @foo() {
  %local = alloca i64
  store i64 2, ptr %local
  %res = call i64 @bar(ptr
%local)
  ret i64 %res
}


define i64 @bar(ptr %local) {
  %val = load i64, ptr %local
  %res = add i64 %val, 2
  ret i64 %res
}
```

</td><td>

```
define i64 @foo() {
  %local = alloca i64
  store i64 2, ptr %local
  %val.i = load i64, ptr %local
  %res.i = add i64 %val.i, 2
  ret i64 %res.i
}


define i64 @bar(ptr %local) {
  %val = load i64, ptr %local, align 4
  %res = add i64 %val, 2
  ret i64 %res
}
```

</td></tr>
</table>

In this example, `@foo` calls `@bar`. Since `@bar` contains only a few instructions, the cost model of the inliner decides to inline this call into `@foo`. As a result, `@foo` does not contain any calls anymore and further optimization opportunities are exposed. `@bar` is kept because its linkage type does not allow the optimization to remove it. Indeed, its linkage type is not `internal`, and as a result, another function from another module may use it.

Each decision to inline is controlled by the `InlineAdvisorAnalysis` pass, which you can customize to your needs. By default, the `InlineAdvisorAnalysis` pass uses the information available through the current `TargetTransformInfo` instance to produce a cost and compare it to a predefined threshold.

There are many more IPO passes but these give you an idea of the kinds of transformations you can find in this part of the LLVM code base.

The next section covers the passes you can find under the `ScalarOpts` library, under `Transforms/Scalar`.

## Scalar optimizations

As already mentioned, the scalar optimizations in LLVM parlance are optimizations that do not deal with vectorization. As such, you will find most of the transformations here.

In this section, we cover a few of them that we chose based on their usefulness and diversity so that you can get an idea of the kinds of things available.

| Dead code elimination | |
| --- | --- |
| `DCEPass (DCELegacyPass)` | `dce` |
| This pass does a simple dead code elimination based on the usage of the SSA values. In other words, if a value is not used and the instruction does not have any side effect, such as memory writes or jumps, the value is removed. | |

```
define i64 @foo(i64 %in) {             define i64 @foo(i64 %in) {
  %dead = add i64 %in, %in               %res = mul i64 %in, 2
  %res = mul i64 %in, 2                  ret i64 %res
  ret i64 %res                         }
}
```

In this example, the value named `%dead` is not used at all and is removed by the dead code elimination pass, since the `add` instruction does not have any side effect.

`TargetLibraryInfo` is used to check whether it is safe to remove values that are defined by library calls and other intrinsics.

| Induction variables simplification | |
|---|---|
| IndVarSimplifyPass (NA) | indvars |

This transformation changes how values derived from induction variables are computed to make the computation more amenable to other optimizations.

```
define i64 @foo(i64 %src, i64
%ub) {
entry:
  br label %loop

loop:
  %iv = phi i64 [0, %entry],
[%iv1, %loop]
  %iv1 = add i64 %iv, 1
  %cond = icmp ult i64 %iv1, %ub
  br i1 %cond, label %loop, label
%end

end:
  %tmp = add i64 %iv1, %src
  %res = add i64 %tmp, %iv1
  ret i64 %res
}
```

```
define i64 @foo(i64 %src, i64 %ub) {
entry:
  br label %loop

loop:
  br i1 false, label %loop, label %end

end:
  %umax = call i64 @llvm.umax.i64(i64
%ub, i64 1)
  %tmp = add i64 %umax, %src
  %res = add i64 %tmp, %umax
  ret i64 %res
}

declare i64 @llvm.umax.i64(i64, i64)
```

The loop trip count (the number of times the loop is going to be executed) in this example can be determined statically. As a result, the optimization pushes the whole computation, represented by the %iv and %iv1 chain, outside of the loop and expresses the result as a function of the upper bound (%ub). The loop body gets transformed into a simple jump that can be simplified by further optimizations.

For this transformation, both the TargetLibraryInfo and TargetTransformInfo classes are used. The former is used to check whether things such as library calls become dead (i.e., do not have side effects) and the latter is used to compute the cost of the new sequence of code versus the original one.

| Loop invariant code motion | |
|---|---|
| LICMPass (LegacyLICMPass) | `licm` |

The **loop invariant code motion** (**LICM**) pass consists of identifying the pieces of code that are not dependent on the loop iteration (i.e., that do not change within a loop body) and moving them out of the loop body.

In other words, it takes the code that is loop invariant and moves it outside of the loop.

<table>
<tr><td>

```
define i64 @foo(i64 %src, i64
%ub, ptr %addr) {
entry:
  br label %loop

loop:
  %iv = phi i64 [0, %entry],
[%iv1, %loop]
  %offset = load i64, ptr %addr
  %iv1 = add i64 %iv, %offset
  %cond = icmp ult i64 %iv1, %ub
  br i1 %cond, label %loop, label
%end

end:
  %res = add i64 %src, %iv1
  ret i64 %res
}
```

</td><td>

```
define i64 @foo(i64 %src, i64 %ub, ptr
%addr) {
entry:
  %offset = load i64, ptr %addr
  br label %loop

loop:
  %iv = phi i64 [ 0, %entry ], [ %iv1,
%loop ]
  %iv1 = add i64 %iv, %offset
  %cond = icmp ult i64 %iv1, %ub
  br i1 %cond, label %loop, label %end

end:
  %iv1.lcssa = phi i64 [ %iv1, %loop ]
  %res = add i64 %src, %iv1.lcssa
  ret i64 %res
}
```

</td></tr>
</table>

In this example, you can see the `%offset` value being loaded at each iteration of the loop. LICM hoists that `load` outside of the loop since the loaded value does not depend on anything tied to the current loop iteration and no memory location is written within that loop (i.e., there is no aliasing issue here).

Notice how the resulting form is using the LCSSA form. As we said, every loop pass gets loops in LCSSA form before running.

This pass uses both the `TargetLibraryInfo` and `TargetTransformInfo` classes. The former is mainly used to perform legality checks and the latter for profitability checks.

| Loop strength reduction | |
| --- | --- |
| LoopStrengthReducePass<br>(LoopStrengthReduce) | loop-reduce |

Strength reduction in compiler terms means replacing a computation with an equivalent and cheaper computation, for instance, x * 2 into x << 1. x << 1 is of lesser strength than x * 2 because the underlying hardware implementation of a shift (<<) is cheaper than a multiply.

The loop strength reduction pass is a transformation that reduces the strength of address computations that are based on the induction variables.

The goal of this pass is to expose address computations that better fit the addressing modes (the way a target can compute an address) of the current target.

For instance, when you access a typical array in C, you write something such as A[i]. This code sequence translates roughly into *(A + i * sizeof(A[0])). In other words, each time you move one element ahead in the array, you move several bytes in the address, hence a multiply is introduced during the lowering. A lot of targets handle that through their addressing modes (the multiplying constant is called the **scaling factor**) and this pass helps get the IR in a shape that will allow the later codegen passes to leverage these addressing modes and hence, lower the memory accesses efficiently.

```
target triple = "aarch64-apple-ios"

define i64 @foo(ptr %arg, i64 %ub) {
bb:
  br label %bb3

bb3:
  %idx = phi i64 [ 0, %bb ], [ %i9,
%bb8 ]
  %i = icmp slt i64 %idx, %ub
  br i1 %i, label %bb4, label %bb10

bb4:
  %i5 = getelementptr inbounds i64,
ptr %arg, i64 %idx
  %i6 = load i64, ptr %i5
  %i7 = icmp ne i64 %i6, 0
  br i1 %i7, label %bb10, label %bb8

bb8:
  %i9 = add nsw i64 %idx, 1
  br label %bb3

bb10:
  %res = phi i64 [ %idx, %bb4 ], [
-1, %bb3 ]
  ret i64 %res
}
```

```
target triple = "aarch64-apple-ios"

define i64 @foo(ptr %arg, i64 %ub) {
bb:
  br label %bb3

bb3:
  %idx = phi i64 [ 0, %bb ], [ %i9,
%bb8 ]
  %i = icmp slt i64 %idx, %ub
  br i1 %i, label %bb4, label
%bb10split

bb4:
  %0 = shl i64 %idx, 3
  %scevgep = getelementptr i8, ptr
%arg, i64 %0
  %i6 = load i64, ptr %scevgep
  %i7 = icmp ne i64 %i6, 0
  br i1 %i7, label %bb4.bb10_crit_
edge, label %bb8

bb8:
  %i9 = add nsw i64 %idx, 1
  br label %bb3

bb10split:
  br label %bb10

bb4.bb10_crit_edge:
  %idx.lcssa1 = phi i64 [ %idx, %bb4
]
  br label %bb10

bb10:
  %res = phi i64 [ %idx.lcssa1,
%bb4.bb10_crit_edge ], [ -1,
%bb10split ]
  ret i64 %res
}
```

This example traverses a given array, represented by the `%arg` pointer, until it reaches the upper bound, `%ub`, or stumbles on a non-zero element and returns the index of the non-zero element.

Loop strength reduction kicks in to simplify `getelementptr` in the loop body (`bb4`).

`getelementptr` for `%i5` would be lowered to `%arg + %idx * 8` due to the `i64` type at the beginning. Put differently, this means `%arg` is interpreted as an array of `i64` elements and `%idx` needs to be scaled accordingly.

Notice how the `%i5` part is replaced by the sequence of instructions `%0` and `%scevgep`. The new sequence applies the scaling factor on `%idx` with a lesser-strength instruction (`shl`), then adds this offset to `%arg`. Notice how the new `getelementptr` uses the `i8` type instead of `i64`. The new `getelementptr` now describes an address calculation with an array of `i8` elements, which means no scaling factor (or, more precisely, a scaling factor of 1 byte, i.e., `%idx * 1`, so something that can be trivially optimized away).

There are also other changes here, such as the LCSSA form and the splitting of the critical edge. These are done by the loop strength reduction pass to make its job simpler.

---

This pass uses the usual suspects, `TargetLoweringInfo` and `TargetTransformInfo`, for legality and profitability checks, respectively. Notice, however, that in our test, we defined a target triple. This is because `TargetTransformInfo` needs to have a real lowering target (represented via the `TargetLowering` base class embedded in the `TargetTransformInfo` class) to be able to query which addressing modes are available.

---

### Loop unrolling

| `LoopUnrollPass (LoopUnroll)` | `loop-unroll` |
| --- | --- |

Loop unrolling consists of expanding the body of loops into a longer sequence of code with fewer iterations. For instance, an unroll factor of 2 would achieve two iterations of the original loop in one iteration of the new loop.

If the trip count is constant, a loop can be completely unrolled and replaced by pure non-looping code with `if` statements. We say that the loop is fully unrolled.

The goals of such optimization are to reduce the overhead of branching and expose new opportunities for later optimizations, such as vectorization or scheduling.

```
define i64 @foo(ptr %arg) {
bb:
  br label %bb3

bb3:
  %idx = phi i64 [ 0, %bb ], [
%i9, %bb8 ]
  %i = icmp slt i64 %idx, 3
  br i1 %i, label %bb4, label
%bb10

bb4:
  %i5 = getelementptr inbounds
i64, ptr %arg, i64 %idx
  %i6 = load i64, ptr %i5
  %i7 = icmp ne i64 %i6, 0
  br i1 %i7, label %bb10, label
%bb8

bb8:
  %i9 = add nsw i64 %idx, 1
  br label %bb3

bb10:
  %res = phi i64 [ %idx, %bb4 ],
[ -1, %bb3 ]
  ret i64 %res
}
```

```
define i64 @foo(ptr %arg) {
bb:
  br label %bb3

bb3:
  br label %bb4

bb4:
  %i6 = load i64, ptr %arg
  %i7 = icmp ne i64 %i6, 0
  br i1 %i7, label %bb10, label %bb8

bb8:
  br label %bb4.1

bb4.1:
  %i5.1 = getelementptr inbounds i64,
ptr %arg, i64 1
  %i6.1 = load i64, ptr %i5.1
  %i7.1 = icmp ne i64 %i6.1, 0
  br i1 %i7.1, label %bb10, label
%bb8.1

bb8.1:
  br label %bb4.2
[...]
bb8.3:
  unreachable

bb10:
  %res = phi i64 [ 0, %bb4 ], [ 1,
%bb4.1 ], [ 2, %bb4.2 ], [ -1, %bb8.2
], [ 3, %bb4.3 ]
  ret i64 %res
}
```

The input IR is the same as the loop strength reduction example except that we set the upper dimension to a constant, 3, to make the effect of loop unrolling easier to follow.

The resulting IR is a fully unrolled version of the loop where each of the three iterations has been expanded. The IR has been cropped but you can see the pattern: the first iteration is expanded in `bb4`, the second in `bb4.1`, and then the same thing happens with `bb4.3` for the third iteration. Finally, the final value, `%res`, gets the right iteration number depending on which iteration block the control flow takes thanks to the `phi` instruction.

This pass uses `TargetTransformInfo` to estimate the cost of the unrolled loop and decide on the unrolling factor. Additionally, targets can override `TargetTransformInfo::getUnrollingPreferences` to control the threshold and so on used in the loop unrolling cost model.

| **Reassociate** | |
| --- | --- |
| `ReassociatePass (ReassociateLegacyPass)` | `reassociate` |

The reassociate pass performs what in mathematics we call reassociation. Reassociation consists of changing the order in which computations are made, for example, turning `(a + b) + c` into `a + (b + c)`.

The difficulty with reassociation is proving that it is legal because changing the order of the computations may change the result since each computation may have rounding errors that would accumulate differently.

The goal of this pass is to simplify computations. It does that by grouping the constants together so that they can be computed as compile time, by putting expressions that cancel each other together, and by exposing common subexpression elimination (a technique that consists of recognizing that some computations are the same and instead of recomputing them, we store the result and reuse it).

```
define i64 @foo(i64 %in0, i64
%in1) {
  %v0 = add i64 %in0, %in1
  %v1 = add i64 %v0, 2
  %v2 = sub i64 %v1, %in1
  ret i64 %v2
}
```

```
define i64 @foo(i64 %in0, i64 %in1) {
  %v2 = add i64 %in0, 2
  ret i64 %v2
}
```

In the input IR, we compute `%in0 + %in1 + 2 - %in1`, which the reassociate pass replaces in `%in0 + %in1 - %in1 + 2` and simplifies in `%in0 + 2`.

Target-specific elements: None

| Control flow graph simplification | |
|---|---|
| `SimplifyCFGPass (CFGSimplifyPass)` | `simplifycfg` |

The **control flow graph** (CFG) simplification pass eliminates useless control flow jumps such as conditional branches with a constant condition.

Its capabilities are also available directly through the `simplifyCFG` APIs from the `TransformUtils` library.

<table>
<tr>
<td>

```
define i64 @foo(i64 %src, i64
%ub) {
entry:
  br label %loop

loop:
  br i1 false, label %loop, label
%end

end:
  %umax = call i64 @llvm.umax.
i64(i64 %ub, i64 1)
  %tmp = add i64 %umax, %src
  %res = add i64 %tmp, %umax
  ret i64 %res
}

declare i64 @llvm.umax.i64(i64,
i64)
```

</td>
<td>

```
define i64 @foo(i64 %src, i64 %ub) {
entry:
  %umax = call i64 @llvm.umax.i64(i64
%ub, i64 1)
  %tmp = add i64 %umax, %src
  %res = add i64 %tmp, %umax
  ret i64 %res
}

declare i64 @llvm.umax.i64(i64, i64)
```

</td>
</tr>
</table>

In the input IR, we have the `entry` block, which jumps directly to the block named `loop` with that unconditional branch. That branch is, in theory, mandatory because `loop` has two predecessors (entry and itself) and entry blocks cannot have predecessors. In practice, the `loop` block uses a conditional branch that always resolves to jumping to `end`. Hence, it can be simplified into an unconditional branch to `end`, and these two blocks can be merged. After this merger, `entry` jumps to `end`, and since `end` has only one predecessor (`entry`), then these two blocks can also be merged, resulting in a single basic block.

This pass uses `TargetTransformInfo` for its cost model.

This concludes our survey of the passes available in this library. Again, there are many more useful optimizations there and we encourage you to take a closer look before writing new optimizations. Chances are, what you need already exists!

Our next and final stop in this chapter is the `Vectorize` library.

# Vectorization

As its name suggests, the Vectorize folder contains all the transformations that deal with vectorization. As already mentioned, vectorization is an optimization that transforms the IR from a scalar version to a vector version using the SIMD programming model.

For instance, given two unrelated scalar additions, a = b + c and d = e + f, we can produce one two-way vectorized addition <a, d> = <b, e> + <c, f>, where the addition is carried out in parallel on each lane.

The vectorize library features passes that perform this kind of transformation but with different focuses and contexts of applications.

| Load store vectorizer | |
|---|---|
| LoadStoreVectorizerPass<br>(LoadStoreVectorizerLegacyPass) | `load-store-vectorizer` |
| The focus of the load store vectorizer is around... loads and stores!<br><br>This pass scans loads and stores and tries to find the longest chain of the same kind of accesses (read for loads and write for stores) to contiguous locations to produce vectorized loads and stores.<br><br>By collapsing loads (or stores) together, this pass reduces the number of instructions and the number of times the memory subsystem of the target is invoked. | |

```
target triple="aarch64-apple-ios"

define void @bar(ptr %src, ptr
%dst) {
  %v0 = load i64, ptr %src
  %src1 = getelementptr i64, ptr
%src, i64 1
  %v1 = load i64, ptr %src1
  store i64 %v0, ptr %dst
  %dst1 = getelementptr i64, ptr
%dst, i64 1
  store i64 %v1, ptr %dst1
  ret void
}
```

```
target triple = "aarch64-apple-ios"

define void @bar(ptr %src, ptr %dst) {
  %1 = load <2 x i64>, ptr %src
  %v01 = extractelement <2 x i64> %1,
i32 0
  %v12 = extractelement <2 x i64> %1,
i32 1
  %2 = insertelement <2 x i64> poison,
i64 %v01, i32 0
  %3 = insertelement <2 x i64> %2, i64
%v12, i32 1
  store <2 x i64> %3, ptr %dst
  ret void
}
```

The input IR performs two loads of i64 values at %src and %src + 1, respectively, hence contiguous accesses, and stores them in %dst in contiguous locations as well.

The load store vectorizer recognizes that and replaces the two loads and two stores with one load of <2 x i64> and one store of <2 x i64>, respectively.

This pass uses TargetTransformInfo to check what vector types the target supports. Note that we need an actual target in this example (hence the directive that specifies the triple at the beginning of the IR, see *Chapter 7* if you are unclear about what the triple represents) because this information is usually carried by the TargetLowering class.

---

### Straight-line program vectorizer

| SLPVectorizerPass (NA) | slp-vectorizer |
|---|---|

The **straight-line program (SLP)** vectorizer takes a sequence of similar scalar instructions and groups them together to form a vectorized sequence.

```
define <2 x i64> @foo(i64 %in0,
i64 %in1) {
  %v0 = add i64 %in0, 2
  %v1 = add i64 %in1, 5
  %partial = insertelement <2 x
i64> poison, i64 %v0, i32 0
  %res = insertelement <2 x i64>
%partial, i64 %v1, i32 1
  ret <2 x i64> %res
}
```

```
define <2 x i64> @foo(i64 %in0, i64
%in1) {
  %1 = insertelement <2 x i64> poison,
i64 %in0, i32 0
  %2 = insertelement <2 x i64> %1, i64
%in1, i32 1
  %3 = add <2 x i64> %2, <i64 2, i64
5>
  ret <2 x i64> %3
}
```

In this example, we compute two different additions (%v0 and %v1) and group them together to compute the two results in one go (%res).

The SLP vectorizer groups the additions under one vector addition (%3) and returns it directly.

This pass uses the usual suspect for legality checks, TargetLibraryInfo, and profitability checks, TargetTransformInfo.

---

### Loop vectorizer

| LoopVectorizePass (NA) | loop-vectorize |
|---|---|

The loop vectorizer pass transforms loop bodies into vectorized variants.

```
target triple = "arm64-apple-
macosx14.0.0"


define void @foo(ptr noalias
noundef %arg, ptr noalias noundef
%arg1, ptr noalias noundef %arg2)
{
[...]
bb3:
  %idx = phi i64 [ 0, %bb ], [
%i14, %bb4 ]
  %i = icmp ne i64 %idx, 24
  br i1 %i, label %bb4, label
%bb15

bb4:
  %i5 = getelementptr inbounds
i16, ptr %arg1, i64 %idx
  %i6 = load i16, ptr %i5
  %i7 = sext i16 %i6 to i32
  %i8 = getelementptr inbounds
i16, ptr %arg2, i64 %idx
  %i9 = load i16, ptr %i8
  %i10 = sext i16 %i9 to i32
  %i11 = add nsw i32 %i7, %i10
  %i12 = trunc i32 %i11 to i16
  %i13 = getelementptr inbounds
i16, ptr %arg, i64 %idx
  store i16 %i12, ptr %i13
  %i14 = add nsw i64 %idx, 1
  br label %bb3
 [...]
```

```
target triple = "arm64-apple-
macosx14.0.0"


define void @foo(ptr noalias noundef
%arg, ptr noalias noundef %arg1, ptr
noalias noundef %arg2) {
[...]
vector.body:
  %index = phi i64 [ 0, %vector.ph ],
[ %index.next, %vector.body ]
  %0 = add i64 %index, 0
  %1 = getelementptr inbounds i16, ptr
%arg1, i64 %0
  %2 = getelementptr inbounds i16, ptr
%1, i32 0
  %wide.load = load <8 x i16>, ptr %2
  %3 = getelementptr inbounds i16, ptr
%arg2, i64 %0
  %4 = getelementptr inbounds i16, ptr
%3, i32 0
  %wide.load1 = load <8 x i16>, ptr %4
  %5 = add <8 x i16> %wide.load,
%wide.load1
  %6 = getelementptr inbounds i16, ptr
%arg, i64 %0
  %7 = getelementptr inbounds i16, ptr
%6, i32 0
  store <8 x i16> %5, ptr %7
  %index.next = add nuw i64 %index, 8
  %8 = icmp eq i64 %index.next, 24
  br i1 %8, label %middle.block, label
%vector.body, !llvm.loop !0
 [...]
```

The input IR computes %arg[i] = %arg1[i] + %arg2[i]. After loop vectorization, each loop iteration computes eight values in parallel. The IR has been cropped to show only the interesting parts.

This pass uses the usual TargetLibraryInfo and TargetTransformInfo classes and the underlying TargetLowering for the actual vector support.

In this section, we saw some of the optimizations offered by the LLVM middle end. You found out what they do with examples, discovered the underlying classes that you can use to add them to your custom pass pipeline, and their CLI option name to experiment with them using opt.

# Summary

In this chapter, you learned how to find out the kinds of optimizations that LLVM has to offer by yourself. To this end, you saw two ways to approach this discovery process:

- **Top-down:** Starting from the opt driver's help message all the way to the implementation
- **Bottom-up:** Starting from the directory structure and filenames to find the implementation and connect that back to opt's CLI

You then learned about some of the critical tools that you can leverage to help you understand what the compiler does: the verifier and printer.

After that, you began building your knowledge of what the middle end features. First, you learned about the analysis passes, then the canonicalization passes, and finally, the optimization passes.

While this chapter just scratched the surface of the LLVM ecosystem, it gave you a broad overview of the kind of things you can find.

We believe that with this newly acquired knowledge, you will now be able to confidently explore the middle end on your own and develop your own middle end by reusing what exists.

The next chapter will take you further along in the target-specific domain by showing you how to connect target-specific constructs in the middle end.

# Further reading

The LLVM website features a list of most of the middle-end passes at https://llvm.org/docs/Passes. html with a short description of what they do. This is slightly more verbose than the help message from opt. You can look at that list to get a better idea of what is available, then use the techniques described in this chapter to add the desired classes to your pass pipeline.

# Quiz time

Now that you have completed reading this chapter, try answering the following questions to test your knowledge:

1. Given the CLI name of an optimization, how can you check whether it is part of the middle end?

   You can use the `print-passes` option from opt to check whether this name is part of one of the `Module`, `Function`, or `Loop` pass categories.

   See the *Leveraging opt* section for more details.

2. Imagine that you have an existing pass that crashes on the output IR of one of your custom passes. What is one of the first things you can try before debugging the existing pass?

   Start by putting the output IR through the verifier. Chances are your custom pass produces an invalid IR and this is what breaks the existing pass, since invalid IR must not be fed to passes.

   See the *The verifier* section for more details.

3. Where would you find the implementation of the **common subexpression elimination (CSE)** pass?

   The CSE transformation is an optimization, hence it will be in one of the subdirectories of `Transforms`. Then, it works at the function level, therefore you can eliminate the IPO directory. Next, it does not deal with vectorization, so you can eliminate the `Vectorize` directory as well. Therefore, it must be in the `Scalar` directory.

   Sure enough, you will find the implementation of CSE in `llvm/lib/Transforms/Scalar/ EarlyCSE.cpp`.

   See the *Using the LLVM code base* section for a breakdown of where to find what.

4. Using the output of the example of the indvars pass, what pass should you run to eliminate the conditional branch instruction left?

   Here, we want to eliminate a conditional branch with a constant condition. This is exactly what the CFG simplification pass is made for; therefore, you can test it by running opt `-passes=simplifycfg`.

   See the *Scalar optimizations* section for more information on this pass.

5. Imagine that you are writing a test for the load store vectorizer, and that test does not produce the IR you normally see when running within your compiler. What could be one of the reasons?

   The vectorizer passes are typically controlled by the low-level information that is carried by the `TargetLowering` pass. If you do not specify the target triple in your test, chances are the vectorizer uses a default target model that does not match the actual preferences of your target.

   See the target-specific elements field of the load store vectorizer in the *Vectorization* section for more details.

## Unlock this book's exclusive benefits now

This book comes with additional benefits designed to elevate your learning experience.

*Note: Have your purchase invoice ready before you begin.*

https://www.packtpub.com/unlock/9781837637782

# 9

# Introducing Target-Specific Constructs

So far, you have seen how the middle-end is structured and how to reuse the existing passes to create your own pass pipeline. In particular, in the previous chapter, you saw that some passes leverage some target-provided **application programming interfaces** (**APIs**) to perform their transformations. In this chapter, you will learn how to bring-up and populate this APIs to connect your target-specific information to the generic passes.

To this end, you will learn the following:

- How to add a new target to the LLVM infrastructure, including the Clang frontend
- How to add intrinsics, which are a mechanism that allows you to expose target-specific constructs at the language level (C, C++, etc.) all the way down to the backend
- How to create your own `TargetTransformInfo` sub-class, which is the API that supplies the information that controls/informs some of the middle-end optimizations
- How to inject your custom passes in the default pipeline

By the end of this chapter, you will have a backend capable of producing the LLVM **intermediate representation** (**IR**), using the default pass pipeline augmented with your target-specific set of LLVM IR passes. It is only much later in this book that this backend will be able to produce assembly code and object files.

Let's now get started with the technical requirements.

# Technical requirements

In this chapter, we will build LLVM from sources, and as such, all the requirements of *Chapter 1* apply. In other words, you need a working version of Git, CMake, Python, and a C++ toolchain. Refer to *Chapter 1* to see how to meet these requirements.

Additionally, in this chapter, we introduce a second repository for all the changes that need to happen directly in LLVM when adding a new backend. This repository is available at `https://github.com/PacktPublishing/LLVM-Code-Generation-by-example`. This repository is a clone of the LLVM open source repository, which we augmented with all the code changes that are required to create a new backend.

In other words, this repository holds the complete code changes that are mentioned in the snippets presented in this chapter, and by looking at the details of each commit, you can see how things connect in the build system, and so on. To look at the details of each commit, you can use the `git log -p` command line on this repository.

In particular, we have created tags for you to make it easy to follow the changes specific to this chapter. These tags are `begin_ch9` and `end_ch9` for, respectively, the first and last commit of this chapter.

Using these tags, you can easily see all the changes made in this chapter in one Git `diff`:

```
$ git diff begin_ch9^..end_ch9
```

You can navigate all the commits made for this chapter:

```
$ git log begin_ch9^..end_ch9
```

And you see all the changes per commit for this chapter:

```
$ git log -p begin_ch9^..end_ch9
```

You should use this repository as a guideline on how to build your own backend. The commits have been sliced such that they are all individually correct, meaning that the code compiles and passes the **LLVM integrated test** (**lit**) checks at each commit, and they also come with detailed commit messages that tell you what is being done and what the state is after the related commit.

When working on your own backend, you will want to create a similar structure to what is shown in this repository in your own fork of LLVM.

Going forward, the backend that we will build is completely made up, meaning that it does not represent real hardware that you can buy. However, we chose its characteristics such that we cover a wide range of use cases, and this should give you enough material to tackle anything that you may encounter in a real backend.

The name of the backend that we will develop, starting in this chapter, is H2BLB, which stands for *how to build an LLVM backend*, and as you learned in *Chapter 1*, this means that the bulk of the changes happen in `${LLVM_SRC}/llvm/lib/Target/H2BLB`, where `${LLVM_SRC}` is the path where you cloned the Git repository mentioned earlier. Going forward, we will describe the directory paths relative to `${LLVM_SRC}` unless otherwise specified.

Now that you are all set, let's get started with adding this new backend to the LLVM build system.

# Adding a new backend in LLVM

In this section, you will learn how to register a new backend in the LLVM build system and plumb the information of that target all the way up to Clang, such that you can enable this target via a Clang invocation.

By the end of this section, you will be able to create a backend that can produce LLVM IR, with the default optimizing and non-optimizing pass pipelines (that is, the O0, O1, and so on options that you regularly use with your favorite compiler toolchain). The optimizations used in these pipelines nevertheless still use the default target information currently.

Let's dive into the details!

## Connecting your target to the build system

Each LLVM backend lives in its own directory under llvm/lib/Target/<MyTarget>, where <MyTarget> is the name of your backend. In our case, we will create an H2BLB directory.

Your first task consists of connecting this new directory to the LLVM build system.

The connection to the build system involves two main tasks:

* Registering your target in CMake
* Providing a few required functions

The registration is straightforward – you simply add an entry to the list of available targets in the CMakeLists.txt file that lives in llvm. To do that, you either add your target to the LLVM_ALL_TARGETS variable or the LLVM_ALL_EXPERIMENTAL_TARGETS variable. The differences between the variables are whether your target is considered experimental or a main target (as the names of the variables imply) or whether it will be built by default. The experimental targets are not built by default.

For H2BLB, we decided to modify the LLVM_ALL_TARGETS variable, which translates to the following snippet:

```
set(LLVM_ALL_TARGETS
  AArch64
  <snip>
  H2BLB
  <snip>
)
```

Next, you need to provide the C functions that allow you to initialize the different elements of your backend.

This is mandatory because when you enable a backend, the LLVM build system automatically populates `InitializeAllTargets`, `InitializeAllTargetMCs`, and so on, with the related `LLVMInitializeXXXTargetYYYs` calls (one per enabled backend), where XXX is the target name and YYY is the component being initialized.

These functions are used by the tools built on top of LLVM (for instance, Clang) to register and initialize the target-specific elements of the related components.

More specifically, to compile your target with the LLVM build system, you must provide the following three C functions, here named for the H2BLB target:

- `void LLVMInitializeH2BLBTargetInfo()`: This function registers the instance of the `Target` class, from the MC library, for this backend. We will describe what the `Target` class is shortly.

- `void LLVMInitializeH2BLBTargetMC()`: This function registers the **machine code (MC)** components of this backend in the instance of the `Target` class of this backend. The MC components represent a low-level description of a target, such as the number of registers it has or how to produce object files. You will discover more about this as we progress through the book.

- `void LLVMInitializeH2BLBTarget()`: This function registers the target-specific `TargetMachine` instance, from the `Target` library, in the instance of the `Target` class of this backend. `TargetMachine` provides methods to enable and control the various pieces of the LLVM codegen infrastructure. We will discuss this in more detail as we progress through the rest of this book.

The `Target` class is a helper class that acts as a factory for the various components that make a target-specific backend. For instance, the `Target::createMCRegInfo` method gets you an instance of the target-specific `MCRegisterInfo` class. In other words, it returns a version of the `MCRegisterInfo` class that exactly models this backend with its specific registers, register classes, and so on.

The role of the `LLVMInitializeXXX` functions is to populate the `Target` instance with the constructors of the related components. The way it works is that each `LLVMInitializeXXX` gets a hold of the same unique `Target` instance that, by construction, represents this backend and uses the mechanism offers by the `TargetRegistry` class, also from the MC library, to register the constructors.

For the sake of connecting your target to the build system, these `LLVMInitiailizeXXX` functions can be left empty to begin with, which is what we do. For now, we will focus on setting up the proper directory structure.

Therefore, as a first step, you will want to create the following structure in your backend directory (in our case, `llvm/lib/Target/H2BLB`):

- `CMakeLists.txt`: The main file that describes your backend to the CMake build system.
- `H2BLBTargetMachine.cpp`: Holds the implementation of the target-specific `TargetMachine` instance. Hence, since we are only creating the structure of the backend at this point, we will provide only the implementation of `LLVMInitializeH2BLBTarget`.

- MCTargetDesc: Holds all the MC components of the backend:

    - CMakeLists.txt: The file that describes the MC components to the build system.
    - H2BLBMCTargetDesc.cpp: Holds the MC target descriptions of the backend. Currently, this is only the LLVMInitializeH2BLBTargetMC function.

- TargetInfo: Holds the information about the Target.
- CMakeLists.txt: The CMake file for the target information.

    - H2BLBTargetInfo.cpp: The implementation of the Target information for this backend. Hence, currently, this is only the implementation of LLVMInitializeH2BLBTargetInfo.

- H2BLBTargetInfo.h: The header for the Target information. This header will be required to get access to the unique Target instance of this backend in the other LLVMInitializeH2BLBXXX functions (for instance, in the H2BLBTargetMachine.cpp file).

Now, let's dive into the details. For the .cpp files, at this stage, just add an empty implementation of LLVMInitializeH2BLBXXX. For instance, for H2BLBTargetInfo.cpp, this looks like the following:

```
#include "llvm/Support/Compiler.h" // For LLVM_EXTERNAL_VISIBILITY.
extern "C" LLVM_EXTERNAL_VISIBILITY void LLVMInitializeH2BLBTargetInfo() {}
```

If you remember from *Chapter 1*, some of the LLVM APIs are exposed as a C API. The LLLVMInitializeXXX functions are part of this C API. As such, you must use extern "C" to keep the LLVMInitializeH2BLBTargetInfo function as a C symbol and not a C++ one. In other words, you must disable the mangling for this function, which means you must disable how symbols are made unique to allow function overloading. For instance, the mangled symbols of the function with the void foo(int) and void foo(float) prototypes are, respectively, __Z3fooi and __Z3foof on macOS. (To get the unmangled name, you can use the c++filt command-line tool.) Note how we used the LLVM_EXTERNAL_VISIBILITY macro to make sure that the related symbol is exported in the current library such that the LLVM build system will be able to link against it.

Next, since this is the first time you have written CMake code in the LLVM infrastructure, let's show you what the CMakeLists.txt files look like. Indeed, the LLVM build system offers additional CMake functions that encapsulate the default CMake functionalities.

So, here is the content of CMakeLists.txt at the root of the H2BLB directory:

```
add_llvm_component_group(H2BLB)

add_llvm_target(H2BLBCodeGen
  H2BLBTargetMachine.cpp


  LINK_COMPONENTS
  H2BLBDesc
  H2BLBInfo
```

```
    Support

    ADD_TO_COMPONENT
    H2BLB
)

add_subdirectory(MCTargetDesc)
add_subdirectory(TargetInfo)
```

In this snippet, you can see the use of a couple of LLVM-specific CMake functions:

- add_llvm_component_group: Creates a new component name that can be used to aggregate dependencies. In this case, we create an LLVM component named H2BLB, which means that the LLVM build system can get all the dependencies of this backend with just one name.
- add_llvm_target: Creates a new CMake build target. The first argument is the name of the target. The next arguments are all the .cpp files that must be built as part of this target. The use of the LINK_COMPONENTS variable means that this target depends on the listed libraries. In this case, we say that the target-specific codegen library (H2BLBCodeGen) depends on the target-specific H2BLBDesc and H2BLBInfo libraries (defined in the subdirectories – see the related CMakeLists.txt files in the related directory to see their names) and the LLVM generic library, Support, which we need, since we included the llvm/Support/Compiler.h file in H2BLBTargetMachine.cpp (that is, one of the files listed in this target). Then, ADD_TO_COMPONENT makes sure this target is added to the LLVM component of the same name, as defined by the add_llvm_component_group function. Finally, this function tells the LLVM build system to add the current directory to the search paths of the include directories.

> **Note**
> If you are curious about the implementation of the LLVM-specific CMake functions, you can find them under llvm/cmake.

The add_subdirectory calls simply tell CMake to scan through the subdirectory to find further CMakeLists.txt files and, thus, more targets. This is a built-in CMake function.

> **Note**
> In this particular case, we could avoid listing Support as one of the dependencies of our H2BLBCodeGen library because LLVM_ATTRIBUTE_VISIBILITY_DEFAULT is just a macro that sets an attribute; thus, it does not pull any symbols from this library. That being said, we believe it is good practice to still list these kinds of dependencies because this may expose some layering issues in the general architecture of the backend. For instance, let's say that libA depends on a header from libB but does not need to link against it, while libB depends on libA for linking. By not listing that libA depends on libB, you may be hiding circular dependencies that, sooner or later, will come back to haunt you.

The content of the CMakeLists.txt file under llvm/lib/Target/H2BLB/TargetInfo looks like this:

```
add_llvm_component_library(LLVMH2BLBInfo
  H2BLBTargetInfo.cpp

  LINK_COMPONENTS
  Support

  ADD_TO_COMPONENT
  H2BLB
  )
```

By now, you should be able to completely grasp what this snippet does. If this is not the case, reread the explanation of the first CMakeLists.txt.

Then, you should be able to write the content of the CMakeLists.txt file for the MCTargetDesc. Feel free to look at the implementation in the repository if you cannot.

Going forward, we will not present the changes in the CMakeLists.txt file unless they require something new. For instance, when we add more code to our backend, additional LLVM libraries will need to be listed in the LINK_COMPONENTS CMake variable. We will not show how and which components needs to be added to this variable, since these are mechanical changes. Your cue that this needs to happen will be when a piece of code uses something from a new library (for instance, when we use the Target class from the MC library, you will need to add a dependency on MC). Also, you can always refer back to the code in the repository to find a concrete example of how to modify this CMakeLists.txt file.

Congratulations! Now, your backend is connected to the LLVM infrastructure. This means you can compile it using the regular LLVM mechanism presented in *Chapter 1*. For instance, for the H2BLB target, you can now build LLVM after having configured it with LLVM_TARGETS_TO_BUILD=H2BLB.

However, currently, your target is actually useless because it is, unsurprisingly, not connected to anything!

Let's fix that by describing the steps to connect your target to Clang.

## Registering your target with Clang

Registering your target with Clang involves three main steps:

1. Create a new Triple entry to identify your architecture.
2. Populate the Target instance of your backend.
3. Teach Clang about this new architecture.

Let's start with how to modify the Triple class.

# Adding a new architecture to the Triple class

In *Chapter 7*, you learned that `Triple` describes the three main characteristics of the target – the architecture, the vendor, and the **operating system (OS)**.

When creating a new backend, you must add an entry in the architectures that `Triple` can describe.

This process is straightforward:

1.  Add an entry to the `ArchType` enumeration in the `Triple` class, in `llvm/include/llvm/TargetParser/Triple.h`.

2.  Add a case for this new enumeration value to all the switches controlled by `ArchType` in `llvm/lib/TargetParser/Triple.cpp` (for instance, in `Triple::getArchTypeName(ArchType Kind)` and `Triple::getArchTypePrefix(ArchType Kind)`).

A few of the switches that you will modify are simple mappings between strings and the new enumeration value. Other switches give some information about the target. For instance, `Triple::isLittleEndian()` returns true if the architecture is a little-endian target.

For the H2BLB target, our `Triple` describes a little-endian 32-bit target with 16-bit pointers that supports several object file formats – **Common Object File Format (COFF)** for Windows, **Mach object file format (Mach-O)** for the Apple system, and **Executable and Linkable Format (ELF)** for the rest (COFF, ELF, and Mach-O are standard object file formats).

We describe the supported object file formats with the following code snippet:

```
static Triple::ObjectFormatType getDefaultFormat(const Triple &T) {
  switch (T.getArch()) {
  case Triple::h2blb:
    switch (T.getOS()) {
    case Triple::Win32:
    case Triple::UEFI:
      return Triple::COFF;
    default:
      return T.isOSDarwin() ? Triple::MachO : Triple::ELF;
    }
    <snip>

unsigned Triple::getArchPointerBitWidth(llvm::Triple::ArchType Arch) {
  switch (Arch) {
  case llvm::Triple::h2blb:
    return 16;
  <snip>
```

```
Triple Triple::get32BitArchVariant() const {
  Triple T(*this);
  switch (getArch()) {
  case llvm::Triple::h2blb:
    // This is already in 32-bit
    return T;
<snip>
```

As you can see in this snippet, describing the aforementioned constraints is mechanical.

Now that `Triple` exists for our architecture, we can use it to populate the `TargetRegistry` object that we mentioned in the previous section.

## Populating the Target instance

Initially, we created empty implementations of the `LLVMInitializeXXX` functions.

Now that we have an `ArchType` value for our backend, we can revisit these implementations to create the related components through the `Target` class instance of our backend.

First, we start by creating a singleton instance of the `Target` class in the `H2BLBInfo` library. As seen in a previous section, remember that the `Target` class comes from the MC library. (This is your hint to update the `CMakeLists.txt` file.) We do that by adding a new function to the `llvm/lib/Target/H2BLB/TargetInfo/H2BLBTargetInfo.cpp` file and by exposing this function in the `llvm/lib/Target/H2BLB/TargetInfo/H2BLBTargetInfo.h` file.

The snippet for the `H2BLBTargetInfo.h` class is as follows:

```
namespace llvm {
class Target;

Target &getTheH2BLBTarget();
} // end namespace llvm.
```

The snippet for `H2BLBTargetInfo.cpp` is as follows:

```
#include "llvm/TextAPI/Target.h" // For Target class.
using namespace llvm;

Target &llvm::getTheH2BLBTarget() {
  static Target TheH2BLBTarget;
  return TheH2BLBTarget;
}
```

Note how the implementation of getTheH2BLBTarget returns a static instance of the Target class. This ensures that the Target instance that we return will be unique across different calls.

> **On thread-safety**
>
> It is okay to implement a singleton pattern like this, as the LLVM infrastructure explicitly states that the target initializations are expected to be done in only one thread. In other words, it is fine to not be thread-safe.

Now that we have the unique instance of the Target class for our backend, we can use it in the relevant LLVMInitializeXXX functions.

To expose our backend to Clang, we need to implement two of the three functions we have presented so far.

The first one, LLVMInitializeH2BLBTargetInfo, in H2BLBTargetInfo.cpp, maps the ArchType value to the Target instance:

```
extern "C" LLVM_EXTERNAL_VISIBILITY void LLVMInitializeH2BLBTargetInfo() {
  RegisterTarget<Triple::h2blb, /*HasJIT=*/false> X(
      getTheH2BLBTarget(), /*Name=*/"h2blb",
      /*Desc=*/"How to build an LLVM backend by example",
      /*BackendName=*/"H2BLB");
}
```

Note that we omitted the include files for conciseness, but you can find the full code in the repository referred to in the *Technical requirements* section.

This snippet uses the TargetRegistry mechanism, from the MC library, to register our instance of the Target class under the Triple::h2blb enumeration. The string arguments are used in various help messages.

The second thing that we need to set up is the TargetMachine instance of our backend. Clang uses it to create the right codegen pipeline.

For now, we do not need to worry about the codegen pipeline; we will address that later in this book – for instance, we can create the skeleton of what is going to be our TargetMachine implementation.

To achieve that, we will create a new H2BLBTargetMachine.h file under llvm/lib/Target/H2BLB, which holds the declaration of our TargetMachine specialization called H2BLBTargetMachine:

```
class H2BLBTargetMachine : public CodeGenTargetMachineImpl {
public:
  H2BLBTargetMachine(const Target &T, const Triple &TT,
                     StringRef CPU,
                     StringRef FS,
                     const TargetOptions &Options,
```

```
                          std::optional<Reloc::Model> RM,
                          std::optional<CodeModel::Model> CM,
                          CodeGenOptLevel OL,
                          bool JIT);
  ~H2BLBTargetMachine() override;
};
```

The arguments of the constructor must match the provided list, irrespective of the backend you are implementing, in order to connect properly with the mechanism provided by the `TargetRegistry` class. In other words, if you do not understand why you need so many arguments for your `TargetMachine` instance, do not worry – we will explain them shortly, and, in any case, they are mandatory to play nice with the rest of the infrastructure.

> **Note**
>
> If you look at the arguments of the constructor of the parent class of our target-specific `TargetMachine` class (that is, the arguments of the constructor of the `CodeGenTargetMachineImpl` class), you will see that the lists for the `H2BLBTargetMachine` and `CodeGenTargetMachineImpl` classes do not match. This is expected because what we are matching here are the requirements of the `TargetRegistry` class (which come from the `TargetRegistry::TargetMachineCtorTy` function pointer). These arguments cover a superset of what is needed for the `CodeGenTargetMachineImpl` class.

Now that we have declared our class, we need to implement it.

We do that in the `H2BLBTargetMachine.cpp` file:

```
static const char *H2BLBDataLayoutStr =
    "e-p:16:16:16-n16:32-i32:32:32-i16:16:16-i1:8:8-f32:32:32-v32:32:32";

H2BLBTargetMachine::H2BLBTargetMachine(const Target &T, const Triple &TT,
                                       StringRef CPU, StringRef FS,
                                       const TargetOptions &Options,
                                       std::optional<Reloc::Model> RM,
                                       std::optional<CodeModel::Model> CM,
                                       CodeGenOptLevel OL, bool JIT)
    : CodeGenTargetMachineImpl(T, H2BLBDataLayoutStr, TT, CPU, FS, Options,
                   // Use the simplest relocation by default.
                   RM ? *RM : Reloc::Static, CM ? *CM : CodeModel::Small,
                   OL) {}

H2BLBTargetMachine::~H2BLBTargetMachine() = default;
```

In this snippet, the bulk of the code simply propagates the constructor arguments to the constructor of the parent class. Things are not as simple for the optional arguments. The parent constructor does not support them, so our target must provide default values. In this case, we use the simplest/most standard modeling – static relocation and small code mode. While this may seem like gibberish for you currently, this is fine, since we have not connected anything useful yet, so the actual values do not matter.

Now, as promised, here is an explanation of the various arguments:

- `T` is the `Target` singleton of our backend.
- `TT` is an instance that represents the `Triple` object for our backend and, based on its value, we may do something differently for instance based on the target OS, and so on.
- `CPU` is the string that represents the name of the CPU we instantiate our backend for. For instance, you may instantiate the X86 backend for different generations of CPUs such as Skylake or Haswell. Different generations of CPUs may have access to different features, so your `TargetMachine` may need to be slightly different to accommodate that. For instance, an old GPU may use 32-bit pointers, whereas a more recent one may use 64-bit pointers.
- `FS` stands for **feature string**. This is a list of different features that the caller of this constructor may want to enable (prefixed with +) or disable (prefixed with -). For instance, from the Clang command line, `-Xclang -target-feature -Xclang +sse2,-sse` would tell the `TargetMachine` to disable the SSE instruction set while enabling the SSE2 instruction set, which are two different X86 instruction extensions of the base instruction set.
- `Options` sets the default behavior for the target, for things such as how are math instructions interpreted (remember our discussion about fast math flags in *Chapter 4*).
- `RM` represents the relocation model for the binary. In a nutshell, this affects how symbols are accessed. For instance, to call the `foo` function, we may have the address of `foo` available directly, which is the static mode. Alternatively, the `foo` function may be placed in memory at runtime, and we need to rely on a dynamically populated relocation table to resolve the address of `foo`. You can imagine that, depending on these two different modes, we could produce different sequences of instructions. In Clang, this is controlled with the `-mrelocation-model` option.
- `CM` represents the code model that codegen targets. This essentially tells the compiler how big you expect your final binary to be. Most targets default to the `small` mode, which means that the program and its symbols must fit in the lower 2 GB of the final executable. This has some implications on the kind of address computation you must generate. For instance, in `small` mode, it may be fine to use relative addressing from the program counter, whereas in `large` mode you must fully compute the address. You can play with this parameter by using `-mcmodel` in Clang.
- `OL` represents the optimization level. In Clang, that would be `-O0`, `-O1`, and so on.
- `JIT` indicates whether codegen is being run in a **just-in-time** (JIT) setting. When using JIT, for instance, the target may want to scale down its pass pipeline to have a better compile time.

Finally, at the beginning of this snippet, you will recognize a data layout string. This string is one of the arguments of the parent constructor, so your backend must provide it.

The details do not matter, and every target has its own data layout. If you want to decode this string, refer to *Chapter 7*. For the purpose of this book, we chose the data layout to make things interesting! If you really want to assess your understanding of this string, you can check out the commit messages in the repository.

Now that we have our `TargetMachine`, we need to register it so that Clang (and other tools) can find it. This is what the following snippet, from `H2BLBTargetMachine.cpp`, does:

```
extern "C" LLVM_EXTERNAL_VISIBILITY void LLVMInitializeH2BLBTarget() {
  RegisterTargetMachine<H2BLBTargetMachine> X(getTheH2BLBTarget());
}
```

Now that these two `LLVMInitializeXXX` functions are implemented, external tools, such as Clang, know that `Triple::h2blb` maps to our `Target` singleton and that `Target` singleton can create our `TargetMachine`.

With the plumbing you just did, you can now see your target in the list of available targets in `llc`, using the `--version` option:

```
$ ${LLVM_BUILD}/bin/llc --version
...
  Registered Targets:
    h2blb - How to build an LLVM backend by example
```

The backend will not do anything useful yet; in fact, it will crash `llc`, which is expected at this stage. We will plug in the missing pieces as we go.

The next step is to connect your backend to the Clang target information.

## Plumbing your Target through Clang

To connect our backend to Clang, we need to specialize the `clang::TargetInfo` class, from the `clangBasic` library, and connect it to the values of the `Triple` object that represents our architecture. All these changes need to happen in the `clang` project.

Specifially, in the `clang/lib/Basic/Targets` directory, you need to create a header file for your target specialization.

The content of the file should resemble this:

```
namespace clang {
namespace targets {
class LLVM_LIBRARY_VISIBILITY H2BLBTargetInfo : public TargetInfo {
public:
  H2BLBTargetInfo(const llvm::Triple &Triple, const TargetOptions &)
      : TargetInfo(Triple) {
    resetDataLayout(/*data layout string*/<snip>);
  }
```

```
    void getTargetDefines(const LangOptions &Opts,
                          MacroBuilder &Builder) const override;
    ArrayRef<Builtin::Info> getTargetBuiltins() const override;
<snip>
```

In a nutshell, this snippet declares the target-specific implementation of the `clang::TargetInfo` class.

This implementation must provide two main elements:

- The data layout string for the target by calling `clang::TargetInfo::resetDataLayout` within the constructor.
- An implementation of the various pure virtual functions of the `clang::TargetInfo` base class (for instance, `getTargetDefines` or `getTargetBuiltins`). The implementation of these functions provides key target-specific information to Clang and, by extension, opens up neat use cases for your user. For instance, in the case of the H2BLB backend, we added a macro that defined the preprocessor variable, `__H2BLB__`, which our users can leverage in preprocessor statements such as `ifdef`.

For the purpose of connecting our backend in Clang, the content of these methods does not matter; therefore, you can focus on creating a minimally viable implementation. For instance, our implementation of the `getTargetBuiltins` method simply returns `std::nullopt`.

However you decide to approach the implementation, if you are struggling to come up with the minimal implementation or are unsure which methods should be overloaded, you can look at what we did with the H2BLB backend in the `clang/lib/Basic/Targets/H2BLBTargetInfo.cpp` file in the repository referred to in *Technical requirements*. Note that we will not cover how to implement these functions beyond what is covered in this chapter.

Also, remember to update the list of the `.cpp` files that are part of the `clangBasic` library in he `clang/lib/Basic/CMakeLists.txt` file.

Currently, you have a `clang::TargetInfo` implementation that represents your backend on the Clang side. The only thing remaining is to connect your backend with `Triple` in the Clang code base.

To do that, you must add a case in the `switch` statement of the `AllocateTarget` function in `clang/lib/Basic/Targets.cpp`. It should resemble something like this:

```
    case llvm::Triple::h2blb:
        return std::make_unique<H2BLBTargetInfo>(Triple, Opts);
```

Remember to include your header for the `H2BLBTargetInfo` class too!

Congratulations! Your backend is now connected to Clang. This means that you can trigger it by using a triple with your architecture (for instance, h2blb-unknown) or by using the print-targets option:

```
$ ${BUILD_LLVM}/bin/clang --print-targets

  Registered Targets:
    ...
    h2blb       - How to build an LLVM backend by example
```

However, note that, at this stage, you cannot generate anything target-specific, and if your compilation pipeline enables any of the backend-specific parts, it will crash.

Concretely, at this point, you can generate LLVM IR for your backend using -emit-llvm but only in O0:

```
$ ${BUILD_LLVM}/bin/clang -target h2blb -O0 -o - -emit-llvm -S input.c
target datalayout = "e-p:16:16:16-n16:32-i32:32:32-i16:16:16-i1:8:8-
f32:32:32-v32:32:32"
target triple = "h2blb"
...
```

In the previous command, we invoked Clang for our backend (-target) without any optimization (-O0) and told it to generate the text representation (-S) of LLVM IR (-emit-llvm). You can see that our backend is correctly connected because the data layout matches what we set up for our target.

To go beyond the non-optimizing pipeline (in other words, to be able to use O1 and upward), you need to create a few different target-specific classes that are used by the optimizers. More specifically, you need to provide an implementation of the following two classes:

- TargetSubtargetInfo: This class exposes several getter functions to access some of the low-level target APIs, such as the target-specific implementation of the TargetLowering class.
- TargetLowering: This class implements the logic to lower LLVM IR to the legacy instruction selector, SelectionDAG.

Similar to what we have been doing so far in this chapter, the implementation of these classes does not need to do anything useful. We just need to provide their skeleton.

Let's start with the target-specific implementation of the TargetLowering class.

This class is usually named XXXTargetLowering and lives in llvm/lib/Target/XXX/XXXISelLowering.<h|cpp>, where XXX is the name of our backend.

Therefore, in our case, the content of H2BLBISelLowering.h looks like this:

```
class H2BLBTargetLowering : public TargetLowering {
public:
  explicit H2BLBTargetLowering(const TargetMachine &TM);
};
```

For conciseness, we have omitted some of the boilerplate code (forward declarations, etc.). As always, refer to the repository link in the *Technical requirements* section to see the actual code.

For the implementation of the `H2BLBTargetLowering` class, we do the strict minimum in `H2BLBISelLowering.cpp`:

```
H2BLBTargetLowering::H2BLBTargetLowering(const TargetMachine &TM)
    : TargetLowering(TM) {}
```

Then, we do exactly the same thing for the `TargetSubtargetInfo` class but this time in the `XXXSubtarget.<h|cpp>` files.

Here is the snippet for `H2BLBSubtarget.h`:

```
class H2BLBSubtarget : public TargetSubtargetInfo {
  virtual void anchor();
  H2BLBTargetLowering TLInfo;
public:
  H2BLBSubtarget(const Triple &TT, StringRef CPU, StringRef FS,
                 const TargetMachine &TM);
  const H2BLBTargetLowering *getTargetLowering() const override {
    return &TLInfo;
  }
};
```

Here is the snippet for `H2BLBSubtarget.cpp`:

```
H2BLBSubtarget::H2BLBSubtarget(const Triple &TT, StringRef CPU, StringRef FS,
                               const TargetMachine &TM)
    : TargetSubtargetInfo(TT, CPU, /*TuneCPU=*/"", FS, /*PF=*/{},
                          /*PD=*/{},
                          /*WPR=*/nullptr,
                          /*WL=*/nullptr,
                          /*RA=*/nullptr, /*IS=*/nullptr,
                          /*OC=*/nullptr, /*FP=*/nullptr),
      TLInfo(TM) {}
```

In all these snippets, there is nothing complicated happening. We have just created target-specific classes of the parent classes that needed targeting. Later in this book, we will populate them with real functionality.

The things to point out relate to the constructor of `H2BLBSubtarget`. In this constructor, you should recognize the arguments that we described for the `TargetMachine` class (for instance, `FS` for the feature string). Also, there is a lot of `nullptr` initialization. Each of these arguments represents some low-level information relating to the scheduling information of the instructions of our sub-target. This information needs to be produced with TableGen, but we do not need it at this point.

Finally, we need to connect our XXXSubtarget to our XXXTargetMachine; we do that by overloading the TargetMachine::getSubtargetImpl function, like so:

```
const H2BLBSubtarget *
H2BLBTargetMachine::getSubtargetImpl(const Function &F) const {
  Attribute CPUAttr = F.getFnAttribute("target-cpu");
  Attribute FSAttr = F.getFnAttribute("target-features");

  StringRef CPU = CPUAttr.isValid() ? CPUAttr.getValueAsString() : TargetCPU;
  StringRef FS = FSAttr.isValid() ? FSAttr.getValueAsString() : TargetFS;

  if (!SubtargetSingleton)
    SubtargetSingleton =
        std::make_unique<H2BLBSubtarget>(TargetTriple, CPU, FS, *this);
  return SubtargetSingleton.get();
}
```

This snippet collects the CPU and feature string requirements from the instance of the instance of the Function class passed as an argument. Then, it creates an instance of our H2BLBSubtarget class with this Function instance. We save this instance in a mutable unique pointer in our TargetMachine object to avoid creating it for each input Function objects. This method is called for each Function object that is compiled in a module.

> **Note**
>
> The proposed implementation is technically too simple to be correct because you may need different instances of the H2BLBSubtarget class for different CPUs or feature strings. In our case, this is fine because we know our target behaves the same way, no matter the content of these inputs. However, generally speaking, you would need to maintain a dictionary of subtargets to match what the Function object passed as argument needs. Look at how the AArch64TargetMachine class does this if you need this functionality.

Let's look back at what we just did. You may wonder why you needed to do all that.

Certain functions have target-specific attributes attached to them. Certain optimizers while compiling these functions ask for the related sub-target, through the TargetMachine instance, to get access to the right TargetLowering information. Different TargetLowering instances may report different costs and push the optimizers in different directions. In other words, what you did is connect the optimizers to the information they need, as illustrated by *Figure 9.1*.

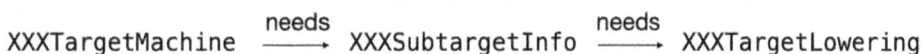

$$XXXTargetMachine \xrightarrow{\text{needs}} XXXSubtargetInfo \xrightarrow{\text{needs}} XXXTargetLowering$$

*Figure 9.1: How optimizers access target information*

After connecting this information, you can now run the default optimizing pipelines. Congratulations!

In this section, you learned how to add a new, mostly empty, backend to LLVM.

You saw how to create the proper directory structure, how to tell to the LLVM build system to take your new backend into account, and which functions and classes you must implement.

You learned how to connect your backend to any tool that uses the built-in `TargetRegistry` mechanism, such as `llc` or `opt`, and then went further by teaching Clang about your backend.

In the next section, you will discover how to thread target-specific constructs, called intrinsics, through Clang.

# Creating your own intrinsics

Intrinsics are special functions that are exposed at the source language level, such as C and C++, that allow to use of target-specific constructs. For instance, the **Advanced Encryption Standard (AES)** instruction set of the AArch64 or X86 backend exposes hardware-accelerated cryptographic instructions that you can leverage to speed up related algorithms.

In this section, you will learn how to expose your own intrinsics to the users of your backend. This task entails teaching Clang about your intrinsics and registering them as valid LLVM IR built-in functions. The connection to the assembly code will be covered in a later chapter, as it requires setting up some infrastructure at the Machine IR level.

In any case, before diving into how to connect such a construct, let's address a high-level question – when do you need an intrinsic?

## The pros and cons of intrinsics

Before you embark on adding an intrinsic, take the time to think about whether you really need one.

On the one hand, intrinsics convey clear semantics, and you can efficiently lower them to the constructs you want. On the other hand, intrinsics are not free!

You have to implement them; most optimization passes cannot do anything with them unless you teach these passes about them, and since they are user-facing, you have to treat them carefully if you want to modify or deprecate them.

Therefore, ask yourself whether you can represent the same semantics with the input language you are targeting. If so, you do not need an intrinsic. You will learn how to pattern-match LLVM IR constructs to specific instructions when reading about instruction selection. Then, if you still think you may need an intrinsic, do not hesitate to play with inline assembly first.

**Inline assembly**, or **inline asm** for short, is a source language level construct that allows you to inject assembly code directly into your program. Using this mechanism, you can quickly check whether using the particular instruction/sequence of instructions you want to achieve is worth plumbing an intrinsic through.

While you can decide that an inline assembly-based solution is good enough for your use case, beware that inline assembly constructs are both a blessing and a curse. Indeed, these constructs are completely opaque to the compiler. Therefore, on the bright side, you can, from the source language, push anything you want through the backend. The backend will just dump that string (modulo inline assembly magic such as register allocation!) in the final assembly code. On the not-so-bright side, the optimizations cannot do anything with inline assembly constructs and must handle them conservatively, which may impact the quality of the surrounding code.

> Note
>
> Inline assembly comes with a predefined syntax. Nevertheless, you can extend it if you have special needs – for example, if you want to expose a particular class of registers differently. These extension points are, in fact, one of the pieces of information that you need to provide when you implement the pure virtual functions of the clang::TargetInfo class that we mentioned in the *Plumbing your Target through Clang* section. Validating your custom assembly constraints must be done in your implementation of the clang::Targ etInfo::validateAsmConstraint method.

In the rest of this section, we will show you how to connect two intrinsics for our H2BLB backend.

These intrinsics will take two 16-bit values, multiply them together, and produce a 32-bit value. The first intrinsic operates on unsigned 16-bit values and the second one on signed 16-bit values.

These intrinsics are expressible in the source language; in C, for instance, the signed variant would look like this:

```
int widening_smul(short a, short b) {
  return a * b;
}
```

Here, the inputs of the multiply are automatically promoted to 32-bit, and thus, the computation does exactly what we want, as opposed to doing the computation on the 16-bit type, for instance.

Therefore, technically, the semantics we want to convey here do not require an intrinsic, and instead, matching the desired sequence of instructions at instruction selection time would yield a better user experience.

However, the mechanism to connect an intrinsic is the same no matter how useful it is, so please indulge the dubious relevance of this particular example!

Before we explain how to make this connection, here is, for completeness, what the inline assembly equivalent of this widening multiply instruction (that is, our intrinsic) would be:

```
int widening_smul(short a, short b) {
  int res;
  asm ("wsmul %0, %1, %2" : "=r" (res) : "r" (a), "r" (b));
```

```
    return res;
}
```

We will not go into the details of the inline asm syntax, but in a nutshell, the statement that starts with the `asm` keyword indicates that what is in parenthesis is an inline assembly statement. The first string is the assembly to be emitted. This string can contain special modifiers (here, %0, %1, and %2), that act as a placeholder for the following arguments – %0 maps to the first argument (res), %1 to the second argument (a), and so on. Note that each argument is decorated with a modifier that specifies their type – =r means a definition in a register, and r means an argument in a register. The colon (:) separates the different types of arguments – first, the result operands, and then the input operands.

After this digression, let's focus on creating an intrinsic.

In the next sections, we will demonstrate a two-part process:

1.  The creation of an intrinsic in LLVM IR (that is, how the backend models this intrinsic).
2.  The generation by Clang of this new intrinsic (that is, how the frontend exposes this intrinsic to the users and how it is connected to the backend intrinsic).

Without further ado, let's see how to create an intrinsic in LLVM IR.

## Creating an intrinsic in the backend

Intrinsics in LLVM IR are represented with the `IntrinsicInst` class, from the IR (Core) library. This class is a sub-class of the `CallInst` class, which is itself a descendant of the `Instruction` class. To cut a long story short, the main distinction between an intrinsic and a function call is that LLVM IR knows that the destination of the call is a built-in function. As such, built-ins come pre-packaged in LLVM IR. In other words, you need to know about them at the **build time** of your compiler. Indeed, intrinsics are identified via `Intrinsic::ID`, which is an enumeration created at build time.

Creating a new intrinsic in the backend means, among other things, adding an entry to this enumeration and describing what the prototype of the intrinsic is so that the parser can reject invalid uses of it.

The implementation is so mechanical and prevalent in LLVM that it has been hidden behind a TableGen backend (invoked with the `gen-intrinsic-enums` option).

In this section, we will teach you how to use the appropriate TableGen classes and definitions to describe your intrinsics, as well as how to invoke the related TableGen backend as part of the build system so that your intrinsics are added to LLVM IR at build time.

*Figure 9.2* shows how the intrinsics' definition for a specific backend fits into the whole LLVM infrastructure.

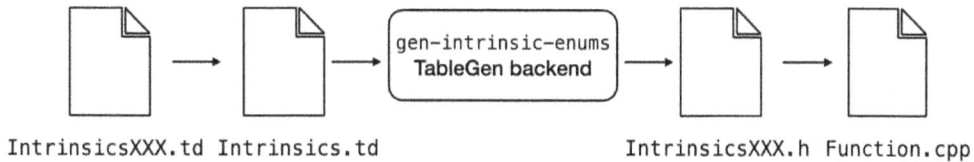

*Figure 9.2: The integration of target-specific intrinsics*

In *Figure 9.2*, you can see that the target-specific intrinsics for the XXX target are put in an IntrinsicsXXX. td file. That file is included in another Intrinsics.td file, located in llvm/include/llvm/IR, that gathers all the intrinsics for all the targets in LLVM. This file is fed to the gen-intrinsic-enums TableGen backend that generates an IntrinsicsXXX.h file, in ${BUILD_DIR}/include/llvm/IR. Finally, this file is included and used in the llvm/lib/IR/Intrinsics.cpp file such that the function definitions at the LLVM IR level know about all the intrinsics.

Now that you know at a high level how to leverage TableGen to produce your intrinsics, you understand that we need to make the following changes:

1.  Add and populate our IntrinsicsXXX.td file.
2.  Include that file in Intrinsics.td.
3.  Hook up the gen-intrinsic-enums TableGen backend to our target.
4.  Include and use the IntrinsicsXXX.h file in the Intrinsics.cpp file.

These mechanical changes should be straightforward and now, we can focus on explaining how to define intrinsics.

## Defining our intrinsics

To define our intrinsics, we need to create a new file, named IntrinsicsH2BLB.td – in our case, in llvm/include/llvm/IR. The content of this file should resemble the following:

```
let TargetPrefix = "h2blb" in {
  def int_h2blb_widening_smul :
  Intrinsic<[llvm_i32_ty], [llvm_i16_ty, llvm_i16_ty]>;
  def int_h2blb_widening_umul :
  Intrinsic<[llvm_i32_ty], [llvm_i16_ty, llvm_i16_ty]>;
} // end TargetPrefix = "h2blb"
```

What you see on the first line of this snippet is a sort of namespace, called TargetPrefix.

If you remember your TableGen syntax from *Chapter 6*, you will know that this effectively sets a TargetPrefix field for all the records (that is, the instances identified with the def keyword) within this block.

Next, you can see that this snippet defines two records named, respectively, `int_h2blb_widening_smul` and `int_h2blb_widening_umul`.

The name of an intrinsic must start with `int_`; otherwise, the TableGen backend will complain when processing them. Then, for target-specific intrinsics, it is recommended to put the target prefix (in this case, `h2blb`) right after the `int_` string. Finally, you have the actual name of the intrinsic – in this case, `widening_smul` and `widening_umul`.

By default, the TableGen backend produces the name of the built-in LLVM IR functions by replacing `int_` with `llvm.` and all the other underscores (`_`) in the name of the record with a dot (`.`). For instance, `int_h2blb_widening_smul` will show up in the textual LLVM IR representation as `llvm.h2blb.widening.smul`. You can change this default by assigning a non-empty string to the name field (the fourth argument) of the `Intrinsic<...>` instance of your record.

The `Intrinsic` class, defined in the `Intrinsics.td` file, takes many more arguments, but only the first argument, which describes the return type of the intrinsic, is mandatory.

We will not go into any more detail; just know that with the other arguments of the `Intrinsic` class , you can specify properties that will affect:

- The optimizers; for instance, the `IntrSpeculatable` property tells the  optimizers that they can move your intrinsic across conditional blocks
- The instruction selector; for instance the `SDNPCommutative` property tells the selector that your intrinsic is commutative

Finally, you also have a way to enable or disable the properties added by default to your intrinsic.

The default properties are gathered from the union of what is defined in `Intrinsics.td` and the backend-specific file (look for `IntrinsicProperty<1>` to find them), which are good properties to have unless you are doing something unconventional (for instance, modeling a trap instruction, which would not satisfy the default `IntrWillReturn` property since it will cause the system to abort).

Back to our snippet – the first two arguments are, respectively, the return type and the list of the type of the arguments of the intrinsic. In our case, both intrinsics use the predefined types (see the next note), return a 32-bit integer, and take two 16-bit integers as input.

`Intrinsics.td` offers a lot of predefined types, but you can always create yours by creating your own records from the `LLVMType` class. This class takes `ValueType` as as parameter, which gives you plenty of existing choices (see `llvm/include/llvm/CodeGen/ValueTypes.td`). Nevertheless, if this is not satisfactory, you can create your own `ValueType` as well.

A family of types

The predefined types provide records to model a family of types. You can find them by looking for the records named llvm_anyxxx_ty. For instance, llvm_anyfloat_ty allows you to define intrinsics that support all the family of floating-point types, such as single precision and double precision, with only one record, as opposed to one record by actual type. In other words, instead of having one record of your intrinsic for the half type, one record for float type, and so on, you only have one record for all of them. This shrinks the number of records you have to write and the number of intrinsics you have to support down the line. However, beware of how you use these types because you may allow inputs that you may not support. For instance, [llvm_anyfloat_ty, llvm_anyfloat_ty] means that you take two inputs of the floating-point family, but in this form, there is nothing that prevents the first argument from having a different type than the second argument. Therefore, this syntax means that you support the cartesian product of all the combinations of these two families of types (that is, (float, float), (float, half), (half, float), etc.). If, instead, you want to state that you support any floating-point type but that both arguments must have the same type, you can use something such as [llvm_anyfloat_ty, LLVMMatchType<0>], which tells TableGen that the type of the second argument must be the same as the type of the first one; otherwise, the intrinsic is invalid. Technically, LLVMMatchType<0> reads as the type of the generic type that appears in index 0 in the list of the generic types used in the intrinsic definition. Read the comments in Intrinsics.td to learn more about this kind of matching and discover other fancy features you can leverage.

So, we have our definitions of our intrinsics; now, we need to add them to the main Intrinsics.td file. This is achieved by adding the following line to this file:

```
include "llvm/IR/IntrinsicsH2BLB.td"
```

Make sure to insert this line where the other backends put their include statements; otherwise, you run into the risk of including your file too early and missing some class definitions.

Let's see how to make the build system feed our intrinsics to the proper TableGen backend.

## Hooking up the TableGen backend

Like everything related to the build system in LLVM, hooking up a TableGen backend in the build system means modifying the related CMakeLists.txt file. In this case, the CMakeLists.txt file that we must modify is in llvm/include/llvm/IR.

You need to add the following line to this file:

```
tablegen(LLVM IntrinsicsH2BLB.h -gen-intrinsic-enums -intrinsic-prefix=h2blb)
```

This line tells the build system to run the LLVM TableGen tool, ${BUILD_DIR}/bin/llvm-tblgen (the first argument), to produce IntrinsicsH2BLB.h (the second argument), using the -gen-intrinsic-enums -intrinsic-prefix=h2blb command-line options (the remaining arguments).

If you paid attention, you will have noticed that this line does not specify the input file. This is expected. The input file was previously specified in `CMakeLists.txt` by setting the proper variable:

```
set(LLVM_TARGET_DEFINITIONS Intrinsics.td)
```

You could technically change this to your `IntrinsicsXXX.td` file and run TableGen only on this file, but you would have to then include the `Intrinsics.td` file in your `IntrinsicsXXX.td` file to get the definition of all the classes you use, so ultimately, it would not simplify anything.

For completeness, if you look at the end of `CMakeLists.txt`, you will find the following line:

```
add_public_tablegen_target(intrinsics_gen)
```

This line tells the build system that all TableGen commands registered so far must be run under the `intrinsics_gen` build target. This means that if you want to only generate the header files for the intrinsics (for instance, for faster iteration on this particular aspect of your development), you can run this one target with the following:

```
$ ninja intrinsics_gen
```

At this stage of the development, we have our intrinsic definitions properly generated in a header file. The next step is to use this header file in `Intrinsics.cpp`.

## Teaching LLVM IR about our intrinsics

The final step to make our intrinsics part of LLVM IR is to plumb through the generated header file, `IntrinsicsH2BLB.h` – in our case, in `Intrinsics.cpp`.

To achieve this, you simply include it in `Intrinsics.cpp`:

```
#include "llvm/IR/IntrinsicsH2BLB.h"
```

And that's it!

At this point, you can write LLVM IR that uses your target-specific intrinsics. They are not connected to the lower part of the LLVM infrastructure yet (Machine IR and below), but this is expected.

Now that we have created a substrate for our intrinsics in LLVM IR, the next step is to teach Clang how to generate these intrinsics from a source language.

## Connecting an intrinsic to Clang

In Clang, you create built-in functions that produce specific LLVM IR constructs. In other words, while this mechanism primarily focuses on exposing intrinsics at the source language level, you can in fact do much more with it. For instance, you can create, at the source language level, your own built-ins to expose a sequence of pure LLVM IR instructions, such as `shufflevector` followed by `atomicrmw`. The point is that this is a powerful mechanism, and we will not cover it entirely. Instead, in this section, we will focus solely on the use case of connecting intrinsics.

Like many things in LLVM, connecting an intrinsic can be done in many ways. In particular, in January 2024, the LLVM infrastructure added a TableGen-driven way of describing intrinsics to produce the right source language-level prototypes.

In this section, we will show you how to use the new and old ways of doing this, as the transition to the new way only applies to the generic Clang built-ins and a handful of targets. In other words, realistically, you still need to understand how the old way works to be able to contribute to existing targets (or work with an older LLVM code base.)

The good news is that the old and new ways are likely to be compatible for a while and can be used interchangeably, as the new way produces under the hood what you used to write manually in the old way. *Figure 9.3* illustrates the differences between the two approaches.

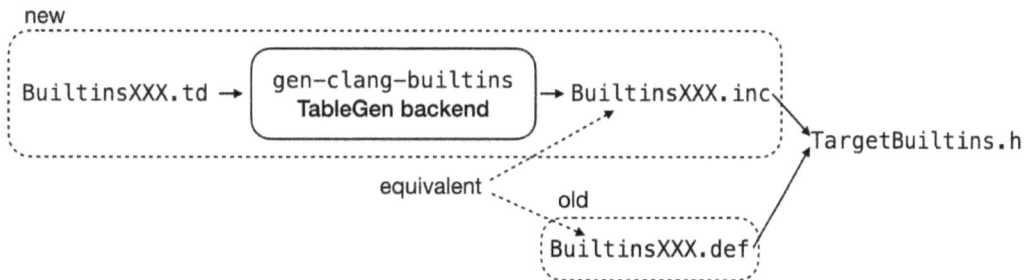

Figure 9.3: The different ways to describe intrinsics in Clang

In *Figure 9.3*, you can see that the new way describes the intrinsics in a .td file. That file is then consumed by the gen-clang-builtins (Clang-)TableGen backend to produce a .inc file that is used in TargetBuiltins.h. Conversely, the old way feeds directly a .def file to TargetBuiltins.h. If you look closer at the content of the produced .inc file and the handwritten content of the .def file, they are equivalent, if not identical. The advantage of the new way is that the syntax is more compact and easier to understand.

To illustrate this, let's implement our H2BLB intrinsics with the old method and then do the same with the new way.

## Writing the .def file by hand

The .def file that describes your target intrinsics is a C++ file that will be directly included in the TargetBuiltins.h file, in the clangBasic library. The content of this file is expected to use three different C macros:

- BUILTIN: Defines intrinsics that are always available for your target. It takes three arguments:
  - ID: The source language-level name that will be exposed to the user
  - TYPE: The types of the result and arguments
  - ATTRS: The attributes, such as whether this intrinsic has side effects or does not return

- **TARGET_BUILTIN**: Defines intrinsics available only for certain target features. It takes the same arguments as the BUILTIN macro and has an additional FEATURE argument that describes the feature string, behind which this intrinsic is hidden. In other words, setting an empty feature string is equivalent to using the BUILTIN macro.
- **LIBBUILTIN**: Defines intrinsics that are exposed only through specific header files and available only for specific source languages. It takes the same arguments as the BUILTIN macro and adds two more:
    - **HEADER**: Where the prototypes are defined. The user must include this header to use them.
    - **LANG**: In which language this intrinsic is available.

The TYPE and ATTRS arguments are the trickiest to set and are the reason why a new approach was added. You will understand why in a minute!

For the H2BLB target, the content of BuiltinsH2BLB.def, located in clang/include/clang/Basic, is as follows:

```
TARGET_BUILTIN(__builtin_h2blb_widening_smul, "SiSsSs", "nc", "")
TARGET_BUILTIN(__builtin_h2blb_widening_umul, "UiUsUs", "nc", "")
```

As you can see, the TYPE arguments (SiSsSs and UiUsUs, respectively) and the ATTRS arguments (nc in both cases) look like gibberish if you do not know how to interpret them.

For the TYPE argument, the string describes the constraints on the result type, followed by the constraints on the argument types using the C-style types. SiSsSs reads as a signed (S) int (i) result, followed by a signed (S) short (s) argument and another signed (S) short (s) argument. In other words, this string describes a prototype that looks in the C, int(short, short). The string for the second built-in reads similarly, except that we used unsigned (U) instead of signed (S).

The TYPE string can become much more complicated as you add decorators for pointer types, and so on.

Now, for the ATTRS argument, the string describes the list of all the function attributes that must be attached to this intrinsic and, thus, which properties this intrinsic has. Each character in this string represents an attribute – n stands for NoThrow (that is, this intrinsic does not throw exceptions), and c stands for Const (that is, this intrinsic is a pure function, meaning that it does not touch anything beyond the arguments that it is given, and when given two different calls to this intrinsic with the same input, it is guaranteed to return the same output).

At this point, you may be wondering where you would find the mapping from these strings to the types/attributes.

Unfortunately, the answer is, by looking at the code of the related parser!

For instance, you can look at the DecodeTypeFromStr function in the clang/lib/AST/ASTContext.cpp file, which is called from the ASTContext::DecodeTypeStr method, or the recent addition, the PrototypeParser::ParseType method in the clang/utils/TableGen/ClangBuiltinsEmitter.cpp file.

In summary, if you can avoid using the old way of describing intrinsics, use the new method; it is much easier to follow, as you will find out in the next section.

## Using the TableGen capabilities

As you saw, coming up with the right string to capture the prototype and attributes of your intrinsic is not a pleasant task, and we guarantee you that when you look at this code in a couple of months, it will take you some time to remember what it does.

Needless to say, the `gen-clang-builtins` TableGen capabilities are a welcome addition for LLVM compiler writers.

In this section, we will show you how to use the new TableGen syntax and enable the related TableGen backend in the build system. However, we will not show you all the bells and whistles that this TableGen backend offers.

All the classes and records used here are defined in `clang/include/clang/Basic/BuiltinsBase.td`. Moreover, the Clang generic built-ins are defined in `clang/include/clang/Basic/Builtins.td`. We encourage you to take a look at the latter, which offers concrete examples of how to leverage things such as the `Template` class for a nice and compact syntax when repeating a prototype for different types.

Let's return to defining H2BLB intrinsics in Clang – instead of writing the `.def` file previously shown, we need to write a `.td` file, `clang/include/clang/Basic/BuiltinsH2BLB.td`.

The content of this file for the first intrinsic should resemble this:

```
def WideningSignedMultiply : TargetBuiltin {
  let Spellings = ["__builtin_h2blb_widening_smul"];
  let Attributes = [NoThrow, Const];
  let Prototype = "int(short, short)";
}
```

As you can see, the syntax itself is more verbose but also easy to understand. You can see the actual names of the attributes (`NoThrow` and `Const`) and the actual C-style prototype (`int(short, short)`) in a field with the related name (`Attributes` and `Prototype`), instead of a cryptic string (`nc` and `SiSsSs`, respectively).

The next and final thing to do is enable the related TableGen backend to produce the `.inc` file that needs to be included in `TargetBuiltins.h`, as shown in *Figure 9.3*.

To do this, add the following lines to the `CMakeLists.txt` file in `clang/include/clang/Basic` around the already existing calls to `clang_tablegen`:

```
clang_tablegen(BuiltinsH2BLB.inc -gen-clang-builtins
  SOURCE BuiltinsH2BLB.td
  TARGET ClangBuiltinsH2BLB)
```

What this snippet does is define a new build target (ClangBuiltinsH2BLB) that will be produced by calling the Clang-TableGen tool (${BUILD_DIR}/bin/clang-tblgen), with the -gen-clang-builtins option and BuiltinsH2BLB.td as an input file and BuiltinsH2BLB.inc as the output file.

Let's now see how to connect the generated .inc file to the TargetBuiltins.h file and do the other required implementations.

## Hooking up the built-in information

Irrespective of how you created your target-specific Clang built-in definitions, you need to hook them up in your clang::TargetInfo class. In this section, we assume you went with the TableGen method, meaning the new way. Hence the snippets in this section use a .inc file. If you used the old method, simply replace .inc with .def in the snippets.

First, we need to teach Clang about the enumeration values that consist of our built-ins. (Note that this enumeration is completely different from the Intrinsic::ID enumeration that we set up in the LLVM IR.) We do this by adding the following lines to TargetBuiltins.h, anywhere within the scope of the clang namespace:

```
namespace H2BLB {
enum {
  LastTIBuiltin = clang::Builtin::FirstTSBuiltin - 1,
#define BUILTIN(ID, TYPE, ATTRS) BI##ID,
#include "clang/Basic/BuiltinsH2BLB.inc"
  LastTSBuiltin
};
} // namespace H2BLB
```

Next, we need to connect these built-ins with the clang::TargetInfo class that we created previously to represent our backend in Clang. To do that, we must implement properly the getTargetBuiltins method that we have left blank so far. We do this in clang/lib/Basic/Targets/H2BLB.cpp with the following snippet:

```
static constexpr Builtin::Info BuiltinInfo[] = {
#define BUILTIN(ID, TYPE, ATTRS)                                    \
  {#ID, TYPE, ATTRS, nullptr, HeaderDesc::NO_HEADER, ALL_LANGUAGES},
#define LIBBUILTIN(ID, TYPE, ATTRS, HEADER)                         \
  {#ID, TYPE, ATTRS, nullptr, HEADER, ALL_LANGUAGES},
#define TARGET_BUILTIN(ID, TYPE, ATTRS, FEATURE)                    \
  {#ID, TYPE, ATTRS, FEATURE, HeaderDesc::NO_HEADER, ALL_LANGUAGES},
#include "clang/Basic/BuiltinsH2BLB.inc"
};

ArrayRef<Builtin::Info> H2BLBTargetInfo::getTargetBuiltins() const {
  return llvm::ArrayRef(BuiltinInfo,
```

```
                              clang::H2BLB::LastTSBuiltin - Builtin::FirstTSBuiltin);
}
```

In this snippet, we create `Builtin::Info` instances for each of our built-ins by leveraging the macros that we saw previously. We recommend defining all three macros (`BUILTIN`, `LIBBUILTIN`, and `TARGET_BUILTIN`) even if you know that you're not using all of them currently. It will save you trouble in the future!

Looking at the definitions of the macros, you can easily identify the main differences:

- `BUILTIN` and `LIBBUILTIN` set `nullptr` for the feature string.
- `BUILTIN` and `TARGET_BUILTIN` set `NO_HEADER` and `ALL_LANGUAGES` to describe that the intrinsics come with the compiler (that is, there's no need to include anything, and they are not specific to the source language).

Finally, we return this information to `H2BLBTargetInfo::getTargetBuiltins` via `ArrayRef`, and we provide the right size of this array by computing the difference of the enum values that we defined in `TargetBuiltins.h` for our target.

Currently, we have all the building blocks set up in Clang; now, we need to connect these intrinsics to the LLVM IR intrinsics that we set up in the backend.

## Establishing the code generation link

In this section, we will explain how to establish the final link between what Clang exposes at the source language level and the LLVM IR intrinsics that we defined previously.

The method presented here works only for intrinsics that have a one-to-one mapping with C-style functions. For instance, an LLVM IR intrinsic using `llvm_anyfloat_ty` does not fall under this category, since several C-style functions can be mapped to it (`float`, `half`, etc.) – that is, this is an $N$-to-one mapping.

> **Going beyond one-to-one mapping**
>
> While establishing an $N$-to-one mapping (or really an $N$-to-$M$ mapping) from source language-level built-ins to LLVM IR constructs is outside the scope of this book, we thought that it is important to get a sense of where this happens so that you know where to start if you ever need to do it. In a nutshell, you need to implement the lowering of your instrinsics through one of the functions called from the `CodeGenFunction::EmitTargetBuiltinExpr` method. Most likely, the path that you are interested in will imply modifying the function called `EmitTargetArchBuiltinExpr` – add an entry for your `Triple` and implement your own `CodeGenFunction::EmitXXXBuiltinExpr` method. There are plenty of examples to choose from!

The one-to-one mapping is completely handled by TableGen. When you define your LLVM IR intrinsic, you only need to have your intrinsic inherit from the `ClangBuiltin` TableGen class, and you are done!

We did some refactoring to our `llvm/include/llvm/IR/IntrinsicsH2BLB.td` file, and here is a snippet of the final result:

```
class H2BLB_Intrinsic<string suffix, list<LLVMType> ret_types,
                              list<LLVMType> param_types>
  : ClangBuiltin<!strconcat("__builtin_h2blb_", suffix)>,
    DefaultAttrsIntrinsic<ret_types, param_types>;


def int_h2blb_widening_smul :
  H2BLB_Intrinsic<"widening_smul", [llvm_i32_ty], [llvm_i16_ty, llvm_i16_ty]>;
```

In a nutshell, we created a new TableGen class called `H2BLB_Intrinsic` that is wrapped around the `ClangBuiltin` class and the intrinsics, with default attributes (the `DefaultAttrsIntrinsic` class).

We then use this new class as the definition of our intrinsic and provide an additional parameter (the first one here), which is the string that represents our built-in in the source language. Note how our call to `ClangBuiltin` prepends `__builtin_h2blb_` to the string we passed to this class.

What happens here is the `ClangBuiltin` class tells the `gen-intrinsic-enums` (LLVM-)TableGen backend to generate the `Intrinsic::getIntrinsicForClangBuiltin` method, mapping the `Intrinsic::ID` value of the LLVM intrinsic with your target prefix and the provided built-in name. Clang calls this function with these arguments (the target prefix and built-in name) to find the `Intrinsic::ID` value to create the related `IntrinsicInst` when producing the LLVM IR.

Finally, you can use your intrinsic in a source language such as C:

```
int widening_signed_multiply(short a, short b) {
  return __builtin_h2blb_widening_smul(a, b);
}
```

Using the previous snippet as input, you can run the following command to see your intrinsic generated in LLVM IR:

```
$ clang -emit-llvm -S -target h2blb -O1 input.c -o -
```

The LLVM IR that you should get should resemble the following:

```
define i32 @widening_signed_multiply(i16 signext %a, i16 signext %b) {
entry:
  %0 = tail call i32 @llvm.h2blb.widening.smul(i16 %a, i16 %b)
  ret i32 %0
}
```

In this section, you learned how to create target-specific intrinsics at the LLVM IR level and how to connect them, all the way up to a source language level, through Clang. This offers your users a unique way to interact with your target.

In the next section, we show you how to set up your `TargetTransformInfo` class. This class allows you to influence optimizers by providing custom cost modeling.

# Adding a target-specific TargetTransformInfo implementation

If you remember what you read in *Chapter 4*, you will know that the `TargetTransformInfo` class, from the `Analysis` library, is used to get some information about the cost of lowering LLVM IR constructs.

In this section, you will learn how to create your own `TargetTransformInfo` implementation to match what your target supports.

## Establishing a connection to your target-specific information

The targeting of `TargetTransformInfo` goes through a helper class, `BasicTTIImplBase`, from the `CodeGen` library, which uses the **curiously recurring template pattern (CRTP)**.

Concretely, you must retarget this helper class and then register it with `TargetTransformInfo` through your `TargetMachine`.

Let's start with the retargeting of `BasicTTIImplBase`.

The following snippet does exactly this:

```
class H2BLBTTIImpl : public BasicTTIImplBase<H2BLBTTIImpl> {
  using BaseT = BasicTTIImplBase<H2BLBTTIImpl>;
  using TTI = TargetTransformInfo;

  friend BaseT;

  const H2BLBSubtarget &ST;
  const H2BLBTargetLowering &TLI;

  const H2BLBSubtarget *getST() const { return &ST; }
  const H2BLBTargetLowering *getTLI() const { return &TLI; }

public:
  explicit H2BLBTTIImpl(const H2BLBTargetMachine *TM, const Function &F)
      : BaseT(TM, F.getDataLayout()), ST(*TM->getSubtargetImpl(F)),
        TLI(*ST.getTargetLowering()) {}
};
```

In this snippet, we create our target-specific `H2BLBTTIImpl` from the `BasicTTIImplBase` class, and we set a few type names (using ...) to make the retargeting easier. Note that we need to make `BaseT` a friend of this class, as CRTP usage in `BasicTTIImplBase` requires that some of the private methods of the target-specific class be accessible to the base class. This snippet lives in `llvm/lib/Target/H2BLB/H2BLBTargetTransformInfo.h`.

Next, we connect this helper class to our `TargetMachine`:

```
TargetTransformInfo
H2BLBTargetMachine::getTargetTransformInfo(const Function &F) const {
  return TargetTransformInfo(H2BLBTTIImpl(this, F));
}
```

This snippet overrides the getter for the `TargetTransformInfo` class using our target-specific implementation. Make sure to update the declaration of the `H2BLBTargetMachine` class accordingly in the `H2BLBTargetMachine.h` file.

At this point, the connection between the LLVM infrastructure and your target-specific `TargetTransformInfo` class is all set.

Next, let's see how we can modify your target-specific `TargetTransformInfo` class to actually provide useful information to the optimizers.

## Introducing target-specific costs

The introduction of target-specific costs in the `TargetTransformInfo` class is as simple as implementing the right overrides in your target-specific implementation of the `BasicTTIImplBase` class.

The methods that you need to override depend on the optimization that you want to influence. Concretely, to know what to override, you have to look at the implementation of an optimizer and check what `TargetTransformInfo` methods it uses.

While this may not be the most efficient way to go about it, this at least gives you a way to prioritize which APIs to focus on first. Indeed, eventually, you will need to override all of them, so just focus on the ones that are the most useful to you first.

To give an example, let's say that we want to influence how the load store vectorizer behaves. Let's say that our target only supports `<2 x i16>` loads and that we do not allow any other form of vector loads to be produced by this optimizer.

To convey this information, we need to add a new public method, `getLoadVectorFactor`, to our `H2BLBTTIImpl` class. The implementation, in `llvm/lib/Target/H2BLB/H2BLBTargetTransformInfo.cpp`, resembles the following snippet:

```
unsigned H2BLBTTIImpl::getLoadVectorFactor(unsigned VF, unsigned LoadSize,
                                           unsigned ChainSizeInBytes,
                                           VectorType *VecTy) const {
  unsigned ElemSize = VecTy->getScalarSizeInBits();
```

```
    if (ElemSize != 16)
      return 0;

    return std::min(VF, 2u);
}
```

In this snippet, we check what vector type the load store vectorizer (or any optimizer that uses this API) wants to produce and reject anything that uses a non-i16 type. (The returned 0 means that we accept only a vector with zero element, hence no vector at all!) For i16 type, we return 2, meaning we allow two-element-wide vectors.

To see this API in action, we can call the load store vectorizer with our target on the following input:

```
define i16 @load_i16x2(ptr %source) {
 %h0 = load i16, ptr %source, align 8
  %idx1 = getelementptr inbounds i16, ptr %source, i64 1
  %h1 = load i16, ptr %idx1, align 8
  %idx2 = getelementptr inbounds i16, ptr %source, i64 2
  %h2 = load i16, ptr %idx2, align 8
  %idx3 = getelementptr inbounds i16, ptr %source, i64 3
  %h3 = load i16, ptr %idx3, align 8
  %add1 = add i16 %h1, %h0
  %add2 = add i16 %h3, %h2
  %res = add i16 %add1, %add2
  ret i16 %res
}
```

This snippet loads four i16 values and does some computation on them. These four loads are next to each other and, thus, coalesce into one <4 x i16> load. However, given that we allow only <2 x i16> load, the load store vectorizer produces two <2 x i16> loads.

You can see this for yourself, using the following command:

```
$ opt -passes=load-store-vectorizer %s -S -mtriple=h2blb input.ll -o -
```

In the repository referred to in the *Technical requirements* section, you can also find an example of how to set up custom costs for your intrinsics. Search for H2BLBTTIImpl::getIntrinsicInstrCost in llvm/lib/Target/H2BLB/H2BLBTargetTransformInfo.cpp.

In this section, you learned how to connect your target-specific TargetTransformInfo implementation. You also saw how you can customize this implementation such that it represents your target accurately.

Our next section teaches you how to inject LLVM IR passes into the default compiler pipeline.

# Customizing the default middle-end pipeline

In *Chapter 5*, you learned how to create your own pass pipeline and manipulate it. Here, we will address a somewhat easier yet equally important use case – how to customize the default pipelines.

What we call the default pipelines are, actually, the sequence of passes that LLVM-based tools such as Clang and opt invoke when you use the optimization options – O0, O1, and so on.

Like in *Chapter 5*, we have to interact with both the legacy and new pass managers.

For this section, we assume that the middle-end part of the pass pipeline is entirely done with the new pass manager, since this is the reality today in LLVM upstream. However, for the default codegen pipeline, we will focus on the legacy pass manager, since it is still the main vehicle for that.

Concretely, when Clang creates the pass pipeline, it uses one pipeline for the optimization sequence at the LLVM IR level and one pass pipeline to go from LLVM IR to assembly code. In other words, the default pass pipeline is composed of two sub-pipelines, the optimization pipeline and the codegen one.

In this section, we will show you how to inject LLVM IR passes into both pipelines.

As an example, we will use the pass that we developed in *Chapter 4* and add it to our backend.

Try to add this pass to the LLVM code base by yourself, which includes modifying the CMakeLists. txt file. If you struggle with this task, look at the commits that touch llvm/lib/Target/H2BLB/ H2BLBSimpleConstantPropagation.cpp in the repository referred to in the *Technical requirements* section.

Now, let's assume that we built an LLVM IR pass that is exposed via H2BLBSimpleConstantPropagati onNewPass for the new pass manager and createH2BLBSimpleConstantPropagationPassForLegacy PM for the legacy pass manager.

Let's now see how to connect that pass to the default pass pipelines with the two pass managers.

## Using the new pass manager

The default pass pipeline with the new pass manager is created via the PassBuilder class, from the Passes library.

This class uses the TargetMachine::registerPassBuilderCallbacks method to inject target-specific passes.

This method serves two purposes:

- Registers target-specific passes so that you can use them on the opt command line
- Inject passes into the default pass pipeline

For the registration part, we leverage the TargetPassRegistry mechanism available at llvm/Passes/ TargetPassRegistry.inc. This file implements macros that expand to the proper C++ sequence to register your function pass, module pass, and so on. You can achieve the same result by writing this code by hand, but this is much more convenient and productive.

To use this mechanism, we first need to create a new file that contains the registry of our target-specific pass. In our case, this file is `llvm/lib/Target/H2BLB/H2BLBPassRegistry.def`.

At this point, we have only one function-pass to register, and the interesting part of the content of the file looks like this:

```
FUNCTION_PASS("h2blb-simple-cst-prop",
              H2BLBSimpleConstantPropagationNewPass())
```

In this macro, we specify the name of the command line option to invoke this pass (`h2blb-simple-cst-prop`) and provide a way to construct the pass, using the new pass manager's construction style.

We encourage you to take a look at the whole file, as it is good practice to include macros for all the different types to make sure that your backend is future-proof.

Now that our pass is registered, we can invoke it with opt, as long as our target is registered (that, we use the right `Triple` value). Try it for yourself!

```
$ opt -mtriple=h2blb -passes=h2blb-simple-cst-prop %s -S input.ll -o -
```

The next step is to inject our pass into the default pass pipeline. To do that, within `TargetMachine::registerPassBuilderCallbacks`, we need to register our pass in the right `PassBuilder` hooks.

The `PassBuilder` class exposes several `registerXXXEPCallback` methods. `EPCallback` stands for the extension point callback, and `XXX` represents a particular point in the default pipeline. What this means is, if you add your pass using the `PassBuilder::registerPeepholeEPCallback`, for instance, your pass is assumed to be a peephole-like pass and will be inserted after every run of the instcombiner.

Deciding where to run your pass depends on what your pass does. For the sake of completeness, here is the code snippet to add our custom pass at the very beginning of the pipeline:

```
void H2BLBTargetMachine::registerPassBuilderCallbacks(PassBuilder &PB) {
<snip>
  PB.registerPipelineStartEPCallback(
      [](ModulePassManager &MPM, OptimizationLevel OptLevel) {
        // Do not add optimization passes if we are in O0.
        if (OptLevel == OptimizationLevel::O0)
          return;
        FunctionPassManager FPM;
        FPM.addPass(H2BLBSimpleConstantPropagationNewPass());
        MPM.addPass(createModuleToFunctionPassAdaptor(std::move(FPM)));
      });
<snip>
```

In this snippet, we call one of the callbacks of the `PassBuilder` class that provides an extension point at the beginning of the pass (hence `PipelineStart` in the name of the callback). We use this extension point to add our custom pass, but only if the optimization level is above O0 (that is, optimizations are enabled). Note that since our pass is a function pass, we have to add it to `FunctionPassManager` and then integrate this manager with `ModulePassManager`, using the related adaptor. This should look familiar from *Chapter 5*.

> **Pass ordering**
>
> To know where a specific extension point adds a pass, or decides which extension point to use in your case, refer to the comments that document the various `PassBuilder` APIs. Ultimately, if you want to see what the pass pipeline looks like and, thus, make sure that you used the right extension point, refer to *Chapter 5* to see how to print the pass pipeline.

You can check that your pass is part of the pass pipeline by running the following:

```
$ opt -O1 -mtriple=h2blb -debug-pass-manager %s -S -o /dev/null
```

The name of your pass should be printed. Similarly, if you run with O0, the pass should not be added, given the check we put around `OptLevel`.

That's it – your pass is now part of the default pass pipeline!

Let's now see how to influence the default codegen pipeline, which needs to interact with the legacy pass manager.

## Using the legacy pass manager

At the time of writing, the default codegen pipeline still uses the legacy pass manager. A version that uses the new pass manager is under development and being tested with `llc`, and it is hooked up via the `TargetMachine::buildCodeGenPipeline` methods. Eventually, this method will be responsible for populating the new pass manager (through the `ModulePassManager` argument of this method) with the passes that make this codegen pipeline.

In the meantime, the codegen pipeline is still created through the `TargetMachine::addPassesToEmitFile` method, which needs to populate an instance of the legacy pass manager.

When reusing the LLVM code generator infrastructure, as we intend to do in this book, your `TargetMachine` needs to inherit from the `CodeGenTargetMachineImpl` class, and thus, it also inherits the implementation of the `CodeGenTargetMachineImpl::addPassesToEmitFile` method.

To customize this implementation of `addPassesToEmitFile`, you need to create a target-specific version of the `TargetPassConfig` class, from the `CodeGen` library, and register it in your `TargetMachine`.

To do that, we will add a declaration of our own, `TargetPassConfig`, in `llvm/lib/Target/H2BLB/`
`H2BLBTargetMachine.h`:

```
class H2BLBPassConfig : public TargetPassConfig {
public:
  H2BLBPassConfig(TargetMachine &TM, PassManagerBase &PM);
};
```

Then, we will implement the constructor of this class and instantiate it in the related method of our
`TargetMachine`:

```
H2BLBPassConfig::H2BLBPassConfig(TargetMachine &TM, PassManagerBase &PM)
    : TargetPassConfig(TM, PM) {}

TargetPassConfig *H2BLBTargetMachine::createPassConfig(PassManagerBase &PM) {
  return new H2BLBPassConfig(*this, PM);
}
```

Make sure to also update the declaration of `H2BLBTargetMachine` to override `createPassConfig`.

Currently, you can override various methods of the `TargetPassConfig` class to inject your target-
specific class into the codegen pipeline.

For instance, the `TargetPassConfig::addIRPasses` method is responsible for inserting into the default
codegen pipeline the LLVM-IR-to-LLVM-IR passes at the beginning of the pipeline.

Therefore, by overriding this method, we can inject our custom pass:

```
void H2BLBPassConfig::addIRPasses() {
  TargetPassConfig::addIRPasses();
  if (getOptLevel() != CodeGenOptLevel::None)
    addPass(createH2BLBSimpleConstantPropagationPassForLegacyPM());
}
```

This snippet adds the default IR passes by calling the parent's class, `addIRPasses`, and then adds our
pass to the pipeline if the optimizations are enabled.

In theory, this is all you need to connect your custom pass in the codegen pipeline. However, at this
stage of the development, we need to take some extra steps to provide a coherent empty shell to the
full codegen pipeline; otherwise, `llc` will crash on our target. This is a one-time setup that will put us
on the right track for the rest of this book.

## A one-time setup – assembling a codegen pipeline

When instantiating a codegen pipeline, LLVM-based tools, such as `llc`, assume that the whole codegen
infrastructure is hooked up. As such, these tools assume that the supported object file format is
specified, the MC information is hooked up, and so on.

In this section, we show you how to create a robust enough skeleton of the codegen pipeline to trick llc into instantiating this pipeline for our target. This pipeline will not do anything relevant codegen-wise, but it does set the foundations for the upcoming developments and allows you to check that your custom passes are, indeed, inserted into the pipeline.

At a high level, here is what we need to do:

- Provide a fake instruction selector; otherwise, the codegen pipeline will be incomplete and not instantiated.

- Provide a fake `TargetLoweringObjectFile` implementation; otherwise, llc crashes because it cannot initialize the lowering of the target.

- Provide a fake `MCAsmInfo` implementation; otherwise, `AsmPrinter`, the class responsible for emitting the final assembly code, cannot be set up, even though it is required by the `CodeGenT argetMachineImpl::addPassesToEmitFile` implementation. The initialization of `MCAsmInfo` in the implementation of the `CodeGenTargetMachineImpl` also requires providing the following components:

    - `MCSubtargetInfo`: We already have an implementation of a child of this class with our `H2BLBSubtarget` class. However, we cannot use it, as it would create a circular dependency in our target-specific library. Indeed, the current parent class of our `H2BLBSubtarget` implementation is `TargetSubargetInfo`. This class is from the CodeGen library, which already depends on the MC library. If we use `H2BLBSubtarget` in our MC implementation, our MC layer would depend on the CodeGen library, hence the circular dependency. Therefore, we need a proper `MCSubtargetInfo` implementation, and this entails using the TableGen infrastructure. In this section, we are showing you how to use the TableGen implementation, but we will merge the two implementations later. It is okay to postpone the merge, since our TableGen implementation is empty for now.

    - `MCInstrInfo`: The low-level information about the target instruction. At this point, we only need to provide a fake implementation.

    - `MCRegisterInfo`: This is the same as `MCInstrInfo` but for the registers.

Let's start adding the fake instruction selector.

## Faking the instruction selector

To fake-add an instruction selector, we must override the `TargetPassConfig::addInstSelector` method in our target-specific implementation, `H2BLBPassConfig`:

```
bool H2BLBPassConfig::addInstSelector() {
  return false;
}
```

What this snippet does is tell the pass manager that there was no error (`return false`) when we added our custom instruction selector to the pipeline. Obviously, since we have not added anything, this will not run, but at least the pass pipeline is tricked into believing that it is well-formed.

Next up is the `TargetLoweringObjectFile` implementation.

# Faking the lowering of the object file

To fake the lowering of the object file, we need to provide an implementation of the TargetLoweringObjectFile class from the Target library.

You need one implementation of this class per the file format you want to support.

For our target, we have decided to support two file formats first – ELF (Linux) and Mach-O (macOS and iOS.) Therefore, we need to implement two classes.

We make the declaration of these classes in llvm/lib/Target/H2BLB/H2BLBTargetObjectFile.h:

```
class H2BLB_ELFTargetObjectFile : public TargetLoweringObjectFileELF {
public:
  H2BLB_ELFTargetObjectFile();
};


class H2BLB_MachoTargetObjectFile : public TargetLoweringObjectFileMachO {
public:
  H2BLB_MachoTargetObjectFile();
};
```

This snippet declares our two classes and has them inherit from the TargetLoweringObjectFile class related to the desired file format. Each parent class comes from the CodeGen library.

The implementation of the constructor is straightforward at this point, but we separated it in the llvm/lib/Target/H2BLB/H2BLBTargetObjectFile.cpp file to already have the proper file structure for future changes.

Next, we create a helper function to instantiate the proper type of object, based on the file format carried by the Triple object carried by the TT variable:

```
static std::unique_ptr<TargetLoweringObjectFile> createTLOF(const Triple &TT) {
  if (TT.isOSBinFormatELF())
    return std::make_unique<H2BLB_ELFTargetObjectFile>();
  if (TT.isOSBinFormatMachO())
    return std::make_unique<H2BLB_MachoTargetObjectFile>();
  // Other format not supported yet.
  return nullptr;
}
```

Here, we create our ELF lowering for the ELF format and the Mach-O lowering for the Mach-O format.

Next, we update our TargetMachine implementation to hold an instance of the TargetLoweringObjectFile class for the file format we are currently compiling for, using the helper function to initialize it.

This translates into modifying the constructor of our `H2BLBTargetMachine`:

```
H2BLBTargetMachine::H2BLBTargetMachine(<snip>)
  : <snip>,
    TLOF(createTLOF(getTargetTriple())) <snip>
```

In this snippet, `TLOF` is a private field that we added to the `H2BLBTargetMachine` class.

Finally, we need to override the related getter in our `TargetMachine` to return this `TLOF`. Here is the related code when inserted directly into the `H2BLBTargetMachine`'s class declaration:

```
TargetLoweringObjectFile *getObjFileLowering() const override {
  return TLOF.get();
}
```

Now, we just need to hook up the low-level MC information.

## Creating a skeleton for the assembly information

To create a minimal skeleton of the assembly information, we need to instantiate the four things that we previously mentioned – `MCAsmInfo`, `MCSubtargetInfo`, `MCInstrInfo`, and `MCRegisterInfo`.

`MCSubtargetInfo` is more involved, so let's start with this one.

First, we create a new TableGen file, `llvm/lib/Target/H2BLB/H2BLB.td`, that will be our placeholder for all the TableGen work for our backend.

The content of this file is as follows:

```
include "llvm/Target/Target.td"
def H2BLBInstrInfo : InstrInfo;
def H2BLB : Target {
  let InstructionSet = H2BLBInstrInfo;
}
```

This snippet includes the class and records that are required to create a backend (`llvm/Target/Target.td`) and creates two records, one for `MCInstrInfo` and one that holds the information for our entry backend. The `Target` TableGen class has several fields, but for now, we will use the default implementation for all of them except the `InstructionSet` one.

Next, we need to hook up this TableGen file to our build system. We achieve this by adding the following lines to our `CMakeLists.txt` file (hence in `llvm/lib/Target/H2BLB`):

```
set(LLVM_TARGET_DEFINITIONS H2BLB.td)
tablegen(LLVM H2BLBGenSubtargetInfo.inc -gen-subtarget)
add_public_tablegen_target(H2BLBCommonTableGen)
```

You should already be familiar with what this does from the *Hooking up the TableGen backend* subsection in the *Creating an intrinsic in the backend* section.

Now that TableGen generates the boilerplate for our `MCSubtargetInfo` implementation, we just need to harvest it.

First, we create a new file, `llvm/lib/Target/H2BLB/MCTargetDesc/H2BLBMCTargetDesc.h`, that holds the declaration of our class by leveraging what TableGen produces:

```
#define GET_SUBTARGETINFO_ENUM
#include "H2BLBGenSubtargetInfo.inc"
```

Then, we enable the implementation of this class in the related `H2BLBMCTargetDesc.cpp`:

```
#define GET_SUBTARGETINFO_MC_DESC
#include "H2BLBGenSubtargetInfo.inc"

static MCSubtargetInfo *
createH2BLBMCSubtargetInfo(const Triple &TT, StringRef CPU, StringRef FS) {
  return createH2BLBMCSubtargetInfoImpl(TT, CPU, /*TuneCPU*/ CPU, FS);
}
```

Finally, we register our sub-target in our MC initializer (that is, we modify `LLVMInitializeH2BLBTargetMC` in the same file):

```
extern "C" LLVM_EXTERNAL_VISIBILITY void LLVMInitializeH2BLBTargetMC() {
  Target &TheTarget = getTheH2BLBTarget();
  TargetRegistry::RegisterMCSubtargetInfo(TheTarget,
                                          createH2BLBMCSubtargetInfo);
}
```

One down and three to go!

For the next two pieces of MC information, `MCRegisterInfo` and `MCInstrInfo`, an empty implementation will suffice for now. Therefore, creating the default implementations in `H2BLBMCTargetDesc.cpp` is enough:

```
static MCInstrInfo *createH2BLBMCInstrInfo() {
  return new MCInstrInfo();
}
static MCRegisterInfo *createH2BLBMCRegisterInfo(const Triple &Triple) {
  return new MCRegisterInfo();
}
```

Then, we just have to register these functions in our MC initializer by adding the following two lines to `LLVMInitializeH2BLBTargetMC`:

```
TargetRegistry::RegisterMCInstrInfo(TheTarget, createH2BLBMCInstrInfo);
TargetRegistry::RegisterMCRegInfo(TheTarget, createH2BLBMCRegisterInfo);
```

Let's move on to the last one, the `MCAsmInfo` class.

For this one, like the lowering of the object file, we need to create one `MCAsmInfo` instance per file format.

We do that by creating a file, `llvm/lib/Target/H2BLB/MCTargetDesc/H2BLBMCAsmInfo.h`, with the following declarations:

```
class H2BLBMCAsmInfoELF : public MCAsmInfoELF {
public:
  explicit H2BLBMCAsmInfoELF(const Triple &TT, const MCTargetOptions &Options);
};


class H2BLBMCAsmInfoDarwin : public MCAsmInfoDarwin {
public:
  explicit H2BLBMCAsmInfoDarwin(const Triple &TT,
                                const MCTargetOptions &Options);
};
```

This snippet declares two classes of `MCAsmInfo`, one for each file format we support. The implementation is trivial and needs to live in `llvm/lib/Target/H2BLB/MCTargetDesc/H2BLBMCAsmInfo.cpp`.

Next, we provide a helper function, in `H2BLBMCTargetDesc.cpp`, to select the correct `MCAsmInfo` implementation based on the file format:

```
static MCAsmInfo *createH2BLBMCAsmInfo(const MCRegisterInfo &MRI,
                                       const Triple &TheTriple,
                                       const MCTargetOptions &Options) {
  MCAsmInfo *MAI;
  if (TheTriple.isOSBinFormatMachO())
    MAI = new H2BLBMCAsmInfoDarwin(TheTriple, Options);
  else if (TheTriple.isOSBinFormatELF())
    MAI = new H2BLBMCAsmInfoELF(TheTriple, Options);
  else
    report_fatal_error("Binary format not supported");
  return MAI;
}
```

Note that to match the signature expected by the initializer of the `MCAsmInfo`, we theoretically need `MCRegisterInfo`. We set that up previously, so we are good!

Finally, we must register how to instantiate our `MCAsmInfo` class with our `Target` in the MC initializer. In other words, we need to add the following line to `LLVMInitializeH2BLBTargetMC`:

```
RegisterMCAsmInfoFn X(TheTarget, createH2BLBMCAsmInfo);
```

Currently, our MC layer is properly registered and supplies the right initializers for our `TargetMachine` to instantiate it.

We enable this last phase by adding the following line to the constructor of our `TargetMachine` class, `H2BLBTargetMachine`:

```
initAsmInfo();
```

Now, the skeleton of our MC layer is completely set up, and it is possible to call the `TargetMachine::addPassesToEmitPasses` method with our `TargetMachine` instance. However, currently, only empty files can be processed, since we did not really implement anything substantial.

However, you can use this setup to check that your `TargetPassConfig` implementation can inject your passes – for instance, by running the following command line on an empty input:

```
$ llc -O1 -mtriple h2blb input.ll -debug-pass=Structure --stop-before=peephole-opt -o /dev/null
```

This command prints the list of passes run by the codegen pipeline and stops the execution before the peephole optimizer. We stop there to make sure that we do not hit the fake MC layer.

In this section, you learned how to modify both the default optimizing pipeline, also known as the middle-end, and the codegen pipeline, also known as the backend, by leveraging the callbacks supplied, respectively, by the `PassBuilder` and the `TargetPassConfig` classes. You also had your first foray into setting up the skeleton of the MC layer for your backend. This task is required to get you started on implementing your backend.

Before we conclude this chapter, let's quickly discuss the backend versus the middle-end.

# Using the right abstraction

As we close our journey with LLVM IR, and before we start digging into Machine IR, we wanted to give you a few recommendations on how to decide if you need to implement your optimization passes in LLVM IR or in Machine IR.

Before you decide whether you should implement something in one IR or the other, step back and think about what you are trying to achieve.

Transformations at the LLVM IR level are easier to reuse across backends and are usually easier to write. Conversely, Machine IR passes have to provide additional mechanisms, such as helper functions and classes, to abstract away target-specific constructs. For instance, things as simple as recognizing an add instruction are not portable across targets in Machine IR, unless you push some logic on the target itself.

In contrast, LLVM IR passes are at the mercy of what later transformations will do, including the Machine IR passes. For instance, computing an estimate of the register pressure of some LLVM IR is relatively easy and straightforward if you assume that the schedule of your input IR will not change. This is not a realistic expectation. Conversely, Machine IR can run after scheduling or register allocation, and as such, it can offer a lot more information about what the final assembly code will look like.

Knowing these facts, you have to balance the trade-offs of how much low-level information you need and the kind of reuse you want when deciding where to implement something.

In this section, we looked at the kind of trade-offs you have to make when deciding at which level of IR it is preferable to implement something.

Our next stop wraps up this chapter.

# Summary

In this chapter, we looked at all the ways you can inject target-specific constructs at the LLVM IR level.

To get started, you saw how to add a target to the LLVM project. The process involved creating a new directory in `llvm/lib/Target` and connecting it to the build system. You learned how to do the same thing with Clang such that it can produce LLVM IR for your backend.

You also discovered how to create your own built-in functions, called intrinsics, and connect them at the source language level via Clang.

Then, you saw how to tell the LLVM optimizers about your target-specific constraints by creating your own implementation of the `TargetTransformInfo` class. While what was presented in this chapter remain toy examples, they gave you concrete illustrations of how to connect things in the LLVM infrastructure.

Finally, you learned how you can inject your own LLVM IR passes into the default pass pipelines, used by tools such as Clang. In the process, you learned how to set up the MC layer for your backend, which is a required step for the upcoming chapters and, ultimately, having a fully functional backend.

The next chapter will teach you how to approach debugging when working with LLVM at the LLVM IR level. After this upcoming chapter, you will be in Machine IR land.

# Further reading

When we discussed the intrinsics, we mentioned that you could experiment with inline assembly first. If you want to know more about inline assembly, we encourage you to read the **GNU Compiler Collection (GCC)** documentation about this: `https://gcc.gnu.org/onlinedocs/gcc/extensions-to-the-c-language-family/how-to-use-inline-assembly-language-in-c-code.html`.

The official LLVM website features a document that explains in broad strokes how to implement an LLVM backend: `https://llvm.org/docs/WritingAnLLVMBackend.html`. If you read that document, you will see that the approach we started in this chapter is more structured and incremental. Indeed, the official documentation essentially says to take an existing backend, clone its content in a new directory, delete what you do not like, and modify the rest. While this is a valid approach, we believe this is not how you gain knowledge about how things work, and as a result, it puts you in a difficult position if you ever have to find issues in things you simply copied and pasted.

# Quiz time

Now that you have finished reading this chapter, try answering the following questions to test your knowledge:

1.  Are intrinsics the only option to experiment with target-specific constructs?

    No, you can start with inline assembly. Inline assembly does not require any change to the compiler, whereas intrinsics do. However, inline assembly puts additional constraints on the optimizers and these constraints may degrade the quality of the generated code.

    See the *The pros and cons of intrinsics* section for more details.

2.  How can you quickly check whether Clang knows about your target?

    Clang can print all the targets it has been built for by using the `--print-targets` option. You can then check whether the target is hooked up by printing some IR with Clang, using `-target <yourTarget> -S -emit-llvm`.

    See the *Plumbing your Target through Clang* section.

3.  How can you inject a pass into the default optimization pipeline?

    You need to use the right `PassBuilder::XXXEPCallBack` method to register your pass where you want in the pipeline. This registration needs to happen within your `TargetMachine::reg isterPassBuilderCallbacks` implementation.

    See the *Using the new pass manager* subsection in the *Customizing the default middle-end pipeline* section.

4.  How can you influence the decisions made by an optimization pass?

    Optimization passes that take target-specific information into account usually do that through the `TargetTransformInfo` class. (You have an overview of which classes use what in *Chapter 8*.) As such, you need to override the methods used by the optimization you are interested in in your target implementation of the `TargetTransformInfo` class.

    See the *Adding a target-specific TargetTransformInfo implementation* section for more details.

5.  You injected a custom pass into the default optimization pipeline for your target, but this pass is not invoked with `opt -O1`. What could be the reason?

    Assuming you hooked up your pass properly, the most likely reason is you did not invoke your target-specific pipeline. By default, `opt` uses the generic default pipeline and only invokes the target-specific one if you specify `-mtriple` on the command line, or if your input IR has a `target triple` string.

    See the *Customizing the default middle-end pipeline* section and the part about hooking up a pass in the middle-end.

## Unlock this book's exclusive benefits now

This book comes with additional benefits designed to elevate your learning experience.

*Note: Have your purchase invoice ready before you begin.*

https://www.packtpub.com/unlock/9781837637782

# 10

# Hands-On Debugging LLVM IR Passes

Before we start diving into machine **intermediate representation** (IR), which is the topic of the next chapter, we thought it was important to provide an overview of the tools the LLVM project offers so that you can debug your compiler.

In this chapter, you'll learn how to do the following:

- Leverage the logging mechanisms that LLVM offers to debug your passes
- Reduce test cases using the tools provided by the LLVM infrastructure
- Enable the sanitizers to identify memory leaks, memory corruptions, or undefined behavior
- Interact with the LLVM code base through a debugger

You'll be able to use this knowledge as a guideline when you're tackling your first compiler issues. This knowledge should also boost your productivity as a lot of the tasks that you must perform to work with a compiler can be automated or sped up by leveraging the tools that will be presented in this chapter.

## Technical requirements

In this chapter, most of the things that we'll show you require a version of LLVM that's been built with assertions enabled. As such, you'll need to build LLVM yourself. If you haven't done so already, please follow the steps provided in *Chapter 1*.

Moreover, in the ch10 folder of this book's GitHub repository (`https://github.com/PacktPublishing/LLVM-Code-Generation`), you'll find examples of how to use the techniques presented here. We encourage you to complete the activities available there when you're done with this chapter/the related sections to solidify your knowledge with hands-on exercises.

Now that you've set everything up, let's start with the logging mechanism in LLVM.

# The logging capabilities in LLVM

One of the nice things that you get for almost free when building components with the LLVM infrastructure is its logging capabilities.

You can use this feature as soon as you've hooked up the LLVM **command-line interface** (**CLI**) in your compiler (see *Chapter 5* on how to do this). The opt developer tool, which you can build within the LLVM project and Clang, is set up to expose these logging capabilities.

Let's start with the first class of logging that you can enable: intermediate dumps.

## Printing the IR between passes

The pass managers expose command-line options to print the IR before and after each pass using the textual representation. You can use the following options to enable this printing:

- `print-before-all`/`print-after-all`: Print the IR before (or after, respectively) each pass in the current pipeline.
- `print-before`/`print-after=PassName1[,PassName2]*`: Print the IR before (or after, respectively) `PassName1`, `PassName2`, and so on, where `PassNameI` is the CLI option name of the related pass (see *Chapter 5* to find out how to find this name). Like all the CLI options that accept comma-separated lists in the LLVM CLI, you can specify this option several times. This is equivalent to providing the concatenated comma-separated list to one instance of the option.

For Clang, make sure you prefix the option with `-mllvm` since these are backend options, not frontend ones. For instance, you can use the following command line to print the IR after each pass for the O3 pipeline in Clang:

```
$ clang -O3 -S input.c -o input.s -mllvm -print-after-all
```

Printer granularity

By default, the printed IR matches the scope of the pass that's run. In other words, passes that run at the loop or with function granularity will only print the related loop or function, not the full module. To print the IR at the module scope, irrespective of the pass' scope, add the `print-module-scope` option.

These dumps are particularly useful when you're tracking why something happened the way it did:

1. Go through the `print-after-all` log to find which pass introduces what you're looking for.
2. Grab the IR that feeds the faulty pass, either by taking the output of the previous pass from the `print-after-all` log or the output of the related pass in the `print-before-all` or `print-before=faultyPass` log.
3. Feed this IR to opt while solely invoking `faultyPass`.

> **Note**
>
> The logs in these steps also show the machine IR for the backend passes. As stated in *Chapter 5*, opt can't consume these. Instead, you must use `llc` in a peculiar way, something we'll describe in *Chapter 12*.

At performing these steps, you have a much faster way to observe what you want to see since you're only running the pass that interests you and bypassing everything that happened before.

> **Note**
>
> Sometimes, a pass doesn't behave the way you want because the IR may miss something or have something that shouldn't be there. The root cause may be that the pass runs too late or too early in your pass pipeline. The bottom line is that when you drill down into a pass, keep in mind that the fix might be somewhere else.

Next, let's see how we can observe why a pass does what it does.

# Printing the debug log

Most of the LLVM passes feature debug logs that help us follow what they do. However, these logs are only available when LLVM is built with assertions enabled (see *Chapter 1* to learn how to set the proper build type or CMake variable).

To print these logs, you can use one of the two command-line options:

- debug: This prints the debug log of all the passes, including the analysis passes, that are run within the current pipeline. Beware that this log is going to be massive!
- debug-only=passName1[,passName2]*: This only prints the debug log for passName1, passName2, and so on. This option allows for a more targeted way to print the debug log and avoid an explosion in the size of the log. This option follows the rule of the comma-separated list options that we mentioned for `print-before=<...>`.

Note

Most of the time, the `passName` value that you give to `debug-only` is the same as the CLI option name of the `opt` invocation of the related pass. However, there's no guarantee that this is the case. To find the name to use with the `debug-only` option for a specific pass, you must go to the pass' implementation (check *Chapter 8* if you don't remember how to do that) and locate the `DEBUG_TYPE` macro. The name that's used to define this macro is the name that you must use with the `debug-only` option. While it's annoying to have to look up this information, this flexibility allows passes to share a `DEBUG_TYPE` value while having a different CLI option name for their `opt` invocation. This is useful if you wish to group the debug log of one conceptual task when it's scattered across several passes. For instance, the debug log for tracing what happens during register allocation spans the register coalescing pass, the register coloring pass (which itself can use a different implementation based on the optimization level and other factors), and the inline spiller helper class. Having to remember all the passes that are involved here is too complicated, so instead, they're all registered under one `DEBUG_TYPE` name: `regalloc`.

At this point, you should have several questions:

- Where do these logs come from?
- How do I produce these for my pass?

Technically, the LLVM infrastructure doesn't offer a logging mechanism per se. Instead, it provides a macro called `LLVM_DEBUG` that produces a block of code that's only executed when the `debug-only` option contains the name currently defined by the `DEBUG_TYPE` macro. What this means is that you can put print statements in that macro. But you can do much more! However, we recommend sticking to simply printing or verifying information; you don't want your program to behave differently when the debug options are used!

So, to start producing debug logs in your pass, you must do the following:

1. Include the `Debug.h`, from the `Support` library, in your pass.
2. Define the `DEBUG_TYPE` macro. We recommend sticking to the same name as the one you used for the CLI option name unless it makes sense to group your debug log with other passes.
3. Use the `LLVM_DEBUG` macro to start performing debug-log-specific tasks such as printing some message or the content of a variable.

For instance, here's a snippet of a code that prints which instruction is about to be processed:

```
#include "llvm/Support/Debug.h"

#define DEBUG_TYPE "my-pass"
...
  LLVM_DEBUG(dbgs() << "Processing: " << Instr << "\n");
```

In this snippet, the LLVM_DEBUG statement is only executed if debug-only contains my-pass, as identified by DEBUG_TYPE. Now, for the content of the LLVM_DEBUG statement itself, this uses the debug stream (dbgs()) declared in Debug.h to print a message followed by the Instr variable. The dbgs() stream redirects its content to the standard error of the system.

> **Note**
>
> While you can put compile-time-intensive checks behind LLVM_DEBUG to check that each value in a function has, at most, two uses per basic block after your pass is done, remember that these checks won't run without user intervention (debug logs are always off when not using -debugxxx). Instead, if you want these checks to be enabled by default while developing your compiler, you can put them behind #ifdef EXPENSIVE_CHECKS. An EXPENSIVE_CHECKS build is only defined when you turn the LLVM_ENABLE_EXPENSIVE_CHECKS CMake variable on. Make sure you turn this CMake variable back off before shipping your toolchain to your end users; otherwise, they will exercise degraded compile time due to the additional checks.

Existing passes use more or fewer LLVM_DEBUG statements. We recommend that you use more such statements than fewer because it helps with debugging passes overall. This is especially true when the person who's debugging the pass isn't the one who wrote it. This happens a lot in open source environments, for instance.

Putting everything together with an example, the following command line runs the **straight-line program** (SLP) vectorizer, an optimization pass in the LLVM pipeline (see *Chapter 8*), while enabling its debug log:

```
$ opt -passes=slp-vectorizer -debug-only=SLP input.ll -S -o output.ll
```

In this command line, notice how the CLI option name (slp-vectorizer) is different than the debug log option name (SLP).

The next and final logging mechanism that we'll cover in this section is statistics.

## Printing high-level information about what happened

The final piece of infrastructure around logging that we want you to know about is statistics.

In essence, statistics offer us a condensed way to know whether a pass was triggered and how often. Like the debug log, by default, statistics are only available when assertions are enabled. You can also override this behavior with the LLVM_FORCE_ENABLE_STATS CMake variable.

Statistics can be printed using the stats CLI option.

For instance, here's a snippet of the statistics that you can get while running Clang:

```
$ clang -o out.s in.c -S -mllvm -stats
<snip>
    1 prologepilog      - Number of functions seen in PEI
    2 regalloc          - Number of copies coalesced
```

Looking at the implementation details, we can see that statistics are sort of global integer variables that you modify in your pass and that are automatically printed at the end of the compilation process.

To use such counters, you need to include `Statistic.h`, from the `ADT` library, and use the `STATISTIC` macro to define your counter.

This macro takes two arguments:

- `NAME`: The name of the variable for your counter.
- `DESC`: The description of what this counter holds. This information will be printed in the final report.

Now, you can use the variable representing your counter directly to capture high-level information, such as the number of bytes you saved by using a different instruction encoding or the number of times you found a specific pattern.

Statistics are an interesting mechanism because they offer an inexpensive way to capture something that's happened. This is particularly valuable when you're iterating on a feature with colleagues, for instance, because you can point them to the relevant statistics to check whether the pass you're developing has an effect as opposed to teaching them how to read the final assembly or interpret some IR.

> Note
>
> The LLVM infrastructure also offers some statistics that are always available, irrespective of whether the statistics were enabled in the build system. To use these, use the `ALWAYS_ENABLED_STATISTIC` macro instead of the `STATISTIC` macro. However, be aware that the counters that are produced through that method aren't automatically reported, so you must report them yourself. At the time of writing, this type of counter has never been used in the backend, though it's used in Clang.

In this section, you learned about the mechanisms you can use to inspect what an LLVM-based compiler does. You learned how to do the following:

- Print the intermediate state of the IR between passes.
- Enable the debug log both globally and for specific passes.
- Print the statistics, which are built-in LLVM counters that the passes can leverage to produce synthetic information.

While doing so, you learned how to implement your own debug logs and statistics.

To play around with these concepts, check out the activity available in this book's GitHub repository in the ch10/debug_capabilities folder.

In the next section, you'll learn how to leverage LLVM-provided tools to reduce the input IR size while keeping some properties intact.

# Reducing the input IR size

One of the challenges that you'll face as a compiler writer is wrestling with the complexity of the input IR.

While sometimes there's nothing you can do about it, at the end of the day, you must compile what the user asked for. When performing certain tasks, it's desirable to scale this complexity back. One effective way to do this is by reducing the input IR size.

The LLVM infrastructure offers several tools that you can use to reduce the input IR size.

The first one is a tool that can be used to extract a subset of the input IR.

## Extracting a subset of the input IR

The llvm-extract tool is a command-line tool that allows us to extract pieces of the input IR and create a new standalone module from it.

For instance, let's assume that we have thousands of lines of IR in an input module, but we're only interested in one function.

Naively copy-pasting the IR of the function may not be enough because this function may call other functions, use custom types, or read from global variables – the list goes on and on. In other words, you need to track all the dependencies of this function and pull them inappropriately while potentially rewriting them from definitions to declarations to cut the dependencies short.

Overall, this isn't something you want to do manually, and you're not alone. This is why llvm-extract exists.

The llvm-extract tool pulls all the dependencies while rewriting to keep the IR as small as possible.

For instance, let's assume we want to extract the foo and bar functions from some input IR. The following command does this for us:

```
$ llvm-extract -S -func=bar -func=foo -o - input.ll
```

In this command, we specify which functions we want to extract with as many -func options as are required, followed by the name of the function that we need. The -S option means that we want to output the result as a textual IR (as opposed to the bitcode format; see *Chapter 7*), while -o - means that we output the result on the standard output.

Using `llvm-extract`, you can extract pieces of IR as small as a basic block using the `-bb` option. This option takes the function and basic block names separated by a colon (`:`). In that mode, the tool creates a small function consisting of this basic block plus some boilerplate code. The boilerplate code is here to make sure that all the values that are used but not defined in that block are available by adding them as input arguments. For the values that are produced but not consumed in that block, they're written in output arguments – that is, a store to an input pointer.

For instance, consider the following input IR:

```
define i32 @bar(i32 noundef %arg) {
<snip>
bb2:
  %i3 = sdiv i32 3, %i
  br label %bb6
<snip>
```

> 💡 **Quick tip**: Enhance your coding experience with the **AI Code Explainer** and **Quick Copy** features. Open this book in the next-gen Packt Reader. Click the **Copy** button (**1**) to quickly copy code into your coding environment, or click the **Explain** button (**2**) to get the AI assistant to explain a block of code to you.
>
> ```
> function calculate(a, b) {
>   return {sum: a + b};
> };
> ```
>                                                                     Copy        Explain
>                                                                      (1)          (2)
>
> 🔒 **The next-gen Packt Reader** is included for free with the purchase of this book. Unlock it by scanning the QR code below or visiting `https://www.packtpub.com/unlock/9781837637782`.

To extract bb2 from bar, you can run the following command:

```
$ llvm-extract -S -o - input.ll -bb=bar:bb2
```

This command yields the following output:

```
define dso_local void @bar.bb2(i32 %i, ptr %i3.out) {
<snip>
bb2:
```

```
    %i3 = sdiv i32 3, %i
    store i32 %i3, ptr %i3.out, align 4
    br label %bb6.exitStub
<snip>
```

In this output, you can see the input value of the original basic block, %i, being promoted to an argument of the new function, @bar.bb2. Likewise, the output value of the %i3 basic block gets stored at the address represented by %i3.out, an argument of the new function.

Extracting regions

The capabilities of llvm-extract are built around the ExtractGVPass and BlockExtractorPass passes from the IPO library. Generally speaking, if you want to extract a region from some IR, this functionality is available in the TransformsUtils library under the CodeExtractor class. This class can be used in the PartialInliner or the LoopExtractor passes.

The llvm-extract tool is great when you know what you're looking for. Sometimes, however, you may have to deal with a massive input IR and not know what needs to be extracted to reproduce the behavior you want. In this case, you need more powerful tools such as llvm-reduce and bugpoint. This is the topic of the next section.

## Shrinking the IR automatically

In this section, we'll look at llvm-reduce and bugpoint, two command-line tools available in the LLVM project (that is, under ${LLVM_SRC}/llvm/tools). When it comes to reducing the input IR, you can use these tools interchangeably. Note that their requirements are slightly different; we'll cover this later.

Both tools work fundamentally the same way: you give them an objective and they rewrite the IR iteratively such that it becomes smaller and smaller until it can't preserve the objective. The objective is simply a status that tells us whether the IR matches the desired properties of whatever is being sought.

To be concrete, let's say that our compiler crashes on some giant IR. What we report to these tools is whether the current iteration of the IR crashes our compiler. Depending on this status, the tool either keeps shrinking the IR or tries a different rewrite rule. In the end, the tool produces the smallest IR their rewrite rules allow them to find while still reproducing the desired properties.

Note

When the IR is fully reduced by one of the tools, it may be possible to reduce it further by hand. At the end of the day, the rewrite rules are applied blindly. This is super useful for doing the heavy lifting, but they may miss the mark. Starting from this reduced IR, chances are you'll be able to understand the problem and tweak the IR toward a smaller reproducer or something different enough that re-running it through the tools may reduce it further.

Now, let's look at the requirements for these tools.

In a nutshell, both tools can be driven by a script that, given the current iteration of the IR, tells us whether the interesting property of the IR still holds (for instance, it still crashes our compiler). The main difference between the tools is that bugpoint expects the script to return non-zero when the IR is interesting while llvm-reduce expects zero when the IR is interesting. In other words, the logic is swapped. That's it!

Now, you may be wondering why LLVM exposes two tools with the same functionality.

As you may have guessed, this is because llvm-reduce is a rewrite of bugpoint, but it doesn't completely replace it. Instead, llvm-reduce focuses on replicating the core use case of this tool, which is reducing the size of the input IR. The other functionalities that bugpoint offers, such as the code generator debugger, are still solely in bugpoint. The reality is that few people were using these functionalities anyway and they can easily be reproduced with some scripting around llvm-extract and the -opt-bisect-limit command-line option (https://llvm.org/docs/OptBisect.html) with opt, for instance.

Let's see llvm-reduce and bugpoint in action!

For the sake of this exercise, imagine that you know nothing about the AArch64 backend and you're wondering how the bfi instruction, which is a bitfield insertion instruction, is matched from your massive IR function.

Essentially, you're trying to learn how the matching is done by debugging the AArch64 backend and you want to have your debug log small enough so that you can follow it.

First, you'd need to write a script that checks whether your compiler, say llc in this case, produces the desired IR:

```
#!/bin/bash
llc $@ -o - | grep 'bfi'
exit $?
```

In this script, we assume that llc is in your path.

This script runs llc on the input IR ($@), prints the assembly code on standard output (-o -), pipes this output to grep to check whether the final assembly contains bfi, and runs the status of the search ($? is zero if found; non-zero otherwise).

After making this script executable (for example, by running the chmod u+x has_bfi.sh command), you can use it with llvm-reduce to reduce your input IR:

```
$ llvm-reduce --test=has_bfi.sh input.ll
```

If the has_bfi.sh script produces a bfi instruction when run on the input.ll file, llvm-reduce will reduce the IR from input.ll such that the final IR (saved in reduced.ll) will still produce this instruction (or more precisely will have has_bfi.sh return zero).

You can try it for yourself on `${LLVM_SRC}/llvm/test/CodeGen/AArch64/aarch64-bit-gen.ll`.

> **Note**
>
> Before trying your script with `llvm-reduce` (or `bugpoint`), make sure that it returns the expected status on your motivating example, as well as a negative example.

If you invert the logic in `has_bfi.sh` – in other words, you ensure it returns non-zero when you find `bfi` and zero when you don't – then the following `bugpoint` command does the same thing, although the reduced IR may look different since both tools use different heuristics:

```
$ bugpoint --compile-command=./has_not_bfi.sh --run-llc --compile-custom input.ll
```

As mentioned previously, we can see that `bugpoint` requires more knowledge to use. Here, we simply say that we're compiling something with `--run-llc` (as opposed to running, for instance), and that we use a custom command line, and that command is represented by the `has_not_bfi.sh` script.

> **Note**
>
> Both tools reduce the IR to exactly what you asked for. The bottom line is, make sure you ask for the right thing! For instance, let's say you have a giant function that makes your compiler assert in a specific way and the script only checks that the compiler crashes. When reducing the IR, the tool may perform unexpectedly: it may reduce to something that crashes (for instance, an empty file if you didn't plan for that), and this may not be the assertion you wanted to exercise or be something useful, such as a not-yet-implemented kind of thing that you're already aware of.

In the `ch10/incorrect_optimization` folder of this book's repository, we've created a faulty optimization that breaks certain construction of the IR. We created this input IR and saved it in `bugged_input.ll` in the same folder. Your job is to use one of these tools to reduce the IR automatically. The answers are in this very folder as well. Look at the related `README.md` file for more details and to see the solution.

In this section, you learned how to leverage `llvm-extract`, `llvm-reduce`, and `bugpoint` to reduce the input IR of a problem. This knowledge will prove invaluable when you're investigating compiler issues, working on providing minimal reproducers to file issues, or creating a unit test to go along with your fix.

In the next section, you'll discover some of the instrumentation that you can enable to make finding issues easier.

# Using sanitizers

Depending on your experience, you may already be familiar with the usage of sanitizers. If you're not familiar with them, then this section is for you!

Sanitizers consist of instrumentation that's automatically injected into your program by the compiler. This instrumentation is used to catch issues such as race conditions, memory leaks, and more.

If your compiler behaves in nondeterministic ways, using a sanitizer may be a good idea as you can take the pulse of the health of your system. Generally speaking, running your compiler with sanitizers enabled from time to time is a good idea.

To enable sanitizers, assuming you're using Clang as the compiler toolchain, you only need to use `-fsanitize=typeOfSanitizer`, where `typeOfSanitizer` is one of the following:

- `address`: Detects invalid address accesses – for instance, use-after-free, out-of-bounds access, and so on
- `memory`: Detects access to valid addresses that haven't been uninitialized yet
- `thread`: Detects race conditions
- `undefined`: Detects pieces of code that rely on undefined behavior
- `leak`: Detects memory leaks

This list isn't exhaustive; you can find more information at `https://clang.llvm.org/docs/index.html`.

Sanitizers are great but you don't want to enable them all the time:

- They slow down your program significantly to the point where your program may not be usable.
- They increase the memory requirements to the point where your program may run out of memory.

However, you can try to use them directly for your programs and they may just work fine.

For the LLVM code base, this is, in theory, more complicated. In practice, the LLVM community did all the preparatory work to make the sanitizers usable with the code base, but you must enable them through a dedicated CMake option: `LLVM_USE_SANITIZER`. This CMake option takes a semi-colon-separated list of the sanitizers you want to enable, where the name of the sanitizers starts with a capital letter (for example, to enable the `address` sanitizer, pass `Address` to the `LLVM_USE_SANITIZER` CMake variable).

> **Note**
>
> The sanitizers only check the paths that your program takes at runtime. Make sure you run the sanitizers with sufficiently diverse inputs to ensure good code coverage.

In the `ch10/undefined_behavior` and `ch10/use_after_free` folders of this book's GitHub repository, we've prepared two examples of broken programs that can easily be diagnosed with the right sanitizer. Please refer to the `README.md` file of the related directory to learn how to test, find the problem yourself, and see the solution.

In this section, you learned about instrumentation techniques that can help you find hard-to-track issues.

Next, we'll briefly cover how to use a debugger before we show you the things you can leverage from LLVM in a debugger to make your debugging sessions more productive.

# A crash course on LLDB

Debuggers are a great tool for inspecting the state of a program at runtime.

LLDB is the LLVM debugger – that is, a debugger built using the LLVM project.

A debugger lets you run a program, stop it at any point, and inspect its state.

Depending on how your program was built, your debug session may be more or less close to the source code. A program built with a lower optimization level (for example, O0) is going to reflect the way the program was written more naturally than a program built with a higher optimization level.

To put it in simple terms, if you want to use a debugger to inspect your program at the source level, you're better off building your program with optimization disabled (-O0) and the debug information enabled (-g). This is exactly what the Debug CMake build type is about.

Beyond that, you may have some information, such as the call stack, but you may not have easy access to symbolic information such as the value of a variable (or more precisely, its location, which is then accessed to print its value).

In any case, you can always use a debugger, but beware that you may only have access to low-level constructs, such as the assembly representation of the program. However, when your program is built right, a debugger offers you an interactive way to evaluate expressions, print the content of variables, and so on, which can be invaluable for pinpointing why a program misbehaves or understanding why it behaves the way it does. The main advantage of the debugger compared to the logging mechanism presented earlier is that you don't have to re-compile your program each time you want to inspect something that hasn't been logged yet. If the right longer-term solution is to improve your logging (with LLVM_DEBUG statements), please do so – it will be useful to someone else!

In this section, we'll focus on teaching you a few basic LLDB commands that will help you get started with debuggers. As you become more familiar with debuggers, you'll be able to leverage more complicated features, such as printing the assembly instructions that are about to be executed, switching threads, and so on. However, this is outside the scope of this book.

The goal of this section is to teach you how to do the following:

- Know where you are in the program
- Stop at specific locations
- Inspect the state of the program

Let's start with how to start the debugger!

# Starting a debugging session

There are several ways you can start a debugging session, depending on the type of use case you have.

The most basic way is to start LLDB by running the `lldb` command-line tool without any options.

This starts an interactive CLI within LLDB where you can use all LLDB commands.

The commands you use now depend on your use case.

For instance, you can attach yourself to a running program using the `attach` command, followed by the process ID of the program (which you can get with the `ps` command-line tool, for instance).

Alternatively, you can run a particular executable directly from LLDB by specifying the executable using the `target create` command. Then, you can use the `run` command, followed by the command-line arguments used to feed this executable, to launch it.

For instance, here are the command lines you should use to start a debug session for the `myExec` executable and run it with `arg0`, `arg1`, and `arg2`:

```
$ lldb
(lldb) target create ./myExec
(lldb) run arg0 arg1 arg2
```

In this snippet, notice how the command-line prompt changes from a dollar sign ($) to the LLDB-specific prompt ((lldb)).

Debugging a command-line tool is LLDB's bread and butter. As such, you can set up the executable and its arguments directly when launching LLDB using `--`.

The following command line starts a debugging session for `myExec` with the `arg0`, `arg1`, and `arg2` arguments. In other words, it's equivalent to the previous snippet:

```
$ lldb -- ./myExec arg0 arg1 arg2
(lldb) run
```

Notice how we didn't pass any argument to the `run` command. This is because, without arguments, the `run` command gets its argument from a global LLDB setting named `target.run-args`. Launching LLDB with a command line after the double dashes (`--`) sets this setting directly.

In other words, the `run` command has two modes:

- **Without arguments:** It reads the arguments from the `target.run-args` setting and launch the executable.
- **With arguments:** It sets the `target.run-args` setting and then launches the executable with them.

You can see this behavior by yourself by running the following commands in LLDB:

```
(lldb) setting show target.run-args
<some value>
(lldb) run arg0 arg1
(lldb) setting show target.run-args
target.run-args (arguments) =
  [0]: "arg0"
  [1]: "arg1"
```

You can read/modify LLDB settings using the `setting show`/`setting set` commands.

Let's step back a little bit and see why starting a debugging session is helpful.

If you try to run the previous commands on a perfectly working program, the debugger is only going to blast through the execution. However, if you run these commands on a program that does something invalid (for instance, a segmentation fault or a bus error), the debugger will stop exactly where this issue is hit, allowing you to inspect the state of the program where it fails.

Irrespective of how the program behaves, the debugger can stop the program wherever you want. We'll show you that in the next section.

# Controlling the execution

One of the strengths of a debugger is its ability to stop the execution anywhere you want and resume the program interactively.

First, let's see how to stop the program.

## Stopping the program

There are mainly two ways to specify when to stop a program:

- Use breakpoints to stop the program when you reach a specific location.
- Use watchpoints to stop the program when some data is read and/or written.

Additionally, both these stopping mechanisms support conditions. This means that they support a mode where they only stop when the specified condition is true.

Let's learn how to set a breakpoint using the **GNU Project Debugger** (GDB) syntax, which is, in our opinion, less powerful than the LLDB syntax but much more intuitive, hence why it's perfect to begin with LLDB.

> GDB syntax
>
> LLBD provides command aliases that are abbreviations of the related LLDB commands. The built-in abbreviations provide a syntax that's compatible with the GDB syntax. The commands to set a breakpoint are one of them. The command aliases are listed at the end of the `help` command within `lldb`, under the `Current command abbreviations` section.

To set a breakpoint, we can use the b command, followed by one of the given patterns:

- `filename:lineNumber`: For instance, `main.cpp:12` to stop at the 12th line in the `main.cpp` file
- `functionName`: For instance, `main` to stop at the beginning of the `main` function (more precisely, after the `main` function's prologue)
- `0xRawAddress`: For instance, `0xf00ba4` to stop at the given program counter, which is represented by a raw address, in hexadecimal format, within the program being debugged

All these variants can also be set using the corresponding `breakpoint set` command with the right command-line options.

> **Getting help**
>
> LLDB provides extensive documentation of its commands through the `help` command. Simply run `help <command>` (for example, `help breakpoint`) within `lldb` to get the help for the given family of commands, then `help <command> <subcommand>` (for example, `help breakpoint set`) for the help message of the specific subcommand. For instance, you can view the exhaustive list of the supported ways to set a breakpoint with the `b` command by using `help b`.

Then, you can modify your breakpoint so that you can set a condition on it using the `breakpoint modify` command. This can be done in one go with the `breakpoint set` command – in other words, you can pass the option to set the condition when you create your breakpoint. However, again, we feel it's easier to approach LLDB step by step.

Let's put everything we've seen so far together with an example.

Imagine that you want to know precisely where the instruction represented by the `sdiv i32 %val, 5` textual IR is created.

You could look at the various logs to try to pinpoint where it happens, but you wouldn't know precisely where this happens in the LLVM code base. But with LLDB, you're one conditional breakpoint away from the answer.

What we need to do is stop on the constructor of `BinaryOperator`, but only if we're creating a signed division instruction with the second argument being the constant five.

This is exactly what we can do with the following LLDB commands:

```
(lldb) b BinaryOperator::BinaryOperator
Breakpoint 8: 2 locations.
(lldb) break modify 8 -c 'iType == llvm::Instruction::BinaryOps::SDiv && S2-
>getValueID() == llvm::Value::ValueTy::ConstantIntVal && ((ConstantInt*)S2)-
>getZExtValue() == 5'
```

In this snippet, we create a breakpoint on the constructor of the `BinaryOperator` class. Invoking the b command sets the breakpoint at the desired location and prints the breakpoint ID of our new breakpoint. In this case, the newly created breakpoint is identified by the number 8.

Next, we modify this breakpoint by providing its ID (`break modify 8`) and by adding a condition (`-c`). This condition is an expression that's going to be run in the context of the location of the breakpoint. In other words, we can use any variable that will be local to this program point, and we'll be served the runtime values of these variables.

In this case, we check that the argument of the constructor that represents the type of the `BinaryOperator` class matches a signed division (`iType == llvm::Instruction::BinaryOps::SDiv`) and that the argument of the constructor that represents the second argument of this division is an instance of the `ConstantInt` class (`S2->getValueID() == llvm::Value::ValueTy::ConstantIntVal`) with a value of 5 (`(((ConstantInt*)S2)->getZExtValue() == 5`).

You can imagine how being able to easily pinpoint when something this specific happens is more valuable than tracking complex issues.

## Command resolution

If you paid attention, you'll have noticed that we used the `break modify` command instead of `breakpoint modify` as initially explained. The reason is that LLDB, like GDB, offers a convenient command-line resolution that expands to the right command if the provided prefix is unambiguous. For instance, `brea mod 8` or `br mod 8` would equally modify the breakpoint with an ID of 8 because each string resolves to `breakpoint modify`.

To finish handling breakpoints, you can enable/disable specific/all breakpoints with the `breakpoint enable`/`breakpoint disable` command, respectively.

You can check which breakpoints are set and enabled and with what conditions with `breakpoint list`.

Finally, you can delete breakpoints with `breakpoint delete`.

Moving on to watchpoints, this concept is mainly the same as breakpoints except that you give either an address or a variable to watch and the mode of watching (`read`, `write`, or `read_write`). Then, the debugger will automatically stop the program when the given variable or address is read and/or written according to the given options.

For instance, let's say that something in your program modifies the content of one of your variables unexpectedly. You've checked with the sanitizers that no memory corruption or race condition occurs, which means something accesses your variable legally, but you can't figure it out. Using a watchpoint, you can make the program stop when the variable gets modified, and you can quickly find which modification shouldn't be there.

For instance, the following LLDB command sets a watchpoint that stops the program every time the `MyVar` variable is modified:

```
(lldb) watchpoint set variable -w write MyVar
```

The syntax is straightforward, and you can always use the `help` command to find out more.

Now, let's see how to resume your program interactively.

## Resuming the execution

All the commands that control the interactive execution of the program are under the `thread main` command. For instance, the `thread continue` command resumes the execution of all the threads of the program. We invite you to look at the help message for this family of commands by running the `help thread` command as this will help deepen your proficiency in LLDB.

In this section, we'll introduce you to the most useful commands you can use to control the execution of the program.

As we did in the previous section, we'll use the abbreviated command, when available, for a shorter description.

Without further ado, here are the main LLDB commands you can use to control the execution:

- `next` (or `n`): Executes the next statement of the program.
- `step` (or `s`): This is like the `next` command but if the statement is a function call, it stops at the first statement in the target function. In contrast, the `next` command simply executes the whole function call.
- `finish` (or `fin`): This executes the program until it finishes executing the current frame. In other words, this command allows us to exit the current function call by executing whatever is left to be executed in this function.
- `thread until <lineNumber>`: This executes the program until the specified `lineNumber` is reached. If the normal execution of the program doesn't go through the specified line number, LLDB stops the program when returning from the current frame.
- `thread return <value>`: This overrides the program's execution by directly returning from the current frame with the provided value. This command illustrates how powerful debuggers are; you can alter the execution of the program however you want. Be aware that the state of the program may be incorrect since you may have skipped a lot of code that's normally executed.

All these commands respect whatever breakpoints/watchpoints you may have set. For instance, let's say that you use the `finish` command to exit the current frame but you have a breakpoint within the related function. This command will stop at either the breakpoint or exit of the current frame – whichever is hit first. This is where disabling breakpoints is handy.

> Note
>
> If you want even finer control than what's provided at the statement level, you can use the `nexti` (`ni`) or `stepi` (`si`) command. These have the same semantics as the `next` and `step` commands, except that they work at the assembly instruction level. In other words, `nexti` executes the next assembly instruction while stepping over calls, whereas `stepi` follows call instructions.

For instance, consider the following snippet and assume that the next statement to be executed is the one with the `-->` symbol:

```
        int foo(int a, int b) {
-->     int c = bar(a);
        return c + b;
    }
```

Now, let's describe what would happen if we executed one of the following commands at this point:

- next: The program will execute until the `return c + b` statement.
- step: The program will execute until it reaches the first statement in `bar`.
- finish: The program will execute until it exits `foo` – that is, it stops at the first statement after the call to `foo` in the caller function.
- thread return 12: This bypasses the normal execution of the program and returns a value of 12 straight away. The program stops at the same point that the `finish` command would have yielded.

Now that controlling the execution of the program is no secret to you, let's show you how you can inspect the state of a program.

## Inspecting the state of a program

One of the main value propositions of a debugger is its ability to inspect the state of a program. As such, LLDB comes with an extensive array of commands (for instance, the family of commands under `dwim-print`, `expression`, `memory`, `register`, and so on) to tackle this problem.

In this section, we'll focus on the following commands, again presented in their abbreviated form:

- print (or p) `<variable|expression>`: This evaluates the given variable or expression and prints the result of the evaluation. This command considers the current frame to evaluate the expression.
- bt: This prints the current backtrace, also known as the call stack. Additionally, you can use the up and down commands to move the backtrace up and down and, hence, change the context of the evaluation of the `print` command.
- x `<address>`: This examines the content of the memory at the given address. The address can also be computed through an expression. For instance, assuming var is a local variable, x `&var + 5` would print the content of the memory at the address of var plus 5. This command is useful for peeking at the raw content of the memory to see how the bits are laid out.
- list (or l): This lists the source code around the point where the program is stopped. Repeated calls to this command keep listing the source code forward (a few lines at a time by default). When used with a dash (for instance, `l -`) the source code is listed backward.

In a typical debug session, your program would stop, at which point you'd use the bt command to see where you are, use the up command to move in the context you want, and then use the print command to display the content of some local variables.

All these commands support a variety of refinements that would be too long to go over here. As always, leverage the `help` command to find out more about these. For instance, the `print` command supports a modifier that you can append to the `print` command itself to change how the result of the evaluation is printed. For example, `p/t expression` will print the result of `expression` using a binary representation, and `p/x expression` will print it in hexadecimal.

Let's stay on the topic of the `print` command – it's an extremely powerful tool!

This command can evaluate any expressions, including ones that modify the state of the program. For instance, let's say that you're looking at how to fix an issue in your program and you notice that the content of a variable is incorrect. Using the `print` command, you can assign a new value to this variable (for instance, by running `p MyVar = fct(OtherVar) + 3`) and then resume the execution of the program. This way, you can see whether your understanding of the problem is accurate without having to implement the fix and re-compile your program!

> **Hitting breakpoints while printing**
>
> With the `print` command, you can execute any function of your program at any time. You can combine this capability with breakpoints. For instance, let's say you want to observe the execution of a function with some specific inputs or you didn't set a breakpoint on that function and, after running the `next` command, you realize this function is misbehaving. You can set a breakpoint on this function and then call it with the `print` command! By default, the evaluation of the expression of a `print` command ignores all breakpoints; however, you can change this behavior by overriding the `ignore-breakpoints-in-expressions` setting under the `target.process` family by running the `setting set target.process.ignore-breakpoints-in-expressions false` LLDB command.

Finally, you can combine the `print` command (or any command, in fact) with a breakpoint to, for instance, print the content of some values when you hit the related breakpoint.

Consider the following LLDB command lines:

```
(lldb) b populate_function.cpp:42
Breakpoint 3: <snip>
(lldb) break command add 3
Enter your debugger command(s).  Type 'DONE' to end.
> p &Foo
> DONE
```

These commands set a breakpoint on the 42nd line of the `populate_function.cpp` file, which creates a breakpoint with an ID of 3. The next command, `break command add`, uses this ID to specify that we want to add commands that will be automatically executed when we hit this breakpoint. In this case, we add a command to print the address of the `Foo` variable.

Before we move on to the next section, here's a useful command to know so that you can learn more about LLDB itself: apropos. By using the apropos command followed by a term, LLDB prints all the commands that may be relevant to what you're trying to achieve – for instance, how to run apropos stack lists, among other things, print the backtrace, step out of the current frame (what the finish command does), change the format that's used to display the stack frames, and so on.

In this section, you learned about the basics of how to use LLDB. You learned how to start a debugging session, control the execution of a program, and inspect its state. Using this tool, you can supercharge your productivity while investigating issues.

In the next section, we'll point out the APIs that you can leverage within a debugger to inspect the state of the LLVM IR efficiently.

# The LLVM code base through a debugger

As you discovered in the previous section, a debugger offers a powerful mechanism to evaluate any expression, including the ability to make function calls. In this section, we'll highlight some of the APIs of the LLVM code base that you can use to easily inspect the state of the LLVM IR.

When built with the right CMake options, which is the case when built in Debug mode, most of the key LLVM classes come with a dump method. This method prints the related object in a human-readable form, similar to what you can see in the textual representation of the LLVM IR. What this means is that by calling this method from the debugger, you can easily visualize what the related object represents.

> Note
>
> By default, the dump methods are only available when LLVM is built with assertions enabled. You can change this behavior by setting the LLVM_ENABLE_DUMP CMake variable to on or off.

Let's see these dump methods in action!

Let's assume that we stopped the program in the debugger as it was performing optimization while this optimization was processing some instructions. At this point, let's say that the Instr variable contains a reference to the instruction that's currently being processed.

The following sequence of LLDB commands shows how to use the right LLVM APIs so that you can better grasp what you're dealing with:

```
(lldb) p Instr
(llvm::Instruction &) 0x<snip>: {
  llvm::User = {
    llvm::Value = {
      SubclassID = '6'
<snip>
(lldb) p Instr.dump()
```

```
  %i = shl i32 5, 3
(lldb) p Instr.getType()
(llvm::Type *) 0x0000000137808c00
(lldb) p *Instr.getType()
(llvm::Type) {
  Context = 0x000000016fdfeec8
<snip>
(lldb) p Instr.getType()->dump()
i32
```

The previous snippet shows how difficult it is to interpret the content of a variable when it's printed directly (p Instr). The next command uses the dump method of the related class, which makes it clear what we're dealing with (%i = shl i32 5, 3). Next, printing the LLVM type of the Instr variable (p Instr.getType()) yields the address of the instance of the Type class, and dereferencing this pointer gives us the raw content of this object. Now, when we use the dump method, the LLVM type becomes easy to read (i32).

Note

When the dump methods have been disabled, you can resort to the print methods. Most of the dump methods are thin wrappers around the print method of the related class. The only difference is that they call the print method with all the right arguments. You can use the print methods directly. The first argument of these methods is always the output stream, hence why dbgs() or errs() works, and the other arguments depend on the object being printed. However, if you don't want to check the method signature, just know that most of them can be set to zero and/or nullptr. For instance, the p Instr.getType()->print(dbgs(),0,0); (void)(dbgs() << '\n') LLDB command yields the same result as Instr.getType()->dump(). In this case, we use dbgs() for the output stream; for the other arguments, we just set zero without worrying about what they represent (in this case, two Boolean values that change what's printed). This second part of this expression just adds a new line in the output stream to make sure we can see what's being printed.

Aside from the dump methods, we encourage you to use getParent, getType, and other methods that you already know about (see *Chapter 7* for a reminder) to get the information you need. For instance, let's say that we're wondering what the IR function of our instruction looks like in the previous debugging session. To do that, we can simply use Instr.getFunction() (or Instr.getParent()->getParent()) and apply the dump method to the resulting value to print the encompassing Function instance.

We encourage you to also add a print method and a dump method (add LLVM_DUMP_METHOD in front of your dump method to comply with the LLVM coding standard) to the class that you design within your compiler. That way, you'll have a consistent debugging experience between your custom code and the open source code.

In this section, you learned about the dump method, which most LLVM key classes expose. We showed you how this method, combined with a debugger, offers a straightforward way to print the state of LLVM objects.

# Summary

In this chapter, you learned about the various pieces of the LLVM infrastructure that you can use to help you debug your compiler.

These pieces are as follows:

- Debug logs and statistics that come built into LLVM passes and that you can enable with the debug-only and stats command-line options
- The llvm-reduce and bugpoint command-line tools, which can automatically shrink the size of the input IR
- The sanitizers that you can enable in your build configuration to catch diverse kinds of problems
- The dump method, which you can use to inspect the state of most LLVM objects

Now, you can approach every problem with the right tool and with confidence!

In the next chapter, we'll begin our journey of lowering the LLVM IR.

# Further reading

You can find the official LLVM documentation for the LLVM tools that were presented at the following links:

- https://llvm.org/docs/CommandGuide/llvm-reduce.html for the llvm-reduce CLI
- https://llvm.org/docs/CommandGuide/bugpoint.html for the bugpoint CLI and https://llvm.org/docs/Bugpoint.html for its fancier use cases
- https://llvm.org/docs/CommandGuide/llvm-extract.html for the llvm-extract CLI
- https://llvm.org/docs/OptBisect.html for an explanation of how to use the opt-bisect-limit command-line option

For the sanitizers offered by Clang, please look at the related documentation pages:

- The address sanitizer: https://clang.llvm.org/docs/AddressSanitizer.html
- The thread sanitizer: https://clang.llvm.org/docs/ThreadSanitizer.html
- The memory sanitizer: https://clang.llvm.org/docs/MemorySanitizer.html
- The undefined behavior sanitizer: https://clang.llvm.org/docs/UndefinedBehaviorSanitizer.html
- The dataflow sanitizer: https://clang.llvm.org/docs/DataFlowSanitizer.html
- The leak sanitizer: https://clang.llvm.org/docs/LeakSanitizer.html

Finally, if you want to learn more about LLDB, you can find the official tutorial at https://lldb.llvm.org/use/tutorial.html.

# Quiz time

Now that you have completed reading this chapter, try answering the following questions to test your knowledge:

1.  You want to enable the debug log for a specific pass using debug-only and your compiler refuses, producing Unknown command line argument '-debug-only=MyPass' as an error message. How would you fix that?

    The debug-only option is only available when you build LLVM with assertions enabled.

    To fix that, rebuild LLVM while enabling assertions.

    See the *Printing the debug log* section for more details.

2.  How can you find the string to pass to the debug-only option for a specific pass?

    The string to use with the debug-only option can be found in the DEBUG_TYPE macro. This is instantiated in the file that implements the pass you're interested in.

    See the *Printing the debug log* section for more details.

3.  Given some input IR, what tool could you use to create a standalone function from a basic block?

    The llvm-extract command-line tool can do that for you. You can simply use the -bb=funcName:bbName command-line option to do that.

    More details can be found in the *Extracting a subset of the input IR* section.

4.  Your compiler crashes on some giant input IR. What can you do to shrink the size of the input IR?

    You can use the llvm-reduce or bugpoint LLVM command-line tool to automatically reduce the size of the input IR.

    See the *Shrinking the IR automatically* section to learn how to do this.

5.  You've reduced your input IR and now you want to investigate the crash. What would be a typical debugging session with LLDB?

    You'd typically start with the following sequence of commands:

```
$ lldb -- myCompiler myOptions myInputIR
(lldb) r
<program crashes>
(lldb) bt
```

    Here, we launched the debugger with the command line that reproduces the issue. Then, we ran the executable (with the r command, which is a shortcut for run).

    After the crash, we printed the call stack with the bt command to find out where the crash occurred.

    You can find more details about how to use LLDB in the *A crash course on LLDB* section.

6. You're debugging a version of LLVM that was compiled without the `dump` methods. What alternative do you have to make your debugging session easier?

You can leverage the `print` methods since these are always available. However, beware that some of them require additional arguments.

See the *The LLVM code base through a debugger* section for more details.

---

**Unlock this book's exclusive benefits now**

This book comes with additional benefits designed to elevate your learning experience.

*Note: Have your purchase invoice ready before you begin.*

https://www.packtpub.com/unlock/9781837637782

# Part 3

# Introduction to the Backend

Now that you are familiar with the LLVM middle-end, you are ready to go deeper into the inner workings of the LLVM infrastructure.

This part introduces you to the backend part of the LLVM infrastructure, where you start dealing almost exclusively with target-specific constructs such as the registers or instructions available.

The backend part of LLVM features its own **intermediate representation** (IR), called the Machine IR, and its own pass pipeline, called the **code generation** (**CodeGen**) pipeline. Unlike the LLVM IR, the Machine IR is fully customizable, and one of the tasks of a backend author is to teach the LLVM infrastructure about the **instruction set architecture** (**ISA**) of their target.

Therefore, this part teaches you the following:

- How to understand the Machine IR
- How to augment the Machine IR with your target-specific instruction
- How to describe the binary representation, called encoding, of your instructions and registers
- How to customize the codegen pipeline

By the end of this part, you will be able to fully describe your ISA in the LLVM infrastructure, manipulate the Machine IR, and customize the codegen pipeline.

This part of the book includes the following chapters:

- *Chapter 11, Getting Started with the Backend*
- *Chapter 12, Getting Started with the Machine Code Layer*
- *Chapter 13, The Machine Pass Pipeline*

# 11

# Getting Started with the Backend

As you discovered in *Chapter 3*, the low-level concepts used by the target independent LLVM code generator are expressed in an **intermediate representation (IR)** called **Machine IR**.

In this chapter, you'll deepen your understanding of this IR by learning about the following topics:

- How to interpret its textual representation
- Which APIs to use beyond the ones you already know
- How to implement the key pieces you need to get started with the code generation, or **codegen**, part of your backend to work at this level of IR
- Which tools to use to interact with it

To get you started on the right foot, let's review what you need for this chapter.

## Technical requirements

As in the previous chapter, you'll need a version of LLVM to play with the Machine IR. You can use either one of the recent LLVM releases – for instance, from LLVM 17 and up – or build LLVM directly from its source code. Please see *Chapter 1* on how to build LLVM if you need help with that.

Additionally, in this book's GitHub repository, which is available at https://github.com/ PacktPublishing/LLVM-Code-Generation, you'll find a folder named ch11 that contains the examples and exercises that we'll be implementing in this chapter.

Later in this chapter, we'll start implementing something in an actual LLVM backend. You can find all the necessary commits and details by looking at the GitHub log available at https://github.com/ PacktPublishing/LLVM-Code-Generation-by-example, between the begin_ch11 and end_ch11 tags. Note that we call this repository the companion repository. The commits that have been referenced between these tags apply what we'll describe in this chapter to the H2BLB backend that we started in *Chapter 9*. Please refer to that chapter to learn how to take full advantage of the GitHub history to better understand what the changes are doing.

Now, let's see when you'll encounter the Machine IR.

# Introducing the Machine IR

In *Chapter 1*, we mentioned that an LLVM backend mainly deals with two levels of IR:

- The LLVM IR for high-level optimizations
- The Machine IR for low-level optimizations and the lowering of the LLVM IR to assembly code

As you saw in *Chapter 9*, the LLVM IR can represent target-specific constructs. Therefore, you might be wondering whether we need two different IRs.

We aren't going to reiterate the history of the LLVM project here, so let's just say that the LLVM IR isn't flexible enough. One of the obvious issues is that target architectures don't operate on the **static single assignment (SSA)** form. The SSA form guided a lot of the design decisions of the LLVM IR and departing from it would have dramatic effects on the **application programming interface (API)** of the core library of the LLVM infrastructure.

The Machine IR embraces the concept of flexibility. It supports both SSA and non-SSA forms and has very few rules when it comes to how things are modeled (for instance, you may remember from *Chapter 3* that a `MachineBasicBlock` instance may have zero to several terminator instructions, whereas a basic block in the LLVM IR requires exactly one terminator instruction!), and it can easily be extended through TableGen to support new instructions.

All this flexibility comes with a price; the Machine IR API is difficult to approach for newcomers and can be confusing when you aren't aware of what's being modeled.

Now that you know why there's a second IR in LLVM, in the next section, you'll discover when the Machine IR appears in the pass pipeline.

# Here comes the Machine IR

If you've already followed the logs that were produced by the `print-before-all` or `print-after-all` option (see *Chapter 10*) to the assembly code, then you've already encountered the Machine IR.

Indeed, any transformation that runs after the instruction selection pass produces the Machine IR. *Figure 11.1* illustrates the whole compilation process and mentions where the Machine IR appears:

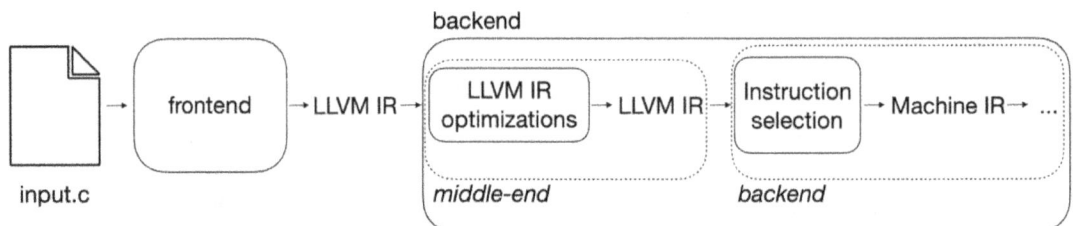

*Figure 11.1: The compilation pipeline and the related IRs*

*Figure 11.1* shows the input file (input.c) going through the frontend and being converted into the LLVM IR. Then, the backend takes over and starts by performing a sequence of LLVM IR to LLVM IR transformations. This sequence is, as you know, called the middle-end. Next, the backend runs the instruction selection pass, which translates the LLVM IR into Machine IR. This marks the beginning of the backend part of the backend (confusing, we know!). From this point forward, all the remaining passes work on the Machine IR until this representation is finally translated into assembly or object code through the transient **machine code** (**MC**) representation.

To summarize, the Machine IR appears as part of the lowering toward assembly code and is introduced during instruction selection.

In the next section, you'll learn how to interpret its textual representation.

# The Machine IR textual representation

Like the LLVM IR, the Machine IR can be represented in a textual format. In this section, we'll describe how this format is structured and how to understand it.

The textual format of the Machine IR is called **MIR** and the related files are suffixed with the .mir file extension.

> On .mir files
>
> The .mir format is intended for developers only. It's used extensively to test specific parts of the backend within the LLVM project but isn't expected to be used beyond that. For instance, it isn't guaranteed to be stable from one LLVM release to another and doesn't offer any compatibility guarantees. The bottom line is this: don't use this format beyond unit testing and debugging!

Let's start by learning how a .mir file is structured.

## The .mir file format

The .mir file format uses **YAML Ain't Markup Language** (**YAML**), a human-readable text format where you can represent structures, lists, and more. The format itself isn't that important and in any case, we don't expect that you'll need to write .mir by hand. Therefore, instead of teaching you the whole YAML syntax, we'll focus on its specific instantiation as a .mir file.

Before we give you the high-level structure of a .mir file, you should note that you'll encounter different flavors of .mir. Setting aside the fact that the content of a .mir file is highly target-specific, the actual information in a .mir file depends on what its intended use is. More specifically, a .mir file contains a lot of information but a lot of it can be (re)computed by the compiler and can be omitted. As such, a pure dump of the MIR format would contain all that information, but a human-written one or a dump from a pass may contain less information. In other words, the format we're about to describe is a guideline and specific instantiations may differ and may only provide a subset of this information.

With no further due, here's an example of the general structure of a pure `.mir` file:

```
--- |
  Textual LLVM IR
...
---
name: funcName
alignment: 4
<...>
registers:
  - { id: 0, class: regClass0, preferred-register: '' }
<...>
frameInfo:
  isFrameAddressTaken: false
  <...>
body: |
  bb.0 (%ir-block.entry):
    successors: %bb.i(0xProba), <...>, %bb.j(0xProba)
    liveins: $phyReg0, <...>, $physRegN
    MachineInstr0
    <...>
  <...>
  bb.N:
  <...>
...
<...> # more Machine function entries.
```

In this snippet, the `<...>` sequence of characters means that we truncated the content and that the same surrounding structure repeats itself.

Now, let's start with a bit of the YAML syntax.

## A primer on the YAML syntax

The exact details of the YAML syntax can be found on the official website: `https://yaml.org/`. In this section, we'll just give you the bare minimum to help you get started with the MIR file format.

The `---` and `...` sequence of characters mark the beginning and the end of a section, respectively.

> **About nomenclature**
>
> For the explanations, we decided to depart from the official YAML terms because we thought they could be confusing for non-YAML people. For instance, what we call a section is called a document in YAML and what we call a file is called a stream.

A pure .mir file is composed of at least two sections: one for the LLVM IR module and one for each MachineFunction instance (that is, an instance of the class that represents a function at the Machine IR level. See *Chapter 3* for more details.) A non-pure .mir file may ditch the LLVM IR section if it follows certain constraints. We'll come back to this in the *Shrinking a .mir file* section.

Next, you can define mappings of fields to values using the field: value syntax. For instance, name: funcName defines a field called name with a value of funcName. The value itself can be a complex object with nested fields. For instance, in our previous MIR snippet, the frameInfo field contains a mapping of fields, with the first one being isFrameAddressTaken, which has a value of false.

Nested fields are easily recognizable by their indentation, but you can also define them between the { and } characters, as seen with the nested values for the registers field.

Focusing on the registers field, notice that each indented line nested below it starts with the dash (-) character. This character means that the related line is an entry in a list. Put differently, the registers field is a list of objects where each object has the id, class, and preferred-register fields. We'll cover the meaning of these fields in the *The semantics of the different fields* section.

While not depicted in the previous snippet, note that lists can also be represented on one line using the [ and ] characters. Some fields use this syntax.

To summarize, the YAML syntax offers two equivalent representations for lists and mappings: one representation that fits on one line and one that has one element per line.

In other words, lists can be represented with either of the following two syntaxes:

```
listFieldInLine: [ elt0, elt1, ...]
listFieldWithOnePerLine:
  - elt0
  - elt1
```

Likewise, mappings can be represented with the following two syntaxes:

```
mappingFieldInLine: { field0: elt0, field1: elt1, ...}
mappingFieldWithOnePerLine:
  field0: elt0
  field1: elt1
```

We have one final bit of syntax to present, after which you'll be able to interpret all the fields in a MIR field.

Fields, or more generally YAML directives, such as ---, can be followed by the pipe (|) character. This character means that within the related scope, YAML must preserve the newlines and not try to interpret the content of the related scope, so long as the lines are properly indented. This means that if you don't indent a line properly within this verbatim directive, YAML will try to resume its parsing to find the end of the section (the ... sequence of characters), for instance.

You see this kind of raw input in action in two instances in a .mir file:

- In the section that describes the LLVM IR: --- |
- In the field that describes the body of a MachineFunction instance: body: |

What this means is that both the content of the LLVM IR section and the field that represents the body of a MachineFunction instance use a custom parser.

> **Comments and custom parsers**
>
> You can add comments to a YAML file by using the # character, followed by applying the comments. However, if you add comments in the raw sections of the .mir file – that is, in the body field or the LLVM IR section of a .mir file – you must use the comment syntax of that related section. For instance, if you add a comment in the textual LLVM IR section, since that section is parsed by the LLVM IR parser, it must use the semicolon character (;) to start a comment. In other words, depending on where you put your comments in a .mir file, the syntax may be different. This is why the check lines that are used for FileCheck in the unit test may not look consistent across tests and/or targets.

At this point, you should be able to understand the structure of the .mir file format. However, you don't know what the underlying semantics is. Let's fix that.

## The semantics of the different fields

Setting aside the textual LLVM IR section that's here so that the MachineFunction instances can refer to the related Function instance, each field of the .mir file is used to populate either the related field of the MachineFunction instance or some of its helper classes, such as the MachineFrameInfo class or the MachineRegisterInfo class.

Let's see how this plays out in detail.

### Mapping the content of a .mir file to the C++ API

Typically, the plain fields, as opposed to the nested ones, are used to populate the MachineFunction instance and the nested ones are used for the helper classes.

For instance, the alignment field in the .mir file is used to set the Alignment variable member of the MachineFunction instance, and the nested fields under the frameinfo field in the .mir file are used to populate the MachineFrameInfo instance – for example, the isFrameAddressTaken nested field populates the information behind the MachineFrameInfo::isFrameAddressTaken method.

In general, the fields' name may not exactly match the related class field's name (for instance, callSites in the .mir file versus the callSitesInfo variable member in the MachineFunction class), but we're confident that you'll manage to connect the dots. Then, looking at the comments on the related class members in the LLVM code base will tell you what they mean!

Here's what you need to remember:

- Plain fields populate the MachineFunction instance
- Fields under frameinfo populate the MachineFrameInfo instance
- Fields (or values, in this case) under the registers field populate the MachineRegisterInfo instance
- Fields under the machineFunctionInfo field populate the MachineFunctionInfo instance

Some of the plain fields map to the MachineFunctionProperties variable member of the MachineFunction instance. These fields identify where in the lowering pipeline the MachineFunction instance is. However, they may not be relevant in all cases. For instance, the regBankSelected field represents a value of the MachineFunctionProperties class but is only set and used when the backend uses the global instruction selector. Most MachineFunctionProperties values are otherwise computed directly from the input .mir file.

> Note
>
> Each MachineFunction object can have a MachineFunctionInfo instance attached to it. The MachineFunctionInfo class and the related target-specific subclasses (for instance, the AMDGPUMachineFunction class) represent some target-specific state or information that's otherwise not available at the machine level. In other words, you can leverage the MachineFunctionInfo class in your backend to attach custom information to each instance of a MachineFunction class. While this is useful and sometimes the only available mechanism, we recommend using analysis passes instead so that you can propagate or keep information around as much as possible. We won't explain how to leverage the MachineFunctionInfo class in this book since its usage is very target-specific and difficult to illustrate with generic problems. If you're interested in this mechanism, look at the implementation of the AMDGPU backend.

Next, the name field is a bit special because technically, a MachineFunction object doesn't have a name. Instead, this object gets its name from the LLVM IR Function instance that's tied to it. Therefore, this field ties the MachineFunction instance to the Function instance with the same name. The Function instance comes from the textual LLVM IR section.

At this point, we've covered all but one field: the body field. This is the topic of the next section.

## A deep dive into the body of a MachineFunction instance

For an easier read, here's a repeat of the general structure of the serialization format of a MachineFunction instance:

```
name: funcName
attribute1: ...
attribute2: ...
body: |
<...>
```

The body field in the .mir file contains almost verbatim what you'd get when you call the MachineFunction::dump method. The only differences are around some pretty printing that doesn't affect how you interpret the output. In other words, with what you're about to learn, you'll be able to understand the .mir file format, the debug logs (see *Chapter 10*), and the calls to the dump methods from the MachineFunction, MachineBasicBlock, and MachineInstr objects equally.

The body field contains the sequence of the MachineBasicBlock instances in the order that they will be emitted in the final assembly code. One such basic block would look like the following serialized format:

```
bb.0 (%ir-block.entry):
  successors: %bb.i(0xProba), <...>, %bb.j(0xProba)
  liveins: $phyReg0, <...>, $physRegN
  MachineInstr0
  <...>
  MachineInstrN
```

The beginning of a basic block is identified by bb.num (prop0, prop1, ...):, where num is the number of the related MachineBasicBlock instance (available through the MachineBasicBlock::getNumber() method) and (prop0, prop1, ...) is a comma-separated list of properties that specifies different attributes or variable members of the related MachineBasicBlock instance. The list of properties is completely optional and if it isn't set, a MachineBasicBlock object uses the default values.

For instance, if a MachineBasicBlock object originates from an LLVM IR basic block, this would be reflected as the %ir-block.blockName property, as seen in the previous snippet (bb.0 (%ir-block. entry):). This means that the MachineBasicBlock::getBasicBlock() method on this instance of MachineBasicBlock yields the LLVM IR BasicBlock instance with the name blockName (here, this is entry).

Other properties include align num, call-frame-size size, machine-block-address-taken, and landing-pad. The point is that you can easily interpret them from the property name, plus you can find the related variable member in the MachineBasicBlock class so that you can read the comments directly from the LLVM code base if you don't understand these property models.

A note on the number variable member of the MachineBasicBlock class

The number variable member is guaranteed to be unique across the MachineBasicBlock objects belonging to the same MachineFunction instance. Moreover, they're guaranteed to be densely assigned, meaning that there's no gap between two basic block numbers. These properties make it easy to create a hash map cheaply with a plain array where the basic blocks are hashed with their number. To allocate the right size of your array, you just need to use the MachineFunction::getNumBlockIDs() method. Additionally, if you're afraid that the actual number of basic blocks may be much smaller than the number of assigned IDs (for instance, because a previous optimization deleted a ton of them), you can repack the IDs using the MachineFunction::RenumberBlocks method.

After the beginning of the basic block and before the first `MachineInstr` instance, you may find the `successors` and/or `liveins` directives. Let's take a closer look at them:

- `successors`: The list of basic blocks that are the successors of the current one. The format of this list is a comma-separated list of `%bb.num(0xProba)`, where `num` is the number of the related basic blocks and `(0xProba)` is a probability defined using a fixed-point format in hexadecimal (for instance, `0x80000000` means 100%, `0x30000000` means 37.5%, and `0x50000000` means 62.5%). We won't describe this format here because we don't expect you will have to write them manually and the debug logs automatically print them in a human-readable form.
- `liveins`: The list of live registers, meaning they carry a useful value, at the beginning of this block. This is a comma-separated list of physical registers.

Both these directives are optional but have a couple of caveats:

- The parser knows how to rebuild the `successors` list from the `MachineInstr` instance within the current basic block. However, when it rebuilds this list, it will use an equal distribution to set the probabilities for each branch. For instance, if a basic block has two successors, this means we have a 50/50 chance to go to one or the other. This is fine but beware that if you try to reproduce specific bugs, such as something that changes the order of the basic blocks based on their probabilities, this may change the behavior of your optimizer. Note that you can also specify the list of successors while leaving the probability out (that is, removing the whole `(0xProba)` part).
- If the `liveins` directive isn't set, the variables that are alive at the beginning of the related basic block will be assumed to be empty.

The next thing you'll find in a basic block is the textual representation of the `MachineInstr` instances. There's one `MachineInstr` instance per line and the syntax looks like this:

```
def0, def1, ... = opcode arg0, arg1, ... :: mem ops
```

All the operands of the `MachineInstr` object – that is, `def0`, `def1`, ..., `arg0`, `arg1`, ... – in this snippet are instances of the `MachineOperand` class.

The type of an operand is identified by the character that prefixes it. Here are the main ones:

- Virtual registers are prefixed with the `%` character (for instance, `%1` or `%myReg`)
- Physical registers are prefixed with the `$` character (for instance, `$w0`)
- Symbols are prefixed with the `@` character (for instance, `@funcBar`)
- Immediate values are plain immediate values (for instance, `3`)

We'll cover these types and more in the *Working with MachineOperand instances* section.

Register operands can be decorated with additional properties that appear before the operand, such as `implicit-def`, `dead`, and so on (for instance, `dead %1`), or after the operand, such as the sub-register index (for instance, `%1.sub_32`), the register class (for instance, `%1:gpr64`), and so on. We'll come back to the concepts of register classes and the sub-register index in the *Working with registers* section. For the other properties, you can easily tie them to the related property in the `MachineOperand` class by looking for their names in the related header file in the `CodeGen` library. We'll cover some of these properties in the *Working with MachineOperand instances* section since a handful of them may be difficult to grasp.

The opcode is target-specific and is generated through TableGen. We'll show you how the TableGen description connects to the printing of the Machine IR in the *Describing instructions* section, but in any case, you need to know the backend and its **instruction set architecture** (**ISA**) to understand what the semantics of a specific opcode is. Most of the opcodes have sensible names, so you may know what they do from the get-go. For instance, if you look at the `%8:gpr32 = ADDWrr %6, %7` string from the AArch64 backend, you can guess that this is an addition instruction that takes two registers and produces one register. The `W` part of the opcode in this case means that it works on `W` registers, which are 32-bit registers on AArch64, and `rr` means that both input operands are registers. Additionally, instructions can have properties. These will show up right in front of the opcode – for instance, we could have `frame-setup` and `reassoc`, which map to the `MachineInstr::getFlags` family of methods.

Finally, the instruction may have some memory operands attached to it. These operands appear at the end of the textual representation of the instruction, after the sequence of double colons (`::`) characters. These operands provide more information about the memory accesses of the instruction, such as the size and location of a store (the location is expressed in terms of an LLVM IR value, such as `store (s16) into %ir.p.addr`, which describes the store of a 16-bit value in the location represented by the `p.addr` LLVM IR value) and are stored in instances of the `MachineMemOperand` class and can be obtained through the `MachineInstr::getMMOs()` method. These operands can be used to query, for instance, the results of the alias analysis performed on the LLVM IR.

Now that you have a basic understanding of the `.mir` file format, let's teach you how you can interact with it.

## Working with a .mir file

As mentioned previously, the main use of `.mir` files is for writing unit tests for the low-level part of the backend. You can also use them to run only specific parts of the backend when you're debugging issues.

Let's get started by showing you how to generate a `.mir` file.

## Generating a .mir file

You can generate a `.mir` file after any pass that runs on a `MachineFunction` instance. Put differently, you can generate a `.mir` file for each of the passes after instruction selection.

Concretely, you can generate a `.mir` file by using the `-stop-before=pass-name` or `-stop-after=pass-name` command-line option, where `pass-name` is the name of the backend pass before (or after, respectively) which you want to dump the Machine IR. This `pass-name` value is the name that has been used to register the pass you're interested in in the pass manager (see *Chapter 5* for more details).

The stop-before and stop-after command-line options are free if you hook up the LLVM **command-line interface (CLI)** in your compiler. The clang and llc binaries offer them by default. Please refer to *Chapter 5* if you're building your own tools and want to connect to the LLVM CLI.

For instance, let's say that we want to print the Machine IR right before the peephole optimizer, which is an optimization pass that runs almost right after the instruction selector.

The command line to do this with clang would be as follows:

```
$ clang -O3 -S -mllvm -stop-before=peephole-opt input.c -o out.mir
```

In this command, notice that you invoke Clang as you would normally do, but you must add the -mllvm option to tell it that you want to pass an option to the backend, after which you pass the necessary option (in this case, -stop-before).

The llc command line looks similar but drops the -mllvm option:

```
$ llc -stop-before=peephole-opt input.ll -o out.mir
```

For both these commands, you end up with a pure .mir file, meaning it matches the general structure we showed you in the *The .mir file format* section. This format is extremely verbose and contains a lot of redundant information.

> **Note**
>
> If the pass that you use for the stop-before/after option isn't run, for instance, it will only run when a specific target feature is enabled, such as when support for the half-precision floating-point type is provided, the .mir file will contain the output of the last MachineFunction pass in the backend.

In the next section, we'll show you what you can do with your .mir file.

## Running passes

Using a .mir file, you can run a custom set of passes using llc.

The set of passes depends on the command-line options you use:

- start-before/after=pass-name: Starts the pass pipeline of the backend before (or after, respectively) the pass registered under the pass-name CLI option. In other words, this option allows you to run a subset of the predefined pass pipeline. Note that this option can be used alongside the stop-before and stop-after options.
- run-pass=pass-name: Runs only the given pass. This option can be specified several times (or pass names can be separated by commas (,) within just one instance of this option) so that only the predefined set of passes is run. In other words, this option completely bypasses the pass pipeline provided by the backend and builds a custom one instead.

For instance, the following command line runs the backend starting at the peephole optimizer:

```
$ llc -start-before=peephole-opt input.mir -o out.s
```

By using the `start-before` option, this command line runs the backend to the assembly code output but starting from the peephole optimizer. This is useful for checking whether a fix that you made in the peephole optimizer still plays nicely with the rest of the backend.

Alternatively, the following command line allows you to run and test the peephole optimizer in isolation:

```
$ llc -run-pass=peephole-opt input.mir -o out.mir
```

Notice how this command spits out a new `.mir` file and not the final assembly code, as identified by the file extension (`.mir` versus `.s`).

> **Note**
>
> Using a `.mir` file and chaining different `llc` commands may yield different results than running the equivalent pipeline in one go. For instance, let's say that you run `llc` with `run-pass=opt1`, followed by `start-after=opt1` on the output of the first invocation. While in theory, this should yield the same results as running `llc` with `start-before=opt1`, this may not be the case. The MIR format doesn't serialize the entire state of the backend and things not captured in the `.mir` file may produce different results. For instance, let's say that our `opt1` pass uses an analysis named `foo` but doesn't invalidate it properly (see *Chapter 5* for a refresher on these concepts) and a later pass, `opt2`, uses it later. When running with the two invocations of `llc` (`run-pass` followed by `start-after`), at the end of the first run, `foo` contains invalid information but `opt2` won't see that because `foo` will be recomputed from scratch when the second invocation of `llc` occurs. In the unique invocation of `llc` (`start-before`), `opt2` will be exposed to the out-of-date information of `foo`. The bottom line is that when you're using `.mir` files, if you don't observe the behavior you expect, chances are you're relying on some information that hasn't been serialized.

Irrespective of the reasons you use a `.mir` file, knowing how to shrink this type of file is an important skill to have. Indeed, to ensure the tests are robust, understandable, and maintainable, it's important to keep `.mir` files as small as possible. Similarly, when reproducing an issue or iterating on something, having smaller inputs allows you to focus on the right things and speed up the whole iteration velocity since fewer things need to be processed by the backend.

In the next section, we'll show you how to shrink the size of a `.mir` file while keeping it valid enough for its intended use.

# Shrinking a .mir file

LLVM comes with automatic ways to shrink a .mir file.

The first one is the simplify-mir CLI option. This option removes the things that use the default values or that can be recomputed from the .mir file's output. For example, in the ch11/mir_format folder of this book's GitHub repository, you can find an example where we generated two .mir files from the same input LLVM IR file – one with the simplify-mir option and one without. The simplified file (simplified-dump.mir) contains 78 lines, whereas the non-simplified one (full-dump.mir) contains 118 lines.

In other words, by adding a single option to the command line that prints out .mir files, you get smaller .mir files:

```
$ llc -stop-before=peephole-opt input.ll -o out.mir -simplify-mir
```

The second way to shrink the size of a .mir file is by using the llvm-reduce command-line tool. We touched on the llvm-reduce tool in *Chapter 10*; using the techniques you learned there, you can use this tool on .mir files as well. In other words, simplify-mir gets rid of the pieces that the compiler can recompute and llvm-reduce gets rid of the pieces that aren't relevant to whatever you're trying to capture. For instance, you would use llvm-reduce to shrink an input file to something that reproduces a bug with the smallest possible input, then use simplify-mir on that file to remove the things that are redundant in the default serialized output.

The third and last way is to slash out the unnecessary part of the .mir file yourself. While this process can be highly dependent on what you're trying to achieve, here are a few things that generally work:

- Removing the LLVM IR section can work. In general, you don't need to have the full LLVM IR around to reproduce an issue, so removing this section is an easy size win. To be able to do that, you have to get rid of all the references to the LLVM IR (usually starting with %ir) from the sections of the different MachineFunction instances: Remove the references of the LLVM IR basic blocks – for instance, bb.0.entry becomes bb.0

- Remove the references of the memory values in the memory operands – for instance, load (s32) from %ir.i7 becomes load (s32). Note that you may lose the information from alias analysis when doing this, so this isn't always possible: Replace the symbols with a dummy value in the machine operands – for instance, BL @_bar becomes BL 0. This technically changes the semantics of the machine instruction since instead of doing something with the address of the bar symbol, you do something with address 0, but most of the time, you don't need the symbol to catch the behavior you want to exercise. See the following note if you need the symbol to reproduce your issue but still want to reduce the size of your .mir file.

- Removing the registers field. Unless you need to keep unreferenced registers (registers not used or defined in the body of the function) or the preferred-register field (which changes how the register allocator assigns physical registers to the related virtual register) to reproduce your issue, the list of elements in the registers field can be recomputed from the body field and be safely removed.

- Removing the liveins, frameInfo, alignment, and other fields from the fields of the function instance. Unless you're doing something with the fields of the function, they're all useless for most of the pass pipeline. The only mandatory fields are name and tracksRegLiveness. For instance, the liveins field is rarely useful unless you're dealing with specific instruction selection issues. Note that you need to keep the liveins information within the body field though, so pay attention to whether the liveins field is nested in the body field before removing it! In any case, you can try to remove a field, see whether what you want to reproduce still happens or not, and repeat. Note that removing a lot of fields may prevent you from generating assembly code with your input file (for instance, the frameInfo field is required to do the frame lowering), but it may be fine to remove it so that you can run a test on an individual pass.

- Removing the successors field in the body field. Successors are recomputed automatically. So, unless you care about the probabilities attached to them, you can remove them. Note that keeping the successors field but without the probabilities is also a good compromise because they help with understanding the **control flow** of the program, without you having to manually inspect the **terminators** of the related basic block (remember that if the last instruction of a block isn't an unconditional jump instruction, then it will fall through to the next basic block in the linear order, meaning the program will continue to the block that's printed after the current one).

Note

If you can't remove all the symbols from your machine code – for instance, you need to keep the name of the function in the call instruction of your body to reproduce an issue – you can shrink the LLVM IR section manually: just define empty functions! The parser for the .mir file will succeed if it finds the symbols in the LLVM IR section. It doesn't try to see whether the function is semantically correct; it only needs to parse correctly. If the LLVM IR section isn't in a .mir file, the parser will create these empty functions for the MachineFunction instances described in the current file automatically. You can see that for yourself; run the llc command-line tool on a .mir file without the LLVM IR section (for instance, shrunk-dump.mir from the ch11 folder) and dump the .mir file (using the -run-pass=peephole-opt option, for instance). You'll see that this will produce a pure .mir file with an LLVM IR section that contains empty functions.

Using all these techniques, you'll end up with compact .mir files that capture the essence of the issue you want to demonstrate. For instance, starting with the simplified-dump.mir file from the ch11/mir_format folder, we can manually reduce it to 29 lines (from 78 lines), assuming the goal was to run only the peephole optimizer pass!

Note

When you remove the LLVM IR section, you also get rid of the target triple field that comes with it. Therefore, make sure you specify it back on your command line using the mtriple option to keep hitting the right backend. Similarly, if what you want to capture depends on some target features, they may have been captured in the attributes metadata, so you'll need to specify them again with the mattr option.

The techniques presented here are mechanical and apply in all the cases. However, there are other things that you can do to further reduce the size of your `.mir` file, such as using implicit operands or transient operations such as the `KILL` instruction. This is the type of thing that you'll pick up as you work on LLVM backends but in any case, they require a deeper knowledge of what a specific backend does to be used, which means they're outside the scope of this book.

In this section, you learned everything you need to know about the textual representation of the Machine IR, called MIR. You learned how to produce it, interpret it, and work with it, including techniques to shrink the size of your `.mir` file to produce easy-to-work-with test cases.

In the next section, we'll focus on the `MachineInstr` class and explain some of the tricky concepts you'll have to deal with while working on the Machine IR.

# The anatomy of a MachineInstr instance

While working in the backend, you'll mainly be manipulating `MachineInstr` instances. As such, it's important to have a good understanding of what they represent and how to make sure what you're doing with them is legal since what you do preserves the semantics of the program.

At a high level, a `MachineInstr` object is a combination of three things:

- An array of `MachineOperand` instances
- Some flags that can be set or queried – for instance, the `fast-math` flags attached to this instruction, whether it's an instruction used for setting up the call frame, and so on (see the `MachineInstr::getFlag/setFlag` family of methods).
- Properties that allow the target independent passes to figure out the effects the instruction may have – for instance, the `MachineInstr::mayLoad` method returns `true` for instructions that can read from memory and the `MachineInstr::isCommutable` method returns `true` if the operands of the instruction are commutative.

In other words, unlike in the LLVM IR, where the diverse types of instructions are implemented as subclasses of the `Instruction` class, in the Machine IR, all the instructions are represented with one unique class. Therefore, specific instructions are immediately identified via their opcode or their properties. For instance, to check whether an instruction is an `add` instruction, you must know which opcodes carry these semantics for your backend. If you want to get this information in a target-independent way, you must expose it as a property and add and/or implement the proper target hooks in the subclass of the `TargetInstrInfo` class of your backend. You can look at how the `MachineInstr::isRegSequenceLike` and `TargetInstrInfo::getRegSequenceInputs` methods work together and are implemented if you need to surface additional semantics.

While this design may look cumbersome, you must remember that the point of the backend is to perform tasks that are highly target-specific. Therefore, unless you're developing pieces of the target-independent code generator infrastructure, you shouldn't need to reason about the abstract semantics of the instructions since, by construction, you should know how to interpret the actual opcodes. Simply put, the properties are here to help the independent pieces of the backend, not your backend itself.

Now, let's dive into the details of the `MachineInstr` class, starting with its properties.

# Introducing the MC layer

The properties of a machine instruction are carried by an immutable instance of an object called `MCInstrDesc`, which is the description of the instruction at the MC level. This class is your first real exposure to the MC layer of the LLVM infrastructure.

The MC layer models the instructions at the assembly code level, such as their encodings, how to assemble and disassemble them, and so on. If you look at the whole `MC` library, you'll find almost a one-to-one mapping between the MC layer and the Machine layer. For instance, the MC layer has the `MCOperand` class, whereas the Machine layer has `MachineOperand` class; similarly, the MC layer has the `MCInst` class, whereas the Machine layer has the `MachineInstr` class, and so on. The Machine layer (or `CodeGen`, if you go by the name of the LLVM library) is built on top of the MC layer, and you'll see a lot of MC concepts being used in the code generation pipeline of the backends. For instance, a lot of the `TargetXXX` classes are subclasses of related `MCXXX` classes, such as the `TargetRegisterInfo` class and the `MCRegisterInfo` class, the `TargetInstrInfo` class and the `MCInstrInfo` class, and so on.

This is expected given how close to the hardware the Machine IR is. The `TargetXXX` classes simply augment what an assembler would need with higher-level helper functions or concepts. For instance, an assembler doesn't need to understand the concept of a basic block since its job is to translate the textual representation of an instruction in a sequence of zeros and ones. Considering the `TargetRegisterInfo` class, an assembler doesn't need to find the intersection of the encoding constraints carried by two different operands, whereas an optimizer does if it wants to check that the same register can be used for a value that's used by two instructions, hence why the `TargetRegisterInfo` class has the `getCommonSubClass` method while the `MCRegisterInfo` class doesn't.

> **Note**
>
> Given how close the Machine and MC representations are, it isn't a surprise that tools have started emerging on the MC representation for link-time optimizations. The bolt project within the LLVM infrastructure is one such project.

Going back to the `MCInstrDesc` class, each machine instruction opcode maps to one `MCInstrDesc` instance. This instance describes the following aspects:

- The properties of the machine instruction (the same ones that are exposed directly through the `MachineInstr` class).
- The number of statically expected operands. Instructions can have more than the statically expected number of operands but not less. We'll explain this in more detail in the *Dealing with explicit and implicit operands* section.
- The operands' types, such as whether an operand is a register or an immediate value, but also whether it's a definition or an argument or an output or input operand, respectively.
- The constraints on the operands, such as the encoding constraints, which are carried by the register class (represented by the `TargetRegisterClass` and `MCRegisterClass` classes). We'll cover this in more detail in the *Working with registers* section while also covering specific concepts such as tied operands and early clobbers.

All in all, you can think of a MachineInstr object as a dynamically sized array of operands and the MCInstrDesc object associated with this object as the contract that the operands must respect to be a valid instruction for the related opcode. For example, the ADDWrr instruction, which we mentioned previously in this chapter, is at the high level of an array of three operands. However, when you look at the related MCInstrDesc instance (for instance, using MCInstrInfo::get(unsigned Opcode) or MachineInstr::getDesc()) you'll see that this array must contain one definition followed by two register operands. If you don't respect this contract, the MachineVerifier pass will reject the instruction, deeming it invalid.

At this point, you know how the completely flat MachineInstr hierarchy is articulated around the opcodes and the MCInstrDesc instances to convey the semantics and constraints of the related machine instruction.

In the next section, we'll take a closer look at the MachineOperand class to help you get comfortable manipulating it.

# Working with MachineOperand instances

Like the MachineInstr class, the MachineOperand class is completely flat, meaning that all types of operands, including registers and symbols, use the same MachineOperand class.

At a high level, a MachineOperand instance is a sort of iterator within the array of operands of the related MachineInstr instance. You can query its position within this array using the MachineOperand::getOperandNo() method and get to the MachineInstr instance using the MachineOperand::getParent() method.

## Unboxing a MachineOperand instance

Like iterators, you must unbox an instance of the MachineOperand class to get to the underlying object that represents the specific type of operand. Indeed, a MachineOperand instance wraps the following:

- A Register instance for register operands
- An MCSymbol instance for symbol operands
- An int64_t instance for immediate values

The general pattern to get to the underlying object is to check the type of the operand using the appropriate MachineOperand::isXXX method (for instance, MachineOperand::isReg for a register, MachineOperand::isImm for an immediate value, and so on). Then, if the operand is of the desired type, you can unbox it using the related MachineOperand::getXXX method (for instance, MachineOperand::getReg for a register and MachineOperand::getImm for an immediate value).

Note

You'll see that in a lot of the backend source code, MachineOperand instances are unboxed without it being checked whether they represent the right type of operand, meaning that the getXXX method gets called without any call to the isXXX method. This is a common and valid pattern because, in a lot of cases, you know what you're dealing with. For instance, if you're dealing with a copy instruction (the MachineInstr::isCopy() method returns true), by construction, this instruction is valid only on a register-to-register copy, so it must have one register definition and one register argument. Beware that if you use the wrong getXXX method, the compiler will crash.

For MachineOperand objects that hold registers, you can also check whether this register is defined by this instruction or only used using the MachineOperand::isDef() method. When this method returns true, the register operand is a definition; otherwise, it's a use. This is an important method to know because you can't determine the role (definition or argument) of a register by its position in the array of operands alone. We'll come back to this in the next section.

Note

Most types of operands are straightforward to understand and, in any case, you should use the comments in the MachineOperand.h file to help you. One of the not-so-obvious ones is the concept of a **register mask**. Register masks are a compact way to list a lot of physical registers. The semantics of a register mask is that all the registers in the mask are expected to be preserved – that is, unmodified – through the related instruction. This is particularly useful if you wish to model the registers that are expected to be left untouched through a function call, for instance. These are known as **callee saved registers** – registers whose content needs to be saved before the register can be modified within a function and restored at the end of the function.

At this point, you know how to get to the underlying object of a MachineOperand instance and you also know how to categorize whether a register operand is a definition or an argument of the instruction. Now, if you were to look at the MachineOperand class, we're sure there are still concepts that would be puzzling to you. The first of these concepts is the distinction between implicit and explicit operands, which you can check with the MachineOperand::isImplicit() method. The next section explains this important distinction.

# Dealing with explicit and implicit operands

Initially, implicit and explicit operands model constraints of the inner workings of the instruction in the hardware. Simply put, **implicit operands** are operands that are used or defined by an instruction, and you have zero control over where they come from. For instance, on the x86 architecture, when you use a comparison instruction to check whether two operands are equal, the instruction will set the result of the comparison in the `eflags` register. In this case, the `eflags` register is an implicit operand because you can't change the destination; it will always be set. In other words, if you want the result of this comparison to be stored in a different register, you must retrieve it from the `eflags` register – there's no way around this as this is how the hardware behaves. **Explicit operands**, on the other hand, are operands that you can set explicitly – for instance, the arguments or the result of an add instruction.

When you instantiate a `MachineInstr` object, you don't have to worry about initializing the implicit operands. They're just there, hence why they're implicit.

To help you make some sense of the array of operands of an instruction, all the `MCInstrDesc` instances come with the following guaranteed order of operands:

- Explicit definitions come first, which by construction can only be registers.
- Explicit arguments come second; the order matches the description of the instruction.
- Implicit operands come last; both definitions and arguments are mixed. The order isn't specified because you can add more implicit operands dynamically.

This order is reflected in the textual Machine IR. For example, here's a conditional move instruction for the x86 architecture:

```
%0:gr64 = CMOV64rr_ND %1, %2, 7, implicit $eflags
```

In this snippet, we can see the definition with a virtual register, `%0`, followed by two explicit register arguments, `%1` and `%2`, an explicit immediate value, `7`, and one implicit use of the physical register, `eflags`. Since explicit definitions appear first in the list, they're placed on the left-hand side of the assignment operator (`=`) to distinguish them from the arguments. On the other hand, the implicit uses and definitions are identified with the `implicit` and `implicit-def` keywords, respectively.

Here's an example of a call instruction being used on the AArch64 architecture where we can see that the implicit uses and definitions are mixed:

```
BL @_bar, csr_darwin_aarch64_aapcs, implicit-def dead $lr, implicit $sp,
implicit $x0, implicit-def $sp, implicit-def $x0
```

In this snippet, we can see that the call has two explicit values: the `bar` symbol and a register mask, `csr_darwin_aarch64_aapcs`. This instruction doesn't define any value explicitly; instead, all the register arguments and definitions are implicit.

What this last example shows is another way that implicit operands are used. Indeed, the implicit operands you can see in this case aren't hardware constraints of the call instruction. Instead, they represent the **application binary interface (ABI)**, which is controlled by the compiler. Yet, these operands are implicit because, in the final assembly code, you wouldn't set these operands explicitly on the call.

This type of use case illustrates another reality of implicit operands: they aren't necessarily known statically. What this means is that everything known statically is encoded in the MCInstrDesc object that's attached to the MachineInstr instance, but you can still add an arbitrary number of implicit operands (both definitions and arguments) to any instruction.

> Note
>
> While you're free to add implicit operands to any machine instructions, be aware that this may prevent some optimizations – for instance, copy instructions are expected to have only two operands (one definition register and one source register) and if you add more operands, the optimizer may bail on trying to remove them. Additionally, remember that these implicit operands won't explicitly be materialized in the final assembly. Therefore, you can use them to convey additional semantics when it makes sense. However, note that they won't appear in the final assembly code automatically.

Now that you know what implicit and explicit operands are and their use cases, let's focus on some of the constraints that are carried by these operands.

## Understanding the constraints of an operand

One of the obvious constraints of an operand is its type (register, symbol, and so on). You already saw how this information is carried by the MCInstrDesc instance that's attached to the instruction.

The next type of constraint is the encoding constraint – for instance, which physical registers you can use for a specific operand or how large an immediate value can be. For the former, this information is carried by the register class and the *Working with registers* section goes into more detail about what this represents. For the latter, this information isn't captured at the Machine IR level. The backend needs to do the right thing during instruction selection to make sure that only properly sized immediate values end up in the related operand. If the backend fails to do this, the value is expected to be rejected by the assembler.

The other constraints are carried by member variables of the MachineOperand class. These are IsKill, IsRenamable, and so on. To understand what each constraint represents, you can read the comments in the MachineOperand.h file. However, we wanted to explain a couple of them that are specifically used when modeling an instruction.

The first constraint describes **tied operands**. This constraint applies exclusively to register operands. Two operands are tied when a physical register for two operands must be the same. This is typically used to model instructions that perform a read-write on one of their operands. For instance, consider the a += b C statement. Here, the a variable is both read and written. Some architectures, such as x86, offer instructions that operate with such read-write semantics. This pattern breaks the SSA form since the a variable is redefined. The concept of tied operands captures this constraint; it models a read-write operand as two separate operands – one read and the other written – but tells the register allocator that both operands must use the same physical register.

The second constraint that we want to cover is **early-clobber**. This constraint only applies to the definition of register operands. When attached to a register definition, this constraint tells the register allocator that the related definition is produced before the arguments of the instructions are read. This departs from the classical expectation that definitions are produced after all the arguments are read. What this means is that the definition with this constraint must not use the same physical registers of the arguments; otherwise, it will clobber their content and produce invalid results. This constraint is typically used to avoid a definition getting assigned to the same register as its inputs for complicated instructions (or inline assembly). For instance, imagine that we use several instructions within a single inline assembly statement, such as a = ...; ... = b + c, which sequentially defines the a value and then reads the b and c values. From the perspective of the register allocator, this inline assembly statement is a single instruction, so without modeling the a variable as an early clobber, we would risk that it gets assigned to the same physical register as either b or c and that it would clobber the related variable.

All these constraints come directly from the TableGen description of your instructions. We'll show you how to create a description of your instructions in the *Describing instructions* section.

In this section, you learned what the constraints that are attached to the MachineOperand objects mean for the optimizers. While we left a lot out in this section, we're confident that the existing comments in the LLVM code base will be sufficient for you to grasp what we didn't cover.

More broadly, this section concludes our overview of the anatomy of the MachineInstr class. You saw that this class is a simple yet powerful object that's used to represent all the instructions across all the backends. You saw that most of the constraints and properties of an instruction are captured in a single object represented with the MCInstrDesc class. You were exposed to the concept of implicit operands and learned about some of the complex modeling that's used on these operands to shoehorn actual architecture constraints in SSA form or capture the effect of inline assembly statements.

The next section focuses on defining the concepts around registers.

# Working with registers

One of the main tasks of the backend is to go from an IR where the input program assumes an infinite number of registers in the SSA form to a program that uses only what's available on the target architecture and that isn't in SSA form.

In the Machine IR, the concept of a register maps to the `Register` class. This class represents both physical and virtual registers. Physical registers represent what the target architecture can offer and are thus limited in number, whereas virtual registers represent the unlimited number of variables that the input program starts with.

We already showed you how to differentiate virtual registers from physical registers in the textual Machine IR; physical registers start with the $ character, whereas virtual registers start with the % character.

Looking at the API, to find out whether you're dealing with a physical or virtual register, you can use the `Register::isVirtual()` or `Register::isPhysical()` method, respectively.

If you scratch the surface a little bit, you'll see that the `Register` class is a thin wrapper around an unsigned value where specific ranges are assigned to physical registers and virtual registers, respectively. While the detail of the implementation shouldn't matter in general, this is still interesting to know because some legacy code may still use the `unsigned` type instead of the `Register` type and use the 0 value instead of the default constructor of the `Register` class to indicate that the register is unknown yet or doesn't matter (this special value gets printed as `noreg` in the textual Machine IR).

> **Note**
>
> The MC layer also has its own class to represent registers: `MCRegister`. However, this class is used exclusively to represent physical registers.

In *Chapter 4*, we showed you how the `def-use` chain for the registers was available in a helper class called `MachineRegisterInfo`. If you look at the API of this class, you'll find that it holds even more information about each register. One such piece of information is the register class of a register, accessible via the `MachineRegisterInfo::getRegClass` method.

> **Note**
>
> You may have noticed that you must manipulate both the `TargetRegisterInfo` and `MachineRegisterInfo` classes in the backend. One way to distinguish one class from the other is to follow the naming convention. Any class with a name that starts with `Machine` (for instance, the `MachineBasicBlock` class) is specific to the current `MachineFunction` instance, whereas any class with a name that starts with `Target` models properties that hold for the current (sub)target. In other words, `Machine` instances represent something that's being compiled and is dynamic by nature, whereas `Target` instances represent facts about the backend and are static (they don't change during the compilation process) by nature.

Let's discover what a register class is.

# The concept of the register class

Registers are grouped in what are called **register classes** in LLVM. Each register can be in zero or several register classes. A register class typically represents some higher-level concept – for example, all registers that can hold 32-bit values, the group of registers that can work with floating-point instructions, and so on. The classes that represent a register class are `TargetRegisterClass` at the Machine IR level and `MCRegisterClass` at the MC level.

The concept of the register class will become clearer with an example. You'll find one when we build register information in the *Describing registers* section.

For now, let's continue looking at the concepts related to registers in LLVM, starting with sub-registers.

# The concept of sub-registers

Most modern target architectures have some sort of register hierarchy where a register is composed of several smaller registers. For instance, in the x86 architecture, the 16-bit ax register is formed by putting together two 8-bit registers, al and ah. In LLVM, this concept is called sub-registers; al and ah are sub-registers of ax. It's important to familiarize yourself with this concept of sub-registers because one of the obvious implications is that modifying a sub-register modifies its parent register and vice versa. This should remind you of the concept of memory aliasing; you shouldn't be surprised to learn that this is called register aliasing. This type of effect is obvious in the Machine IR because the concept of a sub-register is directly exposed in the `MachineOperand` class. For register operands, the `MachineOperand::getSubReg()` method returns the sub-register index of the related operand. When this index is non-zero, this means that the related operand needs to be mapped to a sub-register of the current virtual register.

Let's look at an example.

Consider the following piece of Machine IR that comes from the AArch64 backend:

```
%1:gpr64 = ...
%2:gpr32 = COPY %1.sub_32
```

Here, the virtual register, %1, is defined by a 64-bit instruction, as reflected by its register class, gpr64. Next, %1 – or more precisely, the part that can be addressed via the sub_32 sub-register index (that is, the low 32-bit part of %1, in this case) – is copied into %2. In other words, we copy the low part of %1 into %2.

The interpretation of the sub-register indices is target-specific. We'll show you how to reconstruct this information in the *Describing registers* section.

Note

The concept of a sub-register comes with the concept of a lane mask. In a nutshell, a lane mask captures the parts of the bigger register that are touched by the sub-registers. For instance, let's consider the `ax` register from the previous example. Its lane mask, in binary form, could be `0b11`. Using this representation, the sub-register index that represents `al` would have `0b01`, and the sub-register index for `ah` would be `0b10`. What this tells you is that each sub-register affects half of the bigger register, and they don't overlap; indeed, the intersection of both masks is empty (`0b01 & 0b10 == 0`). You can query the lane mask using the `TargetRegisterInfo::getSubRegIndexLaneMask` method.

Going back to the register hierarchy of the actual physical registers, LLVM offers a rich set of APIs to help you figure out how two different physical registers relate to each other and, more specifically, whether modifying one of them affects the other.

We'll explain how this works and the API you can use at the end of the *The concept of register units* section, but first, let's introduce another related concept that will make it clear why we need to understand the concept of register units.

## The concept of register tuples

Register tuples represent a group of registers that are used together but that are otherwise not bound by any architectural constraints. For instance, let's say that our architecture only contains 32-bit registers, but for some reason, you want to be able to hold 64-bit values in registers that are next to each other (note that this is just an example – we don't recommend using tuples for this!). Let's say you want to hold such values in pairs of 32-bit registers that look like (r0, r1), (r1, r2), and so on, where ri is a 32-bit register. Since your architecture doesn't contain 64-bit registers, you can't use the concept of sub-register and must use the concept of register tuples instead.

Register tuples act as logical super registers, also known as **pseudo-registers**, where the elements that compose them are logical sub-registers. Using the previous example, with this modeling, the backend would have access to logical physical registers named r0_r1, r1_r2, and so on.

From an API perspective, LLVM doesn't make any difference when using logical and real super/sub-registers.

With all these concepts of super and sub-registers – which, by the way, can have as many layers as necessary – it quickly becomes difficult to know whether two registers overlap with each other, meaning that modifying one will modify the other. To avoid this explosion in complexity, LLVM uses the concept of register units.

# The concept of register units

While a modern target has between tens to hundreds of physical registers, this number climbs higher quickly, even to thousands for certain targets, when you add all the pseudo-registers.

What this means is doing anything with all the available registers quickly becomes a compile-time sink.

While enumerating all the registers in LLVM is possible, a better abstraction exists called a **register unit**.

Register units capture the complete set of registers with the smallest number of units. A unit is conceptually a leaf register, but this is an implementation detail. The point is, thanks to this representation, you can quickly determine which registers are available, used, clobbered, and so on while tracking a much smaller number of entities – the register units.

Let's see how this works by looking at an example.

Consider the register hierarchy shown in *Figure 11.2*:

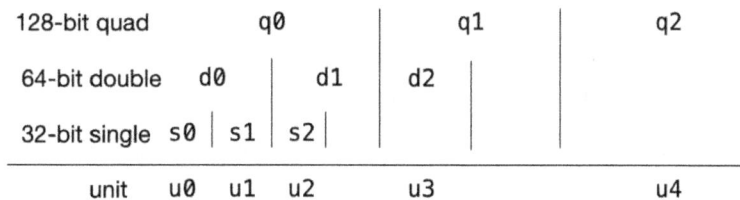

| 128-bit quad | | q0 | | q1 | | q2 |
|---|---|---|---|---|---|---|
| 64-bit double | d0 | | d1 | d2 | | |
| 32-bit single | s0 | s1 | s2 | | | |
| unit | u0 | u1 | u2 | u3 | | u4 |

*Figure 11.2: The concept of register units*

This figure represents a register hierarchy with three levels. At the bottom, there are the single registers (s0, s1, s2). Putting two single registers together makes a double register, which is represented on the middle layer with d0, d1, and d2. Notice that some double registers don't have any corresponding single registers. This is common in register aliasing because the registers that can be addressed at each layer depend on some encoding constraints. For instance, in this example, we can only encode and reach three registers per layer (a non-power of two isn't realistic, but you get the point). Next comes the quad layer, where each register is composed of four single registers or two double registers. For instance, q0 is composed of d0 and d1, and d0 is composed of s0 and s1.

From this figure, you can see that we have nine registers – three per layer. Now, if you look at the units at the very bottom, you'll see that we only need five units (u0 to u4) to capture all the registers. The way the units are computed isn't important; again, this is an implementation detail of the related TableGen backend.

Now, imagine that you want to check whether q0 is available to be allocated. If you were to go by the register hierarchy, you'd need to check that d0, d1, s0, s1, and s2 are all available. That's five checks. If you use the register units, q0 maps to u0 to u2 and you'd need to check whether these units were available, which in this case is only three checks. This example isn't that impressive but when you're factoring all the registers aliases that exist when you have register tuples and/or a deeper register hierarchy, the register units are a compile-time life-saving mechanism. In other words, checking all register aliases can take a while, whereas checking the register units is guaranteed to give you a minimal number of checks.

To give you an idea of how this works, the LLVM infrastructure gives you a mapping from a physical register to the list of all the register units it touches. This list is encapsulated in the `MCRegUnitIterator` class from the `MC` library. In this case, this list would tell us that the `q0` register touches the units from `u0` to `u2`. If you keep track of the available registers using register units (for instance, by using the `LiveRegUnits` helper class), that's enough to check that `q0` is available. For instance, if `d0` was used, it would have taken `u0` to `u1`, so not all units that make `q0` would have been available.

The LLVM infrastructure also provides reverse mapping: from a register unit to all the physical registers that contain it. Gathering information requires more effort as it involves two classes, `MCRegUnitRootIterator` and `MCSuperRegIterator`, but it's readily available anyway. You can use that information to find that the `q0` register clobbers the `s0`, `s1`, `s2`, `d0`, and `d1` registers. We leave that as an exercise for you!

Manipulating register units, represented by the `MCRegUnit` class, may be daunting at first, but the key takeaway is they offer a more efficient way to iterate through your registers and check for interferences, meaning overlaps between registers.

There are several helper classes built around register units that you can leverage to get efficient implementations of common compiler problems.

Here's a list of a few of these problems and the APIs that encapsulate the related solution:

- **Calculating the register pressure:** You can build a solution using the `TargetRegisterClass::getRegXXXPressureSetXXX` and `TargetRegisterClass::getRegXXXWeight` family of methods. You can find an example of the usage of these methods in the `MachineLICM` optimization.
- **Liveness analysis of physical registers:** This is solved by the `LiveRegUnits` class. This class is intended to be used at the basic block level by using the `addLiveOuts` method for initialization and then using the `stepBackward` method to get the register units that are alive.
- **Overlap checks between physical registers:** You can use the `TargetRegisterInfo::regsOverlap` method.

Unlike the last two items, register pressure computation may not be that easy to figure out by using the API alone, so let's explain how it works.

We already explained the concept of register pressure in *Chapter 4*, which boils down to estimating how many registers you need to keep all the values of a region in these registers.

Register units solve this problem by offering a unified way of tracking the register pressure across the layers of the register hierarchy. For instance, going back to *Figure 11.1*, at a high level, a single register consumes one unit, a double two units, and a quad four units. In practice, this is more complicated since there are holes, but you get the idea.

The pressure sets aim to capture the holes by describing different pressure limits (the maximum number of registers per se, as identified by the `TargetRegisterInfo::getRegPressureSetLimit` method) per group of similar things (meaning roughly per register class).

Each element in a register class contributes a cost in terms of unit pressure returned by the `TargetRegisterInfo::getRegClassWeight` method to a given number of pressure sets, which are identified by the list returned by the `TargetRegisterInfo::getRegClassPressureSets` method.

To calculate this register pressure, you must accumulate across all the touched pressure sets the number of units consumed by an element of that register class across all the touched pressure sets (in other words, its cost). If one of the sets goes past its limit, then you don't have enough registers to keep all your values in registers.

> The object that's returned by `TargetRegisterInfo::getRegClassWeight` has two fields: `RegWeight`, which represents the cost in terms of unit of pressure, and `WeightLimit`, which is the old way of computing pressure limits. In other words, don't use the second field when you're computing the register pressure!

In this section, you learned how the LLVM codegen infrastructure abstracts some of the complexity around the register hierarchy with the concept of register units. Now that you know everything about the concepts that can be used to represent registers, let's step back and look at the SSA form versus the non-SSA form that's carried by the registers in the Machine representation.

## The registers and SSA and non-SSA forms

As we mentioned at the beginning of this chapter, the Machine IR needs to represent programs in SSA and non-SSA forms.

We'll learn more about the actual phases of the machine pass pipeline in *Chapter 13*. Here, we'll focus on what to expect from the Machine IR when it comes to SSA and non-SSA forms.

The SSA-ness of the Machine IR is solely carried by the virtual registers. Indeed, like the LLVM IR, other mutable entities (such as the memory and physical registers) aren't considered by the SSA form.

Simply put, the Machine IR is in SSA form so long as all its virtual registers are defined, at most, once.

As soon as a virtual register is defined more than once, the Machine IR isn't in SSA form anymore.

You can check the status of the Machine IR by querying the `IsSSA` property on your `MachineFunction` instance using the `hasProperty` method.

The LLVM target-independent code generator also strives to maintain two other characteristics of the IR while the code is in SSA form:

1. `PHI` instructions are only present when the code is in SSA form.
2. Physical registers have the shortest live-range possible.

The first property ensures that we don't have `PHI` instructions, which are typically associated with the SSA form, in non-SSA programs.

The second property ensures that non-SSA registers (the physical registers) interfere with the least number of virtual registers possible. Breaking this can make the job of the register allocator hard or create unnecessary constraints for the generic optimizer passes.

For instance, consider the following snippet:

```
$r0 = opc1 ...
...
... = opcN $r0
```

In this snippet, you know that you must have the first operand of the opcN instruction in the physical register, r0, so you pine the related definition of the opc1 instruction to r0. This creates a large live range for r0 where the register allocator can't use this register for anything else between the opc1 and opcN instructions. Similarly, using a physical register for the opc1 instruction may disable some optimization that would have otherwise applied to this opcode.

Instead, it's better to generate something like this:

```
%v0 = opc1 ...
...
$r0 = COPY %v0
... = opcN $r0
```

In this new snippet, the first argument of the opcN instruction is still properly pined to r0, but now, the live range of r0 is minimal thanks to the COPY instruction and the opc1 instruction and the v0 virtual register can be optimized freely.

As a backend author, you should also abide by these guidelines; otherwise, the generic optimizations may do unexpected things.

In conclusion, the Machine IR is agnostic as to whether it represents an SSA program or not. This information is carried by the registers and is reflected both in the MachineFunction instance properties and the def-use chains of the virtual registers, as explained in *Chapter 4*.

Before we wrap up this section on registers, let's consider a few tips regarding how to interact with registers in a debugger.

## Interacting with registers in the debugger

In *Chapter 10*, you learned how a debugger can conveniently stop a program at a specific point using a conditional breakpoint. In this section, we'll go over a few tips that you can leverage to easily make use of such capabilities when you're dealing with registers.

As mentioned previously, the concept of a register is modeled as a thin wrapper around an unsigned value. Although you could deconstruct how this wrapping is done to interpret a specific value (for instance, finding which register an MCRegister instance with a value of 123 is), there are a few APIs that you can use directly in the debugger (or your regular C++ code!) to make this effortless:

- To print out a physical register in a human-readable way, use the MCRegisterInfo::getName method. Notice that we said *physical register*. This method won't work for virtual registers. See the next bullet point for a method that works in both cases.

- To print out any register, use the static `TargetRegisterInfo::dumpReg` method. This method requires a few additional parameters (namely a sub-register index and a pointer to an instance of the `TargetRegisterInfo` class), but they're straightforward to figure out.

- To stop on a specific virtual register, say `%123`, you can use the static `Register::virtReg2Index` method to translate the raw `unsigned int` representation into the number that you expect (in this case, 123). For instance, let's say you want to set up a conditional breakpoint when you hit a certain point in the program and the `Reg` variable contains the 123 virtual register. Here, you could use the `Reg.isVirtualRegister() && Register::virtReg2Index(Reg) == 123` condition. Note that the `Register::virtReg2Index` method allows you to use plain arrays as hash tables for your virtual register. The indices that are produced are guaranteed to be between 0 and the value returned by the `MachineRegisterInfo::getNumVirtRegs()` method.

Generally speaking, to print out anything register-related, look at the `TargetRegisterInfo` class (and its super-class, `MCRegisterInfo`). This class contains all the `getXXXName` methods that you can use to get a human-readable version of the different classes that you manipulate. For instance, for the sub-register index, use the `TargetRegisterInfo::getSubRegIndexName` method, for the register class use the `TargetRegisterInfo::getRegClassName` method, and so on.

In this section, you learned about various concepts that are used in the LLVM codegen infrastructure for working with registers.

More specifically, you learned about the following aspects:

- How registers, both physical and virtual, are encapsulated behind the `Register` class
- How you can group them by register class, represented by the `TargetRegisterClass` class, to represent logical sets that share the same properties (for instance, the group of registers used in floating-point instructions)
- How the concept of register tuples can be used to represent logical registers (also known as pseudo-registers) that don't exist in the hardware like pairs of registers that must be used together
- How register hierarchies are conveniently simplified with the concept of sub-registers and register units
- How the definitions of the virtual registers affect the fact that the Machine IR is in SSA or non-SSA form

Finally, we gave you some tips so that you can interact with these concepts through a debugger and, more generally, in any C++ code.

Now that you know what a register is made of, we can put all this knowledge together and learn how to populate `MachineInstr` objects with these registers!

# Creating MachineInstr objects

Like a lot of things in the LLVM infrastructure, there's not one but two ways of building `MachineInstr` objects.

> **Note**
>
> There's actually a third way of creating `MachineInstr` objects: you can use the bare APIs of the `MachineOperand` and `MachineInstr` class – for instance, using the `MachineOperand::CreateXXX` family of methods or the `MachineFunction::CreateMachineInstr` method. We won't describe this way of building these objects because it's very verbose and barely used.

The first way of building such objects is via the `MachineIRBuilder` class, which you briefly used in *Chapter 4*. This class is usually used at the beginning of the `MachineFunction` passes pipeline, when the produced code is still in SSA. Indeed, it abstracts you away from creating the virtual registers (you can still do this if you want to, though) and instead provides an API that feels more like the `IRBuilder` class of the LLVM IR.

We gave you a primer on the `MachineIRBuilder` class in *Chapter 4*, so please refer to that chapter for more information.

The second way of building `MachineInstr` objects is via the `MachineInstrBuilder` class. This is the most prevalent way of building these objects because it's the method that's been around the longest.

Conceptually, a `MachineInstrBuilder` instance is a thin wrapper around a `MachineInstr` instance. This wrapper offers methods to add operands to the currently wrapped `MachineInstr` instance.

A typical build sequence with this API goes through the following phases:

- Create the virtual registers that will be used or defined in the instruction using the `MachineRegisterInfo` instance of the current `MachineFunction` instance. This is equivalent to declaring your variables in your favorite programming language.
- Instantiate a `MachineInstrBuilder` object, typically using one of the `BuildMI` functions. This involves providing an insertion point for the yet-to-be instruction and passing its instruction description (remember the `MCInstrDesc` class). Note that a `MachineInstrBuilder` object can also be instantiated by attaching it to an existing `MachineInstr` object to modify this `MachineInstr` instance.
- Populate the `MachineInstr` instance using the `MachineInstrBuilder::addXXX` methods.

Let's see these steps in action by looking at an example that's been taken from the `${LLVM_SRC}llvm/lib/Target/AArch64/AArch64InstrInfo.cpp` file:

```
Register NewCond = MRI.createVirtualRegister(&AArch64::GPR64commonRegClass);
BuildMI(MBB, MBB.end(), Comp->getDebugLoc(), TII->get(AArch64::CSINCXr))
    .addReg(NewCond, RegState::Define)
    .addReg(CurCond)
```

```
    .addReg(CurCond)
    .addImm(AArch64CC::getInvertedCondCode(CC));
```

In this snippet, we create a virtual register called NewCond and specify its register class, GPR64commonRegClass. Then, we instantiate our MachineInstrBuilder object with the BuildMI function, which anchors the new MachineInstr instance after the provided basic block iterator. So, in this case, the MBB, MBB.end() pair means that we insert the new instruction at the end of MBB. The next parameter provides some metadata about the new instruction – in this case, its debug location (Comp->getDebugLoc()).

> **About the debug location**
>
> When you can, preserving the debug location is a good practice because it will improve the debuggability of the code that your compiler produces. For instance, this is how the online compiler explorer (https://godbolt.org) maps the source code to the final assembly code.

The next parameter of the BuildMI function is the MCInstrDesc instance of the MachineInstr object we want to create (in this case, the instruction identified by the AArch64::CSINCXr opcode). Now that our instruction has been created, we can use the add method of the MachineInstrBuilder wrapper to populate it. First, we add a definition (which defines NewCond), as identified by the provided RegState value, followed by two register uses (the default RegState value that, when it isn't specified, represents a use), and a final immediate value.

> **Note**
>
> The second argument of MachineInstrBuilder::addReg – in other words, the one used to pass the RegState value in the previous example – is a bitfield. The reason this is a bitfield is because the RegState values have been designed to be composed together. For instance, the RegState::Define | RegState::Implicit statement defines an implicit definition.

Putting everything together, this snippet generates something that would resemble the following Machine IR:

```
%NewCond = CSINCXr %CurCond, %CurCond, intValueOfCC
```

That's it!

Take some time to familiarize yourself with the APIs offered by the MachineInstrBuilder and MachineIRBuilder classes. Once you've done this, creating your own instances of MachineInstr class should be a breeze!

In this section, we pointed out the APIs that you can leverage to build MachineInstr instances. You were reminded that MachineIRBuilder is a relatively straightforward way to work with the Machine IR when you come from the LLVM IR world. Then, you saw how to use MachineInstrBuilder to achieve the same kind of IR creation. This API is particularly important to know since most of the backend code uses it.

In the next few sections, we'll focus on the TableGen backends involved in the Machine IR. This will address some of the questions you may have accumulated through the previous sections, such as where to find the necessary opcode or sub-register indices.

# Describing registers

As explained in *Chapter 6*, everything related to modeling a target goes through a TableGen backend. Unsurprisingly, this means that describing the registers of a target goes through this path as well. You'll want to leverage this infrastructure because it will create the skeleton of your backend's MCRegisterInfo and TargetRegisterInfo classes, as well as the iterators and enumerators for manipulating your registers and register classes.

## Writing the target description

The process of modeling registers is supported by two TableGen classes, both defined in the ${LLVM_SRC}/lvm/include/llvm/Target/Target.td file.

The first one, known as the TableGen Register class, describes a register. For low-level modeling, you'll find things such as its assembly name (via the AsmName field) or its encoding (via the HwEncoding field). You'll also find higher-level concepts, such as its sub-registers (via the SubRegs fields) and the related sub-register indices (via the SubRegIndices field). The sub-register indices are modeled through the TableGen SubRegIndex class. This class describes the size of the sub-register in bits and where it starts, meaning an offset in bits from the first bit in the bigger register. We'll see an example of this at the end of this section.

The second one, known as the TableGen RegisterClass class, describes – you guessed it – a register class. This class is only about concepts that the Machine layer cares about, meaning how to generate code. For example, here, you'll find the memory alignment of the register of this register class, which is used to generate the right code to store or load the related registers.

These two TableGen classes alone feature a lot of subtleties that you can leverage to tweak the generic codegen passes. For instance, the isConstant field of the Register class that models registers that can't be modified. We'll cover some of them in the upcoming chapters, but feel free to read the comments of these classes to see what you can model since we won't cover all of them.

> **Note**
>
> A lot of the TableGen classes have a Namespace field. This field is used to define in which C++ namespace the generated code will be. Traditionally, the namespace that's used in that field matches the name of the folder for the related backend. By default, this field is empty.

Let's illustrate how to define a few registers with their sub-registers.

For example, imagine that you want to model the s0, s1, and d0 registers from *Figure 11.2*:

```
def sub32_low: SubRegIndex<32>;
def sub32_high: SubRegIndex<32, 32>;
def s0 : Register<"s0">;
def s1 : Register<"s1">;
def d0 : Register<"d0"> {
  let SubRegIndices = [sub32_low, sub32_high];
  let SubRegs = [s0, s1];
  let CoveredBySubRegs = true;
}
def SINGLES : RegisterClass<"", [f32], 32, (add s0, s1)>;
def DOUBLES : RegisterClass<"", [f64], 64, (add d0)>;
```

What this snippet does is define two records named sub32_low and sub32_high that describe the sub-register index for a 32-bit chunk that starts at offset 0 (0 is the default offset, hence it isn't specified) and a 32-bit chunk that stats at offset 32, respectively. Next, we define two registers, s0 and s1, with the related assembly name passed as a string to the Register class. Note that in this snippet, we didn't specify the encoding field, so it will remain empty. Next comes the record for d0, which describes a register fully covered by its sub-registers, s0 and s1 (defined on the previous lines), at the sub32_low and sub32_high sub-register indices. Finally, we describe two register classes, SINGLES and DOUBLES. The SINGLES record describes the 32-bit registers and pins them on the i32 type (this isn't important at this point) and the DOUBLES record describes the 64-bit registers. The first argument for both classes is the namespace, which we left empty in this case.

Easy, right?

You typically describe your registers and register classes in a file named XXXRegisterInfo.td at the root of the directory of your backend (that is, ${LLVM_SRC}/llvm/lib/Target/XXX), where XXX is the name of your backend.

Before we learn what to do with this file, try to write the target description of the complete hierarchy of registers illustrated in *Figure 11.2*. To do that, go into the ch11/register_units folder of this book's GitHub repository and fill out the target description file named yourTurn-reginfo.td. Then, follow the instructions in the README.md file in that same directory to see whether it builds and generates the same register units as the provided solution. If you get stuck, feel free to look at the solution in the solution-reginfo.td file.

Now that you have the XXXRegisterInfo.td file that describes the register hierarchy of your backend, you need to invoke the gen-register-info TableGen backend to produce the C++ code that you'll use in your backend.

First, you need to add the following line to your `${LLVM_SRC}/llvm/lib/Target/XXX/CMakeLists.txt` file to invoke the related backend:

```
tablegen(LLVM XXXGenRegisterInfo.inc -gen-register-info)
```

This line must be added somewhere between the directive that sets the input file of the TableGen tool (as identified by the `set(LLVM_TARGET_DEFINITIONS XXX.td)` CMake directive in that file) and the `add_public_tablegen_target` CMake function.

If you're unsure about where to add this line, look at the companion repository where we've built the H2BLB backend and look at the changes that have been made in the `CMakeLists.txt` file at the gen-register-info_ch11 tag using the following command line:

```
$ git diff gen-register-info_ch11^..gen-register-info_ch11
```

This command prints the changes that have been made at this exact tag.

> **Note**
>
> The previous Git command can be used with any tag (or commit) to see how the code was modified with this one tag (or commit). Note that we won't call it out explicitly from this point forward. The caret symbol (^) simply means *before* in Git. Therefore, the `git diff hash^..hash` command line shows us the difference between whatever was before the commit identified by `hash` and `hash`. You can pair this command with the `-UNum` CLI option, where `Num` is an arbitrarily large (or small) number, to see the change with more (or less) context. For instance, the `git diff -U999999 hash^..hash` command line shows the difference for the `hash` commit with a context of 999999 lines, which is likely to be all the files involved in this change.

Make sure you include your `XXXRegisterInfo.td` file via the `include` TableGen directive in the main `XXX.td` file of your backend. There are other ways to do this, but this is the standard way to structure your backend in LLVM.

This CMake rule will produce an `XXXGenRegisterInfo.inc` file in your build directory under the `${BUILD}/lib/Target/XXX` folder (where `${BUILD}` is the root of your LLVM build directory) when you build your backend.

This generated file contains four pieces that are guarded by preprocessor macros that enable various things:

- `GET_REGINFO_ENUM`: The enumeration that represents your registers.
- `GET_REGINFO_MC_DESC`: The implementation of `MCRegisterInfo` for your target. In particular, this macro guards the `InitXXXMCRegisterInfo` function, which needs to be used to initialize your `MCRegisterInfo` instance in your `TargetMachine` instance. We left this part out in *Chapter 9*.
- `GET_REGINFO_HEADER`: The class declaration of the `XXXGenRegisterInfo` class.
- `GET_REGINFO_TARGET_DESC`: The implementation of the `XXXGenRegisterInfo` class.

In other words, these four pieces are the header and implementation of the MC layer and the same things for the Machine layer, respectively.

How the description of the registers in the LLVM infrastructure plays with the related TableGen backend is summarized in *Figure 11.3*:

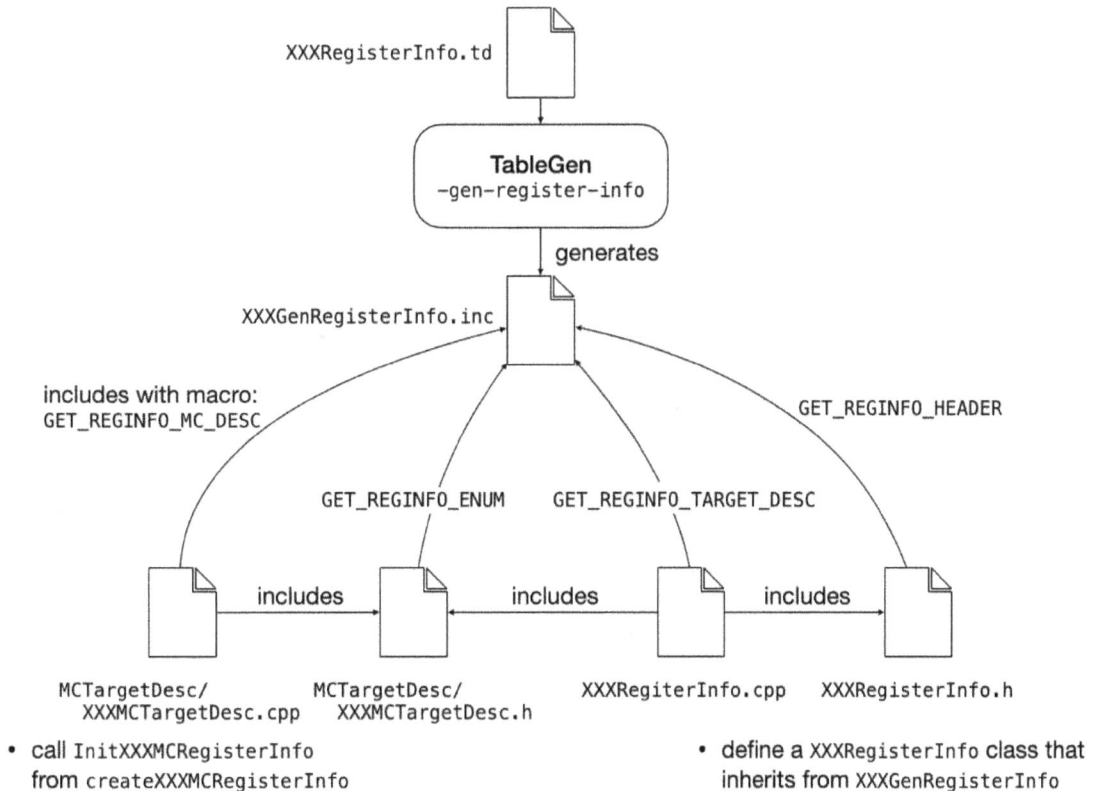

Figure 11.3: How TableGen provides the basic implementation of the register information

Here, you can see how the target description file at the top (.td) is used by the gen-register-info TableGen backend to produce the pieces that you need to pull in your MC and Machine layers. The arrows where GET_XXX is specified tell you which macro you need to define when you include the generated .inc file so that you can pull the right code in the related file. The bullet points under the files point out some of the actions that must be performed manually.

On the TableGen input

*Figure 11.3* – and all the figures regarding TableGen going forward – is a simplification of the actual process. Indeed, all the TableGen backends that deal with low-level information need the records that define the target backend and their related dependencies, starting from the record that implements the TableGen Target class. These records are all aggregated in the XXX.td file and we thought it was better to show which .td file contributes the most to a TableGen backend instead of always showing the XXX.td file as input.

Now that you understand what TableGen generates, let's learn how to connect these pieces to your backend.

If you followed the steps provided in *Chapter 9*, your backend should already contain the XXXMCTargetDesc.h and .cpp files in the MCTargetDesc directory of your backend. Just add the enumeration (guarded by the GET_REGINFO_ENUM macro) to the header file and the implementation (guarded by the GET_REGINFO_MC_DESC macro) to the .cpp file. Alternatively, you could add the related pieces to new files (the header and .cpp files) if you prefer, just remember that these generated pieces need to live in the MC component of your backend to play nicely, in particular with the linking process, with the MC-based LLVM tools such as llvm-mc.

For our H2BLB backend, we need to add the following lines to the H2BLBMCTargetDesc.h file:

```
#define GET_REGINFO_ENUM
#include "H2BLBGenRegisterInfo.inc"
```

We also need to add the following lines to the H2BLBMCTargetDesc.cpp file:

```
#define GET_REGINFO_MC_DESC
#include "H2BLBGenRegisterInfo.inc"
```

These last two lines enable the implementation of the InitXXXMCRegisterInfo function, which you can now use to fill out the MCRegisterInfo instance that you registered with your TargetMachine instance in *Chapter 9* via the createXXXMCRegisterInfo function. The InitXXXMCRegisterInfo function takes two arguments: a pointer to the MCRegisterInfo instance to initialize and the enumerator value of the register that was used as the return address for your backend. For instance, the updated version of createH2BLBMCRegisterInfo would now look like this for the H2BLB backend:

```
static MCRegisterInfo *createH2BLBMCRegisterInfo(const Triple &Triple) {
    MCRegisterInfo *X = new MCRegisterInfo();
    InitH2BLBMCRegisterInfo(X, H2BLB::R7);
    return X;
}
```

If you're having issues following these changes, remember that you can follow each commit one by one in the companion repository. This particular change is tagged with the hook-up-mc-reginfo_ch11 tag so that it's easy to identify.

This takes care of the register description at the MC layer. For the Machine layer, you need to follow similar steps to enable the XXXGenRegisterInfo class. However, this time, you need to create the placeholder for your implementation of the TargetRegisterInfo class. This involves performing five steps:

1. Create the XXXRegisterInfo.h and XXXRegisterInfo.cpp files at the root of your backend directory.

2. Add the proper define directives while including XXXGenRegisterInfo.inc in the respective header and .cpp files.

3. Modify the header file to create an XXXRegisterInfo class that inherits from the generated XXXGenRegisterInfo class.

4. Implement the pure virtual methods of the parent TargetRegisterInfo class to make your XXXRegisterInfo class instantiable.

5. Provide a mock implementation of the XXXFrameLowering class.

*Steps 1* and *2* are mechanical and easy to do. *Step 3* is required because the generated XXXGenRegisterInfo class is only a partial implementation of its super abstract class, TargetRegisterInfo. Therefore, you need to create a subclass of XXXGenRegisterInfo to provide a concrete class of the TargetRegisterInfo class for your backend. *Step 4* makes your XXXRegisterInfo class a concrete class by providing the missing methods: getCalleeSavedRegs, eliminateFrameIndex, and getFrameRegister. At this point, just go with the simplest implementation possible – that is, return some empty values and so on.

Finally, *Step 5* is required so that you can compile the code that's generated by TableGen for the XXXGenRegisterInfo implementation, meaning that TableGen assumes that your backend features an XXXFrameLowering class. This step involves creating a header (typically named XXXFrameLowering.h) and .cpp files for your XXXFrameLowering class at the root directory of your backend. This class must inherit from the TargetFrameLowering class and provide an implementation of all the pure virtual methods: emitPrologue, emitEpilogue, and hasFPImpl. Don't bother with real implementations at this point – just do the simplest ones you can.

Regarding the simplest implementation possible for all the overloaded methods for the XXXFrameLowering and XXXRegisterInfo classes, go with returning nullptr for the pointers, use Register() when a register is required (for example, to use the constructor of the XXXGenRegisterInfo class from the constructor of the XXXRegisterInfo class), and so on. We'll revisit these methods when we need them later in this book.

If you feel overwhelmed, feel free to look at the hook-up-tgt-reginfo_ch11 commit for a full example of *Steps 1* to *4* and the mock-frame-lowering-impl_ch11 commit for an example of *Step 5* in the companion repository.

This concludes our section on describing registers. We understand that what we've done so far may feel abstract and not particularly useful, but remember that you can't build a codegen layer before you can describe your target. Bear with us – the mechanical work is almost over, and you'll see the interest in this scaffolding when we hook up the MC layer to enable some of the tooling of this layer in the next chapter!

In this section, you learned how to model the registers of your target using the existing TableGen infrastructure. This knowledge allows you to interpret the information that you saw in the Machine IR, such as what a particular sub-register describes, or which registers are in a register class. While doing so, you learned how to connect the pieces generated by TableGen to produce the C++ objects that are used to describe your registers at the MC level (via the MCRegisterInfo class) and the Machine level (via the partially generated implementation of the TargetRegisterInfo class.)

Now that your registers are lined up, let's see how they connect with the description of our instructions.

# Describing instructions

To teach the LLVM infrastructure about the instructions of your backend, you need to use yet another TableGen backend. This TableGen backend is available through the gen-instr-info command-line option.

Instructions are simply described by the TableGen Instruction class, which is defined in ${LLVM_SRC}/llvm/include/llvm/Target/Target.td, like most TableGen classes used for the Machine and MC layers.

Most of the fields of the TableGen Instruction class have a default value. This makes it very easy to add the skeleton of a target-specific instruction.

In a nutshell, you only need to define two fields of the TableGen instruction class to instantiate a new record. These fields are OutOperandList and InOperandList, both of which capture a **directed acyclic graph** (**DAG**) that represents the output and input operands of the instruction, respectively. You can ignore the DAG aspect and assume these are lists of operands. DAGs are just how lists with mixed types are represented at this point.

Let's see this in action:

```
def MYINSTR: Instruction<> {
  let OutOperandList = (outs defTy0:$dst0, defTy1:$dst1);
  let InOperandList = (ins opTy0:$src0, opTy1:$src1);
}
```

This TableGen snippet describes an instruction with the MYINSTR opcode – in other words, the name of the TableGen record is the name of the enumeration that you can use in your C++ code to create such an instruction – and the name that's displayed in the Machine IR. This instruction produces two results (as captured via the OutOperandList field) represented by the $dst0 and $dst1 variables of the defTy0 and defTy1 types and reads from two inputs (as captured via the InOperandList field) represented by the $src0 and $src1 variables of the opTy0 and opTy1 types.

> **Note**
>
> The dollar ($) sign here is TableGen syntax – don't mix it up with how the Machine IR prints physical registers.

Zooming into the XXXOperandList fields, the outs and ins strings are keywords that are interpreted by the gen-instr-info TableGen backend. These keywords describe the values that are defined (these values are called nodes in TableGen parlance) and used, respectively.

Next, looking at the xxTy strings, these are the names of the records that describe the types of the related value. The LLVM infrastructure offers a few predefined types that you can find by looking for the OperandType string in the Target.td file. For instance, this file exposes different types for immediate values of various sizes, such as the i1imm type for immediate values that fit in one bit and the i16imm type for the ones that fit in 16 bits. You can create your own types, but we'll cover that in *Chapter 14*, when we will look at how to do instruction selection. Additionally, your target's register classes are automatically included in the list of types that you can use for values with the register type. For instance, looking back at the snippet from the *Describing registers* section, you can use both SINGLES and DOUBLES as types.

Finally, the $xx strings bind the related operand to a variable that you'll be able to reference in other fields, such as the string that this instruction lowers to when emitted to assembly code (the AsmString field.) We'll augment this example by using these variables in the next chapter. As it is, the MYINSTR record can be manipulated by the Machine layer – for instance, you'll be able to instantiate MachineInstr objects that use the MCInstrDesc instance of this opcode, but you won't be able to use the assembler and disassembler capabilities of the MC layer.

Now, it's your turn to try to write your first instruction!

Go to the ch11/instr_info folder in this book's GitHub repository and try to create the records for the instructions described in the comments in the yourTurn-instrinfo.td file. Follow the instructions in the README.md file that's in the same directory to build and run this example. Refer to the solution-instrinfo.td file in this same directory if you want a possible solution.

Now that you know how to describe an instruction with TableGen, next, you'll learn how to connect this description to your C++ code so that you can use it in your backend.

In general, to connect the output of a TableGen backend, something you saw previously, you need to do the following:

- Add the proper TableGen invocation in the related CMakeLists.txt file
- Include the generated .inc file at the right places with the right macro definitions
- Implement the missing pure virtual methods to make your backend-specific class a concrete class

We described these steps for the gen-register-info backend in the previous section. Since this is mechanical, we only capture what needs to happen, as shown in *Figure 11.4*:

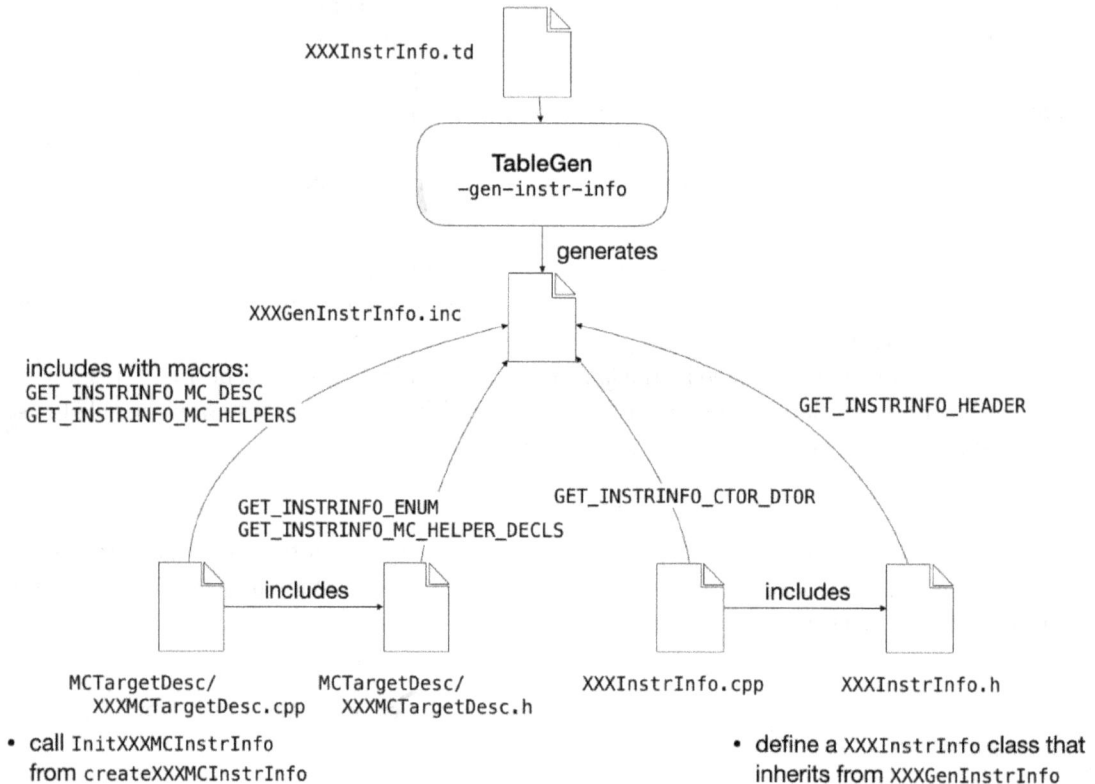

*Figure 11.4: How TableGen provides the basic implementation of the instruction information*

*Figure 11.4* illustrates which TableGen backend you need to invoke to produce the skeleton for your target-specific MCInstrInfo instance and XXXInstrInfo class. It follows the same convention that was shown in *Figure 11.3*.

If you follow the steps that we demonstrated for our H2BLB backend in *Chapter 9*, then XXXInstrInfo.h and .cpp won't exist yet. Make sure you create them and register them in the related CMakeLists.txt file. Finally, *Figure 11.4* calls out the specific action that you need to take to register your MCInstrInfo instance with the TargetMachine instance that represents your backend.

This can be a lot to take in, so to ease this burden, look at the gen-and-connect-mc-instr-info_ch11, and hook-up-tgt-instr-info_ch11 tags in the companion repository for a concrete example of how to do all this.

In this section, you learned how to describe your target instructions so that you can use them in the C++ code of your backend. The instructions' descriptions may feel too abstract at this point. In the next chapter, we'll make this more concrete by showing you how this connects to the final assembly code of your backend.

# Summary

In this chapter, you learned the basics of how to start implementing your backend.

You deepened your understanding of the Machine IR and now understand how its textual representation connects to the target description of your registers, instructions, and other related concepts, such as sub-register indices.

You also learned how these concepts map to the C++ API and its `TargetRegisterInfo` and `TargetInstrInfo` classes, how to create instances of these classes, and how to leverage these APIs to make your debugging sessions more productive.

In the next chapter, you'll learn how to connect the Machine representation to its MC counterpart by augmenting your target description with information about the assembly syntax and encoding.

# Further reading

The Machine IR has a dedicated official page that describes its syntax and gives some tips regarding how to work with it. It's available at `https://llvm.org/docs/MIRLangRef.html`.

Additionally, to get more comfortable with the YAML syntax, you can go through its current specifications at `https://yaml.org/spec/1.2.2/`.

# Quiz time

Now that you have completed reading this chapter, try answering the following questions to test your knowledge:

1. Given the following Machine IR snippet and assuming the `dsub_x` sub-register indices describe sub-registers that don't overlap, is this IR in SSA form?

   ```
   undef %4.dsub_0:dquad = COPY %0
   %4.dsub_1:dquad = COPY %1
   %4.dsub_2:dquad = COPY %2
   %4.dsub_3:dquad = COPY %3
   ```

   The answer is no – this Machine IR isn't in SSA form.

   This was a bit of a trick question because you must think about the virtual register (in this case, %4) as a whole. Irrespective of how the sub-registers are mapped, the reality is that %4 appears more than once on the left-hand side of the assignment operator, which by definition is against the SSA form.

One way to represent something similar in SSA form is shown here:

```
%sub0:... = COPY %0
%sub1:... = COPY %1

...

%4:dquad = REG_SEQUENCE %sub0, %subreg.dsub_0,
                        %sub1, %subreg.dsub_1, ...
```

See the *The registers and SSA and non-SSA forms* section for more details regarding what determines that the Machine IR is in SSA form and the *The concept of sub-register* section for more details on what a sub-register represents.

2.  What's the difference between the `MachineInstrBuilder` and `MachineIRBuilder` classes?

    The `MachineIRBuilder` class offers a slightly higher level of abstraction than the `MachineInstrBuilder` class. This means that coming from the LLVM IR world, it may feel easier to use than the `MachineInstrBuilder` class.

    See the *Creating MachineInstr objects* section to learn more about how to build `MachineInstr` objects.

3.  Consider the following Machine IR snippet. If you were to move the `bb.3` basic block between the `bb.1` and `bb.2` basic blocks without making any further changes, what would happen?

```
bb.1:
  successors: %bb.2


bb.2:
  ...
bb.3:
  ...
```

If you look at the sequence of instructions in `bb.1`, you'll notice that this basic block doesn't end with a terminator instruction (`bb.1` is empty). So, when the program reaches the end of `bb.1`, it's supposed to continue in `bb.2`. By moving `bb.3` between `bb.1` and `bb.2`, you're breaking the program's semantics because now, `bb.1` will reach `bb.3` instead of `bb.2`. The proper way to do that would involve adding a terminator instruction to `bb.1` that would jump to `bb.2`.

See the *Shrinking a .mir file* section for a reminder of the impact that the linear order has on the semantics of the program.

4.  Suppose we run the `llc --start-before opt --stop-after opt` command. What simpler command could you use that would have the same effect?

    With this command, we only care about running the opt pass. A simpler way to do that would be to invoke the `llc` tool with `--run-pass=opt`.

    See the *Running passes* section for more details.

5.  Suppose that you want to optimize the Machine IR in a way that makes it impossible to recompute some information that you need in a later pass. How would you keep this information?

    There are two ways you can go about this.

    The first one is by capturing the information you need in an analysis pass that would run before the optimization – let's call it `foo` – that destroys this information and then makes sure this analysis pass is preserved across all the passes that run between `foo` and where you need this information. See *Chapter 5* if you don't remember how to do that.

    The second one is by leveraging the `MachineFunctionInfo` class: record the information you need in a target specialization of that class and use this target-specialized class later.

    See the *Semantics of the different fields* section for more details on the `MachineFunctionInfo` class.

# 12

# Getting Started with the Machine Code Layer

So far in this book, we started with high-level concepts and progressively, chapter by chapter, we explained how a concept is brought down to the next, lower level of abstraction. In this chapter, we break away from this top-down approach by making a detour to the **machine code (MC)** layer, which is the final stage of an LLVM backend.

We thought it was important to look at this layer now for two reasons.

First, this makes the instruction description you have been doing throughout *Chapter 11* more concrete because you can see the connection to the hardware.

Second, adding the support for the MC layer to your target description (the .td files that you wrote for your registers and instructions) can be disruptive if you did not think it through beforehand. In other words, if you do not consider the MC layer now, you may need to severely rewrite how your instruction records are structured in TableGen. For example, *Figure 12.1* shows a typical grouping of the instructions based on their encoding pattern:

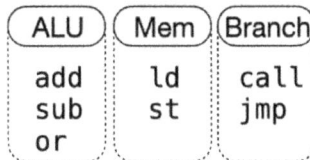

*Figure 12.1: Assembly instructions and their encoding family*

In this figure, you can see that the add, sub, and or instructions are all grouped in the same ALU encoding family and the ld and st instructions are grouped in the Mem family and so on. This grouping can wreak havoc in your TableGen description classes if you do not consider them early on.

All in all, we acknowledge that this may feel like falling off an abstraction cliff, but we believe that this is for the better.

In this chapter, you will learn how to augment the TableGen descriptions of your registers and instructions to produce the foundation of your MC layer.

More specifically, you will learn how to do the following:

- Describe your assembly syntax
- Describe the encoding of your instructions

Using the output generated by TableGen from these descriptions, we will show you how to enable some of the capabilities of the MC layer by building the beginning of an assembly parser and an assembler.

To get you started on the right foot, let us review what you need for this chapter.

# Technical requirements

As you did in the previous chapter, you will need a version of LLVM to play with the Machine **intermediate representation** (IR). You can use either one of the recent LLVM releases – for instance, from LLVM 17 and up – or build LLVM directly from its source code. Please see *Chapter 1* on how to build LLVM if you need help with that.

For the part that involves implementing something in an actual LLVM backend, you will find all the necessary commits and details by looking at the Git log of the `https://github.com/PacktPublishing/` `LLVM-Code-Generation-by-example` repository between the `begin_ch12` and `end_ch12` tags. Note that we call this repository the **companion repository**.

Let us now see when you will encounter the Machine IR.

# The use of the MC layer

The MC layer is used to handle the final representation of the actual instructions of the target. The final representation in the context of a backend compiler is either the textual or binary representation of the object file.

*Figure 12.2* illustrates when the MC layer is used in the LLVM infrastructure:

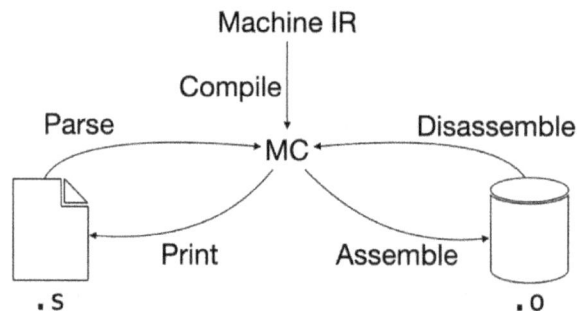

*Figure 12.2: MC, the glue for handling with the final output of the compiler*

Looking closer at *Figure 12.2*, you can see that the Machine IR gets compiled to the MC representation. Then you can print the MC representation to produce assembly files (.s), in other words, the textual representation of an object file, or assemble it to produce the binary file that is typically called the object file (.o). These are the two main output paths used with MC.

Similarly, MC is used as the representation when coming from either an assembly or object file. For assembly files, the LLVM infrastructure parses the textual representation and internally produces the MC representation. For object files, a similar translation happens except that it goes from the binary representation to the MC representation; we disassemble the object file to MC.

> Note
>
> Technically MC is an IR, but we prefer to call it simply a representation because when it comes to handling assembly and object files, it is limited to capturing one instruction at a time. Indeed, the whole IR consists mainly of one transient MCInst instance at a time and we thought it barely fit the definition of an IR. The MCInst class is used to represent an instruction at the MC level and comes with the expected MCOperand class dependency to model the operands to do anything useful with an instruction.

Looking back at *Figure 12.2*, you can see what needs to happen to implement the binary tools that typically come with a compiler toolchain. For instance, let us say that you want to implement an assembler for your target. An assembler takes an assembly file (.s) and produces an object file (.o). The way this works with the LLVM infrastructure is that you need to provide a parser to go from a .s file to the MC representation and then an assembler from MC to the .o file. Both the parser and assembler are partly auto generated in the LLVM infrastructure as you will see in the rest of this chapter.

In this section, we show you how the MC layer is the heart of the LLVM infrastructure for everything related to the binary tools.

Next, we will show you how you populate the information required by this layer by providing the necessary bits in the target description of your backend, in other words, what you need to write in your .td files.

# Connecting the MC layer

Both the registers and the instruction descriptions contribute to defining the MC layer of your backend through the MCRegisterInfo and MCInstrInfo classes. In the examples of *Chapter 11*, we showed the minimal examples for these descriptions to work but they did not contain enough information to really grasp the interest of the MC layer.

In this section, we will show you how to augment these descriptions to be able to tap into the functionalities offered by the MC layer. In other words, now that you have grasped how to define registers and instructions, thanks to *Chapter 11*, we can focus on adding the assembly code and encoding support on top of this knowledge instead of mixing everything all at once.

We keep the plumbing part to the section named *Enabling MC-based tools* and instead focus in this section on how to augment your records with the proper information for MC enablement. Before we see what this looks like, let us step back and answer an obvious question: what are these instructions that you need to describe?

## What instructions to describe

If you have already worked on a compiler backend, the answer is as obvious as the question, but if you are new to writing backends, you may feel overwhelmed.

Therefore, where do you start?

The answer lies with the **instruction set architecture (ISA)** of your backend. The ISA lists explicitly all the instructions that the target supports and, most of the time, provides the encoding for each instruction as well as its assembly syntax. For instance, *Figure 12.3* shows an encoding extracted from the *A64 Instruction Set Encoding* documentation distributed by the Arm company (full pdf available at `https://developer.arm.com/documentation/ddi0487/latest/`):

### SME FP16 widening outer product

```
 31   29                    21|20    16|15 13|12 10|9    5| 4| 3 | 2|1    0
┌─────────────────────────┬───────┬──────┬──────┬──────┬──┬──┬──┬─────┐
│1 0│0 0 0 0 0 1 1 0 1│   Zm  │  Pm  │  Pn  │  Zn  │S│0│0│ZAda│
└─────────────────────────┴───────┴──────┴──────┴──────┴──┴──┴──┴─────┘
```

*Figure 12.3: Encoding of an Arm instruction as described in its ISA document*

In this figure, you can see that the *SME FP16 widening outer product* instruction is a 32-bit instruction, as captured by the numbering of the bits in the table. In this table, Zm, Pm, and so on are the operands of the related instruction. Therefore, the operand Zn, for instance, is encoded with 5 bits, starting at the 5th bit in this instruction encoding.

The takeaway is you do not create instructions out of thin air; the target architecture gives you clear instructions (no pun intended) on what you need to describe.

Now that you know which instructions to create, you may already see the benefits of hooking up the MC layer first. Indeed, with the MC layer, you can enable lower-level tools such as the assembler and disassembler, meaning that with zero compiler support, (early) users can already use your target by developing assembly code directly!

## Augmenting the target description with MC information

As already mentioned in *Chapter 11*, with the default values of the fields of the TableGen `Register` and `Instruction` classes, the information needed to enable the assembler and disassembler tools is completely missing.

If you think about it, to print assembly code that is human-readable, you need to provide a syntax, meaning that you need to map the C++ enumeration value of your registers to a human-readable string. For instance, you need to know that the register represented by the C++ enumeration value XXX::R0 maps to the string r0. Similarly, an assembler must know that the string r0 represents the register identified by the enumeration value XXX::R0.

Finally, the assembler must know how this register is encoded in an instruction, meaning which bits it must set in the sequence of bits of the current instruction to indicate to the hardware where to read/write the value from/to. A disassembler needs the same kind of information but in the opposite direction; that is, if the assembler must know how to encode the information, the disassembler must know how to decode it – for instance, knowing that the string r3 translates in 0b11 in binary for the encoding, and the other way around for the decoding.

That sounds like a lot of information to convey but in practice, the LLVM infrastructure solves that elegantly. In essence, for the common cases, you must provide an assembly syntax in the form of a formatted string and an encoding in the form of a sequence of bits with placeholders for the different operands.

Let us see what this looks like in practice, starting with the registers.

## Defining the MC layer for the registers

For the registers' description, the fields that need to be set are as follows:

- AsmName for the assembly syntax
- HwEncoding for the encoding

For instance, let us say that we have two registers s0 and s1, and that they are encoded respectively as 0 and 1. Their TableGen records would look like the following:

```
let HwEncoding = 0 in
def s0 : Register<"s0">;
let HwEncoding = 1 in
def s1 : Register<"s1">;
```

In other words, we filled out the information for their encoding using the let HwEncoding syntax for each record.

There is a more structured way to do that, as illustrated by the changes we made in *Chapter 11* to our H2BLB backend in the companion repository at the gen-register-info_ch11 tag, but while the syntax we used in this tag is more compact, these are technical details.

Let us now move on to the instructions.

## Defining the MC layer for the instructions

For the instructions, the assembly syntax is super-easy to describe; you just need to set the related AsmString field using the variables that you defined for your operands. Augmenting our example from the previous chapter, the complete description of our MYINSTR instruction would look as follows:

```
def MYINSTR: Instruction<> {
  let OutOperandList = (outs defTy0:$dst0, defTy1:$dst1);
  let InOperandList = (ins opTy0:$src0, opTy1:$src1);
  let AsmString = "$dst0, $dst1 = myinstr $src0, $src1";
}
```

In this snippet, the $xx values are automatically mapped to the operands that we described in the OutOperandList and InOperandList fields (see *Chapter 11* for an explanation of these fields). The AsmString field is a freeform string in the sense that you can arrange the syntax however you want. For instance, here, we decided to put the definitions before an assignment operator (=), but we could have put them right after the opcode (myinstr). Usually, the syntax is described by the ISA document as well, so you are not going to invent it. Instead, you must follow the related specifications. In any case, whatever you do, you will have to write the assembly parser accordingly. The assembly parser is only partially generated, as we will see in the next section.

If you're wondering how this assembly syntax works, here is a quick primer. Essentially, each xxTy type that you set for your operand comes with a print method that fills out the related $xx in the formatted string with the output of that method. You can identify the print method used for a type by looking at the value of the PrintMethod field. These methods are implemented by default in the MCInstPrinter class and for custom types, you need to implement them in your own target-specialized MCInstPrinter class.

In other words, you can view the assembly syntax as an equivalent C-style printf statement that would resemble the following pseudo-code:

```
printf("%s,%s = myinstr %s,%s", defTy0.printMethod(dst0),
                                defTy1.printMethod(dst1), <snip>);
```

In this pseudo-code, the resulting string of each printMethod method is inserted in the corresponding %s placeholder.

All right, enough about the assembly syntax; let us focus on the encoding of the instructions.

The encoding of the instructions is a little bit hidden in the TableGen Instruction class. This is not particularly surprising because not all the instructions that you describe make it to the MC layer. Indeed, it is common to use pseudo-instructions at the Machine level to make certain optimizations easier. For instance, all backends feature PHI and COPY instructions (automatically included by the TableGen backend; well, more precisely, embedded in the Target.td file or one of the files included in this file) that are manipulated at the Machine level by the generic optimizers but must be eliminated before reaching the MC layer. This type of instruction does not need encoding information, and they usually carry the IsPseudo or IsCodeGenOnly property (that is, the related field is set to true in the related TableGen record) to make this obvious.

For all other instructions, the most direct way to set up the encoding information is by adding an Inst field to the records that represent your instructions. This field is not directly present in the TableGen Instruction class but is looked for by the TableGen backend, which is responsible for generating the methods used to do the encoding. In other words, you need to know the implementation of the related TableGen backend to know that you must set such a field, hence we were saying that it is hidden.

The encoding information works exactly the way you would expect; you declare your Inst field has a sequence of bits of the right size. For instance, if your instructions are 32 bits long, you will use the bits<32> type, and you describe each bit one by one for each instruction.

This process is not as tedious as it sounds, because you can set a sequence of bits in one go and you can structure your target description such that you share some common encoding structure between similar instructions. Hence our previous remark about how it is important to know about the MC layering when coming up with the descriptions of your instructions. For instance, all the arithmetic operations may use the same bit pattern to encode their information, and you can factor this logic in a target-specific TableGen Instruction class. Usually in an ISA, the instructions are grouped in some encoding family, and you can replicate this structure in your target description.

> **Note**
>
> It is a widespread practice in LLVM backends to have one file with all the TableGen classes that describes how each family of instructions is encoded and one file with all the records that instantiate these classes. The first file is usually named XXXInstrFormat.td and the second one is named XXXInstrInfo.td, where XXX is the name of the backend.

Let us see how this connects with our MYINSTR example:

```
def MYINSTR: Instruction<> {
  ... // unchanged from previous snippet
  bits<32> Inst;
  let Inst{31-22} = 0b1100100111;
  bits<4> dst0;
  let Inst{21-18} = dst0;
  bits<4> dst1;
  let Inst{17-14} = dst1;
  <snip>
```

In this snippet, we first add the Inst field to our record, then set each bit starting with the 10 most significant ones (from the 31st to the 22nd bit). The binary sequence that we provided in this example is completely made up but would, for instance, represent the opcode that is bound to the myinstr hardware instruction. Next, we declare a new field that represents the sequence of bits required to represent our dst0 operand (bits<4> dst0;). The next line (let Inst{21-18} = dst0;) sets the 18th to 21st bits with the encoding of the dst0 operand. We then continue to describe the encoding for all the operands and bits until the Inst field is completely covered.

> **Note**
>
> The Inst field can be preceded by the field keyword – for instance, field bits<32> Inst – in some existing target description files. The field keyword is deprecated and does not do anything at this point, so you can safely ignore it.

Again, this is a made-up example and the position of the bits to set are specified in the ISA, so you must follow that, but you get the idea, and we assure you it is not as scary as it sounds initially.

Beyond showing how to set the encodings for an instruction, the point of this example is to illustrate two things:

1.  Notice how we set the bits for the Inst field from the most significant bits to the least significant bits; in other words, the syntax describes the bits in decreasing order (Inst{21-18}) instead of increasing order (Inst{18-21}). Both syntaxes are valid, but they mean different things, as explained hereafter.
2.  Notice how the value of variables dst0, dst1, and so on have never been defined. We declared the related field and used it right after, so how is the information connected?

For the first bullet point, if you look at *Figure 12.3* again, notice how the specification is described in decreasing order of the bits as well.

This is typical in ISA because this is how, as humans, we represent numbers. For instance, when you print the number 8 in binary form, you expect to see 0b1000, not 0b0001. For the encoding, this is the same thing; if you encode 8 as 0b1000, this means that when you read this bit pattern from left to right, the first encountered bit (1 in this case) must be encoded at the third position (starting at the 0th bit). Therefore, the encoding is Inst{3-0} = 0b1000. If you were to write Inst{0-3} = 0b1000, then you will be encoding the number 0b0001, since you map 1 to index 0 and all following zeroes to the indices 1, 2, and 3, which would be interpreted as 1, not 8!

This is confusing, but we think that now that you understand how it works, you will be able to clear up that confusion in no time!

For the second bullet point, this is, again, the TableGen backend doing its magic. These dst0, dst1, and so on fields are placeholders for the variables that you described in the OutOperandList and InOperandList fields. In other words, as long as these fields and the $xx variables have the same names, the TableGen backend will fill them with the proper values.

This last statement raises another question that we have not addressed yet: how does the $xx variable get its encoding?

The encoding mechanism of the $xx variables is carried by their xxTy type. Similarly to the assembler syntax, these types come with their own encoding method that is described by the EncoderMethod field. For register operands, this method is automatically derived from the encoding that you set in your Register records (that is, the HwEncoding field).

As for the previous section, you can see an example of how to set up some encodings by looking at the changes carried by the hook-up-mc-codeemitter_ch12 tag of the companion repository.

> **Note**
>
> There is a second, more sophisticated way to specify the encodings of an instruction. This method uses the same principle as the first one, except that you define your encodings on a per-hardware-mode basis. For instance, how you encode myinstr may be different between the 1st generation of your architecture and the 12th generation. We will not describe how to leverage this but in a nutshell, you specify a similar Inst field encoding per hardware mode and the generic infrastructure uses the one specified by the sub-target (as captured by the function attributes attached to the LLVM IR Function instance).

In this section, you learned where to find the encoding of your instructions and how to specify the structure of these encodings in TableGen. You saw how the encodings that you defined for your registers connect with the encoding of your instructions and how this comes together to produce the final sequence of bits that represent a specific instance of your instruction.

Let us now address the final part of connecting the MC layer to your backend.

# Enabling MC-based tools

In this section, you will learn how to connect the assembly syntax and encoding information that you described in the previous sections so that you can use some of the MC-based tools. This section focuses specifically on the llvm-mc command-line tool, which is the LLVM-provided way for developers to test the MC layer of their backend.

For this chapter, we will not enable all the capabilities of the MC layer that you saw in *Figure 12.2*, instead we focus on enabling three MC components that, put together, enable an assembler-like type of experience, meaning that you will be able to test your assembly code syntax and generate encodings from it. Looking back to *Figure 12.2*, we will specifically enable the arrows representing the printing, the parsing, and (some of) the assembling. The reason we need all three components is because we want to enable the testing from .s to .o files (that is, the parsing to assembling), but when using the llvm-mc tool, the printing piece is also involved because llvm-mc prints the encoding (thus the result of the assembling action) next to the textual assembler syntax (thus the result of the printing action).

The three components that we need to enable are as follows:

- **The human-readable assembly code printer**: Represented by the MCInstPrinter base class, this component is responsible for converting MCInst instances to human-readable strings. This component is represented by the *Print* arrow in *Figure 12.2*.
- **The assembly code parser**: Represented by the MCTargetAsmParser base class, this component is responsible for converting a human-readable string into an MCInst instance. This component is represented by the *Parse* arrow in *Figure 12.2*.
- **The binary assembly code printer**: Represented by the MCCodeEmitter base class, this component is responsible for converting MCInst instances to binary code. This component is represented by the *Assemble* arrow in *Figure 12.2*.

With these three components, we will demonstrate a workflow that takes in a human-readable assembly code and outputs the encoding of the instructions in binary form.

To get started, let us cover the TableGen part first.

## Leveraging TableGen

To enable the previously mentioned components, we rely on several TableGen backends to do the heavy lifting. As you probably guessed, since we must generate three components, we need to use three TableGen backends!

The good news is that all three backends take the exact same input as you developed in the previous sections!

*Figure 12.4* shows which TableGen backends to invoke and how to use the produced output:

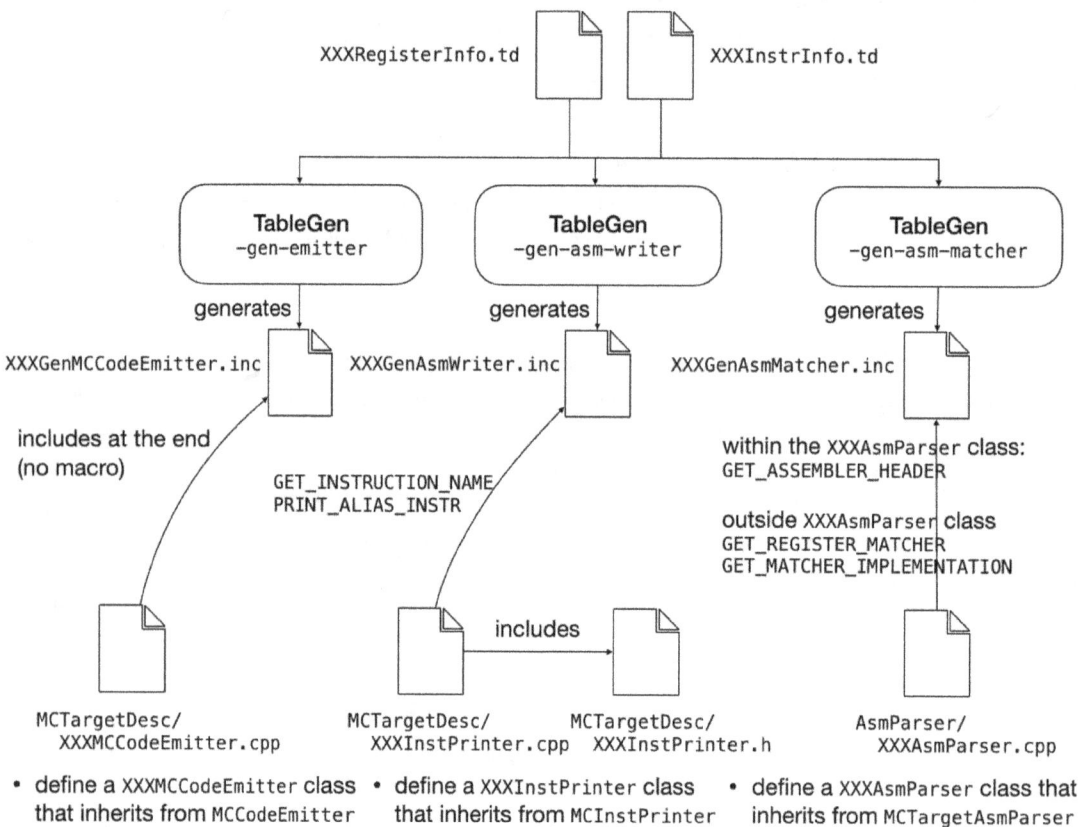

*Figure 12.4: How TableGen provides the basic implementation of different MC components*

To be able to perform the mechanical steps shown in *Figure 12.4*, you need to create the proper directory structure.

This includes the following:

- Creating the .cpp files for the XXXMCCodeEmitter and XXXInstPrinter classes in your MCTargetDesc directory.
- Creating the .h file for the XXXInstPrinter class; this step is not required for the MCCodeEmitter class because it is not reused by anything.
- Creating a new sub-directory named AsmParser at the root of the directory of your target (that is, ${LLVM_SRC}/lib/Target/XXX).

The last bullet point tells you something: we are creating a new target-specific library named LLVMXXXAsmParser that implements the target-specific pieces of what is available in the generic LLVM infrastructure as the MCParser library.

We'll leave the proper plumbing of the CMakeLists.txt file to you, but if you are having trouble connecting the pieces, please look at the different tags that we will mention in the following section to see an example of how to do that.

After you have created your directory structure, you must do the actions listed in *Figure 12.4*. Like in *Chapter 11*, in this figure, the arrows represent the files that you need to include in the related files, and the names on these arrows are the macros that you need to define (with the #define directive) before the #include directive.

When we are done with these actions, there are still some gaps that we need to fill to match TableGen's expectations. Indeed, these TableGen backends generate the implementation of some of the methods, but not necessarily the related prototypes, which means that we must patch up the declarations of our classes to include them.

> **Note**
>
> This kind of manually augmented declaration is atypical of TableGen. Usually, these methods are available through a GET_XXX_HEADER macro that would be suitable to inject directly into the related class, like what you did with GET_ASSEMBLER_HEADER for the XXXAsmParser class. If you feel like fixing this in open source, patches are welcome!

Therefore, concretely, you need to add within the declaration of your XXXInstPrinter class the following static function prototypes:

```
std::pair<const char *, uint64_t> getMnemonic(const MCInst &MI) override;
virtual void printInstruction(const MCInst *MI, uint64_t Address,
                              raw_ostream &O);
virtual bool printAliasInstr(const MCInst *MI, uint64_t Address,
                             raw_ostream &O);
static const char *getRegisterName(MCRegister Reg);
```

Similarly, you need to tweak the declaration of your XXXMCCodeEmitter class by adding the following method prototype:

```
uint64_t getBinaryCodeForInstr(const MCInst &MI,
                               SmallVectorImpl<MCFixup> &Fixups,
                               const MCSubtargetInfo &STI) const;
```

Also, make sure to define the DEBUG_TYPE macro within the XXXMCCodeEmitter.cpp file (for instance, add the following line near the top of the file: #define DEBUG_TYPE "mccodeemitter"), because the code generated by TableGen relies on it.

What is left to do now is the following:

- Provide a proper implementation of the pure virtual methods that you inherited in your target-specific classes.
- Implement the non-virtual methods that TableGen assumes you will provide.
- Create the plumbing with the TargetMachine instance of your backend.

Let us see how to do that.

## Implementing the missing pieces

With the way our target description is set up, TableGen generates most of the implementation of the XXXInstPrinter and XXXMCCodeEmitter classes but not the XXXAsmParser class. There are ways to augment the description of our registers and instructions with callbacks to custom parser methods, but in the end, these methods need to be implemented by hand anyway, so you are on the hook to write a lot of the XXXAsmParser class.

With no further ado, let us start with the missing implementation of the XXXInstPrinter class.

### Implementing your own MCInstPrinter class

There are two methods that must be implemented for you to have a functioning XXXInstPrinter class.

The first one is an override of the pure virtual method MCInstPrinter::printInst.

Thanks to the code generated by TableGen, the implementation is straightforward and looks like this:

```
void XXXInstPrinter::printInst(const MCInst *MI, uint64_t Address,
                               StringRef Annot, const MCSubtargetInfo &STI,
                               raw_ostream &O) {
  if (!PrintAliases || !printAliasInstr(MI, Address, O))
    printInstruction(MI, Address, O);

  printAnnotation(O, Annot);
}
```

In this snippet, we check whether the MCInstPrinter instance is configured such that it needs to print the instruction alias (carried by the member variable PrintAliases), which is an alternative way to print an instruction. For instance, a logical bitwise shift-left instruction could be printed as a multiplication by two. If the PrintAliases member variable is true, we call the printAliasInstr method that is generated by TableGen; otherwise, we call the printInstruction method, which is also generated by TableGen. Finally, we call the method of our superclass that is used to print whatever annotation is attached to this instruction. Annotations can be, for instance, comments attached to the instruction.

The second one that you need to provide is printOperand. This method is called by the code generated by TableGen. This method takes an operand and prints the related assembly string.

A possible implementation for this method is as follows:

```
void XXXInstPrinter::printOperand(const MCInst *MI, unsigned OpNo,
                                  raw_ostream &O) {
  const MCOperand &Op = MI->getOperand(OpNo);
  if (Op.isReg()) {
    unsigned Reg = Op.getReg();
    O << getRegisterName(Reg);
  } else if (Op.isImm()) {
    O << formatImm(Op.getImm());
  } else {
    assert(Op.isExpr() && "unknown operand kind in printOperand");
    Op.getExpr()->print(O, &MAI);
  }
}
```

In this snippet, we check what the type of the MCOperand instance is and call the appropriate superclass method (for instance, formatImm for the immediate value) or a method generated by TableGen (getRegisterName).

Finally, we need to implement the plumbing so that our TargetMachine instance knows about our MCInstPrinter implementation.

To do that, we need to do the following:

- Declare a createXXXMCInstPrinter function in our XXXInstPrinter.h file.
- Implement this createXXXMCInstPrinter function – for instance, in the XXXInstPrinter.cpp file – although most backends implement it directly in the XXXMCTargetDesc.cpp file.
- Call from within the LLVMInitializeXXXTargetMC function (implemented in the XXXMCTargetDesc.cpp file if you followed *Chapter 9*'s steps) the TargetRegistry::RegisterM CInstPrinter function to register our createXXXMCInstPrinter function.

All these steps are mechanical, and we believe that providing the snippets would not be particularly interesting. You can, however, find an example of all this, including the invocation to the related TableGen backend, at the `hook-up-mc-instprinter_ch12` tag in the companion repository.

Let us now look at the `XXXMCCodeEmitter` class.

## Implementing your own MCCodeEmitter class

To get a complete implementation of your `XXXMCCodeEmitter` class, you need to provide the implementation of two methods.

The first one is the implementation of the pure virtual method of the `MCCodeEmitter::encodeInstru ction` superclass. Thanks to TableGen and the helper functions provided by the LLVM infrastructure, a basic implementation of this method is possible in a few lines:

```
void XXXMCCodeEmitter::encodeInstruction(const MCInst &MI,
                                         SmallVectorImpl<char> &CB,
                                         SmallVectorImpl<MCFixup> &Fixups,
                                         const MCSubtargetInfo &STI) const {
  uint64_t Encoding = getBinaryCodeForInstr(MI, Fixups, STI);
  support::endian::write<uint32_t>(CB, Encoding, llvm::endianness::little);
}
```

Before we describe this snippet, let us call out that we made a simplifying assumption: we assumed that our target encodes its instructions with 32 bits (hence the use of the `uint32_t` type) and is little-endian. With these assumptions, the implementation simply leverages the `getBinaryCodeForInstr` method that TableGen produces for us, then calls the `endian::write` function from the Support library with the right parameters to flush out the `Encoding` variable in the array of bytes represented by `CB`.

The second and final method that we need to provide to complete the implementation of our `XXXMCCodeEmitter` class is the `getMachineOpValue` method. Like the previous method, the code generated by TableGen makes it amazingly easy to provide a sensible implementation:

```
unsigned
XXXMCCodeEmitter::getMachineOpValue(const MCInst &MI, const MCOperand &MO,
                                    SmallVectorImpl<MCFixup> &Fixups,
                                    const MCSubtargetInfo &STI) const {
  if (MO.isReg())
    return MCCtxt.getRegisterInfo()->getEncodingValue(MO.getReg());
  return static_cast<unsigned>(MO.getImm());
}
```

In this snippet, we only support register and immediate operands and, for the registers, we call the `MCRegisterInfo::getEncodingValue` method that TableGen generates for our target.

Like the implementation of our target-specific `MCInstPrinter` class, there are a few more steps that we need to take to plumb our `XXXMCCodeEmitter` class with our `TargetMachine` instance.

These steps are as follows:

- Declare the createXXXMCCodeEmitter function, for instance directly in the XXXMCTargetDesc.h file.

- Implement the createXXXMCCodeEmitter function in the XXXMCCodeEmitter.cpp file.

- Call from within the LLVMInitializeXXXTargetMC function the TargetRegistry::RegisterM CCodeEmitter function to register with the createXXXMCCodeEmitter function.

Like in the previous section, we will not show the snippets for these mechanical changes. You can see the full set of changes related to the H2BLB target in the companion repository at the hook-up-mc-codeemitter_ch12 tag if you need an example.

Now, let us conclude this plumbing with the XXXAsmParser class.

## Implementing your own XXXAsmParser class

As we mentioned, the parser is very target-specific and requires a non-trivial amount of work depending on how complex your assembly syntax is.

Since this component is only required to read assembly instructions in a textual format (.s) and put them in the MC layer, this component is not on the critical path of any of the code generator backend work. Indeed, the work of code generation is done, at least with respect to the scope of this book, when the assembly code, either in textual or binary form, is produced. However, this component is still useful to have to test the instruction encodings very early in the development of the compiler, because it means you can use .s files as inputs of your tests instead of waiting for the full code generation pipeline to be there to finally test your assembly code.

This long introduction is to say that we will not go into the details of how to implement the missing methods since they only work for a specific syntax. Instead, we'll provide an example of how to write a basic assembly parser in the companion repository of this book at the basic-asm-parser_ch12 tag.

The syntax that we support for this backend is simpler than what we showed in the *Defining the MC layer for the instructions* section. It does not use the assignment operator and instead sticks to the more widespread assembly syntax that resembles the opcode def0,def1,src0,src1 string; in other words, all the operands are printed behind the opcode and the definitions happen before the arguments.

Now that the parsing of the syntax is taken care of, there is one additional step that we need to take to connect the parser with our TargetMachine instance. By adding the AsmParser library to our backend, we now have one function that we must implement: the LLVMInitializeXXXAsmParser function. This function is called from the InitializeAllAsmParsers function, which is used by all the LLVM tools that need some functionalities of the assembly parser.

The implementation is straightforward and looks like this:

```
extern "C" LLVM_EXTERNAL_VISIBILITY void LLVMInitializeXXXsmParser() {
  RegisterMCAsmParser<XXXAsmParser> Z(getTheXXXTarget());
}
```

In this snippet, you should recognize the patterns that you have already seen in *Chapter 9*. Refer to this chapter for more details on what this type of code does.

With this last component ready, you can now test your MC layer by writing assembly instructions in .s files using whatever syntax you implemented and feeding these files to the llvm-mc tool. Using llvm-mc with the --show-encoding option will print out the binary representation of your instructions and you can check that they match what you expect. You can see this in action by looking at the llvm/test/MC/H2BLB/addi16.s file in the companion repository.

In this section, we gave you an overview of how to enable several MC components that, put together, allow you to test your encodings while starting from the assembly syntax. A lot of the things that we demonstrated in this section are mechanical and we believe that you now understand how to apply the same principles to connect additional MC components, such as the one represented by the MCDisassembler class.

# Summary

In this chapter, you learned how to convey the information about the assembly syntax and the encoding of the instructions of your target.

You saw how to augment the target description of your backend with this information and how to use the different TableGen backends to produce some of the tooling of the MC layer.

You saw how these tools provide you with a way to test the validity of your encodings early in the development of your backend. In other words, thanks to what you learned in this chapter, you do not need to build a full code generator pipeline to start checking that you are accurately modeling the ISA of your target architecture.

Speaking of the code generator pipeline, the next chapter will go over what needs to happen in this pipeline and the expected stages that the Machine IR will go through.

# Quiz time

Now that you have finished reading the chapter, try answering the following questions to test your knowledge:

1.  What field do you have to add to a TableGen instruction record to enable the generation of the encodings?

    The encoding information for an instruction record is primarily carried by the Inst field.

    See the *Defining the MC layer for the instructions* section for more details.

2.  Imagine that you defined the encoding of one of your operands like this: let Inst{0-3} = op. The resulting encoding is incorrect. What is the likely cause?

    The likely cause is that you swapped the order of the bits in the encoding. You likely wanted to use let Inst{3-0} = op instead.

    See the *Defining the MC layer for the instructions* section for more details.

3. Must all the instructions have encodings? Why?

   No; only the instructions that are expected to reach the MC layer must have encodings. This is because the Machine layer may need to use pseudo-instructions, such as `PHI` and `COPY` instructions, to work with the generic part of the backend.

   See the *Defining the MC layer for the instructions* section for more details.

4. What is the responsibility of the `MCCodeEmitter` class?

   The `MCCodeEmitter` class is responsible for translating an `MCInst` instance into a sequence of bytes. In other words, it is responsible for encoding the instructions.

   See the *Enabling MC-based tools* section for more details.

5. Why is it important to think about the MC layer while solely working on the Machine layer?

   At the MC level, it may be beneficial to group the target description of your instructions behind the same family of encoding as usually specified by the ISA document. If you do not consider this while working on the Machine layer, chances are you will miss these groupings and may have to rewrite your target description to account for them.

   See the *Connecting the MC layer* section for more details.

---

## Unlock this book's exclusive benefits now

This book comes with additional benefits designed to elevate your learning experience.

*Note: Have your purchase invoice ready before you begin.*

https://www.packtpub.com/unlock/9781837637782

# 13

# The Machine Pass Pipeline

In the previous chapter, you learned about the **intermediate representation** (IR) that's used in the backend part of the compiler. This IR is called the **Machine IR**. In this chapter, you'll learn about the phases that this IR goes through as it progresses through the backend. These phases are articulated around a pass pipeline (see *Chapter 5*) that we call the Machine pass pipeline. Most backends use the same base pipeline and augment it with their target-specific passes.

In this chapter, you'll learn about the following aspects:

- How to tweak the Machine pass pipeline for your needs
- Which properties the IR must hold throughout the lowering stages of this pipeline
- How to reuse generic passes

The last bullet point is about teaching you how to identify what's needed to use the existing passes and not about what they do. This can seem like a stark difference compared to *Chapter 8*, where you discovered what the LLVM IR passes can do. The reason for this difference is that the default Machine pass pipeline uses most of the Machine IR passes already and that given the constraints on the Machine IR, there's little reason to change that order. Indeed, most of the tweaking of the Machine pass pipeline is expected to happen on the target-specific side, meaning you create new passes and add them to your pass pipeline.

The second reason it isn't that interesting to survey the Machine IR passes is that you should be able to understand them easily already since they're often just a Machine IR version of an existing LLVM IR pass. For instance, the MachineLICM class is an optimization pass that performs the same **loop invariant code motion optimization** as the LLVM IR pass represented by the LICMPass class.

Now that you know what to expect in this chapter, let's start with the technical requirements.

# Technical requirements

For this chapter, we recommend that you have a copy of the LLVM source code so that you can look at the content of the CodeGen library in the llvm/lib/CodeGen and llvm/include/llvm/CodeGen directories. These directories contain passes and helper classes that are used throughout the target-independent code generator. Note that the paths are expressed relative to the root directory of the LLVM code base.

You can find a copy of the LLVM code base at one of the following locations:

- The official LLVM releases website: https://releases.llvm.org
- The official LLVM GitHub repository: https://github.com/llvm/llvm-project
- This book's GitHub repository: https://github.com/PacktPublishing/LLVM-Code-Generation

Additionally, you'll need a version of the LLVM binaries to be able to run the examples that live in the ch13 folder of this book's GitHub repository at https://github.com/PacktPublishing/LLVM-Code-Generation. Either build these binaries from the LLVM sources or use one of the LLVM releases to get them.

Now, let's start with the big picture of the Machine pass pipeline.

# The Machine pass pipeline at a glance

The pass pipeline of a backend is handled by a specialized version of the TargetPassConfig class. This class should be familiar to you because you learned how to specialize and instantiate it for your backend in *Chapter 9*.

By default, the pass pipeline produced by the TargetPassConfig class looks like what's depicted in *Figure 13.1*:

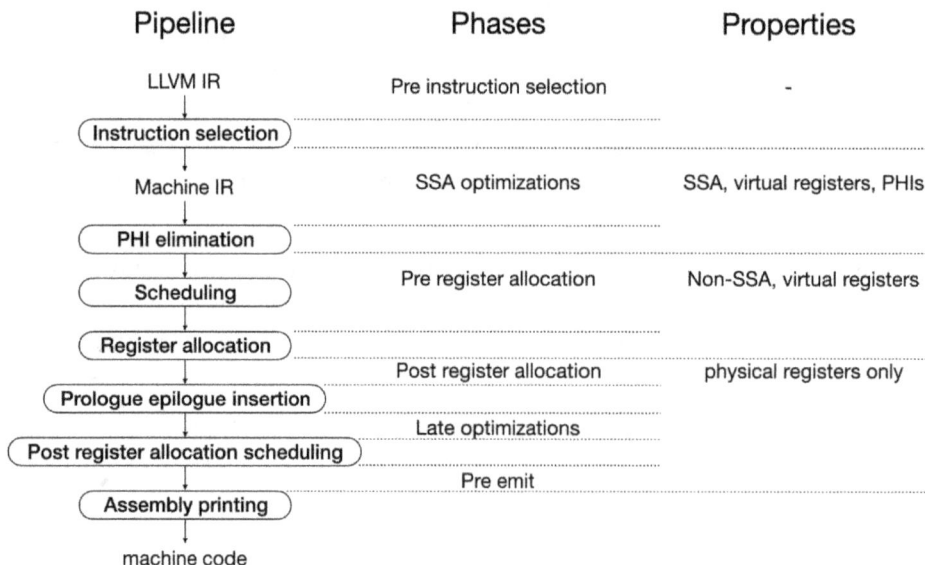

*Figure 13.1: The default Machine pass pipeline*

On the left, in rounded rectangles, you can see the main passes that are used in a backend to lower an input LLVM IR to **machine code (MC)**. On each arrow, each backend can inject more passes, both generic and target-specific.

The middle column of this figure shows the names of the different lowering phases. In the next section, you'll see how they map to the **application binary interfaces (APIs)** of the `TargetConfigPass` class.

Finally, the right column shows the expected properties of the IR that will be manipulated by the passes at this stage of the pipeline. For instance, after the register allocation pass, the Machine IR must only use physical registers. *Table 13.2* provides an example of the different stages of the IR:

| Early | Before Register Allocation | After Register Allocation |
|---|---|---|
| `%1:gpr64sp = PHI`<br>`<...>`<br>`%8:gpr64common =`<br>`ADDXri %1, 1, 0` | `%1:gpr64sp = COPY`<br>`<...>`<br>`%8:gpr64common =`<br>`ADDXri killed %1,`<br>`1, 0` | `# Optimized`<br>`renamable $x8 =`<br>`ADDXri killed`<br>`renamable $x8, 1, 0` |

*Table 13.1: Machine IR at the different lowering stages*

In this table, on the left-hand side, you can see the IR after instruction selection. It contains `PHI` instructions and uses virtual registers such as `%1` and `%8`. After the PHI elimination pass, the IR doesn't contain any `PHI` instructions. Instead, `COPY` instructions have been inserted and the virtual registers may have several definitions. In other words, after this pass, the IR isn't in **static single assignment (SSA)** form anymore. After register allocation, the virtual registers are replaced by physical registers. After the register allocation pass, passes aren't allowed to introduce virtual registers.

You can find an example that shows the stages of the Machine IR in the `ch13` folder of this book's GitHub repository. Follow the instructions in the `README.md` file to produce the IRs.

In this section, you were provided with a high-level view of the pass pipeline that's used by the backends and the implications this pipeline has on the properties of the IR. By knowing this, you'll be able to decide where you should inject your target-specific passes. For instance, imagine that you want to work on the Machine IR while it's still in SSA form. In this case, you'll need to inject your pass somewhere before the PHI elimination pass.

In the next section, we'll show you how to use the `TargetPassConfig` class to do this.

# Injecting passes

By default, the `TargetPassConfig` class sets up a pass pipeline that resembles what we showed in *Figure 13.1*.

This default pipeline is set by the `TargetPassConfig::addMachinePasses` method. While you can overload this method so that you have a completely customized Machine pass pipeline, we recommend that you stick with the default implementation.

Indeed, the hooks that are exposed by the `TargetPassConfig` class allow you to inject passes within the default pass pipeline at distinct stages of the lowering process. If you depart from the default implementation of the `TargetPassConfig::addMachinePasses` method, then these hooks won't be called. Moreover, as mentioned in this chapter's introduction, the default pass pipeline already uses a lot of generic optimizations, so it would be a waste of your time to figure out where in your pass pipeline you should add all these optimizations again.

Zooming into the hooks of the `TargetPassConfig` class, this class defines virtual methods called addXXX, where XXX matches a particular stage of the default pipeline. For instance, by overriding the addPreRegAlloc method in your target-specific implementation of the `TargetPassConfig` class, you can inject passes right before the register allocation pass.

Similarly, by overriding the AddPreISel method, you can inject passes right before the instruction selection pass – that is, while the input IR is still using the LLVM IR.

Using *Figure 13.1* as a reference, you should easily grasp where each overloadable method injects the passes. Now, there are many more injection points than what's shown in this figure; if you want to check where all of them happen, simply look at the implementation of the `TargetPassConfig::addM achinePasses` method in the `llvm/lib/CodeGen/TargetPassConfig.cpp` file. Since you already have the overall picture of the default pass pipeline, thanks to *Figure 13.1*, we believe you should be able to follow the implementation easily.

> **Note**
>
> What we just described should resonate with what you did in *Chapter 9*, where you overloaded the `TargetPassConfig::addIRPasses` method. That method is used to set up all the passes that run before the instruction selection pass. If you want to inject LLVM IR passes on top of the default implementation, a better method to override is the `TargetPassConfig::addPreISel` method. Indeed, overriding the `TargetPassConfig::addIRPasses` method will drop all the IR passes from the default implementation.

In this chapter, we won't show code snippets for injecting passes as we covered this in *Chapter 5* and *Chapter 9*.

In this section, you learned how to use the implementation of the `TargetPassConfig` class of your backend to inject passes into the default Machine pass pipeline. Thanks to this knowledge, you'll be able to choose the right hook so that you can insert your custom or generic passes into the lowering stages of the Machine pass pipeline.

Next, we'll show you how to leverage the generic optimization passes.

# Using the generic Machine optimizations

Although the default Machine pass pipeline comes with a lot of optimizations, some of them may not do a whole lot out of the box.

Indeed, like the LLVM IR passes that rely on the `TargetTransformInfo` class to be able to do their job, some Machine IR passes need the help of the `TargetInstrInfo`, `TargetRegisterInfo`, or `TargetLowering` class, as well as some properties on the instruction themselves to perform their job.

For instance, the `MachineSink` optimization, which pushes down the **control flow graph** (**CFG**) instructions and can be moved in less frequently executed program points, relies on some of the properties that are attached to the `MachineInstr` instances to check whether it's safe to move the instructions (for instance, the memory operations, meaning the instructions with the `mayStore` or `mayLoad` properties are deemed unsafe to move in this pass) and use hooks from the `TargetInstrInfo` class (which you can override) to drive the algorithm (for instance, the `TargetInstrInfo::shouldSink` and `TargetInstrInfo::isSafeToSink` methods).

There are a lot of Machine passes and we believe it wouldn't be particularly useful to explain all of them. Indeed, like we said in the introduction, a lot of the Machine passes are just the counterparts of the same LLVM IR optimization and since we already explained these in *Chapter 8*, there's little interest in going through that again. However, we'll cover the main Machine passes that require non-trivial information and implementation from the backend. These passes are the instruction selector, scheduler, register allocator, and prologue-epilogue inserter, and we'll cover them in *Chapters 14*, *15*, *16*, and *17*, respectively. We leave the rest of the passes for you to check out, but we'll provide a few guidelines.

First, to check whether a generic optimization may exist, check the functions and pass identifiers that are exposed in the `llvm/include/llvm/CodeGen/Passes.h` file. Inside this file, you'll find all the `createXXXPass` functions, as well as all the `XXXPassID` functions that are supported by the generic `CodeGen` library. From there, you can check whether one of the names of the pass may do what you're looking for.

For example, if you look for a dead code elimination pass, you'll find that it's already available under the `DeadMachineInstructionElimID` identifier. Then, you just need to decide where in your pass pipeline you'll run that pass and override the related `TargetPassConfig` method (see the *Injecting passes* section to find the right method). In that method, you just need to call `TargetPassConfig::addPass` with the ID of the pass, and voila – this pass will be injected into your pass pipeline at the right place.

Now, let's say that you found a generic optimization that may match what you need but it doesn't modify the code like you would have hoped.

Start by creating a reduced MIR file with your motivating example and use the `run-pass` command-line option with the `llc` tool to quickly iterate on this pass (see *Chapter 10* if you need help with that). Remember to use the logging capability of the passes to see why this pass may not perform the optimization you wanted. The logs may highlight what's missing (see *Chapter 10* if you need help with that as well).

Next, if the logs aren't enough, open the file that contains the implementation of the pass. If you can't find this file, remember that you can leverage the `git grep` command line to find the source files that contain specific strings.

In that file, look for the usages of the `TargetRegisterInfo`, `TargetInstrInfo`, and `TargetLowering` classes. These classes are usually held in variables named `TRI`, `TII`, and `TLI`, so you can start by looking for them. Similarly, look for usages of the `MachineInstr::isXXX` methods, such as the `isAsCheapAsMove` method; you can specifically look for the sequence of characters – that is, `->is` or `.is` – in the implementation file and look at the ones that are connected to a `MachineInstr` variable (these variables are often named `MI`). Doing these two things will show you which methods you may need to implement in the related `TargetRegisterInfo`, `TargetInstrInfo`, or `TargetLowering` class and which properties your instruction should have.

> Note
>
> Different generic passes work at different lowering stages. Some passes only work in SSA form (for instance, the `MachineCSE` pass), while others only work on register-allocated code (for instance, the `MachineSink` pass). Certain passes also work at any stage (SSA, non-SSA, physical registers, and virtual registers). You can determine where a specific pass can run by looking at the implementation of the `MachineFunctionPass::getRe quiredProperties` method for the related pass. If this method hasn't been overloaded, then it can run anywhere in the Machine pass pipeline (although the pass may behave differently based on the lowering stage); otherwise, the pass can only be run when the related `MachineFunction` carries the specified property (for instance, `IsSSA` means that the pass can only run in the SSA optimizations phase; see *Figure 13.1*).

In this section, we showed you how to discover the optimization passes that are available at the Machine level. Furthermore, you learned what to look for in the implementation of the passes to enable their full potential and how to connect them in your pass pipeline.

In the next section, we'll go over a few passes that can be leveraged by backend authors and that may not be immediately obvious.

# Generic passes worth mentioning

Among the passes that the CodeGen library offers, we wanted to go over the `CodeGenPrepare`, `PeepholeOptimizer`, and `MachineCombiner` passes because they bring something that may not be obvious at first, are particularly useful, and require some backend work to leverage.

The last point is true for most CodeGen passes, but these are less useful than the other ones if you don't put in some work.

Let's start with the `CodeGenPrepare` pass.

## The CodeGenPrepare pass

Despite being part of the `CodeGen` library, the `CodeGenPrepare` pass is an LLVM-IR-to-LLVM-IR pass. This pass is responsible for papering over some of the limitations of the legacy instruction selector called `SelectionDAG`. We'll cover this in more detail in the next chapter, but at this point, the key takeaway is that you may have to perform some transformations at the LLVM IR level for this selector to produce the best possible code.

Among other things, the CodeGenPrepare pass is responsible for producing patterns of instructions that make the instruction selector more effective at producing efficient uses of the addressing modes of the target (the way a target can compute memory addresses while loading or storing data).

A lot of the functionalities of this pass are enabled by the overloaded methods of your target implementation of the TargetLowering class. For instance, for the addressing modes, most decisions are based on the overloadable TargetLowering::isLegalAddressingMode method.

## The PeepholeOptimizer pass

The PeepholeOptimizer pass rewrites certain patterns of instructions into more efficient ones. One of the rewrites massages copy-like instructions to make the register allocation process more efficient.

To enable it, make sure you add the relevant isBitcast, isRegSequenceLike, isInsertSubregLike, or isExtractSubregLike property to your instruction description (see *Chapter 11* if you need help describing your instructions) and implement the related getRegSequenceInputs, getInsertSubregInputs, and getExtractSubregInputs methods in your TargetInstrInfo class.

## The MachineCombiner pass

The MachineCombiner pass offers a framework to replace patterns of instructions with new instructions. You may be wondering what the differences are with the PeepholeOptimizer pass, so let's address this first.

The PeepholeOptimizer pass performs target-agnostic rewrites that are expected to be beneficial across targets. In contrast, the MachineCombiner pass tries to apply target-specific patterns and materializes them only when the length of the critical path is at least as short as the critical path of the original sequence of instructions and the register pressure is as low as the register pressure of the original sequence of instructions. In other words, it comes with a precise profitability model.

Critical path

The **critical path** is something that's used to measure how good the scheduling (or the order) of a sequence of instructions is. It represents the minimal number of processor clock cycles to execute that sequence of code. When an instruction is on the critical path of a sequence of instructions, it means that delaying this instruction will delay the execution of the whole code sequence. For instance, let's say that we have an instruction, a = b + c, and that b is defined by a load from memory and c is defined by another instruction. Let's say that a load is typically three clock cycles – or cycles for short – and the instruction that defines c is one cycle. In this sequence of instructions, b is on the critical path because it has the longest latency of the instructions that feed in a = b + c. Indeed, the definition of c isn't on the critical path because it can be done while waiting for the result of the load of b. In other words, there's no way to reduce the latency of the load and since it takes longer to execute than the definition of c, it's on the critical path.

To use the capabilities of the `MachineCombiner` pass, you must implement several methods in your `TargetInstrInfo` class, starting with the `getMachineCombinerPatterns` and `genAlternativeCodeSequence` methods.

We won't go into more details here, so take a look at the implementation of these methods in the AArch64 backend if you want an example of how to use them.

With that, we've covered a few passes you may be interested in leveraging in your backend. The `CodeGen` library contains many more interesting optimizations, and we encourage you to look at them.

## Summary

In this chapter, you learned how the Machine pass pipeline is structured and the implications of this structure on the IR. You saw that you start from the Machine IR in SSA form with virtual registers, then go to the non-SSA form but still with virtual registers, and finish with pure physical registers before transitioning to the MC layer.

Next, you learned how to inject passes into the Machine pass pipeline at various places using the `TargetPassConfig` class. You also learned how to examine the existing passes of the `CodeGen` passes to see what they need to perform their job.

Finally, you learned about three passes that the `CodeGen` library offers – `CodeGenPrepare`, `PeepholeOptimizer`, and `MachineCombiner` – and got a taste of what you need to do to use these passes to their full potential.

In the next chapter, we'll focus on one of the mandatory steps of the Machine pass pipeline: the instruction selection step.

## Further reading

The official LLVM documentation has a page dedicated to the LLVM target-independent code generator: https://llvm.org/docs/CodeGenerator.html. You can use this page as a refresher for the concepts we've covered so far and as a primer for the pieces we'll cover in the next chapters. Fear not – you don't have to read this page to understand the upcoming chapters.

## Quiz time

Now that you have completed reading this chapter, try answering the following questions to test your knowledge:

1.  What are the three main stages that the Machine IR goes through during the lowering process?

    The Machine IR starts in SSA form with virtual registers, then goes in non-SSA form still with virtual registers, and finally uses only physical registers.

    See the *The Machine pass pipeline at a glance* section for more details.

2. Should you override the `TargetPassConfig::addMachinePasses` method and why?

   Our recommendation is to **not** override this particular method because it creates the backbone of a typical LLVM backend that uses the LLVM target-independent code generator. If you want to use this code generator, you don't want to waste time rediscovering how to build a proper pipeline.

   See the *Injecting passes* section for more details, in particular regarding how to tweak this default pipeline.

3. How can you tell where in the pass pipeline a generic pass can be run?

   Passes that can only be run at specific lowering stages will overload the `MachineFunctionPass::getRequiredProperties` method. Locate this implementation and check what requirements are listed – this will tell you when this pass can run. By default, passes can run everywhere.

   See the *Using the generic Machine optimizations* section for more information.

4. How are the `PeepholeOptimizer` and `MachineCombiner` passes different?

   While the `PeepholeOptimizer` and `MachineCombiner` passes are both optimizations that replace patterns of instructions with new instructions, they differ in that the former applies target-agnostic patterns and the latter applies target-specific patterns.

   See the *Generic passes worth mentioning* section for more details.

5. Let's say you want to reuse the pass identified with the `ExpandPostRAPseudosID` identifier to expand your pseudo-instructions after register allocation. How can you find what this pass needs from your backend?

   In a nutshell, you need to locate the implementation of this pass by using the `git grep ExpandPostRAPseudosID` command line in your LLVM repository, for example, then look at the uses of the `TargetXXX` classes and identify which methods are used. In this case, that would be the `TargetInstrInfo::expandPostRAPseudo` and `TargetInstrInfo::lowerCopy` methods. Then, following further down the implementation of these methods, you would discover that ultimately, you need to implement the `TargetInstrInfo::copyPhysReg` method.

   See the *Using the generic Machine optimizations* section for more details on how to approach generic passes.

---

**Unlock this book's exclusive benefits now**

This book comes with additional benefits designed to elevate your learning experience.

*Note: Have your purchase invoice ready before you begin.*

`https://www.packtpub.com/unlock/9781837637782`

# Part 4

# LLVM IR to Machine IR

Now that the secrets of the Machine **intermediate representation** (**IR**) have been uncovered, you are ready to learn how to produce it from the LLVM IR.

This part focuses on LLVM IR to Machine IR translation. This translation is called **instruction selection** and the LLVM infrastructure features several instruction selection frameworks to choose from.

In this part, you will learn about the different instruction selection frameworks, how to use them, and how to provide the necessary target-specific information that they need to function.

The target-specific information that you will learn to provide includes the **application binary interface** (**ABI**) of your target, which instructions are supported, and how you get from LLVM IR to your target-specific instruction.

By the end of this part, you will be able to write a completely functional instruction selection implementation that will pave the way for the later machine pass optimizations.

This part of the book includes the following chapters:

- *Chapter 14, Getting Started with Instruction Selection*
- *Chapter 15, Instruction Selection: The IR Building Phase*
- *Chapter 16, Instruction Selection: The Legalization Phase*
- *Chapter 17, Instruction Selection: The Selection Phase and Beyond*

# 14

# Getting Started with Instruction Selection

**Instruction selection** (ISel) plays a key role in a **Low Level Virtual Machine** (LLVM) backend. It is responsible for lowering the LLVM **intermediate representation** (IR) down to the Machine IR with the limited set of instructions a backend has to offer.

The set of instructions of a backend is prescribed by the **instruction set architecture** (ISA) of the related architecture, and two different architectures may have very different ISAs. For instance, some architectures support floating-point arithmetic, whereas others do not. Therefore, the way you lower the LLVM IR for one architecture may be completely different for another.

The LLVM target-independent code generator, or **codegen**, provides a lot of infrastructure that you will learn to leverage across the next few chapters to implement your own instruction selector.

In this chapter, we focus on teaching you about the following:

- General ways these selectors work
- How you interact with and manipulate their IR
- Their characteristics
- How to connect them to your pass pipeline

Thanks to this knowledge, you will be able to confidently choose which selector to use, have a general understanding of the work involved in building your selector, and get started with the implementation.

To make things easier to follow, this chapter builds the H2BLB backend that we introduced a few chapters ago. You can refer to the related repository (see the next section) and see full examples of how to implement what we present in this chapter.

Before explaining in more detail what an instruction selector is in LLVM, let's review the technical requirements for this chapter.

# Technical requirements

Building an LLVM backend implies developing directly in the LLVM code base (or a fork of it). As such, you will need all the same tools that we already presented in *Chapter 1*.

Additionally, for all the snippets presented in this chapter, you will find the actual implementation in the https://github.com/PacktPublishing/LLVM-Code-Generation-by-example GitHub repository. We'll call this repository the *companion repository* for the remainder of the chapter.

The changes for this chapter are all included between the begin_ch14 and end_ch14 Git tags of the companion repository. If you are not familiar with Git tags, look at *Chapter 9* for a quick explanation of what you can do with them. Throughout the chapter, we also mention specific tags that we created in this repository for you to easily find the relevant commits.

Note that the code changes made for *Chapter 14* to *Chapter 17* are intertwined. The begin_XXX and end_XXX tags encompass the first and last commits of the related chapter but may also contain unrelated changes. In any case, the commit messages describe what each change is bringing to the table for each chapter.

Let's now get familiar with the concept of instruction selection.

# Overview of the instruction selection frameworks

You can view an instruction selector as a funnel that takes the massive space of a program that can be represented in LLVM IR and narrows it down to an equivalent program that only uses the instructions available for your backend.

The LLVM infrastructure offers two (and a half!) different frameworks to help you solve the **instruction selection (ISel)** problem. The main two frameworks are, respectively, **SelectionDAG** (also known as **SDISel**), which is the legacy instruction selector, and **GlobalISel** (also known as **GISel**), which is the newer selector. There is also a sub-framework called **FastISel**, which is part of the SDISel framework. From this point forward, we will use SDISel, GlobalISel, and FastISel as nouns, since this is what is done in all LLVM documentation.

Therefore, right off the bat, you must choose which selector you want to use for your backend. The frameworks all share some common infrastructure, thanks to TableGen, but for the most part, we are talking about different implementations. We will describe the pros and cons of each framework in the *Which selector to use?* section and will cover all three implementations in the remaining sections, although the implementation of the FastISel framework is kept at a minimum since it is limited but also straightforward.

# How does instruction selection work?

Both SDISel and GlobalISel follow the same overall structure, which consists of the following main phases in this order:

- **IR builder:** Translate the input program in LLVM IR into the IR of the related selector framework.
- **Legalization:** Rewrite IR constructs not supported by the ISA of the backend into something that is supported by the backend.
- **Selection:** Replace the IR of the selector framework with the Machine IR of the backend.

Additionally, some optimizations can happen between these main phases with more or less flexibility depending on the selection framework. You will discover how to add them in *Chapter 17*.

Now, focusing on FastISel, it is a sub-selector that runs inside SDISel. To put it simply, FastISel is a target-specific all-in-one IR builder/legalization/selection phase that goes straight from the LLVM IR to the Machine IR. In other words, FastISel does everything in one step, which means that the compile time is usually faster than the two other frameworks, hence why it is called FastISel.

## Framework complementarity

The LLVM infrastructure features some mechanisms to mix and match the different frameworks. More specifically, since SDISel is the legacy selector, it can be used by the two other selectors (GlobalISel and FastISel) as a fallback mechanism. This means that if GlobalISel cannot select something, for instance, SDISel can be used automatically instead.

The granularity of the fallback mechanism to SDISel is different for FastISel and GlobalISel. Essentially, FastISel can fall back to SDISel in the middle of a basic block, and SDISel will finish the selection of that basic block. On the other hand, if GlobalISel cannot select anything in the input LLVM IR function, it will clean the state of the selection and hand it over to SDISel for a fresh start.

*Figure 14.1* captures visually the fallback mechanism for the selectors in the LLVM infrastructure:

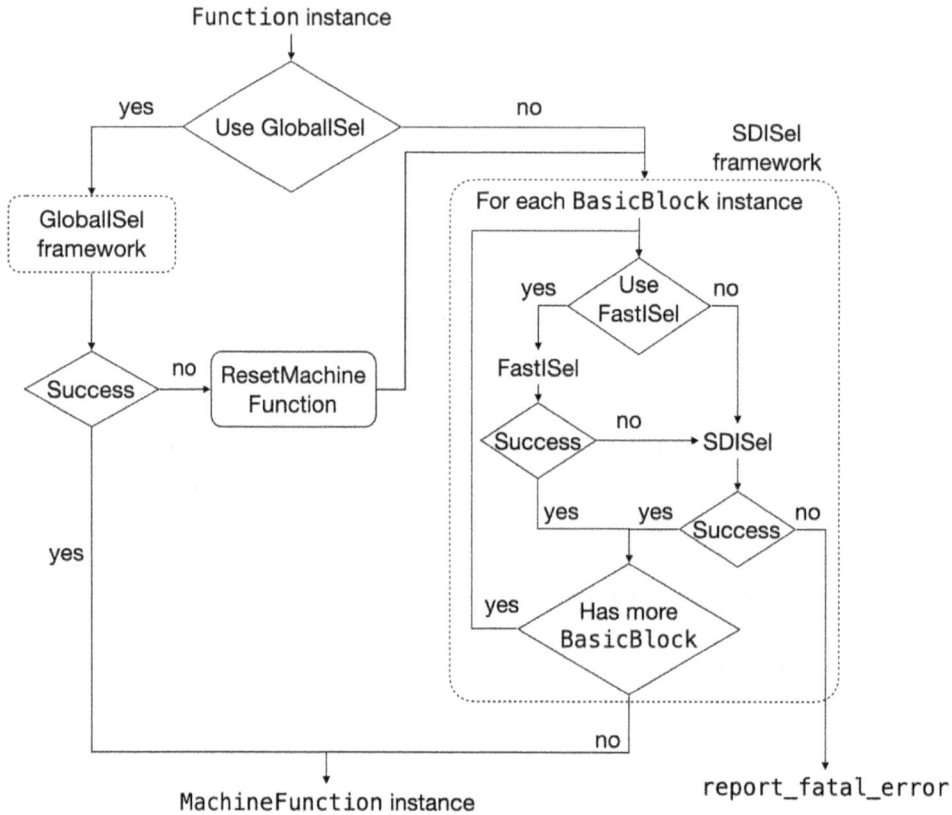

Figure 14.1: How the selectors connect via a fallback mechanism

In *Figure 14.1*, diamonds represent conditions that evaluate to either yes or no, and you can see that if a backend decides to use GlobalISel, the pass manager will first try to select the input LLVM IR function (represented with a Function instance) through that selector. If that selector fails, the state of the MachineFunction object that is being built by the selector is reset by the ResetMachineFunction pass and handed over to SDISel. Within SDISel, each basic block is selected one by one, first by trying to use FastISel on that block, and if FastISel fails at some point, SDISel selects anything that was not selected by FastISel. Naturally, the fallback paths do not exist if the related backend does not provide the involved selectors. For instance, FastISel is not tried if no such selector has been provided.

> **Note**
>
> If your backend does not provide one of the main two selectors, the pass manager will fail to instantiate your pass pipeline for the code generator, and the compilation will fail right away.

While this fallback mechanism may seem like a technicality, we believe it is important to know about its existence for two reasons:

1.  If you do not pay attention, it is easy to go down a fallback path without realizing and then wonder why the code of your selector does not do what it should, whereas it is simply not invoked or has been reset by the `ResetMachineFunction` pass!

2.  You may want to leverage that mechanism when porting an older backend written with SDISel to GlobalISel.

In both cases, we will show you the **application programming interfaces** (**APIs**) and command-line options that you can use to control the pipeline used for instruction selection.

## Overall differences between the selectors

The reason different selectors exist is that while they solve the same instruction selection problem, they do it with a different focus.

Let us see what these focuses are based on different axes.

### Compile time

FastISel is targeted for fast compile time, and what it gains in speed it lacks in generality. When an input LLVM IR goes entirely through FastISel, the compile time is blazing fast. However, most of the time, FastISel has to fall back to SDISel for at least some part of an input function.

SDISel aims at providing the best sequence of instructions for every possible input but does it with a significant increase in compile time compared to FastISel. For instance, it is not uncommon for SDISel to take about 20% of the compile time of the whole backend, where the backend means everything that runs after the frontend in this case, hence this includes the LLVM IR optimization passes.

GlobalISel aims to provide a balanced approach between FastISel and SDISel. At its core, GlobalISel is lean and fast but can be augmented with additional optimizations to produce better sequences of instructions at the expense of compile time. Therefore, GlobalISel can be used to produce unoptimized code for fast compile time (usually what you get with the O0 optimization level), all the way to a heavily optimized code sequence but potentially slow compile time (typically O3 optimization level.) For instance, back in 2019, Apple, in their *LLVM US Dev* talk, reported that GlobalISel was performing as well as SDISel for their GPU backend while being about two times faster. On the other hand, in 2017, we reported that GlobalISel was 1.1 to 1.2 times slower than FastISel on the AArch64 target when no fallback to SDISel was involved, which makes GlobalISel competitive for fast compile time as well.

### Modularity and testability

FastISel and SDISel are part of the same framework that is monolithic in nature. From the LLVM infrastructure point of view, this is a single `MachineFunctionPass` instance that takes the LLVM IR as input and produces the Machine IR as output. Every time you want to test something that happens in that framework, you must reach it through an LLVM IR input and observe the result through the Machine IR output.

For instance, let us say that you want to test some legalization code in SDISel. To do this, you must come up with some LLVM IR that is going to survive all the intermediate optimization steps that SDISel does until it reaches the legalization step. Then, the code you want to test is run, but this is only half the battle. Now, the produced code must survive the later SDISel optimization steps to produce something that you can observe in the selected Machine IR.

While this may not seem like a big deal, in reality, you feel the pain in your productivity every day when you work with this framework. As you get more experienced with this framework, you get used to this gymnastic, but this never gets pleasant.

Since the SDISel framework is a single `MachineFunctionPass` instance, the only way to augment it is through the hooks provided by the various `TargetXXX` classes of your backend.

GlobalISel, on the other hand, was designed from the beginning with modularity and testability in mind. It is built around a set of core `MachineFunctionPass` instances that together form the GlobalISel pipeline. Each core pass comes with hooks to specific target-provided implementation. Like SDISel, it uses the `TargetXXX` classes and new ones, but unlike SDISel, the pipeline itself is completely customizable.

With GlobalISel, testing something in the legalizer, for instance, is as easy as writing a Machine IR test (see *Chapter 11*) for the pass responsible for legalization.

## Scope

The last axis where the selectors differ is on the scope of their optimization. FastISel and SDISel can only look at one basic block at a time, whereas GlobalISel can see through the whole function, which is where the *global* of GlobalISel comes from.

> **Note**
>
> Technically, FastISel can look at more than a basic block at a time since it has access to the whole `Function` instance. However, this is dangerous because if it uses any value outside of the current basic block, it may break the fallback path to SDISel.

Let us see why the scope matters in practice on a contrived example.

Suppose we have the following input LLVM IR:

```
define i32 @smul_widen(i32 %arg, i16 %arg1, i16 %arg2) {
bb:
  %i = icmp eq i32 %arg, 0
  %i3 = sext i16 %arg1 to i32
  %i4 = sext i16 %arg2 to i32
  br i1 %i, label %bb6, label %bb5
bb5:
```

```
   tail call void @bar(i32 %i3, i32 %i4)
   br label %bb6
bb6:
  %i7 = mul nsw i32 %i4, %i3
  ret i32 %i7
}
```

> 💡 **Quick tip**: Enhance your coding experience with the **AI Code Explainer** and **Quick Copy** features. Open this book in the next-gen Packt Reader. Click the **Copy** button (**1**) to quickly copy code into your coding environment, or click the **Explain** button (**2**) to get the AI assistant to explain a block of code to you.

```
                                                          Copy      Explain
function calculate(a, b) {
    return {sum: a + b};                                   1          2
};
```

🔒 **The next-gen Packt Reader** is included for free with the purchase of this book. Unlock it by scanning the QR code below or visiting `https://www.packtpub.com/unlock/9781837637782`.

In this snippet, the %i3 and %i4 values are the sign-extended (sext instruction) version of the %arg1 and %arg2 values. The %i3 and %i4 values are materialized in the basic block named bb while being used in the basic blocks named bb5 and bb6.

Let us say that our backend supports multiplication with widening precision, meaning it can take 16-bit values to produce a full 32-bit value. In other words, the multiplication can perform the sign extension directly. Typically, you would want your selector to generate this type of widening multiply instruction directly from the mul(sext i16 to i32, sext i16 to i32) pattern. This pattern describes two sign-extension instructions from the i16 type to the i32 type feeding into a mul instruction. With a basic block scope, this type of folding is not possible with the given input IR because the selector would need to peek at the bb basic block from the bb6 basic block, which is against the basic block scope.

SDISel has been used for decades, so there are mechanisms to work around these limitations (for instance, duplicating the sext instructions beforehand and sinking them in the related basic blocks, which is the type of things the CodeGenPrepare pass does for addressing modes), but it is a fundamental limitation of SDISel, and sometimes there is no workaround. For instance, SDISel cannot represent values in a loop because it would break its underlying **directed acyclic graph (DAG)** representation, so even if a loop is a single basic block, SDISel cannot represent or look through a PHI instruction since it would break the acyclic property of the graph. We will go through the internal representation of SDISel in the *Understanding the DAG representation* section.

GlobalISel does not have to use workarounds since it has access to the full scope of the function.

This concludes the overview of the selectors in LLVM. In this section, you learned the main steps that are performed by a selector, namely IR building, legalization, and selection. Then, you saw how each selector can interact with the others via a fallback mechanism. Finally, you discovered the three axes that guide the focus of the selectors: compile time, modularity and testability, and scope.

In the next section, we give you some recommendations to decide which selector to implement.

# Which selector to use?

When starting a new backend in the LLVM infrastructure, you must choose which selector framework you want to implement. You can decide to implement all selectors, but this is probably not a good use of your time!

In this section, we try to paint an objective view of the world so that you can decide which selector is the best suited for your case.

## FastISel

FastISel is great if you know that the space of your input LLVM IR is narrow and you want fast compile time. FastISel can also generate great code depending on how much effort you put into it. In other words, you can produce the best selector in the world with just FastISel. The flip side is you are mostly on your own. FastISel is like a complete C++ implementation of a full selector.

Realistically, there is little to no chance that FastISel alone can fit all your needs without significant effort, so having a full implementation of SDISel will be mandatory if you take this road.

## SDISel

SDISel has been the main selector for a couple of decades in LLVM, and everything around instruction selection in the LLVM infrastructure is primarily built for this framework. This means that aside from being the most productive to use, at least at the beginning, it is strong in these decades-long bug shaking and refinements, which makes it smooth to use.

On the flip side, you have little to no control over the optimizations that are performed in this framework, meaning that eventually, you will have to fight the framework to achieve what you want. This lack of flexibility can be seen in the intense compile-time requirements and how difficult it is to write unit tests for it.

Additionally, because of its fundamental limitation around the scope of optimizations, you must resort to pre- or post-instruction selection passes to work around these limitations. Over time, you learn to deal with these issues, but it is always gymnastic.

## GlobalISel

GlobalISel has been built with the goal of removing the rigidity and limitations of SDISel. In that sense, it is the perfect framework to use.

However, the reality is not as bright.

GlobalISel is still missing a lot of quality-of-life features, such as a proper **domain-specific language (DSL)** that allows one to take advantage of the function scope when writing selection patterns or dedicated TableGen backends for various parts of the GlobalISel infrastructure. The available optimizations are not as rich as what SDISel offers, and one can run into surprising gaps.

None of these are blockers, but expect rough edges when working with GlobalISel.

Putting everything together, if you want a future-proof selector and are ready to deal with rough edges, GlobalISel is your choice. It will also give you the opportunity to improve the infrastructure by contributing patches on open source as you develop your backend. If you are, however, not adventurous and would rather enjoy a road that has been taken by many backend authors before you, SDISel is still a valid choice as a selector.

Now that you can make an informed decision on which selector to use, let us dive into their inner workings so that you get a better idea of what it takes to implement one or the other.

## Selectors' inner workings

As we mentioned, overall, the main selectors work the same way and go through three main phases: IR building, legalization, and selection. In practice, the way this materializes is slightly different for each selector.

*Figure 14.2* captures the high-level workings of the two main selectors:

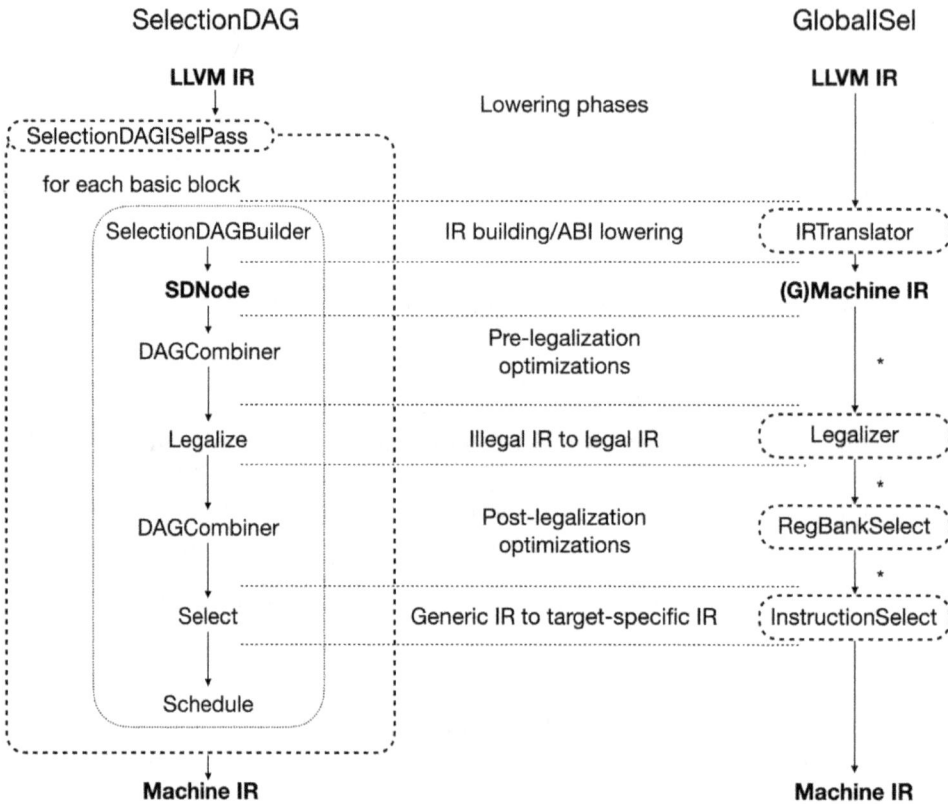

Figure 14.2: Inner workings of SelectionDAG and GlobalISel

The left-hand side of *Figure 14.2* depicts the lowering phases of SDISel. All phases are part of one big `MachineFunctionPass` instance called `SelectionDAGISelPass`. SDISel runs these lowering phases once per basic block. You can see the three main phases of a selector: IR building, legalization, and selection represented respectively with the `SelectionDAGBuilder`, `Legalize`, and `Select` implementations. SDISel also features non-optional pre- and post-legalization optimizations called **DAGCombiners**. After the `Select` phase, SDISel needs to run a mandatory `Schedule` phase that takes the internal DAG representation and turns it into a linear sequence of instructions to create a final `MachineBasicBlock` instance of the Machine IR. The internal representation is represented in bold in the diagram, and its main constituents are represented with `SDNode` instances. We will describe this IR in the *Understanding the DAG representation* section.

Focusing on GlobalISel, the right-hand side of *Figure 14.2*, you can see the main lowering phases represented by the `IRTranslator`, `Legalizer`, and `InstructionSelect` implementations. Unlike SDISel, all these are standalone instances of the `MachineFunctionPass` class. GlobalISel features an additional mandatory pass called `RegBankSelect`. When used in a non-optimizing pipeline (for instance, the O0 optimization level), this pass simply assigns a register bank to all virtual registers. The register banks are vital type information necessary to guide the later InstructionSelect pass. In an optimized build, the RegBankSelect pass performs some rewrites of the IR to minimize cross-register-bank copies. We will go into more detail on this in *Chapter 17*.

Aside from the RegBankSelect pass, the GlobalISel pipeline does not feature any pre- or post-legalization optimizations out of the box. However, since this is a pure machine pass pipeline, backend authors are free to add any MachineFunctionPass instances between any of the core passes, as illustrated with the * character in the diagram. GlobalISel works with an augmented version of the Machine IR called the **generic Machine IR** or **(G)Machine IR** or, simply, **(G)MIR**. We will go over the specificities of this IR in the *Understanding the generic Machine IR* section.

From an implementation point of view, to enable SDISel, one must implement the proper methods in their target-specific specialization of the TargetLowering class and provide a specialized version of the SelectionDAGISel class. We will cover all this in this chapter.

For GlobalISel, since its design is more modular, the APIs are scattered in dedicated target-specific specializations. You need a specialization for the CallLowering, LegalizerInfo, RegBankInfo, and InstructionSelector classes. We will cover these classes in the relevant chapters later in this book.

Finally, to implement a FastISel selector, since this is a sub-selector of SDISel, you need to implement enough pieces of SDISel to make FastISel attainable. Additionally, you need to implement your own specialized version of the FastISel class.

You now have a high-level understanding of the pieces that you need to implement to enable each selector. Before you can get started with the implementation of your selector, you need to familiarize yourself with the IRs you will need to manipulate each of them. This is the topic of our next two sections.

# Understanding the DAG representation

As already mentioned, SDISel uses a DAG representation where each node is an operation and each directed edge a dependency. The dependencies can be one of the following:

- **Data dependency**: The source node reads a value that is produced by the destination node. This is the most prevalent type of dependency and is used to represent the regular use-def chains (see *Chapter 4* if you need a refresher on this concept). This may sound confusing because the representation of the data dependency is flipped in the SDISel representation. Indeed, the direction of the dependency is not the usual def-use chain; it is the use-def chain. You will learn how to print this graph in *Chapter 17*, which will make it easy to visualize it.

- **Scheduling dependency**: The source node must happen before the destination node when the DAG gets linearized as a basic block. This type of dependency is typically used to enforce some ordering between instructions; for instance, between a load and a store where we cannot prove that they do not alias and must assume they do. Therefore, we need an edge between them to make sure they cannot be reordered between themselves. This is called a **chain** in SDISel.

- **Glue dependency**: The source node must remain next to the destination node when the DAG gets linearized as a basic block. This type of dependency is used to force a compact sequence of instructions in the final basic block. This is typically used when introducing uses or definitions of physical registers (for instance, while lowering the **application binary interface** (ABI)) so that their live ranges remain as short as possible.

The DAG representation is implemented with the `SelectionDAG` class (we know this can be confusing since the term *SelectionDAG* is used both to talk about the selector itself and the class that represents its IR), the nodes are implemented via the `SDNode` class and its subclasses (all defined in the `llvm/include/llvm/CodeGen/SelectionDAGNodes.h` file), and the edges are simply pointers between `SDNode` instances. The type of dependency carried by an edge depends on the value type of the source node.

## Textual representation of the SelectionDAG class

Before we describe the main APIs of the classes used by SDISel, let us see an example of what a debug print of a `SelectionDAG` object looks like. That way, it will make sense why there are two main classes that you must manipulate: the `SDNode` and `SDValue` classes.

Here is an example of a debug dump of a `SelectionDAG` object:

```
SelectionDAG has 9 nodes:
  t0: ch,glue = EntryToken
      t2: i16,ch = CopyFromReg t0, Register:i16 %0
      t4: i16,ch = CopyFromReg t0, Register:i16 %1
    t5: i16 = add t2, t4
  t7: ch,glue = CopyToReg t0, Register:i16 $r1, t5
  t8: ch = H2BLBISD::RETURN_GLUE t7, Register:i16 $r1, t7:1
```

In this snippet, each line represents an `SDNode` instance of the printed `SelectionDAG` object. The `tX` instance printed at the beginning of each line is the human-readable name of the `SDNode` object. That name is generated on the fly when printing the DAG and may not be stable from run to run. Next comes the types of each of the values that are produced by the related `SDNode` object (for instance, `ch,glue`). Then, the assignment operator (=) that delimits which operands are definitions and which ones are uses then follows the opcode (for instance, `CopyToReg`.) The opcodes are either generic or target-specific. Generic opcodes are defined and documented in the `llvm/include/llvm/CodeGen/ISDOpcodes.h` file; for instance, `add` is a generic opcode for an integer addition. Target-specific opcodes are, by convention, prefixed with `XXXISD::`, where `XXX` is the backend name, followed by the name of the opcode; for instance, `H2BLBISD::RETURN_GLUE` is an opcode specific to our H2BLB backend. You will learn how to create them in *Chapter 15*.

The arguments of a node (for instance, `t0`, `Register:i16 $r1`) reference either node names (here, `t0`) or special constants prefixed by a type (here, `Register:i16 $r1`). The uses of node names are optionally followed by the index of the value being read. If no index is specified, then the $0^{th}$ value is read; otherwise, the *index-th* value is used. For instance, if you look at the node named t8, you see that it has two uses of the t7 node. The first use is printed with t7, which means it uses the $0^{th}$ value produced by the t7 node, hence the chain (ch) produced by that node. The second use is printed with t7:1, which means it uses the glue value (index 1) produced by the t7 node.

Speaking of types, aside from ch and glue, which represent respectively a chain and a glue dependency, you should feel comfortable interpreting them since they look like the one printed in the LLVM IR. There are, however, a couple of noteworthy changes:

- Floating-point types have shorter names. For instance, float in the textual representation of LLVM IR is f32 in the debug dump of the SelectionDAG instance, half is f16, and so on.
- Vector types are printed using a vXty format, where X is the number of lanes in the vector and ty is the element type. For instance, the <2 x float> LLVM IR type is printed as v2f32.
- Pointer types do not exist in SDISel (this is one of its limitations compared to GlobalISel). All the pointer types are replaced by integer types of the right size during the DAG construction. For instance, pointer types for a backend that uses 64-bit addresses are replaced by i64 types.

> **Note**
>
> The nodes are indented in a best-effort fashion to help visualize parent-children dependencies. The children are more indented than their parents. However, this is best effort only, meaning that if a node has several parents (for instance, a value is used by several other nodes), since each node is printed only once, the indentation will only be correct for the first printed parent. Again, this may sound confusing, but remember that the direction of the parent-children relationship is flipped in SDISel: the use (the parent) points to its definition (the child).

Finally, all SelectionDAG objects start with an EntryToken node that delimits the beginning of the basic block. That node produces a chain and a glue. The chain provides a usable value for all nodes that require a chain as input, such as load instructions. The glue can be used to stick values at the very beginning of the basic block being generated. Additionally, all SelectionDAG objects bring their live-in values via CopyFromReg nodes and push their locally unused live-out values via CopyToReg nodes (or TokenFactor nodes for nodes that do not produce real values, such as store instructions). These Copy<To|From>Reg nodes are the logical glue between the values that flow from one basic block to another, and SDISel automatically maps them internally to be able to generate PHI nodes when producing the final Machine IR. Because of these two Copy<To|From>Reg nodes, all values manipulated in a SelectionDAG instance are always local to the current basic block.

Now that you are familiar with what a DAG looks like in SDISel, let us see the APIs that you must use to manipulate it.

# Manipulating a DAG

Most of the APIs that you will need to work with in SDISel involve instances of the SDNode and SDValue classes and a SelectionDAG object.

Although the SelectionDAG object represents the entirety of the DAG of the basic block being processed, you only use this object as a node factory. In other words, you do not typically traverse the nodes of the DAG; you just process the one that is given to you in the API you override. As a result, the main APIs that you will use from the SelectionDAG class are the getNode (or one of its numerous specialized versions, such as the getCopyToReg or getLoad method), getVTList, ReplaceAllUsesWith, and SelectionDAGRemoveDeadNode methods. Aside from the getVTList method, which is used to create a list of **value type (VT)** to set the result types of a node, the other methods should look familiar to you since this is close to what the LLVM IR API looks like.

> Note
>
> The SelectionDAG::getNode method may return a pointer on an existing object. The SelectionDAG class does something called continuous **common subexpression elimination (CSE)**, which means that if you want to create a node but that node already exists (with the same arguments, of course), then the SelectionDAG object will give you the same node instead of creating a new one. For instance, let us say that the basic block being processed contained two add a, b instructions; the SelectionDAG object will automatically collapse the original two values on one unique SDNode instance.

In its most generic form, the SelectionDAG::getNode method takes an opcode, a debug location, a list of the types of the defined values, and a list of the arguments of the node. All other forms are convenient wrappers around the generic form and let you create nodes more easily without requiring you to wrap your input arguments or return types in a list.

> Note
>
> The debug location is represented with the SDLoc class. When creating a new node, you usually just propagate the debug location of the node you are replacing using the SDLoc(OrigNode) constructor or set an empty location using the SDLoc() empty constructor. Please try to preserve the debug locations when you can, and it makes sense since it will improve the debuggability of the code you generate and make the lives of your users easier!

Looking at the SDValue class, this represents a single result of an SDNode object. To make things more concrete, going back to our textual DAG example, t7 is an SDNode instance, but t7:0 (printed just t7) or t7:1 are instances of the SDValue class. In other words, an SDValue object is a simple class that wraps together an SDNode and an index. Instances of type SDValue are automatically converted to SDNode instances, and the operator* and operator-> methods allow you to directly access SDNode methods. Objects of type SDValue are lightweight objects and are usually passed by value in the API. Additionally,

SDValue instances produced by the default constructor are usually used to signify that an optimization did not take place. Indeed, most of the APIs are about lowering/optimizing a node into a new one, and returning SDValue() means that we did not manage to find a new suitable replacement. You can get the type of an SDValue instance using the getValueType method. This method also exists on the SDNode class but requires you to provide an index to specify which value of the SDNode object you want to query. Since an SDValue instance already encodes this information, getting its type is slightly easier.

Looking at the SDNode class, you will find what you would expect: getOpcode, getOperand, use_begin, and so on. You should feel at home!

Focusing on the types now, SDISel uses two classes to represent the types: the EVT and MVT classes.

The EVT class stands for **extended value type**. Instances of this class are usually used to represent types before legalization since they can represent any non-conventional types, such as a 3-bit integer (i3). The API is straightforward, and the EVT class features all the necessary static member methods to create anything you need.

The MVT class stands for **machine value type**. Instances of type MVT are used to represent the actual types that are held in the target registers. As a result, all the types that are modeled with an MVT instance are fixed, meaning that this is just a sort of a big enumeration of all the types supported by at least one backend in LLVM. Instances of type MVT can be used where EVT instances are expected.

> Note
>
> If you want to modify the set of types that you can model with an MVT instance, you need to change the generic implementation. This involves, among other things, changing the target description of the value types (located in the llvm/include/llvm/CodeGen/ValueTypes.td file). We will not cover how to do that in this book. If you need to do that, we suggest engaging with the open source community not to have to maintain your own set of value types downstream.

Going back to the EVT class for a second, the isSimple method tells you if the current instance is compatible with an MVT instance. Similarly, the isExtended method tells you if it is incompatible.

This concludes our overview of the DAG representation. We understand this is a lot to take in, but we are confident that with the snippets coming in the next sections, things will become clearer. For now, remember that the EVT class represents your types, the SDNode class your instructions, and the SDValue class a particular result of your instruction.

Let us now see how the IR used for GlobalISel differs from the regular Machine IR.

# Understanding the generic Machine IR

GlobalISel works directly on the Machine IR that you learned about in *Chapter 11*, except that it has a slightly different flavor, called generic Machine IR. The goal of the whole GlobalISel pipeline is to remove this generic flavor from the Machine IR to reach plain Machine IR at the end of the InstructionSelect pass.

The generic Machine IR differs from the regular Machine IR in two aspects:

- The virtual registers may not have a register class. Instead, they have a type and, optionally, a register bank. Virtual registers that do not have a register class are called **generic virtual registers**.
- The opcode of `MachineInstr` instances can use generic Machine IR opcodes easily identifiable by their `G_` prefix. For instance, a generic addition instruction uses the `G_ADD` opcode. These opcodes are defined in the `llvm/include/llvm/Target/GenericOpcodes.td` file.

> **Note**
>
> The only difference between a regular and a generic virtual register is that regular virtual registers have a proper register class and, thus, can be used after instruction selection. In other words, as soon as you assign a register class to a generic virtual register, it becomes a regular virtual register, even if it has a type. We will go into more detail on constraints on the Machine IR in the *Lowering constraints of the generic Machine IR* section.

Instances of type `MachineInstr` that use the generic Machine IR flavor can coexist with regular `MachineInstr` instances. In other words, it is perfectly valid to have both virtual registers and generic virtual registers used at the same time.

Instances of type `MachineInstr` that use generic opcodes must, however, reference only virtual registers (generic or not). In other words, generic instructions cannot use immediate operands, for instance. Instead, immediate values need to be materialized in a virtual register first via the `G_CONSTANT` opcode, then that virtual register should be used instead of directly using the immediate value.

## Textual representation of generic attributes

When looking at a `.mir` file or, more generally, at the debug output of a `MachineInstr` instance, it is easy to identify both generic `MachineInstr` instances and generic virtual registers. For the former, their opcode is prefixed with `G_`. For the latter, the generic virtual registers have a register bank or `_` when this one is not set instead of a register class. Moreover, generic virtual registers must have a type.

Here are a few examples of strings that represent the different flavors of a (generic) virtual register:

- `%0:gpr32`: A virtual register. As soon as a register class is set (here, gpr32), a register is considered a regular virtual register.
- `%1:gpr32(s32)`: A virtual register with a scalar type of size 32-bit.
- `%2:_(p0)`: A generic virtual register with no register class or register bank and a pointer type to the address space 0.
- `%3:gprb(<2 x s16>)`: A generic virtual register mapped on the gprb register bank and with the `<2 x s16>` vector type.

> Note
>
> The distinction between a register bank and a register class in the textual representation is based purely on the printed name. Therefore, you must know how the register banks of a backend are printed if you want to distinguish which registers are mapped to a register bank and which ones are mapped to a register class. Usually, the backend authors make the distinction obvious (for instance, they add a b, for the bank, at the end of the name, such as gprb).

A quick word on the types shown in these strings. These strings are the textual representation of **low-level types** (**LLTs**), which are types that are used in the GlobalISel pipeline. We will briefly highlight their APIs in the *APIs to work with the generic Machine IR* section.

## Lowering constraints of the generic Machine IR

As the generic Machine IR progresses through the lowering phases of the GlobalISel pipeline, stricter and stricter rules apply:

- **Before legalization:** Any generic opcode is allowed on any relevant type. For instance, G_ADD can be used on i3, i32, i124, and so on.

  Generic virtual registers may not have a register bank, but they must have a type.

- **After legalization but before register bank selection:** Only legal generic opcodes with legal types are allowed. The legality is determined by the target. We will go into more detail on this in *Chapter 16*.

- **After register bank selection but before instruction selection:** The legalization constraints apply, and alive generic virtual registers must have a register bank.

- **After instruction selection:** No more generic virtual register is allowed. All alive virtual registers must have a valid register class. No more generic opcode is allowed. Only target-specific opcodes all allowed.

*Figure 14.3* summarizes these constraints visually:

| Pass Pipeline | Generic MachineInstr | Generic virtual register | | MachineFunction Properties | | |
|---|---|---|---|---|---|---|
| | | Type | RegisterBank | legalized | regBankSelected | selected |
| **LLVM IR** | | | | | | |
| IRTranslator | | | | | | |
| **(G)Machine IR** | ☑ | ☑ | Optional | false | false | false |
| Legalizer | | | | | | |
| RegBankSelect | ☑ Only legal opcodes | ☑ Only legal types | Optional | true | false | false |
| InstructionSelect | ☑ Only legal opcodes | ☑ Only legal types | Must | true | true | false |
| **Machine IR** | ✗ | ✗ | ✗ | true | true | true |

Figure 14.3: The constraints on generic MachineInstr and virtual registers instances

In *Figure 14.3*, the leftmost column shows the GlobalISel pass pipeline with the core passes. The next two columns summarize the constraints we already mentioned on the MachineInstr instances and the generic virtual register instances. The last column shows the values of the properties of the MachineFunction object being processed through the GlobalISel pipeline. These properties can be queried by the passes that you insert in the GlobalISel pipeline to check where in the lowering phase the pass runs.

## APIs to work with the generic Machine IR

From an API standpoint, the only new things that you must learn for the generic Machine IR compared to the regular Machine IR are the following few things:

- The handling of the generic virtual register is completely encapsulated in the MachineRegisterInfo class. There, you will find methods to create a generic virtual register, get or set its type, get or set its register bank, and so on. The methods are easy to find and self-explanatory; for instance, getType and createGenericVirtualRegister, to name a few.
- The handling of generic MachineInstr instances is even easier. The only thing that changes is the opcode that you use when you create them. In other words, just use a G_ opcode and you have a generic MachineInstr object. You can check if a MachineInstr instance is a generic one by checking whether its opcode returns true when querying the isPreISelGenericOpcode function or directly using the MachineInstr::isPreISelOpcode method.

- The information around register banks is encapsulated in the `RegisterBank` class, and the `RegisterBank` instances of a backend are handled by the target specialization of the `RegisterBankInfo` class. We will show you how to set that up in *Chapter 17*.

- The types themselves use the `LLT` class. This class, defined in the `llvm/include/llvm/CodeGenTypes/LowLevelType.h` file, is straightforward to use, like the `EVT` and `MVT` classes used in SDISel. It features a static member method to create various instances of types. For instance, to create a 32-bit pointer type to the address space 5, you simply use the following statement: `LLT::pointer(5, 32)`. One thing to call out is at the time of the writing scalar types, meaning non-pointer and non-vector types, are all represented with the same type. In other words, integers and floating-point types with the same bit width share the same `LLT` instance. For instance, both 32-bit integer and 32-bit floating-point types are mapped to the 32-bit scalar type (printed as `s32`). The way you disambiguate one from the other is by looking at how they are used. For instance, integer additions are represented with the `G_ADD` opcode, whereas floating-point additions are represented with the `G_FADD` opcode (notice the `F` right after the `G_` prefix). This is currently being reworked because that disambiguation system does not work for types of the same kind and same bit width. For instance, it gets complicated to differentiate a half-precision floating-point type and a brain floating-point type. Both are 16-bit floating-point types, hence the `s16` type in the current system.

This concludes the section on the generic Machine IR, where you learned about how it differs from the regular Machine IR. In particular, you learned that all the APIs of the Machine IR that you know and love are still relevant and that you only need to add generic virtual registers, the `LLT` class, and the `RegisterBank` class into the mix. You also discovered what the generic attributes of the Machine IR look like in the textual representation and what the IR goes through during lowering, from pure generic virtual registers that only have a type all the way to virtual registers with a register class.

Now, you have all the basis to start implementing one of the selectors, but before we get started on that, we need to show you how to wire up the codegen pipeline of your backend so that a frontend such as Clang or an LLVM command-line tool such as `llc` can instantiate it.

# Groundwork to connect the codegen pipeline

Up until this chapter, we connected (and faked) enough pieces to get a frontend such as Clang to invoke our backend on the LLVM IR to LLVM IR passes. To get beyond that point and exercise the instruction selector of a backend, we need to connect (or fake the connection of) the full codegen pipeline.

From the frontend point of view, the codegen pipeline is responsible for taking some LLVM IR as input and generating code in either textual form (assembly `.s` file) or binary form (object `.o` file).

There are three pieces involved in creating this pipeline:

1. You need to build the codegen pass pipeline for your target.
2. You need to provide the LLVM infrastructure with some key target-specific information for the generic codegen passes to work.
3. You need to connect your instruction selector or your instruction selectors if you want to offer more than one selector.

Let us start with the connection of the codegen pass pipeline.

## Instantiating the codegen pass pipeline

Frontends and tools such as the llc command-line tool set up the codegen pipeline by invoking the TargetMachine::addPassesToEmitFile method.

If you used the steps given in this book, which follow LLVM's best practices, your backend TargetMachine class should derive from the LLVMTargetMachine class. The LLVMTargetMachine class offers a default implementation for this addPassesToEmitFile method. The only thing you are missing to make the default implementation work is providing the implementation of your target's AsmPrinter class. This class is responsible for taking some Machine IR input and producing an assembly or object file. You can look at the commit tagged add-asm-printer_ch14 in the companion repository to see a full example of how to do that.

In a nutshell, you need to do the following:

1.  Create a class that inherits from the AsmPrinter class, from the AsmPrinter library. Usually, that class is called XXXAsmPrinter, where XXX is the name of your backend.

2.  Override the emitInstruction method. This method takes a MachineInstr instance and writes it to the MCStreamer object that was given to the constructor of your AsmPrinter class. You already did all the heavy lifting of writing in an MCStreamer object in *Chapter 12*, so the implementation here is almost trivial, and a snippet is given hereafter.

3.  Register your XXXAsmPrinter class with your Target class by implementing the LLVMInitializeXXXAsmPrinter function.

Let us expand on *step 2*: the implementation of the XXXAsmPrinter::emitInstruction method. The rest should be obvious, and if not, you can still look at the commit tagged add-asm-printer_ch14.

As mentioned, the emitInstruction method takes a MachineInstr instance and emits it in an MCStreamer object. The following snippet does this:

```
void XXXAsmPrinter::emitInstruction(const MachineInstr *MI) {
  MCInst TmpInst = MachineInstrToMCInst(*MI);
  EmitToStreamer(*OutStreamer, TmpInst);
}
```

In this snippet, we convert the given MachineInstr instance (the variable named MI) to an MCInst instance (the variable named TmpInst) and call the EmitToStreamer generic method on the MCStreamer instance that was provided to the constructor of our class.

Under the hood, this works thanks to the work we did in *Chapter 12*. More specifically, the EmitToStreamer method invokes indirectly the XXXInstPrinter::printInst method for the assembly output and the XXXMCCodeEmitter::encodeInstruction method for the object output. You implemented both these methods to be able to print assembly instructions with their encoding!

> **Note**
>
> While we do not recommend this, it is totally possible to fake the implementation of your `AsmPrinter` class. Just do nothing in the `emitInstruction` method, and this is enough to instantiate the codegen pipeline.

Going back to the snippet, we cheated a little bit. The `MachineInstrToMCInst` method is something that is not available by default. Here is what it should look like:

```
MCInst XXXAsmPrinter::MachineInstrToMCInst(const MachineInstr &MI) {
  MCInst TmpInst;
  TmpInst.setOpcode(MI.getOpcode());
  for (const MachineOperand &MO : MI.operands()) {
    MCOperand MCOp;
    if (lowerOperand(MO, MCOp))
      TmpInst.addOperand(MCOp);
  }
  return TmpInst;
}
```

In this snippet, we traverse the operands of the input `MachineInstr` instance and convert them to their **machine code** (**MC**) equivalent. The meat of the logic is in the `lowerOperand` method that we provided as well, and that also looks how you would expect:

```
bool XXXAsmPrinter::lowerOperand(const MachineOperand &MO, MCOperand &MCO) {
  switch (MO.getType()) {
  case MachineOperand::MO_Register:
    // Ignore all implicit register operands.
    if (MO.isImplicit())
      return false;
    MCO = MCOperand::createReg(MO.getReg());
    break;
  case MachineOperand::MO_Immediate:
    MCO = MCOperand::createImm(MO.getImm());
    break;
...
```

Essentially, the `lowerOperand` method returns `true` when there is an `MCOperand` instance to be added to the `MCInst` instance and `false` otherwise. Other than that, this is a straightforward `switch` statement that maps the kind of the `MachineOperand` instance to its `MCOperand` instance counterpart.

This is all that is needed to connect the implementation of your AsmPrinter class to the codegen pipeline. Let us now see what key target information you need to provide to satisfy the requirements of the MachineFunctionPass instances that run in this pipeline.

## Providing the key target APIs to the codegen pipeline

The codegen pipeline instances a lot of MachineFunctionPass objects. As you learned in the previous chapters, these passes rely on hooks provided by the TargetXXXInfo classes to perform their job, where XXX can be Instr, Register, and so on.

If you followed the steps in this book, you'll already have all these APIs implemented; however, we did not connect them in a way that made them discoverable by the passes that need them.

Fixing that is straightforward: override the appropriate getXXX methods in your implementation of the Subtarget class.

If you followed the steps in this book, you should only miss the TargetRegisterInfo, TargetInstrInfo, and TargetFrameInfo classes. Therefore, add a member variable of the right type for each missing API and override the related getter.

For instance, for the TargetRegisterInfo class, you would add in your XXXSubtarget class, where XXX is your backend name:

```
class XXXSubtarget : public XXXGenSubtargetInfo {
  XXXRegisterInfo RegisterInfo;
public:
  const H2BLBRegisterInfo *getRegisterInfo() const override {
    return &RegisterInfo;
  }
...
```

If you need help finding the method to override or anything else, feel free to look at the example at the commit tagged connect-tgtinfo-apis_ch14 in the companion repository.

We are now down to the last and final part, which is connecting our instruction selector. The related steps will depend on which selector you want to use, so we'll show how to make the connection in different sections.

## Connecting SDISel to the codegen pipeline

To connect SDISel to the codegen pipeline, you need to override the TargetPassConfig::addInstSelector method in your target-specific implementation of the TargetPassConfig class.

In this method, you need to provide the MachineFunctionPass class that implements the SDISel framework. So, first, we need to create a skeleton of such a pass. We will see in the next sections how to populate it properly.

To create this skeleton, you need to follow these steps:

1.  Run the gen-dag-isel TableGen backend as part of your build system.
2.  Create your target-specific implementation of the SelectionDAGISel class, from the SelectionDAG library.
3.  Integrate the code generated by TableGen into the class that you created.
4.  Create a MachineFunctionPass class that will manage your SelectionDAGISel class.

You can see all these steps in action at the commit tagged add-sdisel-skeleton_ch14 in the companion repository, but we also describe the gist of them hereafter.

The first step should be a breeze for you. Simply add the following line, where all the TableGen invocations sit, in the main CMakeLists.txt file of your backend directory (llvm/lib/Target/XXX, where XXX is your backend name):

```
tablegen(LLVM XXXGenDAGISel.inc -gen-dag-isel)
```

This TableGen backend is responsible for emitting all the code that does the selection phase of SDISel.

Then, create a new file in your backend directory to hold the implementation of your SelectionDAGISel class (this file is usually called XXXDAGTODAGISel.cpp) and fill it with something that resembles the following code that we wrote for our H2BLB backend:

```
class H2BLBDAGToDAGISel : public SelectionDAGISel {
public:
  explicit H2BLBDAGToDAGISel(TargetMachine &TM) : SelectionDAGISel(TM) {}
private:
  void Select(SDNode *N) override;
#include "H2BLBGenDAGISel.inc"
};
```

In this snippet, we declare our derived target-specific class of the SelectionDAGISel class and fill its implementation with what was produced by TableGen by including the H2BLBGenDAGISel.inc file. We also need to override the Select method to avoid our class being a pure abstract class.

Next, we need to provide an implementation for the Select method. We do this with the following snippet:

```
void H2BLBDAGToDAGISel::Select(SDNode *N) {
  if (N->isMachineOpcode())
    return;
  SelectCode(N);
}
```

In this snippet, we bail out from the selection if the given node already represents a valid `MachineInstr` instance opcode. Otherwise, we call the `SelectCode` method, which is what TableGen has generated for us. At this point, the generated `SelectCode` method does not do anything sensible, but it will as we implement the instruction selection phase of SDISel, which we cover in *Chapter 17*.

The only missing piece now is to implement the `MachineFunctionPass` class that manages our `SelectionDAGISel` instance. To do that, you need to inherit from the `SelectionDAGISelLegacy` class and then supply all the boilerplate code for the identifier registration, the initialization, and so on. You should be in known territory and feel comfortable creating this pass. If you need a refresher look at *Chapter 5* and if this is still not enough, remember that you can look at the commit tagged `add-sdisel-skeleton_ch14` in the companion repository for the full example.

In any case, here is what the declaration of your `MachineFunctionPass` class should look like using the legacy pass manager:

```
class H2BLBDAGToDAGISelLegacy : public SelectionDAGISelLegacy {
public:
  static char ID;
  H2BLBDAGToDAGISelLegacy(H2BLBTargetMachine &TM)
      : SelectionDAGISelLegacy(ID, std::make_unique<H2BLBDAGToDAGISel>(TM)) {}
};
```

The only noteworthy piece of this snippet is the fact that we feed our `XXXDAGToDAGISel` class to the parent class's constructor.

Assuming now that you have wrapped the instantiation of your `MachineFunctionPass` class in a function named `createXXXISelDAG`, you would connect it to the codegen pipeline with the following snippet:

```
bool XXXPassConfig::addInstSelector() {
  addPass(createXXXISelDAG(getXXXTargetMachine()));
  return false;
}
```

In this snippet, `XXXPassConfig` is your target implementation of the `TargetPassConfig` class, and `getXXXTargetMachine()` is a getter that returns the `LLVMTargetMachine` instance of your target.

Now that your skeleton of SDISel is connected, let us see how to do the same thing for FastISel.

## Connecting FastISel to the codegen pipeline

Since FastISel is not a standalone selection framework but just a sub-selector of SDISel, before connecting FastISel, you need to connect SDISel first. In other words, before doing what is in this section, you need to perform the steps described in the previous section!

To create a skeleton of FastISel, you need to follow similar steps to what you did for SDISel, except you do them for FastISel:

1. Run the gen-fast-isel TableGen backend.
2. Provide an implementation of the FastISel class.
3. Integrate the code generated by TableGen in your FastISel class.
4. Connect your class to the SDISel framework.

You can find an example of how to do these steps by looking at the commit tagged add-fastisel-skeleton_ch14 in the companion repository.

Now for the details. The first step is straightforward; add the following line in your backend's CMakeLists.txt file:

```
tablegen(LLVM H2BLBGenFastISel.inc -gen-fast-isel)
```

This TableGen backend is responsible for generating the selection code that is derived from the selection patterns. We will cover these patterns in *Chapter 17*.

The second step consists of creating your own specialized class of the FastISel class. Here is the code for the H2BLB backend:

```
class H2BLBFastISel final : public FastISel {
public:
  explicit H2BLBFastISel(FunctionLoweringInfo &FuncInfo,
                         const TargetLibraryInfo *LibInfo)
      : FastISel(FuncInfo, LibInfo, /*SkipTargetIndependentISel=*/true) {}
  bool fastSelectInstruction(const Instruction *I) override;
#include "H2BLBGenFastISel.inc"
};
```

The important pieces in this snippet are the inclusion of the file generated by the TableGen backend, H2BLBGenFastISel.inc, in the body of the class, and the override of the fastSelectInstruction method.

Another thing to point out in this snippet is the setting of the SkipTargetIndependentISel variable to true in the constructor of the parent class. This Boolean determines in which order selection patterns are tried. Setting this variable to true means that fastSelectInstruction is called before the code generated by the TableGen backend and vice versa for false. In our case, we decided to use our custom implementation first because it gives us more opportunity to match complex patterns. If you go with the generated code first, you may end up with the generic code matching simple patterns first and will not be exposed to the more complex ones. Both approaches are valid, and you can always change this setting as you see fit.

So, now, let us look at the implementation of the `fastSelectInstruction` method:

```
bool H2BLBFastISel::fastSelectInstruction(const Instruction *I) {
  if (TLI.fallBackToDAGISel(*I))
    return false;
  switch (I->getOpcode()) {
  default:
    break;
  // insert custom selection here.
  }
  return selectOperator(I, I->getOpcode());
}
```

In this snippet, we first bail out of FastISel if the `TargetLowering` instance of our backend (carried by the `TLI` member variable) says so. Then, we run our custom selection via a switch on the opcode of the input LLVM IR `Instruction` instance (this switch is empty for now) and, finally, use the `selectOperator` method, which was generated by the TableGen backend. If we had set `SkipTargetIndependentISel` to `false` in our constructor, we would not have needed to call the `selectOperator` method because it would have been called by the `FastISel` base class before our custom selector.

The only thing left to do now is to connect our FastISel implementation with our SDISel framework; we do this by overriding the `createFastISel` method of the `TargetLowering` class of our backend:

```
class H2BLBTargetLowering : public TargetLowering {
 public:
  FastISel *createFastISel(FunctionLoweringInfo &FuncInfo,
                           const TargetLibraryInfo *LibInfo) const override {
    return new H2BLBFastISel(FuncInfo, LibInfo);
  }
  ...
```

Thanks to this snippet, SDISel will automatically try to run the FastISel selector before it runs the SDISel one.

Now, the only thing that remains is to show you how to connect GlobalISel to the pass pipeline.

## Connecting GlobalISel to the codegen pipeline

Doing a skeleton for GlobalISel is incredibly simple. You just need to instantiate the four core passes in your target-specific version of the `TargetPassConfig` class by overriding the four related methods, as shown next:

```
bool H2BLBPassConfig::addIRTranslator() {
  addPass(new IRTranslator(getOptLevel()));
  return false;
}
```

```
bool H2BLBPassConfig::addLegalizeMachineIR() {
  addPass(new Legalizer());
  return false;
}
bool H2BLBPassConfig::addRegBankSelect() {
  addPass(new RegBankSelect());
  return false;
}
bool H2BLBPassConfig::addGlobalInstructionSelect() {
  addPass(new InstructionSelect(getOptLevel()));
  return false;
}
```

In this snippet, you register in the legacy pass manager through each of the four `TargetPassConfig` class methods and the related classes that implement the core functionalities. These classes will use some target-specific information that we will set up in the next few sections, but from the pass manager perspective, your job is done. Note that GlobalISel will not do anything sensible at this point. If anything, it should assert/error out that you did not provide the target-specific information if you try to run it.

You can view a full snippet of how to do this connect with the commit tagged `add-gisel-skeleton_ch14`.

Before closing this section on connecting a selector to the codegen pipeline, let us mention how you can switch from one selector to another when your backend features several of them.

## Choosing between different selectors

If your backend has the luxury of offering different selectors, we thought it would be useful to know how you can change which one runs.

Unless overridden by the command-line options, the `TargetPassConfig` class uses SDISel by default.

If you want your target to use a different selector, you need to call the appropriate method from the constructor of your `TargetMachine` class to set the selector you want by default. These methods are `setGlobalISel` for GlobalISel and `setFastISel` for FastISel. You can change these settings from the command line using, respectively, the `global-isel` and the `fast-isel` command-line options. For instance, the `-fast-isel=0` option will disable FastISel altogether.

Additionally, you can set fallback policies for GlobalISel using the `setGlobalISelAbort` method, where you can have GlobalISel fall back silently to SDISel when it cannot process a function, fall back while printing a warning, or not fall back at all. You can change this setting using the `global-isel-abort` command-line option with 0 to fall back silently, 1 to abort on fallbacks, and 2 to emit the warning.

FastISel provides a similar mechanism but only via command-line options. Look at the help message produced by the `help-hidden` command-line option to see how to use the `fast-isel-abort` command-line option, using the `llc` command-line tool, for instance.

In this section, you learned how to connect the `AsmPrinter` class of your backend to be able to instantiate a codegen pipeline. You also learned which connection point you must provide to enable all three selectors. Finally, you saw how to programmatically change which selector is used in your backend and learned how to do the same thing with the command-line options.

Now that your codegen pipeline is all set up, you are all set to start implementing the selector!

# Summary

In this chapter, you learned how to set up an instruction selector using one of the two instruction selection frameworks that the LLVM infrastructure provides.

You learned that the instruction selectors worked by executing different phases: translating the input LLVM IR to a generic IR while introducing elements of the ABI, legalizing this IR toward something that the backend can support, and finally selecting the instructions by producing the Machine IR of your backend.

We presented you with the different characteristics of the selectors and provided recommendations so that you can decide which selector to use based on your use cases and preferences.

You learned the specificities of the generic IR used by each selector, namely the `SelectionDAG` representation for SDISel and the generic Machine IR for GlobalISel, and discovered which APIs to use to manipulate these IRs.

Now that you understand the phases involved in the selectors, we can start going deeper into the implementation of your selector, starting with the IR building phase, the topic of our next chapter.

# Further reading

The 2015, 2017, and 2019 *LLVM Dev* presentations on GlobalISel feature some good material on how SDISel and GlobalISel work, and can be helpful to see what we presented from a different angle. Here are the links to the slides of the different presentations: `https://www.llvm.org/devmtg/2015-10/slides/Colombet-GlobalInstructionSelection.pdf`, `https://llvm.org/devmtg/2017-10/slides/Bougacha-Colombet-GlobalISel.pdf`, and `https://llvm.org/devmtg/2019-10/slides/SandersKeles-GeneratingOptimizedCodewithGlobalISel.pdf`. We also recommend you watch the corresponding recorded YouTube videos of each of the talks.

# Quiz time

Now that you have finished reading this chapter, try answering the following questions to test your knowledge:

1.  What are the two main frameworks that you can use to implement your instruction selection pipeline?

    The two main instruction selection frameworks are SDISel and GlobalISel. They come with different trade-offs and can be both used within the same backend.

For an overview of the frameworks, look at the *Overview of the instruction selection frameworks* section.

2.  What are the three main phases involved in an instruction selection pipeline?

    The three main phases are IR building, legalization, and selection. You can find more details about what each of these phases does in the *How does instruction selection work?* section.

3.  Let us say you want a good mix of generality and compile-time speed. Which selector do you think is the most appropriate?

    GlobalISel offers the most flexibility between supporting a wide range of input IR and generating code fast. You can find more information on what each selector is good at in the *Overall differences between the selectors* and *Which selector to use?* sections.

4.  In SDISel, what is the difference between an `SDNode` instance and an `SDValue` instance?

    An `SDNode` instance represents an instruction in the SDISel IR, and an `SDValue` instance represents one of the results of an instruction. In other words, an `SDValue` instance is a wrapper around an `SDNode` instance and an index in the list of results of this `SDNode` instance.

    Look at the *Understanding the DAG representation* and, more specifically, the *Manipulating a DAG* section for more information on the SDISel IR.

5.  In GlobalISel, what are the two differences between a generic `MachineInstr` instance and a regular `MachineInstr` instance?

    Instances of type `MachineInstr` are considered generic when they use generic opcodes or generic virtual registers; that is, virtual registers that do not have a register class.

    More details are available in the *Understanding the generic Machine IR* section.

# 15

# Instruction Selection: The IR Building Phase

In the previous chapter, you learned how to connect a specific instruction selection framework in your backend. In this chapter, we will study the first phase of the instruction selection pipeline.

The first phase of the instruction selection pipeline consists of lowering the LLVM **intermediate representation** (**IR**) down to the generic IR of the instruction selection framework that you chose. This phase is called the IR building phase.

The LLVM target-independent code generator, or **codegen**, relies on some target hooks to make this IR building suitable for your backend, and in this chapter, you will learn how to supply this information and to leverage the existing infrastructure to be the most productive at it.

More specifically, you will learn how to implement the **application binary interface** (**ABI**) of your backend by doing the following:

- Providing the required target hooks
- Leveraging an existing TableGen backend
- Using the generic infrastructure to write the minimal amount of code required

The lowering of the ABI alone involves a lot of different techniques (indirect passing, by-value passing, tail call promotion, etc.) and could easily fill a book. Therefore, this chapter exposes you to the most common problems and the techniques to solve them while showing you how the LLVM infrastructure works. This way, we believe that you will be able to replicate these solutions and, more importantly, understand and generalize them to tackle any other problems.

To make things more concrete, this chapter builds the H2BLB backend that we introduced a few chapters ago and you can refer to the related repository (see the next section) to see full examples of how to implement different solutions.

Before diving into the responsibilities of the IR building phase, let's review the technical requirements for this chapter.

# Technical requirements

Continuing our effort of building the instruction selection pipeline of our LLVM backend, the same requirements as *Chapter 14* apply.

Additionally, for all the snippets presented in this chapter, you will find the actual implementation in the `https://github.com/PacktPublishing/LLVM-Code-Generation-by-example` GitHub repository. We call this repository the **companion repository** in the remainder of the chapter.

The changes for this chapter are all included between the Git tags `begin_ch15` and `end_ch15` of the companion repository. If you are not familiar with Git tags, look at *Chapter 9* for a quick explanation of what you can do with them. Throughout the chapter, we also mention specific tags that we created in this repository for you to easily find the relevant commits.

Let's now get familiar with what the IR building phase is about in detail.

# Overview of the IR building

The IR building phase of the selectors is conceptually simple except that it is also responsible for materializing the ABI of the input LLVM IR function. In other words, the pure IR building part of this phase is straightforward: one LLVM IR instruction maps to one or several SDNode instances for the **SelectionDAG Instruction Selection (SDISel)** framework or `MachineInstr` instances with generic opcodes for the **Global Instruction Selection (GlobalISel)** framework.

> **Note**
>
> We will use SDISel and GlobalISel as nouns in the rest of this chapter as well as FastISel for the SDISel sub-selector (see *Chapter 14* for more details on how they relate to each other.)

For instance, the add instruction in LLVM IR translates into the `ISD::ADD` SDNode instance and `G_ADD` MachineInstr instance. Also, in SDISel, the IR building phase, implemented with the `SelectionDAGBuilder` class, translates pointer types into integer types of the right size.

The pure translation part is completely generic and there is nothing for you to do here. However, you must provide the target hooks that implement the lowering of the ABI for your selector. Meaning that each selector, including FastISel, has its own target hooks to lower the ABI.

There are four hooks to implement that are responsible for the following, respectively:

- Lowering the arguments from the callee side
- Lowering the return values from the callee side
- Lowering a call to a callee – in other words, preparing the argument of the callee and unpacking its return values
- Checking whether a value is even returnable by a callee

Ignoring the last bullet point for a second, *Figure 15.1* illustrates which hooks produce which sequence of instructions when handling the lowering of a call, both on the callee and the caller side.

**caller**

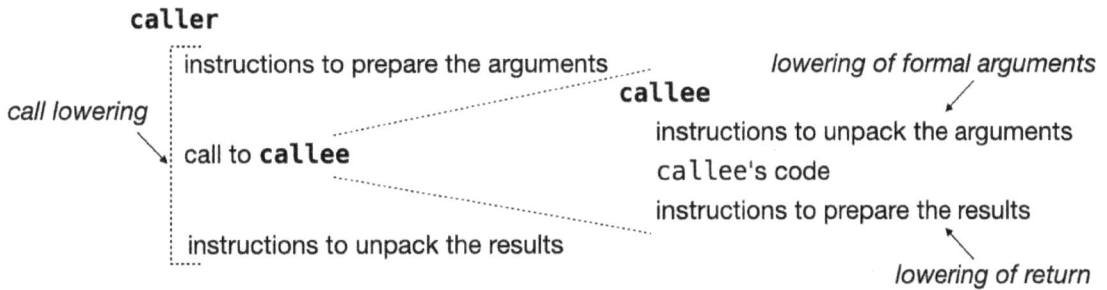

Figure 15.1: Lowering of the ABI with the different target hooks

In *Figure 15.1*, you can see a snippet of the sequence of instructions around a call to a function named callee from a function named caller. The caller function, on the left-hand side, calls the callee function, on the right-hand side. The sequence of instructions of the caller function needs to prepare the arguments for the callee function, then call callee, and finally unpack the result returned by callee. There is one target hook (represented by the *call-lowering* annotation in this picture) that is responsible for the generation of this sequence of instructions. On the right-hand side, the sequence of instructions for the callee function must first unpack the arguments it received. This is encapsulated behind another target hook, and this is called the **lowering of the formal arguments**, as seen in the diagram. After the callee function finishes its execution, it needs to return its results, and the generation of the related sequence of instructions is encapsulated behind yet another target hook responsible for the lowering of the return.

Going back to the last bullet point about the target hook responsible for checking whether a value is returnable by a callee, this hook is used by the target-independent code of SDISel and GlobalISel to handle something called **structure return demotion** or **sret demotion** for short. What sret demotion does is, if a value cannot be returned through the physical registers by the callee (typically, this happens when a structure is too large), then the caller creates a stack slot for the value and passes it to the callee as an additional argument. The callee then uses the stack slot to write the return values. This is a demotion because the returned value is demoted from a fast storage space, the registers, to a slow storage space, the memory. This is illustrated in *Table 15.1*.

| Original code | Equivalent code with sret demotion |
|---|---|
| ```void caller() {     struct BigStruct res =        callee();   ... ``` | ```void caller() {     struct BigStruct res;     callee(&res);   ... ``` |

Table 15.1: With and without sret demotion

In *Table 15.1*, on the left-hand side, the callee function returns a presumably large structure. If that structure cannot be returned via the dedicated physical registers (as defined by the ABI of the target), the signature of the callee function is changed so that it takes the address of the structure where it must write the result.

At this point, you know that your selector(s) will need to implement different target hooks for the IR building phase to work. As part of this lowering, you will need to do two related things:

- Issue the right sequence of instructions
- Read/write from the right location

To elaborate on the last bullet point, imagine that the ABI of your target requires that the first integer argument is passed through the physical register r1. This means that, from the caller's perspective, you must write to r1 when preparing the arguments for the callee. Now, from the callee's perspective, this means that you must read from r1 to get this argument. This sounds easy: you write and read from the same location. Now, imagine having to handle this mapping for tens of different input types and tens of different argument positions (for instance, imagine that after the third integer argument, further arguments are passed through the stack.) Unless you spend the proper amount of time sharing some logic between the code generated for the caller and the callee sides, it is very easy to get these sequences of code out of sync and produce subtle bugs (for instance, writing to a location and reading from a different one). Luckily, you do not have to set up this shared logic yourself. Indeed, this work is mechanical and the LLVM infrastructure abstracted away some of it behind a TableGen backend.

In this section, you learned what the IR building phase is about and what it takes, at a high level, to implement it. You saw that this phase requires you to provide an implementation of four different code sequences around the lowering of the calling convention.

In the next section, we will describe how to use the TableGen backend that we just mentioned and that is shared among all selectors before diving into how to implement the four target hooks.

# Describing the calling convention

Before explaining how to describe a calling convention, let us define what this is.

A **calling convention** is a set of rules that describe how calls are lowered. They represent a subset of the specification of an ABI. Complete ABIs also define how names are mangled, among other things.

It is likely that a given backend must support several calling conventions. For instance, running on different **operation systems (OSs)** may require different lowering rules and it's the same for different input languages (such as Swift or C++.) The bottom line is, when you describe your calling convention, it will be related to a name – for instance, if you look at the specifications of the ABIs of the ARM architecture, called the **ARM architecture procedure call standard (AAPCS)**, you will see that there are different variants for the 32-bit architecture, called **aapcs32**, and the 64-bit architecture, called **aapcs64**. The point is we recommend that you use the name of the calling convention as a lifeline. For instance, prefix all your TableGen records with the name of the calling convention they refer to so that you can easily know which piece belongs to which calling convention.

Now that you know what a calling convention is, let us see how to describe them using the target description mechanism that the LLVM infrastructure offers.

# Writing your target description of the calling convention

To describe your calling convention, you need to produce TableGen records that use the TableGen classes defined in the llvm/include/llvm/Target/TargetCallingConv.td file. The classes in this file are well documented but it may feel overwhelming the first time you look at it.

To help you make sense of what you see in this file, let us give you some guidelines.

The description of the calling convention is articulated around three TableGen classes: the CallingConv class, the CCAction class, and the CalleeSavedRegs class. Your job is to create records of the CallingConv class for each calling convention boundary, populate them with CCAction records, and describe the **callee saved registers** (these are the registers that must be saved before being used) of a function of this calling convention. Let us unpack this.

When you call a function, you need three pieces of information: where its arguments need to be, where its results need to be, and which registers are preserved by this function call, meaning which registers can live through the call of the function without being clobbered. The first two elements of that list are represented by two CallingConv records, one for each, and the third element with a CalleeSavedRegs record.

Now, let's focus on a CallingConv record. Such a record takes a list of CCAction records that are evaluated, in order, to determine where an argument (or result) needs to be. Let us take an example.

Consider the following snippet, which describes the ABI of our H2BLB target:

```
def CC_H2BLB_Common : CallingConv<[
  CCIfType<[v2i16], CCBitConvertToType<i32>>,
  CCIfType<[i16,f16], CCAssignToReg<[R1, R2, R3]>>,
  CCIfType<[i32,f32], CCAssignToReg<[D1]>>,
  CCAssignToStack<2, 2>
]>;
```

This snippet describes a sequence of actions that are evaluated, in order, for each argument. During the evaluation of the actions, the first one that matches is applied to assign the location of the argument.

For instance, let us say we want to lower a call to a function with the following prototype void: @foo(i16, <2 x i16>, i16). We start by trying the first action, CCIfType<[v2i16],..., which checks if the type of the argument is v2i16, and if it is, it does what is described in the next argument. In this case, this does not match (i16 versus v2i16.) The second action, CCIfType<[i16,f16],..., matches – the location of this argument is the R1 Register. Moving to the second argument, the first action applies, and we convert the <2 x i16> type to i32, then move on to the next action, which does not match, then the third action matches, and we end up with the D1 register as the location of this argument. For the final argument, the first action does not match, but the second does; however, the CCAssignToReg action fails because R1, R2, and R3 are all taken (in our example, the registers R2 and R3 alias (in other words, overlap) with the register D1), therefore the second action fails. Moving to the third action, it does not match, and we apply the last action, which says that the location of the argument is a stack slot of a minimum of 2 bytes with an address aligned at 2 bytes.

One thing to notice in this example is that you can compose the CCAction records. For instance, looking at the second action, you can see that the CCIfType record applies another record from a derived CCAction class: CCAssignToReg. The takeaway is that you can nest as many CCAction records as needed to describe how the location of your arguments or results is lowered.

This snippet only covers the arguments of the calling convention. You would need to provide the same kind of list of actions for the return values of the same calling convention.

> **Note**
>
> The CallingConv class features a field named Entry. This Boolean defines whether TableGen will emit the calling convention code in an anonymous namespace (Entry == false) or the llvm namespace (Entry == true). This is useful to toggle that switch when you want to share the description of your calling convention between different allocators within the same backend (for instance, between FastISel and SDISel).

At this point, you should have everything you need to describe the location of your arguments/results. If this is the first time you are doing this and feel lost, there are two situations to consider. First, if you are implementing a well-defined system, you need to find the ABI documentation and simply implement the specification of the ABI. For instance, for aapcs64, you can find the specification at https://github.com/ARM-software/abi-aa/releases/download/2024Q3/aapcs64.pdf. Second, If you are implementing a bespoke system, check if the ABI is already defined somewhere (sometimes the hardware team has some ideas) and implement it. If you must come up with your own ABI, look at an existing one (for instance, aapcs64 again) and follow similar patterns. An ABI is difficult to get right, and it usually takes several iterations to find one that works great.

Now that we have covered the location of the arguments, let us see how to define the list of the preserved registers.

To describe the callee saved registers, simply create a record of the CalleeSavedRegs class and list the registers that are preserved across a call.

For instance, here are the callee saved registers of our H2BLB backend:

```
def CSR : CalleeSavedRegs<(add D2, D3)>;
```

This line means that the D2 and D3 registers are preserved across calls.

To see a more detailed example of how to build your calling convention, look at the commits tagged add-callconv-skeleton_ch15, add-callconv-ret_ch15, add-callconv-fp_ch15, add-callconv-stack_ch15, and add-callconv-vector_ch15 in the companion repository. These commits build our ABI for the H2BLB backend.

Now that you have written your .td file, let us see how to use TableGen to generate the boilerplate code that you need to be able to use your calling conventions in the selectors.

# Connecting the gen-callingconv TableGen backend

To connect the gen-callingconv TableGen backend you need to do the following:

- Add its invocation in the main CMakeLists.txt file of your backend
- Include the generated .inc file in a .cpp file (directly in your selector implementation file, for instance, or a dedicated file)
- Create a header file if you used Entry = true for your CallingConv record to hold the function signatures that will be shared between the selectors

The first two bullet points are trivial and if you need help with them, check the commit tagged add-callconv-skeleton_ch15 in the companion repository. For the third bullet point, the function signature that you need to provide looks like this:

```
bool llvm::XXX(unsigned ValNo, MVT ValVT, MVT LocVT,
               CCValAssign::LocInfo LocInfo, ISD::ArgFlagsTy ArgFlags,
               CCState &State);
```

In this snippet, XXX is the name of the record of your CallingConv class. For instance, for our H2BLB backend, using the previous TableGen snippet of our CallingConv record, that name is CC_H2BLB_Common.

At this point, you've done the groundwork to describe the location of your arguments and results. The functions that you generated match the signature of the type called CCAssignFn, defined in the llvm/include/llvm/CodeGen/CallingConvLower.h file. These functions are the building blocks of the methods of the CCState class. This class is used to compute the locations of all the arguments and results. For instance, in the SDISel, you will use the AnalyzeFormalArguments method, the AnalyzeReturn method, and so on from the CCState class to get the locations of the related arguments and results, then use that information to produce the sequence of instructions that materialize the calling convention.

No matter which selector you use, the general principle remains the same: you will use an instance of the CCState class with an instance of the CCAssignFn class that describes the piece of a calling convention you want to lower (for instance, where to find the arguments of a function or where to find the results of a function). In return, you will get instances of the CCValAssign class that you will use to produce your code sequence in the IR of your selector.

Let us now look more closely at what the CCValAssign class represents.

# Anatomy of the CCValAssign class

The CCValAssign class is your link between the target description of your calling convention and the actual location of a particular argument/result. It is defined in the llvm/include/llvm/CodeGen/CallingConvLower.h file.

When you get an instance of this class, you can check where the corresponding argument/result needs to be read or written using the isXXX method and the related getYYY method – for instance, the isMemLoc and getLocMemOffset methods or the isRegLoc and getLocReg methods.

Additionally, you can check what the original and actual types of the value being lowered are, where the original type is what was set for the related argument/result and the actual type is how the ABI lowers it. For instance, on an architecture with 32-bit registers, passing an 8-bit integer will mean using a full 32-bit value. Therefore, the original type is i8 but the actual type is i32. You can get this information through the getValVT method for the original type and getLocVT for the actual type.

Staying on this notion of original and actual types, the next thing that you need to know is how you go from one to the other. Going back to our 8-bit to 32-bit integers example, we need to know how we get from this 8-bit value to this 32-bit value. Are we sign-extending the 8-bit value, are we zero-extending it, or are we doing something else? The transformation that needs to happen is defined by the getLocInfo method. This method returns an enumeration that represents what you are supposed to do. For instance, the LocInfo::Full value means there is nothing to do, the LocInfo::SExt value means that you must sign-extend the 8-bit value to the 32-bit value, and so on.

To summarize, a CCValAssign instance is the identity card of the location of the related argument or result and your job is to read or write to that location while ensuring you check all the boxes. For instance, if the described location is a register, you must read from or write to (depending on whether you are producing the caller or callee code sequence) this register and if getLocInfo is not LocInfo::Full, you have to materialize the related sequence of instructions to go from getValVT to getLocVT, or the other way around, depending on whether you are reading from the original type or writing to the original type.

In this section, you learned how to describe the location of your results and arguments according to your calling convention. This description is supported by a TableGen backend and the related TableGen classes and is used to generate code that works with the CCState and CCValAssign classes. These classes provide you with the functionalities you need to be able to lower the code sequences that materialize the lowering of the calling conventions.

We understand that everything we just described may look abstract, but you now have all the pieces to implement all the target hooks for any of the three selectors. In the next sections, we will point out what these hooks are, and will show you examples of how to do what we just described. These examples are, however, very basic since, at the end of the day, you must implement the specification of your ABI and this specification likely will not match the examples.

Let us start with SDISel.

# Lowering the ABI with SDISel

To lower the ABI with SDISel, you must implement the four methods of your target-specific version of the TargetLowering class that are responsible for this part of the selector. Specifically, you must implement the LowerFormalArguments, LowerReturn, LowerCall, and CanLowerReturn methods. These methods map exactly to the logic we said you would need to provide at the beginning of the *Overview of the IR building* section.

Concretely, as we hinted previously, the implementation of these methods will rely heavily on the CCState and the CCValAssign classes. More specifically, you need to use one of the CCState::AnalyzeXXX methods with a proper CCAssignFn instance (the one you produced with TableGen) to produce a list of CCValAssign instances. The CCState::AnalyzeXXX method to use depends on what you are trying to achieve:

- AnalyzeFormalArguments: Use this method when producing the sequence of instructions to read the arguments from within a callee function.

- AnalyzeReturn: Use this method when producing the sequence of instructions to write the results from within a callee function.

- AnalyzeCallOperands: Use this method when producing the sequence of instructions to write the arguments before calling a function. In other words, this is the code produced by the caller function before calling the callee function.

- AnalyzeCallResult: Use this method when producing the sequence of instructions to read the results produced by a call of a function. In other words, this is the code produced by the caller function after calling the callee function.

Finally, for checking whether it is possible to lower a returned value without the need to use sret demotion, use the CCState::CheckReturn method.

Let us see how it works with an example.

## Implementing the lowering of formal arguments

Using what we saw in the previous section, let us see how we can assemble an implementation of LowerFormalArguments for our H2BLB backend.

The following snippet gives you a view of the result and you can also find how it was built at the commits tagged add-callconv-fp_ch15 and add-callconv-stack_ch15 in the companion repository. We will break down the important pieces right after this snippet:

```
SDValue H2BLBTargetLowering::LowerFormalArguments(
    SDValue Chain, CallingConv::ID CallConv, bool IsVarArg,
    const SmallVectorImpl<ISD::InputArg> &Ins, const SDLoc &DL,
    SelectionDAG &DAG, SmallVectorImpl<SDValue> &InVals) const {
  ...
  MachineFunction &MF = DAG.getMachineFunction();
  SmallVector<CCValAssign, 16> ArgLocs;
  CCState CCInfo(CallConv, IsVarArg, MF, ArgLocs, *DAG.getContext());
  CCInfo.AnalyzeFormalArguments(Ins, CC_H2BLB_Common);
  for (size_t I = 0; I < ArgLocs.size(); ++I) {
    auto &VA = ArgLocs[I];
    if (VA.isRegLoc()) {
      if (VA.getLocInfo() != CCValAssign::Full)
        report_fatal_error("non-full passing, not yet implemented");
```

```
      EVT RegVT = VA.getLocVT();
      const TargetRegisterClass *DstRC = nullptr;
       ... // Choose right register class based on the type.
      Register VReg = RegInfo.createVirtualRegister(DstRC);
      RegInfo.addLiveIn(VA.getLocReg(), VReg);
      SDValue ArgValue = DAG.getCopyFromReg(Chain, DL, VReg, RegVT);
      InVals.push_back(ArgValue);
    } else {
      ... // Handle stack argument.
    }
  }
  return Chain;
}
```

In this snippet, we show how to lower arguments on the callee side when they are full values (that is, no bitcast, no sign-extension, etc.) and passed in registers.

First, we create a `CCState` object for the function we are lowering:

```
  CCState CCInfo(CallConv, IsVarArg, MF, ArgLocs, *DAG.getContext());
```

The `ArgLocs` argument is our storage for the `CCValAssign` instances that will be populated through the call to the upcoming `AnalyzeFormalArguments` method.

Next, we call the `AnalyzeFormalArguments` method, with the variable `Ins`, which we will describe next, and the `CCAssignFn` instance that represents the calling convention we want to materialize for this lowering, `CC_H2BLB_Common`:

```
  CCInfo.AnalyzeFormalArguments(Ins, CC_H2BLB_Common);
```

The `Ins` argument is given to us by the generic infrastructure of SDISel. It is a list of the `SDNode` instances that represents the input arguments of the function being lowered. Using this list, `AnalyzeFormalArguments` will be able to play out the actions defined by the `CCAssignFn` instance (`CC_H2BLB_Common` in this case) to populate the `ArgLocs` variable. This `ArgLocs` variable was populated within the constructor of the `CCState` instance.

After that call, the `ArgLocs` list contains all the `CCValAssign` instances for all the arguments described by the `Ins` variable.

Therefore, the remainder of the code is a loop over this location that produces the right sequence of instructions for each location description.

Focusing on the implementation within the block after the `if (VA.isRegLoc())` statement, in this block we are dealing with an argument passed through the register. Therefore, we want to produce a sequence of instructions that copy the content of the physical register associated with this `CCValAssign` instance to a virtual register that will be used in the rest of the function.

To do that, we start by looking at the type of physical storage to be able to decide which register class we can use to hold that type and create a virtual register for that:

```
EVT RegVT = VA.getLocVT();
const TargetRegisterClass *DstRC = nullptr;
... // Choose the right register class based on the type.
Register VReg = RegInfo.createVirtualRegister(DstRC);
```

Now, this is a part of SDISel that is convoluted. Instead of directly issuing a copy from the physical register to the virtual register that we created, we tell the MachineRegisterInfo instance of the current function that, first, this physical register is a live-in of the current function (so far, so good), and that this physical register is mapped on the given virtual register. Therefore, we do not materialize a copy yet, just a logical mapping using the following:

```
RegInfo.addLiveIn(VA.getLocReg(), VReg);
```

Next, we materialize this copy in the SDISel IR:

```
SDValue ArgValue = DAG.getCopyFromReg(Chain, DL, VReg, RegVT);
```

Notice that the input of the copy is the previously defined virtual register (the Vreg variable) and not the physical register of the location (the result of the call to VA.getLocReg()). This quirk can be seen in the textual dump of a SelectionDAG object:

```
t2: i32,ch = CopyFromReg t0, Register:i32 %0
```

In this snippet, t2 is the SDNode instance that represents our ArgValue variable and %0 is our virtual register. The MachineRegisterInfo instance knows the mapping of %0 with the actual physical register, thanks to our call to MachineRegisterInfo::addLiveIn. Toward the end of SDISel, the generic code will call MachineRegisterInfo::EmitLiveInCopies to materialize these copies. The reason why we must do this gymnastic is because getCopyFromReg SDNode instances typically do not lower to actual copies. If you remember, they are just a way to materialize the live-in values of a basic block.

Back to the code of our LowerFormalArguments method, we push the SDNode instance that represents the input argument in the InVals list, which is the output parameter of the whole method. In other words, SDISel uses the content of the InVals variable as the values that hold the argument of the currently lowered function in the rest of the selection process.

Lastly, our target hook must return a chain. Here, we did not modify it, so we just return the one that we had been given directly.

For the other target hooks, you will need to use the same kind of logic, except there is an additional complexity that you need to be aware of. SDIsel does not provide generic opcodes for call and return instructions, therefore you must provide a custom description for them to be able to instantiate SDNode objects for these instructions.

Let us see how to achieve that.

# Providing custom description for the SDNode class

When lowering your ABI, there are at least four custom descriptions for the SDNode class that your backend needs to provide: three for the lowering of regular calls (as opposed to calls to intrinsics; intrinsics are lowered differently) and one for the lowering of returns.

The three custom descriptions for calls are the call instruction itself and two marker instructions that delimit the beginning and end of the call sequence. These are mandatory to determine the region where the call frame needs to be properly set up. For instance, if a call requires some stack slots, the pass responsible for the frame lowering (which we will cover in *Chapter 20*) needs to know when the stack needs to be big enough to hold these slots.

To describe a custom description for the SDNode class, you use TableGen and, more specifically, some of the classes defined in the `llvm/include/llvm/Target/TargetSelectionDAG.td` file. Before we get into the details, let us break out the good news: you do not have to connect yet another TableGen backend; the custom descriptions are handled by the `gen-dag-isel` TableGen backend that you connected in *Chapter 14*.

The TableGen class that you need to use for your record is obvious – it is the SDNode TableGen class. This class takes a string that represents how you will instantiate this opcode, a description of the type of the node (number of arguments, number of results, type of each operand, and so on), and the properties of the node.

Let us see what it looks like with the description of the call node of our H2BLB backend:

```
def H2BLBcall : SDNode<"H2BLBISD::CALL",
                       SDTypeProfile<0, -1, [SDTCisPtrTy<0>]>,
                       [SDNPHasChain, SDNPOptInGlue, SDNPOutGlue,
                        SDNPVariadic]>;
```

In this snippet, the `"H2BLBISD::CALL"` string represents the enumeration value that we will use for this opcode. We will have to provide the related C++ definition for this, and we show this hereafter.

> **Note**
>
> You usually define your custom nodes directly in the `XXXInstrInfo.td` file of your backend because this file is already the base of what the `gen-dag-isel` TableGen backend uses. Moreover, these custom nodes are also referenceable in the description of the selection patterns, which usually lives with the target description of the instructions themselves, meaning the `XXXInstrInfo.td` file.

Next comes the type of the node, which is represented with this SDTypeProfile TableGen class: `SDTypeProfile<0, -1, [SDTCisPtrTy<0>]>`. The first argument of SDTypeProfile is the number of explicit results for the current node, so no result here – everything is implicitly returned. The second argument is the number of arguments of the node and `-1` means that this is variadic. This variadic number of arguments is because, unlike the results, we need to pass the arguments to the call instruction explicitly in the SDISel IR. The third argument is a list of constraints that must be matched by the operands of the node.

Here, SDTCisPtrTy<0> means that the $0^{th}$ operand, hence the first argument of the variadic list of arguments, must be a pointer type. This is because a call must have a target function and that target function is an address to where this function resides in the final binary, hence a pointer.

> **Note**
>
> The numbering of the operands in the SDTypeProfile description starts from the results and then the arguments. Therefore, if a node has a result, the $0^{th}$ operand would be that result and not the first argument of the node. This is how operands of the MachineInstr instances are numbered too, if you remember what you learned in *Chapter 11*.

The final argument of the SDNode TableGen class is a list of the properties of the node. Here, the list is made of the following properties: SDNPHasChain, SDNPOptInGlue, SDNPOutGlue, and SDNPVariadic, and their meanings are as follows:

- SDNPHasChain: This node takes a chain as input and produces a chain as output (chains do not count toward the number of results).
- SDNPOptInGlue: This node optionally takes a glue as input. This glue is used to make sure the instructions related to the ABI lowering are next to the call and it is optional because calls with no argument have nothing to stick with.
- SDNPOutGlue: This node produces a glue. This glue can be used by the instructions related to the ABI lowering for retrieving the returned value to make sure they are next to the call.
- SDNPVariadic: This node has a variable number of arguments.

Note that all the properties are defined and documented in the llvm/include/llvm/CodeGen/ SDNodeProperties.td file and you can easily identify that a record is a property because their names start with SDNP for the SDNode property.

That takes care of the TableGen part. Now, we still have to provide the C++ boilerplate to make that description usable in SDISel.

First, we need to provide the enumeration value for our custom node. We do this by adding the following code in our XXXISelLowering.h file:

```
namespace H2BLBISD {
enum NodeType : unsigned {
  FIRST_NUMBER = ISD::BUILTIN_OP_END,
  CALL,
};
}
```

In this snippet, we also introduce a FIRST_NUMBER enumeration value to make sure our custom enumeration values do not collide with the generic ones. The ISD::BUILTIN_OP_END value gives us the last value that is used by the generic code.

Second, we need to tell SDISel how to pretty print our custom node when dumping an SDNode instance that uses that opcode:

```
const char *H2BLBTargetLowering::getTargetNodeName(unsigned Opcode) const {
  switch ((H2BLBISD::NodeType)Opcode) {
  case H2BLBISD::FIRST_NUMBER:
    break;
  case H2BLBISD::CALL:
    return "H2BLBISD::CALL";
  }
  return nullptr;
}
```

In this snippet, we override the TargetLowering::getTargetNodeName method that is used for the textual printing of SDNode instances. This is a straightforward switch that, given the opcode of an SDNode instance, returns the related string to print.

Now that you have set up your custom description, you can use it to create custom SDNode instances. Here is what it would look like for our custom CALL node:

```
SDVTList NodeTys = DAG.getVTList(MVT::Other, MVT::Glue);
Chain = DAG.getNode(H2BLBISD::CALL, DL, NodeTys, Ops);
InGlue = Chain.getValue(1);
```

In this snippet, in the first line, we define the types that are returned by our SDNode instance: MVT::Other for the chain and MVT::Glue for the glue. Next, we create our node using the usual SelectionDAG::getNode method and produce the two values (SDValue instances) we want from the node. The Ops variable represents the list of all the arguments of our call.

You can look at the commits tagged sdisel-call-pseudos_ch15 for the full description of the custom nodes involved in the lowering of calls and sdisel-call-lowering_ch15 for an example of how to use these custom nodes. In the latter commit, you will see that we define opcodes for the call delimiters – respectively, the ISD::CALLSEQ_START and ISD::CALLSEQ_END enumeration values for the beginning and end of a call sequence. These opcodes are special because the LLVM infrastructure expects that every backend provides their TableGen descriptions, while the LLVM infrastructure takes care of the C++ code around them. In other words, you do not have to go through the C++ steps of exposing these opcodes to SDISel for these delimiters; SDISel already knows about them.

The call delimiters take two mandatory integers that respectively represent how big the call frame must be in bytes for this specific call sequence and how many of these bytes are going to be freed by the callee. Unless you are doing tail call optimizations, you can forget about the second integer and just put zero. In any case, these numbers will be important when we do the frame lowering in *Chapter 20*.

Before we move to the next selector framework, let us give you a couple of hints on how to materialize stack locations in your target hooks.

# Handling of stack locations

Eventually, your CCState instances will produce CCValAssing instances with stack locations. When this happens, the CCValAssign instance will contain a memory location (the isMemLoc method returns true.) In this case, you need to use getLocMemOffset to get what this memory location is and create a stack slot for it using the following:

```
unsigned ArgOffset = VA.getLocMemOffset();
unsigned ArgSize = VA.getValVT().getSizeInBits() / 8;
int FrameIdx =
    MFI.CreateFixedObject(ArgSize, ArgOffset, /*IsImmutable=*/true);
```

In this snippet, we get the size and memory offset of the stack location and create a stack slot for it. A stack slot at the machine IR level is just an integer, and we call this integer a **frame index**.

Using this frame index, you can then create an SDNode instance that represents your stack slot:

```
SDValue FrameIdxNode =
  DAG.getFrameIndex(FrameIdx, getPointerTy(DAG.getDataLayout()));
```

You can also create a MachinePointerInfo instance from your frame index:

```
MachinePointerInfo PtrInfo =
  MachinePointerInfo::getFixedStack(MF, FrameIdx);
```

This type of object is required to create SDNode instances that represent load or store instructions – in other words, what you need to read or write your arguments or results at a stack location.

> **Note**
>
> When implementing the lowering of your ABI, start with simple cases. Implement functions without input arguments and no return values, then add the support for register arguments and results. Next, look at stack arguments and results, and finally, implement complex arguments that require extensions and other complicated cases such as variadic arguments, special argument attributes, and so on.

To conclude this section, if you need more examples of how to implement your target hooks, look at the implementation of the other targets, starting with the llvm/lib/Target/H2BLB/H2BLBISelLowering. cpp file of the companion repository (then move on to any other backend implementation!). If you need to see the steps one by one, you can look at the commit tagged add-callconv-stack_ch15 to see how to add the support for stack locations, add-callconv-vector_ch15 to see how to add support for locations that goes beyond the LocInfo::Full support, sdisel-sret-demot_ch15 to see how to enable sret demotion, sdisel-call-lowering_ch15 to see how to add the lowering of calls, sdisel-lowerret_ch15 to see how to add the lowering of returns, or sdisel-call-lowering-stack_ch15 to see how to add stack location support for the lowering of calls.

In this section, you learned how to implement the target hooks required to lower your calling conventions with SDISel. You saw a concrete example of how to do that for the lowering of the formal arguments and learned about the concept of sret demotion in the process.

Now that you know how to implement the lowering of your ABI with SDISel, let us see what this looks like with FastISel.

## Lowering the ABI with FastISel

Aside from the lowering of the formal arguments, the lowering of the ABI in FastISel is intermixed with the selection process itself and, as such, there are fewer target hooks that need to be implemented.

In practice, this means that you must handle the lowering of the ABI yourself when you do the selection of the LLVM IR `call` and `ret` instructions. You will see where this code lives in *Chapter 17*.

For formal arguments, you need to override the `FastISel::fastLowerArguments` method. This method returns `true` if you manage to handle the lowering of the formal arguments or `false` otherwise. When `false` is returned and the fallback mechanism is enabled, SDISel will switch to a selection process based purely on a `SelectionDAG` instance for the current basic block.

In the implementation of `FastISel::fastLowerArguments` (or any FastISel method), you are free to leverage the `CCState` class. However, usually, FastISel is only implemented for very specific cases – for instance, it is implemented only for functions with two 32-bit integer arguments, and it is common that the ABI is hardcoded directly in C++. For instance, as the implementer, you directly assign the registers that you know are used by the ABI in this case. The next snippet gives you a glimpse of such simplified implementations.

Here is a truncated version of what this method looks like in our H2BLB backend:

```
bool H2BLBFastISel::fastLowerArguments() {
  if (!FuncInfo.CanLowerReturn)
    return false;
  const Function *F = FuncInfo.Fn;
  CallingConv::ID CC = F->getCallingConv();
  ... // Do some checks to see if we support this calling convention.
  const DataLayout &DL = F->getDataLayout();
  for (const Argument &Arg : F->args()) {
    Type *ArgTy = Arg.getType();
    ... // Do some checks on the Type of the argument.
  MachineFunction &MF = *FuncInfo.MF;
  for (const Argument &Arg : F->args()) {
    Register SrcPhysReg;
    const TargetRegisterClass *DstRC;
    ... // Find where SrcPhysReg is for the current argument.
    ... // Find a suitable register class for the destination register.
```

```
        Register SrcReg = MF.addLiveIn(SrcPhysReg, DstRC);
        Register ResultReg = createResultReg(DstRC);
        BuildMI(*FuncInfo.MBB, FuncInfo.InsertPt, MIMD, TII.get(TargetOpcode::COPY),
                ResultReg)
            .addReg(SrcReg, getKillRegState(true));
        updateValueMap(&Arg, ResultReg);
    }
    return true;
}
```

In this snippet, we walk through the arguments of the currently processed LLVM IR function and create a `MachineInstr` `COPY` instance for each of the input arguments.

There are a couple of things to mention in this snippet that are generally applicable to FastISel:

- The `FuncInfo` member variable, an instance of the `FunctionLoweringInfo` class, holds relevant information about the LLVM IR function that is currently being selected.
- Since FastISel is part of SDISel, it must use the same quirk as SDISel to lower the copies of the physical register for the formal arguments (the call to `MachineRegisterInfo::addLiveIn` and the `COPY` instruction being from a virtual register instead of being directly from a physical register).
- The `MIMD` member variable is automatically set by the generic code of FastISel. This variable contains the metadata that you need to attach to any `MachineInstr` instances that you may create. In particular, it holds the debug location of what is currently being lowered.

The rest of the snippet should be easy to grasp.

> **Note**
>
> Since FastISel may fall back to SDISel, each time you create a new value that materializes an LLVM IR Value instance, you need to call `FastISel::updateValueMap` so that SDISel knows about what is being used in the FastISel part.

You can look at the commits tagged `fastisel-abi-skeleton_ch15`, `fastisel-ret-val_ch15`, and `fastisel-abi-arg-val_ch15` for the steps that lead to partial but functional support of the lowering of the ABI.

To summarize, you learned that FastISel only exposes one method for the lowering of the calling conventions. This method is the one that handles the lowering of the formal arguments. Everything else in FastISel is custom and is handled directly through the instruction selection phase, which you will discover in *Chapter 17*.

Our next stop covers the last instruction selection framework.

# Lowering the ABI with GlobalISel

The target hooks required to lower the ABI are all gathered in one helper class in GlobalISel. Indeed, to implement the lowering of the ABI in GlobalISel, you need to supply a target-specific version of the CallLowering class, from the GlobalISel library.

To implement this class, you need to override the following four methods: lowerFormalArguments, lowerReturn, lowerCall, and canLowerReturn. Just from their names, you should have an idea of what each of them needs to do!

In the signature of the lowerFormalArguments and lowerReturn methods, you will find an instance of the FunctionLoweringInfo class that, as you know, holds some information about the LLVM IR function being lowered, and for the lowerCall method, an instance of the CallLoweringInfo class, which holds some information about the call instruction being lowered, such as the calling convention used, whether this can be optimized as a tail call, and so on.

Taking each method one by one, here are the high-level expectations of each method:

- lowerFormalArguments: This takes the input LLVM IR function as input and populates the given array of array of virtual registers (ArrayRef<ArrayRef<Register>> VRegs). The first level of the array is indexed by the argument number and the second level represents the list of virtual registers that are required to materialize this argument. For instance, let us say that our target offers only 32-bit registers, but we still want to pass 64-bit values via registers. We will use two registers for one 64-bit register and the related entry of the 64-bit argument will have two 32-bit virtual registers. The exact same thing happens in SDISel, but SDISel breaks down the types before lowering the formal arguments. In GlobalISel, you have full control over how the breakdown is done. The generic code is responsible for stitching the virtual registers of each argument together to produce one big virtual register for each argument. Note that this array of virtual registers also needs to include the sret demoted argument if applicable, as reported by the FuntionLoweringInfo::CanLowerReturn member variable of the given FunctionLoweringInfo instance.
- lowerReturn: This takes the value returned by the input LLVM IR function and populates an array of virtual registers that represents this value.
- lowerCall: This produces the code sequence to call the function described by the CallLoweringInfo instance.
- canLowerReturn: This returns true if the list of provided output values can be lowered directly in the return sequence and false otherwise.

The first three methods take a MachineIRBuilder instance that you should use to create your instructions. This is important to make a habit of using the provided MachineIRBuilder instances, as opposed to creating your own locally, because these objects sometimes come with what we call observer instances that notify the generic infrastructure about changes in the IR. Also, some of them may come with built-in **common subexpression elimination** (CSE) enabled.

Note

The Booleans returned by the lowerXXX methods of the CallLowering class determine whether the IRTranslator pass will succeed or not. This means that if, during a run of the IRTranslator pass, one of these methods returns false, then the whole IRTranslator pass will report a failure, and depending on how your fallback mechanism is configured, this will lead to either a fatal error or a fallback to SDISel.

Focusing on the implementation of the three main methods, you will leverage the CCState class and the CCAssignFn instances that you saw already. However, the usage is slightly different because GlobalISel provides different functionality than SDISel. It is not, strictly speaking, better or worse – it is just different.

Let us see how!

GlobalISel provides methods to find the location of the arguments or results, and then apply this location. Thanks to this, you do not have to traverse the arguments yourself; instead, you just produce the copy, load, or store instruction for one argument or result and the generic code does the rest for you. To interact with the CCState class and CCAssignFn instances that way, you must provide new abstractions called the assigner and the handler.

The assigner is responsible for assigning a location to an argument (using a CCAssignFn instance) and its base class is the CallLowering::ValueAssigner class. In practice, you will likely specialize one of its subclasses: the IncomingValueAssigner or OutgoingValueAssigner class.

The handler is responsible for materializing the location determined by the assigner. Its base class is the CallLowering::ValueHandler class. In practice, you will specialize one of its subclasses – the IncomingValueHandler or OutgoingValueHandler class.

The IncomingValueXXX classes are used to manage the formal arguments and the returned value of a call from the caller's perspective. The OutgoingValueXXX classes are used for the lowering of the arguments of the callee from the caller's perspective and the lowering of the returned value from the callee's perspective. While it may sound confusing to model a returned value as an incoming value and an argument to a callee as an outgoing value, think of the incoming and outgoing values in terms of what flows in and out of the current context of a function. For instance, from the caller's perspective, the arguments to the callee are about to get transferred to an outside context.

Let us see how to use these concepts for the lowering of the formal arguments.

First, we define our IncomingValueAssigner class for our target:

```
struct H2BLBIncomingValueAssigner : public CallLowering::IncomingValueAssigner {
    ...
  bool assignArg(unsigned ValNo, EVT OrigVT, MVT ValVT, MVT LocVT,
              CCValAssign::LocInfo LocInfo,
```

```
                  const CallLowering::ArgInfo &Info, ISD::ArgFlagsTy Flags,
                  CCState &State) override {
    ... // Some checks.
    bool Res = AssignFn(ValNo, ValVT, LocVT, LocInfo, Flags, State);
    StackSize = State.getStackSize();
    return Res;
  }
};
```

In this snippet, we provide the meat of the IncomingValueAssigner class by implementing the assignArg method. What we do here is, after a few checks (omitted for simplicity), we simply call the CCAssignFn instance (remember this is what we produced with TableGen for our calling convention) carried by our member variable, AssignFn, and that was set in our constructor (also omitted for simplicity). We also set the StackSize member variable, which records the total stack size required for the arguments already assigned to the State variable. This information is useful to lower calls. The assigned locations are all registered within the State variable via the call to the AssignFn function.

Now, our IncomingValueHandler class looks like this:

```
struct IncomingArgHandler : public CallLowering::IncomingValueHandler {
  ...
  void assignValueToReg(Register ValVReg, Register PhysReg,
                        const CCValAssign &VA) override {
    ... // Update live-ins of the MachineFunction.
    IncomingValueHandler::assignValueToReg(ValVReg, PhysReg, VA);
  }
  void assignValueToAddress(Register ValVReg, Register Addr, LLT MemTy,
                            const MachinePointerInfo &MPO,
                            const CCValAssign &VA) override {
    MachineFunction &MF = MIRBuilder.getMF();
    LLT ValTy(VA.getValVT());
    LLT LocTy(VA.getLocVT());
    assert(ValTy == LocTy && "extensions not implemented");
    auto MMO = MF.getMachineMemOperand(
        MPO, MachineMemOperand::MOLoad | MachineMemOperand::MOInvariant, MemTy,
        inferAlignFromPtrInfo(MF, MPO));
    MIRBuilder.buildLoad(ValVReg, Addr, *MMO);
  }
  ...
```

In this snippet, we showed only two of the methods that you must override. The first one is the assignValueToReg method. This method is used when the assigner determines that the argument is passed through a register.

The implementation here is simple: we use the parent method while updating the live-in registers for the function (remember we are lowering formal arguments here, meaning values that are coming into the function). The second one is the `assignValueToAddress` method. This one is used when the assigner determines that the argument is passed through memory. The implementation is simple as well: we create a `MachineMemOperand` instance that describes our memory location and build a load operation with the provided address (the `Addr` variable) and the created `MachineMemOperand` instance.

You also need to override one other method, optionally two:

- `getStackAddress`: This returns a virtual register that contains the address of your stack slot. The code for this looks like what you saw already in the *Handling of stack locations* section for creating a frame index.

- `getStackValueStoreType`: This returns the `LLT` instance that must be used for the memory location of this stack slot. For instance, if the argument is an 8-bit value but you can only load or store at a 32-bit granularity, this would return a 32-bit `LLT` instance. This one is optional and, by default, will stick to the input type.

To see the full implementation of these methods, look at the `llvm/lib/Target/H2BLB/GISel/H2BLBCallLowering.cpp` file in the companion repository, or to get the different steps, look at the commits tagged `add-calllowering-initial-version_ch15` and `gisel-calllowering-sret_ch15`.

Let us see how we compose the assigner and handler in our target hook used for the lowering of formal arguments.

The beginning of the method looks like this:

```
bool H2BLBCallLowering::lowerFormalArguments(MachineIRBuilder &MIRBuilder,
                                             const Function &F,
                                             ArrayRef<ArrayRef<Register>> VRegs,
                                             FunctionLoweringInfo &FLI) const {
  ... // Boilerplate to get the MF, MRI, and so on
  SmallVector<ArgInfo, 8> SplitArgs;
  if (!FLI.CanLowerReturn)
    insertSRetIncomingArgument(F, SplitArgs, FLI.DemoteRegister, MRI, DL);
```

We start by checking if our return value can be returned directly, and if not we demote it to an additional pointer parameter using the `insertSRetIncomingArgument` method. The `SplitArgs` variable will in the end contain the list of all the low-level arguments, meaning that it represents the expanded list of arguments when you split the arguments that do not fit in one location (remember the 64-bit to two 32-bit registers example).

Next, we continue by identifying all the arguments we will have at a low level:

```
unsigned i = 0;
for (auto &Arg : F.args()) {
  if (DL.getTypeStoreSize(Arg.getType()).isZero())
    continue;
```

```
    ArgInfo OrigArg{VRegs[i], Arg, i};
    setArgFlags(OrigArg, i + AttributeList::FirstArgIndex, DL, F);
    splitToValueTypes(OrigArg, SplitArgs, DL, F.getCallingConv());
    ++i;
}
```

In this snippet, we walk through all the arguments of the input IR function, and for each argument, first, we skip the arguments that have a size of zero. These arguments do not carry any information. For the other arguments, we create an ArgInfo instance that associates the current argument with the entry in the array of virtual registers. Using the setArgFlags method, we compute all the properties of our ArgInfo instance for later consumption. Then, we call the splitToValueTypes method, which will potentially expand the current argument into several low-level arguments (for instance, a 64-bit value that fits in two 32-bit registers) and record them in the SplitArgs list.

Now that we have our full list of low-level arguments, we can lower them:

```
    ... // some bookkeeping.
    CCAssignFn *AssignFn = CC_H2BLB_Common;
    H2BLBIncomingValueAssigner Assigner(AssignFn, AssignFn);
    IncomingArgHandler Handler(MIRBuilder, MRI);
    SmallVector<CCValAssign, 16> ArgLocs;
    CCState CCInfo(F.getCallingConv(), F.isVarArg(), MF, ArgLocs, F.getContext());
    if (!determineAssignments(Assigner, SplitArgs, CCInfo) ||
        !handleAssignments(Handler, SplitArgs, CCInfo, ArgLocs, MIRBuilder))
      return false;
    ... // some bookkeeping.
    return true;
}
```

This snippet should be straightforward for you at this point. We start by providing our CCAssignFn instance for our calling convention with the CC_H2BLB_Common function. Then we use this instance to create our assigner and create our handler at the same time. Notice that the handler is independent of the assigner. This is expected since it will only materialize the assigner choices. Therefore, the handler does not need to know how these choices were made.

Next, we create our CCState instance and call two helper methods:

- determineAssignments: This runs the assigner on all the provided arguments and fills out the provided CCState instance
- handleAssignments: This runs the handler on the same parameters

At this point, if both methods succeed, your formal arguments are properly lowered!

You can see the full snippet again in the `llvm/lib/Target/H2BLB/GISel/H2BLBCallLowering.cpp` file or the commit tagged `add-calllowering-initial-version_ch15` in the companion repository.

The other target hooks follow the same principles and should be no problem for you! As always, go check the companion repository if you get stuck!

This concludes this section on how to implement the IR building phase for GlobalISel. You saw that the implementation of the lowering of the calling conventions goes through your target-specific implementation of the `CallLowering` class. You learned how to leverage the work you did with the TableGen backend that describes the calling conventions to produce the implementation of the four target hooks that are required to materialize the ABI of your target with this class.

# Summary

In this chapter, you learned that the IR building phase has two goals: building the generic IR used in the related instruction selection framework and lowering the ABI – more specifically, the calling conventions – of your target.

You learned that you need to implement three different lowering paths that correspond to where in the input program the calling convention is lowered (at a function call, to read the formal arguments, and to prepare the returned values) and learned that you need to supply an additional target hook to inform the IR building phase of when to use the sret demotion technique.

Next, you saw how to describe your calling conventions using a TableGen backend, which allows you to share the location information of your arguments and results for all selectors.

Finally, you learned, with examples, how to use the code generated by this TableGen backend to implement the previously mentioned lowering functions in all the instruction selection frameworks.

While we covered a lot in this chapter, it is just the tip of the iceberg. If you need help with advanced constructs such as the lowering of variadic arguments, we suggest you look at the implementation of some open source backend such as AArch64. Although what needs to happen for these types of techniques is more complicated, this chapter covered all the foundations that will allow you to understand them.

Now that you can produce IRs in a generic form with your lowering of the ABI, the next step is to learn how to turn it into something that your target can execute, which is the responsibility of the legalization phase, in the next chapter.

# Further reading

The official LLVM documentation features a section on the calling convention at https://llvm.org/docs/WritingAnLLVMBackend.html#calling-conventions. While the content of this document is rather limited, it could help you solidify some of the knowledge you gained in this chapter.

# Quiz time

Now that you have completed reading this chapter, try answering these questions to test your knowledge:

1.  What target-specific lowering must the IR building phase materialize?

    Aside from building the IR of the related instruction selection framework, the IR building phase is responsible for the lowering of the ABI and specifically the calling convention.

    See the *Overview of the IR building* section for more details.

2.  What are the three code sequences that you need to generate for the lowering of calls?

    You need to be able to produce a code sequence for reading the input arguments of a function, prepare the argument of an outgoing function, and read the returned value of a function.

    Look at the *Overview of the IR building* section for an illustration of what this looks like.

3.  What is the usage of the gen-callingconv TableGen backend?

    This TableGen backend allows you to describe the location of the arguments and results of your functions according to the ABI of your backend. Thanks to the code generated by this TableGen backend, you can use this information independently to read and write to the right locations during the lowering of your calling convention.

    See the *Describing the calling convention* section for more details.

4.  In SDISel, which class is responsible for providing the target hooks to lower the ABI?

    In SDISel, all the hooks responsible for the lowering of the ABI must be implemented in your XXXTargetLowering class.

    More information on how to do that is given in the *Lowering the ABI with SDISel* section.

5.  In FastISel, why do you need to maintain a map of LLVM IR values to virtual registers?

    FastISel is a sub-selector of SDISel. As such, it needs to communicate the values that are used in case it falls back to SDISel.

    You can find more information about how this mapping is set up in practice in the *Lowering the ABI with FastISel* section.

# 16

# Instruction Selection: The Legalization Phase

In instruction selection, the legalization phase is responsible for turning crazy-looking generic **intermediate representations (IRs)** into something that your target can run. For instance, there is little chance that your target can run 3-bit or 13-bit arithmetic natively; instead, these operations have to be emulated on your natively supported operations.

In this chapter, you will learn how to guide the legalization infrastructure of the generic instruction selection frameworks, namely, the **SelectionDAG instruction selection (SDISel)** framework and the **Global instruction selection (GlobalISel)** framework, to support any type of input IR. We will use SDISel and GlobalISel as nouns in the rest of this chapter.

More specifically, you will learn about the following:

- The pieces involved to describe your legalization strategies to the legalization frameworks
- How to implement these strategies in SDISel and GlobalISel

Before going into the general principles of how legalization works, let us point out that the **Fast instruction selection (FastISel)** sub-framework has zero support for legalization. In FastISel, you must hand-code everything in C++ as part of the selection phase (see *Chapter 17*).

As in previous chapters, we will keep using our H2BLB backend as a playground to demonstrate the various concepts. For all the snippets, you can find the implementation with proper tests and comments in the related repository, as described in the next section.

# Technical requirements

Like *Chapter 15*, this chapter builds on what was introduced for instruction selection in *Chapter 14*. As such, this chapter has the same requirements as *Chapter 14*.

All the snippets presented in this chapter live in the `https://github.com/PacktPublishing/LLVM-Code-Generation-by-example` GitHub repository. We call this repository the **companion repository** in the remainder of the chapter.

The changes for this chapter are all included between the Git tags `begin_ch16` and `end_ch16` of the companion repository. If you are not familiar with Git tags, look at *Chapter 9* for a quick explanation of what you can do with them. Throughout the chapter, we also mention specific tags that we created in this repository for you to easily find the relevant commits.

Let's now get started with the concept of legalization in LLVM.

# Legalization overview

In the LLVM infrastructure, legalization is completely driven by the target. This means that the LLVM infrastructure provides some functionalities to do legalization, but it is the target's responsibility to provide the strategies for how these functionalities are used to produce legal code.

> Note
>
> The code produced by the legalization phase is considered legal if you can lower it to an actual sequence of instructions. In other words, the output IR of the legalization phase does not need to be natively supported to be considered legal; it only needs to be supported in your implementation of the selection phase. For instance, if you fancy supplying a complete emulation of the i3 type yourself, you can tell the legalization phase that all the operations on this type are legal but then you will need to be able to handle these operations directly in the selection phase. Therefore, what we call legal code is whatever IR that can be handled by the selection phase.

In practice, for each operation and type pair, you tell the generic infrastructure what action you want the infrastructure to perform with it. Therefore, your job is to funnel all these actions toward the legal code.

Let's take an example before we describe what actions are available to you just to give you an idea of how it works.

Let us say your input IR does a floating-point addition of a half-precision number, meaning that you want to legalize the `fadd half` instruction. Now, assume that you only support 32-bit types and no floating point at all. One strategy could be to extend the 16-bit type to 32-bit so that you land on a storage size that you natively support. Next, you could decide to go with a software emulation of the floating-point arithmetic and convert the instruction to a call. *Table 16.1* shows the steps of such legalization using LLVM IR inputs for simplicity.

| Original code | Widening | Convert to libcall |
|---|---|---|
| `%0 =`<br>`fadd`<br>`half %1,`<br>`%2` | `%t1 = fpext half %1 to float`<br>`%t2 = fpext half %2 to float`<br>`%t0 = fadd float %t1, %t2`<br>`%0 = fptrunc float %to to`<br>`half` | `%t1 = fpext half %1 to float`<br>`%t2 = fpext half %2 to float`<br>`%t0 = call float @float_`<br>`add(float %t1, float %t2)`<br>`%0 = fptrunc float %to to`<br>`half` |

*Table 16.1: Possible legalization steps for a fadd half instruction*

In *Table 16.1*, we see the `fadd half` instruction progressively going to a `fadd float` instruction and then a `call` instruction to an external library. The point of this example is to show you what happens to the surrounding code. You took care of the `fadd half` instruction and, in the process, you created `fpext` and `fptrunc` instructions that you need to handle in your legalization strategies. This type of side effect is unavoidable, and we just wanted you to see it firsthand.

With that said, the expectation is most of these **legalization artifacts** are going to cancel each other out (for instance, a `fptrunc` instruction of a `fpext` instruction is idempotent with these types and can be simplified away, but note that in *Table 16.1*, the artifacts do not cancel each other) as you legalize the chain of computation in your function. When your legalization strategy is complete, the legalization artifacts that survive should be real data movements that your target supports.

Now that you have a general idea of what you need to achieve, let us introduce you to the possible legalization actions that you will need to work with.

# Legalization actions

At its core, the legalization process relies on two main mechanisms that emulate the desired computations. The first emulation mechanism relies on using larger, supported computations – for instance, emulating an `add i13` instruction with an `add i32` instruction. The second emulation mechanism breaks down the computations with smaller, supported computations – for instance, emulating an `add i64` instruction with `add i32` instructions and propagating the `carry` flag.

In practice, you will need to define legalization strategies by listing the actions to apply to different operations and types using the primitives that are summarized in *Table 16.2*.

| Action | Input | Transformed code | Description |
|---|---|---|---|
| Legal | `urem i32` | `urem i32` | Legal operation; nothing to do |
| Narrow scalar | `and i48` | `and i32`<br>`and i16` | Use computations on narrower types |
| Widen scalar | `urem i16` | `urem i32` | Use computations on larger types |

| Action | Input | Transformed code | Description |
|---|---|---|---|
| Fewer elements | `mul <5xi8>` | `mul <2xi8>`<br>`mul <2xi8>`<br>`mul i8` | Break down computation using fewer vector elements |
| More elements | `and <3xi8>` | `and <4 x i8>` | Promote the computation on more vector elements |
| Bitcast | `and <2xi8>` | `and i16` | Compute on a different but same size type |
| Lower | `urem i32` | `udiv i32`<br>`mul i32`<br>`sub i32` | Break down the computation into simpler instructions |
| Libcall | `urem i32` | `call __umodsi3` | Replace the operation with a call to a library |
| Custom | `urem i32` | `fancy sequence` | Replace the operation with a custom sequence |

*Table 16.2: Legalization actions and their results*

In *Table 16.2*, the leftmost column shows the name of the legalization action as you would find it in the LLVM code base. The *Input* column shows an example of instruction in pseudo-LLVM IR that, if considered illegal and flagged as requiring the legalization action of the first column, would be transformed in the sequence shown in the *Transformed code* column. The *Transformed code* column does not show the legalization artifacts that are required to produce a valid sequence of code.

For instance, when using the *Widen scalar* action, the input arguments of the operations need to be extended to the desired wider type (for instance, with a sign-extension or floating-point extension instruction) and the result of the widen instruction needs to be narrowed back down to the original type (for instance, with a truncate operation).

> **Note**
>
> Some of the actions depicted in *Table 16.2* are mixed under a different name in SDISel. For instance, the actions named *Narrow scalar* and *Lower* are grouped under the name **Expand** in SDISel. In SDISel, *Expand* means producing a simpler version of the input computation, and simpler may mean different sequences of instructions or smaller types. Likewise, the *More elements* and *Widen scalar* actions are grouped under the **Promote** name, which reads as using a large type to legalize.

Generally speaking, the legalization artifacts produced by each strategy depend on the source and destination types as well as the instruction being legalized. Typically, the legalization artifacts are as follows:

- **Bitcast:** To change types while keeping the same bitwidth
- **Extension:** To widen a type (sign-, zero-, or floating-point extensions)
- **Truncation:** To narrow a type (including floating-point truncation)
- **Merge values/build vector:** To produce intermediate vector types or larger vector types
- **Unmerge values:** To deconstruct vector types
- **Undef:** To produce values to inject in empty vector lanes
- **Bitwise manipulation/loads and stores:** To extract a continuous sequence of bits (for instance, when breaking down a 48-bit value into a 32-bit and 16-bit value)

For instance, looking at the *More elements* action in *Table 16.2*, the full sequence of instructions, including the legalization artifacts, would turn the `%res = and <3 x i8> %a, %b` instruction into the following pseudo-LLVM IR sequence:

```
%a0, %a1, %a2 = unmerge_values <3 x i8> %a
%moreEltA = build_vector %a0, %a1, %a2, i8 undef
%b0, %b1, %b2 = unmerge_values <3 x i8> %b
%moreEltB = build_vector %b0, %b1, %b2, i8 undef
%moreEltRes = and <4 x i8> %moreEltA, %moreEltB
%res0, %res1, %res2, %res3 = unmerge_values <4 x i8> %moreEltRes
%res = build_vector %res0, %res1, %res2
```

In this snippet, you can see that, at the boundaries, the inputs and the output of the original instruction did not change. The `%a`, `%b`, and `%res` variables are all still mapped on the `<3 x i8>` type. Inside the legalized sequence of instructions, you can see that the vector type has been widened to the `<4 x i8>` type by deconstructing and reconstructing a vector with the original lanes and an undefined element.

The point of this example is to show you the type of legalization artifacts that you may have to deal with.

While the number of legalization artifacts you must support may sound scary, remember that these artifacts are going to cancel each other out as you legalize your code and they should be optimized away as no-op (idempotent operations) by the generic infrastructure. In the end, you must think about where this chain of legalization artifacts originates and finishes for a given chain of computations. When you think about it this way, you realize that you need to be extra careful about how you handle the lowering of your ABI and your loads and stores. These are the points where values ultimately appear and disappear.

In this section, you saw how the legalization phase is articulated around the concept of legalization actions. In the next sections, you will see in practice how to use these actions in SDISel and GlobalISel. Depending on which selector you decide to implement, you can read just the related section since both implementations are completely independent.

# Legalization in SDISel

The legalization phase in SDISel adds another dimension: the *concept of legal types*. The core idea behind this is that you describe to the framework all the types that you natively support and SDISel will figure out how illegal types will be emulated on the legal ones.

> Reminder
>
> The concept of legalization does not exist in FastISel since you must handle the translation from the LLVM IR to the Machine IR in one go in this sub-framework. In other words, when selecting instruction through the FastISel sub-framework, you cannot leverage any of the legalization infrastructure that SDISel provides.

This concept of legal type has a side effect: as soon as you tell SDISel that a type is legal, all the operations on this type are assumed to be legal as well. For instance, imagine that your target can do 64-bit integer additions but not 64-bit integer multiplications. If you mark the 64-bit integer type legal, you must let SDISel know that all 64-bit multiplications are not legal by providing legalization actions for all of them.

The way this is articulated is that SDISel performs the legalization phase in two main steps:

1. **Type legalization:** This step is responsible for bringing all the illegal types to legal types.
2. **Operation legalization:** This step takes the resulting operations on legal types and applies all the legalization actions that you set up.

This approach allows you to focus on providing legalization actions on legal types. The downside is that you have little control over how the types are legalized.

The description of the legal types and legalization actions are all handled in the TargetLowering class of your backend. The constructor of this class is responsible for setting up this information for a pair of TargetMachine and Subtarget instances. The Subtarget instance is particularly important because it carries the features that are available on the actual processor you are compiling for. For instance, when you compile for an X86 target, depending on which processor your code is intended to run on, you have access to different ISA extensions. For instance, you may or may not support 512-bit vectors. This will affect your legal types and legalization actions.

Let us see how you implement this description in practice.

## Describing your legal types

To describe your legal types, you need to call the addRegisterClass method for each of them from your TargetLowering class constructor.

When you are done registering all your legal types, you need to call the computeRegisterProperties method to finalize the registration process and compute all the information that SDISel may need.

To give an example of what we just described, here is a snippet of the constructor of our
H2BLBTargetLowering class:

```
H2BLBTargetLowering::H2BLBTargetLowering(const TargetMachine &TM,
                                         const H2BLBSubtarget &STI)
    : TargetLowering(TM), Subtarget(STI) {
  addRegisterClass(MVT::i16, &H2BLB::GPR16RegClass);
  addRegisterClass(MVT::i32, &H2BLB::GPR32RegClass);
  ...
  computeRegisterProperties(Subtarget.getRegisterInfo());
```

In this snippet, you see that we have to provide a valid register class (as described in your
XXXRegisterInfo.td file) for each legal type that we register. You can find this snippet at the commit
tagged sdisel-lowerret_ch15 in the companion repository (yes, this is tagged ch15, because we had
to sprinkle a little bit of legalization to get going!).

There are additional methods that you can override to influence how the type legalization steps run,
but we will not detail them. You can, for instance, override the TargetLoweringBase::getPreferr
edVectorAction method to change how particular vector types are legalized. For instance, you can
override this method if when you encounter the <2 x i8> type, you would rather legalize it to the <4
x i8> type instead of the <2 x i16> type.

The next step is to describe the legalization actions.

## Describing your legalization actions

As already mentioned, the description of your legalization actions happens in the constructor of your
TargetLowering class. To specify an action, you need to call the related setXXXAction method for the
type of operation you want to legalize, where XXX is the type of operation (for instance, TruncStore)
or just Operation. In other words, you describe the legalization action for most instructions using
setOperationAction, but some instructions have their own flavor, such as a truncating store node
(identifiable programmatically by using the StoreSDNode:: isTruncatingStore method).

The setXXXAction family of methods describes an action using the following:

- An enumeration value, defined by the TargetLoweringBase::LegalizeAction enumeration
- An operation opcode (using the ISD enumeration values)
- A type (using the MVT enumeration values)

The enumeration value for the action maps to what we described in *Table 16.2*.

The following snippet gives you an example of actions that we use in our H2BLB backend:

```
setOperationAction(ISD::FADD, MVT::f32, LibCall);
setTruncStoreAction(MVT::i32, MVT::i16, Expand);
setOperationAction(ISD::MUL, MVT::i32, Custom);
```

In our backend, all three f32, i32, and i16 types are legal, so we have to explicitly teach SDISel how to legalize the instructions that operate on these types and that we do not support directly.

In this snippet, we first describe that for floating-point additions (ISD::FADD opcode) on a single precision type (the MVT::f32 type), we use a library call to implement the functionality. This action will automatically lower all the related SDNode instances into a sequence of instructions that calls, by default, the libm library implementation.

If you want to change which function is called by a LibCall lowering, you can use the setLibcallName method.

Next, we describe the legalization action on a truncating store when the input type is i32 and the stored type is i16. Truncating stores are not represented by a separate opcode; instead, they are just a special flavor of the ISD::STORE node, which is why you cannot use a regular setOperationAction method on them. What this snippet does is tell SDISel that when a truncating store is encountered, we want it to be lowered in a simpler sequence (Expand). For this operation, the simpler sequence consists of a TRUNC node followed by a STORE node.

Finally, our last call to the setOperationAction method tells SDISel that when we encounter a multiplication (ISD::MUL opcode) on the i32 type, we use a custom lowering (the Custom legalization action value). The custom lowering is implemented separately and is the topic of our next section.

Before we go there, you can find examples of setting legalization actions in the commits tagged sdisel-scalarize-lgl_ch16 and sdisel-truncstore-lgl_ch16 for Expand actions, sdisel-libcall-lgl_ch16 for LibCall actions, and sdisel-custom-lgl_ch16 for Custom actions, all in the companion repository. Generally speaking, this is mechanical and there is nothing surprising here. The challenge for you is to discover how you want to legalize each of the operations.

Let us now show you how to set up your custom lowering.

## Implementing a custom legalization action

Custom legalization actions allow you to completely take control of how an operation gets legalized by providing your own C++ implementation.

You already saw in the previous section how to declare a custom action using the setOperationAction family of methods. When you set a custom action, SDISel will automatically call the LowerOperation method of your TargetLowering instance for the related pair of operations and types.

Therefore, your job is to set up your custom lowering from within this method.

For instance, the following snippet demonstrates how we custom legalize ISD::MUL nodes for our H2BLB target where we try to map them to our widening multiplication operation:

```
SDValue H2BLBTargetLowering::LowerOperation(SDValue Op,
                                            SelectionDAG &DAG) const {
  switch (Op.getOpcode()) {
  ...
  case ISD::MUL:
```

```
        return lowerMUL(Op, DAG);
    }
}
```

In this snippet, we look at the opcode of the provided SDValue instance and call another method to custom lower our ISD::MUL node.

The custom method looks like the following:

```
SDValue H2BLBTargetLowering::lowerMUL(SDValue Op, SelectionDAG &DAG) const {
    assert(Op.getOpcode() == ISD::MUL);
    ... // Check if we can custom lower ISD::MUL.
    if (PlainLHS.getValueType() != MVT::i16 ||
        PlainRHS.getValueType() != MVT::i16)
      return SDValue();
    unsigned Opcode =
        isSigned ? H2BLBISD::WIDENING_SMUL : H2BLBISD::WIDENING_UMUL;
    SDValue NewVal = DAG.getNode(Opcode, SDLoc(Op), ValTy, PlainLHS, PlainRHS);
    return NewVal;
}
```

In this truncated snippet (see the commit tagged sdisel-custom-lgl_ch16 in the companion repository for the full snippet), we check whether we can apply our custom legalization for the current node (the Op variable). If we cannot, we return an empty SDValue instance. This tells SDISel that the custom lowering failed.

> **Note**
>
> It is okay to fail to custom lower an operation but be aware that then SDISel will use the Expand strategy for that node, if that fails too, it will use the LibCall strategy and if that fails too, it will abort. This cascade of actions is specific to custom-lowered operations and is not parameterizable. The Expand and LibCall strategies apply the actions that you already know, so make sure to either always succeed in your custom lowering or make sure that the Expand and/or LibCall strategies will do something sensible in the cases you do not support. In any case, make sure to write unit cases for all these cases!

When your custom legalization works, you must return the SDValue instance that represents the equivalent of the input node. SDISel will automatically update all the uses of the original node with your new node; therefore, the number of values that you produce and their types must match the original node.

> **Note**
>
> During custom legalization, if you produce illegal types with opaque nodes, meaning nodes that SDISel does not know (such as `H2BLBISD::WIDENING_SMUL` in the previous snippet since this is a target-specific opcode), you will need to implement the `TargetLowering::ReplaceNodeResults` and/or `TargetLowering::LowerOperationWrapper` methods to handle the type legalization manually. You can find examples of how to implement this in almost all the LLVM backends.

Remember that when you do custom legalization, you likely will need to introduce a custom `SDNode` opcode, as you learned in *Chapter 15*.

In this section, you learned that SDISel breaks down the legalization phase into two phases: the type legalization and the operation legalization. The first phase allows you to narrow down the types that you need to support, and in the second phase, you need to provide legalization actions for all the operations to produce legal operations. You then discovered which **application programming interfaces** (**APIs**) you should use to describe your legal types and the legalization actions and saw an example of how this works.

Let us now see how to do the legalization in GlobalISel.

# Legalization in GlobalISel

In GlobalISel, all the legalization decisions and the implementation of the custom legalization are described with your target-specific instance of the `LegalizerInfo` class.

Your job is to implement that class and to connect it to your `Subtarget` class for the `Legalizer` pass to automatically find it. The connection in your `Subtarget` class simply consists of overriding the `getLegalizerInfo` method:

```
class H2BLBSubtarget : public H2BLBGenSubtargetInfo {
  ...
  std::unique_ptr<LegalizerInfo> Legalizer;
public:
  H2BLBSubtarget::H2BLBSubtarget(/*...*/ {
    Legalizer.reset(new H2BLBLegalizerInfo(*this));
  }
  const LegalizerInfo *getLegalizerInfo() const override {
    return Legalizer.get();
  }
}`
```

In this snippet, we create an `H2BLBLegalizerInfo` instance, our implementation of the `LegalizerInfo` class, in the constructor of our `Subtarget` class and we provide it in the overridden getter.

Focusing on the implementation of your `LegalizerInfo` class, you need to describe all the legalization actions for all the generic `MachineInstr` opcode within the constructor of your `LegalizerInfo` class and then call the `getLegacyLegalizerInfo().computeTables()` method when you are done.

Unlike SDISel, there is no concept of *legal type* in GlobalISel. Instead, you describe your actions in terms of pairs of operation and type. Anything that is not covered by your actions is considered illegal.

At this point, you may be wondering how you can describe all the actions for a massive space of types (for instance, starting with the `i1` type all the way to the `i1942652` type, the smallest and biggest integer types supported by LLVM) and operations with something that looks like a static description. After all, the SDISel approach makes the legal type finite by pinning it down to a few types and making the description of the actions for this space manageable.

The answer is in how the legalization description works in GlobalISel. GlobalISel offers a programmatic way to describe your legalization actions. For instance, unlike SDISel, you can describe that any integer type bigger than `i32` on an integer addition needs to be lowered to a simpler sequence.

Let us see that in action!

## Describing your legalization actions with the LegalizeRuleSet class

To describe your legalization action, you program `LegalizeRuleSet` instances in your `LegalizerInfo` class.

The way it works is you tell your `LegalizerInfo` class that you want to register a new set of actions (or rules) for a specific (list of) opcode(s) and this class will give you a handle on a `LegalizeRuleSet` instance that will be applied to the given opcode(s) using the `getActionDefinitionsBuilder` method.

Then, you configure this `LegalizeRuleSet` instance using the methods provided by this class.

Under the hood, the actions that you describe compose the basic actions that we described in *Table 16.2*. For instance, the `scalarize` method tells the `LegalizeRuleSet` instance that when you encounter a vector type, you want to break it down into individual lanes. This action is just an extreme version of the *Fewer elements* action described in that table, where fewer elements means exactly one element.

The `LegalizeRuleSet` class has a rich set of methods that makes it very powerful and flexible. Additionally, it is well documented (look at its Doxygen page; see *Chapter 3* if you need help with that).

Let us give you an example of what it looks like:

```
H2BLBLegalizerInfo::H2BLBLegalizerInfo(const H2BLBSubtarget &ST) : ST(ST) {
  const LLT p0 = LLT::pointer(0, 16);
  ... // more LLT definitions.
  getActionDefinitionsBuilder({TargetOpcode::G_LOAD, TargetOpcode::G_STORE})
      .legalForTypesWithMemDesc({{s8, p0, s8, 8},
                                 {s16, p0, s8, 8}, // anyext/truncstore
                                 {s16, p0, s16, 8},
                                 {s32, p0, s32, 8}})
```

```
        .clampScalar(0, s16, s32)
        .lowerIf([=](const LegalityQuery &Query) {
          return Query.Types[0].isScalar() &&
                 Query.Types[0] != Query.MMODescrs[0].MemoryTy;
        })
        .legalIf([=](const LegalityQuery &Query) {
          TypeSize Size = Query.Types[0].getSizeInBits();
          return Size == 16 || Size == 32;
        })
        .scalarize(0)
        .lower();
    ...
    getLegacyLegalizerInfo().computeTables();
```

In this snippet, you see the overall structure of the code that we described: we get a `LegalizeRuleSet` object to describe our actions for our load and store instructions (`G_LOAD` and `G_STORE` opcodes) with the `getActionDefinitionsBuilder` method. Then, we program that rule set using its `legalForTypesWithMemDesc` and `legalIf` methods, and finally, we call `getLegacyLegalizerInfo().computeTables()`.

Zooming in on the methods of the `LegalizeRuleSet` object, here is what each of them does:

- `legalForTypesWithMemDesc`: This marks as legal all the types that match the provided `Legali tyPredicates::TypePairAndMemDesc` instances. An instance of this class describes a concrete type, an address type, a stored type, and the alignment of the address. For instance, the {`s16`, `p0`, `s16`, `8`} tuple means that a 16-bit scalar type (`s16`, concrete type) is loaded from or stored to the address space 0 (`p0`, address type) with a memory slot matching a 16-bit scalar (`s16`, stored type) and unaligned access (aligned on 8 bits, each byte-aligned, meaning unaligned). Similarly, the {`s16`, `p0`, `s8`, `8`} tuple means the operation using that type is reading (for the `G_LOAD` opcode, and respectively, writing for the `G_STORE` opcode) a 16-bit scalar value from address space 0 from (respectively, to) a memory slot of 8-bit. This latter tuple describes, respectively, an extending load (read 8-bit from memory and get a 16-bit value in register) for the `G_LOAD` opcode and a truncating store (write 8-bit to memory from a 16-bit value in register) for the `G_STORE` opcode.

- `clampScalar`: This method allows you to specify the range of scalar types that can fit in an instance of the related instruction. The way you read the parameters (here, `0`, `s16`, `s32`) is the type at the given **type index** (more on this in a second) must be between the given two scalar types. The type index is something prevalent in how you describe your legalization rule in the `LegalizeRuleSet` class. It maps to the index in the list of types required to describe a generic instruction. For instance, a `G_ADD` instruction has one type, because its result and its two arguments must have the same type. Hence, for this operation, there is only one type index possible: `0`. Now, if you look at a `G_SEXT` instruction, you need two types: one to describe the input type and one to describe the sign-extended type, hence, two types – so the possible type indexes are 0 (output type) and 1 (input type). You can see the number of supported types and their index for each opcode by looking at the `OutOperandList` and `InOperandList` values in their target description in the `llvm/include/llvm/Target/GenericOpcodes.td` file. In these fields, you should see `type0`, `type1`, and so on, and the digit at the end of each `typeX` keyword is the type index to use in the C++ code.

- `lowerIf`: This applies the lower action (replaces the original instruction with a sequence of simpler instructions) if the given `LegalityPredicate` instance returns `true`. The `LegalityPredicate` object represents functions that take a `LegalityQuery` object as a parameter and return a Boolean that tells whether the related action (*lower* in this case) needs to be applied. A `LegalityQuery` object holds the information about the instance of the instruction that is currently being legalized. Specifically, it holds the opcode of the current operation, its list of types, and for memory operation, some information on the memory descriptions.

- `legalIf`: This is similar to `lowerIf` in that it uses the `LegalityPredicate` object mechanism to determine when to apply the action, but the action itself does nothing except mark the current operation as legal.

- `scalarize`: This method triggers the scalarization of the current operation if the given type index refers to a vector type.

- `lower`: This method triggers the lowering of the current operation. The sequence of instructions produced by a lowering action is operation-specific, for instance, a `G_UREM` operation will be lowered differently from a `G_FNEG` operation.

To step back a little bit, when describing your rule set, consider the following:

- The `LegalizeRuleSet` class holds on the `LegalityPredicate` instance that you attach to each action.

- The various helper functions allow you to compose `LegalityPredicate` instances to produce new, more powerful, ones. For instance, the `LegalityPredicates::any` function allows you to specify an arbitrary number of `LegalityPredicate` instances and apply the related legalization action if any of them returns `true`.

- The `LegalizeMutation` instances allow you to further customize the related legalization action. For instance, you can apply a `lower` action while increasing the number of elements of a vector type to the next power of 2 using the `lowerIf` action with the `moreElementsToNextPow2` `LegalizeMutation` instance.

By composing these classes, you can create extremely powerful legalization rules. The rules that we showed as examples are basic, but you can find elaborated examples in the AMDGPU (in the `llvm/lib/Target/AMDGPU/AMDGPULegalizerInfo.cpp` file) and AArch64 (the `llvm/lib/Target/AArch64/GISel/AArch64LegalizerInfo.cpp` file) backends.

Finally, you can find a breakdown of the previous example and more in the companion repository at the commits tagged `gisel-legalizerinfo_ch16`, `gisel-lower-memop_ch16`, `gisel-vector-memop_ch16`, and `sdisel-libcall-lgl_ch16`.

Let us now cover the one action that requires a bit more work, custom legalization.

# Custom legalization in GlobalISel

Implementing custom legalization in GlobalISel is similar to SDISel. You start by telling `LegalizeRuleSet` that you want to custom-legalize the related operation using one of the `customXXX` methods, where `XXX` can be `If`, `For`, and so on. Then, you need to override the `LegalizerInfo::legalizeCustom` method.

Here is an example of what it looks like with the `G_MUL` instruction in our H2BLB backend.

First, we define the custom rule set in our `H2BLBLegalizerInfo` constructor:

```
getActionDefinitionsBuilder(TargetOpcode::G_MUL)
    .customIf([=](const LegalityQuery &Query) {
      const auto &DstTy = Query.Types[0];
      return !DstTy.isVector() && DstTy.getSizeInBits() == 32;
    });
```

In this snippet, we tell the `LegalizeRuleSet` instance returned by the `getActionDefinitionsBuilder` method that we use a custom legalization action when the type of a `G_MUL` instruction is a scalar (that is, not a vector) and its size is 32 bits.

Then, we need to provide the implementation of this custom legalization in the `H2BLBLegalizerInf oo::legalizeCustom` method:

```
bool H2BLBLegalizerInfo::legalizeCustom(
    LegalizerHelper &Helper, MachineInstr &MI,
    LostDebugLocObserver &LocObserver) const {
  MachineIRBuilder &MIRBuilder = Helper.MIRBuilder;
  MachineRegisterInfo &MRI = *MIRBuilder.getMRI();
  GISelChangeObserver &Observer = Helper.Observer;
  switch (MI.getOpcode()) {
  ...
  case TargetOpcode::G_MUL:
    return legalizeMul(MI, MRI, MIRBuilder, Observer);
  }
  llvm_unreachable("expected switch to return");
}
```

In this snippet, we collect a few instances of different objects that we are going to use in the method that we dedicated to the handling of the custom legalization of the `G_MUL` instruction. The only new things for you in this snippet are the `GISelChangeObserver` and `LegalizerHelper` instances. The former is an object that you use to inform the generic legalization infrastructure about the changes you are making to the IR. The latter is a helper class that features methods that can help you perform legalization actions such as the `reduceLoadStoreWidth` method, which you can use to break down a load or store into smaller pieces.

Finally, the implementation of our `legalizeMul` method is a regular manipulation of the Machine IR:

```
bool H2BLBLegalizerInfo::legalizeMul(MachineInstr &MI, MachineRegisterInfo &MRI,
                                     MachineIRBuilder &MIRBuilder,
                                     GISelChangeObserver &Observer) const {
  assert(MI.getOpcode() == TargetOpcode::G_MUL);
  Register LHS = MI.getOperand(1).getReg();
  Register PlainLHS;
  ...
  if (mi_match(LHS, MRI, m_GSExt(m_Reg(PlainLHS))) &&
      mi_match(RHS, MRI, m_GSExt(m_Reg(PlainRHS))))
    isSigned = true;
  ...
  const TargetInstrInfo &TII = *ST.getInstrInfo();
  unsigned Opcode = isSigned ? H2BLB::WIDENING_SMUL : H2BLB::WIDENING_UMUL;
  Observer.changingInstr(MI);
  MI.setDesc(TII.get(Opcode));
  ...
  constrainSelectedInstRegOperands(MI, TII, *MRI.getTargetRegisterInfo(),
                                   *ST.getRegBankInfo());
  Observer.changedInstr(MI);
  return true;
}
```

The details of this snippet are not particularly important, but we wanted to highlight a couple of things with this. First, you can use the `mi_match` utilities (declared in the `llvm/include/llvm/CodeGen/GlobalISel/MIPatternMatch.h` file) to pattern-match sequences of instructions. In this case, the `mi_match(LHS, MRI, m_GSExt(m_Reg(PlainLHS)))` statement assigns to the `PlainLHS` variable the register argument of a `G_SEXT` instruction if the definition of the `LHS` register is a `G_SEXT` instruction. Note that SDISel offers similar capabilities, since February 2024, through the `sd_match` utilities.

The second thing we wanted to point out is how to use the `GISelChangeObserver` instance. In this snippet, you can see that we notify the observer before starting to morph the `G_MUL` instruction into our final instruction using the `changingInstr` method and notify it again when we are done by using the `changedInstr` method. This is important because the observer propagates this information to all its listeners and this mechanism is used, for instance, to keep the optional CSE map that can be set up in the `MachineIRBuilder` instances updated.

The final thing we wanted to point out is the call to the `constrainSelectedInstRegOperands` method. You need to call this method when you morph a generic instruction into a target-specific one. This method sets all register classes for all the operands and potentially creates copies if the operands of the instructions are not compatible with such register classes. The takeaway is that this is required to produce a well-formed target-specific `MachineInstr` instance.

You can find the full snippet of this example at the commit tagged `gisel-custom-lgl_ch16` in the companion repository.

In this section, you learned how to compose the legalization actions through the API of the `LegalizeRuleSets` class to describe how to handle illegal instructions for your target, and you saw that you need to gather all these rules under a target-specific version of the `LegalizerInfo` class to guide the legalization phase, handled by the `Legalizer` pass, of GlobalISel.

# Summary

In this chapter, you learned how to implement the legalization phase of your instruction selection pipeline. You saw how both SDISel and GlobalISel use legalization actions to describe the transformations that need to happen to go from illegal to legal IR.

You learned that SDISel relies on the concept of legal type to guide the legalization decisions while GlobalISel drives all its legalization decisions through precise legalization actions.

Finally, you learned how to implement each of these legalization actions and, in particular, the most advanced one, the custom legalization for both these frameworks.

What you learned in this chapter is the basis of how to do legalization in LLVM. At this point, you know the APIs and the principles behind them, but writing these legalization strategies is the hard part. We are confident that with your now solid background, you will be able to navigate what is ahead of you. As always, use the existing backends as examples to see how things are done, starting with the H2BLB backend in the companion repository.

In our next chapter, we will cover the last stage of the instruction selection pipeline and some of the related infrastructure.

# Quiz time

Now that you have completed reading this chapter, try answering the following questions to test your knowledge:

1. What is the goal of legalization?

   The goal of the legalization phase is to emulate constructs that are not natively supported in your backend with instructions that are natively supported in your backend.

   See the *Legalization overview* section for more details.

2. How do you drive the legalization decisions?

   You drive the legalization decisions by providing the generic frameworks with a set of rules that tell them the legalization action that needs to happen for a pair of opcode and type.

   See the *Legalization actions*, *Describing your legalization actions*, and *Describing your legalization actions with the LegalizeRuleSet class* sections for an overview of the legalization actions, how you use them in SDISel, and how you use them in GlobalISel, respectively.

3.  In SDISel, what does the concept of legal type capture?

    The concept of legal type captures the types that your backend supports natively.

    More details on the implications of this are in the *Legalization in SDISel* section.

4.  What legalization action can you use if the generic framework does not feature what you need?

    If none of the regular legalization actions does what you need, you can use the `Custom` legalization action to open the legalization to custom C++ implementations.

    More information on how to use this type of action is in the *Implementing a custom legalization action* and *Custom legalization in GlobalISel* sections for SDISel and GlobalISel, respectively.

5.  In GlobalISel, how do you manage the potential explosion of legalization rules given the lack of a legal type concept?

    You can control the explosion of legalization rules by leveraging two things. First, the `LegalizeRuleSet` class provides a rich set of APIs that allows it to programmatically cover all the types. Second, as long as you carefully manage how types are produced at the boundaries of the `def-use` chains, the legalization artifacts should cancel each other out, limiting the amount of code you have to support.

    Look at the *Describing your legalization actions with the LegalizeRuleSet class* section for more details.

# 17

# Instruction Selection: The Selection Phase and Beyond

The instruction selection phase, or selection phase for short, is the last phase of the instruction selection pipeline. It is responsible for translating the generic, yet legal, **intermediate representation (IR)** used by the instruction selection framework to the target-specific incantation of the Machine IR.

In LLVM, this translation can match sequences of instructions to produce highly optimized code right off the bat.

In this chapter, you will learn how to do the following:

- Describe the matching of these sequences of instructions with patterns
- Integrate this matching into all the instruction selection frameworks – that is, the **SelectionDAG instruction selection (SDISel)** framework, the **Fast instruction selection (FastISel)** framework, and the **Global instruction selection (GlobalISel)** framework
- Go beyond these patterns

Aside from the pure selection phase, we also use this chapter to wrap up all the concepts around the instruction selection frameworks and will teach you how to do the following:

- Implement the register bank selection phase that is mandatory in GlobalISel.
- Add optimizations in your instruction selection pipeline.
- Tidy up (or finalize, in LLVM parlance) the MachineFunction instance that you produced so that this instance can be consumed by the later optimization passes. This process is mandatory for all selectors.
- Debug your instruction selectors.

Like all the chapters that covered an aspect of the instruction selection pipeline, this chapter demonstrates the concepts introduced in our H2BLB.

# Technical requirements

This chapter has the same requirements as *Chapter 14*.

Similarly, all the snippets presented in this chapter are available in the `https://github.com/PacktPublishing/LLVM-Code-Generation-by-example` GitHub repository. We call this repository the **companion repository** in the remainder of the chapter.

The changes for this chapter are all included between the Git tags `begin_ch17` and `end_ch17` of the companion repository. If you are not familiar with Git tags, look at *Chapter 9* for a quick explanation of what you can do with them. Throughout the chapter, we also mention specific tags that we created in this repository for you to easily find the relevant commits.

Before we get to the instruction selection phase, we need to address the `RegBankSelect` pass, which is a mandatory phase for GlobalISel between the legalization and the instruction selection phase.

# Register bank selection

The register bank selection phase, represented by the `RegBankSelect` pass, is a mandatory pass in GlobalISel. This phase is responsible for assigning register banks to all the virtual registers of the current `MachineFunction` instance. If you are not using GlobalISel, you can skip this section. However, you may still want to read through it to see what GlobalISel has to offer on something that SDISel cannot do.

## The goal of the register bank selection

The concept of register bank selection came with GlobalISel and solved the problem of optimizing cross-register bank copies. A cross-register bank copy is an instruction that cannot be coalesced (removed) during register allocation because the source and destination of the copy live on different register files or banks. For instance, on an architecture with **general purpose registers (GPRs)** and **vector registers (VRs)**, the GPRs may be used for integer operations and the VRs may be used for vector type operations and a cross-register bank copy would exist any time we go from one type of operation to another. This can happen when you insert an integer value into a vector value or bitcast a vector value into an integer value in the LLVM IR, for instance. The type involved in such copies depends on the underlying architecture. In other words, different architectures will introduce cross-register bank copies with different types.

In SDISel, cross-register bank copies are not optimized at all. Types pin a register class (and by extension, a register bank) period. For instance, if you load a vector value, you get a VR; if you load an integer value, you get a GPR. Now, if that value gets bitcast right away and for some reason that bitcast was not folded with the load, you get a cross-register bank copy.

GlobalISel solves this by scanning how instructions are used, and then it assigns and potentially rewrites the operations to avoid the cross-register bank copy. *Table 17.1* illustrates an example of what such rewrites could look like.

| Original code | Cross-register bank copy free code |
|---|---|
| ```<br>define i32 @foo(i32 %a, i32 %b) {<br>  %vec = insertelement <2 x i32><br>undef, i32 %a, i32 0<br>  %vec1 = insertelement <2 x i32><br>%vec, i32 %b, i32 1<br>  %masked = and <2 x i32> %vec1,<br><i32 127, i32 127><br>  %maskedA = extractelement <2 x<br>i32> %masked, i32 0<br>  %maskedB = extractelement <2 x<br>i32> %masked, i32 1<br>  %res = add i32 %maskedA, %maskedB<br>  ret i32 %res<br>}<br>``` | ```<br>define i32 @foo(i32 %a, i32 %b) {<br><br><br><br><br>  %maskedA = and i32 %a, 127<br>  %maskedB = and i32 %b, 127<br><br><br><br><br>  %res = add i32 %maskedA,<br>%maskedB<br>  ret i32 %res<br>}<br>``` |

*Table 17.1: Code rewritten to avoid cross-register bank copies*

If vector types use one type of register bank and integer types use another type of register bank, on the left-hand side of *Table 17.1*, the LLVM IR contains at least two cross-register bank copies: one to build the vector value (the two insertelement instructions) and one to deconstruct the vector value (the two extractelement instructions). These cross-register bank copies may be avoided by scalarizing the and instruction. This scalarization produces two and instructions, which may be more costly than the original vector and instruction; however, since the cross-register bank copies have been eliminated, the new sequence is more efficient. Of course, this type of transformation is driven by a cost model.

This example demonstrates what the register bank selection phase can achieve. However, for the purpose of this chapter, we will focus on having a simple register bank assignment and we will not explore how to do the rewrites. In other words, we will show you have to implement the mandatory part of the register bank selection phase. You can look at the AArch64 backend in the LLVM infrastructure to see how to achieve these rewrites.

## Describing the register banks

To describe your register bank, you must instantiate records of the RegisterBank TableGen class and then use the related target description with the gen-register-bank TableGen backend to produce the code used in LLVM.

The RegisterBank TableGen class takes a name and the list of register classes that are covered by this register bank.

Here is what it looks like for our H2BLB backend:

```
def GPRBRegBank : RegisterBank<"GPRB", [GPR32, GPR16sp]>;
```

Our backend has only one register bank and it covers all our register classes. Note that you do not have to list all the register classes, only the largest one because the TableGen backend automatically pulls all the smaller register classes. For instance, in this example, we said that our register bank covers the GPR16sp register class but we did not say that it covers the GPR16 register class. This is because the GPR16sp register class is a super set of all the registers contained in the GPR16 register class.

Now, you must integrate the produced code into your implementation file. Let us assume you created a header (.h) file and a .cpp file.

In the header file, you will pull the code that is guarded by the GET_REGBANK_DECLARATIONS macro, and in the .cpp file, the code guarded by the GET_TARGET_REGBANK_IMPL macro.

Finally, you need to integrate the code guarded by the GET_TARGET_REGBANK_CLASS macro in an XXXGenRegisterBankInfo class in your header file:

```
class H2BLBGenRegisterBankInfo : public RegisterBankInfo {
protected:
#define GET_TARGET_REGBANK_CLASS
#include "H2BLBGenRegisterBank.inc"
};
```

> 💡 **Quick tip**: Enhance your coding experience with the **AI Code Explainer** and **Quick Copy** features. Open this book in the next-gen Packt Reader. Click the **Copy** button **(1)** to quickly copy code into your coding environment, or click the **Explain** button **(2)** to get the AI assistant to explain a block of code to you.
>
> ```
>                                              Copy      Explain
> function calculate(a, b) {
>     return {sum: a + b};                      1          2
> };
> ```
>
> 🔒 **The next-gen Packt Reader** is included for free with the purchase of this book. Unlock it by scanning the QR code below or visiting https://www.packtpub.com/unlock/9781837637782.
>
>

In this snippet, we create the placeholder for the code generated by TableGen.

Next, let us see how this code is used to build your XXXRegisterBankInfo class.

# Implementing your RegisterBankInfo class

The RegBankSelect pass relies on the Subtarget class of your backend to provide an instance of the RegisterBankInfo class. This class should inherit from the XXXGenRegisterBankInfo class that you partially generated with TableGen in the previous section.

This RegisterBankInfo class is responsible for describing how the operands of each instruction are mapped to the register banks and how the register classes map to the register banks. In practice, this means that you must implement two methods – getInstrMapping and getRegBankFromRegClass – to fulfill these requirements.

The getIntrMapping method is the hardest to implement because you must understand the concept captured by the InstructionMapping class first since this is what this method returns.

The InstructionMapping class represents a particular register bank assignment for every register operand of an instruction. It also encapsulates a cost and an identifier that are used in the cost model of the RegBankSelect pass, but for the purpose of this chapter, we will ignore them.

The assignment of each register operand is represented with the ValueMapping class, which is a wrapper around an array of PartialMapping instances. To put it simply, a value may span several registers, and this is what is captured with this array. For instance, a value with the <2 x i32> vector type may be mapped on one 64-bit register (for instance, a VR) or two 32-bit registers (for instance, two GPRs).

The PartialMapping class essentially represents how the bits of the original value are mapped across the partial values. Using the <2 x i32> value, the vector mapping would look like one PartialMapping instance – {0, 64, VR} – and the GPR mapping would look like two PartialMapping instances – {0, 32, GPR} and {32, 32, GPR} – where the first element of the tuple is the index of the first bit mapped in the original value, followed by the number of bits mapped from the first index, and finally the register bank used. Therefore, in the first case, we mapped the whole 64-bit value in one go, and in the second case, we first map the 32-bit low half and then the 32-bit high half (that is, starting at the $32^{nd}$ bit).

To help grasp how the InstructionMapping, ValueMapping, and PartialMapping classes work together, look at *Figure 17.1*:

```
%0:_(<2 x s32>) = G_AND %1, %2
```

| Vector InstructionMapping | | | | Scalar InstructionMapping | | |
|---|---|---|---|---|---|---|
| Operand index | #Partial values | PartialMapping | | Operand index | #Partial values | PartialMapping |
| 0 | 1 | {0, 64, VR} | | 0 | 2 | {0, 32, GPR}<br>{32, 32, GPR} |
| 1 | 1 | {0, 64, VR} | | 1 | 2 | {0, 32, GPR}<br>{32, 32, GPR} |
| 2 | 1 | {0, 64, VR} | | 2 | 2 | {0, 32, GPR}<br>{32, 32, GPR} |

*Figure 17.1: Different register bank mappings for a G_AND instruction*

*Figure 17.1* shows a vector (the `<2 x s32>` type) `G_AND` instruction with its expected three operands: one result and two operands. Right below that, we show two different `InstructionMapping` instances. On the left is an `InstructionMapping` instance that describes a vector instruction and, on the right, we can see what an instruction mapping with a scalarization of the `G_AND` instruction would look like. In both cases, you can see that the `InstructionMapping` instances must describe all three operands of the `G_AND` instruction, as seen in the *Operand index* column. Then, for each operand instance, you have one `ValueMapping` instance. A `ValueMapping` instance consists of the number of partial mappings (represented by the *#Partial values* column) needed to fully map the related operand (so 1 for the vector mapping and 2 for the scalarization in this case) and all the `PartialMapping` instances that describe how this mapping is done. Note that the actual implementation of the `InstructionMapping` and related classes uses pointers instead of duplicating similar instances of the related classes.

Since our H2BLB backend has only one register bank, there are no cross-register bank copies to optimize; therefore, we can focus on providing `PartialMapping` instances that always capture the full value.

In our backend, we only support two sizes, 16-bit and 32-bit; therefore, we can produce a compile-time constant instance of `PartialMapping` for each of the sizes:

```
const RegisterBankInfo::PartialMapping PartMappings[] = {
    {0, 16, GPRBRegBank},
    {0, 32, GPRBRegBank},
};
```

This snippet defines two `PartialMapping` instances, one for 16-bit (the first element of the array) and one for 32-bit (the second element of the array). While you can create `PartialMapping` instances on the fly, going with a constant implementation is a common practice because it saves (a lot) on compile-time. The following snippets are also only required if you are after the best compile-time experience for your users; otherwise, you can create your `ValueMapping` instances on the fly.

To make indexing in the array easier, we create symbolic indices:

```
enum PartialMappingIdx {
  PMI_GPRB16 = 0,
  PMI_GPRB32 = 1,
};
```

The `PMI_XXX` values match the index in our `PartMappings` array from the previous snippet.

Now that we have the `PartialMapping` instances lined up, we use them to create our compile-time constant `ValueMapping` instances:

```
const RegisterBankInfo::ValueMapping ValueMappings[] = {
    // Invalid value mapping.
    {nullptr, 0},
    // Maximum 3 GPR operands; 16 bit.
    {&PartMappings[PMI_GPRB16], 1},
```

```
      {&PartMappings[PMI_GPRB16], 1},
      {&PartMappings[PMI_GPRB16], 1},
      // Maximum 3 GPR operands; 32 bit.
      {&PartMappings[PMI_GPRB32], 1},
      {&PartMappings[PMI_GPRB32], 1},
      {&PartMappings[PMI_GPRB32], 1},
};
```

The first ValueMapping instance represents, by convention, an invalid mapping. Next, the trick in this snippet is that we lay out the array of ValueMapping instances such that an instruction with one, two, and three operands (where three is the maximum number of operands we have in our **instruction set architecture (ISA)**) can all reuse the same start address of the ValueMapping instance entry in the array. This makes sure the array does not explode in size. A ValueMapping instance is simply an address to a PartialMapping instance and the number of PartialMapping instances that this address points to. Here, since all our mappings are full mappings, we have exactly one partial mapping per operand.

Finally, we set up symbolic indices in our array of ValueMapping instances:

```
enum ValueMappingIdx {
   InvalidIdx = 0,
   GPRB16Idx = 1,
   GPRB32Idx = 4,
};
```

The value of XXXIdx matches the index of the first ValueMapping instance in the previous array.

Now that our ValueMapping array is set up, we just need to use it in our getInstrMapping method.

First, we check the type of opcode we are dealing with:

```
const RegisterBankInfo::InstructionMapping &
H2BLBRegisterBankInfo::getInstrMapping(const MachineInstr &MI) const {
   const unsigned Opc = MI.getOpcode();
   if (!isPreISelGenericOpcode(Opc) || Opc == TargetOpcode::G_PHI) {
      const InstructionMapping &Mapping = getInstrMappingImpl(MI);
      if (Mapping.isValid())
         return Mapping;
   }
```

In this snippet, if the opcode is not a generic opcode, we check whether the generic implementation can come up with a valid mapping, and if it does, we exit with that mapping. This can happen when an instruction already uses a target-specific MachineInstr instance. In this case, the register class assigned to the instruction will directly give us the mapping.

If this does not work, we must provide the mapping ourselves:

```
... // some boilerplate code to save the indices of the ValueMapping instances.
switch (Opc) {
case TargetOpcode::G_ADD:
case TargetOpcode::G_SUB:
... {
  LLT Ty = MRI.getType(MI.getOperand(0).getReg());
  TypeSize Size = Ty.getSizeInBits();
  const ValueMapping *Mapping =
      Size == 16 ? GPR16ValueMapping : GPR32ValueMapping;
  return getInstructionMapping(DefaultMappingID, 1, Mapping, NumOperands);
}
```

In this snippet, we check the opcode of the given instruction, and for all the opcodes that we know have fewer than three operands, we use our compile-time constant mapping.

Finally, if some instructions have more operands (for instance, a PHI instruction), we build a ValueMapping array on the fly:

```
default: {
  SmallVector<const ValueMapping *, 4> OpdsMapping(NumOperands);
  for (unsigned Idx = 0; Idx < NumOperands; ++Idx) {
    auto &MO = MI.getOperand(Idx);
    if (!MO.isReg() || !MO.getReg())
      continue;
    LLT Ty = MRI.getType(MO.getReg());
    if (!Ty.isValid())
      continue;
    OpdsMapping[Idx] =
        Ty.getSizeInBits() == 16 ? GPR16ValueMapping : GPR32ValueMapping;
  }
  return getInstructionMapping(DefaultMappingID, /*Cost=*/1,
                                 getOperandsMapping(OpdsMapping), NumOperands);
}
```

In this snippet, we walk you through all the operands of the given instruction, and for each register operand, we append a ValueMapping instance of the right size. Then, we return the final InstructionMapping instance using the getInstructionMapping method.

Now, the only thing left to complete our RegisterBankInfo implementation is to provide the getRegBankFromRegClass method.

This method is straightforward, and here is what it looks like for our H2BLB backend:

```
const RegisterBank &
H2BLBRegisterBankInfo::getRegBankFromRegClass(const TargetRegisterClass &RC,
                                              LLT Ty) const {
  switch (RC.getID()) {
  default:
    llvm_unreachable("Register class not supported");
  case H2BLB::GPR16RegClassID:
  case H2BLB::GPR32RegClassID:
  case H2BLB::GPR16spRegClassID:
  case H2BLB::OnlySPRegClassID:
    return getRegBank(H2BLB::GPRBRegBankID);
  }
}
```

In this snippet, we simply have a big switch that maps all our register classes to our unique register bank.

To see the full code of the previously shared snippets, look at the commit tagged `gisel-regbank-mapping_ch17` in the companion repository.

Now that our `RegisterBankInfo` class is complete, we just need to connect it to our `Subtarget` class. This is similar to what you did for the `LegalizerInfo` class, so this should be easy for you. If you need help, look at the commit tagged `gisel-regbank-desc_ch17` in the companion repository.

Now, the only thing left to have a complete instruction selection pipeline is to select your instructions. This is the topic of our next section.

# Instruction selection

The instruction selection phase of the whole instruction selection pipeline is comparatively easier than anything you have done so far. Additionally, the LLVM infrastructure provides a DSL to describe the selection patterns. This DSL, in TableGen, allows us to reuse a lot of the instruction selection description between all three selectors, although, for FastISel, the supported patterns are limited. Obviously, not everything is as easy as writing a few patterns in TableGen, but we will go into these considerations in due time. First, let us introduce how you describe your selection patterns in TableGen.

## Expressing your selection patterns

If you look at the `Instruction` TableGen class, you will notice that it features a `Pattern` field. This field is one of the ways you can describe a selection pattern for a particular instruction. The second way to describe a pattern is by instantiating a record of the `Pat` class. In both cases, you describe a dag instance that represents what needs to be matched, and for the `Pat` class, you also describe a dag instance that represents what you want to generate for the matched input dag instance. A dag object is a built-in type in TableGen that is used to describe the selection patterns, among other things.

## Introduction to the selection patterns

In this section, we show you how to use the previously defined two mechanisms (the `Pattern` field and the `Pat` class) to describe basic selection patterns.

The following snippet shows an example of such a pattern using the `Pattern` field of the `Instruction` class:

```
let Pattern = [(set GPR16:$dst, (add GPR16:$src0, GPR16:$src1))] in
def ADDi16rr : H2BLBBinaryInstruction<"addi16", ...
```

In this snippet, we define the `Pattern` field using the `let` syntax that you learned about in *Chapter 6*. This field is a list of dag instances. The [ and ] characters are the list delimiters and the ( and ) characters are the delimiters of a dag instance. This pattern describes a DAG that sets the `$dst` value. `$dst` is a value that is mapped on the GPR16 register class and is defined by an `add` instruction with two input values, `$src0` and `$src1`, both mapped to the GPR16 register class. You can find this snippet at the commit tagged `isel-add-pat_ch17` in the companion repository.

Thanks to this pattern, any time an `add` instruction reaches instruction selection with a type that matches GPR16 for all three operands, `ADDi16rr` is selected.

At this point, it may sound a bit too magical, so let us break it down to understand it:

- The opcode that is matched is defined by the name of the related `SDNode` instance (add here.) The name of the `SDNode` instances are defined for TableGen consumption in the `llvm/include/llvm/Target/TargetSelectionDAG.td` file; look at the record names of the `SDNode` instances. Note that if you want to match one of your intrinsics, you can simply use the name of the record you used to define your intrinsic (from your `llvm/include/llvm/IR/IntrinsicsXXX.td` file) as the name of the operation to match (for instance, we can use the name `int_h2blb_widening_smul` for our widening multiply instruction.) The commit tagged `isel-wmul-intrinsic-pat_ch17` in the companion repository shows such an example. Similarly, you can match your custom `SDNode` instances by using their record names.
- The types that map to GPR16 are defined by the types that this register class supports per your register class description (in your `XXXRegisterInfo.td` file.) In this case, our GPR16 definition looks like `def GPR16 : RegisterClass<"H2BLB", [i16], ...` *the list of types*; here, [i16] defines the supported types.
- The `$dst`, `$src0`, and `$src1` variables map to the `OutOperandList` and `InOperandList` arguments of your instruction description. These fields are how you describe the output and input operands of your instruction. (Look at *Chapter 11* if you need a refresher on these fields.) This is how the connection is made between the pattern and the final list of operands in the `MachineInstr` instance.

> **Note**
>
> If a register class supports more than one type, you have to help TableGen disambiguate which type you want to match by providing it explicitly. For instance, our H2BLB GPR32 class supports the list of [i32,v2i16,f32] types and if we write a pattern with GPR32, we need to explicitly set which type we are referring to by using the type RegClass syntax, for instance, (set (i32 GPR32:$dst), ... – notice the parenthesis right after the set keyword for this syntax.

The DAG that you match can be as complicated as you like, as demonstrated by the following snippet that uses the Pat class:

```
def : Pat<(i32 (mul (sext GPR16:$src0), (sext GPR16:$src1))),
          (WIDENING_SMUL GPR16:$src0, GPR16:$src1)>;
```

The Pat class takes the pattern to be matched as its first argument and the pattern to produce, both as dag instances, as its second argument. In this snippet, you can see that the pattern that we match is more complicated than just a simple instruction. We match a mul instruction where both its arguments are sext instructions. Then, we fold the sext instructions into our resulting WIDENING_SMUL instruction. The WIDENING_SMUL is the name of the record that you use to define the related Instruction TableGen instance. Notice how you do not use the set keyword when using the Pat class syntax.

Generally speaking, the syntax used in the Pat class and the Pattern field is the same, except that you need to use the set keyword followed by a variable name and then describe your pattern (that is, set type $var, pattern) for the Pattern field, and the Pat class needs to spell out the produced instructions, whereas the produced instruction is implicitly the instruction that is attached to the Pattern field in the other case. You can find this snippet at the commit tagged isel-mul-pat_ch17 in the companion repository.

The matching of patterns can include more than just register types. You can use all the OperandType records defined in the llvm/include/llvm/Target/Target.td file.

For instance, here is a match that uses the existing i16imm type:

```
def : Pat<(H2BLBcall texternalsym:$tgt), (CALL i16imm:$tgt)>;
```

In this snippet, which you can find at the commit tagged isel-ext-call-pat_ch17 in the companion repository, we match our custom H2BLBcall SDNode instance and replace it with our CALL instruction. The match uses the texternalsym type, which describes a target-specific external symbol, and we lower it to an i16imm type. Changing the types on the fly like this is only possible when both the input type (here, the texternalsym type) and the destination type (here, the i16imm type) are equivalent (here, they are equivalent because the texternalsym type is a pointer type and our target uses 16-bit pointers, so they map perfectly). For more complex type conversions, you have to use an SDNodeXForm construct, which we will cover in the following section.

Before moving on to more complex constructs, here is an example of how to generate a sequence of instructions in a pattern:

```
def : Pat<(i32 (shl (i32 GPR32:$src0), (i32 GPR32:$src1))),
          (SHL32rr (i32 GPR32:$src0),
                   (i16 (EXTRACT_SUBREG GPR32:$src1, sub_low16)))>;
```

In this snippet, we match a `shl` (shift left) instruction and produce two instructions: `EXTRACT_SUBREG` and `SHL32rr`. The result of the `EXTRACT_SUBREG` instruction is used as the second argument of the `SHL32rr` instruction. You can use the `Pat` class construct to generate DAG as complicated as you like. In particular, notice that you can also create constant values out of thin air, such as the `sub_low16` constant in this example, which is one of our sub-register indexes. This snippet can be found at the commit tagged `isel-shl-pat_ch17` in the companion repository.

> **Note**
>
> It is very easy to mess up the types in your selection patterns, and the error messages are cryptic to read when this happens. For instance, the `def : Pat<(i16 (trunc (...))),` `(i32 (EXTRACT_SUBREG ...))>;` pattern will fail with a message saying `error: Type set is empty for each HW mode in 'anonymous_XXX'`. This error is just telling you that there is a type mismatch between the input and output patterns! If you look closely, the input pattern defines an `i16` value, whereas the output pattern defines an `i32` value.

Let us see now how to customize the matching even more by introducing more complex constructs.

## Advanced selection patterns

In this section, we introduce advanced selection pattern constructs that allow us to customize the matching constraints and the node formation. We will describe three constructs:

- The `PatFrag` class: This TableGen class allows us to create sub-patterns that can be used to refine other matches. This is useful to capture matches that depend on properties of the operations that are not exposed at the TableGen level.

- The `SDNodeXForm` class: This TableGen class allows us to transform an `SDNode` instance into another one while matching a pattern. This is useful to perform non-trivial type conversions between the input and output patterns for instance.

- The `ComplexPattern` class: This TableGen class allows us to provide custom matching functions in C++. This is useful for capturing target-specific constructs that cannot be expressed with regular patterns.

Starting with the PatFrag class, you can describe a match for only a part (a fragment) of a DAG and reuse that pattern in a bigger pattern. You typically use the PatFrag class when you need to describe a match that cannot be expressed directly with regular patterns. The classic example of PatFrag instances is the extended load and truncating store instructions represented with the extload, truncstore, and so on records. If you look at a load instruction, it is represented by a load SDNode; there is no other instruction to represent extended loads. This means that with a regular pattern that relies on the opcode of the operation, you cannot distinguish whether a load is a regular or an extended load. This is where the PatFrag class comes in.

With the PatFrag class, you can match an arbitrary predicate with C++ code. In the case of an extended load, this means that you can take a regular load instruction in and check whether the underlying LoadSDNode instance returns the EXTLOAD extension type (using the getExtensionType method.) This example is not the most useful one because the TableGen backend responsible for generating the matching code has some special handling for these records, but you get the idea. A more direct use of the PatFrag class is to describe the ranges of the immediate values that you support in your instructions. The reason we started with the extended load example to introduce the PatFrag class is because this class is buried under the ImmLeaf class and you would have missed the general capability of this construct.

So, let us see how to use the ImmLeaf class with an example:

```
def uimm7 : ImmLeaf<i16, [{return Imm >= 0 && Imm < 128;}]>, ...
```

In this shortened snippet, we show how to define a record named uimm7, which represents a pattern fragment that matches when a value of the i16 type has an immediate value comprised in the range [0,128). Now that we have defined our pattern fragment, we can use it in our patterns, for instance, for our load of immediate values:

```
def LD16imm7 : H2BLBInstruction<"ldi16", "$dst, $imm7", ...> {
    ...
    let Pattern = [(set GPR16:$dst, uimm7:$imm7)];
}
```

The only notable thing in this snippet is that you can see the use of uimm7 as the input pattern of one of the operands. This pattern only matches if the related operand matches the pattern fragment defined by the predicate defined by the uimm7 record.

You can look at the commit tagged add-ldimm_ch17 for the introduction of the uimm7 record, and isel-ldimm-pat_ch17 for its use in a selection pattern.

The next construct available in your arsenal for advanced matching is the SDNodeXForm class. Thanks to this class, you can create SDNode instances on the fly.

Consider the following snippet:

```
def : Pat<(i16 (frameindex:$ptr)), (MOVFROMSP (i16 (to_tframeindex $ptr)))>;
```

In this snippet, we match a `frameindex` SDNode instance and produce a `MOVFROMSP` instruction. If you look closer, you will see that we changed the type of the `$ptr` variable from `frameindex` to `to_tframeindex`. This `to_tframeindex` type is an `SDNodeXForm` record that we introduced. Here is what it looks like:

```
def to_tframeindex : SDNodeXForm<frameindex, [{
  return CurDAG->getTargetFrameIndex(N->getIndex(), N->getValueType(0));
}]>;
```

In this snippet, we define a `to_tframeindex` record with the `SDNodeXForm` type that takes a `frameindex` SDNode instance as input and runs the C++ snippet passed as an argument of the `SDNodeXForm` class to produce a new SDNode instance. The code in this C++ snippet will live in your `XXXTargetLowering` class and you can use any method you want from this snippet. If you are wondering why we need `SDNodeXForm` to begin with, this is because the frame index needs to be converted from a generic frame index to a target-specific frame index. The conversion is trivial, as you can see, but required nonetheless.

> **Note**
>
> `SDNodeXForm` is a transformation from one SDNode instance to another SDNode instance and, as such, it makes no sense for the other selectors. Therefore, patterns that use `SDNodeXForm` cannot be used by the other selectors. When such a change of type is required in the other selectors, it is handled directly in C++.

The last advanced construct is the complex pattern construct.

The complex pattern construct defines a sort of pattern fragment (although it does not rely on the `PatFrag` class) that applies some C++ code to match an operand and can produce several operands as a result. A typical use case of complex patterns is when matching the addressing mode of a target. For instance, a load from an address `addr` represented with the `load addr` instruction can, on some architecture, access this address via an addressing mode that performs a computation of the form *base plus offset* where the base is held in a register and the offset is an immediate value. In such case, you would like to produce an instruction that looks like `load reg, imm`, where `reg` is the base and `imm` the offset. To use a complex pattern, you define a record of the `ComplexPattern` TableGen class.

Here is the complex pattern that describes the addressing mode of our H2BLB target:

```
def addrmode : ComplexPattern<iPTR, 2, "selectAddrMode", []>;
```

The first argument is the type of the operand that this complex pattern is applied to, so in this case, this is a pointer type (`iPTR`). The next argument is the number of values this complex pattern will break the input value into – in this case, 2. Next comes the name of the method that implements this complex pattern. This method needs to be implemented manually in your `XXXDAGToDAGISel` class. The next argument is a DAG that, if non-empty, tells the selector that you only want operands that match such DAG. There are additional properties that you can specify in the next argument (here, an empty array, [ ]) but we did not use them here. For instance, the SDNPWantParent property gives you access to the operation that uses the node you are matching.

Then, you can use this record as a node type in your selection pattern; for instance, here is the pattern for the H2BLB load instruction:

```
def : Pat<(v2i16 (load (addrmode GPR16:$addr, uimm4:$offset))),
          (LDR32 $addr, $offset)>;
```

In this snippet, we define the input of the load as being an addrmode instance. The thing that may be confusing at first is that the addrmode instance is followed by two values, whereas we said it matches just one operand. The matching is actually on the operand of the load instruction, which is represented by the full (addrmode ...) expression, hence just one operand. The arguments of the addrmode instance are here for you to give names to your values (here, $addr and $offset) so that you can use them in the resulting pattern (the LDR32 part).

Now, zooming in on the implementation of the custom matcher, as we said, you must implement it in your XXXDAGToDAGISel class. Here is what this looks like for our H2BLB target for this specific complex pattern:

```
bool H2BLBDAGToDAGISel::selectAddrMode(SDValue N, SDValue &Base,
                                       SDValue &OffImm) {
  Base = N;
  OffImm = CurDAG->getTargetConstant(0, dl, MVT::i16);
  return true;
}
```

This particular snippet is a waste in that we are not doing anything fancy; we just replace an address carried by the input SDValue instance N from addr to addr, 0. The interesting things we wanted to highlight here are as follows:

- The first argument is the SDValue object that you are trying your match on.
- All the other arguments are the SDValue instances that you must produce on a successful match, hence why they are passed by reference.
- This method returns true on a successful match and false on a failed match.

You can find the full snippet of this example at the commit tagged sdisel-complex-pattern_ch17 in the companion repository.

At this point, you may be wondering what happens for the other selectors since the implementation of the complex pattern is tied to the SDValue class and to your XXXDAGToDAGISel classes, which are not used by GlobalISel, for instance. For FastISel, the answer is simple: this is not supported. For GlobalISel, you need to set up a bridge in TableGen using the GIComplexPatternEquiv class, but we will address that in the *Importing the selection patterns* section.

Note

When you have several patterns that can match the same pattern, by default, the selector uses the first one it sees, meaning that the one defined first in your `.td` file will be used. You can override this behavior by setting the `AddedComplexity` field on your `Instruction` and `Pat` instances. Patterns with the highest `AddedComplexity` value are tried first. For instance, let us say you have a pattern that matches a load of an address and another one that matches a faster load when you can prove that the address is within a certain range. The second pattern will not be tried at all if you do not increase its complexity to tell the selector that it should be tried first. Usually, the `AddedComplexity` field reflects the number of nodes that you can fold in your output patterns. You can see how this is used in the commit tagged `sdisel-spaddrmode_ch17` in the companion repository.

To see more interesting complex patterns in action, look at the commits tagged `sdisel-spaddrmode_ch17`, `sdisel-addrmode-fold-addimm_ch17`, and `sdisel-improved-spaddrmode_ch17` in the companion repository.

In this section, you learned the basics of how to describe your selection patterns. You saw that these patterns sit next to your `Instruction` TableGen classes with the `Pattern` field or can be described separately with the `Pat` TableGen class. You saw how to perform advanced matching with the `PatFrag`, `SDNodeXForm`, and `ComplexPattern` TableGen classes.

Now that you have seen how to describe your patterns, let us see how they integrate with each selector, starting with SDISel.

## Selection in SDISel

At this point, your SDISel selector is already set up! Indeed, you did all the groundwork in *Chapter 14*. All the patterns that you wrote in TableGen are automatically injected into the generated `SelectCode` method that you connected in that chapter.

If you still want to do some custom selection directly in C++, you can change the `Select` method of your `XXXISelDAGToDAG` class.

## Selection in FastISel

For the FastISel selector, some of the patterns that you wrote in TableGen will automatically get added to the `selectOperator` method generated by TableGen for your `XXXFastISel` class. We already set up the related TableGen backend in *Chapter 14*. The patterns that are brought into FastISel are only simple ones, meaning that they must not have any of the advanced constructs that we discussed in the *Advanced selection patterns* section.

For all the other cases, you must translate the LLVM IR input to the Machine IR manually by implementing the lowering directly in the `fastSelectInstruction` method of your `XXXFastISel` class. When writing this method, you can use the `fastEmitInst_x` methods that are available in the base `FastISel` class and the `fastEmit_x` methods, which are autogenerated from your TableGen selection patterns. The letter x in these methods is the type of argument you want to generate an instruction for: r for register and i for immediate. For instance, `fastEmitInst_ri` means that you want to produce a `MachineInstr` instance with a register and an immediate value operand. The difference between the `fastEmitInst_x` and `fastEmit_x` methods is that the former produces a `MachineInstr` instance with the provided target-specific opcode, so you already know what you want to produce, whereas the latter produces a `MachineInstr` instance by selecting the `MachineInstr` opcode based on the provided types and `ISD` opcode. In other words, the former is a helper function to create `MachineInstr` instances, and the latter uses the patterns that you wrote in TableGen. Beware that `fastEmit_x` may fail, so make sure to check that the returned register does not have the `MCRegister::NoRegister` value.

Finally, given that FastISel may fall back to SDISel, remember to update the mapping between the LLVM IR values and the virtual registers using the `updateValueMap` method. Do not hesitate to look at the AArch64 backend for examples of how to use the `fastEmit_x` methods.

# Selection in GlobalISel

As already mentioned, the selection phase in the GlobalISel pipeline is implemented by the `InstructionSelect` pass. This pass uses the `InstructionSelector` class provided by the target through the `Subtarget` class to perform the selection.

Let us see how to set up a target-specific `InstructionSelector` class.

## Setting up the InstructionSelector class

Like the FastISel and SDISel selectors, we need to set up a TableGen backend specific to GlobalISel to generate the selection code from the selection patterns and implement the boilerplate code for the generated code.

First, the TableGen backend to use is the gen-global-isel one. Invoke it from your CMakeLists.txt file:

```
tablegen(LLVM H2BLBGenGlobalISel.inc -gen-global-isel)
```

This TableGen backend will generate the `selectImpl` method that you need to use in your `XXXInstructionSelector` class.

Let us see how to integrate what TableGen generates to make our `InstructionSelector` class a reality.

Like every TableGen backend, the gen-global-isel one creates different pieces of code in the generated .inc file, each behind a preprocessor macro. These pieces of code need to be integrated in different positions compared to your `XXXInstructionSelector` class. The following list gives you the preprocessor macro to use and where to integrate the related code in the file that defines your `XXXInstructionSelector` class:

- `GET_GLOBALISEL_PREDICATE_BITSET`: Use this macro before including the .inc file before the declaration of your `XXXInstructionSelector` class. This macro guards the definition of the `PredicateBitset` type. That type is used to represent all the features that a target supports, and these features can be used to enable or disable patterns, such as whether the subtarget supports vector operations or not.

- `GET_GLOBALISEL_PREDICATES_DECL`: Use this macro before including the `.inc` file inside the declaration of your `XXXInstructionSelector` class. This macro guards the declaration of all the predicates.
- `GET_GLOBALISEL_TEMPORARIES_DECL`: The same position as the previous macro, but guards temporaries used for the match table. The match table is the structure that is used to select the instructions.
- `GET_GLOBALISEL_IMPL`: Use this macro after the declaration of your class. This macro guards the implementation of the generated methods.
- `GET_GLOBALISEL_PREDICATES_INIT`: Use this macro within the initialization list of your `XXXInstructionSelector` class constructor. This guards the initialization of all the predicates.

The commit tagged `gisel-add-inst-select_ch17` in the companion repository has the full snippet of what this looks like for our H2BLB target.

Next, you must provide the prototype of the `selectImpl` method generated by TableGen:

```
bool selectImpl(MachineInstr &I, CodeGenCoverage &CoverageInfo) const;
```

Finally, you must provide an implementation of the `select` method:

```
bool H2BLBInstructionSelector::select(MachineInstr &I) {
  if (!isPreISelGenericOpcode(I.getOpcode()))
    return true;
  if (selectImpl(I, *CoverageInfo))
    return true;
  return false;
}
```

In this snippet, we return directly with a success (we return `true`) when the given instruction is already selected. Remember that GlobalISel allows us to use a non-generic `MachineInstr` instance anywhere in the pipeline, so instructions may already be selected. You check that by using the `isPreISelGenericOpcode` helper function, which tells you whether the given opcode is a generic opcode that cannot appear after selection or an already selected one. Next, we call the method generated by TableGen, `selectImpl`, and if it succeeds at selecting the given instruction, we return a success; otherwise, we report a failure (we return `false`).

Now that we have our `XXXInstructionSelector` class, we need to register it with our `Subtarget` class. You already know how to do this kind of thing, but if you need help, you can look at the commit tagged `gisel-add-inst-select_ch17` in the companion repository that we mentioned earlier.

Now that our selector is connected to the GlobalISel pipeline of our target, let us see how the selection patterns feed into the generated `selectImpl` method.

## Importing the selection patterns

The selection patterns were developed a while ago with SDISel in mind. GlobalISel uses the same patterns but needs to perform a conversion from the syntax that uses the SDNode instances to the generic MachineInstr instances.

While this import mechanism is automatically done by the gen-global-isel TableGen backend, some patterns may fail to be imported and could lead you to selection errors for something that you thought was already covered by a pattern.

If you are starting directly with GlobalISel, there is little chance you will encounter this problem since you would directly test your new patterns as you add them, but if you are transitioning to GlobalISel, it is important to understand how to check what was imported and if not, why.

Let us show you why this is important.

Consider the following pattern:

```
def : Pat<(vector_extract (v2i16 GPR32:$rs), 0),
          (i16 (EXTRACT_SUBREG $rs, sub_low16))>;
```

In this snippet, you see a simple one-to-one instruction pattern. However, this pattern is not imported by GlobalISel.

To see that in action, run the TableGen backend manually (check *Chapter 1* if you do not remember how to extract the command line from Ninja) and add the --warn-on-skipped-patterns command-line option.

For this pattern, you will get the following:

```
warning: Skipped pattern: unsupported type for Src operand (0:{ *:[iPTR] })
```

What this tells you is that the importer does not know what the type of the operand with the constant value of 0 is. We can fix that by adding a type, i16, to this 0 value:

```
def : Pat<(vector_extract (v2i16 GPR32:$rs), (i16 0)),
          (i16 (EXTRACT_SUBREG $rs, sub_low16))>;
```

When re-running the TableGen backend, now we get a different warning:

```
warning: Skipped pattern: Could not infer class for EXTRACT_SUBREG operand #0
```

What this tells you this time is that the importer has no idea what the register class of $rs is in the output pattern. This is because the importer looks at one pattern at a time: the input pattern first, then the output pattern. Since the output pattern does not repeat the register class, it cannot infer it. To fix this, you simply add a register class to the output pattern like so:

```
def : Pat<(vector_extract (v2i16 GPR32:$rs), (i16 0)),
          (i16 (EXTRACT_SUBREG GPR32:$rs, sub_low16))>;
```

Now, the pattern can be imported.

The takeaway is to double-check that your patterns are imported, and to maximize the chances of a pattern being imported, explicitly set all the types.

Patterns that use complex patterns will always be skipped unless you provide a bridge to a GlobalISel implementation for the C++ matching method. To do that, you use a combination of the `GIComplexOperandMatcher` and `GIComplexPatternEquiv` TableGen classes. The former declares a complex matcher method that you need to implement in your `XXXInstructionSelector` class and the latter tells the importer that this matcher maps to the given `ComplexPattern` TableGen record.

Let us see an example:

```
def gi_addrmode :
  GIComplexOperandMatcher<p0, "selectAddrMode">,
  GIComplexPatternEquiv<addrmode>;
```

In this snippet, we declare a mapping of our GlobalISel complex pattern. This complex pattern is the GlobalISel counterpart of the addrmode SDISel `ComplexPattern` instance.

Next, we need to implement the method we declared in the `GIComplexOperandMatcher` instance in our `XXXInstructionSelector` class:

```
InstructionSelector::ComplexRendererFns
H2BLBInstructionSelector::selectAddrMode(MachineOperand &Root) const {
  Register BaseReg = RootDef->getOperand(0).getReg();
  uint64_t Offset = 0;
  ... // matching code.
  return {{
      [=](MachineInstrBuilder &MIB) { MIB.addReg(BaseReg); },
      [=](MachineInstrBuilder &MIB) { MIB.addImm(Offset); },
  }};
}
```

In this snippet, we skipped most of the code, but we wanted to draw your attention to the returned values. Unlike in SDISel, where the matched values are part of the function signature, in GlobalISel, you return pointers to functions called *renderers*. You need to return one renderer function per operand you must produce. In other words, in this example, a `ComplexPattern` instance was declared as producing two operands; therefore, we must return two renderers.

You can find the full snippet at the commit tagged `gisel-addrmode-cplx_ch17` in the companion repository.

This is all there is to do for complex patterns.

The last thing that needs some work to get imported is the patterns written for your custom `SDNode` instances. This type of connection is as simple as a single TableGen line using the `GINodeEquiv` class.

Here is an example:

```
def : GINodeEquiv<G_EXTRACT_VECTOR_ELT, vector_extract>;
```

In this snippet, we tell the importer that the G_EXTRACT_VECTOR_ELT opcode is equivalent to the vector_extract SDNode instance. You can use any machine opcode and SDNode instance for these mappings, even the target-specific ones. You can find the full snippet at the commit tagged gisel-node-equiv_ch17 in the companion directory.

> **Note**
>
> All generic SDNode instances are mapped to their G_XXX opcode equivalent in the llvm/include/llvm/Target/GlobalISel/SelectionDAGCompat.td file. You do not have to worry about doing this mapping yourself. Therefore, you need to use this construct only if you have custom SDNode instances.

When you use the GINodeEquiv construct, the last GINodeEquiv instance remaps the SDNode instance to the given opcode. Therefore, you cannot have an SDNode instance mapped to several opcodes. In other words, make sure to use only one GINodeEquiv construction per SDNode instance; otherwise, you will have surprising results, or at least likely not what you want!

Now that you have imported all the relevant patterns, let us dig into the pieces that are not captured by patterns.

## Going beyond patterns

If patterns do not work, for instance, because of the SDNodeXForm construct (which is by construction tied to the SDNode instances and, by extension, the SDISel representation), you can always use pure C++ code by augmenting the select method of your XXXInstructionSelector class.

The selection code looks exactly like what you would expect, and here is an example of how we select the G_FRAME_INDEX instruction:

```
bool H2BLBInstructionSelector::select(MachineInstr &I) {
  ... // switch over all the opcodes that we custom select.
  case TargetOpcode::G_FRAME_INDEX: {
    I.setDesc(TII.get(H2BLB::MOVFROMSP));
    return constrainSelectedInstRegOperands(I, TII, TRI, RBI);
  }
}
```

In this snippet, we replace a G_FRAME_INDEX instruction with an H2BLB::MOVFROMSP instruction. Since we go from a generic opcode to a target-specific one, we need to make sure that the register class is properly set, and we call the constrainSelectedInstRegOperands method to do that, which you already know. You can find the full snippet at the commit tagged gisel-select-fi_ch17 in the companion repository.

There is one last quirk that you need to handle in GlobalISel. There are some instructions that are in limbo between generic and target-specific opcodes, such as the COPY, PHI, and so on instructions. These instructions are allowed before and after selection and are thus not part of the selection process. However, since they may have been created by the generic infrastructure, such as the IRTranslator pass, they may not have the proper register classes assigned to their operands, which makes them unsuitable for post-instruction selection passes. You fix that as part of the select method of your XXXInstructionSelector class.

This is what the implementation of the solution of this quirk is:

```
bool H2BLBInstructionSelector::select(MachineInstr &I) {
  unsigned Opc = I.getOpcode();
  if (!isPreISelGenericOpcode(Opc) && Opc != TargetOpcode::PHI &&
      Opc != TargetOpcode::COPY)
    return true;
  ...
  switch (Opc) {
  case TargetOpcode::G_PHI:
    I.setDesc(TII.get(TargetOpcode::PHI));
    [[fallthrough]];
  case TargetOpcode::PHI:
  case TargetOpcode::COPY:
    for (MachineOperand &MO : I.operands()) {
      Register Reg = MO.getReg();
      if (Reg.isPhysical())
        continue;
      const TargetRegisterClass *RC = MRI.getRegClassOrNull(Reg);
      if (RC)
        continue;
      unsigned Size = MRI.getType(Reg).getSizeInBits();
      MRI.setRegClass(Reg, Size == 16 ? &H2BLB::GPR16spRegClass
                                      : &H2BLB::GPR32RegClass);
    }
```

In this snippet, we make sure that the COPY and PHI instructions go through the selection process. The selection process consists of checking whether the register operands have a register class, and if they do not, we assign one.

You can find the full snippet at the commit tagged `gisel-select-cpy_ch17` in the companion repository.

In this section, you learned how to implement the instruction selection phase of the different selectors. You saw that most of the heavy lifting is done by the selection patterns that you wrote in the target description but you can still use custom C++ implementation for maximum flexibility.

The next section covers the finalization of the selection pipeline, irrespective of the selector used.

# Finalizing the selection pipeline

After the instruction selection pipeline, the default machine pass pipeline features a pass, represented by the `FinalizeISel` class, which is responsible for tidying up the Machine IR for the remaining passes.

From a backend perspective, there are two things that you can customize in this finalization:

1.  You can morph instructions using a custom inserter. Custom inserters are target hooks that allow you to modify the instructions that you tagged as requiring a customer inserter. You typically use a custom inserter for pseudo instructions that you want to expand right after instruction selection in the pass pipeline.

2.  You can customize the `TargetLowering::finalizeLowering` method, which is the main method that prepares the current `MachineFunction` instance for processing by the remaining passes. By default, this method just freezes the set of **reserved registers**. Reserved registers are physical registers that cannot be used by register allocation. For instance, you can freeze the register that will hold the stack value to make sure it does not get overridden. The freezing mechanism, by default, uses the `MachineRegisterInfo::freezeReservedRegs` method, which ultimately relies on the `TargetRegisterInfo::getReservedRegs` method. If you are only interested in changing how the registers are frozen, just override the `TargetRegisterInfo::getReserved Regs` of your `XXXRegisterInfo` class.

Let us look at these two mechanisms in more detail.

## Using custom inserters

To use a custom inserter, you need to set the `usesCustomInserter` field to 1 for the related instructions in your target description.

For every instruction with that field set, the `FinalizeISel` pass will automatically call the `TargetLow ering::EmitInstrWithCustomInserter` method when encountering the related opcode.

For instance, let us say that loading an immediate value requires a complicated sequence of instructions and that this sequence depends on the value of the immediate value. This is difficult to capture with a regular selection pattern, so instead, you can use a pseudo instruction to select a pseudo load immediate instruction and then use a custom inserter to have the full flexibility of C++ to expand it in a complex sequence of instructions.

This is exactly what we did in our H2BLB backend.

We start by marking our instruction with a custom inserter in the target description:

```
let usesCustomInserter = true in
def LD16imm16 : H2BLBPseudoInstruction<...
```

Then, we implement this custom inserter for this opcode:

```
MachineBasicBlock *
H2BLBTargetLowering::EmitInstrWithCustomInserter(MachineInstr &MI,
                                                 MachineBasicBlock *BB) const {
switch (MI.getOpcode()) {
  case H2BLB::LD16imm16:
    return emitLDimm(MI);
```

Thanks to this hook, you now have all the freedom you need to expand the instruction in any way required.

You can find examples of custom inserters in the commits tagged `ret-custom-inserter_ch17` for our first customer inserter, which we use for our return instruction to produce Machine IR that passes the checks of the `MachineVerifier` pass, and `ldimm-custom-inserter_ch17` for our load immediate custom inserter.

Let us now look at the `TargetLowering::finalizeLowering` method.

## Customizing the TargetLowering::finalizeLowering method

The `TargetLowering::finalizeLowering` method is a pure C++ function that works on the given `MachineFunction` instance. The reason we wanted to spend a little bit of time on it is to call out a couple of pitfalls when overriding it.

> Pitfalls
>
> When you override the `TargetLowering::finalizeLowering` method, make sure to call the parent method; otherwise, you may miss freezing the reserved registers and you expose yourself to random failures in the remaining machine pass pipeline. Moreover, this method is called twice in the GlobalISel pipeline: once during the instruction selection phase and once during the finalization of the `MachineFunction` instance (that is, within the `FinalizeISel` pass.) As a result, if you make any changes to the IR that may not be safe or would not make sense if applied twice, you must structure your code such that the content of this method is run only once. This is easy to do by leveraging the property of your `MachineFunction` instance.

To give you an example of how to avoid these pitfalls, here is what the overall structure of your customized `TargetLowering::finalizeLowering` method should look like:

```
void H2BLBTargetLowering::finalizeLowering(MachineFunction &MF) const {
  if (MF.getProperties().hasProperty(
```

```
            MachineFunctionProperties::Property::Selected))
    return;
  ... // do your things.
  TargetLowering::finalizeLowering(MF);
}
```

In this snippet, we start by checking whether the `MachineFunction` instance has the `Selected` property. If it does not, that means that we either did not run GlobalISel or we are within the instruction selection phase of GlobalISel. In both cases, this is fine to do the finalization. If we have the `Selected` property, then that means the instruction selection phase of GlobalISel ran and thus we already ran this method, so we have nothing else to do. You can find the full snippet in the commits tagged `finalize-lowering_ch17` and `finalize-lowering-w-gisel_ch17` in the companion repository.

To summarize, the `FinalizeISel` pass offers some customization points in the form of the custom inserters and the `TargetLowering::finalizeLowering` method that you can leverage to perform some final tidying up on the already selected `MachineFunction` instance.

In the next section, we will go over some of the ways you can introduce custom optimizations in the instruction selection pipeline.

# Optimizations

In GlobalISel and SDISel, it is possible to inject your own optimizations within the instruction selection pipeline. In this section, you will learn how to use these infrastructures to insert your own optimizations.

Let us start with SDISel.

## Using the DAGCombiner framework

Since SDISel is a single `MachineFunctionPass` instance, the optimization opportunities are limited to what SDISel exposes as hooks.

Essentially, the only thing that you can do in SDISel is some pattern rewriting using the **DAGCombiner** infrastructure. The `DAGCombiner` infrastructure allows you to run custom pattern rewrites at four predetermined points of the SDISel pipeline, identified by the following `CombineLevel` enumeration values:

- `BeforeLegalizeTypes`: Before legalization
- `AfterLegalizeTypes`: After the legalization of scalar types but before the legalization of vector types
- `AfterLegalizeVectorOps`: After the legalization of vector types but before the legalization of the operations
- `AfterLegalizeDAG`: After legalization

All four hook points call the same `TargetLowering::PerformDAGCombine` method, which you need to override to perform your custom rewrites. To identify when in the selection pipeline this method is called, you need to look at the `DAGCombinerInfo` argument of this method. More specifically, you can check the value of the `CombineLevel` instance returned by the `DAGCombinerInfo::getDAGCombineLe vel` method or use one of the `DAGCombinerInfo::isBeforeLegalize` getters, and so on.

To set up a custom rewrite, you need to do two things:

1.  Tell SDISel that you want to perform a custom rewrite when certain nodes are encountered. To do that, in the constructor of your `TargetLowering` class, you need to call the `TargerLowering ::setTargetDAGCombine` method with the `ISD` opcode of the root node of your custom rewrite.
2.  You need to override the `TargetLowering::PerformDAGCombine` method to provide the custom rewrite for each `ISD` opcode that you previously marked for custom rewrite. In this method, if you return the `SDValue()` value, it means that no rewrites were performed; otherwise, you need to return the new `SDValue` instance that replaces the input node, and SDISel will update the DAG accordingly.

The code to write is straightforward but if you need an example, you can find one in the commit tagged `sdisel-custom-rewrite_ch17` in the companion repository.

> **Note**
>
> Be careful when you provide custom rewrites because they may undo some of the generic rewrites. When that happens, your selector may get stuck in an endless loop because it tries to reach a fixed point that does not exist. For instance, let us say that you want loads for floating-point values to be expressed as a load of integer values followed by a bitcast to the floating-point value. You may want to do that because you want to only provide selection patterns for integer types. If you do this, you will hit the endless loop we were talking about. The generic infrastructure optimizes the bitcast of loads into loads of the destination type, hence the generic infrastructure will undo what you want, and vice versa. To break that cycle, you can introduce custom **SDNode** instances, for instance, a target-specific node that would represent your bitcast. This works because your node is opaque to the generic optimizations, and they cannot modify it. However, this is a double-edged sword because now your custom bitcast node cannot be optimized as a regular bitcast in the generic optimizations.

This covers the main way you can optimize things in SDISel.

Let us now see what is possible in GlobalISel.

## Leveraging the combiner framework

As already mentioned, GlobalISel is a regular machine pipeline and, as such, you can insert as many passes as you would like between the core passes. We will not cover that part here since you already learned how to do that in *Chapter 5*. Instead, in this section, we will focus on a mechanism that leverages `CombinerHelper` and related classes to describe pattern rewrites.

Indeed, GlobalISel features a TableGen backend to create `MachineFunctionPass` classes that perform pattern rewriting optimizations. You still need to produce some boilerplate code to connect the pieces, but the bulk of the pattern rewriting logic is done for you, including traversing the IR, trying to apply matching functions, and applying the rewrites.

This pattern rewrite mechanism involves several components:

- A TableGen backend called `gen-global-isel-combiner`. This backend is responsible for generating the boilerplate code that drives the pattern rewrites.
- The `CombinerHelper` class features methods to help you rewrite your code and holds key instances for all the rewrites, such as the current `GISelChangeObserver` and `MachineIRBuilder` instances.
- The `Combiner` class is the driver for all the pattern rewrite rules.

To use this framework, you start by describing your patterns in TableGen using the `GICombineRule` and `GIDefMatchData` TableGen classes.

The `GICombineRule` class describes the following:

- The operation you want to rewrite
- The match function that you apply
- The rewrite function to use

The `GIDefMatchData` class describes the type of information that you carry between the match function and the rewrite function of your `GICombineRule` instance. The idea is that in your match function, you collect the information that you need to perform the rewrite, and if there is a match, then this information is transferred to the rewrite function; otherwise, it is discarded.

Here is how you can describe one pattern:

```
def registers_matchinfo: GIDefMatchData<"SmallVector<Register>">;
def insertvectorelt_to_build_vector : GICombineRule<
  (defs root:$root, registers_matchinfo:$matchinfo),
  (match (wip_match_opcode G_INSERT_VECTOR_ELT):$root,
        [{ return matchInsertVectorElt(*${root}, ${matchinfo}); }]),
  (apply [{ applyInsertVectorElt(*${root}, ${matchinfo}); }])>;
```

In this snippet, the `GIDefMatchData` record, named `registers_matchinfo`, describes that we are going to carry a list of `Register` instances between the match and apply functions. The type given here must be instantiable.

Now, looking at the `GICombineRule` record, the first argument defines the temporary values that need to be passed to both the match and apply functions. Here, we will provide a root (a `MachineInstr` instance) and custom `registers_matchinfo` (our list of `Register` instances).

Next, we describe the matching function, which says that we should try our match function only when the root is a `G_INSERT_VECTOR_ELT` instruction. The match itself is described in the C++ code right after and will need to be implemented manually.

Finally, we describe the apply function with a block of C++ code.

The code provided for both the match and apply functions will need to be manually implemented somewhere.

To describe our custom combiner, we need to create a GICombiner record in TableGen:

```
def H2BLBMandatoryPreLegalizerCombiner: GICombiner<
  "H2BLBMandatoryPreLegalizerCombinerImpl", [optnone_combines, insertvectorelt_
to_build_vector]> {
}
```

The GICombiner TableGen class takes the name of the Combiner record that will be implemented followed by the list of the record names of all the rules that this combiner will use (each rule is a GICombine instance; the GICombine class is the superclass of the GICombineRule class). This mechanism allows us to share rewrite patterns across different passes. For instance, in this snippet, we reuse the generic patterns defined by the optnone_combines GICombineGroup instance.

Using these TableGen definitions, we can run the gen-global-isel-combiner TableGen backend by adding in our CMakeLists.txt file:

```
tablegen(LLVM H2BLBGenMandatoryPreLegalizeGICombiner.inc -gen-global-isel-
combiner
                -combiners="H2BLBMandatoryPreLegalizerCombiner")
```

This TableGen backend takes additional arguments because you can create as many different combiners as needed, whereas the other TableGen backends create one key class that you use for your whole backend. The combiners option tells the TableGen backend the name to use to prefix all the generated code. The expectation is that you will create a MachineFunctionPass class with this name.

Now that you have generated the .inc file for your combiner pass, let us describe the code that you need to integrate this .inc file in your implementation.

To set the context, your implementation will need to provide the following things:

- The match and apply functions that you referenced in your target description. These functions are usually standalone functions since they can be reused across combiners.
- The skeleton of a class named XXXImpl, which derives publicly from the Combiner class, where XXX is the name that you gave to the combiners option when invoking the TableGen backend in the CMakeLists.txt file.
- A new MachineFunctionPass class that calls into your XXXImpl class. This MachineFunctionPass class is usually named after the combiners option.

Here is a snippet of the skeleton that you need to provide for your XXXImpl class:

```
class H2BLBMandatoryPreLegalizerCombinerImpl : public Combiner {
protected:
  mutable CombinerHelper Helper;
```

```
    const H2BLBMandatoryPreLegalizerCombinerImplRuleConfig &RuleConfig;
    const H2BLBSubtarget &STI;
  public:
    H2BLBMandatoryPreLegalizerCombinerImpl(
        MachineFunction &MF, CombinerInfo &CInfo, const TargetPassConfig *TPC,
        GISelKnownBits &KB, GISelCSEInfo *CSEInfo,
        const H2BLBMandatoryPreLegalizerCombinerImplRuleConfig &RuleConfig,
        const H2BLBSubtarget &STI);
    static const char *getName() { return "H2BLBMandatoryPreLegalizerCombiner"; }
    bool tryCombineAll(MachineInstr &I) const override;
```

All the defined member variables and the `tryCombineAll` method are used or implemented by the code generated by TableGen.

Here is the snippet of the main part of the `MachineFunctionPass` class that you need to write:

```
class H2BLBMandatoryPreLegalizerCombiner : public MachineFunctionPass {
  H2BLBMandatoryPreLegalizerCombinerImplRuleConfig RuleConfig;
public:
  H2BLBMandatoryPreLegalizerCombiner() : MachineFunctionPass(ID) {
    if (!RuleConfig.parseCommandLineOption())
      report_fatal_error("Invalid rule identifier");
  }
  bool runOnMachineFunction(MachineFunction &MF) override {
    ... // Get the Function instance in F, the TargetPassConfig in TPC, and so on.
    CombinerInfo CInfo(/*AllowIllegalOps*/ true, /*ShouldLegalizeIllegal*/
                       false, /*LegalizerInfo*/ nullptr, /*EnableOpt*/ false,
                       F.hasOptSize(), F.hasMinSize());
    CInfo.MaxIterations = 1;
    H2BLBMandatoryPreLegalizerCombinerImpl Impl(MF, CInfo, &TPC, *KB,
                                                /*CSEInfo*/ nullptr, RuleConfig,
                                                ST);
    return Impl.combineMachineInstrs();
  }
...
```

This snippet illustrates that you must call the `parseCommandLineOption` method of your `XXXImplRuleConfig` instance in the constructor of your pass. The `XXXImplRuleConfig` class is generated by TableGen. This class makes sure your combiner can play nice with the command-line options.

The meat of the pass is in the `runOnMachineFunction` method. In this method, you must instantiate a `CombinerInfo` class and then use it to instantiate your `XXXImpl` class and call the `combineMachineInstrs` method of this class. This method does all the work of traversing the current `MachineFunction` instance and matching and applying the rewrite rules.

Let us now focus on integrating the code generated by TableGen.

As usual, the code generated by TableGen is broken down into different pieces guarded behind preprocessor macros.

These macros are as follows:

- `GET_GICOMBINER_DEPS`: Use this macro at the beginning of your `.cpp` file. This guards some global dependencies that are used to selectively enable and disable the rewrite rules via the command-line options.

- `GET_GICOMBINER_TYPES`: Use this macro also at the beginning of your `.cpp` file, but within an anonymous namespace. This guards some types internal to the implementation (the `XXXImpl` class) of your combiner.

- `GET_GICOMBINER_CLASS_MEMBERS`: Use this macro inside the declaration of your `XXXImpl` class to populate the member functions and variables generated by TableGen.

- `GET_GICOMBINER_IMPL`: Use this macro outside of your `XXXImpl` class to bring in the implementation of the methods added with the `GET_GICOMBINER_CLASS_MEMBERS` macro.

- `GET_GICOMBINER_CONSTRUCTOR_INITS`: Use this macro within the initialization list of the constructor of your `XXXImpl` class to initialize the member variables added by the `GET_GICOMBINER_CLASS_MEMBERS` macro.

As soon as you are done with these steps, you have a fully fleshed combiner pass that you can inject into the GlobalISel pipeline, for instance, by overriding the `TargetPassConfig::addPreLegalizeMachineIR` method in your related class.

You can find an example of how to create such combiners at the commits tagged `pre-legalizer-combiner_ch17` for a combiner that runs before legalization and `post-legalizer-combiner_ch17` for a combiner that runs after legalization.

In this section, you learned how to set up and use the combiner frameworks in both SDISel and GlobalISel. The combiners allow you to match patterns and rewrite them in a more efficient code sequence. In SDISel, this capability is provided by hooks that you need to override in your `TargetLowering` class, and in GlobalISel, this capability is provided through a TableGen backend that allows you to create the machinery to power a custom `MachineFunctionPass` class implementing this capability.

At this point, you have a fully functional instruction selector framework, but you are still missing some pieces around the lowering of the stack to be able to generate assembly code. Before we wrap up this chapter, we wanted to give you a few guidelines to help you debug your instruction selection pipeline.

# Debugging the selectors

As you saw throughout this chapter, selectors are complicated pieces of machinery and it is common that they do not behave the way you would expect.

In this section, we will give you some guidelines to help you debug issues that are specific to the selectors.

For starters, everything that you learned so far for debugging LLVM still applies. You need to use the debug-only command-line option and the dump methods to help you inspect the IR.

Let us start with tips that are specific to SDISel.

## Debugging SDISel

When debugging the SDISel issue, you can use the dumpr method of the SDNode instance. This method allows printing the children of a node and the children of its children and so on until the specified depth (and argument of this method) is reached. (Note that such a method also exists on the MachineInstr instances but requires you to provide a MachineRegisterInfo instance.) Moreover, when using the dump or dumpr method on an SDNode instance, you can pass a pointer to the current DAG as well. This is useful when printing SDNode instances that use custom opcodes because the pretty printing of these opcodes can only happen when you provide a SelectionDAG instance.

When running SDISel, you can access the current SelectionDAG instance via the CurDAG member variable of the SelectionDAGISel class. When running a DAG combiner, you can access the SelectionDAG instance by looking at the DAG member variable of the DAGCombinerInfo instance.

Finally, SDISel supports a graphical printing of the DAG with nodes and edges. This printing is behind the command-line options named view-*-dags, which you can find in the llvm/lib/CodeGen/SelectionDAG/SelectionDAGISel.cpp file. For instance, the view-isel-dags option prints all the DAGs just before instruction selection and the view-legalize-dags option prints all the DAGs just before operation legalization. You can also filter which DAGs are printed using the filter-view-dags option. The produced output is a .dot file that you can convert to a .pdf file using the dot command-line tool.

For instance, when you use one of the view-*-dags options, you should see in your output something like this:

```
Writing '/path/to/file.dot'... done.
```

Using the path printed on this line, you can produce a .pdf file with the following command line:

```
dot -Tpdf /path/to/file.dot -o mygraph.pdf
```

This command tells the dot command-line tool to produce a .pdf file from the given .dot file.

*Figure 17.2* shows an example of such a dump:

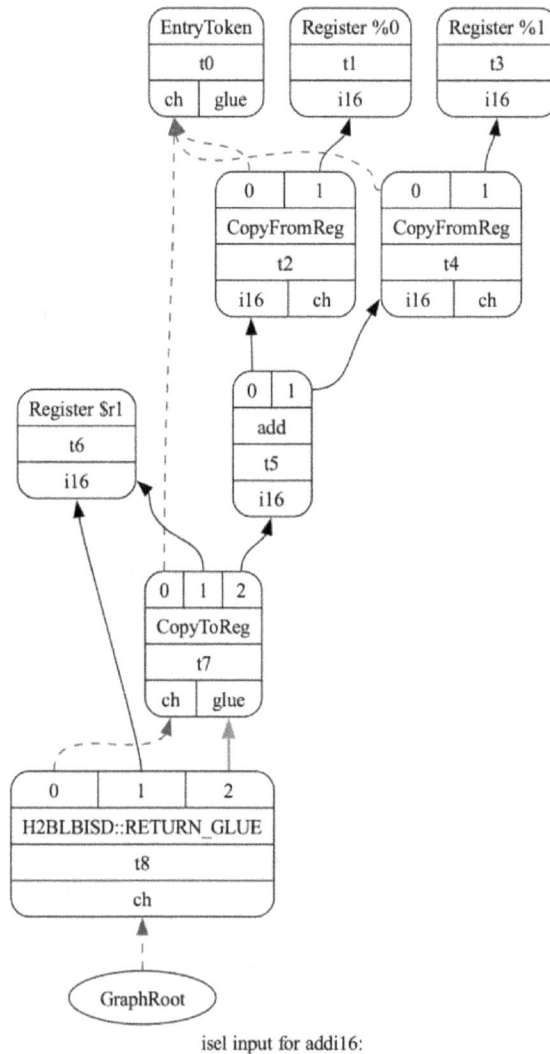

isel input for addi16:

*Figure 17.2: The graphical representation of the SDISel IR*

In *Figure 17.2*, each rectangle with rounded corners is an SDNode instance. Zooming in on the SDNode instances, the top row represents the numbered inputs of the related node, the next row is the opcode (for instance, add), then for regular nodes, the name (regular nodes means non-constant, non-register, and so on), and the last row represents the numbered output values. The (blue) dotted arrows represent chains, the (red) bold arrows (here, only one from the RETURN_GLUE node to the glue value of the CopyToReg node) represent glue, and the solid black arrows are data dependencies.

Lastly, the part of the instruction selection phase that uses the code produced by the TableGen selection patterns is a state machine. When the instruction selection phase fails, you do not want to debug the state machine directly.

Instead, you should look at the output of the debug-only=isel option and you should see something resembling the following:

```
 ISEL: Starting selection on root node: t9: v2i32 = add t2, t2
ISEL: Starting pattern match
  Initial Opcode index to 31041
  Match failed at index 31046
  Continuing at 158464
  ...
```

The number printed on these lines maps to the entries in the match table used by the state machine. TableGen puts these numbers in a comment in the produced XXXGenDAGISel.inc file for you to easily check what is happening.

For instance, in this case, the match table around 31041 is as follows:

```
/* 31041*/  OPC_Scope, 59|128,99|128,7/*127419*/, /*->158464*/ // 130 children
in Scope
/* 31045*/   OPC_MoveChild0,
/* 31046*/   OPC_SwitchOpcode /*2 cases */, 125|128,120|128,3/*64637*/, TARGET_
VAL(ISD::MUL),// ->95689
```

So, we failed to match at 31046, which means the first operand (OPC_MoveChild0) of the input instruction is not an ISD::MUL instruction. Then, we moved to the entry in the match table at 158464 and so on.

## Debugging the GlobalISel match table

GlobalISel is easier to debug than SDISel since all its passes are regular MachineFunctionPass classes.

However, it also uses a state machine for its instruction selection phase but the same principle as SDISel applies to debug the match table, except that the printed indices apply to the element generated in your XXXGenGlobalISel.inc file.

To trace the match table, you must use the following debug-only option: debug-only=instruction-select,xxx, where xxx is the value of what you returned within the getName method of your XXXInstructionSelector class (this is typically the DEBUG_TYPE macro of the related file) – for us, it was h2blb-gisel.

This option enables the following:

- instruction-select: The debug log of the InstructionSelect pass, which is the pass that runs the instruction selection phase
- xxx: The debug log of the code generated by TableGen for your instruction selector

Here is an example of the output produced by the AArch64 backend (the xxx option is aarch64-isel in this case):

```
Selecting:
  %8:gpr(s32) = G_ADD %2:gpr, %3:gpr
10: GIM_SwitchOpcode(MIs[0], [51, 795), Default=357167, JumpTable...) // Got=51
2997: GIM_SwitchType(MIs[0]->getOperand(0), [2, 24), Default=21984,
JumpTable...) // Got=s32
3086: Begin try-block
3093: GIM_CheckType(MIs[0]->getOperand(1), TypeID=2)
```

In this output, the first number gives you the index in the match table of the related entry.

Unfortunately, unlike SelectionDAG, these indices do not appear yet as comments in the generated .inc file, so a little bit of gymnastics is required to know exactly where you are in the match table.

Looking at the AArch64GenGlobalISel.inc file, there are @ annotations that give you the index in the table at this point.

For instance, to find the entry at the index 3086 in the AArch64GenGlobalISel.inc file, we were lucky to find a @ annotation with 3085 and know at this point that our entry sits next to this annotation:

```
// Label 147: @3085
GIM_Try, /*On fail goto*//*Label 161*/ GIMT_Encode4(4607),
  GIM_RootCheckType, /*Op*/1, /*Type*/GILLT_s32,
  GIM_RootCheckType, /*Op*/2, /*Type*/GILLT_s32,
```

Entries reported as try-block in the debug output are usually good for finding your way in the .inc file. Subtract 1 from the value reported for the try-block entry (here, 3086-1=3085) and chances are a @ annotation with that number is right before your try-block entry.

This is not ideal, and it would be nice to fix the TableGen backend to emit these. Consider contributing a patch yourself! (This issue is tracked on GitHub at https://github.com/llvm/llvm-project/issues/119177.)

In this section, you learned a few tips that will help you be more productive should you encounter an issue with one of the selectors. In particular, you learned how to find your way through the match tables, which is a mandatory skill to debug instruction selection issues.

Let us now wrap up this chapter.

# Summary

In this chapter, you learned how to set up and implement the `RegisterBankInfo` class of your target for GlobalISel. You saw that this pass focuses on optimizing cross-register bank copies and that this feature is unique to GlobalISel.

You then focused on the instruction selection phase itself where you learned how to use the selection patterns to describe the matching of your instructions from the generic IR of your selectors – namely, the SelectionDAG IR and the generic Machine IR (and to some extent, the LLVM IR) – to produce your target-specific `MachineInstr` instances.

You saw how these patterns can be augmented with advanced constructs such as pattern fragments that allow you to do partial matching and complex patterns that allow you to describe your matching with pure C++ functions.

Then, you learned how to integrate your patterns in your selectors and saw that you already did the heavy lifting for both SDISel and FastISel in *Chapter 14*. For GlobalISel, you saw how to connect the dedicated TableGen backend to create your target-specific `InstructionSelector` class.

Moving beyond the selection phase, you learned how to inject optimizations in the form of pattern rewrites in both SDISel and GlobalISel. You saw that SDISel's own optimizations may work against you and discovered how to force it to stop doing that. For GlobalISel, you learned how to leverage a dedicated TableGen backend to compose your set of rewriting rules and produce `MachineFunctionPass` instances that run them.

Next, we went over the finalization mechanism and showed you the expectations that this mechanism must fulfill for the other passes to work. You also learned that you could leverage a concept called a custom inserter to do some early pseudo-instruction expansions that are otherwise difficult to capture with selection patterns alone.

Finally, you learned vital skills to debug instruction selection-related issues.

Similar to all the chapters related to the instruction selection phases, remember that we could not cover everything these frameworks have to offer. For instance, SDISel features a mandatory scheduling phase, which you sometimes may want to tweak. However, we left it out of this book because, for most use cases, it is good enough out of the box. Also, there is an art to writing selection patterns, playing nice with legalization, finding the right balance between custom nodes and complex patterns, and so on. These are things that only experience, trial, and error will teach you. We could go on and on about what you should strive to set up, but the trade-offs are subtle and difficult to properly weigh and, ultimately, might go over your head at this point in your journey.

At this point, we feel that you are sufficiently armed with knowledge to go on this journey. Remember that LLVM is a community, and you can always ask for help there; you may even find the author of this book directly! Do not be shy to reach out!

With the instruction selection process completely covered, we can now continue our journey toward producing assembly code and move down the lowering pipeline. Our next stop is the instruction scheduling pass.

# Quiz time

Now that you have completed reading this chapter, try answering the following questions to test your knowledge.

1.  What is the purpose of the register bank selection phase in GlobalISel?

    The register bank selection phase optimizes cross-register bank copies.

    See the *The goal of the register bank selection* section for more details.

2.  What is the main advantage of using the selection patterns as opposed to plain C++ implementations for the different selectors?

    The selection patterns, written in TableGen, offer a declarative way to describe your instruction selection patterns and are portable across the different selection frameworks. The portability has some limitations, but this is the best way to share code across the selectors.

    More information on how to use them is in the *Expressing your selection patterns* and *Importing the selection patterns* sections.

3.  What selection pattern construct can you use to match target-specific addressing modes?

    For complex pattern matching such as addressing modes, you can use the `ComplexPattern` TableGen class construct.

    You can find more information on the advanced patterns in the *Advanced selection patterns* section.

4.  What is the purpose of the concept of a custom inserter?

    A custom inserter allows the production of a code sequence as complex as required right after instruction selection by expanding specific instructions. They are useful to capture custom lowering patterns that are otherwise not expressible through selection patterns.

    See the *Finalizing the selection pipeline* section for more details.

5.  What type of optimization do SDISel and GlobalISel facilitate?

    Both selection frameworks offer a way to plug custom rewriting rules. In SDISel, this is expressed through a few target hooks, and in GlobalISel, you can use a TableGen backend as a factory to build `MachineFunctionPass` classes that implement these custom rewriting rules.

    Both approaches are covered in the *Optimizations* section.

6.  How should you debug the code generated by the selection patterns?

    Selection patterns are used to produce match tables that are interpreted by a state machine. To easily debug what this state machine does, you need to print out the debug log of the instruction selection phase in the related selection framework and use this information to follow the path that the state machine took in the match table produced by TableGen.

    You can find more information on how to do that in the *Debugging the selectors* section.

## Unlock this book's exclusive benefits now

This book comes with additional benefits designed to elevate your learning experience.

*Note: Have your purchase invoice ready before you begin.*

https://www.packtpub.com/unlock/9781837637782

# Part 5

# Final Lowering and Optimizations

At this point, you are able to generate the Machine **intermediate representation (IR)** for your backend from any LLVM IR.

The next and final step is to lower this representation into the final assembly representation with properly assigned registers, stack space, and so on.

This part focuses on the optimization passes that the LLVM infrastructure features to perform this lowering.

More specifically, in this part, you will learn the following:

- How to teach instruction scheduling about the timing of your instructions such that you get the best-performing code out of the LLVM infrastructure
- How to use the LLVM register allocation infrastructure to assign registers to your program
- How to teach the prologue-epilogue inserter how to materialize the stack layout of your target
- How to produce the final binary object

Aside from instruction scheduling, which is an optimization, all these steps are mandatory to produce your final object file.

By the end of this section, you will have a fully functional backend and will be ready to contribute to any existing backend or write your own from end to end!

This part of the book includes the following chapters:

# 18

# Instruction Scheduling

Instruction scheduling is a low-level optimization that improves the sequence of instructions according to different strategies. For instance, it is possible to use this optimization to reduce the register pressure (how many registers you need to allocate) or increase the **instruction-level parallelism** (ILP) (the number of instructions that can be executed in parallel) of your program.

While this optimization is optional in your LLVM backend, we thought it was important to cover it for two main reasons:

- Instruction scheduling can unlock important performance improvements, especially if you are dealing with an in-order processor. In-order processors execute instructions in the order prescribed by the assembly code, whereas out-of-order processors can dynamically adapt the execution of the program while decoding the assembly code.
- Approaching the LLVM instruction scheduling infrastructure can be tricky without some guidance.

In this chapter, you will learn how the instruction scheduling infrastructure is implemented. More specifically, you will learn about the following:

- How to tweak the scheduling heuristics
- How to implement a scheduling model for your target

This knowledge is the foundation to understand and modify the existing scheduling heuristics in the open source LLVM backends and your key to implementing your own scheduling strategies.

Let us start with the technical requirements for this chapter.

# Technical requirements

Similar to the other chapters that built an LLVM backend, you need to develop directly in the LLVM code base (or a fork of it). As such, you will need all the same tools as presented in *Chapter 1*.

Additionally, for all the snippets presented in this chapter, you will find the actual implementation in the GitHub repository at `https://github.com/PacktPublishing/LLVM-Code-Generation-by-example`. We call this repository the **companion repository** in the remainder of the chapter.

The changes for this chapter are all included between the `begin_ch18` and `end_ch18` Git tags of the companion repository. If you are not familiar with Git tags, refer to *Chapter 9* for a quick explanation of what you can do with them. Throughout the chapter, we also mention specific tags that we created in this repository so you can easily find the relevant commits.

Let us now introduce the concepts used for instruction scheduling in LLVM.

# Overview of the instruction scheduling framework

The instruction scheduling framework in LLVM is made up of three main pieces. Let's go through them one by one:

- The data structure that represents the dependencies of the instructions to be scheduled. In the literature, this is called the **data dependency graph** (**DDG**), and in LLVM, it is represented with the `ScheduleDAG` class and its subclasses. At the **code generation** (**codegen**) level, you start with the `ScheduleDAGInstrs` subclass. Similar to what we explained in *Chapter 14* for the **directed-acyclic graph** (**DAG**) instruction selection framework (also known as **SDISel**), this graph represents the producer/consumer data dependencies as well as the ordering constraints of the memory dependencies. In other words, this graph gives a relative order of the instructions, and a schedule is valid if and only if all these constraints are fulfilled. For instance, if there is an edge from node A toward node B, then B must appear before A in the final basic block for the schedule to be valid. To put it differently, the edges represent the **use-def** chain and hence may look counter-intuitive.
- The scheduling strategy that guides all the scheduling decisions. This strategy is represented by the `MachineSchedStrategy` class and its subclasses. More specifically, when implementing your own strategy, you will likely start from the `GenericScheduler` class or the `PostGenericScheduler` class. We will go into more detail regarding what you can do with this concept in the *Changing the scheduling algorithm* section.
- The scheduling model of your subtarget that informs the scheduler about the scheduling events of each instruction, such as the latency of a load, the type of processing unit a specific instruction needs to execute, and how the subtarget executes its instructions, for example, whether the resource is used in order or out of order and how many instructions it can issue in parallel. At the codegen level, the scheduling model is represented with the `TargetSchedModel` class, and at the **machine code** (**MC**) level, it is represented with the `MCSchedModel` class. Like a lot of codegen/MC classes, this codegen class is a wrapper around the MC class with additional logic to make it easier to use by the codegen passes.

> **Note**
>
> You can use the `view-misched-dags` command-line option to print in the dot format the DDG of each region of your input program. To visualize this graph, refer to *Chapter 17* to see how to manipulate dot files.

At a high level, the `MachineScheduler` pass articulates these three pieces by first asking your target to create an instance of the `ScheduleDAGInstrs` class. Then, it schedules it using the strategy and the scheduling model that you attached to your `ScheduleDAGInstrs` instance.

> **Note**
>
> We will explain how to tweak your scheduling strategy and how to create an instance of the `ScheduleDAGInstrs` class in the following sections, but we wanted to highlight that the `MachineScheduler` pass comes with well-written comments that lay out the general principles behind how all these things work together. We will not repeat these comments and we encourage you to read through them in the `llvm/include/llvm/CodeGen/MachineScheduler.h` file.

As we mentioned in the introduction, the scheduling phase is completely optional, and to enable the `MachineScheduler` pass, you must override the related `enableMachineScheduler` and/or `enablePostRAMachineScheduler` method of your `TargetSubtargetInfo` class. Both of these methods return a Boolean that tells the codegen pass pipeline whether the `MachineScheduler` pass needs to be run before register allocation for the first method and after register allocation for the second method. You can find an example of such an override in the commit tagged `enable-misched_ch18` in the companion repository.

> **Note**
>
> When you enable the `MachineScheduler` pass and use SDISel as your instruction selection framework, this framework will use a simpler scheduling heuristic when linearizing the input `SelectionDAG` instance into a basic block. At this point, SDISel relies on the `MachineScheduler` pass to do the heavy lifting. If you still want to use more complex scheduling in SDISel by default, you need to override the `enableMachineSchedDefaultSched` method of your `TargetSubtargetInfo` class and return `false`.

Since you have not tweaked the three main pieces of the scheduling infrastructure yet, at this point, the `MachineScheduler` pass relies on the default scheduling model and heuristics. By default, this does not add much except that now all the instructions marked with the `mayLoad` property are assumed to have a latency of four cycles (as defined by the `MCSchedModel::DefaultLoadLatency` static member variable). Note that the `mayLoad` property is also automatically set on the instructions that are produced by the selection of intrinsics that carries the `mayLoad` property (see *Chapter 17* for more details on these patterns).

Now that you have a general idea of how the different pieces connect, let us see what you can do with each of them, starting with the DDG representation, which is modeled in LLVM with the ScheduleDAGInstrs class.

# The ScheduleDAGInstrs class

The whole scheduling process in the MachineScheduler pass is driven by a ScheduleDAGInstrs instance. The ScheduleDAGInstrs class encapsulates both the DDG and the scheduling strategy used. In other words, this class is responsible for building the DDG and then scheduling it using the scheduling strategy it has been instantiated with.

The MachineScheduler pass acts as a simple driver around the methods of the ScheduleDAGInstrs instance that is provided to it via the MachineScheduler::createMachineScheduler method.

By default, this method creates a ScheduleDAGMILive instance, which is a subclass of the ScheduleDAGInstrs class that is tweaked to schedule MachineInstr instances and keep track of the register liveness (and register pressure) at the same time.

You can change this default by overriding the createMachineScheduler method of your TargetPassConfig class. This override is your main entry point to tweaking the type of ScheduleDAGInstrs subclass that is used, as well as the scheduling strategy. We will cover the scheduling strategy in the next section.

Focusing on the ScheduleDAGInstrs class, one of the main benefits is its capability to accept **mutations**. Mutations are modifications that you can apply to the DDG after it is fully built by the generic algorithm.

Consider the example in *Table 18.1*.

| Input sequence | Default DDG | Mutated DDG |
|---|---|---|
| a = instrA<br>b = instrB a<br>c = instrC a<br>d = instrD b, c | instrA<br>instrB  instrC<br>instrD | instrA<br>instrB<br>instrC<br>instrD |

*Table 18.1: A sequence of instructions, its DDG, and a potential mutated DDG*

The leftmost column of *Table 18.1* shows a sequence of instructions, instrA, instrB, and so on, and the middle column shows the related DDG. In this DDG, you can see that the scheduler is free to pick up either the instrB or instrC instruction after the instrA instruction has been scheduled. Indeed, the instrB and instrC instructions do not have any dependency (represented by the arrows) between them and they can be scheduled freely from one another. Now, let us assume that, for some reason, you know that your target behaves in a more performant way when the instrB instruction is scheduled strictly before the instrC instruction; you can mutate the DDG by adding a constraint between the instrB and instrC instructions, as shown with the dotted arrow in the rightmost column. Thanks to this mutation, the scheduler will have no choice but to schedule the instrB instruction before the instrC instruction.

Note

When applying mutations, make sure you do not create cycles; otherwise, the scheduler will not be able to find a valid solution.

Mutations are represented with the ScheduleDAGMutation class. To create your own mutation, you simply need to create your own specialized version of this class and implement the apply method, which takes a ScheduleDAGInstrs instance and mutates it in place, meaning that the instance of the graph is modified directly.

Then, you need to register your mutations using the addMutation method on the ScheduleDAGInstrs instance of your scheduler. In other words, in your TargetPassConfig::createMachineScheduler method (you will find an example of how to implement this method in the next section), when you create your instance of the ScheduleDAGInstrs subclass, you need to call the addMutation method with your instance of the ScheduleDAGMutation class. You can find plenty of examples of how to do that in open source backends such as AArch64, AMDGPU, or x86, to name a few.

The generic infrastructure also provides mutations that you can use directly, such as one that groups memory operations of the same kind together. These mutations are declared in the llvm/include/llvm/CodeGen/MachineScheduler.h file, and you can use them by registering the createLoadClusterDAGMutation and createStoreClusterDAGMutation functions with calls to the addMutation method.

In this section, you learned that the ScheduleDAGInstrs class represents your DDG and that you can modify it using the concept of mutations. You also learned that this class encapsulates the scheduling heuristics. In the next section, we will show you how you can tweak them.

# Changing the scheduling algorithm

The MachineSchedStrategy class represents the scheduling algorithm used by a ScheduleDAGInstrs class. You set up your strategy while you create your ScheduleDAGInstrs instance in your TargetPassConfig::createMachineScheduler method.

This class offers all the entry points to tweak every aspect of the scheduling algorithm, such as what to do when you start processing a new basic block (with the enterMBB method) and what to do when you pick the next instruction to schedule (with the pickNode method).

This class is a pure abstract class, and if you want to tweak the scheduling algorithm, we recommend that you start from its concrete subclasses that are used by default, respectively, for the pre-register-allocation scheduling with the GenericScheduler class and for the post-register-allocation scheduling with the PostGenericScheduler class.

These classes offer easier-to-override methods thanks to the strategically newly exposed methods. For instance, instead of having to override the `pickNode` method, which would require you to go through the **ready queue** (see the following note for an explanation) yourself and pick the best candidate, these classes expose a `tryCandidate` method that is focused on just checking whether one candidate instruction is better than another one.

> **Ready queue**
>
> In scheduling, the ready queue is the list of instructions that are potential candidates for the next instruction to schedule. They are ready to be scheduled. An instruction is moved into this queue when all its dependencies have been satisfied; that is, for a top-down scheduler (a scheduler that starts scheduling from the top of the DDG), all its successors in the DDG have been scheduled, and in a bottom-up scheduler, all its predecessors have been scheduled.

To make things more concrete, here is an example of the custom scheduling strategy that we used for our H2BLB target. This strategy is used for the pre-register-allocation scheduler (hence it inherits from the `GenericScheduler` class) and prioritizes our widening signed multiply instruction (the `WIDENING_SMUL` opcode) when the candidates are otherwise equivalent:

```
class H2BLBPreRASchedStrategy : public GenericScheduler {
public:
  H2BLBPreRASchedStrategy(const MachineSchedContext *C) : GenericScheduler(C) {}
protected:
  bool tryCandidate(SchedCandidate &Cand, SchedCandidate &TryCand,
                    SchedBoundary *Zone) const override {
    bool BetterCand = GenericScheduler::tryCandidate(Cand, TryCand, Zone);
    if (BetterCand && TryCand.Reason != NodeOrder && TryCand.Reason != NoCand)
      return true;
    if (Zone != nullptr) {
      if (TryCand.SU->getInstr()->mayLoad()) {
        TryCand.Reason = Stall;
        return true;
      }
      unsigned Opc = TryCand.SU->getInstr()->getOpcode();
      if (Opc == H2BLB::WIDENING_SMUL) {
        TryCand.Reason = Stall;
        return true;
      }
    }
    return TryCand.Reason != NoCand;
  }
};
```

In this snippet, we start by using the default heuristic of the GenericScheduler class by calling the tryCandidate method of our super class. The returned Boolean tells us whether the new candidate, represented with the TryCand variable, is better than the original one, represented with the Cand variable. If the new candidate is better, we check why it is better. Indeed, the TryCand variable has a Reason field that tells us why it has been picked up. When the Reason field has either the NoCand or NodeOrder value, this means the pick is not particularly smart, and this is where we tweak the algorithm. Indeed, the NodeOrder value means that the TryCand variable was a better pick because it is simply the next node in the original order of the basic block; in other words, the order is used as a tiebreaker when candidates are equivalent. The NoCand value means there were no other candidates.

It is up to you to decide when to apply your own heuristics, but we wanted to explain our reasoning so you can reproduce it if you think it makes sense.

We then start our own heuristic by checking whether we are in the same **region** with the if (Zone != nullptr) statement. Regions are continuous sequences of instructions that are at most as large as the current basic block. In other words, basic blocks are split into scheduling regions, and this is what you are scheduling. You can influence how the regions are formed by overriding the isSchedulingBoundary method of your TargetInstrInfo class. In any case, you cannot have regions bigger than a full basic block; therefore, there are no super or hyper blocks in LLVM. If you do not know what we are talking about, this is fine since this is not available anyway!

Back to our scheduling strategy snippet, our heuristic is simple: we check whether the new candidate has the mayLoad attribute, and if so, we choose it and report that it was chosen because this instruction may stall (with the TryCand.Reason = Stall statement). Otherwise, we do a similar check with our widening signed multiply instruction providing a similar reason, since we know our instruction has a two-cycle latency.

You can find the full snippet at the commit tagged custom-sched-strategy_ch18 in the companion repository. This is just an example of what you can do with the scheduling strategies; feel free to explore the different methods that you can override.

Now that you have your custom scheduling strategy, let us see how to plug it into your MachineScheduler pass.

As we said at the beginning of this section, the strategy is fed directly to your ScheduleDAGInstrs instance. This means that you simply initialize your ScheduleDAGInstrs instance with your custom strategy, as demonstrated in the following snippet:

```
ScheduleDAGInstrs *
H2BLBPassConfig::createMachineScheduler(MachineSchedContext *C) const {
  ScheduleDAGMILive *DAG = new ScheduleDAGMILive(
      C, std::make_unique<H2BLBPreRASchedStrategy>(C));
  // add DAG Mutations here.
  return DAG;
}
```

In this snippet, we create a `ScheduleDAGMILive` instance, which is one of the concrete classes of the `ScheduleDAGInstrs` class, using our custom `MachineSchedStrategy` instance – the `H2BLBPreRASchedStrategy` class.

You can find the full snippet at the commit tagged `plug-custom-sched-strategy_ch18` in the companion repository.

There is one last thing that you can tweak in the scheduling strategy using the overriding mechanism of the `MachineSchedPolicy` instance in your `TargetSubtargetInfo` class. The `MachineSchedPolicy` class holds some high-level flags that influence the whole processing of the scheduling strategies, such as the direction of the scheduling or whether to track the liveness as part of the scheduling algorithm. You can find the meaning of each field by looking at the comment in the class.

Regarding the scheduling directions, *Figure 18.1* illustrates what this is, in case you are not familiar with this concept:

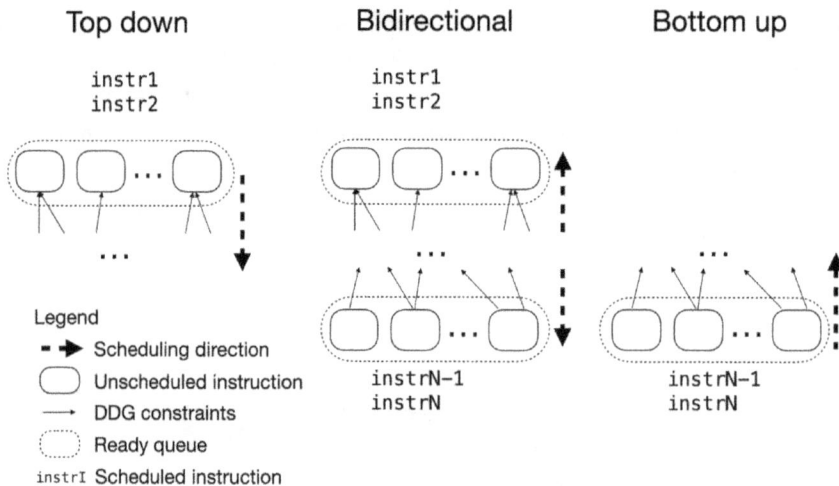

*Figure 18.1: Scheduling directions*

In *Figure 18.2*, all three columns show the same DDG surrounded by the instructions already scheduled. The leftmost column shows the **top-down** scheduling direction. The instructions are scheduled from the beginning of the region (the top) to the end of the region (the bottom). After an instruction is scheduled, the next one is picked from the list of nodes in the DDG that do not have any successor, as illustrated by the dotted rectangle with rounded corners.

The **bottom-up** direction, illustrated in the rightmost column of the diagram, is the opposite of the **top-down** direction. Here, the nodes are scheduled from the end of the region to the beginning of the region and the ready queue is made of the nodes in the DDG that do not have any predecessors.

The **bidirectional** direction is a mixture of both approaches. It picks the next instruction to schedule in either the top or bottom ready queue.

By default, the scheduling policy is set to bidirectional in LLVM. Different directions yield different results and there is no good or bad choice. Which direction to choose is up to you.

To override the `MachineSchedPolicy` instance, among other things, you need to implement the scheduling direction and the `overrideSchedPolicy` method of your `TargetSubtargetInfo` class.

Here is what it looks like for our H2BLB target:

```
void H2BLBSubtarget::overrideSchedPolicy(MachineSchedPolicy &Policy,
                                         unsigned NumRegionInstrs) const {
  Policy.OnlyTopDown = true;
  Policy.OnlyBottomUp = false;
}
```

In this snippet, we modify the `MachineSchedPolicy` instance to always run in the top-down scheduling direction. You can view the full snippet in the commit tagged `sched-policy_ch18` in the companion repository.

In this section, you learned how to inject your own scheduling heuristics by providing your own implementation of the `MachineSchedStrategy` class and attaching it to your `ScheduleDAGInstrs` instance. You also saw that you can change the overall scheduling policy, such as the scheduling direction, by overriding the right method in your `TargetSubtargetInfo` class.

In the next section, we will cover the last piece of the scheduling infrastructure in LLVM, the scheduling model.

# The scheduling model

In the LLVM scheduling infrastructure, the scheduling model is the piece that holds all the information about the resources of the subtarget and how they are used by the various instructions.

> **Note**
>
> We always speak about subtargets when talking about scheduling capabilities. This is because the scheduling capabilities are tied to the microarchitecture of your target, hence its subtarget. For instance, the scheduling capabilities of the x86 target are different for the Haswell and the Sapphire Rapids microarchitectures.

This information is described statically with TableGen and then used by the scheduling infrastructure to make decisions.

In typical LLVM fashion, there are two complementary ways to describe your scheduling model. At the core, both methods model how processor resources are used, such as the **arithmetic logic unit** (**ALU**) and load-store unit, but to simplify it, one does that in terms of scheduling events and the other in terms of itineraries within the instruction pipeline.

In this book, we will only cover the method based on the scheduling events because it is sufficient for most targets. Describing the instruction itineraries is only recommended for in-order **very long instruction word** (VLIW) processors. If you do not know what a VLIW processor is, that is perfect; it means you do not need itineraries, like most people! More seriously, using what you will learn with the scheduling events-based approach, you should be able to approach itineraries modeling by yourself if you ever need it.

In this section, you will learn the pieces involved in a scheduling model, what they represent, and how you can use them to describe the capabilities of your subtarget.

Let's try to understand the scheduling model in more detail.

The scheduling model uses the TableGen classes described in the `llvm/include/llvm/Target/TargetSchedule.td` file and the related included files, such as the `TargetItinerary.td` file for itineraries-based modeling.

These files are extremely well commented but can be hard to approach if you do not know where to start or what you are looking at.

Let's go through how the main pieces are articulated to form a scheduling model. Using this knowledge, we are confident you will be able to then understand all the subtleties that all the other TableGen classes have to offer.

The pieces we will cover are the following:

- **The SchedMachineModel TableGen class:** This class represents the overall scheduling capabilities of the subtarget.
- **The SchedReadWrite TableGen class and subclasses:** These classes represent the scheduling events that are attached to the operands of the instructions.
- **The ProcResourceUnits TableGen class and subclasses:** These classes represent the processing units of a subtarget.
- **The WriteRes and ReadAdvance TableGen classes:** These classes bind the scheduling events with the processing units of a subtarget.

*Figure 18.2* illustrates how these pieces are articulated.

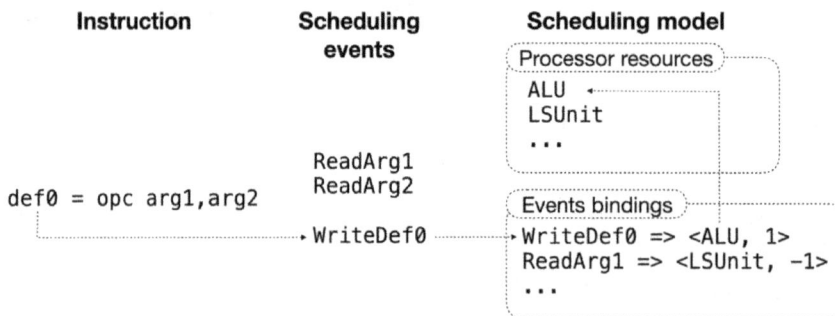

*Figure 18.2: The binding of the scheduling events of an instruction in a scheduling model*

In *Figure 18.2*, the opc instruction on the left produces three scheduling events. In this case, the scheduling events for this instruction are ReadArg1, ReadArg2, and WriteRes0, as listed in the middle column. A scheduling model, represented on the right, defines processor resources (here ALU and LSUnit) and binds the scheduling events on these resources. For instance, let's look at the definition of the opc instruction, def0. This definition is mapped to the WriteDef0 scheduling event. This event is then bound by the scheduling model on the right to the ALU processor resource with a latency of 1. This means that producing this definition costs one cycle of the ALU resource. Resource costs can also be negative (look at ReadArg1, for instance) and represent forwarding paths in this case.

> **Note**
>
> The number of scheduling events for a given instruction is in your control. The only constraint is that you can describe at most one scheduling event per operand and, at a minimum, one (write) scheduling event per explicit definition. In other words, the number of scheduling events that you need to describe per instruction is comprised of [#explicit definitions, #operands], where #operands includes the implicit operands. If you need a refresher on implicit and explicit operands, refer to *Chapter 11*. This range only applies to instructions you want to model in the scheduling model. In other words, if you do not attach any scheduling event to an instruction, this is okay but it will not be covered by the scheduling model.

Now that you have a general idea of how the pieces fit together, let us focus on each of them one by one, starting with the lowest piece of the infrastructure, the scheduling events.

## The scheduling events

As already mentioned, the scheduling events are represented by the SchedReadWrite TableGen class and its subclasses. More precisely, you describe a schedule event by instantiating a record of the SchedRead TableGen class for the arguments (respectively a record of the SchedWrite TableGen class for the definitions) of your instructions.

The only semantics carried by these records is whether they can be attached to a definition or a use. Therefore, you could technically use an instance of the same SchedWrite class for all the definitions of all your instructions, for instance, and the related TableGen backend would be perfectly happy with that. However, this would greatly limit the expressiveness of your scheduling model since you can bind a scheduling event to exactly one resource, so all your instructions would behave the same.

Defining scheduling events in TableGen is straightforward and simply follows what you learned in *Chapter 6*. However, if you need an example, you can look at the commit tagged add-sched-events_ch18 in the companion repository.

Then, you decorate your instructions with the proper scheduling events by doing either of the following:

- Populating the `SchedRW` field on your instructions
- Having your instruction inherit from the `Sched` class with the list of scheduling events as an argument

The following snippet shows an example of both ways that you can do the decoration of your instruction with scheduling events, one using the `SchedRW` field and one using the `Sched` class:

```
let SchedRW = [WriteWUMUL, ReadWUMULArg0, ReadWUMULArg1] in
def WIDENING_UMUL : H2BLBWidenIMul<"wumul", /*isSign=*/0>;
def WIDENING_SMUL : H2BLBWidenIMul<"wsmul", /*isSign=*/1>,
    Sched<[WriteWSMUL, ReadWSMULArg0, ReadWSMULArg1]>;
```

The definition of the `WIDENING_UMUL` record sets the `SchedRW` field of the `Instruction` class using a `let` statement with a list of custom scheduling events that we defined in a separate file (these events are, respectively, instances of the `SchedWrite`, `SchedRead`, and `SchedRead` classes). The second record, `WIDENING_SMUL`, uses the inheritance of the `Sched` class to set the scheduling events. The events are passed directly to the `Sched` class.

> **Note**
>
> Both methods to decorate the instructions with scheduling events just set a `SchedRW` field in the final record of the instruction. The `Sched` class just does it indirectly by stomping on the content of the `SchedRW` field of the instruction, thanks to the inheritance rules of TableGen.

The full snippet can be seen at the commit tagged `add-sched-events_ch18` in the companion repository.

Lastly, we recommend you read the comments set in the `llvm/include/llvm/Target/TargetSchedule.td` file for the `Sched` class because they go into all the details of what the orders of the scheduling events should be, and so on. We have already explained all of this to you at this point, but the comment goes into more detail and may be interesting to read.

# The processing units

At the core, the definition of the processing units relies on the `ProcResourceUnits` TableGen class, which we already mentioned. However, you likely want to compose the instances of this class to achieve an easy-to-maintain or easy-to-extend scheduling model.

Concretely, each instance of the `ProcResourceUnits` TableGen class allows you to model one type of processing unit and specifies how many of this unit your processor has. What and how you model something is up to you. What this means is that you only need to model things that are relevant to what you want to achieve with your scheduler, and you have to model it in a way that makes sense to you and is aligned with your goal.

What we are saying is, for instance, assume that your processor has a floating-point unit and a vector unit. The natural modeling would be to describe them as two different processing units. However, you might want to model them as one unit that encompasses both. There is no right or wrong way here; you need to know the details that you want to model and the impact they have on the flexibility of your whole system.

After describing all your resources, you will want to group them under an instance of the `ProcResGroup` TableGen class to describe your scheduling model efficiently. For instance, let us say that your processor has a memory processing unit and an ALU. Assuming you model these two units as separate resources, you likely will need to bind both resources to all your memory operations because these memory operations need the memory processing unit to read from or write to memory and need the ALU for the addressing modes (that is, for the computation of the address location).

The following snippet demonstrates how this would look in TableGen:

```
def ALURes : ProcResource<1>;
def MemRes : ProcResource<1>;
def MemAndALURes: ProcResGroup<[MemRes, ALURes]>;
```

In this snippet, we start by describing our two resources using one of the subclasses of the `ProcResourceUnits` class, the `ProcResource` class. The parameter given to the `ProcResource` class (here 1 in both cases) describes the number of units available. Next, we group these resources with a `ProcResGroup` instance.

Putting things together, our recommendation is to represent the processing units as close as possible to the actual hardware implementation and then use the grouping mechanism offered by the `ProcResGroup` class to form logical super units that you will use in the bindings of your scheduling model.

You can find plenty of examples of how to use these constructs in open source backends such as AArch64 or x86. Our example in the H2BLB backend, available at the commit tagged `sched-model_ch18` in the companion repository, shows some of them in action but does not demonstrate the use of the `ProcResGroup` class.

We will go into slightly more detail on what you can do with these classes in the *Implementing your scheduling model* section but will remain light on the details. We made this decision because all the TableGen classes involved in the scheduling model are very well documented in the `llvm/include/llvm/Target/TargetSchedule.td` file, as already mentioned, and we do not want to repeat the information that is available there. In particular, the `ProcResourceUnits` TableGen class exposes a `BufferSize` field that can be used to represent different flavors of in-order processors or out-of-order processors.

## The scheduling bindings

As already mentioned, the bindings tie together scheduling events with resource consumption. Every scheduling event must be bound to a processing resource to have a valid scheduling model, but not all instructions need to produce scheduling events.

In other words, when building a scheduling model, you can progressively describe the scheduling events of your instructions until you have covered all of them or are satisfied with the current results. The instructions that have not been explicitly decorated with scheduling events simply use the default values of the scheduling model or the generic infrastructure. For instance, most instructions are assumed to take a single cycle if they are not explicitly covered with scheduling events.

Until you cover all your instructions with bindings, your scheduling model is deemed **incomplete**.

> **Note**
>
> It is okay to have an incomplete scheduling model, but if you strive for a complete one, where all the instructions of your backend are covered in your scheduling model, set the CompleteModel field to true in your SchedMachineModel instance when you think you are done. This will tell the TableGen backend to report errors if some instructions are not modeled. This is particularly useful when several people work on the same backend because it prevents someone from adding, for instance, a new pseudo instruction while forgetting to teach the scheduling model how to deal with it.

The bindings are simple instantiations of the ReadAdvance and WriteRes classes or instantiations of InstRW.

The difference between describing the bindings with the ReadAdvance/WriteRes classes and the InstRW class is where the scheduling events live in your implementation.

For the former, the scheduling events must be attached to the related instructions and then tied to the processing resources using the ReadAdvance/WriteRes classes. So, the scheduling events live with the instructions and the bindings with the scheduling model.

For the InstRW class, the scheduling events are described within the scheduling model using the SchedWriteRes class for the equivalent (WriteRes, SchedWrite) binding and the SchedReadAdvance class for the equivalent (ReadAdvance, SchedRead) binding. Then, the InstRW instances decorate the instructions with this binding.

To summarize, the InstRW method allows you to have both your scheduling events and bindings located within your scheduling model, whereas the ReadAdvance/WriteRes method forces you to mix your instructions with scheduling information and then provide some meaning to this scheduling information in your scheduling model.

We recommend using the InstRW method as it allows for standalone implementations, but both offer different trade-offs and are compatible, meaning that you can mix both within your scheduling model.

The following snippet shows an example of the ReadAdvance/WriteRes methods:

```
let SchedModel = H2BLBDefaultModel in {
let Latency = 2 in
def : WriteRes<WriteWSMUL, [ALURes]>;
```

```
def : ReadAdvance<ReadWSMULArg0, 0>;
def : ReadAdvance<ReadWSMULArg1, 1>;
}
```

In this snippet, you can see three records that represent the three bindings of different scheduling events: WriteWSMUL, ReadWSMULArg0, and ReadWSMULArg1. Given the bindings (the WriteRes or ReadAdvance construct), you should be able to guess which events are records of the SchedWrite class and which ones are records of the SchedRead class.

The first binding registers in the scheduling model, identified by the SchedModel field, that the WriteWSMUL scheduling event takes two cycles (as set by the Latency field) and uses the ALURes processing unit.

Then, the ReadAdvance bindings modulate, if needed, what the reading of the related operands (the one decorated in the description of the instructions with the related scheduling event) does to the scheduling. For the ReadWSMULArg0 event, it does nothing, hence 0 for the second argument, and for ReadWSMULArg1, it absorbs one cycle; that is, there is a forwarding path. What this illustrates is that the ReadAdvance class can be used to model forwarding paths or execution domain penalties. The ReadAdvance class takes an optional argument that specifies the write events after which this bonus or penalty needs to be applied.

The next snippet illustrates how to use the InstRW class:

```
let SchedModel = H2BLBDefaultModel in {
let Latency = 3 in
def DefaultWriteLoad : SchedWriteRes<[MemRes]>;
def : InstRW<[DefaultWriteLoad], (instregex "^LD[^i]*$")>;
}
```

In this snippet, we define a scheduling event and a binding at the same time with the DefaultWriteLoad record using the SchedWriteRes class. This binding is a write event with a latency of 3 cycles that uses the MemRes processing unit. At this point, this binding is not tied to any instruction. The InstRW record that is right after fixes that by decorating all the instructions that match the given regular expression with this scheduling information. The regular expression is matched against the opcode of the instructions (that is, the names of the fully expanded record of your instructions). In this case, we are matching all our load instructions, excluding the load immediate ones.

You can find the full snippet of this example at the commit tagged sched-model_ch18 in the companion repository (see the *Technical requirements* section for the link).

Similar to the previous section, read the comments on all the related TableGen classes to see the full details of what you can model.

# Gluing everything together

The scheduling model, represented by the `SchedMachineModel` TableGen class, glues all the previous information together.

The scheduling model serves two main purposes:

- It provides a home for the processing units exposed by the related hardware implementation and for the bindings of the scheduling events to these processing units. Concretely, all the related classes (`WriteRes`, `ReadAdvance`, and so on) have a `SchedModel` field that needs to be set to the record that represents the scheduling model they describe. You usually do that by setting this field globally with a `let` statement as we did in the last two snippets.

- It defines the overall capabilities of the subtarget, such as the maximum number of micro-operations that can be issued per cycle (complex instructions are usually implemented in the hardware with simpler micro-operations) or the default latency assumed for instructions that have the `mayLoad` property and have not been decorated yet.

> Note
>
> Instructions that do not have their own scheduling information, so the ones that use the default information of the scheduling model, do not benefit (or suffer) from the `ReadAdvance` constructs. For instance, let us say that you have a load instruction that has not been decorated. The LLVM scheduling infrastructure will assume that this load has the default load latency provided by the scheduling model. This is great because the scheduler will try to hide that latency. However, if this load feeds an instruction that has a `ReadAdvance` binding that describes a forwarding path on the related operand, the scheduling infrastructure will ignore it because it will not be able to find the write event that produces this value. Therefore, the scheduler may try to hide too many or too few cycles if you do not provide a complete scheduling model.

Now that your subtarget capabilities are fully described, the LLVM scheduling infrastructure will use its heuristics, with your tweaks, if any, to find the best possible schedule while keeping track of how the different resources of your subtarget are used.

This section concludes the overview of the pieces involved in defining a scheduling model. You saw that you need to describe the processing units, the scheduling events, and the bindings between the units and events, and put all of this under one scheduling model to describe the scheduling capabilities of your subtarget.

In the next section, we will show you how to connect this information to the LLVM infrastructure.

# Implementing your scheduling model

In the previous section, we already covered a lot of the implementation details of the scheduling model while explaining how to understand it.

In this section, we cover what is missing, which is how to connect your scheduling model to the codegen infrastructure, and recommendations of how you should approach the implementation. Notice that we did not speak about running the TableGen backend that produces the scheduling information. This is because you already connected the needed TableGen backend, gen-subtarget, in *Chapter 9*.

Without further ado, let us start with connecting your scheduling model with the codegen infrastructure.

## Connecting your scheduling model

For this section, let us assume you have already implemented your SchedMachineModel TableGen class.

At this point, you need to attach your scheduling model to the related processor model of your target (for instance, Haswell or Sapphire Rapids for x86) and connect the instantiation of your subtarget according to this processor.

### Describing a processor model

Normally, when you build an LLVM backend, you have at least one target processor in mind. Up until now, we have not told you how to describe it, so let us fix this!

The definition of a processor simply uses the ProcessorModel TableGen class.

One of the arguments of this class is the SchedMachineModel instance of the related processor.

The following snippet shows how we defined our processor for our H2BLB target:

```
def : ProcessorModel<"generic", H2BLBDefaultModel, []>;
```

The first argument of the ProcessorModel class, here generic, is the name of the processor. That name is used via the command-line options or metadata in the input LLVM IR to tell the backend which processor, thus subtarget, it should generate the code for.

The second argument is the name of your SchedMachineModel record. If you do not have a scheduling model yet, you can use the NoSchedModel value.

The third argument is the feature set supported by your processor. We will not go into the details of how to use them, but you can look at the comment on the SubtargetFeature TableGen class in the llvm/include/llvm/Target/Target.td file. Other backends have plenty of examples of how to use the subtarget features to gate the codegen of specific instructions, and so on.

Usually, the definition of your ProcessorModel records lives in your llvm/lib/Target/XXX/XXX.td file, where XXX is the name of your backend.

You can find the full snippet for the ProcessorModel definition at the commit tagged skeleton-sched-model_ch18 in the companion repository.

Next, you must connect this processor model to the instantiation of your subtarget.

## Instantiating your subtarget

You already learned how to instantiate your subtarget in *Chapter 14*. However, in that chapter, we did not connect any processor model to the subtarget since you had not yet learned how to implement them.

Connecting your processor model is as easy as passing its name to the constructor of your subtarget. The generic code will take care of finding the related scheduling model based on just this name.

The following snippet shows how to connect your processor model without any refinements:

```
H2BLBSubtarget::H2BLBSubtarget(const Triple &TT, StringRef CPU, StringRef FS,
                               const TargetMachine &TM)
   : H2BLBGenSubtargetInfo(TT, CPU, /*TuneCPU=*/CPU, FS), FrameLowering(*this),
...
```

In this snippet, the third argument passed to the `H2BLBGenSubtargetInfo` constructor (see *Chapter 14* if you do not remember this class), commented here with `TuneCPU`, is the name of your processor model. You can find this snippet at the commit tagged `subtarget-set-sched-model_ch18` in the companion repository.

> **Note**
>
> If the `TuneCPU` argument is empty, the generic code will use the default LLVM scheduling model. This default model is generic to all targets and suitable for none. So, make sure to set this parameter to the right value!

The frontend usually sets the target **central processing unit** (**CPU**) as metadata in the input LLVM IR. Look for a field named `target-cpu` in the attributes of your LLVM IR function to see whether it was properly set.

At this point, your scheduling model is properly set up and connected to your subtarget. Now, let us give you some guidelines on how to approach the implementation of your scheduling model because we realize it can be daunting when doing it for the first time.

## Guidelines to get started with your scheduling model

First, let us come back to our recommendation of using the `InstRW` bindings in favor of the scheduling events description because whether you follow this recommendation will change the order in which you should approach the different elements.

The natural approach when using scheduling events is to first decorate your instructions with them, then bind them in your scheduling model using the `WriteRes` and `ReadAdvance` constructs that you now know. With the `InstRW` bindings, you do not need to go through the decoration step.

The reason we advocate against scheduling events is that you will likely want to share events across different instructions, and that means you will have to think about them globally. This is also true for the InstRW bindings with the SchedWriteRes and SchedReadAdvance classes, but this is less of a problem. Indeed, your InstRW bindings are local to your scheduling model, whereas the scheduling events are global to all scheduling models. Therefore, if you carefully craft your scheduling events for the current set of processors that you support, chances are that the newest generations may invalidate, at least partially, that mapping. For instance, let us say that you defined a WriteFloat event that you use to decorate your fdiv and fmax instructions because they have the exact same characteristics. Now, if the next processor of your architecture changes how these instructions behave, for instance, now the fdiv instruction takes two cycles but fmax only one, then you cannot share the same scheduling events anymore since scheduling events can be bound to only one (set of) resource(s). This is not the end of the world because you can fix your model with dedicated InstRW bindings, but we recommend just going with InstRW bindings everywhere for consistency and ease of reading.

With that out of the way, let us focus on the recommended steps for the InstRW bindings:

1. Start by creating your top-level SchedMachineModel instance.
2. Figure out a good default latency cost for your load instructions.
3. Set up the right issue width and so on.
4. Describe all your processing units, or at least the group of processing units that are useful for your first iteration of the scheduling model. For instance, start by describing the processing resources used in add instructions. Make sure to set the fields of these resources to the right value to achieve the right modeling (for instance, in order versus out of order) of your processor. Again, look at the comments in the llvm/include/llvm/Target/TargetSchedule.td file to help you with that.
5. Focus on creating the scheduling information for one (group of) instruction(s).
6. Create the SchedWriteRes and SchedReadAdvance events for it.
7. Decorate the instruction with these events using the InstRW construct.
8. Write a test case using the .mir file format that only runs the scheduler and that demonstrates a change in scheduling with and without your change.
9. Repeat from step 2 onward until you have described all the resources and instructions.
10. Mark your scheduling model as complete.

Note

All the information about latency, micro-operations, and so on should be provided by your hardware team. Alternatively, you can write microbenchmarks and/or leverage the LLVM llvm-exegesis command-line tool to figure out this information. We have no experience with this tool.

At the end of this process, you are done with your scheduling model. Congratulations!

In this section, you learned how to connect your scheduling model to the codegen infrastructure. Specifically, you saw that you need to tie your scheduling model to a processor description and make sure that the related processor name is correctly passed to the instantiation of your subtarget. Then, we gave you practical advice on how to build your scheduling model while using the knowledge you gained in the *The scheduling model* section.

# Summary

In this chapter, you learned how to leverage the LLVM instruction scheduling infrastructure to customize the scheduling decisions made in your backend.

You saw that the scheduling infrastructure is tied to your subtarget and its customization capabilities hinge on three axes:

- **The mutation of the DDG graph:** This allows you to modify the DDG of your input scheduling region by adding or removing constraints.
- **The tweaking of the scheduling strategy:** This allows you to modify how the overall scheduling algorithm works, such as how it picks its next candidate in the ready queue or in which direction the scheduling algorithm progresses.
- **The definition of your scheduling model:** This provides the scheduling infrastructure with the information it needs to know the resources available in your subtarget and track and optimize their consumption while scheduling the DDGs.

While this chapter scratched only the surface of what you can achieve with these customizations, you built the necessary ground knowledge to explore this design space on your own.

In the next chapter, you will learn about the register allocation infrastructure in LLVM.

# Quiz time

Now that you have completed reading this chapter, try answering the following questions to test your knowledge:

1.  What does a DDG represent?

    The DDG represents all the scheduling constraints of the instructions in a scheduling region. Put differently, it represents the weak order in which the instructions must appear in the linearized sequence of instructions.

    See the *Overview of the instruction scheduling framework* section for more information.

2.  What does the concept of mutations allow you to do to a DDG?

    The concept of mutations allows you to tweak the dependencies of the DDG after it is fully constructed for the current scheduling region. Thanks to this construct, you can, for instance, over-constrain the DDG to limit the freedom that the scheduler has around certain instructions.

    Refer to the *The ScheduleDAGInstrs class* section for more details.

3. Is there a built-in way in LLVM to see the DDG graphically?

   Yes! Use the `view-misched-dags` command-line option for that.

   See the *Overview of the instruction scheduling framework* section for more details.

4. What are the two main steps to add an instruction to a scheduling model with the `InstRW` construct?

   First, you need to describe all the scheduling events of this instruction using the `SchedWriteRes` and `SchedReadAdvance` constructs while setting the `SchedModel` field to your scheduling model. Second, you bind them to your instruction using the `InstRW` construct.

   See the *The scheduling bindings* section for more details.

5. What happens if you do not set the processor model when instantiating your subtarget?

   If you instantiate your subtarget without providing a processor model, the LLVM infrastructure will use its default scheduling model. This means the scheduler will have zero knowledge of the actual capabilities of your subtarget, which will likely result in poor scheduled code.

   For more details on how to pass that information along, see the *Instantiating your subtarget* section.

# 19

# Register Allocation

Register allocation is the process that assigns the unlimited virtual registers used in the input program to the limited number of physical registers available on the target, potentially creating memory access to store and reload the values that cannot be kept in registers.

With the work you have done throughout the previous chapters, the LLVM register allocation infrastructure has almost all the information it needs from your target to perform its work.

The missing pieces are straightforward and, frankly, do not warrant a full chapter. However, the LLVM register allocation infrastructure is special in its own way and we felt that, aside from showing you how to implement the bare minimum to get it to work, it was important to cover some notions that you will inevitably run into if you want to extract the most out of this infrastructure.

In this chapter, you will learn the following:

- How to implement the missing pieces to get the register allocation going seamlessly
- How the LLVM register allocation is structured and, in particular, which code generation (**codegen**) passes contribute to it
- How to understand (and thus use and update) the liveness information featured in this infrastructure

If you do not care about the internal workings of the register allocation infrastructure, which we kept at the minimum, you can focus your attention on the *Enabling the register allocation infrastructure* section and then move on to the next chapter.

Note that we will not cover how the internals of the different allocators that LLVM provides work. This chapter is not aimed at teaching you how to modify or write your own allocator.

Let us start with the technical requirements for this chapter.

# Technical requirements

Similarly to all the chapters that build an LLVM backend, you need to develop directly in the LLVM code base (or a fork of it.) As such, you will need all the same tools as those we presented in *Chapter 1*.

Additionally, for all the snippets presented in this chapter, you will find the actual implementation in the `https://github.com/PacktPublishing/LLVM-Code-Generation-by-example` GitHub repository. We call this repository the **companion repository** in the remainder of the chapter.

The changes for this chapter are scattered around the changes of the previous chapters because we wanted to test a full end-to-end (LLVM IR to assembly code) pipeline before supporting more features. This is how we recommend approaching the implementation of all backends, but obviously, following this flow would not make for a well-structured book! The bottom line is that, for this chapter, we will give you the Git tags for each change, but we do not have the encompassing `begin_chXX` and `end_chXX` Git tags that you saw in the previous chapters. In any case, if you are not familiar with Git tags, look at *Chapter 9* for a quick explanation of what you can do with them.

Let us start with an overview of how register allocation works in LLVM.

# Overview of register allocation in LLVM

In LLVM, register allocation is split into two main optimization passes in the machine pass pipeline. More specifically, after eliminating the **static single assignment** (SSA) form of the input program during the PHI-elimination pass, as you learned in *Chapter 13*, LLVM performs the register coalescing phase and, later, the register assignment phase. The coalescing phase consists of merging variables connected by a `COPY` instruction together. The assignment phase consists of replacing the virtual registers with physical registers or memory locations. *Figure 19.1* illustrates these two phases, while *Figure 19.2* illustrates the register allocation process in LLVM:

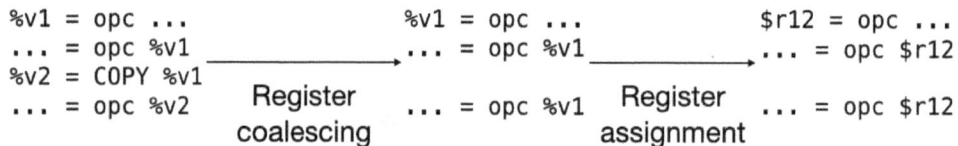

*Figure 19.1: The role of the register coalescing and register assignment phases*

*Figure 19.1* demonstrates how the register coalescing phase simplifies the Machine **intermediate representation** (IR) by merging the `%v1` and `%v2` variables. Thanks to this coalescing, the `COPY` instruction is eliminated, as shown in the middle part of this figure. The register assignment phase then replaces the virtual register, `%v1`, with the physical register, `$r12`:

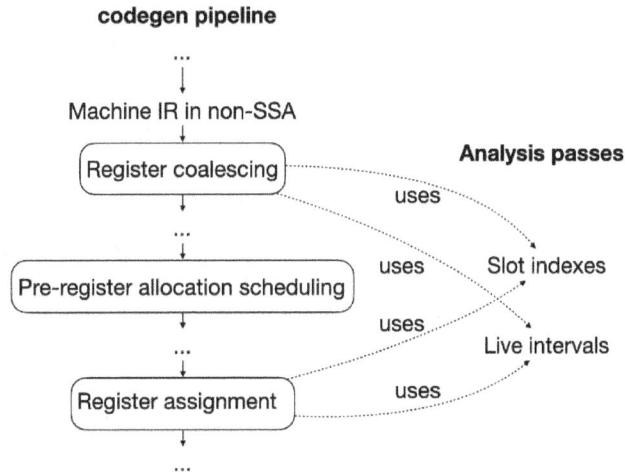

*Figure 19.2: Register allocation in LLVM*

*Figure 19.2* shows, on the left-hand side, the codegen pipeline as typically structured in the LLVM infrastructure. The register coalescer runs on the Machine IR after it has been lowered to a non-SSA form. Then, between the register coalescing and the register assignment phases, the pre-register allocation scheduling is performed. As you learned in *Chapter 18*, the pre-register allocation scheduler may be tweaked with different strategies that will affect how the register assignment phase will perform. For instance, the scheduler can prioritize decreasing the register pressure to minimize the number of registers that are required to allocate the program or can maximize the latency hiding, potentially increasing the number of registers needed to allocate the program.

Then, the register assignment phase takes place. This phase is typically what is referred to as register allocation in LLVM; however, both the register coalescing and register assignment phases contribute to the quality of the final register allocation results.

*Figure 19.2* also highlights a couple of analysis passes that are used in the LLVM infrastructure to drive the coalescing and assignment decisions. These analyses expose two key data structures: the slot indexes and the live intervals, represented respectively with the SlotIndex and LiveInterval classes. We will describe these classes in their dedicated section because they are your lifeline when dealing with **liveness** (refer to *Chapter 4* for a definition of this word) information in your custom passes.

The LLVM register allocation is atypical in several aspects:

1.  The splitting into two phases of the coalescing and assignment tasks is uncommon in register allocation algorithms. At least, it is a departure from the textbook graph coloring approach.

2.  The coalescing phase performs what is called **aggressive coalescing**, and the assignment phase is responsible for splitting the live ranges of the variables to recover from over-aggressive coalescing decisions. In other words, the assignment phase in LLVM is responsible for uncoalescing the variables if needed to reduce the register requirements. Traditionally, register allocation algorithms tend to go with **conservative coalescing**, where variables are coalesced together if, and only if, it is guaranteed that doing so will not increase the number of registers

required to allocate the program. Aggressive coalescing on the overhand eliminates as many COPY instructions as possible, irrespective of what the impact on the number of registers required to allocate the program will be.

3.   While the register allocation in LLVM is performed on a non-SSA form, the SSA representation is maintained in the liveness information. This is a major quirk in the LLVM infrastructure and one of the reasons why understanding how to the liveness information is vital to get you going.

The LLVM register allocation infrastructure is more complex than these two main optimization passes (coalescing and assignment) and the two main analysis passes (slot indexes and live intervals). LLVM features different register allocation schemes (graph coloring, linear scan, and so on) and different spill placement advisors, and it decouples the assignment phase from the rewriting phase, allowing some additional tweaks here. We will not cover this additional complexity as it is not required to get you going. However, we wanted to bring this information forward so that you know it exists in case you want to dig into this.

> **Note**
>
> When debugging register allocation problems, you can use the debug-only=regalloc command-line option. The regalloc debug type covers all the relevant passes, giving you a convenient way to dump all the relevant information with just one option.

Now that you have an overall understanding of how register allocation works in LLVM, let us describe the mandatory steps that you need to take to enable this infrastructure.

# Enabling the register allocation infrastructure

Assuming you use the default machine pass pipeline that we described in *Chapter 13*, the register allocation infrastructure is already up and running. If you did not instantiate the default machine pass pipeline, you will need to manually add the passes involved in the register allocation process yourself, starting with the register coalescer phase (using the RegisterCoalescerID variable), then the register assignment phase (for instance, using the createGreedyRegisterAllocator function), and so on, following what you learned in *Chapter 5*.

Irrespective of how you connect the register allocation infrastructure, as soon as you have something resembling what the default machine pass pipeline does, the whole register allocation process just works with one caveat: you cannot spill any variable.

**Spilling** occurs when the register assignment phase runs out of registers and splitting the live ranges of the variables is not enough to relax the allocation constraints. At this point, the assignment phase must use a memory slot to free some registers for the variables that are alive. Pushing a variable to memory is called spilling.

Spilling a variable means storing to memory the value somewhere after it is defined and reloading it from memory before it is used. In other words, to be able to spill a variable, the register allocator must know how to generate stores to and loads from memory.

To implement this functionality, you must override the following two methods in the target-specific version of your `TargetInstrInfo` class:

- `storeRegToStackSlot`: This method must generate a store of the given register to the given stack slot (represented with a **frame index**, as you learned in *Chapter 15*) at the given instruction iterator.
- `loadRegFromStackSlot`: This method must generate a load from the given stack slot in the given register at the given instruction iterator.

The code may be as complex as you want, but it can be as simple as building the right `MachineInstr` instance, as illustrated with our H2BLB implementation for the method that materializes a store:

```
void H2BLBInstrInfo::storeRegToStackSlot(MachineBasicBlock &MBB,
                                         MachineBasicBlock::iterator MBBI,
                                         Register SrcReg, bool isKill, int FI,
                                         const TargetRegisterClass *RC,
                                         const TargetRegisterInfo *TRI,
                                         Register VReg,
                                         MachineInstr::MIFlag Flags) const {
  MachineFunction &MF = *MBB.getParent();
  MachineFrameInfo &MFI = MF.getFrameInfo();
  MachinePointerInfo PtrInfo = MachinePointerInfo::getFixedStack(MF, FI);
  MachineMemOperand *MMO =
      MF.getMachineMemOperand(PtrInfo, MachineMemOperand::MOStore,
                              MFI.getObjectSize(FI), MFI.getObjectAlign(FI));
  unsigned Opc = TRI->getSpillSize(*RC) == 2 ? H2BLB::STRSP16 : H2BLB::STRSP32;
  MFI.setStackID(FI, TargetStackID::Default);
  BuildMI(MBB, MBBI, DebugLoc(), get(Opc))
      .addReg(SrcReg, getKillRegState(isKill))
      .addFrameIndex(FI)
      .addImm(0)
      .addMemOperand(MMO);
}
```

At this point, all the constructs used in this snippet should be familiar to you. We start by creating the `MachineMemOperand` information that will be required by our `MachineInstr` instance (if you need a refresher, go to *Chapter 11*). Then, we choose the opcode of our store operation based on the size of the register to be spilled and create the `MachineInstr` instance at the right position using the `BuildMI` **application programming interface (API)**.

You can find the complete snippet for both the store and load methods for our H2BLB target at the commit tagged `regalloc-hooks_ch19` in the companion repository.

Note

Some values may be cheaper to recompute than to spill. For instance, it is a waste of memory space and inefficient to spill a constant value if you can just recompute that value cheaply. Recomputing a value instead of spilling it is called **rematerialization**. Rematerialization should just work out of the box in the LLVM infrastructure as long as you set the `isReMaterializable` field in TableGen to `true` on the related instructions. LLVM, however, only supports trivial rematerializations, meaning that the instructions are only rematerializable if they have only trivial (that is, constant) input operands. You can tweak how the rematerialization works by overriding the relevant methods in your `TargetInstrInfo` class. Look for any virtual method with the *rematerialization* word in it.

As soon as you implement these two methods, your register allocation pipeline is complete.

You can, however, still tweak some of the decisions taken in the different optimization phases, such as whether two registers should be coalesced by overriding the `TargetRegisterInfo::shouldCoalesce` method, what the allocation order (the order in which the physical registers are tried when assigning a new variable) is in the target description of your register classes via the `AltOrders` field in the `RegisterClass` TableGen class, what the allocation hints (the preferred registers) are for your virtual registers by overriding the `TargetRegisterInfo::getRegAllocationHints` method, and so on.

We will not cover these topics in this book because, without proper use cases, they are not relevant. Generally speaking, look at the virtual methods of the `TargetRegisterInfo`, `TargetInstrInfo`, and `TargetSubtargetInfo` classes to see what is overridable. In particular, the latter has the overridable `enableSubRegLiveness` method, which you may want to change if your backend uses a lot of subregister indices. This method enables more precise liveness tracking, which yields better register assignment in such cases. It makes dealing with live ranges more complicated if you ever need to maintain them by hand, as we will see in the *Maintaining the live intervals* section.

In this section, you learned what minimal piece of API you need to provide for the default machine pass pipeline to have a fully functional register allocation pipeline. More specifically, you saw that you must implement two methods of the `TargetInstrInfo` class that are responsible for inserting the instructions when the register allocator needs to spill.

In the next section, we will describe the slot index data structure that is used throughout the register allocation pipeline.

# Introducing the slot indexes

If you look at the Machine IR dumps, you will notice that some of them feature numbers in front of the `MachineInstr` instance.

The following snippet shows one such dump:

```
0B bb.0 (%ir-block.1):
...
16B    %3:gpr32 = COPY $w0
...
224B    B %bb.1
240B bb.1 (%ir-block.5):
256B    ADJCALLSTACKDOWN 0, 0, implicit-def dead $sp, implicit $sp
```

These numbers are the slot indexes. Notice how the numbering keeps growing despite the change in the basic block. For instance, the end of the first basic block is at the slot index 224B, and the second basic block starts right after, at 240B.

The slot indexes are a somewhat continuous numbering of all the instructions in the `MachineFunction` instance. Each instruction is assigned a number, a slot index, and that number is guaranteed to increase monotonically with the linear order of the `MachineFunction` instance. In other words, if an instruction, I, has a slot index with a smaller value than another instruction, J, this means I appears before J in the linearized function, that is, the textual representation of the function.

> **Note**
>
> The numbering has holes; for instance, in the previous snippet, the instructions are all spaced by a difference of 16 in the slot index. These holes are there to allow the insertion of new instructions without triggering a renumbering of all the instructions in the `MachineFunction` instance. Renumbering may still happen if too many instructions are inserted.

The slot indexes are computed by and maintained via the `SlotIndexes` class that you get as part of the `SlotIndexesAnalysis` or `SlotIndexesWrapperPass` pass for, respectively, the new pass manager and the legacy pass manager.

Although you can use the slot indexes directly in your algorithm and have them computed via the regular pass manager mechanism (see *Chapter 5*), their main purpose is to model the liveness information. We will detail that in the next section, but let us finish on the slot index first.

When manipulating the slot indexes or, more precisely, when working on a pass that relies on them being correct, you must maintain the mapping held by the SlotIndexes instance between a SlotIndex instance and a MachineInstr instance. In other words, when you are adding or removing instructions, you must call the proper SlotIndexes API:

- When adding an instruction, call the insertMachineInstrInMaps method
- When removing an instruction, call the removeMachineInstrFromMaps method

The SlotIndexes class also features methods to find the basic block for a given SlotIndex instance (getMBBFromIndex), the last SlotIndex instance for a given basic block (getMBBStartIdx), and so on.

Again, all these methods are mainly used for computing and maintaining the liveness information, but they may be useful to you directly, too.

Each SlotIndex instance comes with a slot (represented by the SlotIndex::Slot enumeration) that you can query with the isXXX methods, where XXX is one of the possible values of the slot. The slot is an important concept because it allows us to precisely model when something happens. More precisely, each slot index is broken down into four stages: block, early-clobber, register, and dead, and these stages happen in that order. This means that for a given slot index, the block slot happens before the early-clobber slot, and so on.

These names may be confusing at first, but *Figure 19.3* will help you visualize why they make sense:

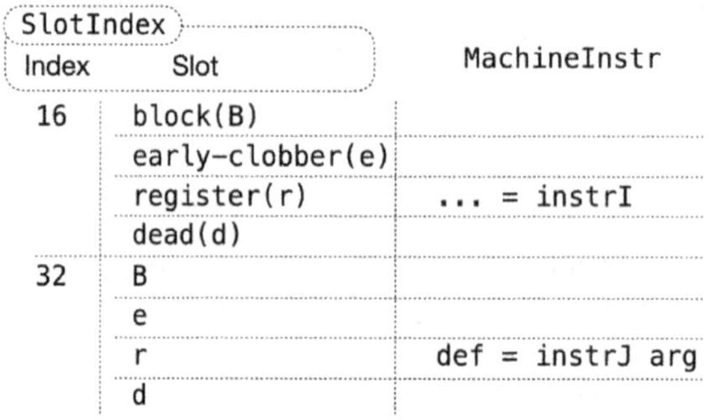

*Figure 19.3: The representation of the slot indexes*

The first two columns in *Figure 19.3* show the SlotIndex instances with their indexes in the first column and their slots in the second. The third column shows the MachineInstr instance that is mapped to the related SlotIndex instance. In this figure, there are two SlotIndex instances, one with an index of 16 and one with an index of 32. Each instance has its four slots (named block, early-clobber, and so on) that are abbreviated with one letter shown in parenthesis (B, e, r, and d). These letters are important to remember because they are used in the printing of the liveness information in the debug logs.

Let us focus on the SlotIndex at index 32 in this picture. To understand the naming of the slots and their meaning, imagine that the instruction is executed from the top to the bottom. At the block(B) slot, you are at the beginning of this execution, and nothing happens. This slot is called block because, for liveness purposes, it is exclusively used to mark the beginning of a basic block. Indeed, at the B slot, nothing interesting happens for an instruction. Next, we move one slot down, to the early-clobber(e) slot. This slot is used to model the early-clobber property, which is when the definitions of an instruction cannot share the same registers as the inputs of this instruction. For instance, to model that the definition, def, is clobbering the argument, arg, we would start the live range of def at slot e. That way, both arg and def are alive at the same time and cannot share the same resource because [32e (that is, the index with the slot abbreviation appended to it) overlaps with the slot where arg is used, 32r. The next slot, register(r), represents the regular execution of the instruction; regular definitions start to live here, and last-used arguments die here. In other words, if we were to represent the live range of the definition of the related instruction, it would look like [32r and the live range of a last use would be 32r). Since the range of the definition is inclusive (the '[' character) and the range of the argument is exclusive (the ')' character), the two ranges do not overlap; therefore, the definition and argument can share the same resources, which is exactly what we want for the register allocator.

Finally, the dead(d) slot is used to represent live ranges for definitions that are dead. They still consume a register, so they must have a non-empty live range, but their live range is kept within the same SlotIndex instance: [32r,32d).

To summarize, the SlotIndex instance represents both an instruction and an execution slot in that instruction and is used to model precisely the live ranges of the registers used or defined by the related instruction.

Note

You can print the SlotIndex instances alongside a MachineFunction instance in your debug logs; just pass the SlotIndexes instance to the MachineFunction::print method. For instance, use the following statement within your optimization pass: MF.print(OutputFileStream, getAnalysisIfAvailable<SlotIndexes>()) where MF is your MachineFunction instance and OutputFileStream your output stream, such as llvm::dbgs() for the standard error output.

In this section, you learned how to interpret what a SlotIndex instance represents. You now have a basic understanding of how live ranges are modeled using the slots in the SlotIndex instances. You also learned the key APIs of the SlotIndexes class, a class that holds all the SlotIndex instances, to make sure you maintain and update the mapping between the SlotIndex instances and the MachineInstr instances of your MachineFunction instance.

In the next section, we will show you how to understand and use the liveness information that is built on top of these SlotIndex instances.

# Introducing the live intervals

The liveness information is represented in LLVM through the concept of live intervals and the related LiveInterval class. Live intervals, at their core, are a set of ranges, described using the slot index representation, that model where a variable is alive in a function.

*Table 19.1* shows an example of the live interval of a virtual register:

| Machine IR | Live interval |
|---|---|
| `0B bb.0` | `# Virtual register` |
| `...` | `%10` |
| `80B    %10:gpr32 = COPY $w0` | `# Segments` |
| `...` | `[80r,320r:0)` |
| `208B   Bcc 1, %bb.2, ...` | `[320r,368B:1)` |
| `224B   B %bb.1` | `[368B,400r:2)` |
| `240B bb.1:` | `# VNInfo` |
| `...` | `0@80r` |
| `320B   %10:gpr32 = ... %10` | `1@320r` |
| `368B bb.2:` | `2@368B-phi` |
| `400B   $w0 = COPY %10:gpr32` | |

*Table 19.1: An example of the live interval representation*

The left column of *Table 19.1* shows a snippet of a function in the Machine IR that has been simplified to include only the basic block boundaries and the uses and definitions of the virtual register, %10. The right column shows the live interval for this virtual register as printed in a debug log but augmented with annotations (prefixed with the # character). A non-modified debug log of a live interval would be printed on one line. As you can see in the right column, you find two related information in the live interval:

- **Segments**: These are ranges where the related virtual register is alive. The number suffixing the colon (:) character at the end of each range is the identifier of the value being held in this segment. In other words, you can view %10 as a variable (that is, an entity with multiple uses and definitions) and the value identified with the number in each range as the original SSA value (hence only one static definition). Notice that the segments happily cover different basic blocks. For instance, the [80r,320r:0) segment spans both the block bb.0 and bb.1. As long as the related value is alive and the indexes are next to each other in the linear order, the segment is uninterrupted.

- **Value number information** (VNInfo): This information shows the location of the definition of each SSA value identified by the number used in the segments. For instance, the value identified with 0 is defined at the slot index 80r, which maps to the %10:gpr32 = COPY $w0 instruction. As you can see, with VNInfo, you also get abstract SSA definitions such as the one represented with 2@368B-phi. If you look at the slot index 368B, you will not see any actual definition of %10; however, when the representation was in the SSA form, a phi must have been at this slot. *Figure 19.4* shows the SSA form that we can reconstruct for %10 from the live interval instance of *Figure 19.3*:

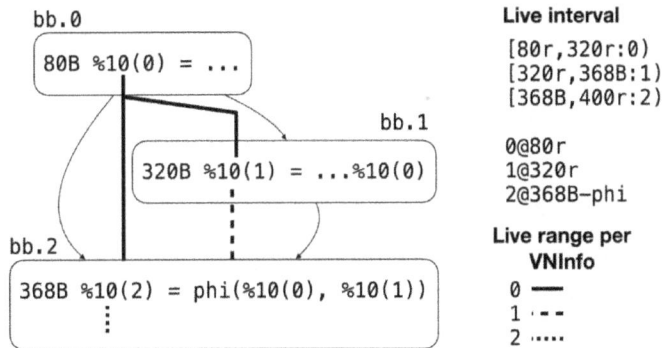

*Figure 19.4: The interpretation of the VNInfo definitions*

*Figure 19.4* shows the three different definitions, one for each VNInfo (or SSA value), of the virtual register, %10. In this diagram, we put in parenthesis the identifier of VNInfo right after the virtual register uses and definitions to easily identify the original SSA form. What this figure shows is that despite the Machine IR being in non-SSA form, the live intervals are still using the SSA form. The thick dashed, dotted, and solid lines show a graphical representation of the live ranges of each SSA value.

The fact that the live intervals maintain the SSA form under the hood allows you to perform certain analyses as if the program were still in SSA form. For instance, let us say you want to know which definitions of %10 are used in the operation at the end of the bb.2 basic block in *Figure 19.3* (or *19.4*). Since the SSA form is not available anymore, you cannot use the use-def chain and you would need to perform a reaching definition analysis. Now, since the live intervals are still in SSA, you can leverage them. More specifically, you can use the LiveInterval instance of your virtual register to recover that information. Let us see how.

To find the reaching definitions of a particular use, you need to do the following:

1. Have an instance of the LiveIntervals class. You can obtain it by adding a dependency on the LiveIntervalsWrapperPass pass for the legacy pass manager or the LiveIntervalsAnalysis pass for the new pass manager (go to *Chapter 5* for how to do that).

2. Query the LiveIntervals object to get the LiveInterval instance of your virtual register using the getInterval method.

3.  Use the getVNInfoAt method on your LiveInterval instance with a SlotIndex instance that matches the location of your use (use the SlotIndexes instance to map your use to a SlotIndex instance or use the wrappers that the LiveIntervals class exposes on top of the SlotIndexes class directly).

4.  Use the isPHIDef method of the returned VNInfo instance to check whether this is an actual definition or a phi definition. If this is not a phi, then this is a reaching definition; use the def field of this VNInfo instance to find the SlotIndex instance of the definition and use the SlotIndexes instance to map it back to the instruction.

5.  If this is a phi, then iteratively check for the reaching definitions of the VNInfo instances that you get from the end of each of the predecessor blocks of this definition. In other words, perform Steps 3 onward with the slot indexes that represent the end of the predecessor block of the block that holds the slot index of the def field of the phi (current) VNInfo instance.

After following these steps, you will get your reaching definitions instead of using a dataflow analysis such as the classical reaching definitions analysis.

Given that the purpose of the LiveInterval class (and its simpler LiveRange super class) is to offer liveness information, you can naturally use the LiveInterval instances to check whether your virtual register is alive at a given program using the liveAt method or check whether it interferes with another virtual register using the overlaps method, just to name a few.

Note

The LiveInterval class also models the live ranges of the individual subregisters of the main live range if you enable the subregister liveness tracking. This information is accessible through the methods related to the subranges, for instance, the hasSubRanges and subranges methods. Subranges are handled transparently, meaning the liveness checks (for instance, when you use the liveAt method) automatically take them into account. If the subregister tracking is enabled, you will see the lane mask preceded with an L being printed in the debug log of the live intervals.

To summarize, live intervals are a powerful abstraction that allows you to reason about the SSA form while not being in SSA anymore.

In this section, you learned what the live intervals represent and how to understand their textual representation. You also learned, through an example that computes the reaching definitions, how to use them. This example only gave you a taste of what the LiveInterval and LiveIntervals APIs are capable of. If you are interested in using them, look closer at the comments in the related header files.

At this point, you may wonder or worry about how you maintain the connection between the Machine IR in non-SSA form and the live intervals in SSA form. We will address this topic in the next section.

# Maintaining the live intervals

If you do not rely on the live intervals within your pass, you could just ignore them because they are automatically recomputed by the regular invalidation mechanism of the pass managers. However, you must actively maintain this information yourself within your pass if you rely on it being correct while modifying the IR. Additionally, if your pass runs in the middle of the register allocation pipeline, you may still want to maintain this representation because, if you invalidate it by modifying the IR, recomputing it may hurt the performance of your compiler since it is compile-time-intensive.

Aside from the updates that you need to perform on the mapping of the SlotIndexes instance, as you saw in the *Introducing the slot indexes* section, you need to use the APIs of the LiveIntervals class to update the live interval of your virtual registers.

Here is an overview of some of the methods of the LiveIntervals class that you will need to use for maintaining the liveness information:

- createEmptyInterval: Use this method when you create a new virtual register and have not yet created its definitions and/or uses.
- createAndComputeVirtRegInterval: Use this method when you have created a new virtual register and its definitions and/or uses.
- shrinkToUses: Use this method after removing uses of your virtual register.
- extendToIndices: Use this method after inserting uses of your virtual register.

> **Note**
>
> Creating subranges is slightly more involved and requires using the subrange-related methods of the LiveInterval class. We will not cover this.

All in all, the APIs to maintain the live intervals are straightforward but it is easy to miss calling them at the right places. To help you catch this kind of mistake, make a habit of running your backend with the machine verifier enabled, for instance, by using the verify-machineinstrs command-line option.

In this section, you learned how to maintain the liveness information yourself. You saw that while you may not need to do that to keep your compiler running correctly, it is recommended to maintain this information when your passes run in the register allocation pipeline to avoid penalizing your compile time.

# Summary

In this chapter, you learned how to implement the necessary target hooks to teach the LLVM register allocation infrastructure how to spill your registers. This is the only mandatory change to use the register allocation infrastructure.

Additionally, you learned how the register allocation pipeline is structured in LLVM with its coalescer and allocator running at two different stages of the codegen pipeline. Note that this is a simplification of how the register allocation pipeline works because, depending on the optimization level set by the frontend, different allocators may be used. For instance, the coalescer is not run when the optimization level is set to 0.

Next, we introduced you to the helper classes that provide the backbone of the liveness information used in LLVM. You learned that the slot indexes are a convenient way to uniquely identify the program points and that they are used to express the live intervals in a compact and intuitive way. The one quirk that you learned is that the liveness information is described in terms of SSA values, whereas the Machine IR is already in the non-SSA form.

Finally, you had a crash course on how to maintain the liveness information if you ever needed to.

The next chapter covers the last piece of infrastructure that you need to be able to generate your assembly code: the lowering of the stack layout.

# Further reading

To see what we presented in this chapter from a different angle, you can look at the excellent slides from *Matthias Braun* in his 2017 LLVM Developers Meeting presentation, `https://llvm.org/devmtg/2017-10/slides/Braun-Welcome%20to%20the%20Back%20End.pdf`, and the related recording, `https://www.youtube.com/watch?v=objxlZg01D0`. More specifically, the second part of the talk focuses on the register allocation framework in LLVM and the liveness representation.

# Quiz time

Now that you have completed reading this chapter, try answering the following questions to test your knowledge:

1.  Is register allocation a monolithic pass in LLVM?

    No, the register allocation infrastructure consists of several passes that work together to perform the register allocation. In an optimized pass pipeline, you can count at least three passes: the coalescer, the allocator, and the virtual register rewriter.

    More details are in the *Overview of register allocation in LLVM* section.

2.  What are the two analysis passes that support the register allocation infrastructure?

    The two analysis passes are the `SlotIndexes` and `LiveIntervals` passes, as explained in the *Overview of register allocation in LLVM* section.

3. What does your target need to provide for the register allocation infrastructure to work?

   Your target needs to implement the hooks that allow the insertion of spilled code.

   See the *Enabling the register allocation infrastructure* section for more details.

4. What `TargetSubtargetInfo` method do you need to override to enable the liveness information for the subregisters?

   The method that you need to override is the `enableSubRegLiveness` method, as described in the *Enabling the register allocation infrastructure* section.

5. In the slot index representation, why are the indexes spaced out instead of being contiguous?

   The indexes are spaced out to offer free indexes for instructions inserted between two already numbered instructions. Without this buffer, each instruction insertion would trigger a costly renumbering of some of the instructions, as explained in the *Introducing the slot indexes* section.

6. In the slot index representation, what does the slot part of the slot index refer to?

   The slot of a slot index represents a stage in the execution of the related instruction. These slots allow us to precisely model the live ranges of the virtual registers.

   See the *Introducing the slot indexes* section for more details.

7. Where do you see the fact that the liveness information is represented in SSA form in the LLVM live intervals representation?

   You can see that the liveness information uses SSA under the hood because the live intervals report the SSA value number that is defined at each definition point as well as at each join point. On the slot index of a join point, you will not see an actual definition of the related register; instead, the live interval information will report a phi definition with a different SSA value number.

   See the *Introducing the live intervals* section for more information.

# 20

# Lowering of the Stack Layout

At this point in this book, the only thing standing between you and a correct textual assembly output of your **code generation (codegen)** pipeline is the lowering of the stack.

In this chapter, you will learn how to drive the LLVM infrastructure so that you can generate the stack layout that is expected for your backend. The **stack layout** describes how you organize the memory space of your target architecture to model the stack of your program. It includes things such as the following:

- The direction in which the stack grows; **upward** means the memory that holds the stack space starts at a low address (for instance, 0) and grows up toward a predefined maximum high address, and **downward** means it starts at a high address and expands downward until it reaches a predefined minimum low address.
- The location of the input/output arguments of a function relative to the beginning of the stack.

The stack layout is a convention that changes from target to target. You will see an illustration of such a convention in *Figure 20.3*.

More specifically, you will learn about the following in this chapter:

- What components are involved in the lowering of the stack
- How to fill in the blanks for the LLVM infrastructure to perform its work
- What you can use to get out of tricky situations

As we did in the previous chapters, we will use our H2BLB backend to illustrate the implementation of the missing bits. As such, the stack layout will follow the layout that we decided to use for this backend, but be aware that this layout may differ from what the **application binary interface (ABI)** of your target dictates. In any case, this chapter gives you enough elements to be able to understand how everything works and we are confident that you will be able to adapt the proposed solutions to your needs.

Without further ado, let us get started by looking at the technical requirements.

# Technical requirements

Similar to the other chapters in which we built an LLVM backend, you need to develop directly in the LLVM code base (or a fork of it). As such, you will need the same tools that we presented in *Chapter 1*.

Additionally, for all the snippets presented in this chapter, you will find the actual implementation in the GitHub repository at https://github.com/PacktPublishing/LLVM-Code-Generation-by-example. We call this repository the **companion repository** in the remainder of the chapter.

For each change presented in this chapter, we highlight a Git tag that you can use to find the full snippet in the companion repository.

If you are unfamiliar with Git tags, refer to *Chapter 9* for a quick explanation of what you can do with them.

Let us start with an overview of how stack lowering works in LLVM.

# Overview of stack lowering

In *Chapter 15*, you learned that stack locations are represented in LLVM with the concept of a **frame index**. As a reminder, a frame index is an identifier for a stack slot. You can think of a stack slot as a chunk of memory that is reserved somewhere in your stack. The purpose of this chunk of memory is to hold some values, for instance, an array local to your function, or a value that was spilled by the register allocator.

Let us start by digging into what this stack slot represents and the type of **application programming interface** (**API**) you can use to handle it.

## Handling of stack slots

Depending on what the stack slot contains, its actual location in your stack may be prescribed by your ABI. In other words, values that are tied to the ABI must appear at an exact location in your stack, for instance, where you lay out the incoming arguments of your next function call. Conversely, values that are not tied to the ABI can be placed more freely in your stack frame, such as where a value is spilled by the register allocator. Put differently, values that cross function boundaries have exact locations in your stack frame, and values local to your stack frame only need to be somewhere in your stack frame.

> **Stack frame**
>
> What we call a stack frame is the region of the memory that is used by the current instantiation of your current function call. Think of it as the local context of your function in your favorite programming language. When you lower the stack, you are effectively creating the stack layout of your stack frame. The stack frame is also called a **call frame**.

Now that you are aware of the constraints of the objects that live on the stack, we can explain how the LLVM infrastructure handles them, and you will understand why it makes sense.

Whether a stack object has a dedicated location or not depends on how you created the related frame index. As you saw in *Chapter 15*, frame indices are created via the `MachineFrameInfo` class. This class features methods to create both fixed stack objects and freely placeable stack objects. When lowering your ABI in *Chapter 15*, you used the method to create fixed stack objects (the `CreateFixedObject` method), since, as you guessed it, these objects are tied to a particular location on the stack. On the other hand, the register allocator uses the `CreateSpillStackObject` method to create a spill location that can be placed more freely in your stack.

The bottom line is that unless you must have specific stack locations for anything that is not ABI-related, the LLVM infrastructure creates the right stack slot out of the box.

> Note
>
> If you ever need to have a spill slot with a specific stack location, for instance, making sure some callee saved registers happen first in your stack frame, you can use the `CreateFixedSpillStackObject` method of the `MachineRegisterInfo` class.

To finish on the `MachineFrameInfo` class, this class maintains the mapping from frame indices to the stack objects or, more generally, their stack slot properties (their size, alignment, and so on) for the current `MachineFunction` instance. This is similar to what the `MachineRegisterInfo` class does for the registers. Like the `MachineRegisterInfo` instance, you get the instance of your `MachineFrameInfo` class from the current `MachineFunction` instance by using the `getFrameInfo` method.

Now that you understand the difference between a fixed stack slot and a non-fixed one, let us see how the whole concept is articulated with the LLVM infrastructure.

# From frame index to stack slot

The purpose of stack lowering in LLVM is to materialize a stack slot for each frame index.

This process hinges on four main components:

- The `MachineFrameInfo` class: As you saw in the previous section, this class holds the mapping from the frame indices to the stack slots.
- The `TargetFrameLowering` class: As its name suggests, this class is responsible for lowering the frame. More specifically, it implements the methods that do the following:
  - Create the stack frame at the beginning of a function (the **prologue**)
  - Destroy the stack frame at the end of a function (the **epilogue**)
  - Set up the stack frame around function calls, if needed
- The `TargetRegisterInfo` class: In addition to what you learned in the previous chapters, this class is also responsible for replacing the frame indices operands of the `MachineInstr` instances with the real address computation. This process typically involves replacing a frame index operand with a stack pointer and offset, but the actual details depend on the target.

- The PEI pass: The **prologue epilogue inserter (PEI)** pass drives the lowering of the stack. It invokes the proper methods from the classes mentioned in the previous bullet points to insert the prologue and epilogue and replace all the frame index operands. After this pass is done, no more frame indices should be used in the codegen pipeline: the stack is lowered.

On top of these components, the StackSlotColoring pass is typically run after register allocation but before the post-register-allocation scheduler to optimize how many stack slots, and ultimately how much stack space, are used for the current stack frame. This pass is part of the default codegen pipeline; hence, it will already run for your backend if you have followed the steps in this book. This pass essentially coalesces frame indices that do not overlap.

> Note
>
> The StackSlotColoring pass only optimizes the stack slots that are used as spill locations. In other words, as you would expect, the location of the fixed stack objects is not optimized. The location of the fixed objects invariably sticks to what you described using the CreateFixedObject method of the MachineFrameInfo class.

Now that you have a general understanding of how the different pieces of the LLVM infrastructure fit together to lower the stack, you will see that we are missing mainly two pieces – the implementation of the TargetFrameLowering class and the implementation of some of the methods of the TargetRegisterInfo class. The next section will focus on the TargetFrameLowering class.

# The lowering of the stack frame

The lowering of the stack frame consists of producing the code sequences that reserve/release the stack space around the function prologue/epilogue and the function calls within the current function. These code sequences are defined in the respective emitPrologue, emitEpilogue, and eliminateCallFramePseudoInstr methods of the TargetFrameLowering class and your job is to implement them for your target.

Before addressing that, let us point out a particularity of the LLVM infrastructure. This is important because this particularity affects the amount of stack space you need to allocate at different points of your program and, ultimately, the implementations of these methods.

## Introducing the reserved call frame

The LLVM infrastructure features two main modes when lowering the stack frame. These modes dictate how the memory space is allocated around function calls and affect how much space you need to reserve in the prologue and, respectively, release in the epilogue of your function. This mode is controlled by the Boolean value returned by the hasReservedCallFrame method of your TargetFrameLowering class.

The reserved mode (that is, when this method returns true) means that you allocate upfront in your prologue the maximum stack space that is required for all the calls in the current function. The non-reserved mode means that you allocate any additional stack space just before the calls that need them and with the right amount.

*Figure 20.1* illustrates the difference between these two modes:

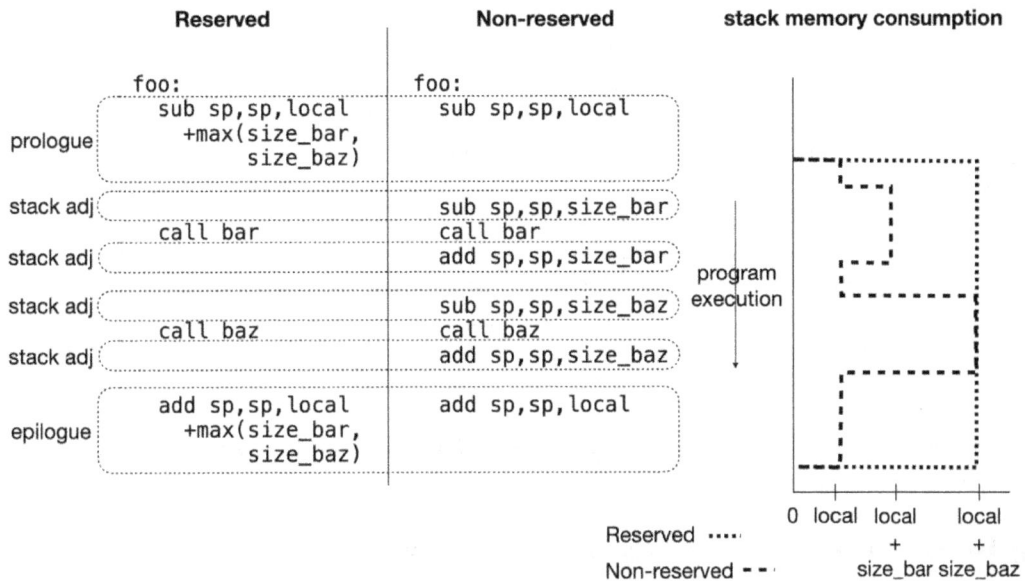

*Figure 20.1: The different modes to handle call frames*

*Figure 20.1* presents the sequence of instructions of the same function called foo lowered with the two different modes of representing the call frames.

With the reserved mode, the stack space of the whole function is computed by taking the size of the local stack requirements (represented by the local value) and the maximum of the call frame requirements for all the functions called from foo. Here, the size_bar and size_baz values represent, respectively, the size requirements of the bar and baz functions. This space is then allocated once in the prologue of the function and released in the epilogue.

With the non-reserved mode, the stack space in the prologue is allocated to accommodate only the size of the local stack. Then, the stack is further adjusted (as highlighted with the **stack adj** rectangles with rounded corners) with the size requirements of the respective call around that call.

The right-hand side of *Figure 20.1* shows the memory consumption for the stack space of foo alongside its execution. The memory consumption implication of the reserved mode is clearly visible in this chart: the area covered by the non-reserved mode (delimited by the dashed line) is smaller than the area covered by the reserved mode (delimited by the dotted line).

Ultimately, you decide which mode to use, but our recommendation is unless you are producing code for devices with a very limited amount of memory, the non-reserved mode is not worth the extra complexity.

By default, the LLVM infrastructure uses the reserved mode whenever your target does not require a **frame pointer**.

Frame pointer versus stack pointer

The frame pointer is something that is required when you want to support the dynamic allocation of objects on the stack (think of C `alloca`). When you support this type of feature, you typically dedicate a register to hold the address of the beginning of the current stack frame. That register is called the frame pointer. In contrast, the stack pointer holds the address of the end of the stack – or, put differently, the address of the next available free space, that is, where the next stack frame will start. Without dynamically allocated objects, you do not need a dedicated frame pointer because you can compute the address of the beginning of the frame statically by doing `sp + frame_size`, where `sp` is the stack pointer and `frame_size` is the size of the (compile-time-known) stack frame. Note that we use + in the previous equation because we assume the stack grows downward. To help you visualize the difference between the frame pointer and stack pointer, take a look at *Figure 20.3*.

Now that you know about the reserved call frame mode, let us see how this translates when generating the lowering of the stack layout.

# Implementing the frame-lowering target hooks

To materialize the layout of your stack frame, you must override four methods in your implementation of the `TargetFrameLowering` class:

- `hasFP`: This method tells whether your stack needs to use a frame pointer for the current function.
- `emitPrologue`: This method is responsible for generating the prologue of the current function. Looking at *Figure 20.1*, this is the code sequence in the prologue area.
- `emitEpilogue`: Similar to the `emitPrologue` method but for the epilogue.
- `eliminateCallFramePseudoInstr`: This method is responsible for lowering the stack adjustments around function calls. Looking at *Figure 20.1*, these are the code sequences in the **stack adj** areas. In other words, if you use the reserved call frame mode, there is nothing to do here.

The following snippet shows you the implementation of the `emitPrologue` method of the `TargetFrameLowering` class for our H2BLB backend:

```
void H2BLBFrameLowering::emitPrologue(MachineFunction &MF,
                                      MachineBasicBlock &MBB) const {
  MachineFrameInfo &MFI = MF.getFrameInfo();
  unsigned NumBytes = MFI.getStackSize();
  if (NumBytes > 0) {
    const TargetInstrInfo *TII = MF.getSubtarget().getInstrInfo();
    BuildMI(MBB, MBB.begin(), DebugLoc(), TII->get(H2BLB::SUBSP), H2BLB::SP)
        .addReg(H2BLB::SP)
        .addImm(NumBytes)
        .setMIFlag(MachineInstr::FrameSetup);
```

```
    }
}
```

In this snippet, using the getStackSize method, we query the MachineFrameInfo instance of the current MachineFunction instance to see how much stack space is needed for this function. Then, we produce the instruction that moves the stack pointer by the related number of bytes, effectively allocating the necessary stack space. The SUBSP instruction is a subtraction, which is in line with the convention that the stack grows downward, for our target. You specify the direction of the growth of your stack in the constructor of your TargetFrameLowering class.

> **Note**
>
> The MachineInstr::FrameSetup flag that we set in the previous snippet on our instruction is optional information that helps identify in the MachineInstr dump which instructions are used for setting up the frame. For the epilogue, we would similarly set the MachineInstr::FrameDestroy flag.

As you can see, the previous snippet is straightforward. However, things can get complicated here when you start supporting things such as dynamic stack objects. For this type of feature, the principles remain the same. That means that these are all the same methods that you need to override, and we invite you to check the existing implementations in the open source backends to see how to implement them.

Focusing on the stack adjustments around the function calls now, with our reserved stack frame mode, there is nothing to do but provide an empty implementation. However, we wanted to point out that the stack adjustments instructions, that is, the ADJCALLSTACKDOWN instruction to grow and the ADJCALLSTACKUP instruction to shrink the stack (when using a downward growing scheme), come with two arguments. The first argument is how much space is needed for the next call (this space is used to store the input and output operands of the next call, as you learned in *Chapter 15*), and the second argument is how much space has been handled already prior to that instruction. While the second parameter may sound confusing, remember that you are producing these instructions during instruction selection (see *Chapter 15*), so unless you already know that you need this feature and know how to handle it, you do not have to worry about it.

You can find the bulk of the implementation of all these methods at the commit tagged stack-lowering_ch20 in the companion repository. Additionally, the following tags identify some refinements on these methods – annotate-frame-instr_ch20, adjust-pseudo-lowering-finalize_ch20, and adjust-pseudo-lowering-init_ch20.

In this section, you learned about the reserved call frame mode that allows you to focus the lowering purely on the prologue and epilogue of your function. Next, you learned how to implement the lowering of your prologues and epilogues and, more generally, which target hooks you need to implement to materialize the layout of your stack frame. At this point, your backend allocates the proper amount of stack space for your function.

The next step is to tie your stack objects to proper address stack addresses – or, to put it differently, to materialize the mapping of your frame indices to actual stack addresses.

## The expansion of the frame indices

In principle, replacing the frame indices that you've used so far is an easy task. As already mentioned, the MachineFrameInfo instance of your function maintains a mapping of the frame indices to an offset in your stack. Therefore, replacing the frame indices with the stack address is as simple as translating each index with its corresponding computation: stack plus offset.

> Note
>
> The offset held by the mapping in the MachineFrameInfo instance is described from the beginning of the stack frame. Therefore, you can use this offset directly if you use a frame pointer, but you need to adjust it to account for the changes made in the prologue if you use a stack pointer. We will come back to this and illustrate it in *Figure 20.3*.

In practice, things get more complicated because materializing your stack-plus-offset value may require you to introduce additional instructions, and since the expansion happens after register allocation, you must produce a sequence of instructions that is properly allocated. *Figure 20.2* illustrates a good and a bad scenario when expanding a frame index:

| Frame index | Good scenario | Bad scenario |
|---|---|---|
| `$r1 = load @Idx1` | `$r1 = load $sp, 32` | `? = add $sp, 32`<br>`$r1 = load ?` |

Table 20.1: The expansion of a frame index

The leftmost column of *Figure 20.2* shows a load instruction from a frame index named @Idx1. In this example, we assume that this index maps to the stack pointer (represented with $sp) plus an offset of 32 bytes. In a good scenario, as represented by the middle column, the addressing mode of the load instruction can fold the computation directly into the instruction itself. In a bad scenario, as in the rightmost column, the load instruction is not able to accommodate the computation directly (for instance, the offset may be too large for its encoding), and a separate instruction must be created, as illustrated with the new add instruction. This creates a situation where we need an intermediate register, represented with the ? character, to hold the result of this computation and feed it to the load instruction.

This example illustrates that you may have to figure out which registers you can use to hold your temporary values. In this case, you may be able to use the result of the load instruction (here, $r1) to hold your temporary value, but this is not generally true. This is why the LLVM infrastructure features a concept called register scavenging.

## Introducing register scavenging

The concept of register scavenging is about finding registers that are not used (in other words, that are dead) at some program points so that they can be used to materialize temporary values.

This concept is materialized in LLVM with the RegScavenger class. You can use this class to get registers available at a given program point.

Working with a RegScavenger instance typically involves the following:

- Initializing the set of registers that are alive by calling the enterBasicBlockEnd method class. This method uses the live-out set to know which registers are available.
- Iterating through the instructions backward to get the liveness information right all the way to the program point you care about using the backward method. In other words, the RegScavenger instance holds the liveness information for one program point at a time and you have to update it as you go.
- Using the FindUnusedReg, isRegUsed, or getRegsAvailable method to find a register that is available. If no register is available at the program point currently tracked by the RegScavenger instance, you can use the scavengeRegisterBackwards method to still get one, but this only works if you provisioned enough space for an emergency spill slot (see the next section).

You can use a RegScavenger instance anywhere after register allocation in your codegen pass pipeline.

For the lowering of the stack, you do not have to explicitly manage a `RegScavenger` instance. Indeed, the PEI manages an instance for you and passes it down to you through the target hooks that you must implement for the expansion of the frame index. Therefore, you just need to use this `RegScavenger` instance when you need it.

## Provisioning an emergency spill slot

An emergency spill slot is a stack slot that you provision in your prologue in case the expansion of your frame indices requires an additional temporary register, and such a temporary register may not exist.

Notice that we said *in case the expansion of your frame indices requires an additional temporary register*. Indeed, due to the ordering of the lowering process, at the time you decide whether you need to reserve some space for your emergency spill slot, you do not know if the expansions will need one since you have not done them yet. Therefore, you do not necessarily know whether you will need this spill slot.

While you may unconditionally create an emergency spill slot, this is not recommended because if you do so, your stack frame will always need a prologue and epilogue to materialize this spill slot even if you have zero frame index to expand. One easy way to be selective when provisioning an emergency spill slot is by checking whether your frame has any stack objects using the `MachineFra meInfo::hasStackObjects` method. If you do not have any stack object, then you will not need any spill slot since by extension, no frame index is in use. Now, if you have some stack object, you might need an emergency spill slot. Using this way of checking whether an emergency spill slot is needed may still overprovision the stack space, but since you must already insert a prologue and epilogue, the additional space is a small price to pay.

You usually instantiate your emergency spill slot by using the `CreateStackObject` method of the `MachineFrameInfo` instance of your function in one of the overridable methods of the `TargetFrameLowering` class that has a `RegScavenger` instance as an argument (for instance, the `determineCalleeSaves` or `processFunctionBeforeFrameFinalized` method). After instantiating such a stack slot, you must register it with your `RegScavenger` instance using the `addScavengingFrameIndex` method.

For our H2BLB backend, we did not use any emergency spill slot because our frame index expansion sequences do not need a temporary register yet. You can find plenty of examples that set an emergency spill slot in the open source backends. For instance, look at the implementation of the `processFunc tionBeforeFrameFinalized` method in the Systemz backend or the `determineCalleeSaves` method in the AArch64 backend.

> **Note**
>
> You need to have as many emergency spill slots as the number of temporary registers that you may need simultaneously in the worst case of the expansion of one frame index.

At this point, you know how to reliably get temporary registers for the expansion of your frame indices. Let us now see how to materialize this expansion.

# Expanding the frame indices

The expansion of the frame indices is handled by your target-specific version of the `TargetRegisterInfo` class. More specifically, you must override the `eliminateFrameIndex` method of this class and implement the replacement of the given frame index with the proper computation of the stack pointer/ frame pointer +/- the offset.

Before we show you an example of how to do that, remember that your stack frame resembles what is depicted in *Figure 20.2*:

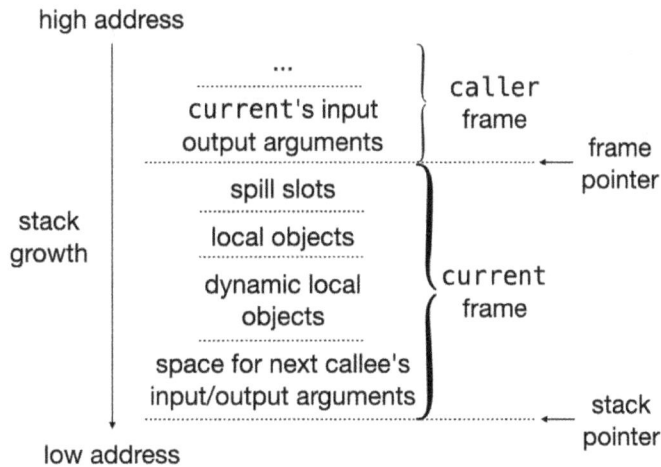

*Figure 20.2: A possible layout of a stack growing downward*

*Figure 20.3* shows one of the ways the layout of the stack can be arranged. The actual layout depends on your ABI. In this case, the input and output arguments of the next call are stored last in the stack frame. For instance, you will find the input and output arguments of the `current` function in the previous stack frame, here identified by the `caller` frame. Similarly, to call a function from the `current` function, the input and output arguments of the function are placed at the end of the `current` function's frame (at the very bottom of the diagram in this example, identified with *next callee's input/output arguments*).

Focusing on the stack frame of the `current` function, you typically place first the stack slots of the objects whose sizes are known at compile time, that is, the static local objects and the spill slots, then the dynamic slots, and finally, the space for the arguments of the next call. Thanks to this layout, you can statically compute from the frame pointer (shown on the right) the address of each local object and the address of the beginning of the region that holds the dynamic objects. Similarly, you can compute statically the address of each input and output argument of the next call from the stack pointer. As you can see, if you do not have any dynamically allocated objects, you can statically compute the frame pointer from the stack pointer and hence do not need to hold that information anywhere.

> **Note**
>
> *Figure 20.3* shows a simplified view of the stack. In particular, we voluntarily collapsed some regions in the stack to make it more approachable. For instance, we did not explicitly separate the space used for the ABI, such as the storage of the link register, the variadic arguments, or the callee saved registers, from the spill slots. In other words, remember that this figure is a high-level view of what a stack layout looks like.

Now that we have defined the layout of the stack, let us see how we implement it in the expansion of the frame indices.

As already mentioned, this expansion happens in the overridden version of the `eliminateFrameIndex` method of your `TargetRegisterInfo` class.

We start this method by collecting the information about the frame index we are expanding:

```
bool H2BLBRegisterInfo::eliminateFrameIndex(MachineBasicBlock::iterator II,
                                    int SPAdj, unsigned FIOperandNum,
                                    RegScavenger *RS) const {
  ...
  MachineOperand &FIOp = MI.getOperand(FIOperandNum);
  int Index = MI.getOperand(FIOperandNum).getIndex();
  int64_t Offset = MFI.getObjectOffset(Index);
```

In this snippet, the `MFI` variable is the `MachineFrameInfo` instance of the `MachineFunction` instance that holds the information we need to update the instruction with the frame index. This instruction is represented by the given `II` argument, but we renamed it to `MI` in the removed boilerplate code. Using this `MFI` variable, we get the offset of the frame index using the `getObjectOffset` method.

Next, since this offset is defined in terms of the frame pointer and we do not use a frame pointer, we need to massage it to describe it in terms of the stack pointer:

```
  Offset += MFI.getStackSize();
```

At this point, the `Offset` variable holds the offset of our frame index from the stack pointer. The next thing we need to do is to replace the frame index with the combo stack pointer plus offset.

The replacement may be different for each instruction that holds a frame index. For instance, expanding the frame index of a `load` instruction may be different than a `move` instruction. Therefore, we do the expansion through a switch on the opcode of the current instruction:

```
  switch (MI.getOpcode()) {
  case H2BLB::LDRSP16:
    FIOp.ChangeToRegister(H2BLB::SP, /*IsDef=*/false);
    Offset += MI.getOperand(2).getImm();
    assert(Offset >= -64 && Offset < 63 && "Offset must fit 7 bits for now");
```

```
    MI.getOperand(2).setImm(Offset);
    break;
```

In this snippet, we turn a load @Idx, Cst instruction into a load SP, Cst+Offset instruction by first turning the operand that holds the @Idx frame index operand into the SP register (the call to the ChangeToRegister method) and then updating the constant offset argument to include the newly computed offset (the call to the setImm method). Notice that we did not bother supporting the case where the offset does not fit into our encoding. Instead, we would assert if it does not fit. This is typically where you will need to use the RegScavenger instance that is passed to the eliminateFrameIndex method (here held by the RS argument). Feel free to modify the code to support that case and remember to add a unit test for it!

Finally, you need to return a Boolean that tells the caller of the eliminateFrameIndex method whether the iterator that was passed for the MachineInstr instance is now invalid – in other words, whether you deleted the input instruction when you performed your expansion. In our case, the answer is no, we did not invalidate the iterator, and we simply returned false.

You can find the complete snippet of this method at the commit tagged stack-lowering_ch20 and one with a slightly more complicated expansion sequence at the commit tagged stack-lowering-extld-movefromsp_ch20. Both of these tags are in the companion repository. Additionally, you can look at the commit tagged sdisel-call-lowering-stack_ch15 for a stress test of the stack lowering. Looking at this stress test, try to verify that the stack layout makes sense to you!

As soon as you have implemented the expansion for each instruction that can use a frame index, you are done with the lowering of your stack. If you are not sure which instructions you should support in this method, look back at the instructions that you generate when lowering the ABI in the instruction selection process and at the instructions that you generate when spilling registers. You should only have to support these opcodes. Indeed, these are the only places where instructions that use frame indices are created, at least by default.

In this section, you learned how to replace your frame index with the actual address used by your program by overriding the related target hook in your TargetRegisterInfo class. You saw that sometimes, this replacement involves temporary variables and that you can use the register scavenger mechanism with its associated emergency spill slot to hold these variables in registers.

# Summary

In this chapter, you learned that the lowering of the stack layout consists of provisioning the stack space for your stack frame and replacing the frame indices with actual stack addresses.

You learned that the whole process is driven by the target-independent PEI pass and that this pass relies on the target-specific versions of the TargetFrameLowering and TargetRegisterInfo classes to perform the lowering. More specifically, you learned which methods you need to provide for both of these classes and saw that the TargetFrameLowering class is responsible for allocating the stack space by providing the code sequences that materialize the prologue and epilogue of your function, as well as that the TargetRegisterInfo class is responsible for the expansion of the frame indices into stack addresses.

Finally, you were exposed to the concept of register scavenging and saw how you can use the related RegScavenger class to obtain the registers that may be necessary to materialize the temporary values that may appear in the expansion of your frame indices into a sequence of stack address computations.

In the next and final chapter, we will cover the pieces that you need to implement to be able to produce an object file.

# Quiz time

Now that you have completed reading this chapter, try answering the following questions to test your knowledge:

1.  What do fixed stack slots represent?

    Fixed stack slots are memory locations on the stack that are created to hold objects that must have a determined stack address. These objects are typically part of the ABI and must have a specific guarantee on where they must be in the stack for the other function (caller or callee) to find it.

    More details can be found in the *Handling of stack slots* section.

2.  What are the four main components involved in the lowering of the stack?

    The four main components involved in the lowering of the stack are the MachineRegisterInfo class, the TargetLoweringInfo class, the TargetRegisterInfo class, and the PEI pass. See the *From frame index to stack slot* section to learn what each of them is responsible for.

3.  What are the pros and cons of the reserved call frame?

    The reserved call frame pushes the allocation and deallocation of the stack space around the calls within a function to the prologue and epilogue. The advantage of such a method is that the produced code sequence is short and thus likely more efficient, but the drawback is that the footprint of the function's stack is bigger across the lifetime of the function.

    See the *Introducing the reserved call frame* section for more information.

4.  Why may you need to scavenge for registers when lowering your frame index?

    When lowering your frame index, you may create additional instructions to materialize the computation of the combination of the stack pointer and offset. This computation may need additional temporary values and you scavenge for registers to hold these values. Take a look at the *The expansion of the frame indices* section for more details.

5.  When lowering the stack, do you have to maintain a RegScavenger instance by yourself?

    No, a RegScavenger instance is maintained for you by the PEI pass. See the *Introducing register scavenging* section.

6. What is an emergency spill slot?

   An emergency spill slot is a stack slot that you provision in case the register scavenging process fails to find a register and needs to spill one to materialize the computation of a frame index.

   Take a look at the *Introducing register scavenging* and *Provisioning an emergency spill slot* sections for more information on emergency spill slots.

---

**Unlock this book's exclusive benefits now**

This book comes with additional benefits designed to elevate your learning experience.

*Note: Have your purchase invoice ready before you begin.*

https://www.packtpub.com/unlock/9781837637782

# 21

# Getting Started with the Assembler

In a compiler toolchain, the assembler is the tool that is responsible for taking assembly code in textual format and producing an object file, that is, a binary file that encodes everything there is to know about this assembly code.

The assembler is at the frontier between a compiler backend and the binary tools, and you could argue that implementing one does not fall within the scope of a compiler engineer.

While there is some truth to this, we wanted to give you a glimpse of what it takes to produce object files with the LLVM infrastructure since you already went through the trouble of learning how to describe the encoding of the instructions in *Chapter 12*. In other words, we wanted to show you how the work you did in *Chapter 12* connects to the bigger picture of a full compiler toolchain.

In this chapter, you will learn how to leverage the LLVM infrastructure to build an assembler. More specifically, we will teach you about the following:

- The steps involved in the translation of a textual assembly file into a binary object file
- The LLVM components involved in building an assembler
- The **application programming interface (API)** you must provide to have a functioning assembler

To set the expectations, the knowledge that you will gain here will give you enough background information for you to understand what you need to do to build your own assembler. However, a lot of the details are kept under the rug and this chapter alone cannot suffice for you to build an assembler from scratch. For instance, we will not cover the specification of the different object file formats, such as the **Executable and Linkable Format (ELF)** or the **Common Object File Format (COFF)**. This is the type of knowledge that is good to have when building an assembler to at least check that your produced object files are correct, and we will not provide it here.

The bottom line is that this chapter gives you guidelines on how to build an assembler with the LLVM infrastructure and highlights the things that you need to be aware of when doing this but leaves out the details that are inherently specific to your binary tools, such as the specification of the relocations and so on. We will define these concepts, but their actual implementations are left out since they are target-specific.

Let us start by seeing what you will need to be able to play with the mock assembler implementation of our H2BLB backend.

## Technical requirements

Similar to all the chapters that build an LLVM backend, you need to develop directly in the LLVM code base (or a fork of it). As such, you will need all the same tools that we presented in *Chapter 1*.

Additionally, for all the snippets presented in this chapter, you will find the actual implementation in the `https://github.com/PacktPublishing/LLVM-Code-Generation-by-example` GitHub repository. We call this repository the **companion repository** in the remainder of the chapter.

For each change presented in this chapter, we highlight a Git tag that you can use to find the full snippet in the companion repository. All changes made in this chapter are between the `begin_ch21` and `end_ch21` Git tags.

If you are not familiar with Git tags, review *Chapter 9* for a quick explanation of what you can do with them.

Let us get started with an overview of the steps involved in producing a binary file from a textual assembly file.

## Overview of the lowering of a textual assembly file

The process of assembling a textual assembly file consists of taking a textual assembly file and turning it into a sequence of bits that comply with the target file format.

During this process, there are two main things that need to happen:

- The encoding of the instructions, which you discovered how to do in *Chapter 12*
- The encoding of the addresses of the symbols, such as the target of a jump or a call

The second point represents the main difficulty in assembling a textual assembly file. Indeed, resolving the address of a symbol may only be possible at (dynamic) link time when all object files and libraries are finally known.

In other words, the assembler needs to resolve all the symbols as best as it can, then leave some directive to the linker, called **relocations**, for the ones it could not resolve.

*Figure 21.1* shows the overall steps that the assembler goes through when lowering assembly code into binary code:

```
                                   call fctA
                                      ↓
                                   call xxxx
                                   fixup: fctA
                                       ↓
                      yes          ╱  Can  ╲          no
              ┌──────────────────╱  resolve  ╲──────────────────┐
              │                   ╲  fctA?  ╱                    │
              │                      ╲    ╱                      │
              │                ╱  Does  ╲                        │
              │      yes      ╱ fctA address ╲    no             │
              │   ┌──────────╱    fit?    ╲──────────┐           │
              │   │           ╲          ╱           │           │
              │   │              ╲    ╱               │           │
              │   │         yes ╱ Can relax ╲  no     │           │
              │   │      ┌─────╱   instr?   ╲─────┐   │           │
         0110 0010       │      ╲          ╱      │               │
                         │         ╲    ╱         │               │
          encode         │                        │               │
                    longerCall xxxxxx        0110 xxxx
                    relax: use longer      relocation: fctA
                        encoding
```

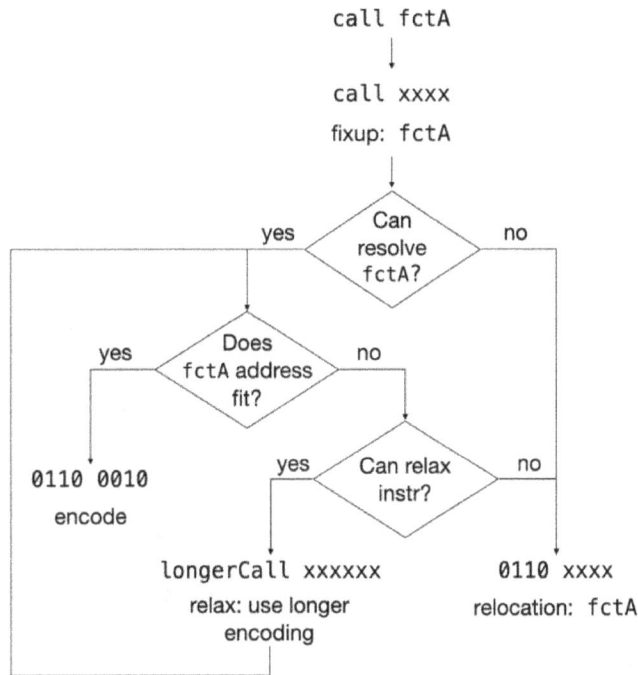

*Figure 21.1: The lowering of a textual instruction into binary code*

At the very top of *Figure 21.1*, we start with an instruction that calls to the fctA function and lowers it to binary code. More specifically, we tell the assembler that we need a **fixup** for the fctA symbol. A fixup is a placeholder for an entry in the instruction that is not yet known. In the preceding figure, xxxx represents the bits that we are trying to fill with a fixup. As the assembler progresses through the lowering of the assembly file, it checks whether it knows this symbol and, thus, whether it can resolve its address. For instance, if the symbol is a call to a function that is defined in the same file, it will be able to eventually find its address; hence, in that case, the address is resolvable. If the address is resolvable, we take the left path and check whether the address of the symbol fits into the encoding of the instruction (the number of bits available in the xxxx sequence). If the address fits, the instruction is fully encoded and, in this example, the opcode is 0110 and the address is 0010. If the address does not fit the available space for the symbol for this instruction (here, the call instruction), the assembler tries to **relax** it. The process of relaxation consists of finding an instruction with the exact same semantics (here, longerCall) but with a larger encoding. This process is target-specific. The goal is to offer more bits to encode the address of the symbol. If such instruction exists, the assembler relaxes the instruction and checks again whether the symbol address can now fit. If it does, then it encodes the full instruction with the new encoding (that is, with the longerCall opcode and the full address of the fctA symbol). If it does not fit, it checks whether the new instruction can be further relaxed, and so on.

If an instruction cannot be relaxed anymore or if the symbol cannot be resolved at assembly time, the assembler records a relocation. A relocation is an entry in a table, called the relocation table, that lives in the final object file. This entry tells the linker that it has some patching to do to produce the final executable. In this case, the patching consists of telling the linker that the instruction at the **program counter (PC)** of the call fctA instruction needs to be updated with the address of the fctA symbol. Relocations are usually target-specific, which means that both the assembler and the linker need to agree on the semantics of the relocations.

In this section, you learned about some of the concepts that are used in the assembly of binary files. More specifically, you learned that the resolution of the address of a symbol goes through a fixup phase and a relocation phase if the fixup cannot be resolved during assembly, either because the encoding is not large enough even with the use of relaxation or because the address of the symbol is not known at assembly time (for instance, when calling an external function).

In the next section, we will see which components in LLVM are responsible for performing these steps.

## Assembling with the LLVM infrastructure

The LLVM infrastructure uses the same overall pipeline for producing both textual assembly files and object files.

In both cases, the process is guided by your target-specific AsmPrinter pass, which you wrote in *Chapter 12*. What changes to produce the different types of files is the actual implementation of the MCStreamer class. *Figure 21.2* captures this difference:

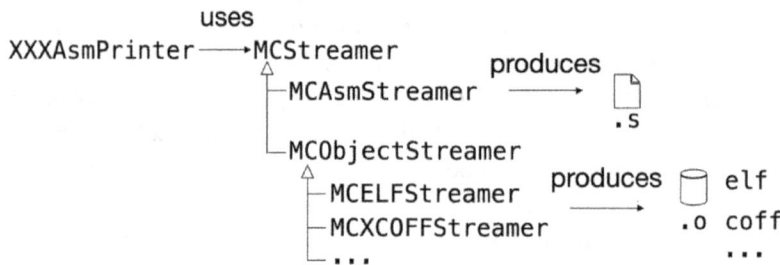

*Figure 21.2: How the target-specific AsmPrinter class produces a textual assembly or binary file*

In *Figure 21.2*, you can see that the abstract MCStreamer class is instantiated with the MCAsmStreamer subclass to produce a textual assembly file (.s) or with one of the MCObjectStreamer subclasses to produce the related binary file format (.o): the MCELFStreamer class for ELF, the MCXCoffStreamer class for COFF, and so on.

The subclasses of the MCObjectStreamer class encapsulate all the logic to produce the layout of the related object file format, including the section that contains the relocation table. You must, however, handle some part of the fixup and relaxation process and produce these relocations.

*Figure 21.3* shows how the different classes articulate to solve this gap in functionality:

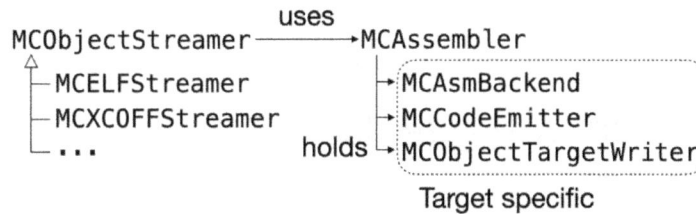

Figure 21.3: How MCObjectStreamer gets the target-specific functionality

At the high level, the MCObjectStreamer class uses a generic helper class called MCAssembler. The MCAssembler class has two main roles:

- It provides the target-specific versions of the MCAsmBackend, MCCodeEmitter, and MCObjectTargetWriter classes, as shown in *Figure 21.3*. Note that the target-specific version of the MCObjectTargetWriter class is likely implemented with one of the MCObjectTargetWriter subclasses that match the desired object format, such as MCELFObjectTargetWriter for ELF and so on.
- It holds the information on the symbols, sections, and so on. That information is used by the MCObjectStreamer class to produce the final binary.

Focusing on the target-specific classes held by the MCAssembler class, here is their respective responsibility:

- The MCAsmBackend class handles the fixups, including the relaxation process. Any fixup not completely encoded in the instruction will be converted to relocations.
- The MCCodeEmitter class handles the encoding of the instructions, including issuing the fixups for any operand that requires some resolution.
- The MCObjectTargetWriter class handles the relocations. In other words, its job is to replace fixups with relocations.

Putting things together, the MCCodeEmitter class issues the fixups while encoding the operands it can. The fixups are then handled by the MCAsmBackend class, which patches the encoding for resolved fixups. Finally, any unresolved fixups are passed to the MCObjectTargetWriter class to record the related relocations in the final object file.

As soon as you have implemented all three classes, you will have a functioning assembler.

In this section, you learned about the different classes involved in the assembling of a binary file. You saw that this process hinges around three target-specific classes (the MCCodeEmitter, MCAsmBackend, and MCObjectTargetWriter classes) that you must provide.

In the next section, we will give you a glimpse of how to implement these target-specific classes.

# Implementing an assembler

As already stated, to get a functioning assembler, you need to provide the implementation of the three previously mentioned classes, starting with the MCCodeEmitter class.

## Providing the MCCodeEmitter class

You already implemented the MCCodeEmitter class in *Chapter 12*. However, at that time, we did not show you how to emit a fixup.

First, we start by defining our target-specific fixups. Fixups are simply enumeration values, and their semantics are up to us.

With the limited instruction set of our H2BLB backend, we support only one type of fixup, and the related declaration looks like the following:

```
enum FixupKind {
  FK_H2BLB_PCRel_11 = FirstTargetFixupKind,
  LastTargetFixupKind,
  NumTargetFixupKinds = LastTargetFixupKind - FirstTargetFixupKind
};
```

Here, we declare an enumeration whose first entry is our target-specific fixup FK_H2BLB_PCRel_11 value. The naming convention follows the recommended LLVM way to start an enumeration: we use the initials of the name of the enumeration, that is, FixupKind, which gives FK. Then, we use the name of our backend, H2BLB, followed by some high-level information on our fixup: it is PC relative, and the fixup is targeted at filling 11 bits in.

Next, we specify some values that will help us handle our fixups (the values of the first and last target-specific fixup and the number of target-specific fixups).

We put this declaration in our target-specific llvm/lib/Target/H2BLB/MCTargetDesc/H2BLBMCFixups.h file, as you can see in the commit tagged fixup-decl_ch21 in the companion repository.

Next, you need to emit the proper fixups in your MCCodeEmitter implementation when you run into a situation where you need them. In our case, we emit our only fixup when we run into our call instruction. We do this as part of the getMachineOpValue method of our MCCodeEmitter class:

```
unsigned
H2BLBMCCodeEmitter::getMachineOpValue(const MCInst &MI, const MCOperand &MO,
                                      SmallVectorImpl<MCFixup> &Fixups,
                                      const MCSubtargetInfo &STI) const {
  // Handle non-symbolic operands, see Chapter 12.
  ...
  // At this point we expect a symbol reference for the branches.
  assert(MO.isExpr());
  const MCExpr *Expr = MO.getExpr();
```

```
    assert(Expr->getKind() == MCExpr::SymbolRef);
    if (MI.getOpcode() == H2BLB::CALL) {
      Fixups.push_back(
          MCFixup::create(0, Expr, (MCFixupKind)H2BLB::FK_H2BLB_PCRel_11));
    }
    ...
```

In this method, when we run into an `MCExpr` instance that is attached to a call instruction (as identified by our `H2BLB::CALL` opcode), we emit a fixup with this `MCExpr` instance and register it with our target-specific kind of fixup using the `FK_H2BLB_PCRel_11` value. The first argument of the `MCFixup::create` method is the offset at which the fixup starts. In our case, this is `0`.

To make the arguments of the `create` method in the previous paragraph feel more concrete, the reason we used our `FK_H2BLB_PCRel_11` fixup is that our `call` instruction is PC relative, meaning that at the time of the execution of the `call` instruction, the address of the target operand of this call is added to the current value of the PC. This computation forms the final called address. The number of bits available for the address of the target operand of our call is 11. In other words, this is the very semantics that our `FK_H2BLB_PCRel_11` fixup captures. Finally, the offset is `0` for the fixup in this case because the 11 bits start at index `0` (from the less significant bit) in the encoding of our `call` instruction.

You can find the full snippet of the `MCCodeEmitter` class changes at the commit tagged `mccodeemitter-emit-fixup_ch21` in the companion repository.

Now that we have told the assembler where we need our fixups, let us see how we apply them with our implementation of the `MCAsmBackend` class.

## Handling the fixups with the MCAsmBackend class

For the generic LLVM infrastructure to work with your backend, your target-specific `MCAsmBackend` class needs to provide three methods:

- The `createObjectTargetWriter` method: This method returns the `MCObjectTargetWriter` instance that implements the recording of the relocation for your target for the desired file format. We will see how to implement it in the next section.
- The `getNumFixupKinds` method: This method returns the number of target-specific fixups that your target has. As soon as this is non-zero, you also need to implement the `getFixupKindInfo` method to provide the characteristics of your target-specific fixup.
- The `applyFixup` method: This method is the meat of the `MCAsmBackend` class. As its name suggests, it applies the given fixup to the given stream of bytes, effectively producing the final encoding in the binary blob that holds this fixup.

Additionally, if your target supports relaxation, you need to implement the `relaxInstruction` method.

Let us focus our attention on the main method of the `MCAsmBackend` class, the `applyFixup` method.

We start the method by checking whether we have anything to do with the given fixup, represented by the Fixup variable:

```
void H2BLBAsmBackend::applyFixup(const MCAssembler &Asm, const MCFixup &Fixup,
                                 const MCValue &Target,
                                 MutableArrayRef<char> Data, uint64_t Value,
                                 bool IsResolved,
                                 const MCSubtargetInfo *STI) const {
  if (!Value)
    return;
  unsigned Kind = Fixup.getKind();
  if (Kind >= FirstLiteralRelocationKind)
    return;
```

In this snippet, we return early if the Value variable contains zero; indeed, this means that the encoding will not be affected since, by default, the bits to be fixed up are set to zero.

The second condition around the Kind variable checks whether we are dealing with a fixup or a relocation. If this is a relocation, then this is not a fixup that we can apply. It will need to be recorded as a relocation and later resolved by the (dynamic) linker.

Next, we collect the information about this fixup and apply it to the value to be encoded:

```
MCFixupKindInfo Info = getFixupKindInfo(Fixup.getKind());
Value <<= Info.TargetOffset;
unsigned NumBytes = (Info.TargetSize + 7) / 8;
uint32_t Offset = Fixup.getOffset();
assert(Offset + NumBytes <= Data.size() && "Invalid fixup offset!");
```

In this snippet, we adjust the Value variable to materialize the offset that is carried by the fixup and check that the blob of bytes, represented by the Data variable, is big enough to accommodate our fixup.

Now, our Value variable contains the fixup the way it is supposed to appear in the final binary, and we just need to emit it in the Data variable at the proper location:

```
for (unsigned i = 0; i != NumBytes; ++i)
  Data[Offset + i] |= static_cast<uint8_t>((Value >> (i * 8)) & 0xff);
```

We do the emission one byte at a time in increasing order of bytes since our target is **little endian**.

All the other methods are straightforward, and if you need help writing them, look at the commit tagged mcasmbackend-impl_ch21 in the companion repository.

Let us now implement the final missing piece, the MCObjectTargetWriter class.

# Recording the relocations with the MCObjectTargetWriter class

You are now in the final stretch of having a functional assembler. The last thing you need to supply is an implementation of the MCObjectTargetWriter class.

For this class, you likely want to base your target-specific version on the subclass that matches the file format that you want to support. For instance, for our H2BLB backend, we want to support the **Mach object (Mach-O)** file format, which is the file format used in macOS; therefore, we base our MCObjectTargetWriter class on the MCMachObjectTargetWriter class. Similarly, if we wanted to support ELF, we would use the MCELFObjectTargetWriter class. If you want to support several file formats, you typically provide one specialized class of the MCObjectTargetWriter class per file format and you select the right instance in the createObjectTargetWriter method of your MCAsmBackend class.

Focusing on the implementation of your MCObjectTargetWriter class, you need to provide the implementation of the recordRelocation method. This method takes an MCObjectWriter instance and populates it with the relocation that matches the given fixup parameter. In other words, for a given fixup, this method records the related relocation.

Let us see an implementation of this method for our H2BLB backend.

> Note
>
> Remember that the code snippets are a mock implementation because, for a target-specific relocation to be valid, all the binary tools need to be taught about it. In particular, the enumeration value used to record the relocations needs to be aligned with all the tools that manipulate them.

We start our method by setting up some values related to the Mach-O format:

```
void H2BLBMachObjectWriter::recordRelocation(
    MachObjectWriter *Writer, MCAssembler &Asm, const MCFragment *Fragment,
    const MCFixup &Fixup, MCValue Target, uint64_t &FixedValue) {
  unsigned IsPCRel = Writer->isFixupKindPCRel(Asm, Fixup.getKind());
  uint32_t FixupOffset = Asm.getFragmentOffset(*Fragment);
  unsigned Log2Size = 1;
  int64_t Value = 0;
  unsigned Index = 0;
  unsigned Type = 0;
  const MCSymbol *RelSymbol = nullptr;
```

We will refine these values along the way, but we started by hardcoding some values since we support only one fixup right now. For instance, the Log2Size variable holds the size of the relocation in the logarithm of 2 of the byte size. We can set it to 1 since we use 11 bits for our unique relocation, meaning that we use two bytes and $\log2(2) == 1$.

The meaning of all these fields can be found in the Mach-O specification and is carried by the `relocation_info` structure in your `reloc.h` Mach-O system header file. Here's a quick introduction:

- The `IsPCRel` variable encodes whether the relocation is PC relative.
- The `index` variable encodes the index of the symbol in the symbol table or the number of the section that this relocation needs to resolve to.
- The `type` variable holds the enumeration value of the relocation as understood by the binary tools.

The other variables are used to compute the information that is emitted in the relocation or returned by this function. For instance, the `Value` variable will be used to compute the value of the `FixedValue` argument that tells the caller that a constant displacement (in other words, an offset (or an **addend** in binary tool parlance)) needs to be applied to the resolved address.

Next, we can start unboxing our fixup and build the related relocation.

The fixup that we need to translate into a relocation is represented with the `MCValue` class. This class conceptually represents an address computation of the form `SymbolA - SymbolB + Constant`. This computation is reflected in the getters of this class: `getSymA`, `getSymB`, and `getConstant`.

Your job is to take the input `MCValue` instance, represented by the `Target` argument, and produce a relocation out of it.

In our case, we support only a simple case where this value is just a symbol since we emit a fixup only for our call instruction. In other words, our `MCValue` instance is made of just a `SymbolA` instance.

With this knowledge, we can start unboxing our `Target` value:

```
const MCSymbol *Symbol = &Target.getSymA()->getSymbol();
const MCSymbol *Base = Writer->getAtom(*Symbol);
```

In this snippet, we only look at the result of the `getSymA` method, as previously explained. Next, we get the encompassing base symbol (which can be the symbol itself) to get the base address of our symbol. This part may be confusing and has to do with how the object file is laid out. The bottom line is that this is why you need some knowledge of the file format to write this type of code.

At this point, you must support two cases: you either get a base symbol or you do not. Here is what the two cases would look like:

```
if (Base) {
  RelSymbol = Base;
  if (Base != Symbol)
    Value += Asm.getSymbolOffset(*Symbol) - Asm.getSymbolOffset(*Base);
} else {
  assert(Symbol->isInSection());
  const MCSection &Sec = Symbol->getSection();
  Index = Sec.getOrdinal() + 1;
  Value += Writer->getSymbolAddress(*Symbol, Asm);
```

```
    if (IsPCRel)
      Value -= Writer->getFragmentAddress(Asm, Fragment) + Fixup.getOffset() +
               (1ULL << Log2Size);
  }
```

In this snippet, when we get a base symbol, we record it as our relative symbol for the relocation by setting the RelSymbol variable to the Base variable. Then, we adjust the offset if the Base symbol is not the same as the target symbol.

Now, looking at the else block, if we did not get a Base symbol, this means we are dealing with a symbol that is within a section. We get the information on this section and set the Index variable to point to this section (sections are numbered starting from one in Mach-O, hence ,+ 1). Next, we adjust the offset based on the symbol address and whether the relocation is PC relative.

Now that we have unboxed the Target value, we can emit our relocation and we do this with the following snippet:

```
  Type = unsigned(MachO::ARM64_RELOC_BRANCH26);
  FixedValue = Value;
  MachO::any_relocation_info MRE;
  MRE.r_word0 = FixupOffset;
  MRE.r_word1 =
      (Index << 0) | (IsPCRel << 24) | (Log2Size << 25) | (Type << 28);
  Writer->addRelocation(RelSymbol, Fragment->getParent(), MRE);
```

We start by setting the type for our relocation; here, we used a dummy value defined by another backend because we wanted to be able to print our relocation with an existing binary tool. Next, we record the addend left by our relocation in the FixedValue variable. This addend will be recorded by our fixup mechanism in the instruction itself, thanks to the implementation of the MCAsmBackend class, and it will automatically be added to the target address when the (dynamic) linker applies the relocation.

Finally, we set up the relocation information in the MCObjectWriter instance.

The left shifts with the different values match the specification of the relocation_info structure, reproduced here for your information:

```
struct relocation_info {
   int32_t r_address;
   uint32_t r_symbolnum : 24, r_pcrel : 1, r_length : 2, r_extern : 1, r_type : 4;
};
```

For instance, the IsPCRel value is shifted by 24 since it occurs right after the r_symbolnum field, which is 24 bits long, and the Log2Size value is shifted by 25 since it is registered in the r_length field, which is right after the r_symbolnum (24-bit) and r_pcrel (1-bit) fields.

This concludes the implementation of our MCObjectTargetWriter class. For more complex cases, we invite you to look at the existing open source backends. In any case, you can find the complete snippet of our H2BLB implementation at the commit tagged mcobjecttgtwriter-impl_ch21 in the companion repository.

Now that you support fixups and record relocations, the only thing remaining is to register your MCAsmBackend class with the LLVM infrastructure. You do this by adding the call to the RegisterMCAsmBackend method to your LLVMInitializeH2BLBTargetMC function. Look at the commit tagged mcasmbackend-impl_ch21 in the companion repository if you need help with that. Using the companion repository, you can look at the test in the llvm/test/MC/H2BLB/asm-backend-external-symbols.ll file to see how to use the llvm-objdump command-line tool to check that your relocations look correct.

## Summary

In this final chapter, you discovered how textual assembly files are lowered into object files and learned how to leverage the LLVM infrastructure to implement this lowering.

More specifically, you learned that the LLVM infrastructure hinges on three classes that you must provide for your target: MCAsmBackend, MCCodeEmitter, and MCObjectTargetWriter. These classes are respectively responsible for handling the fixups, encoding the instructions, and recording the relocations.

While the content of this chapter will not be enough for you to confidently write an assembler, we believe it gives you the necessary background to get you started in your journey as a binary tools writer.

We hope you enjoyed learning with us and wish you good luck in your compiler backend journey or whatever LLVM-related activities you decide to pursue, such as writing your own tools, improving an existing backend, or writing your own backend, to mention a few!

## Further reading

To get a better grasp on the overall design of the **machine code** (MC) layer, you can read the blog post that Chris Lattner wrote when this layer was first introduced in 2010, at https://blog.llvm.org/2010/04/intro-to-llvm-mc-project.html.

To go beyond the guidelines established in this chapter, you can follow Simon Cook's *Implementing LLVM Integrated Assembler* tutorial at https://www.embecosm.com/appnotes/ean10/ean10-howto-llvmas-1.0.html. This tutorial gives some color around the implementation of the MCAsmBackend class and the related classes.

Finally, if you are curious about the Mach-O specifications, look at this document: https://github.com/aidansteele/osx-abi-macho-file-format-reference?tab=readme-ov-file. In particular, it has a section that explains the semantics of the fields of the relocation_info structure.

# Quiz time

Now that you have completed reading this chapter, try answering the following questions to test your knowledge:

1.  What are the main three steps involved in the resolution of addresses in the lowering to binary files?

    The three main steps are the insertion of fixup, the relaxation of the constraints of the instructions, and the recording of the relocations.

    More details are in the *Overview of the lowering of a textual assembly file* section.

2.  What are the three main target-specific components involved in the assembling of an object file?

    The three main target-specific components are the MCAsmBackend, MCCodeEmitter, and MCObjectTargetWriter classes. See the *Assembling with the LLVM infrastructure* section for more details.

3.  What are the responsibilities of the MCAsmBackend class?

    The MCAsmBackend class is responsible for handling the fixups, the relaxation process, and providing the MCObjectTargetWriter class. Refer to the *Assembling with the LLVM infrastructure* section for a refresher.

4.  What target-specific class drives the whole assembly printing for both the textual and binary outputs?

    The AsmPrinter class drives the printing of the assembly. See the *Assembling with the LLVM infrastructure* section.

5.  Which MC component specifies the type of assembly output that is produced by the assembly printing?

    The MC component that determines the type of assembly output is the MCStreamer class. Based on the MCStreamer subclass plugged into the AsmPrinter class, either a textual assembly or a binary output is generated. See the *Assembling with the LLVM infrastructure* section for more details.

---

**Unlock this book's exclusive benefits now**

This book comes with additional benefits designed to elevate your learning experience.

*Note: Have your purchase invoice ready before you begin.*

https://www.packtpub.com/unlock/9781837637782

# 22

# Unlock Your Book's Exclusive Benefits

Your copy of *LLVM Code Generation* comes with the following exclusive benefits:

- Next-gen Packt Reader
- AI assistant (beta)
- DRM-free PDF/ePub downloads

Use the following guide to unlock them if you haven't already. The process takes just a few minutes and needs to be done only once.

## How to unlock these benefits in three easy steps

### Step 1

Have your purchase invoice for this book ready, as you'll need it in *Step 3*. If you received a physical invoice, scan it on your phone and have it ready as either a PDF, JPG, or PNG.

For more help on finding your invoice, visit `https://www.packtpub.com/unlock-benefits/help`.

> **Note:** Bought this book directly from Packt? You don't need an invoice. After completing *Step 2*, you can jump straight to your exclusive content.

## Step 2

Scan the following QR code or visit `https://www.packtpub.com/unlock/9781837637782`:

## Step 3

Sign in to your Packt account or create a new one for free. Once you're logged in, upload your invoice. It can be in PDF, PNG, or JPG format and must be no larger than 10 MB. Follow the rest of the instructions on the screen to complete the process.

## Need help?

If you get stuck and need help, visit `https://www.packtpub.com/unlock-benefits/help` for a detailed FAQ on how to find your invoices and more. The following QR code will take you to the help page directly:

**Note:** If you are still facing issues, reach out to `customercare@packt.com`.

# ‹packt›

packtpub.com

Subscribe to our online digital library for full access to over 7,000 books and videos, as well as industry leading tools to help you plan your personal development and advance your career. For more information, please visit our website.

## Why subscribe?

- Spend less time learning and more time coding with practical eBooks and Videos from over 4,000 industry professionals
- Improve your learning with Skill Plans built especially for you
- Get a free eBook or video every month
- Fully searchable for easy access to vital information
- Copy and paste, print, and bookmark content

At www.packtpub.com, you can also read a collection of free technical articles, sign up for a range of free newsletters, and receive exclusive discounts and offers on Packt books and eBooks.

# Other Books You May Enjoy

If you enjoyed this book, you may be interested in these other books by Packt:

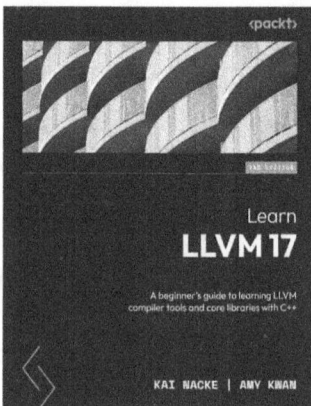

**Learn LLVM 17 — Second Edition**

Kai Nacke, Amy Kwan

ISBN: 978-1-83763-134-6

- Configure, compile, and install the LLVM framework
- Understand how the LLVM source is organized
- Discover what you need to do to use LLVM in your own projects
- Explore how a compiler is structured, and implement a tiny compiler
- Generate LLVM IR for common source language constructs
- Set up an optimization pipeline and tailor it for your own needs
- Extend LLVM with transformation passes and clang tooling
- Add new machine instructions and a complete backend

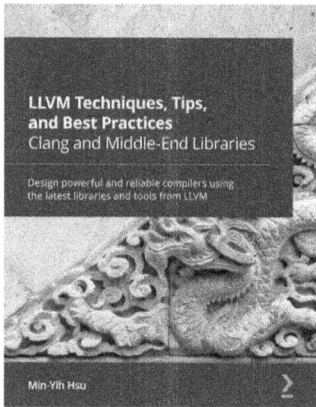

**LLVM Techniques, Tips, and Best Practices Clang and Middle-End Libraries**

Min-Yih Hsu

ISBN: 978-1-83882-495-2

- Find out how LLVM's build system works and how to reduce the building resource
- Get to grips with running custom testing with LLVM's LIT framework
- Build different types of plugins and extensions for Clang
- Customize Clang's toolchain and compiler flags
- Write LLVM passes for the new PassManager
- Discover how to inspect and modify LLVM IR
- Understand how to use LLVM's profile-guided optimizations (PGO) framework
- Create custom compiler sanitizers

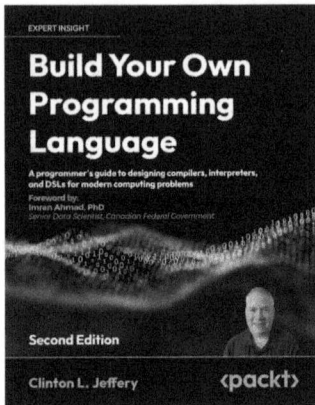

**Build Your Own Programming Language — Second Edition**

Clinton L. Jeffery

ISBN: 978-1-80461-802-8

- Analyze requirements for your language and design syntax and semantics
- Write grammar rules for common expressions and control structures
- Build a scanner to read source code and generate a parser to check syntax
- Implement syntax-coloring for your code in IDEs like VS Code
- Write tree traversals and insert information into the syntax tree
- Implement a bytecode interpreter and run bytecode from your compiler
- Write native code and run it after assembling and linking using system tools
- Preprocess and transpile code into another high-level language

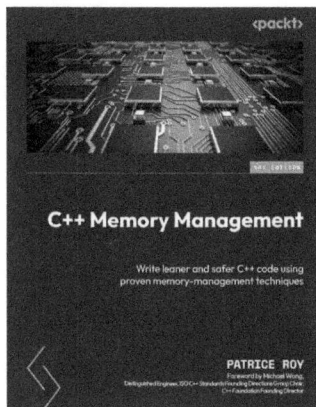

**C++ Memory Management**

Patrice Roy

ISBN: 978-1-80512-980-6

- Master the C++ object model to write more efficient and maintainable code
- Automate resource management to reduce manual errors and improve safety
- Customize memory allocation operators to optimize performance for specific applications
- Develop your own smart pointers to manage dynamic memory with greater control
- Adapt allocation behavior to meet the unique needs of different data types
- Create safe and fast containers to ensure optimal data handling in your programs
- Utilize standard allocators to streamline memory management in your containers

# Packt is searching for authors like you

If you're interested in becoming an author for Packt, please visit authors.packtpub.com and apply today. We have worked with thousands of developers and tech professionals, just like you, to help them share their insight with the global tech community. You can make a general application, apply for a specific hot topic that we are recruiting an author for, or submit your own idea.

# Share your thoughts

Now you've finished *LLVM Code Generation*, we'd love to hear your thoughts! Scan the QR code below to go straight to the Amazon review page for this book and share your feedback or leave a review on the site that you purchased it from.

https://packt.link/r/1837637784

Your review is important to us and the tech community and will help us make sure we're delivering excellent quality content.

# Index

# U

**undef** 179

**undefined behavior (UB)** 100

**use-def chain** 94, 500

  in LLVM IR 94-96

  in Machine IR 97-99

# V

**value**

  replacing 113

**value concept** 86

  def-use chain 94

  dominance 91-93

  SSA form, constructing 88-91

  static single assignment (SSA) 87

  use-def chain 94

**value type (VT)** 400

**vector registers (VRs)** 460

**vectors** 179

**verifier** 207

**very long instruction word (VLIW) processors** 508

**virtual table (vtable)** 63

**Visual Studio Code (VS Code)** 7

**vscale** 179

# W

**WriteRes TableGen class** 508

# Y

**YAML Aint Markup Language (YAML)** 315

  syntax 316-318

www.ingramcontent.com/pod-product-compliance
Lightning Source LLC
Chambersburg PA
CBHW081212220326
41598CB00037B/6753